THE Fostoria VALUE GUIDE

MILBRA LONG & EMILY SEATE

COLLECTOR BOOKS
A Division of Schroeder Publishing Co., Inc.

Acknowledgments

We are grateful to the Lancaster Colony Corporation, Inc., of Columbus, Ohio, for permission to use the materials and logo of the Fostoria Glass Company, Inc.

Deepest thanks to all the dealers who gave unselfishly of their knowledge and experience, especially David and Linda Adams.

We could not have had a better publisher, editor, or designer as partner in creating this value guide from the four Crystal for America books. Our heartfelt appreciation to Billy Schroeder, Gail Ashburn, and Holly Long.

Cover design: Beth Summers
Book design: Holly C. Long
Color photography: Charles R. Lynch
Computer images: Sheré Chamness

Collector Books
P.O. Box 3009
Paducah, KY 42002-3009
www.collectorbooks.com

Milbra Long and Emily Seate
P.O. Box 784
Cleburne, TX 76033-0;784
e-mail: longseat@sbcglobal.net
www.fostoriacrystal.com

Introduction

In preparing this book, our intent was to combine all the listings from the four books in the *Crystal for America* series so that complete patterns would be shown. Thus, a pattern which had stemware and tableware has one listing in this book. The book is intended to be used more for pricing than for identification, although with a little effort, one can use it for both. Each pattern listing includes both stemware and tableware numbers. For example, the Shirley design was etched on 6017 Sceptre stemware, and by looking at Sceptre, one can see the goblet shape in that line.

Page numbers where a pattern may be found in the four books comprising the *Crystal for America* series are included beneath each pattern name so that if you wish to know more about a particular pattern or category, you can find it with ease.

Berry Cutting 188

To determine the values in this book, several criteria were used, including (1) rarity, (2) demand, (3) whether a piece had heavy use or was seldom used, and (4) quality. Some prices have increased since the books in the *Crystal for America* series were first published, and some have decreased. We do feel that the colored, etched ware will continue to increase in value, as will other popular patterns, and we would not be surprised to see an increased interest in cuttings, especially from the 1930s. Cuttings on color have already appreciated in value as collectors discover their beauty. We understand that the American pattern is no longer being made and distributed through the Fostoria outlet stores. This should serve to allay the fears of American collectors regarding reproductions and may affect prices.

Vernon 5000 azure jug

One area that seems to have generated some interest lately is tumblers. We included a tumbler section in Fostoria Stemware, but found some omissions and some new information as we prepared this book. We have used a Tumbler heading to gather all those tumblers in one place, and we have added more specific information. Included at the end of the book are original catalog illustrations of many of the tumblers, some not shown in the previous books.

Blown tumblers were popular items for homes, restaurants, businesses associated with rail traffic, hotels, and bars from 1900 until around 1920. Fostoria produced many numbered tumbler lines, some in eight to ten sizes, during this period. Some of these early lines were listed until around 1928. One wonders at the choices the consumer made when the early crystal tumblers looked so much alike. We have not seen much interest in the crystal flat tumblers unless they have a design added. Even then, most people prefer stemmed or footed pieces. With the introduction of colors in 1924, tumblers became a little more interesting. At first, the 4095 and 5000 lines of footed tumblers dominated the scene. The 5084 footed tumblers were used with 870 stemware, and soon each new stemware pattern had its own flat or footed tumblers. Blank 869 was the first to offer flat tumblers in colors to coordinate with 869 stemware.

American large green boat

Before the advent of the complete dinnerware service, patterns were often a hodgepodge of stemware and tableware. For example, Greek (Etching 45), was used on most of the blanks being made from 1900 to 1920, ultimately comprising more than 170 pieces, including six stemware and tumbler lines and 21 jugs and tankards. We included Greek in Fostoria Stemware because it was still being offered on Blank 880 in 1924. Later, in 1930, it was offered on stemware line 5097 with 5000 tumblers and other complementary pieces as listed.

After the repeal of Prohibition in 1934, barware was once more in great demand. Most tumblers were made in crystal only, although several were made in the colors of that period. In 1934, a few were offered in the "strong" colors of Regal Blue, Empire Green, Burgundy, and Ruby. These and the tumblers in the Wisteria color are probably the most desireable to collectors, as are the etched, colored bar tumblers. The 4132 Standish line was made in azure and gold tint as well as crystal. The 6017 Sceptre stemware line, with Lido etching 329, offered the 4132 tumblers in crystal and azure. These tumblers were also used for some of the carved designs in crystal (see *Fostoria, Useful and Ornamental,* 110 through 131).

Flat tumblers, intended for bar use, usually had "sham" (heavy) bottoms. The 4146 Humpty Dumpty tumblers are exceptions; they are light and delicate. These are shown in *Fostoria, Useful and Ornamental,* page 128, with Toy and Nightmare carvings, and enamel decorations 620 and 621. These have to be rare, because they were only made from 1940 to 1943, during World War II. The 833½ Heatherbell and 4139 Esquire were used primarily for barware. Fuchsia etching 310 used 833 regular optic tumblers, no sham, crystal only, and these tumblers were not called Heatherbell. The 833 tumbler was blown and available even before 1924, optic or no optic, in sizes listed. After 1924, the 8 oz. Table Tumbler continued to be listed with some of the older patterns until around 1928. The 833 tumblers were not listed again until 1934, when they were included with 310 Fuchsia etching in 2 oz., 5 oz., 8 oz., and 12 oz. sizes. They were also available plain or with regular optic in 5 oz., 8 oz., and 12 oz. sizes.

We have attempted to list all the flat and footed tumblers that were shown after 1924. We hope that seeing the tumblers as they were presented on catalog pages by Fostoria will be helpful in visualizing sizes and uses. Some of the older patterns may have tumblers that we do not show or list in the Tumbler category.

When the 5056 American Lady pattern was reintroduced in 1948, there was no longer a 2½ oz. Wine, but a 4 oz. Oyster Cocktail was available for the first time. All pieces were made in crystal and in amethyst, which replaced the earlier burgundy color. A 7", 2337 plate was also added to the line in amethyst. We have included the later catalog page showing the Oyster Cocktail.

Finally, we hope that you will find this book useful, but we would also encourage you to investigate the *Crystal for America* series, where you will find production dates, original drawings or catalog pages for complete patterns, and a host of color.

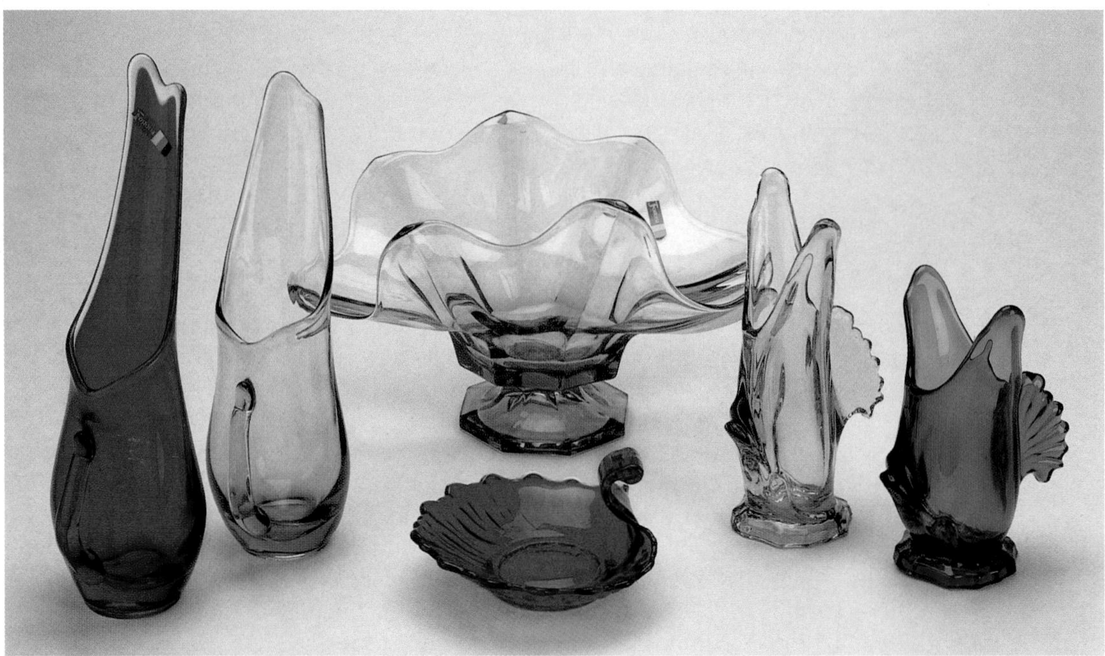

Ruby pitcher vase, lavender pitcher vase, footed basket, Flying Fish; teal Flying Fish, ruby bonbon

Abbreviations Guide

NO –	Narrow Optic	GS –	Ground Stopper
DO –	Dimple Optic	NP –	Nickle Plated
SO –	Spiral Optic	SP –	Silver Plated
RO –	Regular Optic	GF –	Gold Finished
LO –	Loop Optic	CN –	Cut Neck
UDP –	U Drop Prism	Stemware:	*Fostoria Stemware*
CF –	Crystal Footed	Tableware I:	*Fostoria Tableware: 1924 – 1943*
SPT –	Silver Plated Top		
HNT –	Hard Nickel Top	Tableware II:	*Fostoria Tableware: 1944 – 1986*
FGT –	Fostoria Glass Top		
LD –	Line Decoration	Useful and Ornamental:	*Fostoria, Useful and Ornamental*
DS –	Drop Stopper		

- A -

Acanthus, Etching 282

Amber and green

1930 – 1932

Stemware, 68

No.	Item	Price
5098	Goblet	$40.00
5098	Sherbet, high	$35.00
5098	Sherbet, low	$25.00
5098	Parfait	$20.00
5098	Cocktail	$35.00
5098	Claret	$45.00
5098	Wine	$40.00
5098	Cordial	$70.00
5098	Oyster Cocktail	$22.00
5098	Ice Tea, footed	$40.00
5098	Tumbler, 9 oz., footed	$30.00
5098	Juice, footed	$30.00
5098	Whiskey, footed	$40.00

Tableware I, 184

No.	Item	Price
4095	Almond, regular optic	$40.00
2350	Ashtray, small	$38.00
2375	Bonbon	$44.00
2375	Bouillon	$35.00
869	Bowl, finger	$48.00
2283	Plate, 6", regular optic	$48.00
2375	Bowl, 5", fruit	$24.00
2375	Bowl, 6", cereal	$26.00
2375	Bowl, 7", soup	$35.00
2394	Bowl, 6"	$32.00
2375	Bowl, 9", baker	$77.00
2375	Bowl, large, dessert	$85.00
2395	Bowl, 10"	$125.00
2430	Bowl, 11"	$95.00
2375	Bowl, 12"	$95.00
2394	Bowl A, 12"	$95.00
2394	Candlestick, 2", pair	$95.00
2375	Candlestick, 3", pair	$85.00
2375½	Candlestick, pair	$95.00
2395½	Candlestick, 5", pair	$125.00
2430	Candlestick, 9½", pair	$195.00
2430	Jar, candy and cover, ½ pound	$100.00
2375	Celery, 11½"	$52.00
2375	Centerpiece, 12"	$125.00
2375	Cheese and Cracker	$115.00
5098	Comport, 6"	$72.00
2375	Cream Soup and Plate	$85.00
2375½	Cup and Saucer	$40.00
2375	Cup and Saucer, after dinner	$65.00
5082½	Grapefruit and Liner	$85.00
2375	Ice Bucket	$115.00
2430	Jelly, 7"	$35.00
5000	Jug	$450.00
2375	Lemon Dish	$42.00
2375	Mayonnaise, plate and ladle	$110.00
2430	Mint, 5½"	$28.00
2375	Oil, footed	$400.00
2375	Pickle, 8½"	$30.00
2375	Plate, 6"	$12.00
2375	Plate, 7"	$14.00
2375	Plate, 8"	$20.00
2375	Plate, 9"	$28.00
2375	Plate, 10"	$65.00
2375	Plate, 10", grill	$60.00
2375	Plate, 10", cake	$75.00
2375	Plate, 13", chop	$95.00
2375	Platter, 12"	$125.00
2375	Platter, 15"	$150.00
2375	Relish, 8½"	$42.00
2083	Bottle, salad dressing	$400.00
2375	Sauce Boat and Plate	$295.00
2375	Shaker, footed, FGT, pair	$200.00
2375½	Sugar and Cover	$150.00
2375½	Sugar and Cream	$110.00
2375½	Sugar and Cream, Tea	$115.00
2375	Sweetmeat	$46.00
2375	Tray, handled, lunch	$115.00
2417	Vase, 8", regular optic	$300.00
2430	Vase, 8"	$275.00
4105	Vase, 8", regular optic	$295.00

Airdale, Cutting 175

1924 – 1927

Stemware, 36

No.	Item	Price
880	Goblet, 10 oz.	$8.00
880	Saucer Champagne, 5½ oz.	$10.00
880	Sherbet	$9.00
880	Cocktail, 3½ oz.	$9.00
880	Wine, 2¾ oz.	$10.00
701	Tumbler, 13 oz. and Plate	$15.00
820	Tumbler	$10.00
887	Tumbler, 2½ oz.	$8.00
889	Tumbler, 5 oz.	$8.00
4011	Tumbler, 12 oz., handled	$15.00
837	Oyster Cocktail	$9.00
822	Parfait	$14.00

Tableware I, 268

No.	Item	Price
880	Almond	$14.00
880	Bonbon	$18.00
1769	Bowl, finger	$18.00
2283	Plate	$18.00
2219	Jar, candy, ¼ lb. or ½ lb.	$28.00
2250	Jar, candy and cover, ¼ lb. or ½ lb.	$28.00
1697	Carafe	$24.00
4023	Carafe Tumbler, 6 oz.	$6.00
2241	Cologne and Stopper	$52.00
803	Comport, 5"	$16.00
1195	Decanter, large, cut neck	$28.00
945½	Grapefruit and Liner	$22.00
2040/3	Jug	$45.00
303/7	Jug	$95.00
2082-7	Jug	$95.00
803	Nappy, 5", footed	$14.00
803	Nappy, 6", footed	$14.00
701	Plate, 5", tumbler	$4.00
2285	Plate 6"	$4.00
2283	Plate, 7"	$5.00
2290	Plate, 8½"	$6.00
2283	Plate, 11"	$10.00
2263	Salt, individual	$14.00
2235	Shaker, FGT	$16.00
1712	Sugar and Cream	$28.00
880	Sweetmeat	$10.00
2194	Syrup, 12 oz.	$75.00
2287	Tray, lunch	$18.00
4069	Vase, Cut 175½	$35.00

Alaska, Decoration 54

1925 – 1930

Stemware, 31

No.	Item	Price
869	Goblet	$10.00
869	Saucer Champagne	$12.00
869	Fruit	$10.00
869	Parfait	$12.00
869	Cocktail	$10.00
869	Wine	$12.00
4095	Tumbler, 13 oz., footed	$12.00
4095	Tumbler, 10 oz., footed	$10.00
4095	Tumbler, 5 oz., footed	$8.00
4095	Tumbler, 2½ oz., footed	$5.00
5000	Tumbler, 12 oz., footed, RO	$12.00
5000	Tumbler 9 oz., footed, RO	$10.00
5000	Tumbler, 5 oz., footed, RO	$8.00
5000	Tumbler, 2½ oz., footed, RO	$5.00
869	Tumbler, 12 oz., handled	$15.00
869	Tumbler, table	$10.00
869	Tumbler, 5 oz.	$8.00
869	Tumbler, 8 oz.	$10.00
869	Tumbler, 12 oz.	$12.00

Tableware

No.	Item	Price
5078	Comport, 5"	$18.00
766	Bowl, finger	$12.00
945½	Grapefruit and Liner	$22.00
2270	Jug and Cover	$95.00
4095	Jug and Cover	$125.00
2283	Plate, 6"	$5.00
2283	Plate, 7"	$8.00
2283	Plate, 8"	$9.00

Alexis, 1630

1909 – 1925

Stemware, 41

No.	Item	Price
1630	Goblet, 10 oz.	$10.00
1630	Cocktail, 3 oz.	$10.00
1630	Claret, 5 oz.	$12.00
1630	Sherbet, low foot	$8.00
1630	Sherbet, high foot	$10.00
1630	Crème de Menthe, 2½ oz.	$8.00
1630	Champagne, tall, 6 oz.	$10.00
1630	Cordial, 1 oz.	$14.00
1630	Tumbler, 14 oz. and plate	$15.00
1630	Tumbler, split	$12.00
1630	Tumbler, 8½ oz, footed table	$8.00
1630	Tumbler, 10 oz., table	$8.00
1630	Ice Tea, 10 oz., footed	$10.00
1630½	Tumbler, table	$6.00
1630	Tumbler, wine	$6.00
1630	Tumbler, whiskey	$6.00
1630	Wine, 3 oz.	$10.00
1630	Wine, 2 oz.	$8.00

Tableware

No.	Item	Price
1630	Almond, individual	$15.00
1630	Bowl, 4½", high foot	$15.00
1630	Brandy, pousse-café, ¾ oz.	$6.00
1630	Butter and Cover	$28.00
1630	Catsup, ground stopper	$45.00
1630	Celery, tall	$32.00
1630	Tray, celery	$20.00
1630	Cream	$15.00
1630	Cream, Hotel	$15.00
1630	Crushed Ice and Plate	$54.00
1630	Custard	$5.00
1630½	Custard	$5.00
1630	Decanter, ground stopper	$78.00
1630	Egg	$20.00
1630	Bowl, finger	$10.00
1630	Horseradish Jar and Spoon	$48.00
1630	Ice Cream, high foot	$10.00
1630	Ice Jug, 3 quart	$75.00
1630	Ice Jug, ½-gallon	$75.00
1630	Ice Jug, 3 pint	$65.00
1630	Ice Jug, quart	$57.00
1630	Jug	$75.00
1630	Mayonnaise and Plate	$25.00
1630	Molasses Can	
	Ewer nickle top	$75.00
	Ewer silver-plated top	$87.00
	Brittania top	$75.00
1630	Molasses Can Plate	$8.00
1630	Mustard and Cover	$22.00

Alexis, 1630

1630 Nappy, 4½"....$7.00
1630 Nappy, 5"....$7.00
1630 Nappy, 7"....$8.00
1630 Nappy, 8"....$10.00
1630 Nappy, 9"....$12.00
1630 Bowl, nut....$16.00
1630 Oil, 2 oz., drop or ground stopper....$23.00
1630 Oil, 4 oz., drop or ground stopper....$25.00
1630 Oil, 6 oz, drop or ground stopper....$25.00
1630 Tray, olive....$6.00
1630½ Pitcher, tall, ½ gallon....$75.00
1630 Salt, flat, table....$6.00
1630 Salt, flat, individual....$6.00
1630 Shaker No. 1, pair
heavy nickle top....$26.00
silver-plated top....$30.00
non-corrosive top....$30.00
1630 Shaker No. 2, pair
heavy nickle top....$26.00
silverplated top....$30.00
non-corrosive top....$30.00
glass top....$38.00
1630 Spoon....$15.00
1630 Sugar....$15.00
1630 Sugar and Cream....$30.00
1630 Sugar, Hotel....$18.00
1630 Sugar Sifter
silver-plated top....$42.00
1630 Toothpick....$20.00
1630 Water Bottle....$67.00
1630 Vase, 9"....$52.00
1630 Vase, Sweet Pea....$58.00
1630 Vase, Nasturtium....$47.00

Allegro, Cutting 748

1935 – 1943

Stemware, 85

6013 Goblet..$25.00
6013 Goblet, low....$20.00
6013 Saucer Champagne....$22.00
6013 Sherbet, low....$20.00
6013 Cocktail....$20.00
1184 Cocktail, old fashioned, plain....$16.00
6013 Claret....$30.00
6013 Wine....$30.00
6013 Cordial....$40.00
6013 Oyster Cocktail....$18.00
6013 Ice Tea, footed....$20.00
6013 Juice, footed....$18.00
701 Tumbler....$16.00
701 Tumbler, sham, plain....$18.00
1184 Tumbler....$16.00

Tableware I, 287

766 Bowl, finger, plain....$14.00
2533 Bowl, handled, 10"....$45.00
6013 Comport, 5"....$35.00
2533 Candlestick, duo....$65.00
5000 Jug....$225.00
2337 Plate, 6"....$7.00
2337 Plate, 7"....$9.00
2337 Plate, 8"....$10.00

Allegro, Decoration 672

1966 – 1970

Stemware, 132

6107 Goblet....$25.00
6107 Sherbet....$25.00
6107 Clare....$28.00
6107 Wine, tulip....$25.00
6107 Liqueur....$30.00
6107 Ice Tea, footed....$23.00 – 25.00
2337 Plate, 7", narrow optic....$10.00

Aloha, Cutting 805

1940 – 1943

Stemware, 98

6027 Goblet....$20.00
6027 Saucer Champagne....$18.00
6027 Sherbet, low....$14.00
6027 Cocktail....$16.00
6027 Wine....$22.00
6027 Cordial....$30.00
6027 Oyster Cocktail....$12.00
6027 Ice Tea, footed....$18.00
6027 Juice, footed....$12.00

Tableware I, 304

4021 Bowl, finger....$18.00
6023 Candlestick, duo, pair....$75.00
6011 Jug....$175.00
2364 Lily Pond, 12"....$60.00
2337 Plate, 7"....$7.00
2337 Plate, 8"....$10.00

Alta, Cutting 924 2863 Tumbler,

1974 – 1975

Stemware, 152

2863 Old Fashioned, 11 oz., double....$15.00
2863 Highball, 13 oz.....$15.00

Ambassador, Decoration 637

1956 – 1970

Stemware, 112

6065 Goblet....$30.00
6065 Sherbet....$28.00
6065 Cocktail....$30.00
6065 Wine....$30.00
6065 Seafood....$28.00
6065 Cordial....$35.00
6065 Ice Tea, footed....$30.00
6065 Juice, footed....$26.00
2337 Plate, 7"....$10.00
2337 Plate, 8"....$12.00

American, 2056

1915 – 1986

Stemware, 42 – 43

2056 Goblet, low....$16.00
2056 Sherbet, low, flared....$12.00
2056 Sherbet, low, regular....$12.00
2056 Sherbet, handled....$125.00/market
2056 Cocktail, footed....$16.00
2056 Oyster Cocktail....$14.00
2056 Lemonade, handled, footed....$150.00/market
2056 Ice Tea, footed....$20.00
2056 Dessert, hexagon, footed....$16.00
2056 Sundae....$15.00
2056 Tumbler, 9 oz., footed....$14.00
2056 Juice, footed....$18.00
2056 Goblet....$22.00
2056 Sherbet, high, flared....$16.00
2056 Sherbet, high, regular....$14.00
2056 Old Fashioned Cocktail....$17.00
2056 Claret....$67.00
2056 Tumbler, No 141 baby....$400.00/market
2056 Tumbler, ice tea, flared....$24.00
2056 Tumbler, table, flared....$23.00
2056 Tumbler, ice tea, regular
crystal....$22.00
green....$86.00
2056 Tumbler, table, regular
crystal....$18.00
green....$75.00
2056 Tumbler, 5 oz, regular....$14.00
2056 Tumbler, whiskey....$20.00
2056 Wine, footed, hexagon foot..$24.00

Tableware I, 10 – 35; II, 16 – 33

Almond, 3¾", oval....$34.00
Appetizer, individual square..$43.00
Appetizer Set, 7-piece....$395.00
Included 10½", oblong tray and 6 individual square appetizers
Appetizer Set, 7-piece....$445.00
Included 2528 11¾", tray and 6 individual square appetizers
Ashtray, 2⅞", square....$12.00
Ashtray, oval with match stand
crystal....$38.00
ebony....$75.00
2056 Ashtray, 5"....$125.00
Banana Split.... market
Basket, reed handle....$125.00
2056 Mug, beer, reintroduction....$95.00
2056 Bell....$850.00/market
Boat, 8½", small
crystal....$22.00
green....$84.00
Boat, large
crystal....$28.00
green....$110.00
Sauce Boat and plate....$75.00
Bonbon, 3-toed
crystal....$37.00
amber....$135.00
blue....$150.00
canary....$150.00
ruby....$78.00
Bottle, bitters and tube....$157.00
Bottle, catsup and stopper...$160.00
Bottle, cordial and stopper...$195.00
Bottle, water....$700.00/market
Boudoir Set, 5-piece....$1,245.00
Included 10½", oblong tray, quart jug, 7¼", candle, match box, 8 oz. tumbler
Boudoir Set, 5-piece....$650.00
Included 10½", tray, quart jug, 7¼", candle, oval ashtray
Boudoir Set, 8-piece
Included 10", comb and brush tray, bonbon, large cigarette and cover, small cigarette and cover, confection and cover, small cologne, square puff box, 5", oval pin tray
amber....market
blue....market
canary....market
2056 Bowl, baby, No. 142, flared....$65.00
2056 Bowl, baby, No. 150,

straight $65.00
2056 Bowl, handled, serving
crystal $54.00
ruby..................................$98.00
Bowl, 7", cupped...................$75.00
Bowl, finger and plate $96.00
Bowl, 12", footed, fruit $250.00
Bowl, 16", footed, fruit $235.00
Bowl, 8", footed, handled ...$125.00
2056 Bowl, 8", footed, round $135.00
2056 Bowl, 7", footed, square $200.00
Bowl, 8½", handled $74.00
Bowl, 11¾", oval $65.00
Bowl, oval, vegetable $42.00
Bowl, 2-part, vegetable $46.00
Bowl, 14", punch, high foot .$545.00
Bowl, 14", punch, low foot ..$395.00
Bowl, 18", punch, low foot ..$600.00
Bowl, 11½", rolled edge $78.00
Bowl, 3½", rose.....................$35.00
Bowl, 5", rose........................$47.00
Bowl, 13", shallow, fruit......$165.00
Bowl, 10½", 3-toed $48.00
Bowl, 7¼", watercress and
plate, 8"...........................$125.00
2056 Bowl, wedding and cover
crystal $115.00
milk glass $125.00
Box, pomade and cover $695.00
Box, round puff and cover ..$500.00
Box, 3", square puff and cover
crystal $450.00
amber...............................$800.00
blue $900.00
canary $900.00
Box, hair receiver and cover
crystal $800.00
amber............................$1,100.00
blue $1,200.00
canary $1,200.00
Box, 3½", hair pin and
cover.............................$1,000.00
Box, match, same as
hair pin $1,000.00
Box, 4¾"x 3½", cigarette and
cover $95.00
Box, 5½", jewel and cover ..$475.00
Box, 6", handkerchief and
cover $375.00
Box, 9½", glove and cover ..$850.00
Box, cigarette, small
amber...............................$900.00
blue $1,000.00
canary $1,000.00
Box, cigarette, large
amber............................$1,400.00
blue $1,500.00
canary $1,500.00
Box, confection and cover
amber ....$900.00.
blue $1,000.00
canary $1,000.00
Box, 3-part, candy and
cover $125.00
Box, flower $27.00
Butter, oblong and cover $48.00
Butter, round and cover......$125.00
2056 Cake Stand, footed $110.00
Candelabra, duo with UDP,
pair $450.00
Candlestick, duo, pair $345.00
2056 Candlestick, chamber $65.00
Candlestick, 3", pair $46.00
Candlestick, 6", pair $97.00

2056½ Candlestick, 7", pair $300.00
Candlestick, 7¼", pair.........$295.00
Candlestick, twin, pair $158.00
2056 Candy, 7", footed and cover
crystal $64.00
ruby.................................$175.00
Jar, candy and cover.............$64.00
Celery, 6", tall $68.00
Celery, 10"............................$48.00
Centerpiece, 11", 3-cornered...$77.00
Centerpiece, 9½" $65.00
Centerpiece, 11" $95.00
Centerpiece, 15" $225.00
Cheese and Cracker $110.00
Chiffonier, 2¼", x 4½", x 3¼",
........................$3,000.00/market
Coaster, allover design,
3¾"....................................$20.00
2056 Coaster, rayed bottom $16.00
2056½ Cologne, 6 oz., small, DS
crystal $135.00
amber $500.00
blue $700.00
canary $700.00
Cologne, 8 oz., large, DS ...$145.00
Comport, 5", high foot $45.00
Comport and Cover, 5",
high foot $65.00
Comport, 8½"........................$95.00
Comport, 9½"........................$95.00
Condiment Set, 5-piece $250.00
Included 10", oval tray, two 5 oz. oil bottles, DS, two no. 1 shakers, "W" tops
Condiment Set, 6-piece $500.00
Included 9", cloverleaf tray, two 5 oz. oil bottles, DS, 2 no. 2 shakers (FGT), mustard, cover, and spoon
2056 Condiment Bottle and
Stopper $160.00
2056 Cup, 614 punch......................$12.00
Cream, 4¾ oz., individual $15.00
Cream, 9½ oz. $22.00
Cream, 3 oz. tea $14.00
Crushed Fruit and
Cover..............$1,500.00/market
Spoon, crushed fruit.$800.00/market
Cup, custard flared, punch ...$18.00
Cup, custard regular, punch ..$17.00
Cup, footed, coffee $14.00
Decanter and Stopper,
24 oz. $185.00
Decanter Set, 7-piece $295.00
Included 24 oz. decanter and stopper and six 2 oz. whiskeys.
Decanter Set, 8-piece $450.00
Included 10½", oblong tray, 24 oz. decanter and stopper, and six 2 oz. whiskeys.
Floating Garden, 10" $85.00
Floating Garden, 11½"..........$95.00
2056½ Pot, flower, perforated,
cover...............$1,600.00/market
Hotel Cracked
Ice $3,000.00/market
Ice Bucket with metal handle ...$95.00
Ice Cream Tray, 5½".............$67.00
Ice Cream Saucer, 5¼" $67.00
Ice Cream Tray, 3½"
square handled $48.00
Ice Cream Set, 7-piece $450.00
Included 10½", oblong tray and six handled ice creams

Ice Dish, priced with liner $75.00
Liners: tomato juice, crab meat, fruit cocktail
Ice Tub, small and 8", plate....$95.00
Ice Tub, large and 9", plate...$115.00
Jar, jam and cover...............$475.00
2056 Pot, jam and cover $68.00
2056 Jam Pot Set..........................$160.00
2056 Jar, cookie and cover $265.00
Jar, cracker and cover.........$265.00
Jar, pickle and cover...........$475.00
Jar, pretzel and cover $265.00
Jar, straw and cover $325.00
Jelly, footed, flared $110.00
Jelly, footed, regular $35.00
Jelly, footed, regular, cover ..$48.00
Jelly, deep, flared..................$65.00
Jelly, deep, regular $65.00
Jug, 7¼", quart $125.00
Jug, 6½", 3-pint, ice $85.00
Jug, 8", 3-pint.......................$135.00
Jug, 8", ½ gallon $135.00
2056½ Jug, 8¼", ½ gallon, ice
crystal $225.00
green $800.00/market
2056½ Jug, ½ gallon (69 oz.), ice lip..$150.00
Lamp, candle, 3", pair...........$350.00
candle, peg candle insert, wax pot, shade
Lamp, 12", hurricane, base and
chimney, pair.....$800.00/market
Dish, lemon $36.00
Dish, lemon and cover..........$68.00
Lily Pond, 12".......................$95.00
Marmalade, cover and
spoon $145.00
Mayonnaise, 2-part, 2 ladles...$64.00
Mayonnaise, plate, ladle $75.00
2056 Mayonnaise, footed and
ladle..................................$53.00
Molasses Can, 11 oz., ewer
nickel top, glass handle ..market
Molasses Can, 6 oz.,
metal handle ....market
Mug, 12 oz. beer $95.00
2056 Mug, 12 oz. tankard $95.00
2056 Mug, youth........................... $55.00
Mug, Tom and Jerry $55.00
Mustard, cover and spoon $78.00
2056 Napkin Ring $58.00
Nappy, 4¼", regular $35.00
Nappy, 4½", regular
crystal $18.00
green.................................$75.00
Nappy, 4¾", fruit $18.00
Nappy, 5", regular $15.00
Nappy, 5", regular, and cover..$25.00
Nappy, 6", regular $24.00
Nappy, 7", regular $28.00
Nappy, 8", regular
crystal $28.00
green $125.00
Nappy, 8", deep.....................$75.00
Nappy, 10", deep $95.00
Nappy, 4¾", flared................$37.00
Nappy, 6", flared $40.00
Nappy, 7", flared $50.00
Nappy, 8", flared $65.00
Nappy, 9", flared $75.00
Nappy, 10", flared $95.00
Nappy, 4½", handled,
regular $15.00
Nappy, 4½", handled,
square $15.00

Nappy, 5", handled, 3-cornered $15.00
Nappy, 5½", handled, flared $28.00
Nappy, 7", shallow................$65.00
Nappy, 8", shallow................$75.00
Nappy, 10", shallow..............$95.00
Oil, 5 oz., DS, G S.................$64.00
Oil, 7 oz., DS, GS..................$75.00
Olive, 6"..................................$18.00
Old Fashioned Set, 9-piece..$700.00
Included 12", round tray, 24 oz. decanter and stopper, one bitters bottle and tube, and six 6 oz. old fashioned cocktails
Oval, 4½", also known as Almond $32.00
Oval, 9"..................................$75.00
Oval, 10"................................$85.00
Oval, 11½"..............................$95.00
2056 Party Server, 2 spoons..........$40.00
Pickle, 8"................................$22.00
2056 Picture Frame........................$42.00
Pitcher, pint $48.00
Plate, 6", bread and butter....$10.00
Plate, cream soup..................$15.00
Plate, crescent salad.............$98.00
Plate, 6", ice tea $10.00
Plate, 6", syrup......................$10.00
Plate, 6½", finger bowl..........$18.00
Plate, 7", salad.......................$15.00
Plate, 8", salad.......................$20.00
Plate, 8", crushed ice tub......$25.00
Plate, 8", watercress.............$46.00
Plate, 8½", salad $23.00
Plate, 9", sandwich $33.00
Plate, 9", ice tub....................$24.00
Plate 9½", dinner $25.00
2056 Plate, 10", handled, cake
crystal $55.00
ruby..................................$125.00
Plate, 10", square................$225.00
Plate, 10½", sandwich $35.00
Plate, 11½", sandwich $38.00
Plate, 12", footed cake $56.00
Plate, 13½", oval, torte $98.00
Plate, 14", torte $54.00
Plate, 18", torte $175.00
Plate, 20", torte $225.00
Plate, 24", torte....................market
2056 Plate, youth $85.00
Platter, 10½", oval $55.00
Platter, 12", oval $65.00
Preserve, handled and cover.................................$125.00
979 Punch Ladle, plastic.............$20.00
Relish, 2-part.........................$30.00
Relish, 3-part.........................$65.00
2056½ Relish, combination, 3-part...$68.00
Relish, 4-part, square $195.00
2056½ Relish, 4-division $70.00
Salad Set, 3-piece, wooden...$150.00
Included 14" torte plate; 10", deep nappy; salad bowl, and salad fork and spoon
Salt, individual $12.00
Salt, table.............................market
Salver, 10", round $175.00
Salver, 10", square $235.00
Saucer, 6", plain center...........$6.00
Shaker, No. 1, 3", priced as a pair
heavy nickel top................$50.00
heavy silver top................$55.00
Fostoria glass top $75.00
silver plated top $65.00
glass disc with heavy nickel band...................$75.00
2056½ Shaker, No. 2, 3¼", priced as a pair
heavy nickel top................$50.00
heavy silver top.................$55.00
pearl disc, non-corrosive band top........................$75.00
Fostoria glass top $75.00
silver top...........................$65.00
chrome A top $32.00
2056 Shaker Set, individual
Fostoria glass top $95.00
chrome C top $69.00
Shaker, 2", individual, priced as pair
Fostoria glass top $54.00
chrome C top $38.00
Shaker Set, 3-piece
Included individual shaker tray and 2 individual shakers
Fostoria glass top $95.00
silver/chrome tops...........$69.00
2056 Shaker, sugar or cheese $125.00
2056 Shrimp Bowl $425.00
Smoker Set, 5-piece $125.00
Included cigarette box, cover and four 2⅞", square ashtrays
Soup, handled cream $68.00
Spoon.....................................$65.00
Sugar and Cover, 6¼"..........$40.00
Sugar, 5¼", handled and cover $45.00
Sugar, 2½", individual..........$12.00
Sugar and Cream Set, individual, 3-piece...............................$42.00
Included sugar and cream tray, individual sugar and cream
Sugar and Cream Set, tea, 3-piece...............................$48.00
Included sugar and cream tray, tea, sugar and cream
Sugar, 2¼", tea $18.00
2056½ Syrup, 6 oz., screw top, NP ....market
2056 Syrup, 6½ oz., sani-cut server...$195.00
Syrup, 6½ oz., dripcut $87.00
Syrup, 10 oz., cover and plate $300.00
Tid Bit, 3-toed $32.00
Tid Bit Set with metal handle ..$65.00
2056 Toddler Set...........$665.00/market
Tom and Jerry Set, 9-piece...$665.00
Included 12" footed fruit bowl and 8 Tom and Jerry Mugs
Toothpick, 2⅜"......................$22.00
2056 Topper Ashtray
crystal $28.00
milk glass $57.00
2056 Topper, 2½", for matches
crystal $32.00
milk glass $58.00
2056 Topper, 3", cigarette holder
crystal $47.00
milk glass $58.00
2056 Topper, 4"
crystal $74.00
milk glass $125.00
2056 Tray, handled, muffin
crystal $54.00
ruby.................................$125.00
2056 Tray, handled, utility
crystal $54.00
ruby.................................$125.00
Tray, individual, shaker $26.00
Tray, 5", oval, pin ..$300.00/market
Tray, 5½", oval $300.00/market
2056½ Tray, 5", oblong
crystal $250.00
colors $400.00/market
Tray, 5", x 7", candy $300.00
Tray, 6", oval pin...................$65.00
Tray, 9", cloverleaf condiment $250.00
Tray, 10", to 10½", oblong
crystal ....$175.00.
amber..............................$300.00
blue $350.00
canary $350.00
Tray, 10½", oblong.............$175.00
Tray, 10", oval $115.00
2056½ Tray, 10", condiment tray ..$115.00
Tray, 10", square $225.00
Tray, 10½", oval..................$115.00
Tray, 10½", oval, comb and brush or condiment...................$115.00
Tray, 10⅝", ice cream $175.00
Tray, 11½", oval...................market
Tray, 12", oval $65.00
Tray, 12", round $225.00
2056½ Tray, 13½", oval, ice cream..market
Tray, cake with metal handle..$85.00
Tray, handled, lunch $95.00
Tray, sugar and cream..........$18.00
Tricorne, 6½,", 3-toed $96.00
Urn, 6", square......................$75.00
Urn, 7½, square $95.00
2056½ Vase, bagged, ...$1,800.00/market
Vase, 6", footed, cupped, bud..$30.00
Vase, 6", flared......................$52.00
Vase, 7", flared, high foot for punch bowl.................$160.00
Vase, 8", flared $67.00
Vase, 9½", flared.................$250.00
Vase, 10", cupped $225.00
Vase 10", flared.....................$95.00
Vase, small, porch...............market
Vase, large, porch ....market
Vase, 12", square, footed.....market
Vase, 6", straight $68.00
Vase, 8", straight $65.00
Vase, 10", straight $95.00
Vase, 12", straight $145.00
Vase, sweetpea $75.00
Vase, 9", to 12", swung $200.00
Vase, 14", to 16", swung $300.00
Vase, 18", to 20", swung $400.00/market
Vase, 23" to 26", swung $600.00/market
2056 Vase, 6", footed, flared, bud
crystal $30.00
aqua milk glass................$175.00
peach milk glass.............$175.00
milk glass $42.00
ruby...................................$67.00
2056 Vase, 8½", cupped, footed, bud $42.00
2056 Vase, 8½", flared, footed, bud
crystal $42.00
milk glass $75.00
2056 Vase, 9", square, footed
crystal $95.00
milk glass $135.00
Watercress Set, 2-piece.......$125.00
Included 8" plate, and 7¼", 3-toed water cress bowl
2056 Youth Set............................$195.00

American Beauty, Cutting 858

1958 – 1965

Stemware, 115

6077 Goblet..........$35.00
6077 Sherbet................$32.00
6077 Wine/ Cocktail...................$36.00
6077 Cordial....................................$48.00
6077 Ice Tea, footed $35.00
6077 Juice, footed $32.00
2337 Plate, 7" $12.00
2337 Plate, 8" $14.00

American Lady, 5056

1934 – 1971

Stemware, 62

5056 Goblet
 crystal...............$35.00
 burgundy/ amethyst..........$50.00
 regal blue/empire green...........$150.00
5056 Sherbet
 crystal $30.00
 burgundy/amethyst..........$45.00
 regal blue/ empire green.................$125.00
5056 Cocktail
 crystal $32.00
 burgundy/amethyst..........$45.00
 regal blue/empire green ..$95.00
5056 Claret
 crystal $45.00
 burgundy/amethyst..........$55.00
 regal blue/ empire green................$165.00
5056 Wine
 crystal $42.00
 burgundy/amethyst..........$55.00
 regal blue/ empire green................$150.00
5056 Cordial
 crystal $75.00
 burgundy/amethyst..........$95.00
 regal blue/ empire green................$195.00
5056 Oyster Cocktail
 crystal $30.00
 amethyst............................$40.00
5056 Ice Tea, footed
 crystal $35.00
 burgundy/amethyst..........$50.00
 regal blue/ empire green................$150.00
5056 Juice, footed
 crystal $30.00
 burgundy/amethyst..........$45.00
 regal blue/empire green ..$95.00
2337 Plate, 7"
 crystal $10.00
 amethyst............................$30.00
2337 Plate, 8", crystal only.............$12.00

American Milestones

1971 – 1976

Tableware II, 231 – 140

Old Glory $55.00
Star Spangled Banner...$55.00
Washington Crossing the Delaware.....................$55.00
The Spirit of '76......................$55.00
Shrine of Democracy $55.00
One Nation Under God........ $55.00

Amherst, Decoration 58

1926

Tableware I, 325

2297 Bowl A, 10", shallow............$100.00
2324 Bowl, 10" $135.00
2315 Bowl A, 10½", deep.............$125.00
2297 Bowl A, 12", deep $125.00
2324 Candlestick, 4", pair $110.00
2324 Candlestick, 9", pair $200.00
2250 Jar, candy and cover, ½ pound $125.00
2331 Box, candy and cover..........$150.00
2329 Centerpiece, 11" $175.00
2327 Comport, 7"..........................$125.00
2315 Mayonnaise/Grapefruit........$50.00
2283 Plate, 7" $15.00
2283 Plate, 8" $18.00
2283 Plate, 10" $48.00
2283 Plate, 13" $75.00
2315 Sugar and Cream.................$195.00
2287 Tray, handled, lunch $145.00
2276 Vanity Set $350.00

Andover, Decoration 665

1964 – 1974

Stemware, 122

6097 Goblet $38.00
6097 Sherbet $34.00
6097 Cocktail $40.00
6097 Claret $42.00
6097 Cordial....................................$45.00
6097 Ice Tea, footed $38.00
6097 Juice, footed $34.00
6097 Wine...$40.00

Tableware

2337 Plate, 7" $12.00
2337 Plate, 8" $15.00

Anniversary, Decoration 634

1954 – 1970

Stemware, 108

6055½ Goblet......$30.00
6055½ Sherbet $24.00
6055½ Cocktail......................................$26.00
6055½ Claret/Wine $34.00
6055½ Oyster Cocktail...........................$22.00
6055½ Cordial $38.00
6055½ Ice Tea, footed $30.00
6055½ Juice, footed $24.00
2337 Plate, 7" $12.00
2337 Plate, 8" $15.00

Announcement, Decoration 666

1964 – 1982

Stemware, 128

6103 Goblet....$25.00
6103 Sherbet...$22.00
6103 Brandy $26.00
6103 Tulip Wine..............................$27.00
6103 Claret $27.00
6103 Ice Tea, footed $25.00

Tableware II, 195

2785 Bowl, 10", footed...................$35.00
2337 Plate, 7" $9.00
2337 Plate, 8" $12.00
2785 Relish, 2-part $32.00
2785 Relish, 4-part $35.00
2785 Relish, 5-part $42.00
2785 Sugar and Cream, footed......$35.00

Antique, Decoration 56

1926

Color on crystal:
A, yellow and black;
B, red and black;
C, blue and red

Tableware I, 324

2267 Bowl, 7"..$65.00
2324 Bowl, 10" $120.00
2297 Bowl A, 10", shallow..............$90.00
2297 Bowl A, 12", deep $95.00
2324 Candlestick, 2", pair $125.00
2324 Candlestick, 4", pair $95.00
2324 Candlestick, 6"....................$125.00
2324 Candlestick, 9"....................$165.00
2331 Box, candy and cover..........$125.00
2219 Jar, candy and cover, ½ pound $100.00
2250 Jar, candy and cover, ½ pound $95.00
2329 Centerpiece, 11" $125.00
2329 Centerpiece, 13" $150.00
2327 Comport, 7"............................$65.00
2315 Mayonnaise/Grapefruit........$45.00
2283 Plate, 7" $14.00
2283 Plate, 8" $18.00
2283 Plate, 9" $28.00
2283 Plate, 13", cupped.................$68.00
2347 Puff and Cover $150.00
2287 Tray, lunch $125.00
2276 Vanity Set $225.00

Appetizer, Buffet, Relish

1915 – 1970

Useful & Ornamental, 14 – 19

2528 Appetizer Set.......................$400.00
 2528 Appetizer Tray and six 2391 Appetizer Dishes, two each of regal blue, burgundy, and empire green, or six 2056 Appetizer Dishes in crystal
2038 Banana Split $15.00
2517 Bonbon
 crystal $15.00
 regal blue $25.00
 burgundy........................... $25.00
 empire green......................$26.00
 ruby.....................................$26.00
 lavender..............................$28.00
 teal green $28.00
 ruby.................................... $28.00
2661 Buffet Set, 3-piece.................$65.00
 Included: 5-part server, and sauce dish with or without cover
2662 Buffet Set, 3-piece.................$60.00
 Included: 5-part server, and sauce dish with or without cover
2663 Buffet Set: 4-part server and cover $65.00
2375 Canape Set, see Fairfax
2492 Canape Set, see Bar and Refreshment
2276 Cheese and Cracker Set: covered cheese and 11" plate
 crystal $55.00
 amber..................................$58.00

green $65.00
ebony $58.00
2368 Cheese and Cracker
crystal $57.00
rose $68.00
azure $68.00
green $65.00
amber $62.00
blue $95.00
orchid $78.00
topaz $65.00
2511 Cheese and Cracker with or without center board
crystal $34.00
regal blue $85.00
burgundy $78.00
empire green $95.00
amber $65.00
topaz $65.00
2535 Cheese and Cracker with board $48.00
2528 Cocktail Tray, 11¾", x 10¾" ... $200.00
2000 Condiment Tray
rose $32.00
azure $32.00
green $32.00
amber $27.00
blue $38.00
2675 Egg Plate $60.00
4147 Jam Set, 3 pieces $54.00
Included: 4147 oblong tray, two jam pots and covers, cover could be notched for marmalade spoon
2517 Lemon
crystal $15.00
regal blue $25.00
burgundy $25.00
empire green $26.00
ruby $26.00
2287 Tray, lunch, center handled
crystal $34.00
amber $38.00
canary $65.00
green $45.00
rose $45.00
azure $54.00
ebony $40.00
blue $65.00
orchid $65.00
amber, SO $42.00
green, SO $45.00
orchid, SO $68.00
2342 Tray, lunch, octagon, center handled
crystal $34.00
amber $38.00
green $45.00
rose $45.00
azure $54.00
orchid $65.00
blue $65.00
2318 Relish Set, 7 pieces
Included: 13", tray, crimped tumbler, five partitions
crystal $75.00
green $95.00
2462 Relish, 5-part
crystal $55.00
green $65.00
amber $74.00
rose $65.00
topaz/gold tint $65.00
2462 Relish, 5-part, metal handle
crystal $55.00
amber $74.00
green $65.00
rose $65.00
topaz $65.00
2514 Relish, 5-part, square $54.00
2664 Relish, 4-part, server $40.00
2497 Seafood Cocktail
crystal $28.00
regal blue $47.00
burgundy $47.00
empire green $45.00
silver mist $30.00
ruby $47.00
2330 Sherbet and Plate, one piece
amber $18.00
green $18.00
2705 Snack Set, 3-piece $48.00
Included: two snack bowls on satin finished wood tray
4152 Snack Bowl, see Small Bowls, Mints, and Nuts
2015 Spoon Tray $50.00
1851 Sugar and Cream $40.00
2133 Sugar and Cream $32.00
2255 Sugar and Cream
amber $34.00
blue $42.00
green $36.00
2321 Sugar and Cream, see Priscilla
2321 Sugar and Cream set: 2321 sugar, bouillon, 2321 cream, condiment tray
rose $65.00
azure $65.00
green $65.00
amber $60.00
2497½ Sugar and Cream set,
crystal $65.00
regal blue $140.00
burgundy $125.00
empire green $140.00
silver mist $75.00
4020 Sugar and Cream, footed
crystal $45.00
amber base $50.00
green base $50.00
wisteria base $75.00
ebony base $65.00
rose bowl $65.00
topaz bowl $65.00
2517 Sweetmeat
crystal $15.00
regal blue $25.00
burgundy $25.00
empire green $25.00
ruby $28.00
2491 Tea Warmer
crystal $47.00
amber $55.00
topaz/gold tint $58.00
2056 Turntable, 14", wooden $20.00
2056 Turntable, 18", wooden $20.00
2440 Turntable, 13", wooden $20.00
2510 Turntable, 15", wooden $20.00

Apple Blossom, Cutting 866

1918 – 1928

Stemware, 30

863 Goblet, 9 oz $8.00
805 Goblet, 9 oz. $8.00
805 Cocktail $6.00
863 Cocktail, 3½ oz. $6.00
803 Comport, 5", footed and cover $14.00
803 Comport, 5" $10.00
803 Comport, 6" $12.00
805 Saucer Champagne $10.00
863 Saucer Champagne $8.00
805 Sherbet $6.00
863 Wine $8.00
701 Tumbler, 14 oz. and 5" plate $14.00
889 Tumbler, 5 oz. $5.00
833 Tumbler, 8 oz. $6.00
4011 Tumbler, 12 oz. $9.00
127 Tumbler, handled $18.00
4011 Tumbler, 12 oz., handled $18.00
858 Tumbler, 14 oz. $10.00
858 Tumbler, 14 oz., handled $18.00
833 Tumbler, sham, 8 oz. $6.00
4011½ Tumbler, table $6.00
820 Tumbler, table $6.00
858 Tumbler, table $6.00

Tableware

766 Bowl, finger $9.00
766 Plate, 6" $5.00
880 Bonbon, 4½" $8.00
1904 Bonbon and Cover $14.00
2136 Bonbon and Cover $14.00
896 Bowl and Cover $12.00
2219 Jar, candy and cover, ¼ lb. ... $20.00
2219 Jar, candy and cover, ½ lb. ... $22.00
2219 Jar, candy and cover, 1 lb. ... $24.00
1697 Carafe and Tumbler $97.00
1590 Cheese, 4½" and plate $18.00
5051 Cheese and Plate, footed $18.00
2118 Cologne and Stopper $95.00
2241 Cologne and Stopper $95.00
1598 Custard $12.00
863 Almond $18.00
863 Fruit $12.00
1736 Plate, 6", fruit $6.00
945 Grapefruit and Liner $25.00
766 Ice Tea, footed $8.00
300 Jug, 7" $75.00
303 Jug, 7' $50.00
1236 Jug, 6" $76.00
1743 Jug and Cover $95.00
2100 Jug, Cut 138½ $76.00
2104 Jug and Tumbler $95.00
1281 Lemon Dish, 5" $7.00
1733 Marmalade and Cover $18.00
2138 Mayonnaise and Plate $22.00
1831 Mustard and Cover $16.00
803 Nappy, 5", footed $10.00
803 Nappy, 5", footed and cover . $14.00
803 Nappy, 6", footed $12.00
803 Nappy, 7", footed $14.00
453 Nappy, 4½", handled $8.00
1227 Nappy, 4½" $7.00
1227 Nappy, 8" $14.00
1465 Oil, 5 oz. $35.00
1465 Oil, 7 oz., cut neck $37.00
805 Parfait $22.00
2136 Puff and Cover $85.00
1897 Plate, 7", salad $10.00
1719 Plate, 10½", sandwich $18.00
1848 Plate, 9", sandwich $12.00
880 Salt Dip, footed $18.00
2022 Shaker, FGT, pair $28.00
1480 Sugar and Cream $24.00
1712 Sugar and Cream $24.00
858 Sweetmeat $14.00
2194 Syrup, 8 oz., NT $54.00
2194 Syrup, 12 oz., NT $57.00

922 Toothpick $20.00
2137 Vase, brush $67.00
4069 Vase, 9" $49.00
864 Vase, 7½" $68.00
1761 Vase, 10½" $69.00

Apple Blossom, Decoration 516

1939 – 1942

white enamel on regal blue

Tableware I, 329

4116 Bubble Ball, 4" $46.00
4116 Bubble Ball, 5" $50.00
4116 Bubble Ball, 6" $55.00
4116 Bubble Ball, 7" $64.00

April Love, Cutting 866

1958 – 1959

Stemware, 113

6068 Goblet $22.00
6068 Sherbet $20.00
6068 Wine/Cocktail $22.00
6068 Cordial $30.00
6068 Ice Tea, footed $22.00
6068 Juice, footed $20.00
2337 Plate, 7" $9.00
2337 Plate, 8" $10.00

Arbor, Cutting 184

1926 – 1927

Stemware, 31

869 Cocktail
amber $28.00
green $28.00
blue $30.00
869 Goblet
amber $32.00
green $32.00
blue $34.00
869 Sherbet, high
amber $28.00
green $28.00
blue $30.00
869 Sherbet, low
amber $24.00
green $24.00
blue $28.00
869 Oyster Cocktail
amber $22.00
green $22.00
blue $25.00
869 Parfait
amber $32.00
green $32.00
blue $35.00
5000 Tumbler, 12 oz., 9 oz., and 2½ oz., footed
amber $18.00 – 32.00
green $20.00 – 34.00
blue $22.00 – 38.00
869 Wine
amber $34.00
green $36.00
blue $38.00

Tableware I, 269 – 270

869 Bowl, finger, and 2283 plate $25.00
2297 Bowl, A , 10", shallow $30.00
2324 Bowl, 10", footed $48.00
2297 Bowl, A, 12", deep $35.00
2324 Candlestick, 4", pair $35.00
2324 Candlestick, 9", pair $75.00
2327 Comport, 7" $30.00
2331 Box, candy and cover $35.00
2250 Jar, candy and cover $30.00
2329 Centerpiece, 11" $40.00
2329 Centerpiece, 13" $57.00
5000 Jug $195.00
2283 Plate, 7" $9.00
2283 Plate, 8" $9.00
2283 Plate, 13" $38.00
2315 Sugar and Cream $35.00
2287 Tray, handled lunch $38.00
2276 Vanity Set $95.00
2292 Vase, 8" $45.00
4100 Vase, 8" $48.00
2324 Vase, small urn $60.00

Arcady, Etching 326

1936 – 1954

Stemware, 86

6014 Goblet $35.00
6014 Saucer Champagne $32.00
6014 Sherbet, low $25.00
6014 Cocktail $32.00
6014 Claret $46.00
6014 Wine $42.00
6014 Cordial $55.00
6014 Oyster Cocktail $22.00
6014 Ice Tea, footed $35.00
6014 Tumbler, 9 oz., footed $30.00
6014 Juice, footed $25.00

Tableware I, 228

869 Bowl, finger $35.00
2496 Bowl, 10½", handled $95.00
2470½ Bowl, 10½" $95.00
2496 Bowl, 12", flared $94.00
2496 Candlestick, 5½", pair $115.00
2496 Candlestick, duo, pair $135.00
2496 Candlestick, trindle, pair $150.00
2472 Candlestick, duo, pair $150.00
2482 Candlestick, trindle, pair $185.00
2440 Celery, 11½" $48.00
2400 Comport, 6" $50.00
2440 Cup and Saucer $35.00
2375 Ice Bucket $125.00
5000 Jug $575.00
2375 Mayonnaise, plate, ladle $85.00
2496 Mayonnaise, 2-part $48.00
2440 Pickle, 6½" $42.00
2440 Plate, 6" $12.00
2440 Plate, 7" $20.00
2440 Plate, 8" $22.00
2440 Plate, 9" $40.00
2440 Plate, 10", cake $67.00
2496 Plate, 14", torte $95.00
2496 Relish, 2-part $57.00
2496 Relish, 3-part $65.00
2496 Relish, 4-part $85.00
2419 Relish, 5-part, $95.00
2496 Sauce, 6½", oblong $45.00
2375 Shaker, footed, FGT, pair $150.00
2440 Sugar and Cream $78.00
2496 Sweetmeat $38.00
2496 Tray, 8½", oblong $32.00
4121 Vase, 5" $137.00
4128 Vase, 5" $135.00
2470 Vase, 10" $225.00

Archer, Carving 24

1940 – 1942

Useful & Ornamental, 129

315 Bowl, 9" $95.00

Argus, 2770

1963 – 1982

Stemware, 50

2770 Henry Ford Museum Goblet.
crystal $22.00
olive $22.00
smoke $22.00
cobalt $30.00
ruby $35.00
2770 Sherbet
crystal $18.00
olive $18.00
smoke $18.00
cobalt $24.00
ruby $30.00
2770 Wine
crystal $18.00
olive $18.00
smoke $18.00
cobalt $26.00
ruby $30.00
2770 Ice Tea, footed
crystal $22.00
olive $22.00
smoke $22.00
cobalt $30.00
ruby $35.00
2770 Highball
crystal $18.00
olive $18.00
smoke $18.00
cobalt $30.00
ruby $34.00
2770 Old Fashioned
crystal $18.00
olive $18.00
smoke $18.00
cobalt $30.00
ruby $34.00
2770 Juice Tumbler
crystal $18.00
olive $18.00
smoke $18.00
cobalt $30.00
ruby $34.00

Tableware II, 271, 273

2770 Comport and Cover
crystal $95.00
cobalt blue $125.00
olive $65.00
ruby $125.00
2770 Dessert
crystal $24.00
cobalt blue $27.00
olive $24.00
smoke $24.00
ruby $34.00

Argus, 2770

2770 Plate, 8"
crystal $24.00
cobalt blue $30.00
olive $24.00
smoke $24.00
ruby $56.00
2770 Sugar and Cover, cream
crystal $95.00
cobalt blue $135.00
olive $75.00
ruby $150.00

Ariel, Tracing 93

1940 – 1943

Stemware, 40

892 Goblet $25.00
892 Saucer Champagne $22.00
892 Sherbet, low $20.00
892 Cocktail $22.00
892 Claret $28.00
892 Wine $25.00
892 Cordial $38.00
892 Oyster Cocktail $18.00
892 Ice Tea, footed $25.00
892 Juice, footed $20.00
2337 Plate, 7" $8.00

Arlington, Decoration 70

1927

Amber, blue, green

Tableware I, 327

2324 Bowl, 10" $275.00
2297 Bowl A, 10¼", shallow $200.00
2297 Bowl C, 10½", deep $220.00
2315 Bowl A, 10½" $225.00
2297 Bowl A, 12", deep $250.00
2362 Bowl, 12½" $285.00
2362 Candlestick, 3", pair $135.00
2324 Candlestick, 4", pair $125.00
2324 Candlestick, 6", pair $160.00
2324 Candlestick, 9", pair $225.00
2331 Box, candy and cover $150.00
2219 Jar, candy and cover, ½ pound $135.00
2350 Jar, candy and cover, ½ pound $125.00
2329 Centerpiece, 11" $225.00
2371 Centerpiece, 13", oval $300.00
2368 Cheese and Cracker $150.00
2327 Comport, 7" $125.00
2350 Comport, 8" $135.00
2380 Confection and Cover $125.00
2315 Mayonnaise and Plate $48.00
2347½ Puff and Cover $235.00
2287 Tray, lunch $135.00
2276 Vanity Set $375.00
2292 Vase, 8" $150.00

Arlington, 2694 Milk Glass

1954 – 1965

Tableware II, 209

2694 Ashtray, 7"
white $20.00
aqua $26.00
peach $26.00
2694 Ashtray, 9"
white $24.00
aqua $32.00
peach $32.00
2694 Banana Stand, white $145.00
2694 Bowl, lace white $135.00
2694 Candleholder, duo, pair, white $135.00
2694 Comport, belled, white $135.00
2694 Comport and Cover, flared, white $158.00
2694 Comport, flared, white $145.00
2694 Comport, square, white $145.00
2694 Marmalade, cover and crystal spoon, white $47.00
2694 Mustard, cover and crystal spoon, white $37.00
2694 Oil and Stopper white $48.00
2694 Pepper Mill white $48.00
2694 Salver, white $135.00
2694 Shaker, pair, white $40.00
2694 Shaker and Pepper Mill Set, white $88.00
2694 Spoonholder
white $60.00
aqua $75.00
peach $75.00
2694 Spoonholder and Cover, white $70.00
2694 Syrup, dripcut, white $65.00

Arrow, Cutting 142

1919 – 1924

Stemware, 21

766 Goblet $12.00
766 Saucer Champagne $12.00
766 Fruit $8.00
766 Parfait $18.00
766 Cocktail $9.00
766 Ice Tea, footed, handled $15.00
820 Tumbler, table $5.00
4011 Tumbler, 12 oz. handled $10.00
701 Tumbler, 14 oz. $10.00
4011½ Tumbler, table $6.00
4011 Tumbler, 12 oz. $8.00
1697 Tumbler $5.00

Tableware

blanks shown in other patterns

701 Plate, 5" $6.00
766 Bowl, finger $10.00
766 Plate $6.00
766 Bonbon $15.00
1697 Carafe Set $94.00
2219 Jar, candy and cover, ¼ lb. $24.00
2219 Jar, candy and cover, ½ lb. $28.00
2219 Jar, candy and cover, 1 lb. $32.00
2241 Cologne and Stopper $95.00
766 Comport, 5" $10.00
766 Comport, 6" $12.00
300 7 Jug, plain cover $75.00
303 7 Jug $50.00
2100 7 Jug $85.00
2104 Jug and Tumbler, punty $95.00
1733 Marmalade and Cover $22.00
2138 Mayonnaise, plate, ladle $38.00
1831 Mustard and Cover $20.00
766 Nappy, 5", footed $12.00
766 Nappy, 6", footed $14.00
766 Nappy, 7", footed $16.00
453 Nappy, 4½", handled $10.00
1465 Oil, 5 oz., cut neck $34.00
1465 Oil, 7 oz., cut neck $36.00
1719 Plate, 10½" $18.00
2136 Puff and Cover $85.00
2022 Shaker, FGT, pair $28.00
2133 Sugar and Cream $28.00
2214 Sugar and Cover, with cream $32.00
2194 Syrup, 8 oz., NT $54.00
2194 Syrup, 12 oz., NT $58.00
4069 Vase, 9" $49.00

Artisan, 2703

1958 – 1963

Tableware II, 90

2703 Bowl, 12", 3-cornered
crystal $30.00
colors $75.00
2703 Bowl, 4¾", oblong
crystal $40.00
colors $75.00
2703 Plate, 13", square
crystal $40.00
colors $75.00
2570 Bowl, Shell
crystal $47.00
colors $95.00
2570 Vase, Basket
crystal $47.00
colors $95.00

Arvida, Cutting 185

1927

Amber, green, blue and orchid

Tableware

2315 Bowl A, 10½", footed $45.00
2297 Bowl A, 12", deep $48.00
2372 Candle Block, 2", pair $44.00
2374 Candlestick, 4", pair $48.00
2331 Box, candy and cover $68.00
2329 Centerpiece, 11" $75.00
2329 Centerpiece, 13" $85.00
2371 Centerpiece, 13", oval $95.00
2368 Cheese and Plate $56.00
2327 Comport, 7" $48.00
2362 Comport, 11½" $85.00
2378 Ice Bucket, NP handle $67.00
2378 Ice Bucket, NP handle, drainer, tongs $78.00
2350 Plate, 13" $46.00
2287 Tray, handled, lunch $64.00
4100 Vase, 6" $52.00
4100 Vase, 8" $58.00
4100 Vase, 10" $70.00
4100 Vase, 12" $85.00
4103 Vase, 3" $28.00
4103 Vase, 4" $35.00
4103 Vase, 5" $40.00
4103 Vase, 6" $46.00
4103 Vase, 7" $53.00
4103 Vase, 9" $65.00
2269 Vase, 7" $65.00
2269 Vase, 9" $85.00

Aspen, 2861 Tumbler
1974 – 1982
Stemware, 152
2861 Old Fashioned, 11 oz., double..............$15.00
2861 Highball, 13 oz. ...$15.00

Astrid, 6030
1942 – 1974
Stemware, 100
6030 Goblet..................$30.00
6030 Goblet, low.............$28.00
6030 Saucer Champagne...$28.00
6030 Sherbet, low..............$25.00
6030 Cocktail.....................$25.00
6030 Claret......................$30.00
6030 Wine.........................$30.00
6030 Cordial.................................$35.00
6030 Oyster Cocktail.....................$22.00
6030 Ice Tea, footed $28.00
6030 Juice, footed $23.00

Athenian, Cutting 770
1938 – 1943
Stemware, 82
6011 Goblet......$28.00
6011 Saucer Champagne $26.00
6011 Sherbet, low..$22.00
6011 Cocktail $25.00
6011 Claret $30.00
6011 Wine..$30.00
6011 Brandy $36.00
6011 Cordial $36.00
6011 Oyster Cocktail.......................$20.00
6011 Ice Tea, footed $28.00
6011 Tumbler, 10 oz., footed $820.00
6011 Juice, footed $122.00
4132 Tumbler, 14 oz., sham $15.00
4132 Tumbler, 12 oz., sham $14.00
4132 Tumbler, 9 oz., sham $12.00
4132 Tumbler, 5 oz., sham $9.00
4132 Cocktail, 7½ oz., old fashioned, sham $10.00
4132 Whiskey, 1½ oz., sham.........$10.00

Tableware I, 298
1769 Bowl, finger..........................$14.00
4132 Decanter and Stopper $85.00
4132 Ice Bowl.................................$40.00
2337 Plate, 7" $7.00

Athens (Imported Stemware)
1984 – 1986
Stemware
Goblet..........................$17.50
Wine.............................$17.50
Flute...........................$17.50
Ice Tea...................$17.50

Aura (Imported Stemware)
1984 – 1986
Tableware II, 280 – 281
Goblet..........................$16.00
Wine.............................$16.00
Flute............................$16.00
Ice Tea.......................$16.00

Aurora, Decoration 651
1960 – 1974
Stemware, 120
6092 Goblet $30.00
6092 Sherbet $28.00
6092 Wine..$34.00
6092 Cocktail $30.00
6092 Cordial $40.00
6092 Ice Tea, footed $30.00
6092 Juice, footed $26.00

Tableware
2337 Plate, 7" $10.00
2337 Plate, 8" $12.00

Autumn, Cutting 850
1957 – 1958
Stemware, 113
6068 Goblet......$27.00
6068 Sherbet $24.00
6068 Cocktail $24.00
6068 Wine..$26.00
6068 Seafood $24.00
6068 Cordial $36.00
6068 Ice Tea, footed $28.00
6068 Juice, footed $22.00
2337 Plate, 7" $10.00
2337 Plate, 8" $12.00

Avalon, Etching 85
1929 – 1930
Rose or azure bowl
Stemware, 66
5093 Goblet $38.00
5093 Sherbet, high $34.00
5093 Sherbet, low $30.00
5093 Parfait $45.00
5093 Cocktail $34.00
5093 Claret $48.00
5093 Wine...$45.00
5093 Cordial $75.00
5000 Oyster Cocktail.......................$28.00
5082½ Grapefruit and Liner $50.00
5000 Tumbler, 12 oz., footed $38.00
5000 Tumbler, 9 oz., footed $32.00
5000 Tumbler, 5 oz., footed $30.00
5000 Tumbler, 2½ oz., footed........$34.00

Tableware
869 Bowl, finger and plate $30.00
5000 Jug $395.00
2283 Plate, 6" $15.00
2283 Plate, 7" $18.00
2283 Plate, 8" $20.00

Avalon, Cutting 832
1952 – 1954
Stemware, 105
6049 Goblet $22.00
6049 Sherbet, high $20.00
6049 Sherbet, low $18.00
6049 Parfait $20.00
6049 Cocktail $18.00
6049 Claret $25.00
6049 Wine...$25.00
6049 Cordial $30.00
6049 Oyster Cocktail.......................$14.00
6049 Ice Tea, footed $20.00
6049 Juice, footed $14.00
2337 Plate, 7" $10.00
2337 Plate, 8" $12.00

Azelea, Decoration 30
1928
Gold decoration on green
Tableware I, 317
2297 Bowl A, 12", deep $125.00
2394 Bowl, 12" $134.00
2394 Candlestick, 2", pair $125.00
2324 Candlestick, 4", pair $125.00
2329 Centerpiece, 11" $135.00
2331 Box, candy and cover..........$135.00
2391 Box, cigarette and cover
small...................................$68.00
large $97.00
2350 Comport, 8" $65.00
2400 Comport, 8" $70.00
2380 Confection and Cover $125.00
2378 Ice Bucket, GF handle $125.00
2378 Sugar Pail, GF handle $148.00
2287 Tray, handled lunch $95.00
2373 Vase and Cover
small window $200.00
large window...................$250.00
4100 Vase, 8" $145.00
2385 Vase, 8½", footed, fan $265.00
2378 Whip Cream Pail, GF handle $148.00

Aztec, Carving 6
1938 – 1942
Useful & Ornamental
1895½ Vase, 10"..............$125.00

- B -

Ballerina, Cutting 900
1964 – 1967
Stemware, 128
6103 Goblet $26.00
6103 Sherbet $24.00
6103 Claret $28.00
6103 Tulip Wine................................$28.00
6103 Brandy $26.00
6103 Ice Tea, footed $26.00
2337 Plate, 7" ....
2337 Plate, 8" ....

Ballet, Etching 91
1935 – 1944
Stemware, 18
661 Goblet.........................$8.00
661 Saucer Champagne, 5½ oz..................$8.00
661 Fruit/Sherbet, low, 5½ oz................$7.00
661 Cocktail...............$7.00
661 Claret, 4 oz..............$10.00
661 Wine, 2¾ oz. $10.00
661 Cordial $10.00
4095 Oyster Cocktail........................$7.00
4095 Tumbler, 13 oz., footed $9.00
4095 Tumbler, 10 oz., footed $8.00
4095 Tumbler, 5 oz., footed $7.00
1769 Bowl, finger and 6", plate......$12.00
2337 Plate, 7" $6.00
2337 Plate, 8" $7.00

Ballet, Cutting 828

1952 – 1965

Stemware, 103

6036 Goblet $32.00
6036 Sherbet, high.....$28.00
6036 Sherbet, low $22.00
6036 Parfait $32.00
6036 Cocktail $28.00
6036 Claret-Wine $34.00
6036 Cordial $40.00
6036 Oyster Cocktail......................$20.00
6036 Ice Tea, footed $32.00
6036 Juice, footed $22.00
2337 Plate, 7" $8.00
2337 Plate, 8" $10.00

Banner, Carving 45

1941 – 1943

Useful & Ornamental, 131

2577 Vase, 8½"..................$250.00

Bar and Refreshment

1928 – 1943

Useful & Ornamental, 20-34

319 Bar Bottle and Stopper $48.00
322 Bar Bottle and Stopper $40.00
808 Beer Goblet, 8 oz., 4¾", plain or optic $8.00
810 Beer Goblet, 12 oz., 5⅜", plain $9.00
811 Beer Goblet, 14 oz., 5½", plain $10.00
1861 Beer Mug, 11 oz. or 15 oz.
- all crystal $40.00
- crystal with amber............$47.00
- regal blue $60.00
- empire green handle.........$60.00

2435 Beer Mug, 9 oz
- all crystal $40.00
- crystal with amber............$47.00
- regal blue $60.00
- empire green handle.........$60.00

2464 Beer Mug, 10 oz. $35.00
2487 Beer Mug, 12 oz.
- crystal $35.00
- amber.................................$45.00

2487 Beer Mug, 14 oz.
- crystal $44.00
- amber.................................$48.00
- green..................................$50.00
- rose $50.00
- topaz..................................$48.00
- wisteria $95.00

2493 Beer Mug, 14 oz., tavern
- crystal $45.00
- amber.................................$48.00
- topaz..................................$48.00

Bicentennial Tavern Mug
- crystal $45.00
- amber.................................$48.00

2048 Beer Stein, 18 oz...................$30.00
2490 Beer Stein, 16 oz., crystal
- with amber handle $40.00
- with green handle..............$50.00
- with regal blue handle $60.00

4168 Beverage Set, 6 tumbler $95.00
4168 Beverage Set, 12 tumbler in 6 colors $125.00

2494 Bitters Bottle with Tube
- crystal $67.00
- amber.................................$85.00
- regal blue $95.00
- burgundy............................$95.00
- empire green......................$95.00
- ruby..................................$115.00

2518 Bottle, bitters with tube, may not have been made
- crystal $85.00
- regal blue $125.00
- burgundy..........................$110.00
- empire green....................$110.00
- ruby..................................$125.00
- mother-of-pearl $60.00

2492 Canape Set: fish canape plate, and 4115 3 oz. or 4115½ 4 oz. footed cocktail $32.00
1697 Carafe and 4023 Tumbler
- crystal $38.00
- amber.................................$45.00
- green..................................$50.00
- rose $58.00
- azure $58.00

5068 Cocktail (Stemware, 183) $27.00
5069 Cordial (Stemware, 183).......$34.00
2524 Cocktail Mixer
- crystal $35.00
- regal blue $60.00
- burgundy............................$65.00
- empire green......................$60.00

4169 Cocktail Mixer, used with 4168 sets............................$47.00
2518 Cocktail Shaker, metal top
- crystal $95.00
- regal blue $145.00
- burgundy..........................$145.00
- empire green....................$145.00
- ruby..................................$175.00

2518½ Cocktail Shaker, 7⅜", gold top
- crystal $95.00
- regal blue $145.00
- burgundy..........................$145.00
- empire green....................$145.00
- ruby..................................$145.00

2525 Cocktail Shaker, gold top
- crystal $75.00
- regal blue $145.00
- burgundy..........................$135.00
- empire green....................$175.00
- ruby..................................$145.00

2525½ Cocktail Shaker, gold top
- crystal $75.00
- regal blue $95.00
- ruby....................................$95.00

2528 Cocktail Tray $200.00
2429 Cordial Tray, 12", see Twenty-Four Twenty-Nine
- crystal $125.00
- regal blue $200.00
- burgundy..........................$200.00
- empire green....................$200.00
- silver mist........................$135.00

2429 Cordial Set: 2429 Cordial Tray, 2494 Cordial Bottle, and six 4024 Cordials
- crystal $385.00
- regal blue $650.00
- burgundy..........................$650.00
- empire green....................$650.00
- silver mist........................$395.00

2494 Bottle, cordial
- crystal $85.00
- amber.................................$95.00
- regal blue $150.00
- burgundy..........................$150.00
- empire green....................$160.00
- ruby..................................$175.00
- silver mist..........................$85.00
- mother-of-pearl $85.00

2494 Cordial Set: cordial bottle and six 4024 Cordials
- crystal $260.00
- amber...............................$300.00
- regal blue $435.00
- burgundy..........................$425.00
- empire green....................$450.00
- ruby..................................$475.00
- silver mist........................$265.00

2518 Cordial Bottle, crystal stopper, may not have been made.
- crystal $95.00
- regal blue $135.00
- burgundy..........................$125.00
- empire green....................$125.00

423 Custard, handled $7.00
300 Decanter and Stopper, pint or quart, plain or optic $40.00
1918 Decanter and Stopper $48.00
1918 Decanter and Stopper, handled.............................$58.00
1928 Decanter and Stopper, pinched.............................$48.00
2052 Decanter and Stopper, pinched.............................$48.00
2439 Decanter and Stopper
- crystal................$300.00/market
- amber $400.00/market
- topaz $475.00/market
- rose....................$600.00/market
- azure,.................$600.00/market
- green $600.00/market

2439 Decanter Set: 2439 Decanter, and six 5098 2½ oz. footed Tumblers
- crystal................$500.00/market
- amber $550.00/market
- topaz $700.00/market
- rose....................$850.00/market
- azure..................$850.00/market
- green $850.00/market

2494 Decanter and Stopper
- crystal, RO.......................$150.00
- amber, RO $200.00
- regal blue $275.00
- burgundy..........................$275.00
- empire green....................$275.00
- ruby..................................$300.00
- mother-of-pearl $150.00

2502 Decanter and Stopper
- crystal $125.00
- regal blue $165.00
- burgundy..........................$175.00
- empire green....................$195.00

2502 Decanter Set: decanter and six 2 oz. whiskeys
- crystal $225.00
- regal blue $325.00
- burgundy..........................$300.00
- empire green....................$325.00

2510 Decanter, see Sunray

2518 Decanter and crystal Stopper
crystal $95.00
regal blue $195.00
burgundy $175.00
empire green $195.00
ruby $195.00

2525 Decanter, crystal stopper
crystal $125.00
regal blue $275.00
burgundy $225.00
empire green $275.00

4020 Decanter
crystal $495.00/market
green base $600.00/market
amber base $565.00/market
ebony base $565.00/market
rose bowl $625.00/market
topaz bowl $625.00/market

4101 Decanter and Stopper, quart
amber $125.00
topaz $150.00
green $150.00
rose $175.00
azure, ...$175.00

4101 Decanter Set: decanter and six whiskey tumblers, see Blank 4101
amber $195.00
topaz $250.00
green $250.00
rose $250.00
azure $275.00

4132 Decanter and Stopper. $54.00

6011 Decanter and Stopper
crystal $250.00
amber base $325.00
regal blue bowl $750.00
burgundy bowl $750.00
empire green bowl $750.00

701 Highball, 10 oz., NO or plain
crystal $20.00
regal blue $35.00
burgundy $35.00
empire green $35.00
ruby $35.00

701 Highball, 12 oz., NO or plain
crystal $20.00
ruby $40.00

4098 Hollow Stem Beer, 12 oz.
crystal $25.00
amber base $35.00
burgundy base $37.00
empire green base $40.00
regal blue base $40.00

863 Champagne, hollow stem $18.00

1554 Champagne, hollow stem $22.00

4132 Ice Bowl $37.00

4140 Ice Tea Set, same as 414 water set 7 pieces: Jug and six 12 oz. Tumbler

2443 Ice Tub
crystal $45.00
rose $67.00
azure $67.00
green $58.00
ebony $45.00
topaz $56.00

2464 Jug, ice
crystal $225.00
amber $280.00
green $325.00
rose $325.00
topaz $325.00

2503 Jug, quart wine, colored handle
crystal $75.00
regal blue handle $95.00
burgundy handle $95.00
empire green handle $95.00

2518 Jug, crystal, handled, wine
crystal $95.00
regal blue $135.00
burgundy $125.00
empire green $125.00

4101 Jug
amber $65.00
topaz $75.00
green $75.00
rose $85.00
azure $85.00

4118 Jug, 60 oz.
crystal $145.00
regal blue $300.00
burgundy $300.00
empire green $300.00
ruby $300.00

2283 Luncheon Set, SO, see Plates, Cups, and Saucers $12.00
Plate, 6" $4.00
Plate, 7" $5.00
Plate, 8" $5.00
Plate, 9" $7.00
Plate, 10" $9.00
Plate, 13" $15.00

2255 Sugar and Cream, see Appetizer, Buffet, and Relish

1184 Old Fashioned Cocktail, 3⅜", NO or plain
crystal $12.00
rose $22.00
azure $22.00
amber $18.00
green $20.00
topaz $20.00
wisteria $35.00

1185 Old Fashioned Cocktail, 8 oz.
crystal $12.00
regal blue $32.00
burgundy $32.00
empire green $32.00

2510 Pilsner $64.00

2464 Refreshment Set: jug and six tumblers
crystal $295.00
rose $500.00
green $500.00
amber $425.00
topaz $450.00

4101 Refreshment Set: Jug and six Tumbler
amber $125.00
topaz $125.00
green $125.00
rose $150.00
azure $150.00

4118 Refreshment Set: 60 oz. jug, with crystal handle and six 4118 Tumblers, 12 oz.
crystal $295.00
regal blue $525.00
burgundy $525.00
empire green $525.00
ruby $575.00

4141 Refreshment Set: 4141 Jug and six 10 oz. or six 12 oz. 4141 Tumblers
crystal $150.00
amber $195.00
azure $235.00
regal blue $300.00

4142 Refreshment Set: 4142 Jug and six 10 oz. or six 12 oz. 4142 Tumblers
crystal $150.00
amber $195.00
azure $235.00
regal blue, ...$300.00

2706/599
Salad/Punch Bowl, wood base with ebony finish $50.00

2706/615
Cup, punch $7.00

2464 Tumbler
crystal $25.00
amber $32.00
green $32.00
rose $35.00
topaz $32.00

4118 Tumbler, 12 oz.
crystal $25.00
regal blue $38.00
burgundy $38.00
empire green $38.00
ruby $45.00

4132 Tumbler , see Standish

4140 Tumbler, 10 oz., 12 oz., see Blank 4140

4140 Water Set, 7 pieces: jug and six 10 oz. or 12 oz. Tumbler
crystal $200.00
azure $300.00
amber $285.00
regal blue $345.00

2033 Tray, water, 12", ...$22.00

2106 Tray, water, 10" $25.00

887 Whiskey, 1¾ oz., plain, see Blank 887 Tumbler

887 Whiskey, 1¾ oz., RO, see Blank 887 Tumbler

887 Whiskey, 2½ oz., 2¼", see Blank 887 Tumbler

887 Whiskey Sham, 2⅛", see Blank 887 Tumbler

4122 Whiskey Sham, 1½ oz $18.00

889 Whiskey Sour, 5 oz. plain, see Blank 887 Tumbler

1185 Whiskey Sour, 5 oz $20.00

2502 Whiskey, 2 oz.
crystal, ...$18.00
regal blue $25.00
burgundy $25.00
empire green $25.00

2518 Wine, 5 oz. and whiskey, 2 oz.
crystal $20.00
regal blue $30.00
burgundy $32.00
empire green $30.00
ruby $30.00

2494 Wine Set: Decanter and six 4024 Sherries
crystal $300.00
amber $350.00
regal blue $550.00
burgundy $465.00
empire green $465.00
ruby $625.00

2460 Goblet, 10 oz. $18.00
2460 Sherbet, 6 oz., low $15.00
2460 Oyster Cocktail, 4 oz. $15.00
2460 Ice Tea, 13 oz., footed $18.00

Barcelona, Cutting 705

Rose and azure
Year

Tableware

2375 Bonbon $25.00
2394 Bowl, 6" $28.00
2375 Bowl, large dessert $47.00
2297 Bowl A, 12" $68.00
2324 Candlestick, 4", pair $45.00
4100 Vase, 8" $75.00
2430 Vase, 8" $75.00
2287 Lunch Tray, 11" $68.00
2430 Jelly, 7" $28.00
2375 Comport, 7" $57.00
2331-3 Box, candy and cover $95.00
2375 Cake, 10" $60.00
2375 Dish, lemon $22.00
2375 Sweetmeat $25.00
2375 Whip Cream $25.00
2375½ Sugar and Cream $68.00

Barcelona, Crystal Print 27

1971 – 1973

Stemware. 128

6103 Goblet $28.00
6103 Sherbet $26.00
6103 Tulip Wine $30.00
6103 Ice Tea, footed $28.00
2337 Plate, 7" $10.00

Baroness (Imported Stemware)

1984 – 1986

Tableware II, 280, 282

Goblet $20.00
Wine $20.00
Flute $20.00
Ice Tea $20.00

Baronet, Etching 92

1926 – 1943

Stemware, 32

870 Goblet $24.00
870 Sherbet, high $22.00
870 Sherbet, low $18.00
870 Cocktail $20.00
870 Claret $26.00
870 Wine $24.00
870 Cordial $28.00
5084 Oyster Cocktail $18.00
5084 Tumbler, 12 oz. footed $24.00
5084 Tumbler, 9 oz. footed $20.00
5084 Tumbler, 5 oz. footed $18.00
869 Bowl, finger, and plate $22.00
2337 Plate, 7" $10.00
2337 Plate, 8" $12.00

Baronet, Cutting 847

1956 – 1965

Stemware, 112

6065 Goblet $35.00
6065 Sherbet $32.00
6065 Cocktail/Wine/Seafood $34.00
6065 Cordial $40.00
6065 Ice Tea, footed $35.00
6065 Juice, footed $28.00
2337 Plate, 7" $10.00
2337 Plate, 8" $12.00

Baroque, 2496

1937 – 1965

Stemware, 47

2496 Goblet
crystal $27.00
azure $45.00
gold tint $45.00

2496 Sherbet
crystal $18.00
azure $35.00
gold tint $30.00

2496 Cocktail, footed
crystal $10.00
azure $25.00
gold tint $25.00

2496 Old Fashioned Cocktail
crystal $25.00
azure $80.00
gold tint $54.00

2496 Ice Tea, footed
crystal $45.00
azure $75.00
gold tint $65.00

2496 Tumbler, 9 oz., footed
crystal $30.00
azure $45.00
gold tint $45.00

2496 Ice Tea, 14 oz., flat
crystal $52.00
azure $85.00
gold tint $80.00

2496 Tumbler, 9 oz.
crystal $30.00
azure $60.00
gold tint $60.00

2496 Tumbler, 5 oz.
crystal $25.00
azure $50.00
gold tint $55.00

Tableware I, 86-96

Ashtray, oblong
crystal $12.00
azure $18.00
gold tint $16.00

Bonbon, 3-toed
crystal $52.00
azure $85.00
gold tint $75.00

Bowl, nut, 3-toed
crystal $64.00
azure $87.00
gold tint $85.00

Bowl, rose, 3½"
crystal, ...$75.00
azure $135.00
gold tint $125.00

Bowl, 5", fruit
crystal $20.00
azure $32.00
gold tint $32.00

Bowl, 7", cupped
crystal $96.00
azure $125.00
gold tint $110.00

2484 Bowl, 10", handled
crystal $95.00
amber $135.00
azure $195.00
topaz/gold tint $150.00
green $145.00
silver mist $110.00

Bowl, 10½", salad
crystal $68.00
azure $85.00
gold tint $75.00

Bowl, 10½", handled
crystal $87.00
azure $165.00
gold tint $145.00

Bowl, 11", rolled edge
crystal $87.00
azure $125.00
gold tint $125.00

Bowl, 12", flared
crystal $68.00
azure $87.00
gold tint $75.00

Bowl, punch, footed, 1½ gallon
crystal $475.00
azure $1,200.00

Cake, 10", handled
crystal $68.00
azure $85.00
gold tint $85.00

Candlestick, 4", pair
crystal $45.00
azure $135.00
gold tint $135.00

Candlestick, 5½", pair
crystal $60.00
azure $150.00
gold tint $150.00

Candlestick, duo, priced each
crystal $34.00
azure $52.00
gold tint $50.00
silver mist $38.00

Candlestick, trindle, priced each
crystal $52.00
amber $150.00
azure $150.00
burgundy $150.00
empire green $150.00
green $150.00
regal blue $175.00
ruby $175.00
topaz/gold tint $145.00
silver mist $65.00

2484 Candlestick, 7¾", UDP Lustre, priced each
crystal $75.00
azure $250.00
gold tint $175.00

2484 Candlestick, 2-light, candle drips
silver mist, priced each...$135.00
2484 Candelabra, 2-light, UDP, pair
crystal...$250.00
azure...$500.00
topaz/gold tint...$450.00
2484 Candelabra, 3-light, UDP, pair
crystal...$300.00
azure...$550.00
Candy, 3-part and cover
crystal...$115.00
azure...$195.00
gold tint...$175.00
Celery, 11"
crystal...$35.00
azure...$65.00
gold tint...$65.00
Box, cigarette and cover
crystal...$135.00
azure...$250.00
gold tint...$250.00
Cheese and Cracker
crystal...$75.00
azure...$125.00
gold tint...$125.00
Comport, 5½"
crystal...$47.00
azure...$78.00
gold tint...$75.00
Comport, 6½", tall
crystal...$75.00
azure...$135.00
gold tint...$125.00
Condiment Set, 4-piece:
regular shakers, mustard, tray
crystal...$225.00
azure...$375.00
gold tint...$365.00
Cream Soup and Plate
crystal...$64.00
azure...$125.00
gold tint...$95.00
Cup and Saucer
crystal...$28.00
azure...$45.00
gold tint...$45.00
Cup, punch
crystal...$22.00
azure...$34.00
Floating Garden, 10"
crystal...$95.00
azure...$135.00
Ice Bucket and tongs, chrome handle
crystal...$125.00
azure...$165.00
gold tint...$145.00
Jelly
crystal...$47.00
azure...$75.00
gold tint...$85.00
Jelly and Cover
crystal...$125.00
azure...$225.00
gold tint...$225.00
Jug, 3-pint
crystal...$195.00
azure...$1,200.00
gold tint...$1,200.00
Jug, 3-pint, ice
crystal...$225.00
azure...$695.00
gold tint...$800.00
Mayonnaise, 6½", 2-part
crystal...$54.00
azure...$95.00
gold tint...$95.00
2496½ Mayonnaise, plate, crystal ladle
crystal...$85.00
azure...$135.00
gold tint...$125.00
Mint, handled
crystal...$42.00
azure...$47.00
gold tint...$48.00
Mustard, cover, spoon
crystal...$85.00
azure...$125.00
gold tint,...$95.00
Oil, 3½ ounces
crystal...$125.00
azure...$575.00
gold tint...$350.00
Nappy, handled, regular
crystal...$24.00
azure...$48.00
gold tint...$48.00
Nappy, handled, flared
crystal...$24.00
azure...$48.00
gold tint...$48.00
Nappy, handled, 3-cornered
crystal...$24.00
azure...$48.00
gold tint...$48.00
Nappy, handled, square
crystal...$24.00
azure...$48.00
gold tint...$48.00
Pickle, 8"
crystal...$25.00
azure...$48.00
gold tint...$48.00
Plate, 6"
crystal...$16.00
azure...$20.00
gold tint...$20.00
Plate, 7"
crystal...$15.00
azure...$22.00
gold tint...$22.00
Plate 8"
crystal...$20.00
azure...$25.00
gold tint...$25.00
Plate, 9"
crystal...$34.00
azure...$65.00
gold tint...$65.00
Plate, 14", torte
crystal...$55.00
azure...$125.00
gold tint...$125.00
Platter, 12", oval
crystal...$60.00
azure...$125.00
gold tint...$150.00
Preserve and Cover
crystal...$195.00
azure...$285.00
gold tint...$275.00
Relish, 2-part
crystal...$36.00
azure...$67.00
gold tint...$68.00
Relish, 3-part
crystal...$47.00
azure,...$95.00
gold tint...$84.00
Relish, 4-part
crystal...$65.00
azure...$125.00
Salad Set: 10½", bowl, 14", torte,
and wooden fork and spoon
crystal...$125.00
azure...$195.00
gold tint...$185.00
Sauce, 6½", oblong
crystal...$46.00
azure...$98.00
gold tint...$85.00
Serving Dish, 8½"
crystal...$35.00
azure...$50.00
gold tint...$56.00
Shaker, FGT, set
crystal...$95.00
azure...$235.00
gold tint...$225.00
Shaker, individual, FGT
crystal...$90.00
azure...$200.00
gold tint...$200.00
Smoker Set: cigarette box and
4 ashtrays
crystal...$154.00
azure...$225.00
gold tint...$225.00
ebony...$250.00
Sugar and Cream, footed
crystal...$35.00
azure...$85.00
gold tint...$80.00
Sugar and Cream, individual
crystal...$35.00
azure...$85.00
gold tint...$80.00
Sugar, cream and tray
crystal...$68.00
azure...$135.00
gold tint...$135.00
Sweetmeat
crystal...$38.00
azure...$57.00
gold tint...$64.00
Tid Bit, 3-toed
crystal...$36.00
azure...$68.00
gold tint...$68.00
Tray, 6½", sugar and cream
crystal...$34.00
azure...$45.00
gold tint...$50.00
Tray, 8", oblong
crystal...$35.00
azure...$95.00
gold tint,...$68.00
Tray, 11", oval
crystal...$65.00
azure...$95.00
gold tint...$95.00

2484 Vase, 7"
- crystal $87.00
- azure $195.00
- gold tint $150.00

Vase, 8"
- crystal $95.00
- azure $225.00
- gold tint $150.00

Vegetable Dish, 9½"
- crystal $54.00
- azure $95.00
- gold tint $95.00

Beacon, Cutting 767
1937 – 1954

Stemware, 89

6017 Goblet....$30.00
6017 Sherbet, high $28.00
6017 Sherbet, low $24.00
6017 Cocktail $28.00
6017 Claret $35.00
6017 Wine....$35.00
6017 Cordial $45.00
6017 Oyster Cocktail....$22.00
6017 Tumbler, 14 oz., footed $32.00
6017 Ice Tea, footed $30.00
6017 Tumbler, 9 oz., footed $24.00
6017 Juice, footed $22.00
4132 Old Fashioned Cocktail, 7½ oz., sham $14.00
4132 Tumbler, 14 oz., sham $20.00
4132 Tumbler, 12 oz., sham $18.00
4132 Tumbler, 9 oz., sham $16.00
4132 Tumbler, 7 oz., sham $14.00
4132 Tumbler, 5 oz., sham $12.00
4132 Tumbler, 4 oz., sham $8.00
4132 Whiskey, 1½ oz., sham....$12.00

Tableware I, 297

766 Bowl, finger....$14.00
2496 Bowl, 8½", serving $60.00
2496 Bowl, 10½", handled $75.00
2496 Bowl, 12", flared $65.00
2545 Bowl, 12½", oval....$65.00
2545 Candelabra, 2-light, B prisms pair $200.00
2496 Candlestick, 4", pair $45.00
2496 Candlestick, 5½", pair....$55.00
2496 Candlestick, duo, pair $75.00
2545 Candlestick, duo, pair $125.00
2496 Candlestick, trindle, pair $95.00
2496 Celery, 11"....$27.00
2496 Cheese and Cracker....$65.00
2496 Comport, 5½"....$30.00
2496 Comport, 6½", tall $65.00
4132 Decanter and Stopper $95.00
4132 Ice Bowl....$48.00
2496 Ice Bucket, gold handle....$54.00
6011 Jug....$225.00
2496 Mayonnaise, 2-part....$28.00
2496½ Mayonnaise, plate, ladle $48.00
2496 Pickle, 8" $22.00
2337 Plate, 6" $7.00
2337 Plate, 7" $9.00
2337 Plate, 8" $12.00
2496 Plate, cake $48.00
2496 Plate, 14", torte $65.00
2496 Relish, 2-part....$28.00
2496 Relish, 3-part....$40.00
2496 Sauce and Tray, oblong $62.00
2496 Sugar and Cream....$47.00
2496 Sugar and Cream, individual ..$47.00
2496 Tray, sugar and cream $24.00
2496 Sweetmeat....$28.00
2496 Tid Bit, 3-toed $32.00

Beacon Hill, Cutting 917
1968 – 1970

Stemware, 129

6104½ Goblet....$30.00
6104½ Sherbet....$28.00
6104½ Claret....$34.00
6104½ Wine....$34.00
6104½ Cordial $42.00
6104½ Ice Tea, footed $30.00
2574 Plate, 7" $10.00
2574 Plate, 8" $12.00

Bells
1977 – 1986

Useful & Ornamental, 35 – 38

American....$800.00/market
Angel, silver mist....$47.00
Cameo, crystal $35.00
Christmas
- 1977....$95.00
- 1978....$95.00
- 1979....$95.00
- 1980....$95.00
- 1981, ruby with silver mist handle....$125.00
- 1982.... $95.00
- Silent Night, cobalt blue, silver metal handle $25.00
- Peace on Earth, flashed ruby, gold metal handle....$25.00
- Silent Night, cobalt blue, silver metal handle $25.00
- Merry Christmas, gold metal handle $25.00

Coca Cola, gold metal handle $75.00
Fostoria Commemorative, gold metal handle.... $45.00
Kimberly, gold metal handle $35.00
Love Bell
- 1980-1982.... $95.00
- 1986.... $25.00

Love Birds, flashed ruby, gold metal handle $25.00
Love Always, Fostoria Outlet Store flashed ruby, gold metal handle $35.00
Mother's Day
- 1978....$95.00
- 1979....$95.00

Navarre
- crystal $95.00
- blue $125.00
- pink $110.00
- Avon....$135.00

Richmond $40.00
Serenity
- crystal $85.00
- yellow.... $95.00
- blue $125.00

Sheffield....$36.00
6020 Twisted Handle, SO $70.00
Valentine $95.00
Wedding Bell, crystal and silver mist, NO $95.00
Wilma, pink, special order....$85.00

Bellwether (Imported Stemware)
1984 – 1986

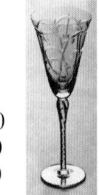

Tableware II, 280 – 281

Goblet....$17.50
Wine....$17.50
Flute....$17.50
Ice Tea....$17.50

Beloved, Decoration 647
1960 – 1973

Stemware, 119

6089 Goblet....$35.00
6089 Sherbet....$32.00
6089 Wine/Cocktail $38.00
6089 Brandy $42.00
6089 Ice Tea, footed....$35.00
6089 Juice, footed $30.00
2337 Plate, 7" $10.00
2337 Plate, 8" $12.00

Bennington, BE04
1983 – 1986

Stemware, 187

BE04 Goblet, 10 oz....$20.00
BE04 Champagne, 8 oz....$18.00
BE04 Wine, 7 oz....$20.00
BE04 Flute/Parfait, 8 oz....$26.00
BE04 Ice Tea, 14 oz., footed $20.00
BE04 Old Fashioned, double.... $16.00
BE04 Highball....$16.00

Berkeley, Cutting 909
1966 – 1967

Stemware, 131

6106 Goblet....$30.00
6106 Sherbet....$28.00
6106 Claret $35.00
6106 Tulip Wine....$35.00
6106 Liqueur $42.00
6106 Ice Tea, footed $30.00
2337 Plate, 7" $10.00
2337 Plate, 8" $12.00

Berkshire, 6105
1965 – 1974

Stemware, 130

6105 Goblet....$22.00
6105 Sherbet....$22.00
6105 Claret....$22.00
6105 Wine....$22.00
6105 Cordial....$27.00
6105 Ice Tea, footed $22.00
2337 Plate, 7" $8.00
2337 Plate, 8" $10.00

Berry, Cutting 188

1928 – 1929
Green and rose

Stemware, 69

5098 Goblet........$60.00
5098 Sherbet, high $50.00
5098 Sherbet, low $32.00
5098 Parfait $45.00
5098 Cocktail $44.00
5098 Wine..$58.00
5098 Oyster Cocktail......................$30.00
5098 Ice Tea, footed $60.00
5098 Tumbler, 9 oz., footed $38.00
5098 Juice, footed...........................$38.00
5098 Whiskey, footed $55.00
5082½ Grapefruit and Liner $54.00

Tableware I, 271

869 Bowl, finger and2283 Plate.... $28.00
2342 Bowl A, 12"........................... $48.00
2394 Bowl, 12" $57.00
2394 Candlestick, 2", pair $56.00
2324 Candlestick, 4", pair $57.00
2331 Box, candy and cover............$74.00
2329 Centerpiece, 11" $65.00
2329 Centerpiece, 13" $72.00
2368 Cheese and Cracker............. $70.00
2400 Comport $40.00
2378 Ice Bucket, NP handle..........$70.00
5000 Jug...................................... $250.00
2315 Mayonnaise and Plate...........$35.00
2394 Mint $16.00
2283 Plate, 7" $9.00
2283 Plate, 8" $9.00
2315 Plate, 13" $27.00
2350½ Sugar and Cream................. $48.00
2378 Sugar Pail, NP handle........ $145.00
2342 Tray, handled, lunch $60.00
4103 Vase, 6", optic $60.00
4105 Vase, 6", optic $60.00
4105 Vase, 8", optic $75.00
4100 Vase, 8", optic $75.00
2369 Vase, 7", optic $85.00
2369 Vase, 9", optic $95.00
2373 Vase, small, window and cover...............................$150.00
2373 Vase, large, window and cover $175.00
2378 Pail, whip cream, NP handle....................... $145.00

Berry, 2721 Milkglass

1957 – 1965

Tableware II, 212

2721 Bowl, 4½", berry
- white $20.00
- aqua $28.00
- peach $28.00

2721 Bowl, 6½", shallow
- white $30.00

2721 Bowl, 7½", cupped
- white $35.00
- aqua $47.00
- peach $47.00

2721 Bowl, 8", berry
- white $38.00
- aqua $54.00
- peach $54.00

2721 Candle, flora, pair
- white $54.00

2721 Candy and Cover
- white $56.00

2721 Jelly, footed
- white $22.00
- aqua $30.00
- peach $30.00

2721 Nappy, 4½", 3-cornered
- white $18.00
- aqua $24.00
- peach $24.00

2721 Nappy, 4½", oblong
- white $18.00
- aqua $24.00
- peach $24.00

2721 Plate, 8"
- white $20.00
- aqua $27.00
- peach $27.00

2721 Sugar and Cream, individual
- white $48.00
- aqua $100.00
- peach $100.00

2721 Tray, sugar and cream
- white $20.00
- aqua $25.00
- peach $25.00

2721 Vase, 8", bud
- white $42.00
- aqua $57.00
- peach $57.00

Betrothal, Decoration 673

1966 – 1971

Stemware, 132

6107 Goblet.......................$30.00
6107 Sherbet.....................$28.00
6107 Claret........................$35.00
6107 Tulip Wine............................$35.00
6107 Liqueur...............................$42.00
6107 Ice Tea, footed $30.00
2337 Plate, 7" $10.00

Betsy Ross, 2620 Milkglass (see also Wistar)

1954 – 1965

Stemware, 48

2620 Goblet..................$20.00
2620 Sherbet...............$18.00
2620 Tumbler, 12 oz.......$22.00
2620 Tumbler, 5 oz.........................$20.00

Tableware II, 205

Basket, 11½"
- white $37.00
- peach $65.00
- aqua $65.00

Bowl, 8½", cupped, white.... $38.00
Bowl, 10½", flared, white......$38.00
Bowl, 10¾", fruit, white $42.00

Candlestick, 3", pair
- white $40.00
- peach $65.00
- aqua $65.00

Hurricane Lamp, crystal chimney
- white $45.00
- peach $55.00
- aqua $55.00

Nappy, handled, square
- white $20.00

Nappy, 3-cornered, white......$20.00
Plate, 8", white $25.00
Sugar and Cream, white $48.00

Beverly, Etching 276

1927 – 1933

Stemware, 67

5097 Goblet
- crystal.......$30.00
- amber................................$35.00
- green.................................$35.00

5097 Sherbet, high
- crystal $28.00
- amber $30.00
- green $30.00

5097 Sherbet, low
- crystal $22.00
- amber................................$25.00
- green.................................$25.00

5097 Parfait
- crystal $30.00
- amber................................$38.00
- green.................................$38.00

5097 Cocktail
- crystal $28.00
- amber................................$28.00
- green.................................$28.00

5097 Claret
- crystal $34.00
- amber................................$40.00
- green.................................$40.00

5097 Wine
- crystal $30.00
- amber................................$35.00
- green.................................$35.00

5097 Cordial
- crystal $38.00
- amber................................$55.00
- green.................................$55.00

5000 Oyster Cocktail, 4½ oz. $25.00
5097½ Grapefruit and 945½ Liner ...$50.00
5000 Ice Tea, 12 oz., footed $32.00
5000 Tumbler, 9 oz., footed...........$26.00
5000 Juice, 5 oz. $25.00
5000 Whiskey, 2½ oz. $25.00

Tableware I, 162 – 163

2350 Ashtray, small
- crystal $20.00
- amber................................ $22.00
- green................................. $24.00

2350½ Bouillon, footed
- crystal $14.00
- amber................................ $16.00
- green................................. $18.00

869 Bowl, finger and 2283 6" Plate
- crystal $22.00
- amber................................$25.00
- green................................. $28.00

2350 Bowl, 5", fruit
- crystal $22.00
- amber................................ $24.00
- green................................. $27.00

2350 Bowl, 6", cereal
- crystal $25.00
- amber................................$27.00
- green................................. $30.00

2350 Bowl, 7", soup
- crystal $26.00
- amber................................ $28.00

green $32.00
2350 Bowl, 8", nappy
crystal $34.00
amber $37.00
green $42.00
2350 Bowl, 9", bake
crystal $40.00
amber $48.00
green $52.00
2297 Bowl A, deep
crystal $85.00
amber $94.00
green $98.00
2324 Bowl, 10", footed
crystal $85.00
amber $96.00
green $115.00
2350 Bowl, 10", salad
crystal $75.00
amber $86.00
green $94.00
2329 Bowl, 11", centerpiece
crystal $85.00
amber $95.00
green $100.00
2329 Bowl, 13", centerpiece
crystal $95.00
amber $125.00
green $135.00
2324 Candlestick, 4", pair
crystal $75.00
amber $85.00
green $90.00
2331 Box, candy and cover
crystal $94.00
amber $110.00
green $115.00
2350 Celery
crystal $38.00
amber $43.00
green $45.00
2368 Cheese and Cracker
crystal $85.00
amber $110.00
green $125.00
2327 Comport, 7"
crystal $58.00
amber $67.00
green $75.00
2350 Cream Soup
crystal $28.00
amber $34.00
green $36.00
2350½ Cream Soup, footed
crystal $30.00
amber $36.00
green $40.00
2350 Plate, cream soup
crystal $12.00
amber $14.00
green $15.00
2350 Cup and Saucer
crystal $22.00
amber $26.00
green $30.00
2350½ Cup and Saucer
crystal $22.00
amber $26.00
green $30.00
2350 Cup and Saucer, AD
crystal $28.00
amber $35.00
green $38.00
2315 Grapefruit
crystal $28.00
amber $34.00
green $42.00
2378 Ice Bucket
crystal $88.00
amber $100.00
green $110.00
5000 Jug
crystal $258.00
amber $275.00
green $295.00
2350 Pickle
crystal $26.00
amber $30.00
green $34.00
2350 Plate, 6"
crystal $12.00
amber $16.00
green $18.00
2350 Plate, 7"
crystal $12.00
amber $18.00
green $120.00
2350 Plate, 8"
crystal $14.00
amber $20.00
green $22.00
2350 Plate, 9"
crystal $24.00
amber $30.00
green $35.00
2350 Plate, 10"
crystal $30.00
amber $45.00
green $48.00
2350 Plate, 13", chop
crystal $64.00
amber $75.00
green $80.00
2350 Platter, 10½"
crystal $42.00
amber $48.00
green $58.00
2350 Platter, 12"
crystal $48.00
amber $57.00
green $68.00
2350 Platter, 15"
crystal $75.00
amber $87.00
green $98.00
2350 Sauce Boat and Plate
crystal $64.00
amber $75.00
green $78.00
2350½ Sugar and Cream, footed
crystal $60.00
amber $68.00
green $74.00
2292 Vase, 8"
crystal $175.00
amber $225.00
green $250.00

Bianca, Crystal Print 22

1969 – 1970

Stemware, 126

6102 Goblet $32.00
6102 Sherbet $30.00
6102 Claret $35.00
6102 Tulip Wine $35.00
6102 Brandy $35.00
6102 Ice Tea, footed $32.00
2337 Plate, 7" $10.00
2337 Plate, 8" $12.00

Billow, Cutting 118

1913 – 1917

Stemware, 25, 29

858 Goblet, 11 oz. $8.00
858 Goblet, 10 oz. $8.00
858 Goblet, 9 oz. $8.00
858 Goblet, 8 oz. $8.00
858 Saucer Champagne,
7 oz. $8.00
5½ oz. $8.00
858 Sherbet $6.00
858 Fruit $6.00
858 Cocktail $6.00
858 Claret, 6½ oz. $8.00
858 Claret, 4½ oz. $8.00
858 Wine, 3½ oz. $8.00
858 Wine, 2¾ oz. $8.00
858 Sherry $6.00
858 Crème de Menthe $6.00
858 Brandy $12.00
858 Cordial $15.00
858 Oyster Cocktail $5.00
858 Champagne,
hollow stem $10.00
tall $10.00
long stem $18.00
858 Bass Ale $15.00
858 Hot Whiskey $6.00
863 Goblet, 10½ oz. $8.00
863 Goblet, 9 oz. $8.00
863 Goblet, 7 oz. $8.00
863 Goblet, 5½ oz. $8.00
863 Saucer Champagne $8.00
863 Fruit $6.00
863 Cocktail, 3½ oz. $6.00
863 Claret $8.00
863 Rhine Wine $8.00
863 Wine $8.00
863 Sherry $6.00
863 Crème de Menthe $6.00
863 Brandy, pousse-café $8.00
863 Cordial $15.00
863 Champagne, hollow stem $8.00
tall $8.00
863 Roemer, 5½ oz. $18.00
863 Roemer, 4½ oz. $18.00
1389 Oyster Cocktail $8.00
945/945½
Grapefruit and Liner $25.00
4061 Lemonade, handled $18.00
701 Tumbler $4.00 – 8.00
820 Tumbler $4.00 – 8.00
833 Tumbler $4.00 – 8.00
858 Tumbler $4.00 – 8.00

887 Tumbler....$4.00 – 8.00
889 Tumbler....$4.00 – 8.00

Tableware

863 Almond....$14.00
880 Bonbon....$16.00
1904 Bonbon....$16.00
803 Comport, 5"....$14.00
803 Comport, 6"....$16.00
481 Custard....$8.00
300 Decanter, quart....$50.00
48 Flower Set, 3-piece....$95.00
1132 Horseradish....$47.00
1718 Ice Tub, 6"....$34.00
300 Jug....$75.00
303 Jug....$50.00
724 Jug....$85.00
1851 Jug....$75.00
1733 Marmalade and Cover....$22.00
1831 Mustard and Cover....$28.00
803 Nappy, 5"....$14.00
803 Nappy, 6"....$16.00
803 Nappy, 7", footed....$18.00
1227 Nappy, 4½"....$10.00
1227 Nappy, 8"....$16.00
300½ Oil, small....$30.00
1465 Oil, 7 oz., cut neck....$32.00
1666 Puff and Cover....$35.00
1227 Punch Bowl and Stand....$125.00
1478 Lavender Salts and Stopper....$45.00
1848 Sandwich Plate, 9", cut star....$10.00
1165½ Shaker, pearl top, pair....$26.00
2022 Shaker, FGT....$26.00
1478 Sugar and Cream....$43.00
1480 Sugar and Cream....$45.00
1759 Sugar and Cream....$42.00
1851 Sugar and Cream....$42.00
2194 Syrup, 12 oz., nickle top....$67.00
2194 Syrup, 8 oz., nickle top....$64.00
300 Tankard....$75.00
1761 Tankard....$75.00
1787 Tankard....$75.00
1852 Tankard....$75.00
1743 Tankard and Cover....$85.00
1741 Tea Caddy and Cover....$68.00
922 Toothpick....$15.00
1558 Bottle, water, cut neck....$34.00
725 Vase, 10"....$45.00
725 Vase, 8"....$37.00
1895 Vase, 10"....$45.00

Biscayne, 6122

1971 – 1973

Stemware, 139

6122 Goblet
- blue....$24.00
- nutmeg....$24.00
- gold....$24.00
- snow....22.00
- onyx....$22.00

6122 Sherbet
- blue....$20.00
- nutmeg....$20.00
- gold....$20.00
- snow....$22.00
- onyx....$22.00

6122 Wine
- blue....$24.00
- nutmeg....$24.00
- gold....$24.00
- snow....$24.00
- onyx....$24.00

6122 Ice Tea, footed
- blue....$24.00
- nutmeg....$24.00
- gold....$24.00
- snow....$24.00
- onyx....$24.00

6122 Highball
- blue....$20.00
- nutmeg....$20.00
- gold....$20.00
- snow....$22.00
- onyx....$22.00

6122 On the Rocks
- blue....$20.00
- nutmeg....$20.00
- gold....$20.00
- snow....$22.00
- onyx....$22.00

Black and Gold, Decoration 23

1923 – 1924

Stemware, 18

660 Goblet....$45.00
660 Saucer Champagne....$45.00
660 Sherbet, low....$35.00
660 Parfait....$45.00
660 Cocktail....$35.00
660 Claret....$55.00
660 Wine....$45.00
660 Cordial....$64.00
945 Grapefruit and Liner....$54.00
889 Tumbler....$18.00 – 30.00

Tableware I, 315

2246 Candlestick, 8¼", pair....$185.00
2219 Jar, candy and cover, ¼ pound....$85.00
2219 Jar, candy and cover, ½ pound....$95.00
2250 Jar, candy and cover, ¼ pound....$85.00
2250 Jar, candy and cover, ½ pound....$95.00
2241 Cologne, drip stopper....$300.00
1743/4 Jug and Cover....$400.00
300/7 Tankard....$450.00
896 Nappy and Cover, 6½", footed....$65.00
1897 Plate, 7"....$38.00
2283 Plate, 8¼"....$42.00
2283 Plate, 11"....$56.00
1851 Sugar and Cream....$125.00

Blackberry, Etching 205

1908 – 1909

Stemware, 23

858 Goblet, 11 oz....$10.00
858 Goblet, 10 oz....$6.00
858 Goblet, 9 oz....$6.00
858 Goblet, 8 oz....$6.00
858 Saucer Champagne, 7 oz....$6.00
- 5½ oz....$6.00

858 Sherbet....$6.00
858 Fruit....$6.00
858 Parfait....$18.00
858 Cocktail....$6.00
858 Claret, 6½ oz....$6.00
858 Claret, 4½ oz....$6.00
858 Wine, 3½ oz....$6.00
858 Wine, 2¾ oz....$6.00
858 Sherry....$6.00
858 Crème de Menthe....$6.00
858 Brandy....$8.00
858 Cordial....$15.00
858 Oyster Cocktail....$7.00
858 Champagne
- hollow stem....$15.00
- tall....$15.00
- long stem....$25.00

858 Champagne, long stem, Cutting R....$25.00
858 Bass Ale....$20.00
858 Hot Whiskey....$10.00

Black Border, Decoration 20

1920s

Stemware, 26

858 Goblet, 9 oz....$40.00 – 45.00
858 Saucer Champagne, 5½ oz....$40.00 – 45.00
858 Fruit....$40.00 – 45.00
858 Cocktail....$40.00 – 45.00
766 Ice Tea, footed, handled....$45.00
701 Tumbler....$35.00
820 Tumbler....$35.00

Tableware I, 313

2136 Bonbon and Cover, 5"....$195.00
2083 Bottle, salad, lettered....$195.00
2090 Bottle, 6 oz., toilet....$125.00
2118 Bottle, 6 oz., toilet....$125.00
858 Bowl, finger and plate....$45.00
1490 Candlestick, 8", pair....$250.00
2245 Candlestick, 8¼", pair....$200.00
2219 Jar, candy and cover, ¼ pound....$75.00
2219 Jar, candy and cover, ½ pound....$85.00
2219 Jar, candy and cover, pound....$95.00
2250 Jar, candy and cover, ¼ pound....$75.00
2250 Jar, candy and cover, ½ pound....$85.00
2250 Jar, candy and cover, pound....$95.00
1697 Carafe Set, 3 pieces....$165.00
2241 Cologne, 2¼ oz., drip stopper....$165.00
2242 Cologne, 3¼ oz., drip stopper....$145.00
2243 Cologne, 2¼ oz., drip stopper....$145.00
803 Comport, 5", tall....$53.00
1848 Dish, 7", salad, matt star base....$38.00
2104 Jug....$450.00
1743/5 Jug and Cover....$200.00
1743/7 Jug and Cover....$300.00
1968 Marmalade and Cover....$65.00
2138 Mayonnaise Set, 2 pieces....$65.00
127 Mug, handled....$45.00
803 Nappy, 5", LD....$40.00

1848 Plate, 9", sandwich, matt star base $40.00
1719 Plate, 10½", sandwich, matt star base $45.00
2091 Soap and Cover $135.00
2199 Tray, gold edge only $30.00
2208 Vase, 5" $65.00
2137 Vase, brush $150.00
1957 Vase, 7", center $85.00

Blank 660

1922 – 1943

Stemware, 17 – 18

660 Goblet
- crystal $6.00
- orchid $25.00

660 Saucer Champagne
- crystal $5.00
- orchid $25.00

660 Sherbet, low
- crystal $5.00
- orchid $20.00

660 Parfait
- crystal $5.00
- orchid $25.00

660 Cocktail
- crystal $5.00
- orchid $20.00

660 Claret
- crystal $6.00
- orchid $25.00

660 Wine
- crystal $5.00
- orchid $20.00

660 Cordial
- crystal $6.00
- orchid $30.00

Blank 661

1922 – 1928

Stemware, 18 – 19

661 Goblet $4.00
661 Saucer Champagne $4.00
661 Fruit/Sherbet, low $4.00
661 Parfait $4.00
661 Cocktail $4.00
661 Claret $4.00
661 Wine $4.00
661 Cordial $8.00

Blank 766

1898 – 1928

Stemware, 20 – 22

766 Goblet, 9 oz. $10.00
766 Goblet, 7 oz $10.00
766 Saucer Champagne $10.00
766 Sherbet $7.00
766 Fruit $7.00
766 Parfait $14.00
766 Cocktail $7.00
766 Claret $10.00
766 Rhine Wine $12.00
766 Wine $10.00
766 Burgundy $12.00
766 Sherry $12.00
766 Crème de Menthe $10.00
766 Brandy, pousse-café $12.00
766 Cordial $12.00
766 Sorbet $7.00
766 Ice Tea, footed, handled $15.00
766 Custard, handled, $7.00
766 Grapefruit and Liner $25.00
766 Whiskey Tumbler $6.00
766½ Parfait $18.00

Blank 858 (see 858 Tumbler)

1904 – 1927

Stemware, 22

858 Goblet, 8 oz $7.00
858 Goblet, 9 oz $7.00
858 Goblet, 10 oz. $8.00
858 Goblet, 11 oz. $8.00
858 Saucer Champagne, 5½ oz. $7.00
858 Saucer Champagne, 7 oz. $8.00
858 Sherbet $7.00
858 Cocktail $7.00
858 Claret, 6½ oz. or 4½ oz. $8.00
858 Wine, 3½ oz. or 2¾ oz. $8.00
858 Sherry $8.00
858 Crème de Menthe $7.00
858 Brandy $8.00
858 Cordial $8.00
858 Oyster Cocktail $6.00
858 Parfait $10.00
858 Fruit $7.00
858 Champagne, tall, hollow stem $8.00
858 Champagne, long stem $15.00
858 Hot Whiskey $8.00
858 Ale $12.00
858 Custard $7.00
858 Tumbler, 5 oz., flat $5.00
858 Tumbler, 3½ oz., flat $5.00
858 Tumbler, 16 oz., table $6.00
858 Tumbler, 14 oz., table $6.00
858 Tumbler, 12 oz., table $6.00
858 Tumbler, 10 oz., table $5.00
858 Tumbler, 8 oz., table $5.00
858 Tumbler, 6½ oz., table $5.00

Blank 863

1898 – 1927

Stemware, 26

863 Goblet, 10½ oz. $7.00
863 Goblet, 9 oz., short stem $7.00
863 Goblet, 7 oz., long stem $7.00
863 Goblet, 5½ oz $7.00
863 Saucer Champagne $7.00
863 Fruit $7.00
863 Cafe Parfait $22.00
863 Roemer, 5½ oz., cocktail, tall $8.00
863 Roemer, 4½ oz., cocktail, tall $8.00
863 Cocktail, 3½ oz. $7.00
863 Cocktail, 3 oz. $7.00
863 Claret $7.00
863 Rhine Wine $7.00
863 Wine $7.00
863 Sherry $7.00
863 Crème de Menthe $7.00
863 Brandy, pousse-café $7.00
863 Cordial $15.00
863 Champagne, hollow stem, CF $12.00
863 Champagne, tall $7.00

Blank 867, 867½

1925 – 1930

Stemware, 30

867 Goblet, 10 oz. $8.00
867 Goblet, 9 oz. $8.00
867 Saucer Champagne $8.00
867 Fruit $8.00
867 Sherbet $8.00
867 Cocktail $8.00
867 Claret $8.00
867 Wine $8.00
867 Sherry $8.00
867 Cordial $12.00

Blank 869

1925 – 1939

Stemware, 31

869 Goblet
- crystal $22.00
- amber $26.00
- green $26.00
- blue $30.00

869 Saucer Champagne
- crystal $20.00
- amber $22.00
- green $22.00
- blue $26.00

869 Sherbet, high
- crystal $20.00
- amber $22.00
- green $22.00
- blue $26.00

869 Sherbet, low
- crystal $15.00
- amber $20.00
- green $20.00
- blue $23.00

869 Fruit
- crystal $15.00
- amber $20.00
- green $20.00
- blue $23.00

869 Parfait
- crystal $22.00
- amber $25.00
- green $25.00
- blue $30.00

869 Cocktail
- crystal $20.00
- amber $22.00
- green $22.00
- blue $26.00

869 Claret
- crystal $22.00
- amber $25.00
- green $25.00
- blue $30.00

869 Wine
- crystal $22.00
- amber $25.00
- green $25.00
- blue $30.00

869 Cordial
crystal $24.00
amber $28.00
green $28.00
blue $35.00
869 Oyster Cocktail
crystal $12.00
amber $15.00
green $15.00
blue $20.00
869 Tumbler, 2 oz., flat
crystal $10.00
amber $15.00
green $15.00
869 Tumbler, 5 oz.
crystal $12.00
amber $15.00
green $15.00
blue $20.00
orchid $20.00
869 Tumbler, 8 oz.
crystal $12.00
amber $15.00
green $15.00
blue $20.00
orchid $20.00
869 Tumbler, 12 oz.
crystal $14.00
amber $18.00
green $18.00
blue $25.00
orchid $25.00
869 Tumbler, 12 oz.
handled, ...$18.00

Blank 870, see 5084 Tumbler

1926 – 1942

Stemware, 32

870 Goblet
crystal $20.00
mother-of-pearl $20.00
amber $25.00
green $25.00
rose $35.00
blue $35.00
870 Sherbet, high
crystal $12.00
mother-of-pearl $12.00
amber $22.00
green $22.00
rose $32.00
blue $32.00
870 Sherbet, low
crystal $10.00
mother-of-pearl $10.00
amber $20.00
green $20.00
rose $28.00
blue $28.00
870 Parfait
crystal $22.00
mother-of-pearl $22.00
amber $26.00
green $26.00
rose $38.00
blue $38.00
870 Cocktail
crystal $10.00
mother-of-pearl $10.00
amber $22.00
green $22.00
rose $30.00
blue $30.00
870 Claret
crystal $114.00
mother-of-pearl $14.00
amber $28.00
green $28.00
rose $38.00
blue $38.00
870 Wine
crystal $14.00
mother-of-pearl $14.00
amber $26.00
green $26.00
rose $35.00
blue $35.00
870 Cordial
crystal $25.00
mother-of-pearl $25.00
amber $34.00
green $34.00
rose $45.00
blue $45.00
870 Oyster Cocktail
crystal $9.00
mother-of-pearl $9.00
amber $18.00
green $18.00
rose $28.00
blue $28.00

Blank 877, see Repeal, Blown Stemware

1927 – 1942

Stemware, 33

877 Goblet
crystal $25.00
mother-of-pearl $25.00
amber $35.00
green $35.00
orchid $58.00
azure $58.00
empire green $125.00
regal blue $125.00
877 Sherbet, high
crystal $22.00
mother-of-pearl $22.00
amber $32.00
green $32.00
orchid $50.00
azure $50.00
empire green $95.00
regal blue $95.00
877 Sherbet, low
crystal $20.00
mother-of-pearl $20.00
amber $30.00
green $30.00
orchid $40.00
azure $40.00
empire green $60.00
regal blue $60.00
877 Parfait
crystal $27.00
mother-of-pearl $27.00
amber $40.00
green $40.00
orchid $50.00
azure $50.00
877 Cocktail
crystal $20.00
mother-of-pearl $20.00
amber $32.00
green $32.00
orchid $50.00
azure $50.00
empire green $68.00
regal blue $68.00
877 Claret
crystal $28.00
mother-of-pearl $28.00
amber $40.00
green $40.00
orchid $65.00
azure $65.00
empire green $125.00
regal blue $125.00
877 Wine
crystal $28.00
mother-of-pearl $28.00
amber $40.00
green $40.00
orchid $60.00
azure $60.00
877 Cordial
crystal $32.00
mother-of-pearl $32.00
amber $48.00
green $48.00
orchid $75.00
azure $75.00
empire green $125.00
regal blue $125.00
877 Oyster Cocktail
crystal $18.00
mother-of-pearl $18.00
amber $28.00
green $28.00
orchid $30.00
azure $30.00
empire green $45.00
regal blue $45.00
877 Grapefruit and Liner
crystal $35.00
mother-of-pearl $25.00
amber $45.00
green $45.00
orchid $65.00
azure $65.00
877 Ice Tea, footed
crystal $22.00
mother-of-pearl $22.00
amber $32.00
green $32.00
orchid $55.00
azure $55.00
empire green $95.00
regal blue $95.00
877 Tumbler, 9 oz., footed
crystal $18.00
mother-of-pearl $18.00
amber $28.00
green $28.00
orchid $35.00
azure $35.00
empire green $60.00

regal blue $60.00
877 Juice, footed
crystal $18.00
mother-of-pearl $18.00
amber....$28.00
green....$28.00
orchid....$30.00
azure $30.00
empire green....$55.00
regal blue $55.00
877 Whiskey, footed
crystal $20.00
mother-of-pearl $20.00
amber....$30.00
green....$30.00
orchid....$35.00
azure $35.00

Blank 879

1916 – 1928

Stemware, 34

879 Goblet
crystal.....$20.00
orchid....$35.00
879 Saucer Champagne
crystal...$18.00
orchid....$30.00
879 Fruit
crystal $14.00
orchid....$28.00
879 Cocktail
crystal $18.00
orchid....$28.00
879 Claret
crystal $22.00
orchid....$40.00
879 Wine
crystal $20.00
orchid....$38.00
879 Sherry
crystal $18.00
orchid....$30.00
879 Crème de Menthe
crystal $18.00
orchid....$25.00
879 Brandy, pousse-café
crystal $22.00
orchid....$38.00
879 Cordial
crystal $25.00
orchid....$45.00

Blank 880

pre-1900 – 1926

Stemware, 35, 36

880 Goblet, 11 oz.........$8.00
880 Goblet, 10 oz..........$8.00
880 Goblet, 9 oz..............$8.00
880 Goblet, 8 oz..........$8.00
880 Saucer Champagne, 7 oz. $7.00
880 Saucer Champagne, 5½ oz.....$7.00
880 Sherbet $7.00
880 Cocktail, 3½ oz. $8.00
880 Cocktail, 3 oz....$8.00
880 Claret, 6½ oz. $8.00
880 Claret, 4½ oz. $8.00
880 Rhine Wine....$8.00
880 Wine, 3½ oz....$8.00
880 Wine, 2¾ oz....$8.00
880 Sherry....$8.00
880 Crème de Menthe $8.00
880 Brandy, pousse-café, 1 oz....$12.00
880 Brandy, pousse-café, ¾ oz. $12.00
880 Cordial, 1 oz. $12.00
880 Cordial, ¾ oz. $12.00
880 Champagne, hollow stem.....$12.00
880 Champagne, tall....$8.00
880 Grapefruit, tall and liner $35.00
880½ Grapefruit, short and liner $30.00
880 Hot Whiskey $7.00
880 Ale, tall....$8.00

Blank 882

1914 – 1924

Stemware, 37

882 Goblet, 11 oz..........$8.00
882 Goblet, 10 oz.............$8.00
882 Goblet, 9 oz...........$7.00
882 Goblet, 8 oz..........$7.00
882 Saucer Champagne, 7 oz....$8.00
882 Saucer Champagne, 5½ oz.....$8.00
882 Sherbet $7.00
882 Cocktail, 3½ oz. $7.00
882 Cocktail, 3 oz....$7.00
882 Claret, 6½ oz....$12.00
882 Claret, 4½ oz....$8.00
882 Rhine Wine, 4 oz....$8.00
882 Wine, 3½ oz. $8.00
882 Wine, 2¾ oz. $8.00
882 Sherry, 2 oz....$8.00
882 Crème de Menthe, 2½ oz. $7.00
882 Brandy, pousse-café, 1 oz....$15.00
882 Cordial, 1 oz. $15.00
882 Cordial, ¾ oz....$15.00
882 Champagne, hollow stem....$8.00
882 Champagne, tall....$8.00
882 Grapefruit and Liner $25.00
882 Custard $6.00
882 Hot Whiskey $7.00
882 Ale, tall....$8.00

Blank 890

1929 – 1932

Stemware

890 Goblet
crystal....$20.00
green....$35.00
rose....$35.00
burgundy.............$45.00
890 Saucer Champagne
crystal $16.00
green....$30.00
rose $30.00
burgundy....$40.00
890 Sherbet, low
crystal $8.00
green....$24.00
rose $24.00
burgundy....$30.00
890 Parfait
crystal $22.00
green....$34.00
rose $34.00
burgundy....$45.00
890 Cocktail
crystal $14.00
green....$25.00
rose $25.00
burgundy....$35.00
890 Claret Wine
crystal $20.00
green....$36.00
rose $36.00
burgundy....$45.00
890 Cordial
crystal $24.00
green....$40.00
rose $40.00
burgundy....$58.00
890 Oyster Cocktail
crystal $7.00
green....$18.00
rose $18.00
burgundy....$28.00
890 Ice Tea, footed
crystal $18.00
green....$32.00
rose $32.00
burgundy....$40.00
890 Tumbler, footed, 9 oz.
crystal $12.00
green....$22.00
rose $22.00
burgundy....$28.00
890 Juice, footed
crystal $12.00
green....$22.00
rose $22.00
burgundy....$30.00
890 Whiskey, footed
crystal $12.00
green....$24.00
rose $24.00
burgundy....$34.00
890 Jug....
crystal $125.00
green....$250.00
rose $250.00

Blank 891

1933 – 1939

Stemware, 39

891 Goblet
crystal................$20.00
topaz..................$35.00
891 Sherbet, high
crystal.............$16.00
topaz....$32.00
891 Sherbet, low
crystal $9.00
topaz....$28.00
891 Cocktail
crystal $14.00
topaz....$32.00
891 Claret
crystal $20.00
topaz....$38.00
891 Cordial
crystal $25.00
topaz....$45.00
891 Oyster Cocktail
crystal $7.00

topaz....................................$26.00
891 Ice Tea, footed
crystal....................................$18.00
topaz....................................$32.00
891 Tumbler, 9 oz., footed
crystal....................................$15.00
topaz....................................$28.00
891 Juice, footed
crystal....................................$15.00
topaz....................................$28.00

Blank 945/945½ Grapefruits

Stemware, 163

945 Grapefruit and 945½ Liner ...$35.00
945½ Grapefruit and Liner $30.00

Blank 4020

1929 – 1943

Stemware, 57 – 59

4020 Goblet
crystal.............$40.00
ebony base....$40.00
amber base....$40.00
green base...........$40.00
rose bowl....................................$40.00
topaz bowl....................................$40.00
wisteria bowl....................................$55.00
4020 Sherbet, high
crystal....................................$35.00
ebony base....................................$35.00
amber base....................................$35.00
green base....................................$35.00
rose bowl....................................$35.00
topaz bowl....................................$35.00
wisteria bowl....................................$47.00
4020 Sherbet, 7 oz., low
crystal....................................$30.00
ebony base....................................$30.00
amber base....................................$30.00
green base....................................$30.00
rose bowl....................................$30.00
topaz bowl....................................$30.00
wisteria bowl....................................$35.00
4020 Sherbet, 5 oz., low
crystal....................................$30.00
ebony base....................................$30.00
amber base....................................$30.00
green base....................................$30.00
rose bowl....................................$30.00
topaz bowl....................................$30.00
wisteria bowl....................................$35.00
4020 Cocktail, 3½ oz.
crystal....................................$30.00
ebony base....................................$30.00
amber base....................................$35.00
green base....................................$35.00
rose bowl....................................$35.00
topaz bowl....................................$35.00
wisteria bowl....................................$45.00
4020 Claret
crystal....................................$45.00
ebony base....................................$45.00
amber base....................................$45.00
green base....................................$45.00
rose bowl....................................$45.00
topaz bowl....................................$45.00
wisteria bowl....................................$65.00
4020 Wine
crystal....................................$45.00
ebony base....................................$45.00
amber base....................................$45.00
green base....................................$45.00
rose bowl....................................$45.00
topaz bowl....................................$45.00
wisteria bowl....................................$65.00
4020 Ice Tea, 16 oz., footed
crystal....................................$40.00
ebony base....................................$40.00
amber base....................................$45.00
green base....................................$45.00
rose bowl....................................$45.00
topaz bowl....................................$45.00
wisteria bowl....................................$55.00
4020 Tumbler, 13 oz., footed
crystal....................................$40.00
ebony base....................................$40.00
amber base....................................$40.00
green base....................................$40.00
rose bowl....................................$40.00
topaz bowl....................................$40.00
wisteria bowl....................................$55.00
4020 Tumbler, 10 oz., footed
crystal....................................$35.00
ebony base....................................$35.00
amber base....................................$38.00
green base....................................$38.00
rose bowl....................................$38.00
topaz bowl....................................$38.00
wisteria bowl....................................$40.00
4020 Juice, footed
crystal....................................$30.00
ebony base....................................$30.00
amber base....................................$30.00
green base....................................$30.00
rose bowl....................................$30.00
topaz bowl....................................$30.00
wisteria bowl....................................$40.00
4020 Whiskey, footed
crystal....................................$30.00
ebony base....................................$30.00
amber base....................................$30.00
green base....................................$30.00
rose bowl....................................$30.00
topaz bowl....................................$30.00
wisteria bowl....................................$45.00

Tableware

4020 Almond, individual
crystal....................................$22.00
green base....................................$27.00
amber base....................................$25.00
ebony base....................................$27.00
rose bowl....................................$32.00
topaz....................................$30.00
wisteria bowl....................................$45.00
4021 Bowl, finger
crystal....................................$26.00
green base....................................$30.00
amber base....................................$30.00
ebony base....................................$30.00
rose bowl....................................$35.00
topaz/gold tint bowl..........$35.00
wisteria bowl....................................$64.00
4020 Decanter, footed and stopper
crystal................$495.00/market
green base $600.00/market
amber base $565.00/market
ebony base.........$565.00/market
rose bowl...........$625.00/market
topaz bowl.........$625.00/market
4020 Jug, footed
crystal....................................$150.00
ebony base....................................$195.00
green base....................................$250.00
amber base....................................$225.00
wisteria base....................................$495.00
green bowl....................................$350.00
rose bowl....................................$350.00
topaz bowl....................................$350.00
wisteria bowl....................................$700.00
4020 Shaker, FGT, pair
crystal....................................$77.00
amber base....................................$98.00
green base....................................$125.00
rose bowl....................................$125.00
topaz bowl....................................$125.00
ebony base....................................$110.00
wisteria base....................................$145.00
4020 Sugar and Cream
amber base....................................$98.00
green base....................................$125.00
rose bowl....................................$137.00
topaz bowl....................................$125.00
ebony base....................................$125.00
wisteria base....................................$145.00

Blank 4101 (see Barware)

1936 – 1940

Stemware, 180

Useful & Ornamental, 22

4101 Decanter
rose........$125.00
azure........$150.00
green...........$150.00
amber....................................$175.00
topaz....................................$175.00
4101 Jug
rose....................................$85.00
azure....................................$85.00
green....................................$75.00
amber....................................$65.00
topaz....................................$75.00
4101 Tumbler, 13 oz.
rose....................................$14.00
azure....................................$14.00
green....................................$12.00
amber....................................$10.00
topaz....................................$12.00
4101 Tumbler, 9 oz.
rose....................................$10.00
azure....................................$10.00
green....................................$8.00
amber....................................$8.00
topaz....................................$8.00
4101 Tumbler, 2½ oz.
rose....................................$14.00
azure....................................$14.00
green....................................$12.00
amber....................................$10.00
topaz....................................$12.00

Blank 4140 (see Barware)

1938 – 1940

Stemware, 181

Useful & Ornamental, 24

4140 Jug
crystal............$65.00
azure.............$80.00

amber..........$70.00
regal blue..........$125.00

4140 Tumbler, 12 oz.
crystal..........$10.00
azure..........$14.00
amber..........$12.00
regal blue..........$18.00

4140 Tumbler, 10 oz.
crystal..........$10.00
azure..........$14.00
amber..........$12.00
regal blue..........$18.00

Blank 4141 (see Barware)

1938 – 1942

Stemware, 182
Useful & Ornamental, 24

4141 Jug
crystal..........$65.00
azure..........$80.00
amber..........$70.00
regal blue..........$125.00

4141 Tumbler, 12 oz.
crystal..........$10.00
azure..........$14.00
amber..........$12.00
regal blue..........$18.00

4141 Tumbler, 10 oz.
crystal..........$10.00
azure..........$14.00
amber..........$12.00
regal blue..........$18.00

Blank 4142

1938 – 1940

Stemware, 182
Useful & Ornamental, 24

4140 Jug
crystal..........$65.00
azure..........$80.00
amber..........$70.00
regal blue..........$125.00

4140 Tumbler, 12 oz.
crystal..........$10.00
azure..........$14.00
amber..........$12.00
regal blue..........$18.00

4140 Tumbler, 10 oz.
crystal..........$10.00
azure..........$14.00
amber..........$12.00
regal blue..........$18.00

Blank 5001

1906 – 1927

Stemware, 61

5001 Goblet, 11 oz..........$10.00
5001 Goblet, 8¾ oz..........$8.00
5001 Goblet, 7½ oz..........$8.00
5001 Saucer Champagne..........$8.00
5001 Cocktail, 4 oz..........$8.00
5001 Cocktail, 3 oz..........$8.00
5001 Cocktail, 2½ oz..........$8.00
5001 Claret, 5½ oz..........$10.00
5001 Claret, 4¾ oz..........$10.00
5001 Rhine Wine, 4 oz..........$10.00
5001 Rhine Wine, 2½ oz..........$10.00
5001 Wine, 3½ oz..........$10.00
5001 Wine, 2 oz..........$10.00
5001 Sherry, 2½ oz..........$8.00
5001 Sherry, 2 oz..........$8.00
5001 Sherry, 1½ oz..........$8.00
5001 Brandy, ¾ oz..........$10.00
5001 Cordial, 1 oz..........$10.00
5001 Cordial, ¾ oz..........$10.00
5001 Champagne, 5¾ oz., tall..........$10.00
5001 Hot Whiskey, 5 oz..........$8.00

Blank 5061

1903 – 1914

Stemware, 63

5061 Goblet, 11 oz..........$10.00
5061 Goblet, 10 oz..........$10.00
5061 Goblet, 9 oz..........$8.00
5061 Goblet, 8 oz..........$8.00
5061 Saucer Champagne..........$10.00
5061 Sherbet..........$8.00
5061 Cocktail..........$8.00
5061 Claret, 6½ oz..........$10.00
5061 Claret, 4½ oz..........$10.00
5061 Rhine Wine..........$10.00
5061 Wine..........$10.00
5061 Sherry..........$10.00
5061 Crème de Menthe..........$8.00
5061 Brandy, pousse-café..........$10.00
5061 Cordial..........$10.00
5061 Champagne, hollow stem..........$10.00
5061 Champagne, tall..........$10.00
5061 Hot Whiskey..........$10.00

Blank 5070

1913 – 1927

Stemware, 63

5070 Goblet, 10 oz..........$10.00
5070 Goblet, 9 oz..........$9.00
5070 Goblet, 8 oz..........$9.00
5070 Saucer Champagne..........$10.00
5070 Sherbet..........$8.00
5070 Cocktail, 3½ oz..........$8.00
5070 Cocktail, 3 oz..........$8.00
5070 Claret, 6 oz..........$10.00
5070 Claret, 4½ oz..........$10.00
5070 Rhine Wine..........$10.00
5070 Wine..........$10.00
5070 Sherry..........$10.00
5070 Crème de Menthe..........$9.00
5070 Brandy, pousse-café, 1 oz..........$12.00
5070 Brandy, pousse-café, ¾ oz..........$12.00
5070 Cordial, 1 oz..........$12.00
5070 Cordial, ¾ oz..........$12.00
5070 Champagne, hollow stem..........$10.00
5070 Champagne, tall..........$9.00
5070 Hot Whiskey..........$8.00

Blank 5082

1924 – 1943

Stemware, 64, 65

5082 Goblet
crystal..........$34.00
amber..........$34.00
green..........$34.00
rose..........$35.00
azure..........$35.00
blue..........$40.00

5082 Sherbet, high
crystal..........$30.00
amber..........$30.00
green..........$30.00
rose..........$32.00
azure..........$32.00
blue..........$35.00

5082 Sherbet, low
crystal..........$25.00
amber..........$25.00
green..........$25.00
rose..........$27.00
azure..........$27.00
blue..........$30.00

5082 Parfait
crystal..........$35.00
amber..........$35.00
green..........$35.00
rose..........$35.00
azure..........$35.00
blue..........$38.00

5082 Cocktail
crystal..........$28.00
amber..........$28.00
green..........$28.00
rose..........$28.00
azure..........$28.00
blue..........$30.00

5082 Claret
crystal..........$35.00
amber..........$35.00
green..........$35.00
rose..........$38.00
azure..........$38.00
blue..........$45.00

5082 Wine
crystal..........$30.00
amber..........$30.00
green..........$30.00
rose..........$34.00
azure..........$34.00
blue..........$40.00

5082 Cordial
crystal..........$40.00
amber..........$40.00
green..........$40.00
rose..........$42.00
azure..........$42.00
blue..........$65.00

5082 Grapefruit
crystal..........$45.00
amber..........$45.00
green..........$45.00
rose..........$50.00
azure..........$50.00
blue..........$60.00

Blank 5083

1925 – 1932

Stemware, 65

5083 Goblet
crystal..........$20.00
green..........$20.00
amber..........$20.00
blue..........$22.00

5083 Sherbet, high
crystal..........$20.00
green..........$20.00
amber..........$20.00

blue $22.00
5083 Sherbet, low
crystal $18.00
green....................................$18.00
amber....................................$18.00
blue $20.00
5083 Parfait
crystal $20.00
green....................................$20.00
amber....................................$20.00
blue $22.00
5083 Cocktail
crystal $18.00
green....................................$18.00
amber....................................$18.00
blue $20.00
5083 Wine
crystal $22.00
green....................................$22.00
amber....................................$22.00
blue $25.00

Blank 5093

1926 – 1940

Stemware, 66

5093 Goblet
amber.................$34.00
green.................$34.00
mother-of-pearl
......................$34.00
rose $38.00
azure $38.00
blue $65.00
5093 Sherbet, high
amber....................................$30.00
green....................................$30.00
mother-of-pearl $30.00
rose $35.00
azure $35.00
blue $60.00
5093 Sherbet, low
amber....................................$25.00
green....................................$25.00
mother-of-pearl $25.00
rose $30.00
azure $30.00
blue $50.00
5093 Parfait
amber....................................$35.00
green....................................$35.00
mother-of-pearl $35.00
rose $38.00
azure $38.00
blue $65.00
5093 Cocktail
amber....................................$30.00
green....................................$30.00
mother-of-pearl $30.00
rose $35.00
azure $35.00
blue $60.00
5093 Claret
amber....................................$37.00
green....................................$37.00
mother-of-pearl $37.00
rose $45.00
azure $45.00
blue $75.00
5093 Wine
amber....................................$35.00
green....................................$35.00
mother-of-pearl $35.00
rose $42.00
azure $42.00
blue $65.00
5093 Cordial
amber....................................$45.00
green....................................$45.00
mother-of-pearl $45.00
rose $68.00
azure $68.00
blue $95.00

Blank 5097

1927 – 1943

Stemware, 67

5097 Goblet
crystal...............$25.00
amber................$35.00
green...............$35.00
mother-of-pearl
......................$25.00
rose $45.00
orchid....................................$55.00
5097 Sherbet, high
crystal $22.00
amber....................................$30.00
green....................................$30.00
mother-of-pearl $22.00
rose $40.00
orchid....................................$48.00
5097 Sherbet, low
crystal $20.00
amber....................................$23.00
green....................................$23.00
mother-of-pearl $20.00
rose $30.00
orchid....................................$35.00
5097 Parfait
crystal $22.00
amber....................................$35.00
green....................................$35.00
mother-of-pearl $22.00
rose $42.00
orchid....................................$48.00
5097 Cocktail
crystal $20.00
amber....................................$30.00
green....................................$30.00
mother-of-pearl $20.00
rose $35.00
orchid....................................$40.00
5097 Claret
crystal $25.00
amber....................................$38.00
green....................................$38.00
mother-of-pearl $25.00
rose $45.00
orchid....................................$58.00
5097 Wine
crystal $25.00
amber....................................$35.00
green....................................$35.00
mother-of-pearl $25.00
rose $40.00
orchid....................................$55.00
5097 Cordial
crystal $35.00
amber....................................$45.00
green....................................$45.00
mother-of-pearl $35.00
rose $58.00
orchid....................................$68.00
5097½ Grapefruit and 945½ Liner
crystal $35.00
amber....................................$38.00
green....................................$40.00
mother-of-pearl $35.00
rose $40.00
orchid....................................$45.00

Blank 5098

1928 – 1943

Stemware, 68, 69

5098 Goblet
crystal................$25.00
amber...............$38.00
green..............$38.00
topaz................$38.00
rose..................$48.00
azure $48.00
wisteria $95.00
5098 Sherbet, high
crystal $22.00
amber....................................$35.00
green....................................$35.00
topaz....................................$35.00
rose $44.00
azure $44.00
wisteria $75.00
5098 Sherbet, low
crystal $20.00
amber....................................$28.00
green....................................$28.00
topaz....................................$28.00
rose $35.00
azure $35.00
wisteria $50.00
5098 Parfait
crystal $25.00
amber....................................$38.00
green....................................$38.00
topaz....................................$38.00
rose $45.00
azure $45.00
5098 Cocktail
crystal $22.00
amber....................................$35.00
green....................................$35.00
topaz....................................$35.00
rose $44.00
azure $44.00
wisteria $65.00
5098 Claret
crystal $25.00
amber....................................$45.00
green....................................$45.00
topaz....................................$45.00
rose $50.00
azure $50.00
wisteria $125.00
5098 Wine
crystal $24.00
amber....................................$40.00
green....................................$40.00
topaz....................................$40.00
rose $45.00
azure $45.00
wisteria $95.00

5098 Cordial
- crystal $35.00
- amber $48.00
- green $48.00
- topaz $48.00
- rose $55.00
- azure $55.00
- wisteria $150.00

5098 Oyster Cocktail
- crystal $20.00
- amber $25.00
- green $25.00
- topaz $25.00
- rose $30.00
- azure $30.00
- wisteria $50.00

5098 Ice Tea, footed
- crystal $25.00
- amber $38.00
- green $38.00
- topaz $38.00
- rose $48.00
- azure $48.00
- wisteria $85.00

5098 Tumbler, 9 oz., footed
- crystal $20.00
- amber $30.00
- green $30.00
- topaz $30.00
- rose $32.00
- azure $32.00
- wisteria $55.00

5098 Juice, footed
- crystal $20.00
- amber $30.00
- green $30.00
- topaz $30.00
- rose $30.00
- azure $30.00
- wisteria $55.00

5098 Whiskey, footed
- crystal $22.00
- amber $32.00
- green $32.00
- topaz $32.00
- rose $35.00
- azure $35.00
- wisteria $65.00

Blank 5099

1928 – 1943

Stemware, 70

5099 Goblet
- green $45.00
- rose $45.00
- azure $45.00
- topaz $45.00
- wisteria $95.00

5099 Sherbet, high
- green $40.00
- rose $40.00
- azure $40.00
- topaz $40.00
- wisteria $75.00

5099 Sherbet, low
- green $34.00
- rose $34.00
- azure $34.00
- topaz $34.00
- wisteria $50.00

5099 Parfait
- green $45.00
- rose $45.00
- azure $45.00
- topaz $45.00

5099 Cocktail
- green $35.00
- rose $35.00
- azure $35.00
- topaz $35.00
- wisteria $70.00

5099 Claret
- green $54.00
- rose $54.00
- azure $54.00
- topaz $54.00
- wisteria $125.00

5099 Wine
- green $45.00
- rose $45.00
- azure $45.00
- topaz $45.00
- wisteria $125.00

5099 Cordial
- green $58.00
- rose $58.00
- azure $58.00
- topaz $58.00
- wisteria $150.00

5099 Oyster Cocktail
- green $30.00
- rose $30.00
- azure $30.00
- topaz $30.00
- wisteria $45.00

5099 Ice Tea, footed
- green $45.00
- rose $45.00
- azure $45.00
- topaz $45.00
- wisteria $85.00

5099 Tumbler, 9 oz., footed
- green $34.00
- rose $34.00
- azure $34.00
- topaz $34.00
- wisteria $50.00

5099 Juice, footed
- green $30.00
- rose $30.00
- azure $30.00
- topaz $30.00
- wisteria $50.00

5099 Whiskey, footed
- green $48.00
- rose $48.00
- azure $48.00
- topaz $48.00
- wisteria $75.00

Blank 6000

1931 – 1943

Stemware, 72

6000 Goblet
- crystal.,,,,,,,,,$24.00
- amber $34.00
- green $34.00
- topaz $34.00

6000 Sherbet, high
- crystal $22.00
- amber $30.00
- green $30.00
- topaz $30.00

6000 Sherbet, low
- crystal $18.00
- amber $25.00
- green $25.00
- topaz $25.00

6000 Cocktail
- crystal $18.00
- amber $28.00
- green $28.00
- topaz $28.00

6000 Wine
- crystal $30.00
- amber $35.00
- green $35.00
- topaz $35.00

6000 Oyster Cocktail
- crystal $14.00
- amber $22.00
- green $22.00
- topaz $22.00

6000 Ice Tea, footed
- crystal $22.00
- amber $34.00
- green $34.00
- topaz $34.00

6000 Juice, footed
- crystal $18.00
- amber $24.00
- green $24.00
- topaz $24.00

Blank 6002

1931 – 1933

Stemware, 73

- 6002 Goblet $45.00
- 6002 Sherbet, high $38.00
- 6002 Sherbet, low $34.00
- 6002 Claret $54.00
- 6002 Wine $50.00
- 6002 Cordial $75.00
- 6002 Oyster Cocktail $32.00
- 6002 Ice Tea, footed $45.00
- 6002 Tumbler, 10 oz., footed $37.00
- 6002 Juice, footed $30.00
- 6002 Whiskey, footed $50.00

Blank 6003

1931 – 1938

Stemware, 74

6003 Goblet
- crystal $26.00
- wisteria $65.00
- green $35.00
- topaz $35.00

6003 Sherbet, high
- crystal $22.00
- wisteria $60.00
- green $30.00
- topaz $30.00

6003 Sherbet, low
- crystal $20.00
- wisteria $50.00
- green $25.00
- topaz $25.00

6003 Cocktail
- crystal $22.00
- wisteria $60.00

green $30.00
topaz $30.00

6003 Cordial
crystal $28.00
wisteria $125.00
green $75.00
topaz $70.00

6003 Oyster Cocktail
crystal $20.00
wisteria $45.00
green $25.00
topaz $25.00

6003 Ice Tea, footed
crystal $26.00
wisteria $65.00
green $38.00
topaz $35.00

6003 Tumbler, 10 oz., footed
crystal $20.00
wisteria $54.00
green $30.00
topaz $30.00

6003 Juice, footed
crystal $20.00
wisteria $54.00
green $30.00
topaz $30.00

6003 Whiskey, footed
crystal $25.00
wisteria $76.00
green $45.00
topaz $45.00

Blank 6004

1933 – 1943

Stemware, 75

6004 Goblet
crystal $34.00
green $48.00
wisteria $95.00

6004 Sherbet, high
crystal $30.00
green $42.00
wisteria $85.00

6004 Sherbet, low
crystal $20.00
green $30.00
wisteria $60.00

6004 Parfait
crystal $38.00
green $54.00
wisteria $85.00

6004 Cocktail
crystal $30.00
green $42.00
wisteria $78.00

6004 Claret
crystal $40.00
green $54.00
wisteria $125.00

6004 Wine
crystal $40.00
green $54.00
wisteria $125.00

6004 Cordial
crystal $42.00
green $65.00
wisteria $135.00

6004 Oyster Cocktail
crystal $20.00
green $30.00
wisteria $47.00

6004 Ice Tea, footed
crystal $35.00
green $48.00
wisteria $45.00

6004 Tumbler, 9 oz., footed
crystal $25.00
green $35.00
wisteria $54.00

6004 Juice, footed
crystal $22.00
green $32.00
wisteria $54.00

6004 Whiskey, footed
crystal $34.00
green $45.00
wisteria $85.00

Blank 6005

1933 – 1943

Stemware, 76

6005 Goblet
crystal $30.00
topaz $48.00
green $48.00
mother-of-pearl $30.00

6005 Sherbet, high
crystal $28.00
topaz $42.00
green $42.00
mother-of-pearl $28.00

6005 Sherbet, low
crystal $20.00
topaz $30.00
green $30.00
mother-of-pearl $20.00

6005 Parfait
crystal $30.00
topaz $54.00
green $54.00
mother-of-pearl $30.00

6005 Cocktail
crystal $25.00
topaz $42.00
green $42.00
mother-of-pearl $25.00

6005 Claret
crystal $35.00
topaz $54.00
green $54.00
mother-of-pearl $35.00

6005 Wine
crystal $32.00
topaz $52.00
green $52.00
mother-of-pearl $32.00

6005 Cordial
crystal $40.00
topaz $67.00
green $67.00
mother-of-pearl $40.00

6005 Oyster Cocktail
crystal $15.00
topaz $30.00
green $30.00
mother-of-pearl $15.00

6005 Ice Tea, footed
crystal $30.00
topaz $45.00
green $45.00
mother-of-pearl $30.00

6005 Tumbler, 9 oz., footed
crystal $16.00
topaz $34.00
green $34.00
mother-of-pearl $16.00

6005 Juice, footed
crystal $16.00
topaz $34.00
green $34.00
mother-of-pearl $16.00

6005 Whiskey, footed
crystal $25.00
topaz $47.00
green $47.00
mother-of-pearl $25.00

Blank 6007

1933 – 1943

Stemware, 77

6007 Goblet
crystal $35.00
wisteria $125.00
amber $50.00
green $50.00
topaz 50.00

6007 Sherbet, high
crystal $32.00
wisteria $90.00
amber $48.00
green $48.00
topaz $48.00

6007 Sherbet, low
crystal $28.00
wisteria $68.00
amber $40.00
green $40.00
topaz $40.00

6007 Cocktail
crystal $30.00
wisteria $75.00
amber $42.00
green $42.00
topaz $42.00

6007 Claret
crystal $40.00
wisteria $125.00
amber $56.00
green $56.00
topaz $56.00

6007 Wine
crystal $40.00
wisteria $125.00
amber $54.00
green $54.00
topaz $54.00

6007 Cordial
crystal $48.00
wisteria $150.00
amber $75.00
green $75.00
topaz $75.00

6007 Oyster Cocktail
crystal $28.00
wisteria $56.00
amber $34.00
green $34.00
topaz $34.00

Blank 6007

6007 Ice Tea, footed
- crystal $35.00
- wisteria $100.00
- amber $50.00
- green $50.00
- topaz $50.00

6007 Tumbler, 9 oz., footed
- crystal $30.00
- wisteria $68.00
- amber $38.00
- green $38.00
- topaz $38.00

6007 Juice, footed
- crystal $30.00
- wisteria $68.00
- amber $38.00
- green $38.00
- topaz $38.00

6007 Whiskey, footed
- crystal $34.00
- wisteria $75.00
- amber $47.00
- green $47.00
- topaz $47.00

Blank 6008

1933 – 1943

Stemware, 78

6008 Goblet
- crystal $35.00
- topaz $48.00
- wisteria $125.00

6008 Sherbet, high
- crystal $32.00
- topaz $45.00
- wisteria $95.00

6008 Sherbet, low
- crystal $28.00
- topaz $38.00
- wisteria $75.00

6008 Cocktail
- crystal $30.00
- topaz $44.00
- wisteria $85.00

6008 Wine
- crystal $40.00
- topaz $55.00
- wisteria $135.00

6008 Cordial
- crystal $48.00
- topaz $75.00
- wisteria $150.00

6008 Oyster Cocktail
- crystal $28.00
- topaz $32.00
- wisteria $58.00

6008 Ice Tea, footed
- crystal $35.00
- topaz $48.00
- wisteria $100.00

6008 Tumbler, 9 oz., footed
- crystal $30.00
- topaz $38.00
- wisteria $65.00

6008 Juice, footed
- crystal $30.00
- topaz $40.00
- wisteria $65.00

Blank 6009, see Camelot

1933 – 1957

Stemware, 79

6009 Goblet
- crystal $32.00
- amber $40.00
- rose $40.00

6009 Sherbet, high
- crystal $30.00
- amber $36.00
- rose $36.00

6009 Sherbet, low
- crystal $25.00
- amber $30.00
- rose $30.00

6009 Cocktail
- crystal $30.00
- amber $36.00
- rose $36.00

6009 Claret-Wine
- crystal $36.00
- amber $45.00
- rose $45.00

6009 Cordial
- crystal $42.00
- amber $55.00
- rose $55.00

6009 Oyster Cocktail
- crystal $24.00
- amber $28.00
- rose $28.00

6009 Ice Tea, footed
- crystal $32.00
- amber $40.00
- rose $40.00

6009 Tumbler, 9 oz., footed
- crystal $25.00
- amber $32.00
- rose $32.00

6009 Juice, footed
- crystal $25.00
- amber $32.00
- rose $32.00

Blank 6010

1933 – 1939

Stemware, 80

- 6010 Goblet $30.00
- 6010 Sherbet, high $26.00
- 6010 Sherbet, low $22.00
- 6010 Cocktail $26.00
- 6010 Claret-Wine $35.00
- 6010 Cordial $40.00
- 6010 Oyster Cocktail $20.00
- 6010 Ice Tea, footed $30.00
- 6010 Tumbler, 9 oz., footed $22.00
- 6010 Juice, footed $22.00

Blank 6013

1935 – 1943

Stemware, 85

6013 Goblet
- crystal $30.00
- regal blue $75.00
- ruby $75.00
- burgundy $75.00

6013 Goblet, low
- crystal $28.00

6013 Saucer Champagne
- crystal $28.00
- regal blue $64.00
- ruby $64.00
- burgundy $64.00

6013 Sherbet, low
- crystal $22.00

6013 Cocktail
- crystal $28.00
- regal blue $60.00
- ruby $60.00
- burgundy $60.00

6013 Claret
- crystal $35.00

6013 Wine
- crystal $34.00
- regal blue $78.00
- ruby $78.00
- burgundy $78.00

6013 Cordial
- crystal $45.00

6013 Oyster Cocktail
- crystal $20.00

6013 Ice Tea, footed
- crystal $28.00
- regal blue $68.00
- ruby $68.00
- burgundy $68.00

6013 Juice, footed
- crystal $22.00

Blank 6014, 6014½, see Wavecrest

1935 – 1958

Stemware, 86

6014 Goblet
- crystal $30.00
- azure $38.00
- gold tint $38.00

6014 Saucer Champagne
- crystal $28.00
- azure $34.00
- gold tint $34.00

6014 Sherbet, low
- crystal $22.00
- azure $30.00
- gold tint $30.00

6014 Cocktail
- crystal $28.00
- azure $34.00
- gold tint $34.00

6014 Claret
- crystal $35.00
- azure $42.00
- gold tint $42.00

6014 Wine
- crystal $35.00
- azure $42.00
- gold tint $42.00

6014 Cordial
- crystal $45.00
- azure $52.00
- gold tint $52.00

6014 Oyster Cocktail
- crystal $20.00
- azure $28.00
- gold tint $28.00

6014 Ice Tea, footed
- crystal $28.00
- azure $35.00

gold tint $35.00
6014 Tumbler, 9 oz., footed
crystal $24.00
azure $34.00
gold tint $34.00
6014 Juice, footed
crystal $22.00
azure $30.00
gold tint $30.00

Blank 6031
1942 – 1957
Stemware, 101
6031 Goblet....................$25.00
6031 Goblet, low..............$25.00
6031 Saucer Champagne
............................$25.00
6031 Sherbet, low..........$20.00
6031 Cocktail..................$22.00
6031 Claret-Wine $28.00
6031 Cordial $35.00
6031 Oyster Cocktail......................$18.00
6031 Ice Tea, footed $25.00
6031 Juice, footed $20.00

Block, Etching 38½
1915 – 1927
Stemware, 26 – 30, 34
863 Goblet,
10½ oz. ....$ 7.00
863 Goblet, 9 oz. $7.00
863 Saucer Champagne,
5½ oz. $7.00
863 Fruit $7.00
863 Cocktail, 3 oz...........................$7.00
863 Claret $7.00
863 Rhine Wine................................$7.00
863 Wine..$7.00
863 Sherry $7.00
863 Crème de Menthe $7.00
863 Brandy, pousse-café $7.00
863 Cordial $7.00
863 Champagne, hollow stem,
CF..$7.00
863 Champagne, tall $7.00
879 Goblet $10.00
879 Saucer Champagne $10.00
879 Fruit $9.00
879 Cocktail $9.00
879 Claret $15.00
879 Wine...$15.00
879 Sherry $10.00
879 Crème de Menthe $10.00
879 Brandy, pousse-café $15.00
879 Cordial $15.00
945 Grapefruit and Liner $25.00
945½ Grapefruit and Liner $25.00
4061 Lemonade, handled...................$18.00
899 Parfait $22.00
701 Tumbler ....$5.00 – 8.00
820 Tumbler ....$5.00 – 8.00
833 Tumbler ....$5.00 – 8.00
858 Tumbler ....$5.00 – 8.00
300 Tankard $76.00
724 Tankard $85.00
1787 Tankard $75.00
303 Jug..$50.00
1236 Jug $75.00

Block, Decoration 608
1931 – 1932
Silver on ebony
Tableware I, 331
2350 Ashtray, large........................$22.00
2430 Bowl, 11" $45.00
2430 Candlestick, 9½", pair.........$150.00
2383 Candlestick, trindle, pair $145.00
2430 Jar, candy and cover,
½ pound $95.00
2427 Box, cigarette and cover.....$125.00
2430 Jelly, 7" $22.00
2430 Mint, 5½" $16.00
2430 Vase, 8"..................................$22.00

Blue Border, Decoration 19
1920s
Stemware, 26
858 Goblet, 9 oz $45.00
858 Saucer Champagne,
5½ oz. $45.00
858 Fruit $45.00
858 Cocktail $45.00
766 Ice Tea, footed, handled, ...$45.00
701 Tumbler.....................................$35.00
820 Tumbler.....................................$35.00
Tableware I, 312
2136 Bonbon and Cover, 5".........$195.00
2083 Bottle, salad, lettered $195.00
2090 Bottle, 6 oz., toilet...............$125.00
2118 Bottle, 6 oz., toilet...............$125.00
858 Bowl, finger and plate $45.00
1490 Candlestick, 8", pair $250.00
2245 Candlestick, 8¼", pair.........$200.00
2219 Jar, candy and cover,
¼ pound $75.00
2219 Jar, candy and cover,
½ pound $85.00
2219 Jar, candy and cover,
pound..................................$95.00
2250 Jar, candy and cover,
¼ pound $75.00
2250 Jar, candy and cover,
½ pound $85.00
2250 Jar, candy,and cover,
pound..................................$95.00
1697 Carafe Set, 3 pieces $165.00
2241 Cologne, 2¼ oz.,
drip stopper.....................$145.00
2242 Cologne, 3¼ oz.,
drip stopper.....................$145.00
2243 Cologne, 2¼ oz.,
drip stopper.....................$145.00
803 Comport, 5", tall.....................$53.00
1848 Dish, 7", salad,
matt star base....................$38.00
2104 Jug...$450.00
1743/5 Jug and Cover $200.00
1968 Marmalade and Cover $65.00
2138 Mayonnaise Set, 2 pieces $65.00
127 Mug, handled..........................$48.00
803 Nappy, 5", LD.........................$40.00
1897 Plate, 7" $24.00
1848 Plate, 9", sandwich,
matt star base....................$40.00
1719 Plate, 10½", sandwich,
matt star base....................$45.00
2091 Soap and Cover...................$135.00
2208 Vase, 5"..................................$68.00

2137 Vase, brush $150.00
1957 Vase, 7", center $85.00

Blue Meadow, Crystal Print 8
1958 – 1962
Stemware, 155
4180 Tumbler, 12 oz., flat,
sky blue $12.00
4180 Juice, 7 oz., flat,
sky blue $12.00
4180 Tumbler, Casual Flair,
sky blue $12.00

Bookends
Year1939 – 1980
Useful & Ornamental, 39, 40
2564 Horse, pair
crystal $145.00
silver mist....................... $195.00
ebony,
feasibility........ $800.00/market
2580 Elephant, pair
crystal $295.00
silver mist....................... $350.00
ebony,
feasibility........ $850.00/market
2585 Eagle, pair
crystal $400.00
silver mist....................... $450.00
2585 Eagle with Stars carving, pair
silver mist...........................$450.00
2601 Lyre, crystal, pair............... $150.00
2615 Owl, pair
crystal $600.00
ebony,
feasibility........ $800.00/market
2641 Seahorse, crystal, pair.........$450.00
2636 Plume, pair
crystal $195.00
ebony $250.00
2626 Chinese, Decoration 522, pair
ebony with gold $650.00
2825 Seashell, small, pair
crystal $150.00
2825 Seashell, large, pair
crystal $185.00
2856 Serendipity 139, pair
crystal $110.00
2856 Serendipity 140, pair
crystal $110.00
2856 Serendipity 141, pair
crystal $150.00

Bordeaux, Cutting 758
1936 – 1943
Stemware, 86
6014 Goblet $30.00
6014 Saucer Champagne
....$27.00
6014 Sherbet, low $22.00
6014 Cocktail $27.00
6014 Claret $35.00
6014 Wine...$34.00
6014 Cordial $45.00
6014 Oyster Cocktail.......................$20.00
6014 Ice Tea, footed $30.00
6014 Tumbler, 9 oz., footed $25.00
6014 Juice, footed $25.00

Bordeaux, Cutting 758

Tableware I, 292

869 Bowl, finger $12.00
2470½ Bowl, 10½" $40.00
2472 Candlestick, duo, pair $70.00
2400 Comport, 6" $27.00
2375 Ice Bucket, NP handle $43.00
2451 Ice Dish, liner, plate $42.00
5000 Jug $185.00
2337 Plate, 6" $6.00
2337 Plate, 7" $7.00
2337 Plate, 8" $8.00
4121 Vase, 5" $55.00
4128 Vase, 5" $55.00
2470 Vase, 10" $95.00

Boudoir Accessories and Jewelry

pre-1924 – 1986

Useful & Ornamental, 41 – 48

1478 Lavender Salt and Stopper, optic,
  crystal $75.00
1666 Puff and Cover, optic, crystal $65.00
1697 Bedroom Set, 2 pieces: carafe and 4023 Tumbler
  crystal $95.00
  green, SO $125.00
  amber, SO $110.00
  rose, SO $145.00
  azure, SO $135.00
1886 Box, pin and cover, see milk glass
1886 Tray, pin and cover, see milk glass
1904 Bonbon and Cover, optic,
  crystal $75.00
2056 Cologne and Stopper, see American
2106 Match and Cover, Vogue pattern
  crystal $68.00
  amber $87.00
  green $95.00
  canary $150.00
2118 Cologne, crystal $95.00
2135 Hair Receiver, optic
  crystal $95.00
  ebony $95.00
2135 Puff and Cover, optic, crystal $95.00
2136 Pomade and Cover, 2"
  crystal $75.00
  amber $75.00
  green $85.00
  canary $125.00
  blue $125.00
2136 Cold Cream and Cover, 3"
  crystal $75.00
  amber $75.00
  green $85.00
  canary $125.00
  blue $125.00
2136 Bonbon and Cover, 5"
  crystal $78.00
  amber $85.00
  green $95.00
  canary $150.00
  blue $150.00
2137 Brush Vase, crystal $67.00
2183 Puff and Cover, see Colonial Prism
  amber $268.00
  blue $350.00
  canary $350.00
2241 Cologne, Engravings D and E, Etchings 253 and 261
  crystal $125.00
  amber $140.00
  green $145.00
  canary $175.00
  blue $175.00
2242 Cologne, Engravings 14 and C, Etchings 253 and 262 $95.00
2243 Cologne, Engravings A and B, Etchings 253 and 263 $95.00
2276 Vanity Set
  crystal $95.00
  ebony $150.00
  amber $145.00
  green $165.00
  canary $275.00
  blue $250.00
  orchid $250.00
2276 Vanity, cut or engraved $125.00
2286 Tray, 5", pin
  ebony $25.00
  amber $28.00
2286 Tray, 10½", comb and brush
  ebony $45.00
  amber $54.00
2289 Vanity Set
  crystal $95.00
  ebony $150.00
  amber $145.00
  green $165.00
  canary $275.00
  blue $250.00
2322 Cologne
  crystal $125.00
  ebony $125.00
  amber $135.00
  green $145.00
  blue $165.00
2323 Cologne
  crystal $95.00
  ebony $115.00
  amber $115.00
  green $124.00
  blue $150.00
2338 Puff and Cover
  crystal $46.00
  ebony $57.00
  amber $52.00
  green $58.00
  canary $75.00
  blue $67.00
2347 Puff and Cover
  crystal $98.00
  ebony $115.00
  amber $115.00
  green $125.00
  canary $175.00
  blue $150.00
2347½ Puff and Cover
  crystal $95.00
  ebony $115.00
  amber $115.00
  green $125.00
  canary $175.00
  blue $150.00
2359½ Puff and Cover
  crystal $48.00
  ebony $57.00
  amber $55.00
  green $60.00
  blue $68.00
2519 Cologne and Stopper, see milk glass
2519 Puff and Cover, see milk glass
2561 Bottle, bath
  crystal $97.00
  silver mist $110.00
  carved $125.00
2561½ Bottle, bath, wide mouth
  crystal $97.00
  silver mist $110.00
  carved $125.00
2562 Bottle, bath
  crystal $95.00
  silver mist $110.00
  carved $125.00
  gold band $110.00
2562½ Bottle, bath, wide mouth
  crystal $95.00
  silver mist $110.00
  carved $125.00
2698 Cologne and Cover, small
  marine $47.00
  bark $47.00
  pink clover $58.00
  milk glass $47.00
2698 Cologne and Cover, large
  marine $54.00
  bark $54.00
  pink clover $65.00
  milk glass $52.00
2698 Bath Salts and Cover
  marine $125.00
  bark $125.00
  pink clover $150.00
  milk glass $125.00
2698 Puff and Cover, small
  marine $56.00
  bark $52.00
  pink clover $75.00
  milk glass $54.00
2698 Puff and Cover, large
  marine $65.00
  bark $56.00
  pink clover $85.00
  milk glass $56.00
2699 Apple and Cover
  marine $125.00
  bark $125.00
  pink clover $150.00
  avocado $140.00
2699 Pear
  marine $125.00
  bark $100.00
  pink clover $150.00
  amethyst $125.00
2699 Melon
  marine $135.00
  bark $110.00
  pink clover $150.00
  amethyst $125.00
2743/133
  Windsor Crown Bottle and Stopper, see Crown
HO04/292
  Mini-Box, hinged cover $45.00
JE01/293
  Box, jewelry and cover,
  crystal $25.00
PE05/873
  Pendant, heart $25.00
PE06/873
  Pendant, rose $25.00

PE07/873
Pendant, cameo $25.00
RI02/865
Ring Holder, silver or gold trim, crystal $25.00
SA05/293
Satin Ribbons $25.00
CA16/293
Captiva $25.00

Bouquet, Etching 342

1949 – 1971

Stemware, 102

6033 Goblet $35.00
6033 Goblet, low $30.00
6033 Saucer Champagne $25.00
6033 Sherbet, low $34.00
6033 Cocktail $28.00
6033 Claret/Wine $38.00
6033 Cordial $45.00
6033 Oyster Cocktail $18.00
6033 Ice Tea, footed $35.00
6033 Juice, footed $26.00

Tableware II, 144 – 145

2630 Basket, reed handle $120.00
2630 Bonbon, 3 -toed $38.00
2630 Bowl, fruit $22.00
2630 Bowl, cereal $26.00
2630 Bowl, 4½", handled, nappy $26.00
2630 Bowl, snack $28.00
2630 Bowl, 8", flared $36.00
2630 Bowl, 8½", salad $38.00
2630 Bowl, 9", lily pond $47.00
2630 Bowl, handled, serving $52.00
2630 Bowl, handled, utility $54.00
2630 Bowl, oval, vegetable $45.00
2630 Bowl, 10½", salad $50.00
2630 Bowl, 10¾", footed, flared $65.00
2630 Bowl, 11", rolled edge $68.00
2630 Bowl, 11¼", lily pond $58.00
2630 Bowl, 12", flared $68.00
2630 Butter and Cover, oblong $57.00
2630 Candlestick, 4½", pair $56.00
2630 Candlestick, duo, pair $75.00
2630 Candlestick, trindle, pair $125.00
2630 Jar, candy and cover $85.00
2630 Cheese and Cracker $85.00
2630 Comport $46.00
2630 Condiment Set, 3-piece $157.00
2630 Cup and Saucer $28.00
2630 Ice Bucket, metal handle $135.00
2630 Jug, 3-pint, ice $225.00
2630 Jug $145.00
2630 Mayonnaise, plate, ladle $65.00
2630 Mayonnaise, 2-part, 2 ladles $65.00
2630 Mustard, cover, and spoon $64.00
2630 Oil, DS, 5 oz. $62.00
2630 Pickle, 8¾" $24.00
2630 Pitcher, pint, cereal $75.00
2630 Plate, 6" $16.00
2360 Plate, 7" $18.00
2360 Plate, 8" $22.00
2360 Plate, 9" $34.00
2630 Plate, 10½", dinner $52.00
2630 Plate, crescent, salad $50.00
2630 Plate, 8", party and cup $42.00
2630 Plate, handled, cake $65.00
2630 Plate, 14", torte $75.00
2630 Plate, 16", torte $75.00
2630 Platter, 12", oval $68.00
2630 Preserve and Cover $65.00
2630 Relish, 2-part $36.00
2630 Relish, 3-part $54.00
2630 Salad Set, 10½", 3-piece $115.00
2630 Salver $110.00
2630 Shaker, chrome top B, pair $65.00
2630 Sugar and Cream, regular $65.00
2630 Sugar and Cream, individual $58.00
2630 Tray, sugar and cream $27.00
2630 Tid Bit, 3-toed $37.00
2630 Tid Bit, 2-tier, metal handle $56.00
2630 Tray, handled, lunch $68.00
2630 Tray, handled, muffin $65.00
2630 Tray, handled, utility $65.00
2630 Tray, 10½", snack $52.00
2630 Tricorne, 3-toed $47.00
4121 Vase, 5", no optic $68.00
2630 Vase, 6", bud $45.00
4143 Vase, 6", footed $67.00
6021 Vase, 6", footed, bud $58.00
2630 Vase, 7½", handled $85.00
5092 Vase, 8", bud $85.00
2660 Vase, 8", flip $85.00
2630 Vase, 8½", oval $85.00
2470 Vase, 10", footed $125.00

Bouquet, Cutting 756

1935 – 1938

Stemware, 85

6013 Goblet $32.00
6013 Goblet, low $30.00
6013 Saucer Champagne $30.00
6013 Sherbet, low $26.00
6013 Cocktail $30.00
6013 Claret $45.00
6013 Wine $40.00
6013 Cordial $55.00
6013 Oyster Cocktail $24.00
6013 Ice Tea, footed $30.00
6013 Juice, footed $24.00

Tableware I, 292

766 Bowl, finger $12.00
2527 Bowl, 9", footed $48.00
2527 Candelabra, 2-light, UDP, pair $125.00
6013 Comport, 5" $32.00
5000 Jug $200.00
2337 Plate, 6" $6.00
2337 Plate, 7" $7.00
2337 Plate, 8" $8.00

Bowls, Centerpieces, and Console Bowls

1923 – 1972

Useful and Ornamental, 49-75

315 Bowls, 4½", 5", 6", 7", 8", 9", plain or 24-point cut star bottom, 24-point cut star bottom, and cut beaded edge $10.00 – 25.00
315 Berry Set: 9" bowl and six 4½" bowls $65.00
2267 Bowl, 7", footed, console
crystal $26.00
amber $28.00
blue $35.00
green $30.00
canary $35.00
ebony $28.00
2267 Bowl, 9", footed, console
crystal $28.00
amber $30.00
blue $40.00
green $32.00
canary $45.00
2267 Bowl, 10", console, rolled edge
crystal $30.00
amber $32.00
blue $47.00
green $38.00
canary $50.00
2267 Console Sets: included 2269 6" Candles or 2275 7" or 9" Candles
2297 Bowl D, 7½", shallow, regular
amber $35.00
green $35.00
blue $40.00
canary $45.00
2297 Bowl D, 7½", deep, plain
crystal $35.00
amber $35.00
green $45.00
blue $54.00
canary $65.00
orchid $54.00
rose $54.00
2297 Bowl D, 7½", deep, SO
amber $40.00
green $45.00
blue $65.00
orchid $60.00
2297 Bowl B, 9¾", shallow, cupped, plain
crystal $32.00
amber $35.00
green $38.00
blue $54.00
canary $65.00
2297 Bowl C, 9¾", rolled edge
amber $35.00
green $38.00
blue $54.00
canary $65.00
2297 Bowl B, 10½", deep, cupped, plain
crystal $30.00
amber $40.00
green $44.00
blue $57.00
canary $68.00
orchid $60.00
rose $48.00
2297 Bowl B, 10½", deep, cupped, SO
amber $45.00
green $48.00
blue $60.00
orchid $60.00
2297 Bowl A, 10½", shallow, flared, plain
crystal $35.00
amber $40.00
green $45.00
blue $54.00
canary $65.00
ebony $45.00
orchid $54.00
2297 Bowl C, 10½", deep, rolled edge
crystal $35.00
amber $40.00

green...$44.00
blue...$65.00
canary...$75.00
orchid...$65.00
rose...$55.00
2297 Bowl C, 10½", deep, rolled edge, SO
amber...$40.00
green...$45.00
blue...$65.00
ebony...$54.00
orchid...$60.00
rose...$54.00
2297 Bowl A, 12", deep, flared
crystal...$30.00
amber...$40.00
green...$45.00
blue...$60.00
canary...$75.00
ebony...$50.00
orchid...$60.00
rose...$54.00
azure...$60.00
2297 Bowl A, 12", deep, SO
crystal...$30.00
amber...$40.00
green...$45.00
blue...$60.00
orchid...$60.00
rose...$57.00
2297 Bowl E, 12½", cabarette
crystal...$35.00
amber...$40.00
green...$45.00
blue...$58.00
canary...$75.00
ebony...$40.00
orchid...$60.00
rose...$56.00
2297 Bowl E, 12½", SO
amber...$45.00
green...$48.00
blue...$65.00
orchid...$60.00
rose...$58.00
2305 Base, 4½", ebony...$22.00
2309 Flower Block, 3" or 3¾"
crystal...$15.00
green...$28.00
amber...$25.00
rose...$35.00
blue...$48.00
2309 Flower Block, 5", green...$35.00
2309 Flower Block, 4½", oval
crystal...$18.00
green...$28.00
amber...$25.00
rose...$32.00
azure...$36.00
2314 Base, 3½", ebony...$18.00
2315 Bowl, see Twenty-Three Fifteen
2320 Bowl A, 11", flared, open edge
amber...$35.00
green...$40.00
blue...$54.00
canary...$65.00
ebony...$36.00
2320 Bowl A, 12", flared, open edge
amber...$35.00
green...$40.00
blue...$54.00
canary...$65.00
ebony...$36.00
2320 Bowl B, 10", cupped, open edge
amber...$35.00
green...$40.00
blue...$54.00
canary...$65.00
ebony...$35.00
2320 Bowl B, 11", cupped, open edge
amber...$35.00
green...$40.00
blue...$57.00
canary...$68.00
ebony...$37.00
rose...$54.00
2324 Bowl, 10", footed, console
crystal...$75.00
amber...$85.00
blue...$125.00
green...$95.00
canary...$150.00
orchid...$135.00
2324 Bowl, 12" or 13", footed, console
crystal...$82.00
amber...$84.00
blue...$135.00
green...$95.00
2324 Bowl, small, footed, urn, 7"
crystal...$74.00
amber...$85.00
blue...$135.00
green...$115.00
canary...$165.00
orchid...$150.00
2324 Bowl, large, footed, urn, 10"
amber...$95.00
blue...$145.00
green...$115.00
2324 Console Sets used 2324 9", and 12" Candlesticks
2329 Centerpiece, 11"
crystal...$38.00
crystal, SO...$40.00
amber...$38.00
amber, SO...$40.00
blue...$50.00
blue, SO...$57.00
green...$45.00
green, SO...$48.00
canary, plain...$65.00
ebony, plain...$38.00
rose...$48.00
rose, SO...$50.00
azure...$48.00
azure, SO...$54.00
orchid...$48.00
orchid, SO...$50.00
2329 Centerpiece, 13 to 14"
crystal...$40.00
crystal, SO...$44.00
amber...$42.00
amber, SO...$45.00
blue...$55.00
blue, SO...$65.00
green...$48.00
green, SO...$54.00
ebony...$44.00
rose...$48.00
rose, SO...$57.00
2333 Bowl, 11", footed, console
crystal...$68.00
amber...$75.00
blue...$95.00
green...$84.00
2339 Bowl D, 7¼", regular
crystal...$30.00
amber...$34.00
green...$38.00
blue...$47.00
orchid...$44.00
canary...$58.00
2339 Bowl A, 10½", flared
amber...$35.00
green...$40.00
blue...$50.00
orchid...$48.00
canary...$65.00
2339 Bowl B, 10¾", cupped
crystal...$35.00
amber...$42.00
green...$46.00
blue,...$58.00
orchid...$50.00
canary...$75.00
2339 Bowl C, 10½", rolled edge
crystal...$35.00
amber...$42.00
green...$46.00
blue...$57.00
orchid...$50.00
canary...$75.00
2339 Bowl E, 12"
crystal...$35.00
amber...$42.00
green...$46.00
blue...$57.00
orchid...$50.00
canary...$75.00
ebony...$38.00
2339 Bowl A, 10½", SO
amber...$38.00
green...$40.00
blue...$54.00
orchid...$50.00
rose...$50.00
azure...$50.00
2342 Bowl A, 12½", octagon
crystal...$30.00
amber...$34.00
green...$48.00
blue...$56.00
orchid...$50.00
rose...$48.00
azure...$48.00
2342 Bowl, 12", salad
amber...$35.00
green...$48.00
blue...$56.00
orchid...$50.00
rose...$48.00
2362 Bowl, 12"
amber...$46.00
blue...$64.00
green...$52.00
rose...$60.00
orchid...$60.00
2362 Comport, 11" and 2362 9" Candlesticks
crystal...$65.00
amber...$65.00

blue $95.00
green....................................$75.00
ebony $60.00
orchid...................................$75.00
2364 Bowl, see Sonata
2367 Bowl, 7", bulb
amber....................................$30.00
green....................................$30.00
blue $35.00
ebony $30.00
2367 Bowl, 8", bulb
amber....................................$30.00
green....................................$35.00
blue $40.00
ebony $30.00
2371 Flower Holder with colored top and plain glass bottom
crystal $45.00
rose $60.00
azure $60.00
green....................................$60.00
amber....................................$50.00
orchid...................................$55.00
2371 Centerpiece, 13", oval
crystal, plain...........................$54.00
green....................................$65.00
green, SO $65.00
amber....................................$60.00
amber, SO $60.00
blue $70.00
orchid...................................$65.00
orchid, SO $65.00
2375 Bowls, see Fairfax
2375 Berry Set, Fairfax: 8" nappy and six fruit bowls
crystal $134.00
rose $185.00
azure $185.00
green...................................$175.00
amber...................................$145.00
orchid..................................$185.00
topaz...................................$153.00
2390 Bowl, 12", footed
amber....................................$65.00
green....................................$75.00
rose $75.00
azure $80.00
orchid...................................$75.00
2390 Centerpiece, 11"
amber....................................$54.00
green....................................$60.00
orchid...................................$65.00
2393 Centerpiece, 12"
amber....................................$85.00
green....................................$95.00
rose $95.00
azure $125.00
2394 Bowl, 12", flared
crystal $40.00
amber....................................$48.00
regal blue $125.00
green....................................$57.00
burgundy................................$115.00
empire green............................$125.00
rose $54.00
azure $65.00
orchid...................................$65.00
topaz/gold tint $60.00
ruby....................................$125.00
2394 Bowl D, 7½"
crystal $38.00
amber....................................$45.00
green....................................$48.00
rose $50.00
azure $54.00
topaz....................................$50.00
2395 Bowl, 10"
crystal $65.00
amber....................................$68.00
green....................................$70.00
ebony $70.00
rose $75.00
azure $85.00
topaz/gold tint $74.00
2398 Bowl, 11", Cornucopia
crystal $58.00
amber....................................$85.00
green....................................$95.00
orchid..................................$150.00
rose $135.00
azure $135.00
2402 Bowl, 9"
crystal $25.00
amber....................................$30.00
green....................................$35.00
ebony $38.00
rose $38.00
azure $38.00
topaz/gold tint $30.00
2402 Bowl, 11"
crystal $26.00
amber....................................$30.00
green....................................$40.00
ebony $46.00
rose $40.00
azure $40.00
topaz....................................$40.00
2415 Bowl, combination
green...................................$125.00
ebony $125.00
rose $125.00
azure $135.00
topaz...................................$125.00
2424 Bowl, 8", RO, later part of Kent pattern in crystal only
crystal, see Kent $28.00
amber....................................$42.00
green....................................$48.00
rose $57.00
topaz....................................$54.00
wisteria $125.00
2424 Bowl, 9 to 9½", flared
crystal, see Kent $34.00
amber....................................$44.00
green....................................$50.00
rose $58.00
topaz....................................$54.00
wisteria $135.00
2425 Bowl, 13", oblong
crystal $28.00
amber....................................$34.00
green....................................$34.00
ebony $34.00
rose $38.00
azure $40.00
topaz....................................$37.00
2426 Bowl, 12", oval
regal blue $75.00
burgundy.................................$75.00
empire green.............................$85.00
2428 Bowl, 7", round
amber....................................$54.00
green....................................$60.00
rose $65.00
ebony $60.00
topaz....................................$65.00
wisteria, ...$150.00
2430 Bowl, see Diadem
2434 Bowl, 13"
amber....................................$95.00
green....................................$95.00
2432 Bowl, 11"
burgundy.................................$75.00
regal blue $95.00
empire green.............................$95.00
2441 Bowl, 12"
crystal $48.00
amber....................................$55.00
green....................................$55.00
rose $60.00
azure $60.00
topaz....................................$58.00
2443 Bowl, 10", oval
crystal $45.00
amber....................................$54.00
green....................................$57.00
ebony $57.00
rose $65.00
azure $70.00
topaz....................................$65.00
2445 Bowl, 8½"
crystal $68.00
amber....................................$77.00
green....................................$80.00
rose $85.00
azure $95.00
ebony $75.00
topaz....................................$85.00
2455 Bowl, 11"
crystal $75.00
amber....................................$80.00
green....................................$85.00
rose $85.00
topaz....................................$85.00
2458 Bowl, 11½", flared
regal blue $125.00
burgundy................................$125.00
empire green............................$125.00
2466 Plateau
crystal $52.00
green....................................$58.00
topaz....................................$58.00
ebony $55.00
2470/2470½
see Twenty-Four Seventy
2481 Bowl, 11", oblong
crystal $38.00
amber....................................$45.00
green....................................$47.00
ebony $45.00
rose $50.00
topaz/gold tint $48.00
2484 Bowl, 10", handled, see Baroque
2496 Bowl, see Baroque
2527 Bowl, 9", footed........................$65.00
2533 Bowl, 9", handled $95.00
2535 Bowl, 7", cupped........................$65.00
2535 Bowl, 9", flared $65.00

2536 Bowl, 9", handled
crystal $60.00
regal blue $95.00
burgundy $95.00
empire green $95.00
ruby $95.00
2538 Salad Set: 11" bowl and six 6" nappies
crystal $85.00
topaz/gold tint $110.00
silver mist $95.00
2538 Berry Set: 11" bowl and six 4½" nappies
crystal $85.00
topaz/gold tint $110.00
2545 Bowl, see Flame
2546 Quadrangle
crystal $25.00
azure $38.00
2547 Bowl, 6½", oblong
crystal $57.00
azure $65.00
gold tint $65.00
2563 Bowl, 9½", handled, Viking $95.00
2570 Bowls, see Artisan
2594 Bowl, 10", handled $92.00
2596 Bowl, 7½", square $75.00
2596 Bowl, 11", shallow, oblong $85.00
2598 Bowl, 11", oval $85.00
2600 Bowl, 9½", footed, Acanthus $135.00
2601 Bowl, 10½", lyre $95.00
2634 Bowl, 13", centerpiece for mermaid $125.00
2639 Bowl, 11", ivy $125.00
2639 Bowl, 13½", oval $70.00
2640 Garden Center Set: 14 lily pond, flower block, and six candleholders $350.00
2651 Bowl, 11", handled $95.00
2652 Bowl, 13½", handled $125.00
2666 Salad Set with 9" Contour
crystal $80.00
ebony $95.00
2666 Salad Set with 11" Contour
crystal $90.00
ebony $100.00
2667 Bowl, 7", footed, blown $34.00
2667 Bowl, 9¼", footed, blown $43.00
2697 Bowl, flared, wood base $36.00
2697 Bowl, floating, wood base $36.00
2697 Bowl, salad, wood base $36.00
2703 Bowls, see Artisan
2706 Bowl, salad/punch, 14", on ebony wooden base $48.00
cup $8.00
2719 Salad Set, 10", see Jamestown
2722 Table Charms
Sets 1 and 2
crystal $145.00
pink $295.00
yellow $350.00
Sets 3 and 4
crystal $125.00
pink $250.00
yellow $300.00
2785 Bowl, salad, 10", footed, see Gourmet
2806 Bowl, salad/punch, 11½", see Pebble Beach
4024 Bowl, 10½", Victorian
regal blue $165.00
burgundy $150.00
empire green $175.00
4171 Bowl, 10¼", crystal, charcoal, bark, and spruce, with wood stand and ebony finish $34.00
6023 Bowl, 9¼", blown, footed $87.00

Bracelet, Cutting 838

1953 – 1956

Stemware, 106

6051½ Goblet $30.00
6051½ Sherbet $26.00
6051½ Cocktail $24.00
6051½ Claret-Wine $34.00
6051½ Cordial $38.00
6051½ Oyster Cocktail $20.00
6051½ Ice Tea, footed $30.00
6051½ Juice, footed $24.00
2337 Plate, 7" $10.00
2337 Plate, 8" $12.00

Bracelet, Decoration 694

1976 – 1982

Stemware, 54

2916 Goblet $15.00
2916 Champagne $15.00
2916 Wine $15.00
2916 Ice Tea, footed $15.00
2916 Cordial $15.00

Bridal Belle, Decoration 639

1957 – 1973

Stemware, 114

6072 Goblet $35.00
6072 Sherbet $32.00
6072 Cocktail/Wine/Seafood $35.00
6072 Cordial $48.00
6072 Ice Tea, footed $35.00
6072 Juice, footed $32.00
2337 Plate, 7" $10.00
2337 Plate, 8" $12.00

Bridal Crown, Cutting 882

1961 – 1965

Stemware, 119

6089 Goblet $32.00
6089 Sherbet $30.00
6089 Wine/Cocktail $36.00
6089 Brandy $40.00
6089 Ice Tea, footed $32.00
6089 Juice, footed $28.00
2337 Plate, 7" $8.00
2337 Plate, 8" $10.00

Bridal Shower, Cutting 768

1937 – 1938

Stemware, 89

6017 Goblet $30.00
6017 Sherbet, high $28.00
6017 Sherbet, low $24.00
6017 Cocktail $28.00
6017 Claret $35.00
6017 Wine $35.00
6017 Cordial $45.00
6017 Oyster Cocktail $22.00
6017 Tumbler, 14 oz., footed $34.00
6017 Ice Tea, footed $30.00
6017 Tumbler, 9 oz., footed $24.00
6017 Juice, footed $22.00

Tableware I, 297

766 Bowl, finger $12.00
2545 Bowl, 12½" $57.00
2545 Candelabra, 2-light pair $175.00
2545 Candlestick, duo pair $95.00
6011 Jug $175.00
2337 Plate, 6" $6.00
2337 Plate, 7" $7.00
2337 Plate, 8" $8.00
2350½ Sugar and Cream $30.00

Bridal Shower, Cutting 897

1963 – 1970

Stemware, 126

6102 Goblet $32.00
6102 Sherbet $30.00
6102 Claret $35.00
6102 Tulip Wine $35.00
6102 Brandy $35.00
6102 Ice Tea, footed $32.00
2337 Plate, 7" $10.00
2337 Plate, 8" $12.00

Bridal Wreath, Cutting 833

1952 – 1965

Note: Price guides put this cutting on Blank 6049 Windsor, but it is actually on Blank 6051½ Courtship

Stemware, 106

6051½ Goblet $25.00
6051½ Sherbet, high $22.00
6051½ Sherbet, low $18.00
6051½ Parfait $25.00
6051½ Cocktail $18.00
6051½ Claret $28.00
6051½ Wine $28.00
6051½ Cordial $38.00
6051½ Oyster Cocktail $16.00
6051½ Ice Tea, footed $22.00
6051½ Juice, footed $16.00

Tableware II, 179-181

2630 Bonbon $45.00
2630 Bowl, 10½", salad $65.00
2630 Bowl, 10¾", footed, flared $77.00
2630 Bowl, 11¼", lily pond $68.00
2630 Candlestick, 4½", pair $65.00
2630 Candlestick, duo, pair $87.00
2630 Cup and Saucer $27.00
6011 Jug $250.00
2630 Mayonnaise, plate, ladle $64.00
2666 Pitcher, quart $165.00
2337 Plate, 7" $12.00
2337 Plate, 8" $16.00
2630 Plate, cake $57.00
2630 Plate, 14", torte $65.00
2630 Relish, 2-part $34.00
2630 Relish, 3-part $45.00
2630 Salad Set, 4-piece $125.00
2630 Shaker, chrome top B, pair $85.00
2630 Sugar and Cream $57.00
2630 Sugar and Cream, individual, tray $64.00
2630 Tray, handled, lunch $58.00

Bridesmaid, Decoration 658
1962 – 1970
Stemware, 124
6100 Goblet $35.00
6100 Sherbet $32.00
6100 Claret $38.00
6100 Tulip Wine $38.00
6100 Brandy $38.00
6100 Ice Tea, footed $35.00
2337 Plate, 7" $10.00
2337 Plate, 8" $12.00

Brighton, Cutting 801
1940 – 1954
Stemware, 94
6023 Goblet $25.00
6023 Saucer Champagne $23.00
6023 Sherbet, low $20.00
6023 Cocktail $22.00
6023 Claret-Wine $28.00
6023 Cordial $38.00
6023 Oyster Cocktail $18.00
6023 Ice Tea, footed $25.00
6023 Tumbler, 9 oz., footed $20.00
6023 Juice, footed $20.00
Tableware II, 168
766 Bowl, finger $22.00
2574 Bowl, 9½", handled $38.00
2574 Candlestick, duo, pair $87.00
6023 Comport, 5" $35.00
6011 Jug $250.00
2337 Plate, 7" $8.00
2337 Plate, 8" $10.00

Bristol, Cutting 710
1933 – 1938
Stemware, 77
6007 Goblet $35.00
6007 Sherbet, high $32.00
6007 Sherbet, low $28.00
6007 Cocktail $30.00
6007 Claret $38.00
6007 Wine $35.00
6007 Cordial $48.00
6007 Oyster Cocktail $28.00
6007 Ice Tea, footed $34.00
6007 Tumbler, 9 oz., footed $28.00
6007 Juice, footed $28.00
6007 Whiskey, footed $30.00
Tableware I, 276
2470 Bowl, 12" $45.00
2470 Candlestick, 5½", pair $58.00
2470 Comport, 6" $48.00
2451 Dish, ice and plate $28.00
2470 Plate, 10", cake $45.00
2440 Plate, 13", torte $45.00
2283 Plate, 7" $10.00
2283 Plate, 8" $12.00

Bristol, Cutting 880
1960 – 1962
Stemware, 121
6093 Goblet $28.00
6093 Sherbet $26.00
6093 Wine $32.00
6093 Cocktail $26.00
6093 Cordial $42.00
6093 Ice Tea, footed $28.00
6093 Juice, footed $25.00
2337 Plate, 7" $8.00
2337 Plate, 8" $10.00

Brocade, Crystal Print 30
1971 – 1973
Stemware, 141
6124 Goblet $35.00
6124 Sherbet $35.00
6124 Wine $35.00
6124 Ice Tea, footed $35.00
2337 Plate, 7" $10.00

Brocade, Decoration 674
1966 – 1970
Stemware, 131
6106 Goblet $32.00
6106 Sherbet $30.00
6106 Claret $35.00
6106 Tulip Wine $35.00
6106 Liqueur $45.00
6106 Ice Tea, footed $32.00
2337 Plate, 7" $10.00
2337 Plate, 8" $12.00

Brunswick, Etching 79
1926 – 1932
Stemware, 32
870 Goblet
- crystal $22.00
- amber $28.00
- green $28.00
- blue $38.00

870 Sherbet, high
- crystal $20.00
- amber $26.00
- green $26.00
- blue $34.00

870 Sherbet, low
- crystal $18.00
- amber $24.00
- green $24.00
- blue $32.00

870 Parfait
- crystal $25.00
- amber $28.00
- green $28.00
- blue $40.00

870 Cocktail
- crystal $20.00
- amber $26.00
- green $26.00
- blue $32.00

870 Claret
- crystal $22.00
- amber $30.00
- green $30.00
- blue $40.00

870 Wine
- crystal $22.00
- amber $28.00
- green $28.00
- blue $38.00

870 Cordial
- crystal $28.00
- amber $40.00
- green $40.00
- blue $48.00

870 Oyster Cocktail
- crystal $16.00
- amber $22.00
- green $22.00
- blue $30.00

869 Tumbler
- crystal $8.00
- amber $12.00
- green $12.00
- blue $16.00

5084 Tumbler
- crystal $14.00
- amber $18.00
- green $18.00
- blue $22.00

Tableware
869 Bowl, finger and plate
- crystal $16.00
- amber $18.00
- green $22.00
- blue $26.00

2270 Jug
- crystal $185.00
- amber $195.00
- green $210.00
- blue $245.00

5084 Jug
- crystal $185.00
- amber $195.00
- green $225.00
- blue $250.00

2283 Plate, 6"
- crystal $9.00
- amber $10.00
- green $12.00
- blue $14.00

2283 Plate, 7"
- crystal $10.00
- amber $12.00
- green $14.00
- blue $16.00

2283 Plate, 8"
- crystal $10.00
- amber $12.00
- green $15.00
- blue $18.00

Bubble Baby, Carving 28
1940 – 1943
Useful & Ornamental, 129
4116½ Vase, 5", ball $125.00

Buckingham, Cutting 721
1933 – 1934
Stemware, 79
6009 Goblet $34.00
6009 Sherbet, high $32.00
6009 Sherbet, low $28.00
6009 Cocktail $32.00
6009 Claret-Wine $38.00
6009 Cordial $47.00
6009 Oyster Cocktail $24.00

Buckingham, Cutting 721

6009 Ice Tea, footed $32.00
6009 Tumbler, 9 oz., footed $26.00
6009 Juice, footed $25.00

Tableware I, 279

869 Bowl, finger..........................$12.00
2470½ Bowl, 10½" $45.00
2470½ Candlestick, 5½", pair..........$54.00
2400 Comport, 6" $27.00
2337 Plate, 6" $6.00
2337 Plate, 7" $7.00
2337 Plate, 8" $8.00
4112 Vase, 8½" $85.00

Burgundy, Cutting 879

1960 – 1968

Stemware, 120

6092 Goblet $35.00
6092 Sherbet $33.00
6092 Wine/Cocktail $38.00
6092 Cordial $42.00
6092 Ice Tea, footed $35.00
6092 Juice, footed $30.00
2337 Plate, 7" $10.00
2337 Plate, 8" $12.00

Burnished Gold Highlights, Decoration 631

1953 – 1957

Tableware II, 198-199

2513 Jar, candy and cover....$150.00
2519 Cologne and Stopper $150.00
2519 Puff and Cover $145.00

Buttercup, Etching 340

1942 – 1959

Stemware, 100

6030 Goblet....$38.00
6030 Goblet, low $34.00
6030 Saucer Champagne $36.00
6030 Sherbet, low $26.00
6030 Cocktail $34.00
6030 Claret-Wine $43.00
6030 Cordial $58.00
6030 Oyster Cocktail.......................$24.00
6030 Ice Tea, footed $38.00
6030 Juice, footed $28.00

Tableware II, 134-138

2364 Ashtray ,individual $42.00
1769 Bowl, finger...........................$34.00
2364 Bowl, 6", baked apple............$54.00
2364 Bowl, 9", salad........................$65.00
6023 Bowl, 9", footed...................$125.00
2594 Bowl, 10", handled $150.00
2364 Bowl, 10½", salad $75.00
2364 Bowl, 12", flared $78.00
2364 Bowl, 12", lily pond................$78.00
2364 Bowl, 13", fruit........................$84.00
2324 Candlestick, 4", pair $58.00
2324 Candlestick, 6", pair $77.00
2594 Candlestick, 5½", pair $125.00
6023 Candlestick, duo, pair $125.00
2594 Candlestick, trindle, pair $175.00
2364 Jar, candy and cover $225.00/market
2350 Celery, 11"............................$45.00
2364 Cheese and Cracker...........$125.00
2364 Cigarette Holder....................$75.00
6030 Comport, 5"...........................$78.00
2364 Comport, 8"..........................$125.00
2350½ Cup and Saucer......................$34.00
2666 Jug, 1 quart...........$500.00/market
6011 Jug...$495.00
2364 Mayonnaise, plate, ladle.........$88.00
2350 Pickle, 8" $35.00
2337 Plate, 6" $18.00
2337 Plate, 7" $22.00
2337 Plate, 8" $25.00
2337 Plate, 9" $45.00
2364 Plate, crescent, salad.............$55.00
2364 Plate, 11", sandwich $50.00
2364 Plate, 14", torte $75.00
2364 Plate, 16", torte $85.00
2364 Relish, 2-part $75.00
2364 Relish, 3-part $65.00
2083 Bottle, salad dressing $450.00/market
2364 Salad Set, 9" $150.00
2364 Salad Set, 10½" $175.00
2586 Syrup, sani-cut $500.00/market
2364 Shaker, 2¼", pair...................$75.00
2350½ Sugar and Cream...................$75.00
2364 Tray, handled, lunch $125.00
6021 Vase, 6", bud $165.00
4143 Vase, 6", footed $245.00
4143 Vase, 7½", footed.................$325.00
2614 Vase, 10"...............................$475.00

Butterfly, Decoration 508

1931

Tableware I, 328

2350 Ashtray, large........$48.00
2430 Jar, candy and cover, ½ pound............................$145.00
2427 Box, cigarette and cover.....$225.00
2419 Jelly $48.00
2419 Dish, lemon $48.00
2419 Mayonnaise..............................$75.00
2419 Plate, cake $125.00
2419 Tray, handled, lunch $150.00
4108 Vase, 6"...................................$135.00
2430 Vase, 8"...................................$160.00
4107 Vase, 9"...................................$175.00

- C -

Cabot, Blank 6025, 6025½

1939 – 1959

Stemware, 96

6025 Goblet, no optic....$20.00
dimple optic....$24.00
6025 Sherbet, no optic $18.00
dimple optic $18.00
6025 Cocktail, no optic...................$15.00
dimple optic $18.00
6025 Claret-Wine, no optic $20.00
dimple optic $24.00
6025 Cordial, no optic $25.00
dimple optic $35.00
6025 Oyster Cocktail, no optic $12.00
dimple optic $14.00
6025 Ice Tea, footed, no optic $20.00
dimple optic $24.00
6025 Juice, footed, no optic $14.00
dimple optic $18.00

Tableware

2337/1 Plate, dimple optic, 7" $12.00

Cadence, Cutting 806

1940 – 1943

Stemware, 98

6027 Goblet...$25.00
6027 Saucer Champagne $24.00
6027 Sherbet, low $20.00
6027 Cocktail $24.00
6027 Wine...$28.00
6027 Cordial $35.00
6027 Oyster Cocktail.......................$16.00
6027 Ice Tea, footed $25.00
6027 Juice, footed $20.00

Tableware I, 304

4021 Bowl, finger...........................$18.00
6023 Candlestick, duo, pair $65.00
6011 Jug...$195.00
2364 Lily Pond, 12"........................$65.00
2337 Plate, 7" $7.00
2337 Plate, 8" $8.00

Camden, Etching 84

1928 – 1930

Amber and green

Stemware, 68

5098 Goblet $40.00
5098 Sherbet, high $35.00
5098 Sherbet, low $30.00
5098 Parfait $40.00
5098 Cocktail $35.00
5098 Claret $45.00
5098 Wine..$40.00
5098 Cordial $50.00
5098 Oyster Cocktail.......................$30.00
5098 Ice Tea, footed $40.00
5098 Tumbler, 9 oz., footed $30.00
5098 Juice, footed $30.00
5098 Whiskey, footed.....................$35.00
5082½ Grapefruit, 945½ liner...........$48.00

Tableware I, 122

869 Bowl, finger;...........................$22.00
5098 Comport, 5";...........................$38.00
4095 Jug, footed, solid color........$395.00
5098 Nappy, 6" $45.00
2283 Plate, 6" $12.00
2283 Plate, 7" $15.00
2283 Plate, 8" $20.00
5000 Jug...$395.00

Camelia, Etching 344

1952 – 1965

Stemware, 103

6036 Goblet........................$32.00
6036 Sherbet, high $28.00
6036 Sherbet, low $20.00
6036 Parfait $30.00
6036 Cocktail $26.00
6036 Claret-Wine $35.00
6036 Cordial $40.00
6036 Oyster Cocktail.......................$20.00
6036 Ice Tea, footed $32.00
6036 Juice, footed $22.00

Tableware II, 148-152

2630 Basket, reed handle $125.00
2630 Bonbon, 3-toed.......................$38.00
2630 Bowl, 4½", nappy..................$22.00
2630 Bowl, fruit...............................$22.00

2630 Bowl, cereal ... $26.00
2630 Bowl, snack ... $28.00
2630 Bowl, 8", flared ... $36.00
2630 Bowl, 8½", salad ... $38.00
2630 Bowl, 9", lily pond ... $47.00
2630 Bowl 10½", salad ... $50.00
2630 Bowl, handled, serving ... $52.00
2630 Bowl, oval, vegetable ... $45.00
2630 Bowl, oval, utility ... $64.00
2630 Bowl, 10¾", footed ... $65.00
2630 Bowl, 11", rolled edge, footed ... $88.00
2630 Bowl, 11¼", lily pond ... $58.00
2630 Bowl, 12", flared ... $68.00
2630 Butter, oblong ... $57.00
2630 Candlestick, 4½", pair ... $56.00
2630 Candlestick, duo, pair ... $75.00
2630 Candlestick, trindle, pair ... $125.00
2630 Jar, candy and cover ... $85.00
2630 Cheese and Cracker ... $85.00
2630 Comport, 4¾" ... $46.00
2630 Condiment Set, 3-piece ... $157.00
2630 Cup and Saucer ... $28.00
2630 Ice Bucket, metal handle ... $135.00
2630 Jug, 3-pint, ice ... $165.00
2630 Mayonnaise, plate, ladle ... $65.00
2630 Mayonnaise, 2-part, 2 ladles ... $65.00
2630 Mustard, cover, spoon ... $64.00
2630 Oil, D.S., 5 oz. ... $62.00
2630 Pickle, 8¾" ... $24.00
2630 Pitcher, 1-pint, cereal ... $75.00
2630 Plate, 6" ... $16.00
2630 Plate, 7" ... $18.00
2630 Plate, 8" ... $22.00
2630 Plate, 9" ... $34.00
2630 Plate, 10½" ... $52.00
2630 Plate, crescent, salad ... $55.00
2630 Plate, 8", party and cup ... $42.00
2630 Plate, handled, cake ... $65.00
2630 Plate, 14", torte ... $75.00
2630 Plate, 16", torte ... $75.00
2630 Platter, 12", oval ... $68.00
2630 Preserve, footed and cover ... $65.00
2630 Relish, 2-part ... $36.00
2630 Relish, 3-part ... $54.00
2630 Salad Set, 10½" ... $125.00
2630 Salver ... $110.00
2630 Shaker, chrome top B, pair ... $65.00
2630 Sugar and Cream ... $65.00
2630 Sugar and Cream, individual ... $58.00
2630 Sugar and Cream Set, individual, tray ... $75.00
2630 Tidbit, 3-toed ... $36.00
2630 Tidbit Set, 3-piece ... $68.00
2630 Tray, handled, lunch ... $65.00
2630 Tray, handled, muffin ... $65.00
2630 Tray, 10½", snack ... $54.00
2630 Tray, handled, utility ... $65.00
2630 Tricorne, 3-toed ... $45.00
2630 Vase, 6", bud ... $45.00
2630 Vase, 7½", handled ... $85.00
2630 Vase, 8½", oval ... $85.00
4121 Vase, 5" ... $68.00
4143 Vase, 6", footed ... $67.00
6021 Vase, 6", footed, bud ... $58.00
2660 Vase, 8", flip ... $85.00
5092 Vase, 8", footed, bud ... $95.00
2470 Vase, 10", footed ... $125.00
2657 Vase, 10½", footed ... $175.00

Camelot, CA13/CA14 Blank 6009

1979 – 1980

Stemware, 79

CA13/CA14
Goblet, 13 oz.
crystal ... $34.00
blue ... $38.00

CA13/CA14
Wine, 9 oz.
crystal ... $32.00
blue ... $36.00

CA13/CA14
Dessert/Champagne, 9 oz.
crystal ... $22.00
blue ... $30.00

CA13/CA14
Magnum,, 16 oz.
crystal ... $45.00
blue ... $55.00

CA13/CA14
Ice Tea, 16 oz., footed
crystal ... $38.00
blue ... $43.00

Cameo, Crystal Print 28

1971 – 1982

Stemware, 140

6123 Goblet ... $28.00
6123 Sherbet ... $25.00
6123 Wine ... $28.00
6123 Ice Tea, footed ... $28.00
2337 Plate, 7", green mist ... $10.00

Cameo, Etching 88

1933 – 1940

Stemware, 79

6009 Goblet ... $32.00
6009 Sherbet, high ... $30.00
6009 Sherbet, low ... $25.00
6009 Cocktail ... $30.00
6009 Claret-Wine ... $35.00
6009 Cordial ... $40.00
6009 Oyster Cocktail ... $21.00
6009 Ice Tea, footed ... $32.00
6009 Tumbler, 9 oz., footed ... $25.00
6009 Juice, footed ... $24.00
701 Tumbler ... $10.00 – 16.00
887 Tumbler ... $10.00 – 16.00
1184 Tumbler ... $10.00 – 16.00
4122 Whiskey Sham ... $10.00

Candle Parts

Useful & Ornamental, 103

4 Bobache, UDP ... $50.00
5 Bobache, cut, tear drop prisms ... $40.00
21 Candle Holder with metal threaded peg to screw into candelabra candle arms ... $36.00
21 Bobache, wired, 4^13^⁄16" outside; ⅞" inside ... $25.00
26 Candle Lamp Base ... $20.00
*26 Candle Lamp Base with peg ... $25.00
26 Candle Lamp Chimney ... $65.00
26 Candle Lamp Pot ... $5.00
26 Ferrule, used to adapt ... $10.00
26 Candle Lamp Shade ... market
121 Bobache with UDP ... $50.00
122 Bobache with UDP ... $50.00
188 Bobache with UDP ... $50.00
1640 Bobache, wired, uses 6" Colonial Prisms, plain, cut, or etched ... $50.00
1941 Bobache or Candle Drip ... $15.00
2279 Candleholder/Bobache crystal ... $15.00
2308 Bobache, wired amber and green ... $65.00
2311 Candleholder/Bobache/Lustre with 4" Colonial Prisms
crystal ... $75.00
amber ... $85.00
green ... $85.00
2482 Bobache, 3⅞" outside, 1⅜" inside, wired for 8 prisms ... $35.00
2482½ Candle Drip, 3¼" ... $20.00
2484½ Candle Drip, 3½", crystal or silver mist ... $20.00
2484 Bobache, 4¼" outside, 1⁷⁄16" inside, wired for 8 UDP ... $45.00
2527 Bobache and UDP or 2" B prisms, same as 2545 Bobache ... $45.00
2545 Bobache, UDP or B prisms ... $45.00
2546 Bobache, square, 7 B prisms ... $75.00
2762 Bobache, 3¾" outside, 1⅛" inside, wired for 8 UDP ... $60.00
2763 Candle Lamp Shade, 5" ... $20.00
2765 Bobache, 4½" outside, 1¾" inside, wired for 10 UDP ... $60.00
2767 Candle Lamp Shade, 9" ... $30.00
2769 Bobache, 4⅞" outside, 2¾" inside, wired for 10 prisms ... $50.00
30 Prism, Spearhead ... $3.50
35 Prism, U Drop (UDP) ... $2.50
40 Prisms, Colonial or flat, may be cut or etched ... $6.00
Prism, 2", B ... $4.00
Prism, tear drop ... $4.00

Candlesticks, Candelabra, Lustres & Candle Lamps, and Candle Vases

1888 – 1982

Useful & Ornamental, 76-102

Tableware II, 285-287

No. 1 Candelabra, 26", 3-light, used 7" vase for top bobache, plain arms ... $675.00
No. 1 Candelabra, 4-light ... $650.00
No. 2 Candelabra, 4-light ... $400.00
No. 3 Candelabra, 7-light, banquet ... $800.00/market
No. 3 Candelabra, 4-light, banquet ... $400.00
No. 4 Lustre Candlestick ... $125.00
No. 5 Candlestick, single, handled ... $45.00
No. 5A Candelabra, 2-light ... $300.00
No. 6 Candlestick, single, ribboned ... $95.00
No. 7 Candelabra, 5-light ... $500.00
4-light ... $300.00
3-light ... $275.00
6-light ... $600.00
7-light ... $700.00/market
No. 8 Candelabra, crucifix, 3-light ... $350.00
No. 8 Candelabra, crucifix, 4-light ... $450.00
No. 9 Candelabra, 4-light ... $400.00
No. 10 Candelabra, 6-light ... $600.00
No. 11 Candelabra, floral ... market
No. 12 Candelabra, Arabian light ... market
No. 13 Candelabra
3-light ... $275.00
4-light ... $400.00
5-light ... $500.00

6-light $600.00
7-light $700.00
low, 4-light, pink holders....$600.00
low, 5-light, pink holders ...$700.00
low, 6-light, pink holders ...$800.00
No. 14 Candelabra, low, 6-light $500.00
No. 15 Candelabra, 2-light $225.00
No. 16 Candelabra
4-light $395.00
5-light $450.00
6-light $500.00
No. 16 Candlestick, cut star and fan ..$95.00
No. 17 Candlestick $150.00
No. 17 Candelabra
5-light $500.00
4-light $400.00
3-light $300.00
6-light $600.00
7-light $700.00
No. 18 Candlestick, single $87.00
No. 18 Candelabra, 4-light $400.00
No. 19 Candlestick, 10", 12", 15", 18", or 7",
single, column ....$65.00 – 165.00
No. 19 Candlestick, single, handled ..$48.00
No. 21 Candlestick, lustre..............$125.00
No. 22 Candelabra, 2-light $225.00
No. 23 Candelabra, 3-light $325.00
No. 24 Candelabra, 4-light, 21"
prisms $350.00
No. 25 Candelabra, 5-light, 24"
prisms $600.00
No. 25½
Candelabra, 5-light, etched,
w/ Spearhead and Colonial
prisms $700.00
No. 26 Candle Lamp Parts, see Parts,
Lustres, Candelabra, Candle Lamps
No. 32 Candelabra, 2-light, with candle
lamps and shades ....market
No. 33 Candelabra, 3-light, with candle
lamps and shades ....market
No. 34 Candelabra, 4-light, with candle
lamps and shades ....market
No. 35 Candelabra, 5-light, with candle
lamps and shades ....market
112 Candlestick, 9" $54.00
112 Candelabra with mirror,
3-light...............................market
121 Bobache, see Parts, Lustres,
Candelabra, Candle Lamps
122 Bobache, see Parts, Lustres,
Candelabra, Candle Lamps
140 Candlestick, Chamber $48.00
161 Candlestick, 6½", 7", single..$47.00
188 Bobache or Candle Drip, see Parts,
Lustres, Candelabra, Candle Lamps
737 Candlestick, single $125.00
1064 Candlestick, 8", single $58.00
1081 Candlestick, 8", single $58.00
1103 Candlestick, 9½", single $67.00
1103 Candlestick, 14½", lustre,
see Queen Anne $125.00
1103 Candlestick, 18½", lustre... $175.00
1103 Candlestick, 22½", lustre....$235.00
1204 Candlestick, 8½", single $75.00
1204 Candlestick, 8½", deep, etched,
D $75.00
1205 Candlestick, 8", single $68.00
1218 Candlestick, 8", single $68.00
1218 Candlestick, 8", deep, etched,
A, Cut 72 ....$75.00
1372 Candlesticks , see Coin
1453 Candlestick, 11", single $95.00
1485 Candlestick, 8", single,
etched B $67.00
1485 Candlestick, 8", lustre 120.00
1485 Candlestick, 9½", single $85.00
1485 Candlestick, 11", single $95.00
1485 Candlestick, 8", Cut 160....... $72.00
1490 Candlestick, 8", single $67.00
1490 Candlestick, 15", single,
plain or etched $150.00
1490 Candlestick, 15", lustre, plain
or etched prisms.............$175.00
1490 Candlestick, 8", Cutting 162.. $72.00
1490 Candlestick, 8", Etched C-2 .. $75.00
1490 Candlestick, 15", etched $150.00
1513 Candlestick, single, saucer...$36.00
1513 Candlestick, chamber $45.00
1612 Candlestick, 5", Christmas ...$34.00
1639 Candlestick, 8", single $68.00
1639 Candlestick, 8", deep, etched,
D.. $75.00
1640 Candlestick, 8½", single $75.00
1640 Candlestick, 11½", lustre, plain or
etched Colonial Prisms...$150.00
1642 Candlestick 8", single $67.00
1643 Candlestick, 9", single $74.00
1666 Candlestick, chamber $45.00
1842 Candlestick, 8½", single $68.00
1843 Candle Lamp, single handled, with
or without shade $48.00
1856 Candlestick, 8", single,
plain or etched $67.00
1856 Candlestick, 8", Cutting 163.. $72.00
1856 Candlestick, 8", deep, etched.. $85.00
1962 Candlestick, 9", 2-handled, single,
plain, or etched $125.00
1962 Candlestick, 9", deep,
etched $125.00
1963 Candlestick, 9", single, plain or
etched $75.00
1963 Candlestick, 9", deep etched.. $95.00
1964 Candlestick, 9", single, plain, or
etched $75.00
1964 Candlestick, 9", deep etched .. $95.00
1965 Candlestick, 8", single, plain, or
etched $67.00
1965 Candlestick, 8", Cutting 164 .. $65.00
1965 Candlestick, 8", deep, etched...$85.00
2056 Candlesticks, see American
2063 Candlestick, 2 3/16", chamber
crystal $32.00
amber................................$38.00
green.................................$40.00
blue $48.00
2080 Candlestick, 6½", single $58.00
2108 Candlestick, single $48.00
2183 Candlestick, see Milk Glass...$24.00
2183 Hurricane Lamp,
see Milk Glass $38.00
2183 Flora Candle, see Heirloom
2244 Candlestick, 6", single, etched,
D..$65.00
2244 Candlestick, 6", deep etched.. $67.00
2244 Candlestick, 8", single, Cut 165,
etched D $77.00
2244 Candlestick, 8", deep, etched .. $85.00
2244 Candlestick, 8¼", single, Decorations
12, 17, 20, 21, 31, and 32....$85.00
2245 Candlestick, 6", single
crystal $40.00
amber................................$55.00
canary $85.00
green................................ $60.00
blue $85.00
ebony $70.00
2245 Candlestick, 6", deep etched.. $62.00
2245 Candlestick, 8¼", single
crystal $58.00
amber................................$65.00
canary $95.00
green................................ $70.00
blue $95.00
ebony $75.00
2245 Candlestick, 8¼", deep
etched $75.00
2246 Candlestick, 8¼", single $52.00
2246 Candlestick, 8¼", deep
etched $85.00
2247 Candlestick, 8½", single $58.00
2268 Candlestick, 6", single,
deep etched.......................$68.00
2269 Candlestick, 6", single
crystal $45.00
amber................................$52.00
green.................................$56.00
canary $65.00
blue $60.00
ebony $52.00
2269 Candlestick, 6", deep etched .. $55.00
2275 Candlestick, 7½", single
crystal $45.00
amber................................$52.00
green.................................$56.00
canary $65.00
blue $60.00
ebony $52.00
2275 Candlestick, 9", single
crystal $50.00
amber............................... $56.00
green................................ $60.00
canary $75.00
blue $70.00
ebony $55.00
2275 Candlestick, 9", deep etched..$90.00
2279 Candleholder/Bobache, 4½" dia.,
pegged with prisms $35.00
2297 Candlestick, 7", single
crystal $45.00
amber............................... $50.00
green.................................$54.00
blue $65.00
canary $75.00
ebony $50.00
2298 Candlestick, 3½", single
crystal $26.00
amber................................$30.00
green................................ $35.00
canary $54.00
blue $54.00
ebony $35.00
2299 Candlestick, 5", single, oval base
crystal $40.00
amber................................$50.00
green.................................$50.00
canary $65.00
blue $65.00
ebony $50.00
2311 Candlestick, 7", single
crystal $50.00
amber................................$75.00
green.................................$85.00
canary $125.00
2311 Candlestick, 9", lustre
canary with crystal
bobache $225.00
all amber..........................$185.00
all green.......................... $195.00
2311 Candleholder/Bobache with 4"
Colonial or UDP

crystal $85.00
amber....$85.00
green....$85.00
2324 Candlestick, 2"
crystal $15.00
amber.... $18.00
green....$25.00
canary $40.00
blue $35.00
ebony $18.00
2324 Candlestick, 4", single
crystal $15.00
amber....$18.00
green.... $20.00
canary $45.00
blue $34.00
orchid.... $28.00
rose $22.00
azure $24.00
ebony $18.00
2324 Candlestick, 4", etched $20.00
2324 Candlestick, 9", single
crystal $30.00
amber.... $35.00
green....$43.00
canary $75.00
blue $64.00
ebony $40.00
2324 Candlestick, 9", etched $95.00
2324 Candlestick, 12", single
crystal $50.00
amber....$58.00
green.... $65.00
ebony $58.00
2324 Candlestick, 12", etched $125.00
2324½ Candlestick, 4, candle socket is 1½" diameter, for larger candle
crystal $32.00
amber.... $35.00
green.... $38.00
canary $45.00
blue $45.00
ebony $35.00
2324 Candlestick, 6", single
crystal $20.00
amber.... $22.00
green.... $24.00
canary $50.00
blue $45.00
orchid....$45.00
ebony $22.00
light blue $25.00
2326 Candle Vase, see Lead Crystal Giftware
2333 Candlestick, 8", single
amber....$54.00
green....$58.00
blue $65.00
2333 Candlestick, 11", single
amber....$65.00
2352 Candlestick, Lily
crystal $45.00
amber....$54.00
green....$65.00
blue $75.00
orchid....$75.00
2362 Candlestick, 3", single
green.... $25.00
blue $35.00
orchid.... $28.00
2362 Candlestick, 9", single
green....$65.00
blue $75.00
orchid....$70.00
2372 Candlestick, 2", block, plain, or spiral optic
crystal $15.00
amber.... $20.00
green....$24.00
blue $30.00
orchid....$30.00
rose $25.00
2375 Candlestick, 3", see Fairfax
crystal $12.50
amber....$15.00
green.... $20.00
orchid....$24.00
rose $20.00
azure $20.00
topaz/gold tint $17.50
ebony $18.00
2375½ Candlestick, Mushroom
crystal $20.00
amber.... $22.50
green....$25.00
orchid.... $32.50
rose $25.00
azure $25.00
topaz....$25.00
2383 Candlestick, trindle
crystal $45.00
amber.... $48.00
green.... $54.00
rose $54.00
azure $54.00
topaz/gold tint $50.00
ebony $48.00
2390 Candlestick, 3"
amber.... $27.00
green....$30.00
rose $40.00
azure .... $40.00..
orchid.... $40.00
2393 Candlestick, 2", crimped, spiral optic
amber....$65.00
green....$70.00
rose $70.00
azure $100.00
2394 Candlestick, 2", 3-toed
crystal $36.00
amber....$40.00
green....$45.00
orchid....$54.00
rose $50.00
azure $50.00
topaz/gold tint $48.00
wisteria $95.00
regal blue $95.00
burgundy....$95.00
empire green....$95.00
2395 Candlestick, 3"
crystal $35.00
amber....$40.00
green....$45.00
rose $45.00
azure $57.00
ebony $45.00
2395½ Candlestick, 5½"
crystal $35.00
amber....$38.00
green....$45.00
rose $48.00
azure $55.00
topaz/gold tint $45.00
ebony $45.00
2402 Candlestick, 2"
crystal $20.00
amber....$22.00
green....$24.00
rose $24.00
azure $26.00
topaz/gold tint $24.00
ebony $24.00
2424 Candlestick, see Kent
2425 Candlestick, 2"
crystal $28.00
amber....$34.00
green....$36.00
rose $36.00
azure $38.00
topaz....$36.00
ebony $36.00
2430 Candlesticks, see Diadem
2433 Candlestick, see Twenty-Four Thirty-Three
2436 Candlestick, 9", lustre
crystal $125.00
amber....$145.00
green....$150.00
rose $168.00
topaz....$150.00
ebony $168.00
wisteria $225.00
2443 Candlestick, 4"
crystal $25.00
amber....$28.00
green....$32.00
rose $32.00
azure $35.00
topaz/gold tint $32.00
ebony $32.00
wisteria $57.00
ruby....$65.00
2446 Candlestick
crystal $35.00
amber....$38.00
green....$42.00
rose $42.00
azure $50.00
topaz....$50.00
ebony $50.00
2447 Candlestick, duo
crystal $38.00
amber....$43.00
green....$48.00
rose $54.00
azure $65.00
topaz/gold tint $48.00
ebony $54.00
ruby....$125.00
wisteria $125.00
2449 Candlestick, 6", see Hermitage
2453 Candlestick, 7½", lustre
crystal $100.00
amber....$125.00
green....$150.00
topaz....$135.00
ebony $150.00
wisteria $225.00
2455 Candlestick, 6"
crystal $45.00
amber....$54.00
green....$60.00
rose $60.00
topaz....$60.00
2466 Candlestick, 3"
crystal $24.00
amber....$26.00
green....$28.00
topaz....$28.00
ebony $25.00
2470 Candlestick, see Twenty-Four Seventy
2470½ see Twenty-Four Seventy

2472 Candlestick, duo
crystal $54.00
amber....$57.00
green....$60.00
rose $60.00
topaz/gold tint $55.00
ebony $55.00
2481 Candlestick, 5"
crystal $40.00
amber....$45.00
green....$50.00
rose $50.00
topaz/gold tin $45.00
ebony $45.00
2482 Candlestick, trindle
crystal $68.00
amber....$75.00
green....$85.00
rose $87.00
topaz....$75.00
ebony $70.00
2482 Candelabra
crystal $80.00
amber....$87.00
green....$95.00
rose $100.00
topaz....$95.00
ebony $95.00
2484 Candlesticks, see Baroque
2496 Candlesticks, see Baroque
2510 Candlesticks, see Sunray
2521 Bird Candleholder, see Lead Crystal Giftware
2527 Candelabra, 2-light, 2527 Bobache, 16 UDP $150.00
2533 Candlestick, duo....$68.00
2533 Candelabra, duo with 2527 Bobache, 2" B prisms, crystal $125.00
2535 Candlestick, 5½", single
crystal $45.00
regal blue $65.00
burgundy....$65.00
empire green....$65.00
ruby....$65.00
2545 Candlesticks, see Flame
2546 Candlestick, duo....$95.00
2546 Candelabra, duo with square bobache, 7 B prisms....$200.00
2546 Candlestick, quadrangle
crystal $150.00
azure $225.00
2546 Candelabra, quadrangle, square bobache, B Prisms
crystal....$400.00/market
azure....$425.00/market
2547 Candlestick, trindle
crystal $95.00
azure $150.00
gold tint $135.00
2550 Candlesticks, see Spool
2560 Candlesticks, see Coronet
2563 Candlestick, 4½", Viking $56.00
2574 Candlesticks, see Raleigh
2592 Candlesticks, see Myriad
2596 Candlestick, 5"....$47.00
2594 Candlestick, trindle $75.00
2598 Candlestick, duo....$125.00
2600 Candlestick, trindle, Acanthus....$175.00
2600 Candelabra, 3-light, 2545 bobache, UDP $325.00
2601 Candlestick, duo, lyre $75.00
2620 Candlestick, see Wistar
2636 Candlestick, Plume $85.00
2636 Candlestick, duo, Plume....$115.00
2638 Candlestick, see Contour, Ebony Glass
2639 Candlestick, duo....$125.00
2640 Garden Center....$350.00
2652 Candlestick, trindle....$95.00
2653 Candlestick, trindle....$95.00
2655 Candlestick, 4-light....$165.00
2655 Candelabra and 3- or 4-light, 2527 Bobache....$250.00
2666 see Contour
2667 Candlestick, 2½"
crystal $18.00
ebony $25.00
2667 Candlestick, 6"....$40.00
2668 Candlestick
crystal $38.00
ebony $48.00
2668 Hurricane Lamp Complete: 2668 Candlestick, 2668 Hurricane Lamp Chimney, crystal....$65.00
ebony base $75.00
2702 Candleholder/Vase, 6¾", brass and glass....$22.00
2702 Candleholder/Vase, 8", brass and glass....$25.00
2702 Candleholder/Vase, 9½", brass and glass....$28.00
2708 Candleholder/Brass, 8"....$35.00
2708 Candleholder, duo....$45.00
2722 Table Charms, see Bowls, Centerpieces, and Console Bowls
2742 Candlestick, see Sculpture
2749 Candlesticks, see Crown
2752 Candlestick, see Facets
2757 Candle Twist, see Sculpture
2761 Candlestick, 10½", Lustre, 8 5", flat prisms....$125.00
2762 Candelabra, 2-light, 12", 2762 Bobache with 8 4" flat prisms....$175.00
2763 Candlestick, 9"....$125.00
2763 Candle Lamp, 13½" 2763 9" Candlestick, 2763 5" Candle Lamp Shade ..$160.00
2765 Candelabra, 3-light, 11¼" 2765 bobache, 10 4", flat prisms ...$225.00
2767 Candle Lamp, 17½" 2763 candlestick, 2767 9" shade....$165.00
2767 Candlestick, 9", lustre, 2769 bobache with 10 flat prisms....$175.00
2767 Candle Lamp Lustre, 17½": 2763 9" candlestick, 2769 bobache wired with 10 4" flat prisms, 2767 shade 9"....$250.00
2768 Candlestick, 3-light....$150.00
2768 Candelabra, 3-light, 12" 2768 candlestick, 2765 Bobache (3), 30 Spearhead Prisms....$290.00
2776/2777
Candlesticks, see Henry Ford Museum
2782 Candleholder, 3½" $20.00
2782 Candle Lamp, 12¼" $40.00
2864 Candleholder B....$7.00
2883 Candlestick, 6"....$10.00
3008 Candlestick, see Holly and Ruby Giftware
4024 Candlestick, 6"
crystal $47.00
regal blue bowl $78.00
burgundy bowl....$78.00
empire green bowl $78.00
4113 Candlestick, 6"
regal blue $78.00
burgundy....$78.00
empire green....$78.00
6023 Candlestick, duo....$35.00

GL06/313
Candleholder, 2", stackable, Glacier, pair.... $9.00
GL06/757
Vase, 6", bud, Glacier.... $9.00
HI01/308
Candle, 3", votive, highlight .. $6.50
HI01/754
Vase, 5", Highlight $6.50
FL05/756
Candle/Vase, 6", flora, Flame .. $6.75
FL03/317
Candleholder, 4", Flame $6.00
FL03/757
Vase, 6", bud, Flame $6.75
CA10/325
Candlestick, 8", pair $75.00
CA10/314
Candlestick, 3", Colony, pair .. $40.00
CA10/326
Candlestick, 9", Colony, pair...$75.00
CA10/332
Candlestick, duo, pair $85.00
CA10/327
Candle Lamp, 9", blown shade, pair $300.00
CA11/314
Candlestick, 3", 2324, pair $40.00
CA11/319
Candlestick, 6", 2324, pair $57.00
CA12/314
Candlestick, 3", Kent, pair....$40.00
CA12/323
Candlestick, 7", pair $72.00
CA10/461
Shade, 9", blown $35.00
CA12/337
Candlestick, 3-light....$125.00
CA12/337
Candelabra, 3-light $220.00
CA12/132
Bobache, wired....$25.00
TR02/981
Prism, 3⅛", Spearhead $6.00

Candlelight, Decoration 652

1961 – 1971

Stemware, 123

6099 Goblet....$28.00
6099 Sherbet....$26.00
6099 Wine/Cocktail....$30.00
6099 Cordial....$36.00
6099 Ice Tea, footed $28.00
6099 Juice, footed $24.00
2337 Plate, 7" $10.00
2337 Plate, 8" $12.00

Candy Jars and Boxes

1915 – 1981

Useful & Ornamental, 104-109

1229 Frisco, see Milk Glass and Centennial II
1372 Coin, see Coin Glass
1904 Bonbon and Cover $65.00
2056 American, see American
2136 Bonbon and Cover, 5"
crystal $54.00
amber....$60.00
green.... $65.00
blue $78.00
canary $85.00
2219 Jar, candy and cover, footed
crystal $42.00

amber ... $48.00
green ... $54.00
blue ... $58.00
canary ... $65.00

2250 Jar, candy and cover, ¼, ½, and 1 pound sizes
crystal ... $40.00
amber ... $45.00
green ... $50.00
blue ... $55.00
canary ... $64.00

2328 Box, candy and cover, 7", oblong
crystal ... $38.00
amber ... $45.00
green ... $54.00
blue ... $65.00
canary ... $95.00

2331 Box, candy and cover, no compartments
crystal ... $40.00
amber ... $47.00
green ... $54.00
blue ... $64.00
canary ... $85.00

2331-3 Box, candy and cover, 3 compartments
crystal ... $35.00
amber ... $45.00
green ... $50.00
blue ... $56.00
canary ... $85.00
ebony ... $45.00
orchid ... $60.00

2364 Jar, candy and cover, see Sonata

2380 Confection and Cover, plain or SO
crystal, plain ... $34.00
amber, plain ... $40.00
amber, SO ... $42.00
green, plain ... $42.00
green, SO ... $45.00
blue, plain ... $50.00
orchid, plain ... $55.00
rose, plain or SO ... $55.00
azure, plain ... $55.00

2394 Jar, candy and cover, ½ pound
crystal ... $42.00
amber ... $45.00
green ... $50.00
rose ... $60.00
azure ... $65.00
topaz ... $65.00

2395 Confection and Cover, oval
amber ... $65.00
green ... $75.00
rose ... $75.00
azure ... $85.00
topaz ... $75.00

2412 Colony, see Colony

2413 Urn and Cover, footed
amber ... $95.00
green ... $125.00
rose ... $150.00
azure ... $150.00

2424 Kent, see Kent

2430 Diadem, see Diadem

2456 Jar, candy and cover
crystal ... $65.00
amber ... $75.00
green ... $87.00
rose ... $90.00
ebony ... $75.00

2496 Baroque, see Baroque

2510 Sunray, see Sunray

2513 Grape Leaf, see Grape Leaf

2545 Flame, see Flame

2546 Box, candy and cover, quadrangle
crystal ... $62.00
azure ... $95.00
gold tint ... $85.00

2592 Myriad, see Myriad

2616 Box, candy and cover, oval .. $125.00

2630 Century, see Century

2711 Diamond Sunburst, see Milk Glass

2712 Berry, see Milk Glass

2713 Vintage, see Milk Glass

4095 Jar, candy and cover, ½ pound, 5" nappy, pound, 6" nappy
amber, LO ... $95.00
amber foot, LO ... $95.00
green, SO ... $110.00
green foot, SO ... $110.00
blue, RO ... $135.00
blue foot, RO ... $125.00

4095½ Jar, candy and cover, ½ pound, tall
amber, LO ... $95.00
amber foot, LO ... $95.00
green, SO ... $110.00
green foot SO ... $110.00
blue, RO ... $135.00
blue foot, RO ... $125.00

4099 Jar, candy and cover
crystal ... $125.00
regal blue ... $175.00
burgundy ... $175.00
empire green ... $175.00

4117 Jar, candy and cover, Bubble
crystal ... $67.00
ruby ... $165.00
regal blue ... $150.00
burgundy ... $165.00
empire green ... $165.00

5084 Jar, candy and cover, RO
crystal ... $135.00
amber ... $150.00
amber foot ... $150.00
green ... $165.00
green foot ... $165.00
blue ... $195.00
blue foot ... $195.00

Cantata, Cutting 907

1965 – 1970

Stemware, 130

6105 Goblet ... $30.00
6105 Sherbet ... $28.00
6105 Claret ... $35.00
6105 Wine ... $35.00
6105 Cordial ... $40.00
6105 Ice Tea, footed ... $30.00
2337 Plate, 7" ... $8.00
2337 Plate, 8" ... $10.00

Canterbury, Cutting 716

1933 – 1935

Stemware, 78

6008 Goblet ... $35.00
6008 Sherbet, high ... $32.00
6008 Sherbet, low ... $28.00
6008 Cocktail ... $32.00
6008 Wine ... $38.00
6008 Cordial ... $48.00
6008 Oyster Cocktail ... $28.00
6008 Ice Tea, footed ... $34.00
6008 Tumbler, 9 oz., footed ... $28.00
6008 Juice, footed ... $28.00

Tableware I, 278

2470½ Bowl, 10½" ... $48.00
2470½ Candlestick, 5½", pair ... $52.00
2482 Candlestick, trindle, pair ... $100.00
2430 Candy and Cover, ½ pound ... $54.00
2400 Comport, 6" ... $27.00
2451 Dish, ice with liner, plate ... $42.00
2283 Plate, 7" ... $7.00
2283 Plate, 8" ... $8.00
2364 Plate, 16", torte ... $48.00
2419 Relish, 4-part ... $26.00
2440 Sugar and Cream ... $45.00
2467 Vase, 7½" ... $75.00
4107 Vase, 9" ... $95.00

Capri, 6045

1952 – 1965

Stemware, 104

6045 Goblet ... $22.00
6045 Sherbet ... $20.00
6045 Cocktail ... $20.00
6045 Claret-Wine ... $22.00
6045 Cordial ... $25.00
6045 Ice Tea, footed ... $22.00
6045 Juice, footed ... $20.00
2665 Plate, 7" ... $8.00
2665 Plate, 8" ... $10.00

Captiva, CA16

1983 – 1986

crystal, light blue, peach

Stemware, 187

Tableware II, 242, 279, 294

CA16 Goblet/Ice Tea, 13 oz. ... $22.00
CA16 Wine/Juice, 8 oz. ... $22.00
CA16 Mug/Cup, 9 oz. ... $22.00
CA16/512 Bowl, 6" ... $15.00
CA16/550 Plate, 8" ... $15.00
CA16/554 Plate, 10" ... $20.00
CA16/783 Tray ... $22.00
CA16/973 Ice Bucket ... $35.00
CA16/888 Highball ... $18.00
CA16/339 Old Fashioned ... $18.00
CA16/293 Box, jewel and cover ... $25.00
CA16/293 Place Card Holder ... $12.00

Caribbean, 2808

1969 – 1970

Tableware II, 102

2808/194 Bowl, 9", footed ... $35.00
2808/347 Candy and Cover, 10", footed ... $52.00
2808/318 Candleholder, 5½", footed, pair ... $56.00
2808/829 Urn and Cover, 15", footed ... $65.00
2808/830 Vase, 13", footed ... $57.00

Carillon, Cutting 915

1967 – 1968

Stemware, 129

6104 Goblet ... $28.00

Carillon, Cutting 915

6104 Sherbet $26.00
6104 Claret $30.00
6104 Wine $30.00
6104 Cordial $40.00
6104 Ice Tea, footed $28.00
2337 Plate, 7" $8.00
2337 Plate, 8" $10.00

Carlisle, Cutting 715

1933 – 1935

Stemware, 78

6008 Goblet........$35.00
6008 Sherbet, high $32.00
6008 Sherbet, low $28.00
6008 Cocktail $32.00
6008 Wine $38.00
6008 Cordial $48.00
6008 Oyster Cocktail $28.00
6008 Ice Tea, footed $34.00
6008 Tumbler, 9 oz., footed $28.00
6008 Juice, footed $28.00

Tableware I, 277

2470 Bonbon $18.00
2470½ Bowl, 10½" $45.00
2481 Bowl, 11", oblong $40.00
2481 Candlestick, 5", pair $50.00
2470½ Candlestick, 5½", pair $50.00
2451 Dish, ice with liner, plate $42.00
2470 Dish, lemon $18.00
2283 Plate, 7" $7.00
2283 Plate, 8" $8.00
2470 Plate, cake $34.00
2440 Plate, 13", torte $35.00
2419 Relish, 5-part $35.00
2440 Sugar and Cream $34.00
2470 Sweetmeat $20.00
4107 Vase, 9" $95.00

Carmel (Imported Stemware)

1984 – 1986

Tableware II, 280, 282

Goblet $20.00
Wine $20.00
Flute $20.00
Ice Tea $20.00

Carnival, Carving 7

1938 – 1943

Useful & Ornamenal, 113

4128½ Vase, 5" $65.00

Carousel, Cutting 863

1958 – 1975

Stemware, 116

6080 Goblet $35.00
6080 Sherbet $32.00
6080 Cocktail $32.00
6080 Claret-Wine $40.00
6080 Cordial $45.00
6080 Ice Tea, footed $35.00
6080 Juice, footed $32.00
6080 Claret, 8 oz., large $42.00
6080 Claret, 6 oz., large $42.00
2337 7", Plate $8.00
2337 8", Plate $10.00

Cascade, Decoration 8

pre-1924 – 1928

Stemware, 21

766 Goblet $15.00
766 Saucer Champagne $15.00
766 Sherbet $15.00
766 Fruit $15.00
766 Parfait $22.00
766 Cocktail $22.00
766 Claret $22.00
766 Wine $22.00
766 Cordial $22.00
766 Ice Tea, footed, handled $22.00
766 Grapefruit and Liner $25.00

Tableware I, 310

766 Almond $28.00
766 Bonbon $18.00
766 Bowl, finger $15.00
2219 Jar, candy and cover, ¼ pound $27.00
2219 Jar, candy and cover, ½ pound $30.00
2219 Jar, candy and cover, pound $34.00
766 Comport, 5", footed $22.00
300 Decanter, quart, cut neck $58.00
303/7 Jug $95.00
766 Nappy, 7", footed $24.00
1897 Plate, 7" $10.00
701 Plate, 5", tumbler $8.00
4011 Tumbler ....$10.00 – 12.00

Cascade, Decoration 636

1956 – 1965

Stemware, 111

6064½ Goblet $34.00
6064½ Champagne $30.00
6064½ Sherbet, low $26.00
6064½ Cocktail $28.00
6064½ Claret $36.00
6064½ Wine $35.00
6064½ Cordial $42.00
6064½ Seafood Cocktail $25.00
6064½ Ice Tea, footed $34.00
6064½ Juice, footed $26.00
2337 Plate, 7", narrow optic $12.00

Castle, Etching 87

1933 – 1943

Stemware, 77

6007 Goblet....$35.00
6007 Sherbet, high $32.00
6007 Sherbet, low $30.00
6007 Cocktail $32.00
6007 Claret $40.00
6007 Wine $40.00
6007 Cordial $50.00
6007 Oyster Cocktail $30.00
6007 Ice Tea, footed $35.00
6007 Tumbler, 9 oz., footed $32.00
6007 Juice, footed $30.00
6007 Whiskey, footed $34.00
2283 Plate, 6" $7.00
2283 Plate, 7" $8.00
2283 Plate, 8" $10.00

Catalina, 6046 Tumbler

1957 – 1958

Stemware, 156

6046 Juice/Cocktail $14.00
6046 Sherbet/Old Fashioned $14.00
6046 Water/Scotch and Soda $14.00
6046 Ice Tea/Highball $14.00

Cathedral, Cutting 792

1939 – 1943

Stemware, 93

6023 Goblet $25.00
6023 Saucer Champagne $23.00
6023 Sherbet, low $20.00
6023 Cocktail $22.00
6023 Claret-Wine $28.00
6023 Cordial $38.00
6023 Oyster Cocktail $18.00
6023 Ice Tea, footed $25.00
6023 Tumbler, 9 oz., footed $20.00
6023 Juice, footed $20.00

Tableware I, 302

766 Bowl, finger $12.00
6023 Bowl, footed $54.00
2324 Candlestick, 6", pair $45.00
6023 Comport, 5" $28.00
6011 Jug $175.00
2337 Plate, 6" $6.00
2337 Plate, 7" $7.00
2337 Plate, 8" $8.00

Cavendish, Cutting 754

1935 – 1939

Stemware, 86

6014 Goblet $30.00
6014 Saucer Champagne $27.00
6014 Sherbet, low $22.00
6014 Cocktail $27.00
6014 Claret $35.00
6014 Wine $34.00
6014 Cordial $45.00
6014 Oyster Cocktail $20.00
6014 Ice Tea, footed $30.00
6014 Tumbler, 9 oz., footed $25.00
6014 Juice, footed $22.00

Tableware I, 290

869 Bowl, finger $12.00
2470½ Bowl, 10½" $40.00
2472 Candlestick, duo, pair $70.00
5000 Jug $185.00
2337 Plate, 6" $6.00
2337 Plate, 7" $7.00
2337 Plate, 8" $8.00

Celebration, Decoration 698

1981 – 1982

Stemware, 145

6147 Goblet $21.00
6147 Champagne $21.00
6147 Wine $21.00
6147 Ice Tea, footed $21.00

Celebrity, 6106

1966 – 1971

Stemware, 131

6106 Goblet $22.00
6106 Sherbet $22.00
6106 Claret $22.00
6106 Tulip Wine $22.00
6106 Liqueur $27.00
6106 Ice Tea, footed $22.00

Celebrity, Cutting 749
1935 – 1943

Stemware, 72

6000 Goblet..........$32.00
6000 Sherbet, high........................$30.00
6000 Sherbet, low..........................$24.00
6000 Cocktail................................$30.00
6000 Wine......................................$35.00
6000 Oyster Cocktail.....................$20.00
6000 Ice Tea, footed......................$30.00
6000 Juice, footed..........................$28.00

Tableware I, 287

869 Bowl, finger...........................$12.00
2424 Bowl, 8", RO..........................$40.00
2481 Candlestick, 5", pair $45.00
5000 Jug.......................................$200.00
2337 Plate, 6"..................................$6.00
2337 Plate, 7"..................................$7.00
2337 Plate, 8"..................................$8.00
2337 Plate, 11", service.................$30.00

Celeste, 6072
1957 – 1973

Stemware, 114

6072 Goblet.................$25.00
6072 Sherbet.................$22.00
6072 Cocktail/Wine/Seafood $27.00
6072 Cordial...............$32.00
6072 Ice Tea, footed $25.00
6072 Juice, footed..........................$22.00

Celestial
1985

Tableware II, 288

318 Candle, 5".........$12.00
179 Bowl, 11"......$12.00
506 Bowl, 5"..........$10.00
554 Platter, 11"............................$18.00
757 Vase, 8"..................................$25.00

Celestial, Cutting 731
1934 – 1937

Stemware, 81

6011 Goblet $35.00
6011 Saucer Champagne..............$30.00
6011 Sherbet, low..........................$25.00
6011 Cocktail.................................$30.00
6011 Claret.....................................$40.00
6011 Rhine Wine............................$40.00
6011 Wine.......................................$38.00
6011 Sherry....................................$38.00
6011 Crème de Menthe.................$34.00
6011 Brandy....................................$47.00
6011 Cordial....................................$50.00
6011 Oyster Cocktail......................$27.00
6011 Ice Tea, footed.......................$32.00
6011 Tumbler 10 oz., footed,.........$26.00
6011 Juice, footed..........................$26.00
6011 Whiskey, footed....................$40.00
795 Champagne, hollow stem..........$18.00 – 20.00
863 Champagne, hollow stem..........$18.00 – 20.00
906 Brandy Inhaler..........$18.00 – 20.00
701 Tumbler.......................$6.00 – 14.00
887 Tumbler.......................$6.00 – 14.00
1184 Tumbler.......................$6.00 – 14.00
4122 Tumbler.......................$6.00 – 14.00

Tableware I, 280

1769 Bowl, finger...........................$14.00
4024 Bowl, 10", footed.................. $35.00
4024 Candlestick, 6", pair $45.00
6011 Decanter..............................$155.00
6011 Jug.......................................$195.00
2337 Plate, 6"................................. $6.00
2337 Plate, 7"..................................$7.00
2337 Plate, 8"..................................$8.00

Cellini, 6024
1938 – 1970

Stemware, 95

6024 Goblet......................$32.00
6024 Saucer Champagne....$28.00
6024 Sherbet, low...............$24.00
6024 Cocktail....................$28.00
6024 Claret.......................$38.00
6024 Wine.......................................$32.00
6024 Cordial...................................$48.00
6024 Oyster Cocktail......................$22.00
6024 Ice Tea, footed.......................$32.00
6024 Tumbler, 9 oz., footed...........$26.00
6024 Juice, footed...........................$26.00

Centennial II
1970 – 1972

Tableware II, 243-246

2864/123
Ashtray, 5½"............$5.00

2864/145
Ashtray A, 3"..........$4.00

2864/147
Ashtray B, 2¾".........$4.00

2864/148
Ashtray C, 3⅛..........................$4.00

1913/127
Basket, 11", Flemish...........$195.00

675/178
Bowl, 8" serving, round........$18.00

1704/517
Bowl, 7½", Rosby.................$18.00

1497/521
Bowl, 8½", Cresap................$18.00

1300/217
Bowl, 10½", Drape, cobalt blue.......................$250.00

1827/211
Bowl, 10½", salad, Rambler, ruby.................................$195.00

2377/355
Bowl, 5⅝", snack................. $15.00

2864/327
Candle B, 2½".......................$10.00

2521/327
Candleholder, bird $16.00

2883/319
Candleholder, 6", pair...........$24.00

2326/312
Candle Vase, 4¾"..................$10.00

2377/354
Box, candy, and cover...........$40.00

1229/676
Box, candy and cover, Frisco................................$42.00

2865/377
Coaster A, 3½", set of 4.........$12.00

2865/378
Coaster B, 3½", set of 4........$12.00

2865/379
Coaster C, 3½", set of 4 .... $12.00

2864/380
Coaster, 5½", wine..................$6.00

1121/219
Comport, 9", footed, Louise..$35.00
ruby................................ $175.00

1467/509
Hostess Server with chrome spoon, same as Sweetmeat........... $12.00

2377/447
Jelly and Cover, 8½", footed...$32.00

2377/448
Jelly, 5⅝", footed...................$24.00

2183/475
Marmalade and Ladle, Colonial Prism................. $24.00

2867/493
Napkin Ring A, 2", set of 4....$20.00

2867/494
Napkin Ring B, 2", set of 4....$20.00

1704/499
Nappy, 4¾", regular, handled..$15.00

1704/501
Nappy, 5", 3-cornered, handled............................ $15.00

1467/516
Nappy, 6½", shallow, Virginia..$12.00

2183/506
Nappy, 5", Colonial Prism.....$12.00

1467/540
Pickle, 8½", Virginia $14.00

2377/454
Pitcher, 7½", quart................$27.00

2538/543
Place Card Holder/Ashtray ...$9.00

1704/554
Plate, 10", serving, Rosby.....$15.00

1704/592
Preserve, 3½", footed, Rosby .$15.00

1704/451
Preserve, 3½", square, footed, Rosby............................... $15.00

2679/591
Preserve and Cover..............$22.00

1704/360
Tray, relish, 10¼", Rosby.....$18.00

2867/623
Salt Dip, 2", set of 4..............$16.00

1641/630
Salver, 10", round, Sovereign
crystal........................... $145.00
ruby............................... $350.00

2183/297
Server and Cover, Colonial Prism $47.00

1871/649
Shaker, chrome top F, pair...$28.00

2883/654
Shaker, chrome top F, pair...$20.00

1704/676
Sugar, Rosby.........................$18.00

1704/680
Cream, Rosby $14.00

2377/677
Sugar......................................$12.00

2377/680
Cream....................................$12.00

2710/687
Sugar, individual, Daisy and Button...............$12.00

2710/688
Cream, individual, Daisy and Button..............$12.00

1467/512
Sweetmeat, 5½", Virginia $8.00

2869/583
Tid Bit, handled, 7½" $24.00
2000/710
Toothpick $22.00
2377/76
Tumbler, 4½" $12.00
2883/329
Urn and Cover, 7⅝", footed..$24.00
272/754
Vase/Candleholder, 5" $9.00
272/785
Vase/Candleholder, 8" $11.00
1300/217
Vase, 4½", Drape...................$30.00
1605/601
Vase, 7¾", square, Sherwood, cobalt blue $395.00/market
1827/801
Vase, 9", footed, Rambler, ruby..................................$250.00
2377/785
Vase, 8"..................................$18.00
2883/757
Vase, 6⅜", bud.......................$12.00
2883/761
Vase, 6", footed $22.00
2883/162
Bowl, wedding and cover, 8"..$28.00

Centerpieces, see Bowls, Centerpieces and Console Bowls

Century, 2630

1949 – 1982

Stemware, 48

2630 Goblet......$25.00
2630 Sherbet $14.00
2630 Cocktail $14.00
2630 Wine.....................................$22.00
2630 Oyster Cocktail.....................$14.00
2630 Ice Tea, footed $25.00
2630 Juice, footed $14.00

Tableware II, 65-72

2630 Ashtray, individual $20.00
2630 Basket, Reed handle $94.00
2630 Bonbon, 3-toed.......................$28.00
2630 Bowl, nappy, 4½", handled...$18.00
2630 Bowl, 5", fruit $20.00
2630 Bowl, 6", cereal.......................$28.00
2630 Bowl, 8", flared $30.00
2630 Bowl, 10¾", footed, flared ... $55.00
2630 Bowl, 12", flared $50.00
2630 Bowl, 11", rolled edge, footed, flared..................................$58.00
2630 Bowl, serving, handled $40.00
2630 Bowl, 10", large..................... $40.00
2630 Bowl, oval, utility $38.00
2630 Bowl, oval, vegetable $26.00
2630 Bowl, 8½", salad $30.00
2630 Bowl, 10½", salad $40.00
2630 Bowl, 6", small $28.00
2630 Bowl, snack............................$27.00
2630 Butter, oblong........................$65.00
2630 Cake, handled........................$48.00
2630 Candlestick, 4½", pair.......... $48.00
2630 Candlestick, duo, pair $125.00
2630 Candlestick, trindle, pair ... $165.00
2630 Jar, candy and cover.............$58.00
2630 Cheese and Cracker..............$58.00
2630 Comport, 4⅜"....................... $34.00
2630 Condiment Set, 3-piece $145.00
2630 Cup and Saucer.................... $22.00
2630 Ice Bucket, metal handle, tongs $95.00
2630 Jug, 9½", 3-pint $175.00
2630 Jug, 3-pint, ice $125.00
2630 Lily Pond, 9"...........................$46.00
2630 Lily Pond, 11¼" $52.00
2630 Mayonnaise, plate, ladle $54.00
2630 Mayonnaise, 2-part set..........$57.00
2630 Mustard, cover, spoon $48.00
2630 Oil, 5 oz................................. $68.00
2630 Pickle, 8¾" $18.00
2630 Pitcher, pint, cereal $67.00
2630 Plate, 6" $14.00
2630 Plate, 7" $16.00
2630 Plate, 8" $20.00
2630 Plate, 9" $32.00
2630 Plate, 10½" $50.00
2630 Plate, crescent, salad........... $47.00
2630 Plate, party, and cup............ $40.00
2630 Plate, 14", torte $40.00
2630 Plate, 16", torte $50.00
2630 Platter, 12", oval.....................$65.00
2630 Preserve and Cover...............$47.00
2630 Relish, 2-part $34.00
2630 Relish, 3-part $38.00
2630 Salad Set, 3-piece $80.00
2630 Salver, cake $95.00
2630 Shaker, regular, chrome top B, pair..$26.00
2630 Shaker, individual, chrome top C, pair $22.00
2630 Shaker, individual set with tray $37.00
2630 Sugar and Cream, regular ... $28.00
2630 Sugar and Cream, individual.. $28.00
2630 Sugar and Cream, individual set....................................... $40.00
2630 Tid Bit, 3-toed $28.00
2630 Tid Bit, 2-tier, metal handle. $85.00
2630 Tray, handled, lunch $65.00
2630 Tray, handled, muffin.......... $65.00
2630 Tray, handled, utility $65.00
2630 Tray, 10½", snack..................$45.00
2630 Tricorne, 3-toed $32.00
2630 Vase, 6", bud $35.00
2630 Vase, 7½", handled...............$95.00
2630 Vase, 8½", oval.......................$85.00

Chain, Etching 42

1898 – 1927

Stemware, 20, 26

766 Goblet $10.00
766 Saucer Champagne $10.00
766 Fruit $7.00
766 Cocktail $10.00
766 Claret $10.00
766 Ice Tea, footed, handled $11.00
863 Goblet, 10½ oz.........................$7.00
863 Goblet, 9 oz. $7.00
863 Saucer Champagne $7.00
863 Fruit $7.00
863 Cocktail $7.00
863 Wine...$7.00
863 Sherry $7.00
863 Crème de Menthe $7.00
863 Cordial $15.00
701 Tumbler.........................$5.00 – 8.00
820 Tumbler.........................$5.00 – 8.00
833 Tumbler.........................$5.00 – 8.00
858 Tumbler.........................$5.00 – 8.00
887 Tumbler.........................$5.00 – 8.00
889 Tumbler.........................$5.00 – 8.00
4011 Tumbler.........................$5.00 – 8.00
300 Jug...$75.00
303 Jug...$50.00
318 Jug...$75.00
1236 Jug...$75.00

Chalice, 6029

1941 – 1943

Stemware, 99

6029 Goblet.......................$20.00
6029 Saucer Champagne $18.00
6029 Cocktail.....................$16.00
6029 Claret.......................$23.00
6029 Wine.........................$23.00
6029 Cordial.................................. $30.00
6029 Oyster Cocktail.....................$14.00
863 Champagne, hollow stem, CF.......................................$15.00.
833½ Tumbler........................$5.00 – 8.00

Chalice, 6059

1955 – 1965

Stemware, 109

6059 Goblet
crystal.........$30.00
ebony............$38.00
6059 Sherbet
crystal.........$28.00
ebony............$34.00
6029 Cocktail/Wine/Seafood
crystal $30.00
ebony $38.00
6059 Cordial
crystal $40.00
ebony $45.00
6059 Ice Tea, footed
crystal $30.00
ebony $38.00
6059 Juice, footed
crystal $26.00
ebony $34.00

Chanticleer, Carving 41

1940 – 1943

Useful & Ornamental, 130

2516 Ashtray...........$30.00

Chapel Bells, Cutting 888

1961 – 1974

Stemware, 123

6099 Goblet $34.00
6099 Sherbet............$32.00
6099 Wine/Cocktail $38.00
6099 Cordial $42.00
6099 Ice Tea, footed $34.00
6099 Juice, footed $30.00
2337 Plate, 7" $10.00
2337 Plate, 8" $12.00

Chateau, 6087

1959 – 1969

Stemware, 118

6087 Goblet.......................$25.00
6087 Sherbet......................$23.00
6087 Wine/Cocktail.........$28.00
6087 Cordial.................$32.00
6087 Ice Tea, footed $25.00
6087 Juice, footed $22.00

Chateau, Etching 315

1933 – 1939

Stemware, 78

6008 Goblet......$45.00
6008 Sherbet, high...........$42.00
6008 Sherbet, low..........................$35.00
6008 Cocktail..................................$42.00
6008 Wine.......................................$54.00
6008 Cordial...................................$74.00
6008 Oyster Cocktail.....................$32.00
6008 Ice Tea, footed......................$45.00
6008 Tumbler, 9 oz., footed...........$35.00
6008 Juice, footed..........................$35.00

Tableware

2470 Bonbon................................ $42.00
1769 Bowl, finger...........................$38.00
2470½ Bowl, 10½"............................$95.00
2481 Bowl, oblong....................... $125.00
2481 Candlestick, 5", pair...........$125.00
2470½ Candlestick, 5½", pair....... $120.00
2472 Candlestick, duo, pair.........$150.00
2482 Candlestick, trindle, pair ... $175.00
2440 Celery, 11½"..........................$50.00
2470 Comport, 6", low...................$52.00
2440 Cream Soup..........................$50.00
2440 Cup and Saucer.................... $35.00
2451 Dish, ice with liner, plate..... $65.00
2470 Lemon................................... $40.00
2440 Olive, 6½"..............................$35.00
2440 Pickle, 8½"..............................$40.00
2440 Plate, 6"................................. $12.00
2440 Plate, 7"................................. $16.00
2440 Plate, 8"................................. $22.00
2440 Plate, 9"................................. $45.00
2470 Plate, cake............................ $75.00
2440 Plate, 13", torte..................... $95.00
2419 Relish, 4-part......................... $65.00
2440 Sugar and Cream................... $78.00
2470 Sweetmeat............................. $42.00
2467 Vase, 7½"............................$135.00

Chatham, Cutting 829

1952 – 1960

Stemware, 103

6036 Goblet ..$32.00
6036 Sherbet, high $28.00
6036 Sherbet, low..........................$22.00
6036 Parfait....................................$28.00
6036 Cocktail..................................$28.00
6036 Claret-Wine...........................$34.00
6036 Cordial...................................$40.00
6036 Oyster Cocktail.....................$20.00
6036 Ice Tea, footed......................$32.00
6036 Juice, footed..........................$22.00
2337 Plate, 7".................................$10.00
2337 Plate, 8".................................$12.00

Chatteris, Cutting 197

1929 – 1930

Stemware, 33

877 Goblet.........$25.00
877 Sherbet, high $20.00
877 Sherbet, low..........................$16.00
877 Parfait....................................$22.00
877 Cocktail..................................$18.00
877 Claret.....................................$24.00
877 Wine.......................................$22.00
877 Cordial...................................$30.00
877 Oyster Cocktail.....................$15.00
877 Ice Tea, footed......................$20.00
877 Tumbler, 9 oz., footed...........$15.00
877 Juice, footed..........................$16.00
877 Whiskey, footed....................$16.00

Tableware I, 273

869 Bowl, finger, and 2283 Plate, 6"..........................$22.00
2394 Bowl, 12"..............................$45.00
2394 Candlestick, 2", pair............ $45.00
2324 Candlestick, 4", pair.............$45.00
2329 Centerpiece, 11"....................$35.00
2375 Cheese and Cracker.............$38.00
2400 Comport, 6"...........................$22.00
2378 Ice Bucket, NP handle..........$38.00
2315 Mayonnaise and Plate.......... $28.00
2283 Plate, 6"..................................$6.00
2283 Plate, 7"..................................$7.00
2283 Plate, 8"..................................$8.00
2350½ Sugar and Cream..................$30.00
2375 Tray, handled, lunch........... $32.00
2369 Vase, 7"................................. $38.00
2417 Vase, 8"................................. $45.00
4105 Vase, 8"................................. $45.00

Chelsea, Cutting 783

1938 – 1943

Stemware, 58

4020 Goblet $30.00
4020 Sherbet, high $30.00
4020 Sherbet, low, 7 oz. $28.00
4020 Sherbet, low, 5 oz. $28.00
4020 Cocktail, 4 oz..........................$28.00
4020 Cocktail, 3½ oz.......................$28.00
4020 Claret.....................................$35.00
4020 Wine.......................................$35.00
4020 Tumbler, 13 oz., footed.........$30.00
4020 Tumbler, 10 oz., footed.........$28.00
4020 Juice, footed..........................$28.00
4020 Whiskey, footed....................$30.00
4020 Jug.......................................$225.00
2419 Mayfair, 7", plate...................$15.00
2419 Mayfair, 8", plate...................$18.00

Cherish, Decoration 681

1969 – 1982

Stemware, 128

6103 Goblet $26.00
6103 Sherbet.................................$24.00
6103 Claret.....................................$28.00
6103 Tulip Wine.............................$28.00
6103 Brandy...................................$28.00
6103 Ice Tea, footed......................$26.00
2337 Plate, 7".................................$12.00

Chintz, Etching 338

1940 – 1973

Stemware, 97

6026 Goblet $38.00
6026 Goblet, low............................$30.00
6026 Saucer Champagne...............$34.00
6026 Sherbet, low..........................$26.00
6026 Cocktail..................................$34.00
6026 Claret-Wine...........................$42.00
6026 Cordial...................................$52.00
6026 Oyster Cocktail.....................$26.00
6026 Ice Tea, footed......................$38.00
6026 Juice, footed..........................$30.00

Tableware I, 257

2496 Bonbon.................................$58.00
869 Bowl, finger...........................$55.00
2496 Bowl, 5", fruit....................... $38.00
2496 Bowl, flared, handled, nappy...............................$27.00
2496 Bowl, 3-cornered, handled, nappy............................... $27.00
2496 Bowl, 8½", serving.............. $75.00
6023 Bowl, 9", footed................. $165.00
2496 Bowl, 9½", vegetable......... $150.00
2484 Bowl, 10", handled.............$110.00
2496 Bowl, 10½", handled...........$150.00
2496 Bowl, 12", flared...................$95.00
2496 Candlestick, 4", pair...............$84.00
2496 Candlestick, 5½", pair.........$125.00
2496 Candlestick, duo, pair.........$135.00
2496 Candlestick, trindle, pair ... $250.00
6023 Candlestick, duo, pair.........$195.00
2496 Box, candy and cover..........$135.00
2496 Celery.................................. $87.00
2496 Cheese and Cracker.......... $115.00
2496 Comport, 5½"...................... $68.00
2496 Cream Soup and Plate..........$78.00
2496 Cup and Saucer.................... $35.00
2496 Ice Bucket, chrome handle..$150.00
2496 Jelly and Cover................. $145.00
5000 Jug.......................................$565.00
2496½ Mayonnaise, plate, ladle...... $95.00
2496 Mayonnaise, 2-part.............. $60.00
2496 Oil, 3½ oz...........................$200.00
2496 Pickle.....................................$50.00
2666 Pitcher, quart.................... $325.00
2496 Plate, 6"................................$14.00
2496 Plate, 7"................................$18.00
2496 Plate, 8"................................$24.00
2496 Plate, 9"................................$65.00
2496 Plate, cake..............................$85.00
2496 Plate, 14", torte.................. $110.00
2364 Plate, 16", torte..................$150.00
2496 Platter, 12", oval................. $150.00
2496 Relish, 2-part........................ $48.00
2496 Relish, 3-part........................ $75.00
2419 Relish, 5-part...................... $150.00
2083 Bottle, salad dressing $500.00/market
2586 Syrup, sani-cut.......$700.00/market
2496 Sauce, oblong......................$135.00
2364 Shaker, chrome top C, pair..$75.00
2496 Shaker, FGT, pair............... $200.00
2496 Sugar and Cream..................$75.00
2496 Sugar and Cream, individual.. $75.00
2496 Sugar, cream, tray set........ $125.00
2496 Tid Bit, 3-toed...................... $58.00
2496 Tray, 8", oblong.................. $85.00
2375 Tray, handled, lunch.......... $115.00
4121 Vase, 5"...............................$185.00
4128 Vase, 5"............................... $195.00
4143 Vase, 6", footed..................$225.00
4143 Vase, 7½", footed............... $450.00
2660 Vase, 8", flip...................... $400.00
2470 Vase, 10", footed...............$495.00

Chippendale, CH05

1983 – 1986

Note: Etching similar to Navarre

Stemware, 186

CH05 Goblet, 10 oz...$25.00
CH05 Champagne, 8 oz. ...$22.00

Chippendale, CH05

CH05 Wine, 7 oz. $27.00
CH05 Flute/Parfait, 8 oz. $34.00
CH05 Ice Tea, 14 oz., footed $25.00

Chippendale, Cutting 788

1939 – 1943

Stemware, 93

6023 Goblet $25.00
6023 Saucer Champagne $23.00
6023 Sherbet, low $20.00
6023 Cocktail $22.00
6023 Claret-Wine $28.00
6023 Cordial $38.00
6023 Oyster Cocktail $18.00
6023 Ice Tea, footed $25.00
6023 Tumbler, 9 oz., footed $20.00
6023 Juice, footed $20.00

Tableware I, 302

766 Bowl, finger $12.00
6023 Bowl, footed $54.00
2324 Candlestick, 6", pair $45.00
6023 Comport, 5" $28.00
6011 Jug $175.00
2337 Plate, 6" $6.00
2337 Plate, 7" $7.00
2337 Plate, 8" $8.00

Christiana, Cutting 814

1942 – 1969

Stemware, 100

6030 Goblet $36.00
6030 Goblet, low $34.00
6030 Saucer Champagne $34.00
6030 Sherbet, low $26.00
6030 Cocktail $34.00
6030 Claret-Wine $42.00
6030 Cordial $54.00
6030 Oyster Cocktail $22.00
6030 Ice Tea, footed $36.00
6030 Juice, footed $27.00

Tableware , 303

1769 Bowl, finger $15.00
6023 Bowl, footed $65.00
6023 Candlestick, duo, pair $65.00
6011 Jug $225.00
2337 Plate, 7" $8.00
2337 Plate, 8" $10.00

Christine, Cutting 798

1939 – 1943

Stemware, 40

892 Goblet $38.00
892 Saucer Champagne $28.00
892 Sherbet, low $25.00
892 Cocktail $25.00
892 Claret $32.00
892 Wine $30.00
892 Cordial $38.00
892 Oyster Cocktail $20.00
892 Ice Tea, footed $30.00
892 Juice, footed $25.00

Tableware I, 303

1769 Bowl, finger $15.00
6023 Bowl, footed $65.00
6023 Candlestick, duo, pair $65.00
6011 Jug $225.00
2337 Plate, 7" $8.00
2337 Plate, 8" $10.00

Christmas Nativity

1979 – 1981

Useful & Ornamental, 132

The Holy Family, first edition $250.00
The Magi, second edition $250.00
The Shepherds, third edition $250.00

Christmas Ornaments

1976 – 1978

Useful & Ornamental, 132

Christmas Tree $15.00
Snowflake $15.00
True Holly $15.00
Wreath $15.00
Bells $15.00
Partridge, crystal mist $18.00
Sphere $15.00
Turtle Doves, crystal mist $18.00

Chrysanthemum, Cutting 133

1918 – 1928

Stemware, 29

863 Goblet, 9 oz. $8.00
863 Saucer Champagne $8.00
863 Fruit $6.00
863 Cocktail, 3½ oz. $6.00
863 Wine $8.00
4061 Lemonade, handled $20.00
701 Tumbler $4.00 – 10.00
820 Tumbler $4.00 – 10.00
833 Tumbler $4.00 – 10.00
889 Tumbler $4.00 – 10.00

Circlet, Cutting 840

1954 – 1969

Stemware, 108

6055½ Goblet $24.00
6055½ Sherbet $20.00
6055½ Cocktail $20.00
6055½ Claret-Wine $28.00
6055½ Cordial $30.00
6055½ Oyster Cocktail $16.00
6055½ Ice Tea, footed $24.00
6055½ Juice, footed $18.00

Tableware II, 186

2666 Bowl, oval $38.00
2666 Candle, flora, pair $48.00
2666 Mayonnaise, plate, ladle $52.00
2337 Plate, 7" $10.00
2337 Plate, 8" $12.00
2666 Plate, canape $22.00
2666 Plate, 10", snack $24.00
2666 Plate, 14", serving $35.00
2666 Relish, 2-part $30.00
2666 Relish, 3-part $38.00
2364 Shaker, large, chrome top B, pair $55.00
2666 Sugar and Cream $48.00
2666 Sugar and Cream, individual and tray $55.00

Classic Gold, Decoration 641

1958 – 1982

Stemware, 116

6080 Goblet $35.00
6080 Sherbet $32.00
6080 Cocktail $32.00
6080 Claret-Wine $38.00
6080 Cordial $42.00
6080 Ice Tea, footed $35.00
6080 Juice, footed $30.00
6080 Claret, 8 oz. $40.00
6080 Claret, 6 oz. $40.00
2337 Plate, 7" $10.00
2337 Plate, 8" $12.00

Clock Sets

1925 – 1927

Useful & Ornamental, 133

2298 Clock Set: St. Clair Clock and two 3½" candlesticks
- blue $600.00
- amber $425.00
- green $500.00
- canary $750.00
- ebony $425.00

2299 Clock Set: St. Alexis Clock and two 5" candlesticks, oval base
- blue $700.00
- amber $500.00
- green $600.00
- canary $850.00
- ebony $525.00

Clover, Cutting 132

1918 – 1928

Stemware, 29

863 Goblet, 9 oz $8.00
863 Saucer Champagne $8.00
863 Fruit $6.00
863 Cocktail, 3½ oz. $6.00
863 Claret $8.00
863 Wine $8.00
863 Sherry $6.00
805 Parfait $22.00
837 Oyster Cocktail $6.00
701 Tumbler $4.00 – 8.00
820 Tumbler $4.00 – 8.00
833 Tumbler $4.00 – 8.00
889 Tumbler $4.00 – 8.00
4011 Tumbler $4.00 – 8.00
303 Jug $50.00
1124 Jug $75.00
1236 Jug $75.00
1793 Jug $75.00
2104 Jug $88.00

Cloverleaf (large), Etching 47

pre-1900 – 1927

Stemware, 17, 22, 61

114 Goblet, 10 oz. $4.00
114 Champagne $4.00
114 Claret $4.00
114 Wine $4.00
114 Cordial $5.00
858 Goblet, 9 oz. $8.00
858 Saucer Champagne, 5½ oz. $8.00
858 Fruit $8.00

858 Wine, 2¾ oz. $8.00
5001 Goblet, 11 oz. $12.00
5001 Goblet, 8¾ oz. $10.00
5001 Goblet, 7½ oz. $10.00
5001 Saucer Champagne $10.00
5001 Cocktail, 4 oz. $10.00
5001 Cocktail, 3 oz. $10.00
5001 Cocktail, 2½ oz. $10.00
5001 Claret, 5½ oz. $12.00
5001 Claret, 4¾ oz. $12.00
5001 Rhine Wine, 4 oz. $12.00
5001 Rhine Wine, 2½ oz. $12.00
5001 Wine, 3½ oz. $12.00
5001 Wine, 2 oz. $12.00
5001 Sherry, 2½ oz. $12.00
5001 Sherry, 2 oz. $12.00
5001 Sherry, 1½ oz. $12.00
5001 Brandy, ¾ oz. $12.00
5001 Cordial, 1 oz. $12.00
5001 Cordial, ¾ oz. $12.00
5001 Champagne, 5¾ oz., tall $10.00
5001 Hot Whiskey, 5 oz. $10.00
701 Tumbler ....$4.00 – 10.00
858 Tumbler ....$4.00 – 10.00
724 Tankard $100.00
300 Jug $65.00
303 Jug $48.00
316 Jug $75.00
317½ Jug $65.00
318 Jug $75.00
1227 Jug $65.00
1236 Jug $75.00
2018 Jug $65.00

Cloverleaf (small), Etching 67

1898 – 1927

Stemware, 27

863 Goblet, 10½ oz. $8.00
863 Goblet, 9 oz. 8.00
863 Goblet, 7 oz. $8.00
863 Goblet, 5½ oz. $8.00
863 Saucer Champagne $8.00
863 Fruit $8.00
863 Cocktail, 3½ oz. $8.00
863 Cocktail, 3 oz. $8.00
863 Claret $8.00
863 Rhine Wine $8.00
863 Wine $8.00
863 Sherry $8.00
863 Créme de Menthe $8.00
863 Brandy, pousse-café $8.00
863 Cordial $15.00
863 Champagne, hollow stem $8.00
863 Champagne, tall $8.00
810 Tumbler ....$4.00 – 8.00

Club Design A, Decoration 603

1929 – 1930

Stemware, 59

4020 Goblet $40.00
4020 Sherbet, high $40.00
4020 Sherbet, low,
7 oz. $40.00
5 oz. $40.00
4020 Cocktail, 3½ oz. $40.00
4020 Ice Tea, footed $40.00
4020 Tumbler, footed,
13 oz. $40.00
10 oz. $40.00
4020 Juice, footed $40.00
4020 Whiskey, footed $40.00

Tableware I, 330

4121 Bowl, finger $26.00
2350 Cream soup $24.00
2350 Cup and Saucer, after dinner $34.00
2419 Saucer, after dinner $14.00
2350½ Cup and 2350 Saucer $20.00
2419 Saucer $8.00
2350 Plate, 6" $8.00
2350 Plate, 7" $10.00
2350 Plate, 9" $20.00
2419 Plate, 6" $8.00
2419 Plate, 7" $10.00
2419 Plate, 8" $16.00

Club Design B, Decoration 604

1929 – 1932

Black with gold line

Stemware, 59

4020 Goblet $45.00
4020 Sherbet, high $45.00
4020 Sherbet, 7 oz., low $40.00
4020 Sherbet, 5 oz., low $40.00
4020 Cocktail, 3½ oz. $40.00
4020 Ice Tea, footed $45.00
4020 Tumbler, footed,
13 oz. $45.00
10 oz. $40.00
4020 Juice, footed $40.00
4020 Whiskey, footed $40.00

Tableware I, 330

2350 Ashtray $15.00
4021 Bowl, finger $28.00
2430 Bowl, 11" $45.00
2297 Bowl A, 12", deep $48.00
2324 Candlestick, 4", pair $45.00
2430 Jar, candy and cover $95.00
2427 Box, cigarette and cover $120.00
2400 Comport, 6" $34.00
2350 Cream Soup $27.00
2350 Cup and Saucer, after dinner $38.00
2419 Saucer, after dinner $15.00
2350½ Cup and 2350 Saucer $24.00
2419 Saucer $10.00
2430 Jelly, 7" $22.00
2375 Dish, lemon $22.00
2430 Mint, 5½" $16.00
2350 Plate, 6" $8.00
2350 Plate, 7" $10.00
2350 Plate, 9" $20.00
2419 Plate, 6" $8.00
2419 Plate, 7" $10.00
2419 Plate, 8" $18.00
2375 Plate, cake $65.00
2350½ Sugar and Cream $65.00
2404 Vase, 6" $52.00
2409 Vase, 7½" $67.00
2387 Vase, 8" $85.00
2430 Vase, 8" $85.00
4105 Vase, 8" $85.00
2421 Vase, 10½" $165.00
2373 Vase, window and cover
small $195.00
large $225.00

Club Design C, Decoration 611

1931 – 1932

Solid crystal with green enamel lines (see B)

Stemware, 59

4020 Sherbet, 7 oz., low $42.00
4020 Ice Tea, footed $42.00
4020 Tumbler, footed
13 oz. $42.00
10 oz. $42.00
4020 Juice, footed $42.00
4020 Whiskey, footed $42.00

Club Design D, Decoration 612

1931 – 1932

Solid crystal with orange enamel lines (see B)

Stemware, 59

4020 Sherbet, 7 oz., low $35.00
4020 Ice Tea, footed $35.00
4020 Tumbler, footed
13 oz. $35.00
10 oz. $35.00
4020 Juice, footed $35.00
4020 Whiskey, footed $35.00

Coasters

pre-1924-1982

Useful & Ornamental, 134

1590 Coaster $8.00
2056 Coaster, see American
2106 Coaster
crystal $5.00
amber $6.00
green $6.00
2272 Coaster
amber $5.00
green $5.00
blue $8.00
rose $5.00
azure $7.00
topaz/gold tint $5.00
orchid $7.00
2442 Coaster
crystal $6.00
amber $7.00
green $7.00
rose $7.00
ebony $6.00
topaz/gold tint $7.00
2510 Coaster, see Sunray
2584 Coaster $6.00
2650 Coaster, see Horizon
2803 Coaster, see Sea Shells
4186 Coaster, see Mesa

Cockatoo, Decoration 505

1931 – 1932

Gold and ebony

Tableware I, 327

2430 Bowl, 11" $135.00
2297 Bowl A, 12", deep $135.00
2324 Candlestick, 4", pair $84.00
2430 Candlestick, 9½", pair $150.00
2447 Candlestick, duo, pair $150.00
2430 Jar, candy and cover, ½ pound $130.00
2427 Box, cigarette and cover $125.00
2419 Jelly $42.00
2430 Jelly, 7" $42.00
2430 Mint, 5½" $35.00
2419 Plate, cake $135.00
2430 Vase, 8" $150.00
2385 Vase, 8½", fan $375.00

Cocktail Shakers, see Bar and Refreshment

Coin, 1372

1958 – 1981

Stemware, 41

1372 Goblet
- olive...$45.00
- ruby..$125.00
- crystal $45.00

1372 Sherbet
- olive....$40.00
- ruby....$95.00
- crystal $40.00

1372 Wine
- olive....$45.00
- ruby....$125.00
- crystal $45.00

1372 Ice Tea
- olive....$50.00
- ruby....$125.00
- crystal $50.00

1372 Double Old Fashioned
- olive....$45.00
- ruby....$95.00
- crystal $45.00

1372 Water/Scotch and Soda
- crystal $45.00

1372 Juice/Old Fashioned
- crystal $45.00

Tableware II, 9 – 15

Ashtray, small, round
- crystal $32.00
- amber....$38.00
- blue $54.00
- green....$75.00

Ashtray, 4", oblong
- crystal $30.00
- amber.... $35.00
- olive green.... $35.00
- blue $45.00
- green....$75.00

Ashtray, 5", one coin
- crystal $15.00
- amber.... $18.00
- olive green....$18.00
- blue $28.00
- ruby.... $24.00
- green....$75.00

Ashtray, 7½", four coin
- crystal $20.00
- amber....$22.00
- olive green.... $22.00
- blue $35.00
- ruby....$25.00
- green.... $78.00

Ashtray, 7½", center coin
- crystal $28.00
- amber.... $28.00
- olive green.... $28.00
- ruby....$25.00

Ashtray, 10", large
- crystal $34.00
- amber.... $37.00
- olive green....$37.00
- blue $45.00
- green....$95.00

Bowl, 8", round
- crystal $38.00
- amber.... $40.00
- olive green....$40.00
- blue $68.00
- ruby.... $64.00
- green.... $125.00

Bowl, 8½", footed
- crystal $64.00
- amber.... $70.00
- olive green.... $70.00
- blue $110.00
- ruby.... $85.00
- green....$195.00

Bowl, 8½", footed and cover
- crystal $125.00
- amber.... $125.00
- blue $175.00
- green....$265.00

Bowl, 9", oval
- crystal $55.00
- amber.... $55.00
- olive green.... $55.00
- blue $75.00
- ruby.... $72.00
- green.... $165.00

Bowl, wedding and cover
- crystal $85.00
- amber....$84.00
- olive green....$84.00
- blue $195.00
- ruby....$125.00
- green....$325.00
- gold coin.... $265.00

Candlestick, 4½", pair
- crystal $58.00
- amber.... $58.00
- olive green.... $58.00
- blue $65.00
- ruby.... $65.00
- green.... $150.00

Candlestick, 8", pair
- crystal $125.00
- amber.... $125.00
- olive green....$125.00
- ruby.... $135.00

Box, candy and cover
- crystal $58.00
- amber.... $60.00
- olive green....$60.00
- blue $125.00
- ruby.... $95.00
- green.... $175.00

Jar, candy and cover
- crystal $40.00
- amber.... $42.00
- olive green.... $42.00
- blue $95.00
- ruby....;$75.00
- green....$175.00
- gold coin.... $150.00

Box, cigarette and cover
- crystal $195.00
- amber.... $195.00
- blue $225.00
- green....$275.00
- gold coin.... $275.00

Holder, cigarette and cover
- crystal $195.00
- amber.... $195.00
- blue $225.00
- green.... $295.00

Urn, cigarette
- crystal $42.00
- amber....$45.00
- olive green.... $45.00
- blue $75.00
- ruby....$58.00
- green....$125.00

Condiment Set: cruet, shakers and tray
- crystal $195.00
- amber.... $195.00
- olive green.... $195.00
- blue $295.00
- green.... $500.00

Condiment Tray, 9⅝"
- crystal $35.00
- amber....$40.00
- olive green....$40.00
- blue $75.00

Cream
- crystal $28.00
- amber.... $32.00
- olive green....$32.00
- blue $50.00
- ruby....$35.00
- green.... $60.00

Cruet and Stopper, 7 oz.
- crystal $95.00
- amber.... $95.00
- olive green.... $95.00
- blue $135.00
- green.... $250.00

Decanter and Stopper
- crystal $185.00
- amber.... $225.00
- olive green.... $225.00
- blue $250.00
- green.... $350.00
- gold coin....$300.00

Jelly
- crystal $32.00
- amber....$38.00
- olive green....$38.00
- blue $50.00
- green.... $75.00

Lamp, coach, electric
- crystal $150.00
- amber....$150.00
- blue $225.00

Lamp, coach, oil
- crystal $150.00
- amber....$150.00
- blue $225.00

Lamp, handled, courting, electric
- amber.... $135.00
- blue $150.00

Lamp, handled, courting, oil
- amber.... $135.00
- blue $150.00

Lamp, tall, patio, electric
- crystal $195.00
- amber.... $225.00
- blue $285.00

Lamp, tall, patio, oil
- crystal $200.00
- amber.... $250.00
- blue $295.00

Pitcher, quart
- crystal $95.00
- amber.... $95.00
- olive green.... $95.00
- blue $175.00
- ruby.... $125.00
- green.... $250.00

Nappy, 4½", round
- crystal $54.00

Nappy, 5⅜", handled
- crystal $22.00
- amber....$22.00
- olive green.... $22.00
- blue $38.00
- ruby....$34.00
- green.... $48.00

Plate, 8"
- crystal $75.00
- olive green.... $95.00

ruby $150.00
Punch Bowl, 14"
crystal $375.00
Punch Bowl Foot
crystal $150.00
Punch Cup
crystal $45.00
Salver, cake
crystal $125.00
amber $145.00
olive green $145.00
blue $250.00
green $350.00
Shaker, chrome top E, pair
crystal $65.00
amber $70.00
olive green $70.00
blue $95.00
ruby $95.00
green $150.00
Smoker Set, 3-piece: cigarette holder, 2 ashtray covers
crystal $275.00
amber $295.00
blue $325.00
green $375.00
Sugar and Cover
crystal $38.00
amber $42.00
olive green $42.00
blue $65.00
ruby $50.00
green $120.00
Urn, 12¾", footed and cover
crystal $125.00
amber $125.00
olive green $125.00
blue $175.00
ruby $150.00
green $300.00
Vase, 8", bud
crystal $38.00
amber $38.00
olive green $38.00
blue $65.00
ruby $56.00
green $125.00
Vase, 10", footed
crystal $125.00

Coin Gold Band, Decoration 1

1906 – 1929

Stemware, 18

660 Goblet $12.00
660 Saucer Champagne $9.00
660 Sherbet, low $8.00
660 Parfait $9.00
660 Cocktail $9.00
660 Claret $10.00
660 Wine $10.00
660 Cordial $15.00

Coin Gold Band, Decoration 2

1906 – 1914

Stemware, 25

858 Goblet, 11 oz. $6.00
858 Goblet, 10 oz. $6.00
858 Goblet, 9 oz. $6.00
858 Goblet, 8 oz. $6.00
858 Saucer Champagne, 7 oz. $6.00
858 Sherbet $6.00
858 Fruit $6.00
858 Cocktail $6.00
858 Claret, 6½ oz. $6.00
858 Claret, 4½ oz. $6.00
858 Wine, 3½ oz. $6.00
858 Wine, 2¾ oz. $6.00
858 Sherry $6.00
858 Crème de Menthe $6.00
858 Brandy $12.00
858 Cordial $15.00
858 Champagne, hollow stem $10.00
858 Champagne, tall $10.00
858 Bass Ale $15.00
858 Hot Whiskey $6.00
863 Rhine Wine $6.00
858 Table Tumbler $5.00
303 Jug $50.00

Coin Gold Band, Decoration 6

1909 – 1929

Stemware, 25

858 Goblet, 10 oz. $6.00
858 Saucer Champagne, 5½ oz. $6.00
858 Sherbet $6.00
858 Fruit $6.00
858 Cocktail $6.00
858 Claret, 4½ oz. $6.00
858 Wine, 3½ oz. $6.00
858 Sherry $6.00
858 Crème de Menthe $6.00
858 Brandy, pousse-café $0.00
858 Cordial $10.00
858 Champagne, hollow stem $10.00
858 Champagne, tall $8.00
766 Grapefruit and Liner $25.00
766 Ice Tea, footed, handled $16.00
858 Tumbler $4.00 – 8.00
300 Tankard $75.00
303 Jug $50.00

Coin Gold Band, Decoration 7

1906 – 1928

Stemware, 25

858 Goblet, 9 oz. $6.00
858 Saucer Champagne, 5½ oz. $6.00
858 Fruit $6.00
858 Wine, 2¾ oz. $6.00
858 Oyster Cocktail $6.00
766 Parfait $8.00
945½ Grapefruit and Liner $22.00
858 Tumbler $4.00 – 8.00

Tableware I, 310

5051 Almond, large $14.00
1499 Bowl, finger, and plate $18.00
2219 Jar, candy and cover, ¼ pound $27.00
2219 Jar, candy and cover, ½ pound $32.00
2219 Jar, candy and cover, pound $35.00
2250 Jar, candy and cover, ¼ pound $27.00
2250 Jar, candy and cover, ½ pound $32.00
2250 Jar, candy and cover, pound $35.00
1697 Carafe and 4023 Tumbler $34.00
880 Comport, 5" $20.00
803 Comport, 5" $20.00
803 Comport, 6" $22.00
803 Comport and Cover, 5", gold knob $20.00
880 Comport and Cover, 5", gold knob $20.00
2252 Dish, 6", salad $10.00
1848 Dish, 7", salad, matt star base $12.00
825 Jelly $18.00
825 Jelly and Cover, gold knob $24.00
1236/6 Jug $75.00
1968 Marmalade and Cover $23.00
803 Nappy, 5", footed $20.00
803 Nappy and Cover, 5", footed, gold knob $20.00
803 Nappy, 6" $16.00
1897 Plate, 7" $10.00
1848 Plate, 9", cracker, matt star base $12.00
2258 Plate, 11", sandwich $15.00
2258 Relish, 6" $14.00
2258 Relish, 8" $18.00
2258 Relish, 10" $26.00
880 Salt, footed $15.00
858 Sweetmeat $18.00

Coin Gold Band, Decoration 15

1920s

Stemware, 22

766 Goblet $10.00
766 Saucer Champagne $10.00
766 Sherbet $8.00
766 Fruit $8.00
766 Parfait $20.00
766 Cocktail $9.00
766 Ice Tea, footed, handled $18.00
4011 Tumbler $10.00 – 12.00
303 Jug $57.00

Colfax, 6023

1940 – 1973

Stemware, 93

6023 Goblet $20.00
6023 Saucer Champagne $18.00
6023 Sherbet, low $15.00
6023 Cocktail $16.00
6023 Claret-Wine $20.00
6023 Cordial $25.00
6023 Oyster Cocktail $12.00
6023 Ice Tea, footed $20.00
6023 Tumbler, 9 oz., footed $16.00
6023 Juice, footed $16.00

Colonial, Colonial Tea Room Service, 2222

1920 – 1932

Stemware, 45

2222 Goblet
crystal $10.00
amber $13.00
green $13.00
2222 Sherbet, high
crystal $10.00
amber $13.00
green $13.00
2222 Sherbet, 4½ oz., low
crystal $8.00
2222 Sherbet, 3 oz., low
crystal $7.00

amber..........$10.00
green..........$10.00
2222 Fruit Cocktail
crystal..........$8.00
amber..........$10.00
green..........$10.00
2222 Wine..........$10.00
2222 Tumbler, wine
crystal..........$10.00
amber..........$12.00
green..........$12.00
2222 Tumbler, 14 oz., ice tea, regular
crystal..........$10.00
amber..........$15.00
green..........$15.00
2222 Tumbler, 12 oz., ice tea, flared
crystal..........$10.00
2222 Tumbler, table, regular
crystal..........$8.00
amber..........$12.00
green..........$12.00
2222 Parfait
amber..........$18.00
green..........$18.00
2222 Tumbler, table, flared
crystal..........$8.00
2222 Oyster Cocktail, footed
crystal..........$8.00
amber..........$10.00
green..........$10.00

Tableware I, 37

2222 Ice Jug, 3 quart..........$70.00
2222 Jug, ½ gallon..........$65.00
2222 Plate, 7"..........$6.00
2222 Plate, 8"..........$7.00
2222 Bowl, finge, and plate..........$15.00
2222½ Sugar and Cover..........$15.00
2222 Cream, individual, no handle..........$11.00
2222 Oil, 4 oz., GS..........$24.00
2222 Oil, 6 oz., GS..........$30.00
1372 Oyster Cocktail and Liner..........$12.00
713½ Shaker, FGT, pair..........$22.00
2222½ Water Bottle..........$32.00

Colonial Dame 5412

1948 – 1965

Crystal and empire green

Stemware, 71

5412 Goblet..........$35.00
5412 Sherbet..........$28.00
5412 Cocktail..........$30.00
5412 Claret-Wine..........$38.00
5412 Cordial..........$45.00
5412 Oyster Cocktail..........$30.00
5412 Ice Tea, footed..........$35.00
5412 Juice, footed..........$30.00
2337 Plate, 7", empire green..........$30.00

Colonial Mirror, Etching 334

1934 – 1944

Stemware, 93

6023 Goblet..........$32.00
6023 Saucer Champagne..........$30.00
6023 Sherbet, low..........$27.00
6023 Cocktail..........$30.00
6023 Claret-Wine..........$36.00
6023 Cordial..........$45.00
6023 Oyster Cocktail..........$24.00
6023 Ice Tea, footed..........$32.00
6023 Tumbler, 9 oz., footed..........$26.00
6023 Juice, footed..........$26.00

Tableware II, 127-129

2574 Bonbon..........$34.00
766 Bowl, finger..........$26.00
2574 Bowl, 8½", serving..........$45.00
6023 Bowl, 9¼", footed..........$57.00
2574 Bowl, 9½", handled..........$58.00
2574 Bowl, 12", flared..........$54.00
2574 Bowl, 13", fruit..........$58.00
2574 Candlestick, 4", pair..........$68.00
2324 Candlestick, 6", pair..........$68.00
2574 Celery, 10½"..........$38.00
2574 Comport, 5"..........$58.00
6023 Comport, 5"..........$58.00
2574 Cup and Saucer..........$28.00
2574 Ice Tub..........$48.00
2574 Lemon..........$30.00
2574 Mayonnaise, plate, ladle..........$65.00
2574 Oil, 4½ oz., G.S...........$85.00
2574 Olive, 6"..........$20.00
2574 Pickle, 8"..........$25.00
6011 Jug..........$275.00
2574 Plate, 6"..........$12.00
2574 Plate, 7"..........$18.00
2574 Plate, 8"..........$20.00
2574 Plate, 9"..........$42.00
2574 Plate, 10", cake..........$54.00
2574 Plate, 14", torte..........$65.00
2574 Relish, 3-part..........$58.00
2574 Shaker, FGT, pair..........$85.00
2574 Sugar and Cream..........$65.00
2574 Sugar and Cream, individual..........$65.00
2574 Sweetmeat..........$34.00
2574 Tray, handled, muffin..........$54.00
2574 Whip Cream..........$34.00

Colonial Prism, 2183

1918 – 1927

Stemware, 44

2183 Tumbler, table..........$8.00
2183 Tumbler, ice tea..........$8.00
2183 Tumbler, handle..........$15.00
2183 Sherbet, regular..........$8.00
2183 Sherbet, flared..........$8.00
2183 Grapefruit and Liner..........$15.00

Tableware I, 36; II, 288, 289

2183 Boat, 8½", small..........$12.00
2183 Boat, 11", large..........$16.00
2183 Bowl, 6½", footed, crimped..........$15.00
2183 Bowl, 6½", footed, flared..........$18.00
2183 Bowl, 8½", combination, nut..........$18.00
2183 Bowl, 8½", orange..........$15.00
amber..........$28.00
blue..........$37.00
green..........$30.00
canary..........$37.00
2183 Bowl, 12", cabarette..........$20.00
amber..........$25.00
blue..........$45.00
green..........$25.00
canary..........$60.00
orchid..........$30.00
azure..........$35.00
rose..........$30.00
Bowl, 12", fruit..........$20.00
Bowl, 14¾", fruit..........$25.00
Bowl, punch and foot..........$150.00
2183½ Butter and Cover, 2-handled..........$85.00
Celery, 6", tall..........$22.00
Tray, 10", celery..........$18.00
2183½ Tray, 12", celery..........$20.00
Comport, 5½"..........$24.00
Comport and Cover, 5½"..........$32.00
Condiment Set: 2-6 oz. oil, 2 shakers, condiment tray..........$95.00
Tray, condiment..........$12.00
Cream..........$10.00
Cream, hotel..........$8.00
2183½ Cream..........$12.00
Custard..........$6.00
Custard, flared..........$6.00
Bowl, finger and plate..........$11.00
Fruit Salad..........$6.00
Grapefruit Plate..........$5.00
Ice Tub, 4½"..........$15.00
Ice Tub, 6½"..........$18.00
Plate, ice tub..........$12.00
Ice, hotel, 9¾", crushed..........$45.00
Jar and Cover, footed..........$50.00
Jelly and Cover, 4", footed..........$30.00
Jelly, 5", footed..........$22.00
Jug, quart..........$50.00
Jug, ½ gallon..........$65.00
Jug, ½ gallon, ice..........$65.00
Jug, 3-quart, ice..........$65.00
Dish, lemon..........$15.00
Dish, lemon and cover..........$20.00
Dish, lemon, 6", flared..........$10.00
Pitcher, milk, 10 oz...........$18.00
Nappy, 3¼", regular..........$6.00
Nappy, 4½", regular..........$6.00
Nappy, 4½", 3-cornered, handled..........$7.00
Nappy, 4½", handled, flared..........$7.00
Nappy, 4½", handled, square..........$7.00
Nappy, 5", regular..........$7.00
Nappy, 6", regular..........$7.00
Nappy, 7", regular..........$8.00
Nappy, 8", regular..........$8.00
Nappy, 4¾", flared..........$9.00
Nappy, 6", flared..........$7.00
Nappy, 7", flared..........$8.00
Nappy, 8", flared..........$8.00
Nappy, 9", flared..........$12.00
Nappy, 7", shallow..........$7.00
Nappy, 8", shallow..........$8.00
Nappy, 8", regular, deep..........$10.00
Nappy, 10", flared, deep..........$15.00
Olive, 5¾"..........$8.00
Oil, 5½ oz., DS or GS..........$28.00
Oil, 6½ oz., DS or GS..........$28.00
Oval, 6"..........$8.00
Oval, 7½"..........$10.00
Oval, 9"..........$12.00
Oval, 10½"..........$15.00
Dish, 8", pickle..........$10.00
2183½ Tray, 10", pickle..........$12.00
Jar, pickle and cover..........$48.00
Plate, 9¼"..........$10.00
Plate, 4½", ice tea..........$4.00
Preserve and Cover, 5½", handled..........$25.00
Puff and Cover
amber..........$268.00
blue..........$350.00
canary..........$350.00
Shakers, HNT, SPT, pearl top, glass top..........$25.00
Sugar and Cover, squat..........$18.00
Sugar and Cover..........$18.00

Sugar and Cover, hotel $15.00
2183½ Sugar and Cover, 2-handled $15.00
Tankard, footed $50.00
Toothpick $22.00
Vase, 8" $28.00
Vase, 10" $32.00
Vase, 12" $40.00
Vase, 12", swung....................$45.00
2183½ Vase, 13", swung....................$55.00

Colony, 2412

1940 – 1973

Stemware, 46

2412 Goblet..............$25.00
2412 Sherbet...........$20.00
2412 Cocktail..........$20.00
2412 Wine.............$25.00
2412 Oyster Cocktail $18.00
2412 Ice Tea, footed $27.00
2412 Juice, footed $20.00
2412 Tumbler, 12 oz., flat $35.00
2412 Tumbler, 9 oz., flat $28.00
2412 Tumbler, 5 oz., flat $24.00

Tableware II, 38-50

2412 Almond, footed $28.00
2412 Ashtray, 3", square $10.00
2412 Ashtray, 3½", square.............$12.00
2412 Ashtray, 4½", square.............$20.00
2412 Ashtray, 3", round $15.00
2412 Ashtray, 4½", round $15.00
2412 Ashtray, 6", round $20.00
2412 Ashtray Set, 3-piece, square .$42.00
2412 Ashtray Set, 3-piece, round ..$50.00
2412 Bonbon, 5"...............................$22.00
2412 Bonbon, 3-toed........................$54.00
2412 Bonbon, footed $34.00
2412 Bowl, 4½", ice $75.00
2412 Bowl, 4½", round, nappy $12.00
2412 Bowl, 4¾", finger...................$18.00
2412 Bowl, 5", round, nappy......... $14.00
2412 Bowl, 7¼", ice $125.00
2412 Bowl, 8", cupped.................... $40.00
2412 Bowl, 8¼", flared $40.00
2412 Bowl, 8½", serving $45.00
2412 Bowl, 9", rolled edge $45.00
2412 Bowl, 9¾", salad $45.00
2412 Bowl, 10", fruit $48.00
2412 Bowl, 10½", fruit.....................$48.00
2412 Bowl, 10½", oval, vegetable..$38.00
2412 Bowl, 10½", 2-part, oval, vegetable $40.00
2412 Bowl, 11", footed oval............$75.00
2412 Bowl, 11", flared $50.00
2412 Bowl, 14", fruit...................... $75.00
2412 Bowl, high, footed $225.00
2412 Bowl, low, footed $125.00
2412 Bowl, 3-toed, nut.....................$54.00
2412 Bowl, ice cream, square........$57.00
2412 Bowl, punch...........$500.00/market
2412 Bowl, rose $37.00
2412 Bowl, tricorne, 3-toed............$54.00
2412 Butter and Cover $65.00
2412 Candelabra, 2-light, pair......$150.00
2412 Candle, duo, pair $115.00
2412 Candle, 6", lustre, pair $125.00
2412 Candle, 7½", lustre, pair $125.00
2412 Candle, 14½", lustre, 1103, pair $300.00
2412 Candle, Lustre No. 4, pair.. $175.00
2412 Candlestick, 3", pair $45.00
2412 Candlestick, 7", pair $95.00
2412 Candle Lamp........................ $145.00
2412 Box, candy and cover........... $95.00
2412 Celery, 9⅝" $54.00
2412 Celery, 11½" $58.00
2412 Celery, 10½", rectangle $65.00
2412 Centerpiece, 13" $70.00
2412 Cheese and Cracker..............$75.00
2412 Box, cigarette and cover.... $225.00
2412 Comport, low and cover........$65.00
2412 Comport, low, plain and cover $85.00
2412 Cream Soup $57.00
2412 Cup and Saucer..................... $18.00
2412 Cup, punch $16.00
2412 Jelly, footed and cover $54.00
2412 Jug, 3-pint $195.00
2412 Jug, 2-quart.......................... $195.00
2412 Lemon, 6½"........................... $22.00
2412 Lily Pond, 9"......................... $40.00
2412 Lily Pond, 10"........................$40.00
2412 Lily Pond, 13"....................... $57.00
2412 Mayonnaise, plate, ladle, plain $75.00
2412 Mayonnaise, plate, ladle $47.00
2412 Oil and Stopper.......................$58.00
2412 Olive, 6¼"..............................$18.00
2412 Olive, 6½", rectangle............ $24.00
2412 Olive, 7" $20.00
2412 Pickle, 8", rectangle $30.00
2412 Pickle, 8" $22.00
2412 Pickle, 9½" $25.00
2412 Pitcher, cereal.........................$85.00
2412 Plate, 6" $10.00
2412 Plate, 7" $12.00
2412 Plate, 8", ...$14.00
2412 Plate, 9" $37.00
2412 Plate, 13", torte $57.00
2412 Plate, 15", torte $75.00
2412 Plate, 18", torte $125.00
2412 Plate, handled, cake $47.00
2412 Platter, 12½" $57.00
2412 Relish, 7¼", rectangle $42.00
2412 Relish, 10", rectangle $54.00
2412 Relish, 2-part $30.00
2412 Relish, 3-part $35.00
2412 Salad Set, 3-piece $100.00
Included: salad bowl, 13", torte, wooden fork and spoon
2412 Salver, 12", cake $150.00
2412 Shaker, pair
chrome top B $36.00
silver top B $36.00
glass top F $48.00
2412 Shaker Set, 3-piece, individual
chrome top C $52.00
silver top C $30.00
glass top F $65.00
2412 Sugar and Cream...................$34.00
2412 Sugar and Cream, individual...........................$30.00
2412 Sweetmeat, 5" $24.00
2412 Sweetmeat, divided, rectangle...........................$36.00
2412 Tid Bit, 3-toed $54.00
2412 Tid Bit, 7", footed $75.00
2412 Tray, sugar and cream $26.00
2412 Tray, handled, lunch $65.00
2412 Tray, muffin............................$57.00
2412 Tray, 10½", snack $40.00
2412 Urn and Cover, footed $125.00
2412 Urn and Cover, footed, plain $165.00
2412 Vase, flared, bud................... $22.00
2412 Vase, 7", cupped, footed $87.00
2412 Vase, 7½", flared, footed $87.00
2412 Vase, 9¼", cornucopia $147.00
2412 Vase, 12" $195.00
2412 Vase, 14" $225.00
2412 Whip Cream, 4¾" $22.00

Comet, Cutting 702

1930 – 1942

Stemware, 58

4020 Goblet
crystal...........$35.00
green/ebony $45.00
4020 Sherbet, high
crystal $35.00
green/ebony $40.00
4020 Sherbet, 7 oz., low
crystal $30.00
green/ebony $36.00
4020 Sherbet, 5 oz., low
crystal $30.00
green/ebony $35.00
4020 Cocktail, 4 oz. (4020½)
crystal $30.00
green/ebony $36.00
4020 Cocktail, 3½ oz.
crystal $30.00
green/ebony $35.00
4020 Claret
crystal $35.00
green/ebony $50.00
4020 Wine
crystal $35.00
green/ebony $50.00
4020 Ice Tea, footed
crystal $35.00
green/ebony $45.00
4020 Tumbler, 13 oz., footed
crystal $35.00
green/ebony $45.00
4020 Tumbler, 10 oz., footed
crystal $30.00
green/ebony $40.00
4020 Juice
crystal $30.00
green/ebony $40.00
4020 Whiskey
crystal $35.00
green/ebony $45.00

Tableware I, 274

4021 Bowl, finger
crystal $22.00
4020 Jug
crystal $175.00
ebony base $200.00
green base $250.00
2419 Plate, 6"
crystal $6.00
2419 Plate, 7"
crystal $8.00
2419 Plate, 8"
crystal $10.00
2419 Cup and Saucer
crystal $22.00
2419 Cup and Saucer, after dinner
crystal $26.00
4020 Sugar and Cream
crystal $35.00
ebony base $40.00
2430 Vase, 8"
crystal $75.00

Comports, Nappies, and Jellies

Pre-1924 – 1971

Useful & Ornamental, 135-140

766 Nappy, 5", footed $15.00
803 Nappy, 5", footed
regal blue $38.00
empire green $38.00
burgundy $38.00
803 Nappy, 6", footed
regal blue $45.00
empire green $45.00
burgundy $45.00
803 Nappy, 7" $20.00
825 Jelly and Cover $25.00
1372 Jelly, Nappies, see Coin
1861½ Jelly
crystal $30.00
amber $32.00
blue $45.00
green $38.00
canary $50.00
rose $38.00
azure $38.00
2056 Comport, Nappy, Jelly, see American
2183 Comport, Nappies, Jelly, see Colonial Prism
2327 Comport, 7", regular
crystal $30.00
blue $65.00
canary $65.00
orchid $54.00
rose $54.00
azure $54.00
green $54.00
amber $46.00
ebony $35.00
2327 Comport, 7", salver
blue $68.00
canary $78.00
green $57.00
amber $54.00
2350 Comport, 8", see Pioneer
2362 Comport, 11", see Bowls, Centerpieces, and Console Bowls
crystal $78.00
blue $135.00
orchid $125.00
green $125.00
amber $115.00
ebony $95.00
2364 Comport, see Sonata
2374 Comport, 6", see small Bowls, Mints, and Nuts
crystal $28.00
rose $45.00
azure $45.00
amber $40.00
green $45.00
2375 Comport, 7", see Fairfax
2400 Comport, 6"
crystal $25.00
topaz/gold tint $32.00
rose $36.00
azure $42.00
green $36.00
amber $36.00
ebony $34.00
wisteria $65.00
2400 Comport, 8"
crystal $40.00
rose $57.00
azure $60.00
green $57.00
amber $52.00
orchid $65.00
2412 Comport, Jelly, see Colony
2419 Comport, Jelly, see Mayfair
2424 Comport, see Kent
2430 Jelly, see Diadem
2433 Comports, see Twenty-Four Thirty-Three
2449 Comport, see Hermitage
2470 Comports, see Twenty-Four Seventy
2496 Comport, Jelly, Nappies, see Baroque
2510 Comport, Jelly, see Sunray
2538 Nappy, 4½"
crystal $10.00
topaz/gold tint $14.00
2538 Nappy, 6", see Bowls, Centerpieces, and Console Bowls
crystal $12.00
topaz/gold tint $16.00
2538 Nappy, 11", see Salad Sets
crystal $50.00
topaz/gold tint $65.00
2550 Comport, handled, Nappy, see Spool
2560 Comport, see Coronet
2574 Comport, see Raleigh
2592 Jelly, see Myriad
2620 Nappies, see Wistar
2630 Comport, see Century
2650 Nappy, see Horizon
2667 Comport, 6", blown, crystal . $32.00
2692/388
Comport, 6½"
crystal $34.00
ruby $42.00
2708 Comport, shallow and deep, brass and glass $34.00
2718 Jelly, see Fairmont
2788 Comport, see Henry Ford Museum
2719 Jelly, see Jamestown
4024 Comport, 5"
crystal $36.00
regal blue $55.00
burgundy $55.00
empire green $60.00
ruby $60.00
4095 Nappy, 4½", with or without cover
crystal, RO $14.00
amber foot, LO $20.00
green, SO $18.00
green foot, SO $18.00
blue foot, RO $22.00
rose bowl, RO $22.00
azure bowl, RO $25.00
green bowl, RO $22.00
4095 Nappy, 5", with or without cover
crystal $16.00
amber foot, LO $22.00
green foot, SO $24.00
blue foot, RO $27.00
4095 Nappy, 6", with or without cover
crystal $18.00
amber foot, LO $27.00
green foot, SO $30.00
blue foot, RO $34.00
4095 Nappy, 7", with or without cover
crystal $20.00
amber foot, LO $30.00
green foot, SO $34.00
blue foot, RO $37.00
4119 Nappy, 4", footed
regal blue $42.00
empire green $42.00
burgundy $42.00
5078 Comport, 5", and cover $14.00
5078 Comport, 6" $14.00
5078 Nappy, low foot, with or without cover, 5", 6", 7", 8" $14.00
5098 Comport, 5"
crystal $37.00
rose $55.00
azure $58.00
topaz $54.00
amber $47.00
green $54.00
5098 Nappy, 6"
crystal $65.00
amber $75.00
green $125.00
rose $125.00
azure $135.00
topaz $125.00
5099 Comport, 6"
topaz $56.00
rose $65.00
azure $70.00
green $68.00
6013 Comport, 5", colored bowl
crystal $48.00
regal blue $75.00
burgundy $65.00
ruby $75.00
6023 Comport, 5", blown
crystal $35.00
6030 Comport, 5", blown
crystal $40.00

Congo, 4162 Tumbler

1955 – 1965

Stemware, 154

4162 Juice, 6 oz.
crystal $12.00
pink $13.00
smoke $13.00
marine $13.00
amber $13.00
4162 Beverage, 14 oz.
crystal $13.00
pink $14.00
smoke $14.00
marine $14.00
amber $14.00
4162 Cooler, 21 oz.
crystal $14.00
pink $15.00
smoke $15.00
marine $15.00
amber $15.00
4162 Bowl, dessert/finger
crystal $10.00
pink $12.00
smoke $12.00
marine $12.00
amber $12.00
4162 Plate, dessert
crystal $10.00
pink $12.00
smoke $12.00
marine $12.00
amber $12.00

Console Bowls, see Bowls, Centerpieces, and Console Bowls

Continental, 6052½
1953 – 1971

Stemware, 107

6052½ Goblet ... $22.00
6052½ Sherbet ... $20.00
6052½ Cocktail ... $20.00
6052½ Claret-Wine ... $25.00
6052½ Cordial ... $30.00
6052½ Oyster Cocktail ... $16.00
6052½ Ice Tea, footed ... $22.00
6052½ Juice, footed ... $18.00

Contour, 2638, 2666, 6060
1955 – 1971

Stemware, 110

6060 Goblet
 pink ... $35.00
 crystal ... $26.00
6060 Sherbet
 pink ... $30.00
 crystal ... $22.00
6060 Cocktail/Wine/Seafood
 pink ... $40.00
 crystal ... $26.00
6060 Cordial
 pink ... $50.00
 crystal ... $35.00
6060 Ice Tea, footed
 pink ... $35.00
 crystal ... $26.00
6060 Juice, footed
 pink ... $30.00
 crystal ... $22.00

Tableware II, 73-78

2638 Ashtray, 6", 3 lips ... $12.00
2638 Ashtray, 7", 1 lip ... $15.00
2638 Ashtray, 7", 2 lips ... $15.00
2638 Bowl, 5½" ... $20.00
2638 Bowl, 5½", square ... $20.00
2638 Bowl, 7", deep ... $20.00
2638 Bowl, 7½", 3-cornered ... $22.00
2638 Bowl, 8½", oval ... $22.00
2638 Bowl, 8½", square ... $24.00
2638 Bowl, 10½", oblong ... $25.00
2638 Candlestick, 4½", pair
 crystal ... $95.00
 ebony ... $150.00
2638 Tray, 7" ... $18.00
2666 Ashtray, 6½" ... $12.00
2666 Bonbon ... $18.00
2666 Bowl, 8¼", oval
 crystal ... $35.00
 silver mist ... $38.00
 ebony ... $38.00
2666 Bowl, 9", salad
 crystal ... $35.00
 ebony ... $40.00
2666 Bowl, 11", salad
 crystal ... $40.00
 ebony ... $45.00
2666 Bowl, individual, salad ... $15.00
2666 Butter, oblong ... $22.00
2666 Butter Pat ... $10.00
2666 Candle, flora, pair
 crystal ... $34.00
 ebony ... $38.00
2666 Celery ... $14.00
2666 Coaster, utility ... $10.00
2666 Cup and Saucer ... $18.00
2666 Mayonnaise, plate, ladle
 crystal ... $55.00
 ebony ... $55.00
2666 Oil and Stopper ... $55.00
2666 Pickle ... $10.00
2666 Pitcher, pint ... $30.00
2666 Pitcher, 3-pint ... $55.00
2666 Pitcher, quart ... $45.00
2666 Plate, 7" ... $10.00
2666 Plate, 10" ... $20.00
2666 Plate, party and cup ... $26.00
2666 Plate, canape ... $30.00
2666 Plate, 10", snack ... $24.00
2666 Plate, 14", serving ... $47.00
2666 Preserve, handled ... $28.00
2666 Relish, 2-part ... $24.00
2666 Relish, 3-part ... $32.00
2666 Salver, cake ... $50.00
2666 Pitcher, sauce ... $30.00
2666 Plate, sauce, oval ... $10.00
2666 Salad Set, 9"
 crystal ... $80.00
 ebony ... $94.00
2666 Salad Set, 11"
 crystal ... $90.00
 ebony ... $100.00
2666 Shaker, chrome top, pair ... $48.00
2666 Sugar and Cream, regular ... $35.00
2666 Sugar and Cream, individual .. $34.00
2666 Tray, individual, sugar and cream ... $10.00
2666 Vase, Pitcher, see Groups: Decorator Collection

Contrast, 6120
1970 – 1972

Stemware, 138

6120 Goblet ... $55.00
6120 Sherbet ... $55.00
6120 Claret ... $55.00
6120 Liqueur ... $80.00
6120 Ice Tea, footed ... $55.00
2337 Plate, 7"
 crystal ... $10.00
 onyx ... $12.00
2337 Plate, 8", crystal only ... $12.00

Coral Pearl, Decoration 623
1940 – 1960

Stemware, 95

6024 Goblet ... $40.00
6024 Saucer Champagne ... $35.00
6024 Sherbet, low ... $30.00
6024 Cocktail ... $34.00
6024 Claret ... $44.00
6024 Wine ... $40.00
6024 Cordial ... $50.00
6024 Oyster Cocktail ... $27.00
6024 Ice Tea, footed ... $40.00
6024 Tumbler, 9 oz., footed ... $30.00
6024 Juice, footed ... $32.00
2337 Plate, 6", LO ... $8.00
2337 Plate, 7", LO ... $10.00
2337 Plate, 8", LO ... $12.00

Cordelia, Etching 82
1927 – 1930

Stemware, 33

877 Goblet
 orchid ... $65.00
 green ... $35.00
877 Sherbet, high
 orchid ... $55.00
 green ... $30.00
877 Sherbet, low
 orchid ... $46.00
 green ... $25.00
877 Parfait
 orchid ... $65.00
 green ... $35.00
877 Cocktail
 orchid ... $50.00
 green ... $28.00
877 Claret
 orchid ... $65.00
 green ... $35.00
877 Wine
 orchid ... $60.00
 green ... $30.00
877 Cordial
 orchid ... $75.00
 green ... $42.00
877 Oyster Cocktail
 orchid ... $35.00
 green ... $24.00
877 Grapefruit and Liner
 orchid ... $75.00
 green ... $48.00
877 Ice Tea, footed
 orchid ... $56.00
 green ... $42.00
877 Tumbler, 9 oz., footed
 orchid ... $35.00
 green ... $28.00
877 Juice, footed
 orchid ... $35.00
 green ... $28.00
877 Whiskey, footed
 orchid ... $35.00
 green ... $28.00
5000 Jug
 orchid ... $400.00
 green ... $350.00
2283 Plate, 7" ... $20.00
2283 Plate, 8" ... $22.00

Cornucopia, Carving 46
1941 – 1943

Useful & Ornamental, 126

2364 Bowl, 12", lily pond ... $95.00
2364 Bowl, 13", fruit ... $95.00
6023 Candlestick, duo, pair ... $125.00
2364 Plate, 14", torte ... $115.00
2364 Plate, 16", torte ... $125.00
2577 Vase, 8½" ... $175.00

Coronada, Decoration 49
1925 – 1927

Tableware I, 322

2324 Bowl, 10", console ... $250.00
2297 Bowl A, 10¼", shallow ... $195.00
2315 Bowl A, 10½", console ... $225.00
2297 Bowl A, 12", deep ... $225.00
2324 Candlestick, 2" ... $125.00
2324 Candlestick, 4" ... $98.00
2324 Candlestick, 9" ... $250.00
2250 Jar, candy and cover, ½ pound ... $125.00

2331 Box, candy and cover..........$195.00
2329 Centerpiece, 11"..........$225.00
2322 Cologne..........$350.00
2323 Cologne..........$325.00
2327 Comport, 7"..........$125.00
2315 Grapefruit/Mayonnaise..........$95.00
2283 Plate, 7"..........$20.00
2283 Plate, 8"..........$25.00
2283 Plate, 10"..........$45.00
2316 Plate, 8", soup..........$65.00
2290 Plate, 13"..........$95.00
2338 Box, puff and cover..........$250.00
2315 Sugar and Cream..........$265.00
2287 Tray, handled, lunch..........$225.00
2276 Vanity Set..........$600.00

Coronet, 2560

1938 – 1959

Tableware II, 52-58

2560 Bonbon, 2 handles..........$26.00
2560 Bonbon, 3-toed....$34.00
2560 Bowl, 5", fruit......$18.00
2560 Bowl, 6", cereal.......$20.00
2560 Bowl, 3-toed nut, cupped..........$34.00
2560 Bowl, 8½", handled, serving..$38.00
2560 Bowl, 8½", cupped..........$47.00
2560 Bowl, 10", salad..........$45.00
2560 Bowl, 2-part, salad..........$65.00
2560 Bowl, 11", handled..........$65.00
2560 Bowl, 11½", crimped..........$65.00
2560 Bowl, 12", flared..........$65.00
2560 Bowl, 13", fruit..........$68.00
2560 Cake, 10½", handled..........$42.00
2560 Candlestick, 4", pair..........$36.00
2560 Candlestick, 4½", pair..........$48.00
2560 Candlestick, duo, pair..........$54.00
2560 Celery, 11"..........$28.00
2560 Cheese and Cracker..........$48.00
2560 Comport, 6"..........$34.00
2560 Cup and Saucer..........$18.00
2560 Ice Bucket, chrome handle..$57.00
2560 Dish, lemon, 2 handles..........$18.00
2560 Mayonnaise, plate, ladle..........$37.00
2560 Mayonnaise, 2-part, 2 ladles.$58.00
2560 Oil and Stopper, 3 oz..........$47.00
2560 Olive, 6¾"..........$18.00
2560 Pickle, 8¾"..........$20.00
2560 Plate, 6"..........$7.00
2560 Plate, 7"..........$9.00
2560 Plate, 8"..........$12.00
2560 Plate, 9"..........$20.00
2560 Plate, 14", torte..........$50.00
2560 Relish, 2-part..........$28.00
2560 Relish, 3-part..........$37.00
2560 Relish, 4-part..........$46.00
2560 Relish, 5-part..........$48.00
2560 Salad Set..........$95.00
2560 Salad Bowl, 10" and torte, 14"
2560 Salad Fork and Spoon, wooden
2560 Shaker, FGT, pair..........$35.00
2560 Sugar and Cream..........$34.00
2560 Sugar and Cream, individual..$34.00
2560 Sugar and Cream Set..........$49.00
individual sugar and cream..$10.00
sugar and cream tray..........$10.00
2560 Sweetmeat, 2-handled..........$26.00
2560 Tid Bit, 3-toed..........$34.00
2560 Tray, handled, muffin..........$42.00
2560 Tray, 11½", lunch..........$58.00
2560 Tray, sugar and cream..........$14.00
2560 Vase, 3¾", pansy..........$37.00
2560 Vase, 6", handled..........$75.00
2560 Whip Cream, 2 handles..........$26.00

Coronet, Decoration 656

1962 – 1970

Stemware, 125

6101 Goblet..........$36.00
6101 Sherbet..........$32.00
6101 Wine/Cocktail..........$38.00
6101 Cordial..........$48.00
6101 Ice Tea, footed..........$36.00
6101 Juice, footed..........$32.00
2337 Plate, 7"..........$10.00
2337 Plate, 8"..........$12.00

Corsage, Etching 325

1935 – 1959

Stemware, 86

6014 Goblet..........$35.00
6014 Saucer Champagne..........$32.00
6014 Sherbet, low..........$24.00
6014 Cocktail..........$27.00
6014 Claret..........$45.00
6014 Wine..........$42.00
6014 Cordial..........$50.00
6014 Oyster Cocktail..........$22.00
6014 Ice Tea, footed..........$35.00
6014 Tumbler, 9 oz., footed..........$28.00
6014 Juice, footed..........$24.00

Tableware I, 226

2496 Bonbon, 3-toed..........$45.00
869 Bowl, finger..........$45.00
2527 Bowl, 9", footed..........$135.00
2536 Bowl, 9", handled..........$87.00
6023 Bowl, 9", footed..........$135.00
2484 Bowl, 10", handled..........$125.00
2496 Bowl, 12", flared..........$100.00
2545 Bowl, 12½", oval..........$125.00
2527 Candelabra, 2-light, pair......$300.00
2545 Candelabra, 2-light, pair......$395.00
2496 Candlestick, 5½", pair..........$95.00
2535 Candlestick, 5½", pair..........$125.00
2496 Candlestick, duo, pair..........$125.00
2545 Candlestick, duo, pair..........$150.00
2496 Candlestick, trindle, pair...$150.00
2545 Candlestick, lustre, pair.....$195.00
2496 Candy, 3-part and cover......$125.00
2440 Celery..........$48.00
2496 Cheese and Cracker..........$95.00
2496 Comport, 5½"..........$67.00
2440 Cup and Saucer..........$32.00
2496 Ice Bucket, chrome handle..$125.00
5000 Jug..........$475.00
2440 Mayonnaise, 2-part..........$48.00
2496½ Mayonnaise, plate, ladle......$85.00
2496 Nappy, regular handled..........$26.00
2496 Nappy, flared handled..........$20.00
2496 Nappy, square handled..........$26.00
2496 Nappy, 3-cornered, handled..$20.00
4119 Nappy, 4", footed..........$34.00
2496 Bowl, nut, 3-toed..........$57.00
2440 Pickle..........$42.00
2666 Pitcher, quart..........$250.00
2337 Plate, 6"..........$10.00
2337 Plate, 7"..........$15.00
2337 Plate, 8"..........$20.00
2337 Plate, 9"..........$40.00
2496 Plate, 10", handled, cake.......$68.00
2440 Plate, 10½", handled, cake...$75.00
2440 Plate, 13", torte..........$95.00
2364 Plate, 16"..........$125.00
2440 Relish, 2-part..........$40.00
2440 Relish, 3-part..........$58.00
2419 Relish, 4-part..........$60.00
2419 Relish, 5-part..........$86.00
2496 Relish, 2-part..........$40.00
2496 Relish, 3-part..........$75.00
2496 Relish, 4-part..........$80.00
2440 Sauce, 6½", oval,..........$45.00
2375 Shaker, footed, F top, pair..$175.00
2440 Sugar and Cream..........$88.00
2496 Sugar and Cream, individual..........$75.00
2496 Sugar, cream, tray..........$125.00
2496 Tid Bit, 3-toed..........$42.00
2440 Tray, 8½", oval..........$32.00
2496 Tray, ½", individual, sugar and cream..........$48.00
5092 Vase, 8", bud..........$75.00
2470 Vase, 10"..........$225.00

Corsage Plum, 6126

1973 – 1974

Stemware, 142

6126 Goblet..........$26.00
6126 Champagne..........$24.00
6126 Wine..........$28.00
6126 Ice Tea, footed..........$26.00
2337 Plate, 7", plum..........$12.00

Cotillion, Cutting 892

1962 – 1970

Stemware, 124

6100 Goblet..........$24.00
6100 Sherbet..........$22.00
6100 Claret..........$30.00
6100 Tulip Wine..........$30.00
6100 Brandy..........$30.00
6100 Ice Tea, footed..........$24.00
2337 Plate, 7"..........$10.00
2337 Plate, 8"..........$12.00

Countess (Imported Stemware)

1984 – 1986

Tableware II, 280, 282

Goblet..........$22.00
Wine..........$22.00
Flute..........$22.00
Ice Tea..........$22.00

Country Garden, Crystal Print 13, 4180 Casual Flair Tumbler

1958 – 1962

Stemware, 155

4180 Tumbler, 12 oz., flat, sky blue..........$12.00
4180 Juice, 7 oz., flat, sky blue..........$8.00

Courtship, 6051½

1953 – 1976

Stemware, 106

6051½ Goblet..........$22.00
6051½ Sherbet..........$20.00
6051½ Cocktail..........$20.00
6051½ Claret-Wine..........$25.00
6051½ Cordial..........$30.00

6051½ Oyster Cocktail $16.00
6051½ Ice Tea, footed $22.00
6051½ Juice, footed $18.00

Coventry, 2834

1970 – 1971

Tableware II, 104

135 Bonbon
- crystal $12.00
- honey gold $14.00

191 Bowl, 8"
- crystal $16.00
- honey gold $20.00

195 Bowl, 9"
- crystal $16.00
- honey gold $20.00

300 Butter and Cover, oblong
- crystal $34.00
- honey gold $38.00

540 Pickle, 8"
- crystal $12.00
- honey gold $14.00

560 Plate, 12", square
- crystal $18.00
- honey gold $22.00

567 Plate, 14", service
- crystal $22.00
- honey gold $26.00

620 Relish, 8", 2-part
- crystal $18.00
- honey gold $20.00

651 Shaker, chrome top E, pair
- crystal $22.00
- honey gold $26.00

677 Sugar and Cream
- crystal $30.00
- honey gold $34.00

Coventry, Cutting 807

1940 – 1943

Tableware I, 304

2596 Bowl, 7½", square $45.00
2364 Bowl, 10½", salad $55.00
2596 Bowl, 11", shallow, oblong $74.00
2364 Bowl, 12", lily pond $62.00
2364 Bowl, 13", fruit $65.00
2596 Candlestick, 5", pair $65.00
2324 Candlestick, 6", pair $65.00
6023 Candlestick, duo, pair $75.00
2364 Plate, 14", torte $60.00
2364 Plate, 16", torte $64.00
2577 Vase, 6" $67.00
4143½ Vase, 6", footed $67.00
2567 Vase, 7½", footed $78.00
4143½ Vase, 7½", footed $75.00
2567 Vase, 8½", footed $95.00
2577 Vase, 8½" $85.00
4126½ Vase, 11", footed $125.00

Crest, Cutting 843

1955 – 1962

Stemware, 110

6061 Goblet $32.00
6061 Sherbet $28.00
6061 Cocktail/Wine/Seafood $28.00
6061 Cordial $38.00
6061 Ice Tea, footed $32.00
6061 Juice, footed $26.00

Tableware II, 189

2691 Ashtray, individual $18.00
2666 Bowl, oval $38.00
2666 Candle, flora, pair $48.00
2691 Holder, cigarette, individual $22.00
2337 Plate, 7" $10.00
2337 Plate, 8" $12.00
2364 Plate, 11", sandwich $24.00
2364 Plate, 14", torte $35.00
2691 Preserve, handled $22.00
2691 Bowl, sauce, with plate and ladle $45.00
2691 Server, 2-part $30.00
2691 Server, 3-part $38.00
2691 Shaker, chrome top A, pair $48.00
2691 Sugar and Cover $24.00
2691 Sugar and Cream $35.00
2691 Tray, sugar and cream, individual $45.00

Criterion, Decoration 65

1926

Amber and green

Stemware

870 Goblet $30.00
870 Saucer Champagne $30.00
870 Fruit $27.00
870 Parfait $34.00
870 Wine $34.00
870 Cocktail $27.00
870 Cordial $50.00
5084 Tumbler
- 12 oz. $30.00
- 9 oz. $28.00
- 5 oz. $26.00
- 2½" $26.00

945½ Grapefruit and Liner $26.00

Tableware I, 325

2350 Bouillon $15.00
869 Bowl, finger and 2283 Plate $25.00
2350 Bowl, fruit $15.00
2350 Bowl, cereal $18.00
2350 Bowl, 9", oval, baker $28.00
2350 Bowl, 10½", oval, baker $37.00
2324 Bowl, 10" $48.00
2297 Bowl A, deep $45.00
2350 Butter and Cover $77.00
2324 Candlestick, 4", pair $45.00
2324 Candlestick, 9", pair $95.00
2350 Celery $38.00
2329 Centerpiece, 11" $95.00
2327 Comport, 7" $46.00
2350 Cream Soup $20.00
2350 Cup and Saucer $18.00
2350½ Cup, footed $14.00
5084 Jug, footed $175.00
2315 Mayonnaise $22.00
2350 Pickle $14.00
2350 Plate, 6" $6.00
2350 Plate, 7" $7.00
2350 Plate, 8" $9.00
2350 Plate, 7", soup $12.00
2350 Plate, 9" $18.00
2350 Plate, 10" $22.00
2350 Plate, 15", round $45.00
2350 Platter, 10½" $25.00
2350 Platter, 12" $30.00
2350 Platter, 15" $48.00
2350 Sugar and Cover $30.00
2350 Sugar and Cream $47.00
2287 Tray, handled, lunch $45.00

Crown Collection

Tableware II, 247 – 249

Hapsburg 2750

386 Chalice and Cover, 9¼", footed
- crystal $125.00
- royal blue $165.00
- gold $135.00
- ruby $175.00

388 Chalice, 7¼", footed
- crystal $75.00
- royal blue $130.00
- gold $95.00
- ruby $135.00

676 Candy and Cover, 5¾"
- crystal $65.00
- royal blue $125.00
- gold $85.00
- ruby $125.00

677 Candy, 3¾"
- crystal $55.00
- royal blue $95.00
- gold $65.00
- ruby $95.00

Luxemburg 2766

311 Bowl, 7¼", trindle, candle
- crystal $85.00
- royal blue $158.00
- gold $130.00
- ruby $160.00

Navarre 2751

195 Bowl, 9"
- crystal $85.00
- royal blue $115.00
- gold $95.00
- ruby $125.00

198 Bowl and Cover, 8½"
- crystal $98.00
- royal blue $125.00
- gold $110.00
- ruby $125.00

199 Bowl, 9", footed
- crystal $110.00
- royal blue $160.00
- gold $125.00
- ruby $165.00

203 Bowl and Cover, 12⅛", footed
- crystal $140.00
- royal blue $195.00
- gold $175.00
- ruby $200.00

Windsor 2749

133 Bottle and Stopper
- crystal $128.00
- royal blue $175.00
- gold $145.00

314 Candleholder, 3½", pair
- crystal $125.00
- royal blue $175.00
- gold $150.00

386 Chalice and Cover, 8½", footed
- crystal $110.00
- royal blue $135.00
- gold $125.00
- ruby $175.00

388 Chalice, 6¾", footed
- crystal $95.00
- royal blue $160.00
- gold $125.00
- ruby $165.00

676	Candy and Cover, 5½"	
	crystal	$75.00
	royal blue	$97.00
	gold	$88.00
	ruby	$110.00
677	Candy, 3¾", open	
	crystal	$55.00
	royal blue	$78.00
	gold	$67.00
	ruby	$90.00

Crown, Decoration 504

1930 – 1932

Ebony with gold decoration

Note: See also 2430 Diadem

Tableware I, 69

2430	Bowl, 11"	$94.00
2430	Jar, candy and cover	$125.00
2430	Jelly, 7"	$45.00
2430	Vase, 8"	$95.00

Crystal Twist, 6101

1962 – 1970

Stemware, 125

6101	Goblet	$28.00
6101	Sherbet	$22.00
6101	Wine/Cocktail	$30.00
6101	Cordial	$35.00
6101	Ice Tea, footed	$28.00
6101	Juice, footed	$22.00

Cumberland, Cutting 762

1936 – 1939

Stemware, 88

6016	Goblet	$30.00
6016	Saucer Champagne	$27.00
6016	Sherbet, low	$24.00
6016	Cocktail	$27.00
6016	Claret	$35.00
6016	Wine	$34.00
6016	Cordial	$45.00
6016	Oyster Cocktail	$22.00
6016	Ice Tea, footed	$28.00
6016	Tumbler, 10 oz., footed	$25.00
6016	Juice, footed	$24.00

Tableware I, 290

869	Bowl, finger	$12.00
2470½	Bowl, 10½"	$40.00
2472	Candlestick, duo, pair	$70.00
2400	Comport, 6"	$27.00
5000	Jug	$185.00
2337	Plate, 6"	$6.00
2337	Plate, 7"	$7.00
2337	Plate, 8"	$8.00

Cupid, Brocade Etching 288

1927 – 1928

Tableware I, 128 – 129

2297	Bowl A, 12", deep	
	blue	$450.00
	green	$375.00
	ebony	$400.00
2324	Candlestick, 4", priced as pair	
	blue	$450.00
	green	$375.00
	ebony	$400.00
2298	Candlestick, priced as pair	
	blue	$475.00
	green	$450.00
	ebony	$450.00
2329	Centerpiece, 11"	
	blue	$475.00
	green	$450.00
	ebony	$450.00
2329	Centerpiece, 13"	
	blue	$550.00
	green	$500.00
	ebony	$500.00
2298	Clock	
	blue	$600.00
	green	$525.00
	ebony	$550.00
2298	Clock Set: clock and 2 candlesticks	
	blue	$1,000.00/market
	green	$900.00/market
	ebony	$900.00/market
2322	Cologne	
	blue	$875.00
	green	$800.00
	ebony	$800.00
2359½	Puff and Cover	
	blue	$750.00/market
	green	$700.00/market
	ebony	$750.00/market
2276	Vanity Set	
	blue	$1,000.00/market
	green	$900.00/market
	ebony	$900.00/market

Cutting 4

1903 – 1916

Stemware, 21, 28, 63

766	Goblet	$12.00
766	Saucer Champagne	$12.00
766	Sherbet	$10.00
766	Fruit	$10.00
766	Parfait	$10.00
766	Cocktail	$10.00
766	Claret	$12.00
766	Rhine Wine	$12.00
766	Wine	$12.00
766	Burgundy	$14.00
766	Sherry	$12.00
766	Crème de Menthe	$12.00
766	Brandy	$15.00
766	Cordial	$15.00
766	Sorbet	$8.00
766	Ice Tea, footed, handled	$15.00
766	Custard, handled	$7.00
863	Goblet, 10½ oz.	$9.00
863	Goblet, 9 oz.	$9.00
863	Goblet, 7 oz.	$8.00
863	Saucer Champagne	$8.00
863	Cocktail	$7.00
863	Claret	$8.00
863	Rhine Wine	$8.00
863	Wine	$8.00
863	Sherry	$7.00
863	Crème de Menthe	$8.00
863	Brandy, pousse-café	$10.00
863	Cordial	$15.00
863	Champagne, hollow stem	$10.00
863	Champagne, tall	$8.00
863	Roemer	$12.00
5061	Goblet, 9 oz.	$10.00
5061	Saucer Champagne	$10.00
5061	Sherbet	$8.00
5061	Cocktail	$8.00
858	Tumbler	$4.00 – 8.00
945	Grapefruit and 945½ Liner	$22.00
822	Parfait	$20.00
300	Tankard	$75.00
303	Jug	$50.00
1236	Jug	$85.00

Cutting 77

1904 – 1913

Stemware, 24

858	Goblet, 11 oz.	$10.00
858	Goblet, 10 oz.	$9.00
858	Goblet, 9 oz.	$9.00
858	Saucer Champagne, 7 oz.	$6.00
858	Sherbet	$6.00
858	Fruit	$6.00
858	Cocktail	$6.00
858	Claret, 6½ oz.	$6.00
858	Claret, 4½ oz.	$6.00
858	Wine, 3½ oz.	$6.00
858	Wine, 2¾ oz.	$6.00
858	Sherry	$6.00
858	Crème de Menthe	$6.00
858	Brandy	$15.00
858	Cordial	$15.00
858	Champagne, CF, hollow stem	$12.00
858	Champagne, tall	$12.00
858	Champagne, long stem	$18.00
858	Hot Whiskey	$6.00
833	Tumbler	$5.00 – 8.00
887	Tumbler	$5.00 – 8.00
889	Tumbler	$5.00 – 8.00
300	Tankard	$75.00
303	Tankard	$50.00
724	Tankard	$95.00
1236	Tankard	$75.00
1743	Tankard and Cover	$84.00

Cutting 110

1913 – 1924

Stemware, 28

863	Goblet, 10½ oz.	$7.00
863	Goblet, 9 oz.	$7.00
863	Goblet, 7 oz.	$7.00
863	Saucer Champagne	$7.00
863	Fruit	$5.00
863	Cocktail, 3½ oz.	$5.00
863	Claret	$7.00
863	Rhine Wine	$7.00
863	Wine	$7.00
863	Sherry	$5.00
863	Crème de Menthe	$5.00
863	Brandy, pousse-café	$7.00
863	Cordial	$7.00
863	Champagne, tall	$7.00
945½	Grapefruit and Liner	$28.00
701	Tumbler	$4.00 – 8.00
820	Tumbler	$4.00 – 8.00
833	Tumbler	$4.00 – 8.00
887	Tumbler	$4.00 – 8.00
889	Tumbler	$4.00 – 8.00
300	Tankard	$75.00
300½	Tankard	$87.00

724 Tankard $87.00
303 Jug $50.00
317 Jug $75.00
1227 Jug $75.00
1236 Jug $85.00

Cutting 125

1915 – 1917

Stemware, 21, 29

766 Goblet $12.00
766 Saucer Champagne $12.00
766 Sherbet $10.00
766 Fruit $10.00
766 Parfait $20.00
766 Cocktail $12.00
766 Claret $12.00
766 Rhine Wine $12.00
766 Wine $12.00
766 Burgundy $12.00
766 Sherry $12.00
766 Créme de Menthe $12.00
766 Brandy $15.00
766 Cordial $20.00
766 Sorbet $8.00
766 Ice Tea, footed, handled $15.00
766 Custard, handled, $7.00
766 Grapefruit and Liner $28.00
863 Goblet, 10½ oz. $10.00
863 Goblet, 9 oz. $10.00
863 Saucer Champagne $10.00
863 Fruit $8.00
863 Cocktail, 3½ oz. $8.00
863 Claret $10.00
863 Rhine Wine $10.00
863 Wine $10.00
863 Sherry $8.00
863 Créme de Menthe $8.00
863 Brandy, pousse-café $20.00
863 Cordial $22.00
863 Champagne, hollow stem, C.F. $10.00
863 Champagne, tall $10.00
945½ Grapefruit and Liner $25.00
899 Parfait $20.00
701 Tumbler $4.00 – 8.00
820 Tumbler $4.00 – 8.00
833 Tumbler $4.00 – 8.00
887 Tumbler $4.00 – 8.00
889 Tumbler $4.00 – 8.00
4077 Tumbler $4.00 – 8.00
300 Tankard $75.00
303 Jug $60.00

Cutting 129

1918 – 1928

Stemware, 29

863 Goblet, 9 oz. $8.00
863 Saucer Champagne $8.00
863 Fruit $6.00
863 Cocktail, 3½ oz. $6.00
863 Claret $8.00
863 Wine $8.00
822 Parfait $22.00
805 Parfait $22.00
766½ Parfait $22.00
837 Oyster Cocktail $6.00
945½ Grapefruit and Liner $25.00
406 Lemonade, handled $18.00
701 Tumbler $4.00 – 8.00
820 Tumbler $4.00 – 8.00
833 Tumbler $4.00 – 8.00
4011 Tumbler $4.00 – 8.00
300 Jug $75.00
303 Jug $50.00
1124 Jug $75.00
1236 Jug $78.00
1743 Jug $75.00
2100 Jug $75.00

Cynthia, Cutting 170

1924 – 1928

Stemware, 19

661 Goblet $10.00
661 Saucer Champagne $10.00
661 Fruit $8.00
661 Sherbet, low $8.00
661 Parfait $12.00
661 Cocktail $10.00
661 Wine $10.00
661 Cordial $15.00
837 Oyster Cocktail $10.00
945½ Grapefruit and Liner $26.00
4085 Tumbler $6.00 – 12.00
4095 Tumbler $6.00 – 12.00
4011 Tumbler $6.00 – 12.00

Tableware I, 267

880 Bonbon $18.00
1769 Bowl, finger and plate $18.00
2250 Jar, candy and cover, ¼ pound $20.00
2250 Jar, candy and cover, ½ pound $26.00
2250 Jar, candy and cover, pound $30.00
1697 Carafe $28.00
4023 Carafe Tumbler, 6 oz. $7.00
5078 Comport, 5" $16.00
5078 Comport, 6" $17.00
300 Decanter, 2-quart, cut neck $28.00
825 Jelly $18.00
825 Jelly and Cover $25.00
2270 Jug $95.00
2270 Jug and Cover, cover not cut $125.00
303/3 Jug $45.00
1852/6 Jug $65.00
724/7 Jug, Tankard $125.00
4087 Marmalade and Cover $28.00
1769 Mayonnaise, plate, ladle $45.00
5078 Nappy, 5" $12.00
5078 Nappy, 6" $14.00
5078 Nappy and Cover, 5" $20.00
5078 Nappy and Cover, 6" $20.00
1465 Oil, 5 oz., cut neck $30.00
1465 Oil, 7 oz., cut neck $30.00
2283 Plate, 6" $4.00
1897 Plate, 7" $5.00
2337 Plate, 7" $5.00
2337 Plate, 8" $8.00
2238 Plate, 8¼", salad $8.00
1848 Plate, 9", sandwich $12.00
2235 Shaker, FGT or pearl top, pair $36.00
2133 Sugar and Cream $28.00

Cynthia, Cutting 785

1938 – 1965

Stemware, 90, 158

6017 Goblet $32.00
6017 Sherbet, high $28.00
6017 Sherbet, low $22.00
6017 Cocktail $28.00
6017 Claret $38.00
6017 Wine $36.00
6017 Cordial $45.00
6017 Oyster Cocktail $20.00
6017 Ice Tea, footed $32.00
6017 Tumbler, 9 oz., footed $24.00
6017 Juice, footed $24.00

Tableware I, 299

2560 Bonbon $38.00
2560 Bonbon, 3-toed $35.00
766 Bowl, finger $16.00
2560 Bowl, 11", handled $78.00
2560 Bowl, serving $60.00
2560 Bowl, 2-part, salad $78.00
2560 Bowl, 11½", crimped $70.00
2560 Bowl, 13", fruit $75.00
2560½ Candlestick, 4", pair $65.00
2560 Candlestick, 4½", pair $65.00
2560 Candlestick, duo, pair $87.00
2560 Celery, 11" $32.00
2560 Cheese and Cracker $75.00
2560 Comport, 6" $46.00
2560 Cup and Saucer $32.00
2560 Ice Bucket, chrome handle $75.00
2560 Tongs, ice, chrome $35.00
6011 Jug $245.00
2560 Lemon $24.00
2560 Mayonnaise, plate, ladle $75.00
2560 Mayonnaise, 2-part, 2 ladles $87.00
2560 Oil, 3 oz. footed, and stopper $125.00
2560 Olive, 6¾" $28.00
2560 Pickle, 8¾" $28.00
2666 Pitcher, quart $250.00
2337 Plate, 6" $7.00
2337 Plate, 7" $9.00
2337 Plate, 8" $11.00
2560 Plate, 10½", cake $56.00
2560 Plate, 14", torte $70.00
2560 Relish, 2-part $34.00
2560 Relish, 3-part $60.00
2560 Relish, 4-part $85.00
2560 Relish, 5-part $95.00
2560 Sugar and Cream, individual $60.00
2560 Sugar and Cream $57.00
2560 Sweetmeat $34.00
2560 Tid Bit, 3-toed $38.00
2560 Tray, muffin $65.00
2560 Whip Cream $34.00
2560 Tray, 11½", handled, lunch $65.00
2567 Vase, 7½", footed $125.00
5100 Vase, 10" $125.00

Cyrene, Cutting 763

1937 – 1943

Stemware, 84

6012 Goblet $28.00
6012 Sherbet, high $26.00
6012 Sherbet, low $22.00
6012 Cocktail $22.00
6012 Claret $28.00
6012 Wine $28.00
6012 Cordial $38.00
6012 Oyster Cocktail $18.00
6012 Ice Tea, footed $27.00
6012 Tumbler, 10 oz., footed $20.00
6012 Juice, footed $18.00

Cyrene, Cutting 763

Tableware I, 297

1769 Bowl, finger $14.00
2496 Bowl, 10½", handled $77.00
2496 Candlestick, 5½", pair $54.00
6011 Jug $185.00
2337 Plate, 6" $6.00
2337 Plate, 7" $7.00
2337 Plate, 8" $8.00
2350½ Sugar and Cream $35.00

- D -

Daisy, Decoration 17

1920s

Stemware, 25

858 Goblet, 5 oz. $45.00
858 Saucer Champagne, 5½ oz. $45.00
858 Fruit $45.00
858 Cocktail $45.00

Tableware I, 312

1904 Bonbon and Cover $225.00
2136 Bonbon and Cover $195.00
2090 Bottle, 6 oz., toilet $125.00
2118 Bottle, 6 oz., toilet $125.00
858 Bowl, finger and plate $45.00
1490 Candlestick, 8", pair $250.00
2244 Candlestick, 8¼", pair $300.00
2245 Candlestick, 8¼", pair $200.00
2219 Jar, candy and cover, ¼ pound $75.00
2219 Jar, candy and cover, ½ pound $85.00
2250 Jar, candy and cover, ¼ pound $75.00
2250 Jar, candy and cover, ½ pound $85.00
2250 Jar, candy and cover, pound $95.00
1697 Carafe Set, 2 pieces $150.00
2136 Cold Cream and Cover, 3" $145.00
2241 Cologne, 2¼ oz., drip stopper $165.00
2242 Cologne, 3¼ oz., drip stopper $145.00
2243 Cologne, 2¼ oz., drip stopper $145.00
803 Comport, 5", tall $53.00
724/7 Jug $450.00
2104 Jug $450.00
2138 Mayonnaise Set, 2 pieces $65.00
803 Nappy, 5", LD $40.00
1848 Plate, 9", sandwich, matt star base $40.00
1719 Plate, 10½", sandwich, matt star base $45.00
2136 Pomade and Cover, 2" $125.00
1666 Puff and Cover $148.00
2135 Puff and Cover $135.00
2091 Soap and Cover $135.00
2137 Vase, brush $150.00
701 Tumbler $30.00
820 Tumbler $30.00

Daisy, Etching 324

1935 – 1943

Stemware, 85

6013 Goblet $35.00
6013 Goblet, low $30.00
6013 Saucer Champagne $30.00
6013 Sherbet, low $25.00
6013 Cocktail $30.00
6013 Claret $45.00
6013 Wine $40.00
6013 Cordial $57.00
6013 Oyster Cocktail $25.00
6013 Ice Tea, footed $32.00
6013 Juice, footed $26.00

Tableware I, 225

766 Bowl, finger $28.00
2533 Bowl, 9", handled $165.00
2536 Bowl, 9", handled $125.00
2535 Candlestick, 5½", pair $135.00
2533 Candlestick, duo, pair $165.00
2535 Cheese and Cracker $87.00
6013 Comport, 5" $56.00
2550½ Cup and Saucer $34.00
5000 Jug $365.00
2375 Mayonnaise, plate, ladle $75.00
2440 Mayonnaise, 2-part $52.00
2337 Plate, 6" $10.00
2337 Plate, 7" $12.00
2337 Plate, 8" $16.00
2440 Plate, 10½", oval, cake $65.00
2440 Plate, 13", torte $95.00
2364 Plate, 16" $110.00
2440 Sauce, 6½", oval $42.00
2350½ Sugar and Cream $75.00
2419 Relish, 4-part $54.00
2528 Tray, cocktail $125.00
2440 Tray, 8½", oval $35.00
2470 Vase, 8" $137.00
5090 Vase, 8", bud $75.00
5092 Vase, 8", bud $75.00
2470 Vase, 10" $200.00
760 Vase, 12" $240.00

Daisy and Button, 2710 Milk Glass

1957 – 1965

Tableware II, 210

2710 Butter and Cover
white $52.00
2710 Nappy, 3-cornered
white $18.00
aqua $24.00
peach $24.00
2710 Nappy, square
white $18.00
aqua $24.00
peach $24.00
2710 Sugar and Cream, individual
white $65.00
aqua $100.00
peach $100.00
2710 Tray, sugar and cream
white $20.00
aqua $25.00
peach $25.00

Daphne, Cutting 797

1939 – 1943

Tableware

2424 Ashtray $24.00
2424 Bowl, 8", regular $60.00
2424 Bowl, 9½", flared $74.00
2424 Bowl, 11½", fruit $85.00
2424 Candlestick, 3½", pair $50.00
2424 Jar, candy and cover $68.00
2424 Box, cigarette and cover $68.00
2424 Mayonnaise, plate, ladle $75.00
2424 Plate, 12" $75.00
2424 Sweetmeat, 7" $40.00
2424 Vase, 6½", footed, urn, flared $95.00
2424 Vase, 7½", footed, urn, regular $95.00

Dawn, 2670 Tumbler

1953 – 1965

Stemware, 151

2670 Tumbler, 12½ oz., ice tea, flat
crystal $10.00
lime $18.00
tokay $18.00
honey $18.00
2670 Tumbler, 10½ oz., water, flat
crystal $8.00
lime $16.00
tokay $16.00
honey $16.00
2670 Tumbler, 5 oz., juice, flat
crystal $8.00
lime $15.00
tokay $15.00
honey $15.00
2670 Tumbler, 6 oz., dessert, flat
crystal $8.00
lime $15.00
tokay $15.00
honey $15.00

Debutante, 6100

1962 – 1982

Stemware, 124

6100 Goblet $24.00
6100 Sherbet $22.00
6100 Claret $30.00
6100 Tulip Wine $30.00
6100 Brandy $30.00
6100 Ice Tea, footed $24.00

Tableware

2337 Plate, 7", gray mist $10.00

Decanters (See Bar and Refreshment)

Decoration 22, Blue and Gold/ Rose and Gold

1924

Tableware I, 314

1904 Bonbon and Cover $225.00
2244 Candlestick, 8¼", pair $200.00
2245 Candlestick, 8¼", pair $195.00
2219 Jar, candy and cover, ¼ pound $68.00
2219 Jar, candy and cover, ½ pound $75.00
2250 Jar, candy and cover, ¼ pound $68.00
2250 Jar, candy and cover, ½ pound $75.00
1697 Carafe Set $125.00
2091 Box, cigarette and cover $95.00
2241 Cologne, 2¼ oz. $145.00
2242 Cologne, 3¼ oz. $135.00
2090 Cologne, 6 oz. and stopper $150.00

2118 Cologne, 6 oz. and stopper $170.00
2135 Hair Receiver and Cover $165.00
127 Mug, handled $48.00
2283 Plate, 8¼", salad $30.00
2283 Plate, 11", sandwich $35.00
1616 Puff and Cover $125.00
2135 Puff and Cover, 5" $150.00
2091 Soap and Cover $125.00
725 Vase, 5" $60.00
2208 Vase, 5" $68.00
725 Vase, 8" $75.00
2137 Vase, 4⅞", x 2¼", brush $125.00

Decoration 35, Encrusted Gold

1924

Tableware I, 318

2252 Dish, 6", salad $24.00
2258 Dish, 6", relish $26.00
2258 Dish, 8", relish $34.00
2258 Dish, 10", relish $45.00
2258 Plate, 11", sandwich $45.00

Decoration 46, Tinted Bands in Gold

1927

Tableware I, 321

2267 Bowl, 7", console $67.00
2297 Bowl C, 9¾", shallow $68.00
2324 Bowl, 10" $95.00
2297 Bowl A, 10¼", shallow $88.00
2297 Bowl C,10½", deep $95.00
2315 Bowl A, 10½" $85.00
2339 Bowl A, 10½", with ebony base $125.00
2297 Bowl A, 12", deep $115.00
2339 Bowl C, 19½", with ebony base $125.00
2324 Candlestick, 4", pair $90.00
2324 Candlestick, 6", pair $110.00
2324 Candlestick, 9", pair $125.00
2331 Box, candy and cover $95.00
2219 Jar, candy and cover, ½ pound $85.00
2250 Jar, candy and cover, ½ pound $75.00
2329 Centerpiece, 11" $100.00
2368 Cheese and Cracker $110.00
2327 Comport, 7" $65.00
2350 Comport, 8" $68.00
2380 Box, confection and cover $80.00
2315 Mayonnaise and 2332 Plate $48.00
2283 Plate 7" $12.00
2283 Plate 8" $14.00
2290 Plate, 13", deep, salad $45.00
2338 Puff and Cover $97.00
2287 Tray, lunch $75.00
2276 Vanity Set $300.00
2292 Vase, 8" $125.00

Decoration 53, Orange Band on Ebony

1925 – 1926

Tableware I, 323

2267 Bowl, 7", console $38.00
2297 Bowl A, 10¼", shallow $48.00
2297 Bowl A, 12", deep $57.00
2324 Candlestick, 4", pair $45.00
2299 Candlestick, 5", pair $50.00
2269 Candlestick, 6", pair $64.00
2297 Candlestick, 7", pair $68.00
2331 Box, candy and cover $75.00
2329 Centerpiece, 11" $75.00
2349 Holder, cigarette and ashtray $54.00
2327 Comport, 7" $45.00
2290 Plate, 7" $7.00
2290 Plate, 8" $10.00
2306 Smoker Set, 4-piece $54.00
2276 Vanity Set $135.00
1491 Vase, 6", small $47.00
1491 Vase, 8¼", large $58.00
1681 Vase, wall pocket $135.00
2288 Vase, Tut $85.00

Decoration 55, Tinted Bands on Crystal, etc.

1926

Tableware I, 323

2267 Bowl, 7" $68.00
2324 Bowl, 1 $125.00
2297 Bowl A, 10", shallow $95.00
2297 Bowl A, 12", deep $110.00
2324 Candlestick, 2", pair $85.00
2324 Candlestick, 4", pair $85.00
2324 Candlestick, 6", pair $95.00
2324 Candlestick, 9", pair $150.00
2331 Box, candy and cover $115.00
2219 Jar, candy and cover, ½ pound $100.00
2250 Jar, candy and cover, ½ pound $95.00
2329 Centerpiece, 11" $95.00
2329 Centerpiece, 13" $135.00
2327 Comport, 7" $60.00
2315 Mayonnaise/Grapefruit $40.00
2283 Plate, 7" $12.00
2283 Plate, 8" $15.00
2283 Plate, 9" $26.00
2283 Plate, 13", cupped $67.00
2347 Puff and Cover $145.00
2287 Tray, lunch $110.00
2276 Vanity Set $225.00

Decoration 512, Gold Bands on Crystal

1935 – 1938

Useful & Ornamental, 25

2518 Cocktail Shaker $95.00
2518 Decanter $95.00
2518 Whiskey $20.00
2518 Wine, 5 oz. $20.00

Decoration 518, White Enamel on Regal Blue

1940 – 1942

Tableware I, 329

4123 Vase, Pansy, Decoration 518A $45.00
4130 Vase, Violet, Decoration 518B $45.00
4137 Vase, 3¾", Decoration 518C $45.00
4138 Vase, 3½", Decoration 518D $45.00

Decoration 519, Colored Flowers on Crystal

1940 – 1943

Tableware I, 329

4123 Vase, Pansy, Decoration 519A $45.00
4130 Vase, Violet, Decoration 519B $45.00
4137 Vase, 3¾", Decoration 519C $45.00
4138 Vase, 3½", Decoration 519D $45.00
4144 Vase, 3", Decoration 519E $45.00
4145 Vase, 3", Decoration 519F $45.00

Decorator Collection

1964 – 1970

Teal or lavender

Tableware II, 250

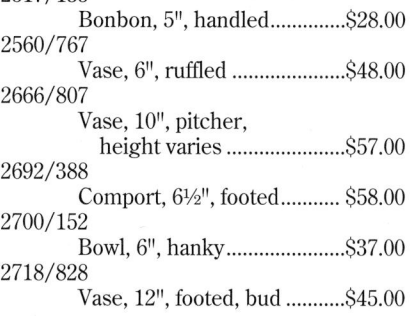

2424/179 Bowl, 6¾", footed, petal $65.00
2424/795 Basket, 10", footed $125.00
2497/787 Vase, height varies, Flying Fish $64.00
2517/135 Bonbon, 5", handled $28.00
2560/767 Vase, 6", ruffled $48.00
2666/807 Vase, 10", pitcher, height varies $57.00
2692/388 Comport, 6½", footed $58.00
2700/152 Bowl, 6", hanky $37.00
2718/828 Vase, 12", footed, bud $45.00

Decorator Pattern, 2691

1955 – 1957

Tableware II, 87, 88

2691 Ashtray $14.00
2691 Cigarette Holder, individual $20.00
2691 Cup and Saucer $16.00
2691 Cup and Saucer, demitasse $25.00
2691 Dessert, 4⅞" $12.00
2691 Plate, 7" $10.00
2691 Preserve, handled $16.00
2691 Bowl, sauce, with plate and

ladle $34.00
2691 Server, 2-part $20.00
2691 Server, 3-part $27.00
2691 Shaker, chrome top A, pair $20.00
2691 Soup $14.00
2691 Sugar and Cream $32.00
2691 Sugar and Cover $18.00
2691 Tray, sugar and cream $12.00

Delphian, Etching 272

1925 – 1927

Stemware, 64

5082 Goblet $54.00
5082 Sherbet, high $45.00
5082 Sherbet, low $35.00
5082 Parfait $55.00
5082 Cocktail $40.00
5082 Wine $55.00
5082 Cordial $75.00
4095 Tumbler .... $28.00 – 45.00

Tableware I, 149

4095 Bowl, finger $34.00
4095½ Jar, candy and cover $95.00
4095 Nappy, 4½", Decoration 51 only $37.00
4095 Nappy, 5" $34.00
4095 Nappy, 6" $36.00
4095 Nappy, 7" $42.00
4095 Nappy and Cover, 5" $42.00
4095 Nappy and Cover, 6" $55.00
4095 Nappy and Cover, 7" $87.00
4095/7 Jug $395.00
4095½ Vase, 8" $395.00
2283 Plate, 6" $14.00
2283 Plate, 7" $18.00
2283 Plate 8" $22.00

Delphine, Cutting 199

1931

Stemware, 69

5098 Goblet $24.00
5098 Sherbet, high $22.00
5098 Sherbet, low $18.00
5098 Parfait $24.00
5098 Cocktail $22.00
5098 Claret $28.00
5098 Wine $28.00
5098 Cordial $32.00
5098 Ice Tea, footed $24.00
5098 Tumbler, 9 oz., footed $16.00
5098 Juice, footed $18.00
5098 Whiskey, footed $22.00
2283 Plate, 8" $10.00

Designer Collection

(see Images, Impressions, Interpretations)

Devon, Cutting 876

1960 – 1962

Stemware, 119

6089 Goblet $32.00
6089 Sherbet $30.00
6089 Wine/Cocktail $36.00
6089 Brandy $40.00
6089 Ice Tea, footed $32.00
6089 Juice, footed $28.00
2337 Plate, 7" $8.00
2337 Plate, 8" $10.00

Diadem, 2430

1938 – 1942

Tableware I, 69-71

Bowl, 11"
- crystal $46.00
- rose $75.00
- azure $75.00
- green $75.00
- amber $64.00
- ebony $65.00
- topaz $75.00

Candlestick, 2", pair
- crystal $45.00
- ebony $58.00

Candlestick, 9½", pair
- crystal $125.00
- rose $195.00
- azure $195.00
- green $195.00
- amber $184.00
- ebony $184.00
- topaz $195.00

Jar, candy and cover, ½ pound
- crystal $45.00
- rose $85.00
- azure $85.00
- green $78.00
- amber $72.00
- ebony $80.00
- topaz $85.00
- wisteria $175.00

Jelly, 7"
- crystal $24.00
- rose $38.00
- azure $38.00
- green $38.00
- amber $28.00
- ebony $34.00
- topaz $38.00

Mint, 5½"
- crystal $18.00
- rose $32.00
- azure $32.00
- green $32.00
- amber $28.00
- ebony $28.00
- topaz $32.00

Vase, 3¾"
- crystal $34.00

Vase, 8"
- crystal $48.00
- rose $75.00
- azure $75.00
- green $70.00
- amber $60.00
- ebony $65.00

Diadem, 6056

1954 – 1965

Stemware, 109

6056 Goblet $28.00
6056 Sherbet $25.00
6056 Cocktail $26.00
6056 Claret-Wine $30.00
6056 Cordial $38.00
6056 Oyster Cocktail $20.00
6056 Ice Tea, footed $28.00
6056 Juice, footed $26.00

Diamond Sunburst, 2711 Milkglass

1957 – 1965

Tableware II, 211

2711 Candy and Cover, footed
- white $47.00
- aqua $58.00
- peach $58.00

2711 Planter
- white $35.00
- aqua $42.00
- peach $42.00

2711 Sugar and Cream
- white $65.00
- aqua $85.00
- peach $85.00

Directoire, Cutting 736

1935 – 1939

Stemware, 82

6011 Goblet $30.00
6011 Saucer Champagne $25.00
6011 Sherbet, low $22.00
6011 Cocktail $25.00
6011 Claret $30.00
6011 Rhine Wine $30.00
6011 Wine $30.00
6011 Sherry $28.00
6011 Crème de Menthe $24.00
6011 Brandy $32.00
6011 Cordial $34.00
6011 Oyster Cocktail $20.00
6011 Ice Tea, footed $28.00
6011 Tumbler, 10 oz., footed $24.00
6011 Juice, footed $24.00
6011 Whiskey, footed $30.00

Tableware I, 281

1769 Bowl, finger $14.00
4024 Bowl, 10", footed $30.00
4024 Candlestick, 6", pair $35.00
4117 Jar, candy and cover $67.00
2525 Cocktail Shaker $95.00
2525 Decanter $80.00
6011 Decanter $95.00
2337 Plate, 6" $6.00
2337 Plate, 7" $7.00
2337 Plate, 8" $8.00
2337 Plate, 11" $20.00
2235 Shaker, FGT, pair $45.00
2350½ Sugar and Cream $30.00

Display and Window

1924

Useful & Ornamental, 141

SHOE

1103½ Plate and Stand, 17" $175.00
1103½ Plate and Stand, 21" $200.00
1103½ Plate and Stand, 25" $250.00
1739½ Plate and Stand, 10" $95.00
1739½ Plate and Stand, 13" $150.00
1739½ Plate and Stand, 15" $185.00
1739½ Plate and Stand, 18" $225.00
1981 Shoe Rest $65.00
1981½ Shoe Rest $65.00
2205 Shoe Rest $65.00

JEWELRY

1738 Plate and Stand, 10½" $150.00
Plate and Stand, 13" $165.00
Plate and Stand, 16" $175.00

CANDLE COLUMN OR PEDESTAL

19 Candle, 7" $34.00

19 Candle, 10", $40.00
19 Candle, 12", $48.00
19 Candle, 15", $60.00
19 Candle, 18", $75.00
1103 Pedestal, 11", flat only $75.00
1103 Pedestal, 15", flat only $85.00
1103 Pedestal, 19", flat only $95.00

Distinction, 6125

1972 – 1982

Stemware, 141

6125 Goblet
- crystal/blue $27.00
- plum $32.00
- ruby $48.00
- cobalt $48.00

6125 Champagne
- crystal/blue $25.00
- plum $28.00
- ruby $44.00
- cobalt $44.00

6125 Wine
- crystal/blue $27.00
- plum $32.00
- ruby $52.00
- cobalt $52.00

6125 Ice Tea, footed
- crystal/blue $27.00
- plum $32.00
- ruby $48.00
- cobalt $48.00

2337 Plate, 7"
- crystal $10.00
- blue $12.00
- plum $12.00

Dog Show, Carving 49

1940 – 1943

Useful & Ornamental, 127

2427 Ashtray, oblong $22.00
4132 Decanter $125.00
4139 Tumbler, 1¾ oz. whiskey $25.00
4139 Tumbler, 5 oz. $25.00
4139 Tumbler, 7 oz., old fashioned cocktail $27.00
4139 Tumbler, 10 oz. $30.00
4139 Tumbler, 12 oz. $35.00
4139 Tumbler, 14 oz. $35.00

Dolly Madison, Cutting 786

1939 – 1973

Stemware, 93

6023 Goblet $25.00
6023 Saucer Champagne $23.00
6023 Sherbet, low $20.00
6023 Cocktail $22.00
6023 Claret-Wine $28.00
6023 Cordial $35.00
6023 Oyster Cocktail $18.00
6023 Ice Tea, footed $25.00
6023 Tumbler, 9 oz., footed $20.00
6023 Juice, footed $20.00
846 Sherry $22.00
833½ Tumbler $10.00 – 15.00
4132 Decanter $75.00
6011 Jug $175.00
2337 Plate, 6" $7.00
2337 Plate, 7" $8.00
2337 Plate, 8" $10.00

Dolphin, Carving 27

1940 – 1943

Useful & Ornamental, 129

2577 Vase, 8½" $165.00

Doncaster, Cutting 718

1933 – 1943

Stemware, 79

6009 Goblet $34.00
6009 Sherbet, high $32.00
6009 Sherbet, low $28.00
6009 Cocktail $32.00
6009 Claret-Wine $38.00
6009 Cordial $47.00
6009 Oyster Cocktail $24.00
6009 Ice Tea, footed $32.00
6009 Tumbler, 9 oz., footed $26.00
6009 Juice, footed $25.00

Tableware I, 278

869 Bowl, finger $12.00
2470½ Bowl, 10½" $45.00
2470½ Candlestick, 5½", pair $45.00
2400 Comport, 6" $27.00
2337 Plate, 6" $6.00
2337 Plate, 7" $7.00
2337 Plate, 8" $8.00
2440 Plate, 13", torte $40.00
4112 Vase, 8½" $85.00

Dresden, Decoration 12

1920s

Stemware, 25

858 Goblet, 9 oz. $45.00
858 Saucer Champagne, 5½ oz. $45.00
858 Fruit $45.00
858 Cocktail $45.00
858 Claret, 4½ oz. $45.00
127 Tumbler $45.00
701 Tumbler $35.00
820 Tumbler $35.00
4061 Lemonade, footed, handled, $45.00

Tableware I, 311

1904 Bonbon $125.00
2090 Bottle, 6 oz., toilet $95.00
2118 Bottle, 6 oz., toilet $95.00
858 Bowl, finger and plate $38.00
1490 Candlestick, 8", pair $200.00
2244 Candlestick, 8¼", pair $250.00
2245 Candlestick, 8¼", pair $195.00
2219 Jar, candy and cover, ¼ pound $75.00
2219 Jar, candy and cover, ½ pound $88.00
2219 Jar, candy and cover, pound $97.00
2250 Jar, candy and cover, ¼ pound $75.00
2250 Jar, candy and cover, ½ pound $88.00
2250 Jar, candy and cover, pound $97.00
1697 Carafe Set, 3 pieces $125.00
2241 Cologne, 2½ oz., drip stopper $135.00
2242 Cologne, 3¼ oz, drip stopper $140.00
2243 Cologne, 2¼ oz., drip stopper $135.00
803 Comport, 5", tall $47.00
1848 Dish, 7", salad, matt star base $38.00
724/7 Jug $395.00
1743-5 Jug and Cover $350.00
2138 Mayonnaise Set, 2 pieces $67.00
803 Nappy, 5", LD $42.00
1897 Plate, 7" $24.00
1848 Plate, 9", sandwich, matt star base $38.00
1719 Plate, 10½", sandwich, matt star base $40.00
2135 Puff and Cover $125.00
2235 Shaker, pair $95.00
2091 Soap and Cover $135.00
1957 Vase, 7", center $85.00
2137 Vase, brush $150.00
2208 Vase $88.00

Duchess, Decoration 51

1925 – 1927

Stemware, 65

5082 Goblet $57.00
5082 Sherbet, high $48.00
5082 Sherbet, low $37.00
5082 Parfait $58.00
5082 Cocktail $37.00
5082 Wine $58.00
5082 Cordial $85.00
4095 Tumbler $45.00 – 50.00

Tableware I , 149

4095 Nappy, 4½" $37.00
4095/7 Jug $495.00
2283 Plate, 6" $18.00
2283 Plate, 7" $22.00
2283 Plate 8" $28.00

Duchess, Cutting 853

1957 – 1958

Stemware, 113

6068 Goblet $22.00
6068 Sherbet $20.00
6068 Cocktail/Wine/Seafood $22.00
6068 Cordial $30.00
6068 Ice Tea, footed $22.00
6068 Juice, footed $20.00
2337 Plate, 7" $8.00
2337 Plate, 8" $10.00

Dusk, 2671 Tumbler

1953 – 1965

Stemware, 151

2671 Tumbler, 12½ oz., ice tea, flat
- crystal $10.00
- lime $18.00
- tokay $18.00
- honey $18.00

2671 Tumbler, 10½ oz., water, flat
- crystal $8.00
- lime $16.00
- tokay $16.00
- honey $16.00

2671 Tumbler, 5 oz., juice, flat
- crystal $8.00
- lime $15.00
- tokay $15.00

honey $15.00

2671 Tumbler, 6 oz., dessert, flat
crystal $8.00
lime $15.00
tokay $15.00
honey $15.00

- E -

Eaton, Cutting 713
1933 – 1938
Stemware, 77
6007 Goblet $35.00
6007 Sherbet, high $32.00
6007 Sherbet, low $28.00
6007 Cocktail $30.00
6007 Claret $38.00
6007 Wine $35.00
6007 Cordial $48.00
6007 Oyster Cocktail $28.00
6007 Ice Tea, footed $34.00
6007 Tumbler, 9 oz., footed $28.00
6007 Juice, footed $28.00
6007 Whiskey, footed $30.00
Tableware I, 277
2470 Bonbon $18.00
2470½ Bowl, 10½" $40.00
2481 Bowl, 11", oblong $40.00
2481 Candlestick, 5", pair $45.00
2470½ Candlestick, 5½", pair $45.00
2472 Candlestick, duo, pair $68.00
2451 Dish, ice with liner, plate $42.00
2470 Dish, lemon $18.00
Plate, 6" $6.00
Plate, 7" $7.00
Plate, 8" $8.00
2470 Plate, 13", torte $35.00
2419 Relish, 4-part $26.00
2440 Sugar and Cream $34.00
2470 Sweetmeat $20.00
2440 Vase, 7" $65.00

Eilene, Etching 83
1928 – 1932
Stemware, 64
5082 Goblet
crystal $34.00
green $34.00
rose $40.00
azure $40.00
5082 Sherbet, high
crystal $30.00
green $30.00
rose $40.00
azure $40.00
5082 Sherbet, low
crystal $22.00
green $22.00
rose $30.00
azure $30.00
5082 Parfait
crystal $30.00
green $30.00
rose $45.00
azure $45.00
5082 Cocktail
crystal $25.00
green $25.00
rose $32.00
azure $32.00
5082 Claret
crystal $35.00
green $35.00
rose $45.00
azure $45.00
5082 Wine
crystal $30.00
green $30.00
rose $40.00
azure $40.00
5082 Cordial
crystal $35.00
green $35.00
rose $65.00
azure $65.00
5082 Grapefruit
crystal $40.00
green $40.00
rose $60.00
azure $60.00
837 Oyster Cocktail $15.00
4095 Oyster Cocktail $15.00
4095 Tumbler ....$15.00 – 35.00
Tableware I, 122
869 Bowl, finger, colors $22.00
5098 Comport, 5", colors $38.00
4095 Jug, footed, solid color $395.00
5098 Nappy, 6", colors $45.00
2283 Plate, 6", colors $14.00
2283 Plate, 7", colors $16.00
2283 Plate, 8", colors $20.00

Elegance, 6064½
1956 – 1970
Stemware, 111
Narrow Optic
6064½ Goblet $30.00
6064½ Champagne $27.00
6064½ Sherbet, low $25.00
6064½ Cocktail $27.00
6064½ Claret $34.00
6064½ Wine $32.00
6064½ Cordial $35.00
6064½ Seafood Cocktail $24.00
6064½ Ice Tea, footed $30.00
6064½ Juice, footed $25.00

Elephant, Carving 36
1940 – 1943
Useful & Ornamental, 130
4148 Ashtray, 2½", individual $22.00
4148 Cigarette Holder $35.00

Eloquence, 6120
1970 – 1974
Stemware, 138
6120 Goblet
crystal $35.00
onyx $35.00
6120 Sherbet
crystal $35.00
onyx $35.00
6120 Claret
crystal $35.00
onyx $35.00
6120 Liqueur
crystal $60.00
onyx $60.00
6120 Ice Tea, footed
crystal $35.00
onyx $35.00

Eloquence Gold, Decoration 686
1970 – 1974
Stemware, 138
6120 Goblet $35.00
6120 Sherbet $35.00
6120 Claret $35.00
6120 Liqueur $60.00
6120 Ice Tea, footed $35.00

Eloquence Platinum, Decoration 687
1970 – 1974
See Eloquence Gold illustration
Stemware, 138
6120 Goblet $35.00
6120 Sherbet $35.00
6120 Claret $35.00
6120 Liqueur $60.00
6120 Ice Tea, footed $35.00

Elsinore, Etching 89
1934 – 1943
Stemware, 60
4024 Goblet, 10 oz. $25.00
4024 Saucer Champagne $25.00
4024 Sherbet $22.00
4024 Cordial $38.00
4024 Oyster Cocktail $18.00
4024 Ice Tea, footed $25.00
4024 Tumbler, 8 oz., footed $20.00
4024 Juice, footed $20.00
701 Tumbler, 10 oz. $15.00
887 Whiskey Sham, 1¾ oz. $10.00
1184 Old Fashioned Cocktail, 7 oz. $10.00
4122 Whiskey Sham, 1½ oz. $12.00

Embassy, 6083
1959 – 1971
Stemware, 117
6083 Goblet $24.00
6083 Sherbet $22.00
6083 Wine/Cocktail $26.00
6083 Cordial $28.00
6083 Ice Tea, footed $24.00
6083 Juice, footed $20.00
2337 Plate, 7" $8.00
2337 Plate, 8" $10.00

Embassy, Cutting 728
1933 – 1937
Stemware, 60
4024 Goblet, 11 oz. $28.00
4024 Goblet, 10 oz. $28.00
4024 Saucer Champagne $28.00
4024 Sherbet $24.00
4024 Cocktail $24.00
4024 Claret-Wine $30.00
4024 Rhine Wine $30.00
4024 Sherry $30.00
4024 Cordial $35.00
4024 Oyster Cocktail $20.00
4024 Ice Tea, footed $28.00
4024 Tumbler, 8 oz., footed $20.00

4024 Juice, footed $20.00
4024 Whiskey, footed $35.00
701 Tumbler, 10 oz. $15.00
887 Whiskey Sham, 1¾ oz. $10.00
1184 Old Fashioned Cocktail, 7 oz. $10.00

Tableware I, 280

869 Bowl, finger $12.00
4024 Bowl, 10", footed $30.00
4024 Candlestick, 6", pair $40.00
4024 Comport, 5" $20.00
6011 Decanter $135.00
6011 Jug $175.00
2337 Plate, 6" $6.00
2337 Plate, 7" $7.00
2337 Plate, 8" $8.00
2337 Plate, 11" $10.00

Embrace, Cutting 887

1961 – 1965

Stemware, 123

6099 Goblet $28.00
6099 Sherbet $26.00
6099 Wine/Cocktail $30.00
6099 Cordial $36.00
6099 Ice Tea, footed $28.00
6099 Juice, footed $26.00
2337 Plate, 7" $8.00
2337 Plate, 8" $10.00

Empire, Etching 238

1915 – 1927

Stemware, 23

858 Goblet, 10 oz. $6.00
858 Goblet, 9 oz. $6.00
858 Saucer Champagne, 5½ oz. $6.00
858 Sherbet $6.00
858 Fruit $6.00
858 Cocktail $6.00
858 Claret, 6½ oz. $6.00
858 Claret, 4½ oz. $6.00
858 Wine, 3½ oz. $6.00
858 Wine 2¾ oz. $6.00
858 Sherry $6.00
858 Crème de Menthe $6.00
858 Brandy $12.00
858 Cordial $12.00
858 Oyster Cocktail $7.00
858 Champagne, hollow stem $10.00
858 Champagne, tall $15.00
822 Parfait $20.00
4061 Lemonade, footed, handled $20.00
833 Tumbler, 8 oz. $5.00
701 Tumbler, 14 oz. $10.00
858 Tumbler $5.00 – 10.00
945½ Grapefruit and Liner $28.00

Tableware

863 Almond $18.00
803 Comport, 5" $20.00
803 Comport, 6" $22.00
303 Jug $95.00
318 Jug $98.00
803 Nappy, 5", footed $22.00
803 Nappy, 6", footed $27.00
803 Nappy, 7", footed $28.00
1227 Nappy, 4½" $20.00
1227 Nappy, 8", footed $30.00
1968 Marmalade and Cover $30.00
1831 Mustard and Cover $27.00
1848 Plate, 9", sandwich $10.00
300½ Oil, small $44.00
1465 Oil, 7 oz., cut neck $47.00
1480 Sugar and Cream $35.00
300 Tankard $95.00
724 Tankard $95.00

Empire, Cutting 908

1966 – 1969

Stemware, 131

6106 Goblet $25.00
6106 Sherbet $25.00
6106 Claret $25.00
6106 Tulip Wine $25.00
6106 Liqueur $30.00
6106 Ice Tea, footed $25.00
2574 Plate, 7", Raleigh, $8.00
2574 Plate, 8", Raleigh, $10.00

Empress, Cutting 861

1958 – 1970

Stemware, 116

6079 Goblet $34.00
6079 Sherbet $32.00
6079 Cocktail $32.00
6079 Claret-Wine $36.00
6079 Cordial $42.00
6079 Ice Tea, footed $34.00
6079 Juice, footed $28.00
2337 Plate, 7" $8.00
2337 Plate, 8" $10.00

Empress, Decoration 29

1924 – 1929

Stemware, 19

661 Goblet $15.00
661 Saucer Champagne $12.00
661 Fruit/Sherbet, low $12.00
661 Parfait $15.00
661 Cocktail $12.00
661 Claret $15.00
661 Wine $12.00
661 Cordial $15.00

Tableware I, 316

863 Almond $32.00
1769 Bowl, finger, and plate $20.00
2245 Candlestick, 8¼" $135.00
1697 Carafe Set $125.00
5051 Cheese, large $45.00
1848 Plate, 9", cracker, matt star base $30.00
803 Comport, 5", footed $45.00
825 Jelly and Cover $40.00
1968 Marmalade and Cover $38.00
2138 Mayonnaise, plate, ladle $47.00
803 Nappy, 5", deep, footed $30.00
803 Nappy, 6", deep, footed $34.00
701 Plate, 5", tumbler $8.00
840 Plate, 5", sherbet $8.00
1867 Plate, 7" $10.00
2238 Plate, 8¼" $12.00
2238 Plate, 11" $14.00
2083 Bottle, salad dressing $120.00
1759 Sugar and Cream $75.00
1852/6 Tankard $250.00
4095 Table Tumbler $16.00
4095 Tumbler, 13 oz. $24.00
4095 Tumbler, 13 oz., handled $28.00
945½ Grapefruit and Liner $32.00

Enamel and Gold, Decoration 21

1920s

Stemware, 26

858 Goblet, 9 oz. $50.00
858 Saucer Champagne, 5½ oz. $50.00
858 Fruit $50.00
701 Tumbler, 14 oz., punty and 5", plate $35.00
820 Tumbler, table, punty $35.00
4023 Tumbler, 6 oz., punty $35.00

Tableware I, 313, 314

2136 Bonbon and Cover $195.00
858 Bowl, finger, and plate $45.00
2244 Candlestick, 8¼", pair $300.00
2245 Candlestick, 8¼", pair $200.00
2250 Jar, candy and cover ¼ pound $85.00
2250 Jar, candy and cover ½ pound $94.00
2250 Jar, candy and cover pound $95.00
2228 Jar, candy and cover pound square $125.00
1697 Carafe Set, 2 pieces $150.00
2136 Cold Cream and Cover, 3" $135.00
803 Comport, 5", footed $50.00
803 Comport and Cover, 5", footed $78.00
880 Comport, 5", footed $50.00
880 Comport and Cover, 5", footed $65.00
1848 Dish, 7", salad $38.00
2252 Dish, 6", salad $24.00
825 Jelly $35.00
825 Jelly and Cover $45.00
1968 Marmalade and Cover $58.00
2138 Mayonnaise, plate, ladle $75.00
803 Nappy, 5", footed $40.00
803 Nappy and Cover, 5", footed $50.00
1848 Plate, 9", sandwich $40.00
2258 Plate, 11", sandwich $47.00
2136 Pomade and Cover $125.00
2135 Puff and Cover $125.00
2258 Relish, 6" $32.00
2258 Relish, 8" $45.00
2258 Relish, 10" $57.00
1957 Vase, 7", center $95.00

Enchantment, 6074

1958 – 1965

Stemware, 115

6074 Goblet $28.00
6074 Sherbet $25.00
6074 Cocktail/Wine $28.00
6074 Cordial $35.00
6074 Ice Tea, footed $28.00
6074 Juice, footed $22.00

Encore, Cutting 860

1958 – 1959

Stemware, 115

6077 Goblet $34.00
6077 Sherbet $32.00
6077 Cocktail/Wine $34.00
6077 Cordial $38.00
6077 Ice Tea, footed $34.00

Encore, Cutting 860

6077 Juice, footed $30.00
2337 Plate, 7" $10.00
2337 Plate, 8" $12.00

Engagement, Decoration 648

1960 – 1982

Stemware, 120

6092 Goblet $34.00
6092 Sherbet $32.00
6092 Wine/Cocktail $40.00
6092 Cordial $42.00
6092 Ice Tea, footed $34.00
6092 Juice, footed $32.00
2337 Plate, 7" $10.00
2337 Plate, 8" $12.00

Envoy, 6027

1940 – 1957

Stemware, 98

6027 Goblet $24.00
6027 Saucer Champagne..$22.00
6027 Sherbet, low......$18.00
6027 Cocktail.....$22.00
6027 Wine.....$27.00
6027 Cordial $32.00
6027 Oyster Cocktail $15.00
6027 Ice Tea, footed $24.00
6027 Juice, footed $18.00

Esquire, 4139 Tumblers

1938 – 1943

Value Guide, Tumbler section

4139 Tumbler, 16 oz., sham $10.00
4139 Tumbler, 14 oz., sham $8.00
4139 Tumbler, 12 oz., sham $8.00
4139 Tumbler, 10 oz., sham $9.00
4139 Water Tumbler, 9 oz., sham $7.00
4139 Old Fashioned Cocktail, 7 oz., sham $6.00
4139 Whiskey, sham, 1¾ oz. $6.00

Etching 32

Pre-1900 – 1920

Stemware, 17

114 Goblet, 10 oz. $4.00
114 Champagne $4.00
114 Claret $4.00
114 Wine $4.00
114 Cordial $5.00

Etching 46

1900 – 1920

Stemware, 17

114 Goblet, 10 oz. $4.00
114 Champagne $4.00
114 Claret $4.00
114 Wine $4.00

Etching 210

1910 – 1927

Stemware, 27

863 Goblet, 10½ oz. $10.00
863 Goblet, 9 oz. $10.00
863 Goblet, 7 oz. $10.00
863 Saucer Champagne $10.00
863 Fruit $8.00
863 Cocktail, 3½ oz. $8.00
863 Claret $10.00
863 Rhine Wine $10.00
863 Wine $10.00
863 Sherry $8.00
863 Crème de Menthe $8.00
863 Brandy, pousse-café $10.00
863 Cordial $20.00
863 Champagne, hollow stem, CF $10.00
863 Champagne, tall $10.00
822 Café Parfait $10.00
5039 Oyster Cocktail and Liner $35.00
945½ Grapefruit $25.00
858 Tumbler .....$5.00 – 8.00
300 Tankard $75.00
724 Tankard $85.00
303 Jug $50.00
317 Jug $75.00
1227 Jug $75.00

Etching 212

1910 – 1928

Stemware, 27

863 Goblet, 10½ oz. $10.00
863 Goblet, 9 oz.........$10.00
863 Goblet, 7 oz.........$10.00
863 Saucer Champagne $10.00
863 Fruit $8.00
863 Cocktail, 3½ oz. $8.00
863 Claret $10.00
863 Rhine Wine $10.00
863 Wine $10.00
863 Sherry $8.00
863 Crème de Menthe $8.00
863 Brandy, pousse-café $10.00
863 Cordial $20.00
863 Champagne, hollow stem, CF $10.00
863 Champagne, tall $10.00
5054 Parfait $22.00
945½ Grapefruit and Liner $28.00
701 Tumbler .....$5.00 – 8.00
820 Tumbler .....$5.00 – 8.00
833 Tumbler .....$5.00 – 8.00
858 Tumbler .....$5.00 – 8.00
887 Tumbler .....$5.00 – 8.00
889 Tumbler .....$5.00 – 8.00
300 Tankard $75.00
724 Tankard $85.00
303 Jug $50.00
318 Jug $75.00
1236 Jug $75.00

Etching 214

1910 – 1927

Stemware, 27

863 Goblet, 10½ oz.....$8.00
863 Goblet, 9 oz.........$8.00
863 Goblet, 7 oz...........$8.00
863 Saucer Champagne $8.00
863 Fruit $6.00
863 Cocktail, 3½ oz. $6.00
863 Claret $8.00
863 Rhine Wine $8.00
863 Wine $8.00
863 Sherry $6.00
863 Crème de Menthe $6.00
863 Brandy, pousse-café $8.00
863 Cordial $8.00
863 Champagne, CF, hollow stem $8.00
863 Champagne, tall $8.00
945½ Grapefruit and Liner $28.00
833 Tumbler .....$5.00 – 8.00
858 Tumbler .....$5.00 – 8.00
300 Tankard $75.00
300½ Tankard $85.00
724 Tankard $95.00
1236 Jug $75.00

Etching 215

1910 – 1927

Stemware, 23

858 Goblet, 11 oz. $6.00
858 Goblet, 10 oz. $6.00
858 Goblet, 9 oz. $6.00
858 Saucer Champagne, 7 oz. $6.00
858 Sherbet $6.00
858 Fruit $6.00
858 Cocktail $6.00
858 Claret, 6½ oz. $6.00
858 Claret, 4½ oz. $6.00
858 Wine, 3½ oz. $6.00
858 Wine, 2¾ oz. $6.00
858 Sherry $6.00
858 Crème de Menthe $6.00
858 Brandy $8.00
858 Cordial $15.00
858 Champagne, hollow stem $10.00
858 Champagne, tall $10.00
858 Champagne, long stem $18.00
858 Hot Whiskey $8.00
701 Tumbler .....$5.00 – 8.00
820 Tumbler .....$5.00 – 8.00
833 Tumbler .....$5.00 – 8.00
858 Tumbler .....$5.00 – 8.00
5036 Parfait $22.00
5054 Parfait $22.00
300 Tankard $75.00
724 Tankard $95.00
303 Jug $50.00

Evangeline, Cutting 752

1935 – 1938

Tableware I, 290

2470½ Bowl, 10½" $45.00
2472 Candlestick, duo, pair $75.00
2482 Candlestick, trindle, pair $125.00
2440 Celery $27.00
2440 Mayonnaise, 2-part $28.00
2440 Pickle $22.00
2440 Plate, cake $45.00
2440 Plate, 13", torte $50.00
2364 Plate, 16" $55.00
2440 Relish, 2-part $24.00
2440 Relish, 3-part $28.00
2419 Relish, 4-part $35.00
2419 Relish, 5-part $60.00
2514 Relish, 5-part $67.00
2440 Sauce, 6½", oval $28.00
2440 Tray, 8½", oval $24.00
2467 Vase, 7½" $72.00
2470 Vase, 10" $95.00

Evening Breeze, Cutting 891

1962 – 1965

Stemware, 124

6100 Goblet.........$28.00
6100 Sherbet.........$26.00
6100 Claret.............$32.00
6100 Tulip Wine.............$32.00
6100 Brandy.............$32.00
6100 Ice Tea, footed.............$28.00
2337 Plate, 7".............$8.00
2337 Plate, 8".............$10.00

Evening Star, Cutting 869

1959 – 1965

Stemware, 118

6087 Goblet.............$26.00
6087 Sherbet.............$24.00
6087 Wine/Cocktail...$30.00
6087 Cordial.............$37.00
6087 Ice Tea, footed.............$26.00
6087 Juice, footed.............$24.00
2337 Plate, 7".............$8.00
2337 Plate, 8".............$10.00

Exeter, 6109

1967 – 1971

Stemware, 133

6109 Goblet
crystal.............$42.00
amethyst.............$56.00
6109 Sherbet
crystal.............$40.00
amethyst.............$52.00
6109 Wine
crystal.............$48.00
amethyst.............$65.00
6109 Sherry/Liqueur
crystal.............$48.00
amethyst.............$65.00
6109 Ice Tea, footed
crystal.............$42.00
amethyst.............$56.00
2337 Plate, 7"
crystal.............$8.00
amethyst.............$35.00
2337 Plate, 8".............$10.00

- F -

Facets, 2752

1962 – 1967

Tableware II, 97, 99

2752/120
Ashtray, 8"
crystal.............$22.00
pink.............$27.00
2752/124
Ashtray, 11", oblong
crystal.............$22.00
pink.............$34.00
2752/189
Bowl, 9", oval
crystal.............$25.00
pink.............$38.00
gold.............$38.00
2752/211
Bowl, 10"
crystal.............$30.00
pink.............$40.00
2752/347
Bowl, footed and cover
crystal.............$45.00
pink.............$60.00
2752/350
Bonbon and Cover
crystal.............$38.00
pink.............$45.00
gold.............$42.00
2752/314
Candlestick, 3½", pair
crystal.............$48.00
pink.............$75.00
gold.............$75.00
2752/354
Box, candy and cover
crystal.............$58.00
pink.............$75.00
2752/374
Box, cigarette, oblong and cover
crystal.............$46.00
pink.............$64.00
2752/653
Shaker, chrome top A, pair
crystal.............$48.00
pink.............$67.00

Fairlane, 2916

1976 – 1982

Stemware, 54

2916 Goblet.............$12.00
2916 Champagne.............$12.00
2916 Wine.............$12.00
2916 Ice Tea, footed.............$12.00
2916 Cordial.............$15.00
2916 Old Fashioned, double.............$10.00
2916 Highball.............$10.00

Fairmont, 2718

1958 – 1965

Stemware, 49

2718 Goblet
crystal.............$8.00
amber/blue.............$15.00
green.............$15.00
2718 Sherbet
crystal.............$7.00
amber/blue/green.............$12.00
2718 Ice Tea, footed
crystal.............$8.00
amber/blue/green.............$15.00
2718 Juice, footed
crystal.............$7.00
amber/blue/green.............$12.00

Tableware II, 91

360 Celery, 9¼"
crystal.............$14.00
amber/blue/green.............$18.00
421 Dessert, 5"
crystal.............$12.00
amber/blue/green.............$14.00
447 Jelly and Cover, 6"
crystal.............$25.00
amber/blue/green.............$35.00
540 Pickle, 7¾"
crystal.............$12.00
amber/blue/green.............$14.00
550 Plate, 8"
crystal.............$8.00
amber/blue/green.............$10.00
630 Relish, 2-part
crystal.............$15.00
amber/blue/green.............$20.00
635 Dish, sauce and cover
crystal.............$18.00
amber/blue/green.............$24.00
679 Sugar and Cream
crystal.............$30.00
amber/blue/green.............$38.00

Fairfax, 2375

1927 – 1945

Tableware I, 46 – 56

2375 Ashtray
crystal...$16.00
rose.........$22.00
azure.............$22.00
green.............$20.00
amber.............$18.00
orchid.............$26.00
2375 Bonbon, 2 handles
crystal.............$22.00
rose.............$27.00
azure.............$27.00
green.............$26.00
amber.............$23.00
orchid.............$30.00
topaz/gold tint.............$26.00
ebony.............$24.00
mother-of-pearl.............$22.00
2375 Bottle, salad dressing
crystal.............$95.00
rose.............$175.00
azure.............$175.00
green.............$165.00
amber.............$150.00
topaz/gold tint.............$150.00
2375 Bouillon, footed
crystal.............$12.00
rose.............$18.00
azure.............$18.00
green.............$15.00
amber.............$15.00
orchid.............$18.00
topaz/gold tint.............$15.00
Bowl, 5", fruit
crystal.............$20.00
rose.............$35.00
azure.............$42.00
green.............$32.00
amber.............$28.00
orchid.............$42.00
topaz.............$32.00
mother-of-pearl.............$16.00
Bowl, 6", cereal
crystal.............$22.00
rose.............$42.00
azure.............$47.00
green.............$42.00
amber.............$37.00
orchid.............$42.00
topaz/gold tint.............$40.00
mother-of-pearl.............$20.00
Bowl, 7", soup
crystal.............$28.00
rose.............$45.00
azure.............$50.00
green.............$45.00
amber.............$40.00
orchid.............$45.00
topaz/gold tint.............$45.00
Bowl, 9", oval, baker
crystal.............$40.00
rose.............$64.00
azure.............$70.00
green.............$62.00

amber $60.00
orchid $75.00
topaz/gold tint $60.00
Bowl, 10½", oval, baker
crystal $47.00
rose $70.00
azure $75.00
green $70.00
amber $60.00
orchid $74.00
topaz $70.00
Bowl, 12"
crystal $45.00
rose $57.00
azure $65.00
green $60.00
amber $54.00
orchid $60.00
topaz/gold tint $57.00
mother-of-pearl $35.00
Bowl, dessert, large
crystal $40.00
rose $60.00
azure $65.00
green $60.00
amber $47.00
topaz $60.00
Butter and Cover
crystal $85.00
rose $135.00
azure $165.00
green $135.00
amber $115.00
orchid $165.00
topaz/gold tint $125.00
Cake, 10", handled
crystal $40.00
rose $65.00
azure, $74.00
green $65.00
amber $55.00
topaz/gold tint $65.00
ebony $60.00
Canape Set: canape plate, 4101
2 oz. footed tumbler
crystal $38.00
rose $58.00
azure $65.00
green $58.00
amber $54.00
topaz $58.00
ebony $54.00
Candlestick, 3", pair
crystal $30.00
rose $56.00
azure $60.00
green $56.00
amber $45.00
orchid $60.00
topaz/gold tint $56.00..
mother-of-pearl $25.00
Candlestick, 2375½, pair
crystal $40.00
rose $64.00
azure $68.00
green $64.00
amber $58.00
orchid $64.00
topaz $67.00
mother-of-pearl $40.00
Celery, 11½"
crystal $32.00
rose $42.00
azure $48.00
green $42.00
amber $38.00
orchid $45.00
topaz/gold tint $42.00
mother-of-pearl $20.00
Centerpiece, 12", round
crystal $45.00
rose $60.00
azure $67.00
green $60.00
amber $48.00
orchid $75.00
topaz $60.00
mother-of-pearl $45.00
Centerpiece, 15", round
rose $80.00
azure $95.00
green $80.00
amber $65.00
orchid $85.00
2375½ Centerpiece, 13", oval and
flower holder
crystal $125.00
rose, $165.00
azure $200.00
green $165.00
amber $150.00
orchid $225.00
2371 Flower Holder, top piece in color;
plain glass bottom
crystal $35.00
rose $57.00
azure $65.00
green $57.00
amber $50.00
orchid $65.00
2375 Cheese and Cracker
crystal $58.00
rose $84.00
azure $88.00
green $85.00
amber $77.00
topaz/gold tint $84.00
2375 Comport, 7"
rose $60.00
azure $74.00
green $60.00
amber $48.00
orchid $74.00
2375 Cream Soup and Plate
crystal $38.00
rose $62.00
azure $62.00
green $62.00
amber $48.00
orchid $62.00
topaz/gold tint $55.00
mother-of-pearl $34.00
2375 Cup and Saucer
crystal $16.00
rose $22.00
azure $23.00
green $22.00
amber $18.00
orchid $23.00
2375½ Cup, footed and saucer
crystal $16.00
rose $22.00
azure $23.00
green $22.00
amber $18.00
orchid $23.00
topaz/gold tint $22.00
mother-of-pearl $12.00
2375 Cup and Saucer, after dinner
crystal $34.00
rose $56.00
azure $60.00
green $54.00
amber $42.00
orchid $60.00
topaz/gold tint $50.00
2375 Ice Bucket, NP handle
crystal $50.00
rose $95.00
azure $100.00
green $92.00
amber $85.00
topaz/gold tint $95.00
2375 Dish, lemon, 2 handles
crystal $24.00
rose $32.00
azure $35.00
green $32.00
amber $26.00
orchid $35.00
topaz/gold tint $32.00
ebony $26.00
2375 Plate, mayonnaise
crystal $52.00
rose $74.00
azure $65.00
green $68.00
amber $52.00
orchid $75.00
topaz/gold tint $64.00
mother-of-pearl $38.00
2375 Ladle, mayonnaise
crystal $22.00
amber $37.00
green $45.00
rose $48.00
azure $60.00
topaz/gold tint $56.00
orchid $75.00
2375 Nappy , 7", round
crystal $36.00
rose $42.00
azure $50.00
green $42.00
amber $36.00
topaz/gold tint $40.00
2375 Nappy, 8", round
crystal $38.00
rose $45.00
azure $52.00
green $40.00
amber $34.00
orchid $57.00
topaz $45.00
2375 Oil, footed
crystal $125.00
rose $175.00
azure $200.00
green $175.00
amber $150.00
topaz/gold tint $175.00
2375 Pickle, 8½"
crystal $27.00
rose $32.00
azure $38.00
green $32.00
amber $28.00
orchid $38.00
topaz/gold tint $30.00
2375 Plate, 6"
crystal $8.00
rose $14.00

azure $16.00
green $14.00
amber $12.00
orchid $16.00
topaz/gold tint $14.00
mother-of-pearl $8.00

2375 Plate, 7"
crystal $10.00
rose $16.00
azure $20.00
green $16.00
amber $14.00
orchid $22.00
topaz/gold tint $16.00
mother-of-pearl $10.00

2375 Plate, 8"
crystal $12.00
rose $20.00
azure $25.00
green $18.00
amber $16.00
orchid $25.00
topaz/gold tint $18.00

2375 Plate, 9"
crystal $20.00
rose $34.00
azure $45.00
green $35.00
amber $30.00
orchid $45.00
topaz/gold tint $35.00
mother-of-pearl $18.00

2375 Plate, 10"
crystal $35.00
rose $54.00
azure $58.00
green $50.00
amber $40.00
orchid $55.00
topaz/gold tint $50.00
mother-of-pearl $30.00

2375 Plate, canape
crystal $18.00
rose $30.00
azure $34.00
green $30.00
amber $22.00
topaz $30.00
ebony $22.00

2375 Plate, 10", grill
crystal $35.00
rose $55.00
azure $60.00
green $55.00
amber $40.00
topaz/gold tint $55.00

2375 Plate, 12", oval, bread
crystal $47.00
green $65.00
amber $45.00
orchid $65.00

2375 Plate, 13", chop
crystal $47.00
rose $65.00
azure $68.00
green $60.00
amber $50.00
orchid $65.00
topaz/gold tint $60.00
mother-of-pearl $47.00

2375 Platter, 10½", oval
crystal $47.00
rose $65.00
azure $75.00
green $65.00
amber $50.00
orchid $85.00
topaz/gold tint $65.00

2375 Platter, 12", oval
crystal $47.00
rose $65.00
azure $75.00
green $65.00
amber $45.00
orchid $65.00
topaz/gold tint $65.00
mother-of-pearl $47.00

2375 Platter, 15", oval
crystal, ...$65.00
rose $77.00
azure $95.00
green $75.00
amber $65.00
orchid $110.00
topaz $95.00

2375 Relish, 8½"
crystal $34.00
rose $42.00
azure $46.00
green $42.00
amber $40.00
orchid $48.00
topaz/gold tint $42.00
mother-of-pearl $32.00

2375 Relish, 11½"
crystal $38.00
rose $48.00
azure $54.00
green $47.00
amber $42.00
orchid $54.00
topaz/gold tint $48.00

2375 Sauce Boat and Plate
crystal $95.00
rose $125.00
azure $125.00
green $110.00
amber $95.00
orchid $135.00
topaz/gold tint $125.00

2375 Shaker, footed, FGT, pair
crystal $85.00
rose $125.00
azure $135.00
green $125.00
amber $95.00
orchid $165.00
topaz/gold tint $125.00
ebony $110.00

2375 Sugar and Cream
crystal $47.00
green $68.00
amber $58.00
orchid $95.00

2375 Sugar and Cream, footed
crystal $48.00
rose $68.00
azure $75.00
green $68.00
amber $60.00
orchid $125.00
topaz/gold tint $68.00
mother-of-pearl $48.00

2375 Sugar Cover
crystal $35.00
rose $48.00
azure $48.00
green $42.00
amber $40.00
orchid $65.00
topaz/gold tint $45.00

2375 Sugar and Cream Set (includes 2429 service tray with insert)
crystal $175.00
rose $250.00
azure $250.00
green $250.00
amber $200.00
topaz $250.00

2375 Sugar and Cream, Tea
crystal $58.00
rose $75.00
azure $75.00
green $68.00
amber $64.00
topaz/gold tint $68.00
ebony $64.00
ruby $96.00

2375 Sweetmeat, 2 handles
crystal $24.00
rose $32.00
azure $35.00
green $32.00
amber $27.00
orchid $38.00
topaz/gold tint $32.00
mother-of-pearl $24.00

2375 Tray, handled, lunch
crystal $45.00
rose $95.00
azure $95.00
green $95.00
amber $75.00
orchid $125.00
topaz/gold tint $95.00
mother-of-pearl $45.00

2375 Whipped Cream
crystal $26.00
rose $34.00
azure $38.00
green $38.00
amber $32.00
orchid $45.00
topaz/gold tint $34.00
mother-of-pearl $26.00

Fairfax, Cutting 167

1922 – 1928

Stemware, 30

863 Goblet, 9 oz...$8.00
863 Saucer Champagne.....$8.00
863 Fruit $6.00
863 Cocktail, 3½ oz. $6.00
863 Wine $8.00
863 Café Parfait $8.00
837 Oyster Cocktail $6.00
820 Tumbler, table $5.00
701 Tumbler, 14 oz. $8.00
701 Tumbler, 12 oz. and 5", tumbler plate $8.00
4011½ Tumbler, table $4.00
4011 Tumbler, 12 oz., table $8.00
4011 Tumbler, 12 oz., handled $8.00

Tableware I, 264

880 Bonbon $18.00
1769 Bowl, finger and 1736 Plate ...$18.00
2219 Jar, candy and cover, ¼ pound $22.00

2219 Jar, candy and cover, ½ pound $26.00
2219 Jar, candy and cover, pound ..$30.00
1697 Carafe $24.00
4023 Carafe Tumbler, 6 oz....$6.00
803 Comport, 5" $16.00
803 Comport, 6" $17.00
803 Comport and Cover, 5" $23.00
803 Comport and Cover, 6" $24.00
825 Jelly $18.00
825 Jelly and Cover $25.00
303 Jug (1712½º....$95.00
2040/3 Jug....$65.00
2082/7 Jug....$95.00
2230/7 Jug and Cover $125.00
1968 Marmalade and Cover $28.00
2138 Mayonnaise, plate, and ladle ..$45.00
803 Nappy, 5" $12.00
803 Nappy, 6" $14.00
803 Nappy, 7" $15.00
803 Nappy and Cover, 5" $20.00
300½ Oil, small $27.00
840 Plate, 5", sherbet $5.00
2238 Plate, 8¼", salad $6.00
880 Salt Dip, footed $14.00
2263 Salt, individual $14.00
2236 Shaker, FGT....$15.00
1712 Sugar and Cover $16.00
1712½ Cream $14.00
2194 Syrup, 8 oz., nickel top....$37.00
2194 Syrup, 12 oz., nickel top....$42.00
4069 Vase, 9" $35.00

Fantasy, Cutting 747

1935 – 1936

Stemware, 85

6013 Goblet $32.00
6013 Goblet, low $30.00
6013 Saucer Champagne $30.00
6013 Sherbet, low $26.00
6013 Cocktail $30.00
6013 Claret $45.00
6013 Wine....$40.00
6013 Cordial $56.00
6013 Oyster Cocktail....$24.00
6013 Ice Tea, footed $30.00
6013 Juice, footed $24.00

Tableware I, 287

766 Bowl, finger....$14.00
2533 Bowl, 9", handled $45.00
2533 Candlestick, duo, pair $50.00
6013 Comport, 5" $32.00
5000 Jug....$185.00
2337 Plate, 6" $7.00
2337 Plate, 7" $8.00
2337 Plate, 8" $10.00
701 Tumbler, 10 oz. $16.00
1184 Old Fashioned Cocktail, 7 oz....$14.00

Fantasy, Crystal Print 17

1959 – 1965

Stemware, 118

6086 Goblet....$28.00
6086 Sherbet $25.00
6086 Wine/Cocktail $30.00
6086 Cordial $38.00
6086 Ice Tea, footed $28.00
6086 Juice, footed $23.00
2337 Plate, 7" $8.00
2337 Plate, 8" $10.00

Fascination, 6080

1958 – 1982

Stemware, 116

6080 Goblet
crystal....$25.00
lilac....$38.00
ruby....$65.00
6080 Sherbet
crystal $23.00
lilac....$35.00
ruby....$58.00
6080 Cocktail
crystal $23.00
lilac....$35.00
ruby....$60.00
6080 Claret-Wine
crystal $30.00
lilac....$40.00
ruby....$75.00
6080 Cordial
crystal $35.00
lilac....$52.00
ruby....$95.00
6080 Ice Tea, footed
crystal $25.00
lilac....$38.00
ruby....$62.00
6080 Juice, footed
crystal $30.00
lilac....$35.00
ruby....$54.00
6080 Claret, 8 oz., large
crystal $34.00
lilac....$45.00
6080 Claret, 6 oz., large
crystal $30.00
lilac....$45.00
2337 Plate, 7",
crystal $10.00
lilac....$35.00
2337 Plate, 8", crystal only....$12.00

Federal, Cutting 771

1937 – 1943

Stemware, 91

6019 Goblet $26.00
6019 Sherbet $23.00
6019 Parfait $26.00
6019 Cocktail $23.00
6019 Claret $28.00
6019 Wine....$26.00
6019 Oyster Cocktail....$16.00
6019 Ice Tea, footed $26.00
6019 Juice, footed $20.00
4132 Tumbler, 14 oz., sham $16.00
4132 Highball, 12 oz. $14.00
4132 Scotch and Soda, 9 oz. $12.00
4132 Tumbler, 5 oz., sham $10.00
4132 Old Fashioned Cocktail, 7½ oz. $12.00
4132 Whiskey, 1½ oz. $18.00

Tableware I, 298

766 Bowl, finger....$12.00
4132 Bowl, ice $40.00
2496 Bowl, 10½", handled $75.00
2430 Bowl, 11" $65.00
2430 Candlestick, 2", pair $65.00
2496 Candlestick, 5½", pair $48.00
4132 Decanter and Stopper $85.00
2430 Jelly, 7" $28.00
2430 Mint, 5½" $22.00
2337 Plate, 6" $6.00
2337 Plate, 7" $7.00
2337 Plate, 8" $8.00
2430 Vase, 8"....$60.00

Fern, Decoration 501

1929 – 1933

Tableware I, 202 – 203

2375 Bonbon $38.00
2395 Bowl, 10" $250.00
2415 Bowl, combination....$295.00
2497 Bowl A, 12", deep $135.00
2324 Candlestick, 4", pair $110.00
2395 Candlestick, 5", pair $145.00
2427 Box, cigarette and cover....$150.00
2400 Comport, 6"....$75.00
2375 Dish, lemon $38.00
2375 Plate, 10", cake $95.00
2409 Vase, 7½" $225.00
4105 Vase, 8", regular optic....$225.00
2373 Vase, large window and cover $450.00
2385 Vase, 8½", fan $485.00

Fern, Etching 305

1928 – 1933

Stemware, 57, 69

4020 Goblet
crystal....$38.00
ebony base....$38.00
4020 Sherbet, high
crystal....$38.00
ebony base $38.00
4020 Sherbet, 7 oz., low
crystal $30.00
ebony base $30.00
4020 Sherbet, 5 oz., low
crystal $30.00
ebony base $30.00
4020½ Cocktail, 4 oz.
crystal $30.00
ebony base $30.00
4020 Cocktail, 3½ oz.
crystal $30.00
ebony base $30.00
4020 Ice Tea, footed
crystal $38.00
ebony base $38.00
4020 Tumbler, 13 oz., footed
crystal $38.00
ebony base $38.00
4020 Tumbler, 10 oz., footed
crystal $30.00
ebony base $30.00
4020 Juice, footed
crystal $30.00
ebony base $30.00
4020 Whiskey, footed
crystal $35.00
ebony base $35.00
5098 Goblet
crystal $35.00
rose $55.00
5098 Sherbet, high
crystal $32.00
rose $48.00
5098 Sherbet, 7 oz., low
crystal $25.00
rose $34.00
5098 Parfait
crystal $35.00
rose $54.00

5098 Cocktail
crystal $32.00
rose $42.00
5098 Claret
crystal $38.00
rose $65.00
5098 Wine
crystal $35.00
rose $55.00
5098 Cordial
crystal $45.00
rose $95.00
5098 Oyster Cocktail
crystal $22.00
rose $30.00
5098 Ice Tea, footed
crystal $35.00
rose $50.00
5098 Tumbler, 9 oz., footed
crystal $28.00
rose $35.00
5098 Tumbler, juice
crystal $28.00
rose $32.00
5098 Whiskey, footed
crystal $32.00
rose $55.00

Tableware I, 202

2375 Bonbon
crystal $34.00
rose $40.00
869 Bowl, finger
crystal $32.00
rose $38.00
4021 Bowl, finger, crystal $35.00
2395 Bowl, 10"
crystal $150.00
rose $245.00
2415 Bowl, combination
crystal $165.00
2297 Bowl A, 12", deep
crystal $95.00
rose $125.00
2324 Candlestick, 4", pair
crystal $75.00
rose $110.00
2395½ Candlestick, 5", pair
crystal $115.00
rose $150.00
2427 Box, cigarette and cover.....$150.00
2400 Comport, 6"
crystal $62.00
rose $75.00
2350½ Cup, footed, crystal $26.00
2419 Saucer
crystal $9.00
rose $12.00
2419 Cup, rose $33.00
2350 Cup and Saucer, after dinner
crystal $52.00
2375 Dish, lemon
crystal $34.00
rose $40.00
4020 Jug
crystal $400.00
ebony base $425.00
5000 Jug
crystal $425.00
rose $495.00
2283 Plate, 6", finger bowl, regular optic
crystal $12.00
rose $15.00
2419 Plate, 6", crystal $9.00
2419 Plate, 7"
crystal $12.00
rose $15.00
2419 Plate, 8"
crystal $20.00
rose $25.00
2375 Plate, 10", cake
crystal $72.00
rose $95.00
4020 Sugar and Cream
crystal $75.00
ebony base $85.00
2409 Vase, 7½" $195.00
4105 Vase, 8", regular optic
crystal $195.00
rose $235.00
2373 Vase, large window and
cover $265.00
2385 Vase, 8½", fan $265.00
5082½ Grapefruit and Liner $50.00

Festival, Etching 45

1981 – 1982

Stemware, 145

6147 Goblet.........$28.00
6147 Champagne
...................$26.00
6147 Wine...................$28.00
6147 Ice Tea, footed $28.00

Festive, 6127

1975 – 1982

Stemware, 142

6127 Goblet......................$24.00
6127 Champagne................$22.00
6127 Wine.........................$24.00
6127 Ice Tea, footed.........$24.00

Festoon, Cutting 738

1934 – 1939

Stemware, 83

6012 Goblet.........$30.00
6012 Sherbet,
high..........$28.00
6012 Sherbet, low $22.00
6012 Cocktail $28.00
6012 Claret $35.00
6012 Rhine Wine...........................$35.00
6012 Wine......................................$34.00
6012 Sherry $34.00
6012 Crème de Menthe $28.00
6012 Brandy $35.00
6012 Cordial $42.00
6012 Oyster Cocktail......................$20.00
863 Champagne, hollow stem $18.00
6012 Ice Tea, footed $30.00
6012 Tumbler, 10 oz., footed $24.00
6012 Juice, footed $24.00
701 Tumbler, 12 oz. $18.00
701 Tumbler, 10 oz. $16.00
1185 Old Fashioned Cocktail
Sham $14.00
4122 Whiskey, 1½ oz. $18.00

Tableware I, 281

319 Bottle, bar.............................$48.00
4024 Bowl, 10", footed $47.00
1769 Bowl, finger...........................$14.00
4117 Jar, candy and cover,
Bubble $68.00
4024 Candlesticks, 6", pair $64.00
2525 Cocktail Shaker $95.00
2400 Comport, 6" $27.00
2525 Decanter................................$95.00
6011 Decanter................................$95.00
6011 Jug.......................................$185.00
2337 Plate, 6" $6.00
2337 Plate, 7" $7.00
2337 Plate, 8" $8.00
2364 Plate, 16" $70.00
2440 Plate, 13" $60.00
2350½ Sugar and Cream..................$30.00
2350½ Sugar and Cream..................$60.00
2470 Vase, 10"................................$75.00

Fifth Avenue, 114

Pre-1900 – 1920

Stemware, 17

114 Goblet, 11½ oz.........$3.00
114 Goblet, 11 oz............$3.00
114 Goblet, 10 oz...........$3.00
114 Champagne...........$3.00
114 Claret.....................$3.00
114 Wine..$3.00
114 Cordial $3.00

Figurals

1935 – 1973

Useful & Ornamental, 141 – 147

2497 Seafood Cocktail,
see Appetizers
2521 Bird, see
Shakers and Open Salts
2531 Penguin
crystal $125.00
topaz/gold tint $175.00
silver mist........................$150.00
2531 Pelican
crystal $125.00
topaz/gold tint $125.00
silver mist........................$150.00
2531 Polar Bear
crystal $125.00
topaz/gold tint $175.00
silver mist........................$150.00
2531 Seal
crystal, ...$125.00
topaz.................................$175.00
silver mist........................$150.00
2566 Ashtray, fish, see Smoker items
2589 Colt, standing
crystal $54.00
silver mist..........................$65.00
2589½ Colt, reclining
crystal $54.00
silver mist..........................$65.00
2589 Deer, standing
crystal $54.00
silver mist..........................$65.00
milk glass $65.00
2589½ Deer, reclining
crystal $54.00
silver mist..........................$65.00
milk glass $65.00
2595 Sleigh, see Milk Glass
2629 Chanticleer
crystal $375.00
ebony $600.00
Decoration 522,
ebony with gold..............market
2631 Squirrels A & B, 2 pieces,
priced each
crystal $54.00
amber.................................$57.00

olive green.....$57.00
cobalt.....$70.00
amber mist.....$64.00
olive green mist.....$64.00
cobalt mist.....$65.00

2623 Duckling Set: Mama Duck, Ducklings A, head back; B, walking; and C, head down
crystal.....$125.00
amber.....$135.00
olive green.....$135.00
cobalt.....$150.00
amber mist.....$135.00
olive green mist.....$135.00
cobalt mist.....$150.00

2633 Fish Set
Fish A (vertical), crystal..$145.00
Fish B (horizontal), crystal.....$175.00

2634 Mermaid, crystal.....$195.00

2634 Floating Garden, 13", base for Mermaid, crystal.....$125.00

2635 Madonna, offered with lighted base
crystal.....$95.00
silver mist.....$125.00
lighted base.....$25.00

2626 Chinese Lute, 12"
silver mist.....$350.00
Decoration 522, ebony with gold.....$700.00

2626½ Chinese Lotus, 12"
silver mist.....$350.00
Decoration 522, ebony with gold.....$700.00

2676 Hen and Nest, see Milk Glass

2680 Stage Coach, see Milk Glass

2782 Nappy, fish, see Milk Glass

2715 St. Francis, offered with lighted base
silver mist.....$450.00
lighted base.....$35.00

2797 Sacred Heart, offered with lighted base
silver mist.....$500.00
lighted base.....$35.00

2798 Madonna and Child, offered with lighted base
silver mist.....$550.00
lighted base.....$35.00

2821/304
Stork
crystal.....$37.00
lemon.....$40.00
olive green.....$40.00
silver mist.....$37.00
lemon mist.....$40.00
olive green mist.....$40.00

2821/357
Cat
crystal.....$35.00
lemon.....$40.00
olive green.....$40.00
silver mist.....$37.00
lemon mist.....$40.00
olive green mist.....$40.00

2821/410
Dolphin
crystal.....$35.00
lemon.....$45.00
olive green.....$45.00
silver mist.....$45.00
lemon mist.....$45.00
olive green mist.....$45.00

2821/420
Frog
crystal.....$35.00
lemon.....$45.00
olive green.....$45.00
silver mist.....$40.00
lemon mist.....$45.00
olive green mist.....$45.00

2821/452
Lady Bug
crystal.....$45.00
lemon.....$50.00
olive green.....$50.00
silver mist.....$50.00
lemon mist.....$50.00
olive green mist.....$50.00

2821/527
Owl
crystal.....$35.00
lemon.....$40.00
olive green.....$40.00
silver mist.....$40.00
lemon mist.....$40.00
olive green mist.....$40.00

2321/627
Baby Rabbit
crystal.....$22.00
lemon.....$25.00
olive green.....$25.00
silver mist.....$25.00
lemon mist.....$25.00
olive green mist.....$25.00

2821/628
Mama Rabbit
crystal.....$35.00
lemon.....$45.00
olive green.....$45.00
silver mist.....$40.00
lemon mist.....$45.00
olive green mist.....$45.00

4165 Santa Claus, see Milk Glass..market

Finger Bowls

Pre-1924 – 1970

Useful & Ornamental, 148 – 149

766 Bowl, finger and 1736 6" Plate, plain
crystal.....$15.00
regal blue.....$45.00
burgundy.....$45.00
empire green.....$45.00

858 Bowl, finger and 2283 6" Plate..$15.00

869 Bowl, finger and 2283 6" Plate
crystal.....$15.00
colors.....$35.00 – 45.00

890 Bowl, finger
crystal.....$15.00
rose.....$35.00
green.....$35.00

1769 Bowl, finger and 2283 6" Plate
crystal, RO.....$15.00
crystal, DO.....$28.00
topaz, DO.....$42.00
wisteria, DO.....$54.00
regal blue, burgundy, empire green, ruby, no optic.....$48.00

4095 Bowl, finger (made from the 4095 4½" footed Nappy) and 2283 6" Plate
crystal, RO.....$20.00
green, SO.....$25.00
blue foot, RO.....$28.00
green foot, SO.....$25.00
amber foot, LO.....$25.00
rose bowl, RO.....$28.00
azure bowl, RO.....$30.00
green bowl, RO.....$30.00

4021 Bowl, finger
crystal.....$26.00
green foot.....$30.00
amber foot.....$30.00
ebony foot.....$30.00
rose bowl.....$35.00
topaz/gold tint bowl.....$35.00
wisteria bowl.....$64.00

4185/495
Bowl, dessert/finger.....$18.00

6002 Bowl, finger
green base.....$38.00
ebony base.....$38.00
rose bowl.....$42.00
topaz bowl.....$42.00

Firelight, Decoration 657

1935 – 1987

Stemware, 116

6080½ Goblet.....$38.00
6080½ Sherbet.....$30.00
6080½ Claret-Wine.....$40.00
6080½ Cordial.....$45.00
6080½ Ice Tea, footed.....$35.00
6080½ Juice, footed.....$24.00
2337 Plate, 7", LO.....$12.00

Firenze, Decoration 502

1929 – 1932

Tableware I, 183

2375 Bonbon.....$56.00
2395 Bowl, 10".....$195.00
2394 Bowl, 12".....$150.00
2394 Candlestick, 2", pair.....$110.00
2395½ Candlestick, 5", pair.....$125.00
2375 Cheese and Cracker.....$150.00
2427 Box, cigarette and cover.....$150.00
2415 Bowl, combination.....$335.00
2400 Comport, 6".....$85.00
2375 Ice Bucket, gold plated handle, tongs.....$160.00
2375 Dish, lemon.....$54.00
2375 Plate, 10", cake.....$95.00
2375 Tray, handled, lunch.....$110.00
2417 Vase, 8".....$525.00
4105 Vase, 8".....$525.00

First Love, Cutting 918

1968 – 1970

Stemware, 135

6111 Goblet.....$28.00
6111 Sherbet.....$28.00
6111 Claret.....$32.00
6111 Wine.....$35.00
6111 Cordial.....$42.00
6111 Ice Tea, footed.....$28.00
2337 Plate, 7".....$10.00
2337 Plate, 8".....$12.00

Flame, 2545

1936 – 1958

Tableware I, 108 – 109

2545 Bowl, 12½", oval
crystal.....$68.00
azure.....$95.00
gold tint.....$95.00

2545 Candelabra, 2-light, priced each
crystal.....$135.00
azure.....$175.00
gold tint.....$175.00

2545 Candle Lamp
crystal $47.00
azure $60.00
2545 Candlestick, 2"
crystal $15.00
azure $26.00
gold tint $26.00
ebony $22.00
2545 Candlestick, 4½"
crystal $22.00
azure $35.00
gold tint $30.00
2545 Candlestick, duo
crystal $78.00
azure $125.00
gold tint $110.00
2545 Candlestick, lustre
crystal $100.00
azure $150.00
gold tint $125.00
2545 Box, candy and cover
crystal $95.00
azure $145.00
gold tint $145.00
2545 Sauce Boat and Plate
crystal $75.00
azure $125.00
gold tint $95.00
2545 Tray, 12", handled, lunch
crystal $75.00
azure $125.00
gold tint $125.00
2545 Vase, 10"
crystal $77.00
azure $185.00
gold tint $185.00

Flemish, Plate Etching 319

1933 – 1938

Tableware I, 218, 220

2440 Bonbon, 5", handled $22.00
4099 Jar, candy and cover..............$95.00
2440 Lemon, 5", handled $22.00
2440 Mayonnaise, 2-part...............$32.00
2440 Plate, 10½", cake $55.00
2440 Relish, 2-part $32.00
2440 Relish, 3-part $38.00
2440 Sauce and Tray $54.00
2440 Sugar and Cream and Tray ..$90.00
2440 Sweetmeat, 4½" $22.00

Fleurette, Crystal Print 26

1972 – 1974

Stemware, 126

6102 Goblet............. $32.00
6102 Sherbet $30.00
6102 Tulip Wine.............................$35.00
6102 Ice Tea, footed $32.00
2337 Plate, 7" $10.00

Florentine, Etching 311

1933 – 1943

Stemware, 76

6005 Goblet
crystal......$42.00
topaz/gold tint $54.00
6005 Sherbet, high
crystal $38.00
topaz/gold tint $48.00
6005 Sherbet, low
crystal $32.00
topaz/gold tint $35.00
6005 Parfait
crystal $42.00
topaz/gold tint $57.00
6005 Cocktail
crystal $36.00
topaz/gold tint $44.00
6005 Claret
crystal $55.00
topaz/gold tint $65.00
6005 Wine
crystal $52.00
topaz/gold tint $62.00
6005 Cordial
crystal $65.00
topaz/gold tint $75.00
6005 Oyster Cocktail
crystal $30.00
topaz/gold tint $35.00
6005 Ice Tea, footed
crystal $42.00
topaz/gold tint $54.00
6005 Tumbler, 9 oz., footed
crystal $34.00
topaz/gold tint $40.00
6005 Juice, footed
crystal $32.00
topaz/gold tint $40.00
6005 Whiskey, footed
crystal $42.00
topaz/gold tint $48.00
4005 Tumbler, 12 oz. $40.00
4005 Tumbler, 9 oz. $35.00
4005 Tumbler, 5 oz. $30.00
4005 Tumbler, 2½ oz. $40.00

Tableware I, 210

2470 Bonbon
crystal $38.00
topaz/gold tint $52.00
869 Bowl, finger
crystal $35.00
topaz/gold tint $40.00
2470½ Bowl, 10½"
crystal $135.00
topaz/gold tint $165.00
2470 Bowl, 12"
crystal $175.00
topaz/gold tint $225.00
2470 Candlestick, 5½", pair
crystal $165.00
topaz....................................$225.00
2470½ Candlestick, 5½", pair
crystal $125.00
topaz/gold tint $150.00
2470 Comport, low
crystal $75.00
topaz....................................$95.00
2470 Comport, tall
crystal $175.00
topaz....................................$225.00
2440 Cup and Saucer
crystal $37.00
topaz/gold tint $44.00
2470 Dish, lemon
crystal $42.00
topaz....................................$50.00
2440 Plate, 6"
crystal $15.00
topaz/gold tint $18.00
2440 Plate, 7"
crystal $20.00
topaz/gold tint $24.00
2440 Plate, 8"
crystal $22.00
topaz/gold tint $26.00
2440 Plate, 9"
crystal $60.00
topaz....................................$75.00
2440 Plate, 10", cake
crystal $95.00
topaz/gold tint $125.00
2440 Plate, 13", torte
crystal $98.00
2470 Relish, 3-part, round
crystal $64.00
topaz/gold tint $75.00
2440 Sugar and Cream
crystal $115.00
topaz/gold tint $135.00
2470 Sweetmeat
crystal $45.00
topaz....................................$52.00
2470 Tray, sugar and cream
crystal $38.00
topaz....................................$45.00

Florid, Etching 256

1920 – 1927

Stemware, 24

858 Goblet, 9 oz...$12.00
858 Saucer Champagne, 5½ oz.........$12.00
858 Sherbet $10.00
858 Fruit $10.00
858 Cocktail $10.00
858 Wine 2¾ oz. $12.00
858 Sherry $10.00
805 Parfait $24.00
766 Ice Tea, footed, handled $20.00
701 Tumbler, 14 oz. and 5" plate ..$12.00
820 Tumbler, table $8.00
833 Tumbler, 8 oz. $8.00
858 Tumbler, 14 oz. $12.00
858 Tumbler, 12 oz. $10.00
858 Tumbler, 8 oz. $8.00
858 Tumbler, 5 oz. $5.00
4011 Tumbler, 12 oz., handled, ...$15.00
945 Grapefruit, ½, and liner $30.00

Tableware

858 Bowl, finger, 1736 6", Plate...$22.00
858 Sweetmeat.............................$27.00
880 Bonbon $22.00
1697 Carafe and Tumbler $65.00
803 Comport, 5"............................$20.00
803 Comport, 6"............................$22.00
300 Jug, 7 ....$75.00
303 Jug, 7 ....$54.00
317 Jug, ½ and Cover.....................$85.00
318 Jug, 7 ....$78.00
1236 Jug, 6 ....$95.00
1968 Marmalade and Cover $34.00
2138 Mayonnaise, plate, ladle $45.00
1831 Mustard and Cover $30.00
803 Nappy, 5"................................$22.00
803 Nappy, 6"................................$24.00
803 Nappy, 7", footed $27.00
1227 Nappy, 4½"..............................$18.00
1227 Nappy, 8"................................$25.00
896 Bowl, candy and cover...........$26.00
2219 Jar, candy and cover, ¼ lb.....$56.00
2219 Jar, candy and cover, ½ lb $60.00

2219 Jar, candy and cover, 1 lb. $65.00
1465 Oil, 5 oz., cut neck $45.00
1465 Oil, 7 oz., cut neck $47.00
1897 Plate, 7", salad $7.00
1848 Plate, 9", sandwich $12.00
1719 Plate, 10½", sandwich...........$14.00
2238 Plate, 8¼", salad $10.00
2238 Plate, 11", salad $14.00
2083 Bottle, salad dressing $54.00
2099 Bowl, sandwich and cover....$54.00
2022 Shaker, FGT, pair.................$45.00
2023 Shaker, FGT, pair.................$45.00
1478 Sugar and Cream..................$38.00
2194 Syrup, 8 oz., nickle top..........$65.00
2194 Syrup, 12 oz., nickle top........$76.00

Florin, Decoration 619

1940 – 1943

Stemware, 98

6027 Goblet........$24.00
6027 Saucer Champagne $23.00
6027 Sherbet, low $18.00
6027 Cocktail $22.00
6027 Wine.......................................$27.00
6027 Cordial....................................$32.00
6027 Oyster Cocktail......................$15.00
6027 Ice Tea, footed $24.00
6027 Juice, footed $18.00

Tableware II, 194

4021 Bowl, finger.......................... $18.00
6023 Bowl, 9", footed...................... $65.00
2364 Bowl, 10½", salad $35.00
2527 Candelabra, 2-light UDP, pair ..$125.00
6023 Candlestick, duo, pair $64.00
6011 Jug..$150.00
2337 Plate, 6" $9.00
2337 Plate, 7" $12.00
2337 Plate, 8" $15.00
2364 Plate, 14", torte $45.00
4143 Vase, 6", footed $55.00
4143 Vase, 7½", footed..................$65.00

Flower Girl, Decoration 659

1962 – 1967

Stemware, 124

6100 Goblet....................................$35.00
6100 Sherbet..................................$32.00
6100 Claret.....................................$38.00
6100 Tulip Wine..............................$38.00
6100 Brandy....................................$38.00
6100 Ice Tea, footed $35.00
2337 Plate, 7" $10.00
2337 Plate, 8" $12.00

Flower Song, Cutting 894

1962 – 1966

Stemware, 125

6101 Goblet.................$35.00
6101 Sherbet..............$32.00
6101 Wine/Cocktail $38.00
6101 Cordial....................................$45.00
6101 Ice Tea, footed $35.00
6101 Juice, footed $30.00
2337 Plate, 7" $10.00
2337 Plate, 8" $12.00

Forever, Cutting 904

1964 – 1965

Stemware, 128

6103 Goblet............$26.00
6103 Sherbet $24.00
6103 Claret $28.00
6103 Tulip Wine..............................$28.00
6103 Brandy $26.00
6103 Ice Tea, footed $26.00
2337 Plate, 7" $8.00
2337 Plate, 8" $10.00

Formal Garden, Cutting 700

1930

Stemware, 58

4020 Goblet
crystal.......$27.00
ebony base $40.00

4020 Sherbet, high
crystal $27.00
ebony base $40.00

4020 Sherbet, 7 oz., low
crystal $20.00
ebony base $35.00

4020 Sherbet, 5 oz., low
crystal $20.00
ebony base $35.00

4020 Cocktail, 3½ oz.
crystal $20.00
ebony base $35.00

4020 Whiskey
crystal $20.00
ebony base $40.00

4020 Tumbler, ice tea, 16 oz., footed
crystal $27.00
ebony base $40.00

4020 Tumbler, 13 oz., footed
crystal $27.00
ebony base $40.00

4020 Tumbler, 10 oz., footed
crystal $20.00
ebony base $35.00

4020 Tumbler, 5 oz., footed
crystal $20.00
ebony base $35.00

4021 Bowl, finger
crystal $24.00
ebony base $30.00

Tableware I, 273

2419 Plate, 6", crystal only..............$6.00
2419 Plate, 7", , crystal only............$7.00
2419 Plate, 8", , crystal only............$8.00
2350½ Cup, crystal only...................$16.00
2419 Saucer, crystal only $6.00
2350 Cup, after dinner,
crystal only.........................$18.00
2419 Saucer, after dinner
crystal only...........................$6.00

Formality, Cutting 818

1942 – 1951

Stemware, 101

6032 Goblet $34.00
6032 Saucer Champagne $32.00
6032 Sherbet, low $28.00
6032 Cocktail $30.00
6032 Claret.....................................$36.00
6032 Wine.......................................$36.00
6032 Cordial....................................$42.00
6032 Oyster Cocktail......................$24.00
6032 Ice Tea, footed $34.00
6032 Juice, footed $26.00
2337 Plate, 6" $8.00
2337 Plate, 7" $10.00
2337 Plate, 8" $12.00
6011 Jug.......................................$175.00

Fostoria Wheat, Cutting 837

1953 – 1963

Stemware, 106, 162

6051½ Goblet......$32.00
6051½ Sherbet............$28.00
6051½ Cocktail $26.00
6051½ Claret-Wine $38.00
6051½ Cordial..................................$45.00
6051½ Oyster Cocktail.....................$22.00
6051½ Ice Tea, footed $32.00
6051½ Juice, footed $26.00

Tableware II, 185

2666 Bonbon $26.00
4185 Bowl, dessert/finger.............$24.00
2666 Bowl, oval $38.00
2666 Bowl, 10½", salad $45.00
2666 Butter and Cover, oblong $48.00
2666 Candle, flora, pair $54.00
2666 Cup and Saucer......................$25.00
2666 Mayonnaise, plate, ladle $58.00
2666 Pitcher, quart......................$665.00
2337 Plate, 7" $10.00
2337 Plate, 8" $12.00
2666 Plate, 10", snack $27.00
2666 Plate, 14", serving..................$45.00
2666 Relish, 2-part $30.00
2666 Relish, 3-part $38.00
2666 Salad Set, 4-piece $95.00
2685 Salver.....................................$75.00
2364 Shaker, large, chrome top B,
pair $65.00
2666 Sugar and Cream..................$52.00
2666 Sugar and Cream, individual
and tray..................................$60.00

Fountain, Etching 307

1929 – 1930

Stemware, 58

4020 Goblet
crystal...$35.00
green base.........................$40.00

4020 Sherbet, high
crystal $32.00
green base.........................$40.00

4020 Sherbet, 7 oz., low
crystal $30.00
green base.........................$35.00

4020 Sherbet, 5 oz., low
crystal $30.00
green base.........................$35.00

4020 Cocktail, 3½ oz.
crystal $30.00
green base.........................$35.00

4020 Ice Tea, footed
crystal $35.00
green base.........................$40.00

4020 Tumbler, 13 oz., footed
crystal $35.00
green base.........................$40.00

4020 Tumbler, 10 oz., footed
crystal $30.00
green base.........................$35.00

4020 Juice, footed
crystal $30.00
green base.........................$35.00

4020 Whiskey, footed
crystal $30.00
green base.........................$35.00

Tableware I, 204
4021 Bowl, finger
crystal $25.00
green base $32.00
2350½ Cup and Saucer $28.00
2350 Cup and Saucer, after dinner $30.00
2350 Cream Soup $22.00
2350 Plate, 6" $6.00
2350 Plate, 7" $8.00
2350 Plate, 9" $28.00
2419 Plate, 6" $6.00
2419 Plate, 7" $8.00
2419 Plate, 8" $24.00

Fountain, Cutting 901
1964 – 1965
Stemware, 128
6103 Goblet $26.00
6103 Sherbet $24.00
6103 Claret $28.00
6103 Tulip Wine $28.00
6103 Brandy $26.00
6103 Ice Tea, footed $26.00
2337 Plate, 7" $8.00
2337 Plate, 8" $10.00

Fresno, Etching 78
1925 – 1930
Stemware, 30
867½ Goblet, 9 oz. $12.00
867½ Saucer Champagne $10.00
867½ Fruit $10.00
867½ Cocktail $10.00
867½ Wine $10.00
701 Tumbler, 13 oz. $10.00
820 Tumbler, table $8.00
4095 Tumbler, 10 oz. $10.00
318 Jug, 7 $88.00

Frisco, 1229 Milkglass
1954 – 1965
Tableware II, 203
1229 Jar, candy and cover, 6½" $50.00
aqua $65.00
peach $65.00
1229 Spoon Holder, 3⅞" $40.00
aqua $54.00
peach $54.00
1229 Toothpick, 2¼"
1229 Vase, 6", bud $24.00
aqua $36.00
peach $36.00
1229 Vase, 10", swung $48.00
aqua $64.00
peach $64.00

Fruit, Plate Etching 320
1933 – 1938
Tableware I, 221
2440 Bonbon $24.00
2499 Jar, candy and cover $95.00
2440 Lemon, handled $22.00
2440 Mayonnaise, 2-part $37.00
2397 Plate, 8" $20.00
2449½ Plate, crescent, salad $35.00
2440 Plate, 10½", cake $68.00
2440 Plate, 13", torte $85.00
2440 Relish, 2-part $42.00
2440 Relish, 3-part $48.00
2419 Relish, 5-part $85.00
2440 Sauce and Tray $75.00
2440 Sugar and Cream $75.00
2440 Sweetmeat, 4½" $22.00
2440 Tray, sugar and cream $25.00

Fruit and Flowers Decoration 523, Milkglass
1955 – 1958
Tableware II, 205
2620 Plate, 8"
apple $30.00
peach $30.00
grape $30.00
pear $30.00
raspberry $30.00
cherry $30.00
1704 Jar, pickle and cover
daisy $65.00
redbud $65.00

Fuchsia, Etching 310
1933 – 1943
Stemware, 75
6004 Goblet
crystal $65.00
wisteria $150.00
6004 Sherbet, high
crystal $55.00
wisteria $125.00
6004 Sherbet, low
crystal $46.00
wisteria $69.00
6004 Parfait
crystal $75.00
wisteria $135.00
6004 Cocktail
crystal $52.00
wisteria $84.00
6004 Claret
crystal $75.00
wisteria $165.00
6004 Wine
crystal $75.00
wisteria $150.00
6004 Cordial
crystal $95.00
wisteria $185.00
6004 Oyster Cocktail
crystal $40.00
wisteria $64.00
6004 Ice Tea, footed
crystal $65.00
wisteria $140.00
6004 Tumbler, 9 oz., footed
crystal $50.00
wisteria $75.00
6004 Juice, footed
crystal $48.00
wisteria $72.00
6004 Whiskey, footed
crystal $56.00
wisteria $125.00
833 Tumbler, 12 oz., crystal only $32.00
833 Tumbler, 8 oz., crystal only $27.00
833 Tumbler, 5 oz., crystal only $24.00
833 Tumbler, 2 oz., crystal only $22.00
Tableware I, 208
2470 Bonbon $45.00
869 Bowl, finger $35.00
2395 Bowl, 10" $175.00
2470½ Bowl, 10½" $150.00
2440 Bowl B, 10½" $125.00
2470 Bowl, 12"
crystal $195.00
wisteria base $400.00
2375 Candlestick, 3", pair $88.00
2395½ Candlestick, 5", pair $150.00
2470 Candlestick, 5½", pair
crystal $250.00
wisteria base $495.00
2470½ Candlestick, 5½", pair $200.00
2470 Comport, 6", low
crystal $75.00
wisteria base $135.00
2470 Comport, 6", tall
crystal $175.00
wisteria base $275.00
2440 Cup and Saucer $36.00
2470 Dish, lemon $45.00
2440 Plate, 6" $20.00
2440 Plate, 7" $24.00
2440 Plate, 8" $27.00
2440 Plate, 9" $65.00
2470 Plate, 10", cake $120.00
2440 Sugar and Cream $125.00
2470 Sweetmeat $45.00

Functional Sculptures/Ashtrays
1980 – 1981
Useful & Ornamental, 147
FU01/116 Lion $54.00
FU02/116 Ram $55.00
FU03/116 Hound $54.00

- G -

Gadroon, Cutting 816
1942 – 1956
Stemware, 100
6030 Goblet $27.00
6030 Goblet, low $25.00
6030 Saucer Champagne $25.00
6030 Sherbet, low $20.00
6030 Cocktail $22.00
6030 Claret-Wine $30.00
6030 Cordial $38.00
6030 Oyster Cocktail $18.00
6030 Ice Tea, footed $25.00
6030 Juice, footed $20.00
Tableware I, 303
1769 Bowl, finger $15.00
6023 Bowl, footed $65.00
6023 Candlestick, duo, pair $75.00
6011 Jug $175.00
2337 Plate, 6" $7.00
2337 Plate, 7" $8.00
2337 Plate, 8" $10.00

Gala, 6147
1981 – 1982
Stemware, 145
6147 Goblet $20.00
6147 Champagne $18.00
6147 Wine $20.00
6147 Ice Tea, footed $20.00

Garden Center Items
1960 – 1964
Tableware II, 253 – 255

4166/151
Bowl, 5", footed
silver mist $18.00
2666/189
Bowl, 8¼", oval
crystal $15.00
silver mist $15.00
4166/199
Bowl, 9", footed
silver mist spruce $28.00
2368/220
Bowl, 10½", oblong
crystal $21.00
2596/215
Bowl, oblong, shallow
silver mist $20.00
2703/189
Bowl, 14¾", oblong
amethyst $45.00
silver mist amethyst $45.00
silver mist spruce $37.00
2692/234
Bowl, footed, fruit
silver mist $22.00
silver mist amethyst $25.00
4116/291
Bubble Ball, 4"
cinnamon $12.00
1121/389
Comport, 5¾"
silver mist milk glass $20.00
silver mist amber $22.00
2364/197
Lily Pond, 9"
crystal $18.00
silver mist $18.00
2364/251
Lily Pond, 12"
crystal $20.00
silver mist $20.00
834/70
Pitcher, Jenny Lind
silver mist amber $54.00
silver mist milk $45.00
2703/191
Plate, 13", square, buffet
crystal $24.00
marine $30.00
amethyst $30.00
2725/761
Urn, 5¾", handled
silver mist $10.00
silver mist spruce $12.00
2692/760
Urn, 6", handled
silver mist $20.00
2692/828
Urn, 12", handled
silver mist $47.00
2693/162
Urn, Franklin and cover
silver mist milk glass $42.00
4152/751
Vase Bowl, 3⅞"
silver mist $10.00
silver mist spruce $10.00
4121/754
Vase, 5"
crystal, ... $12.00
spruce $12.00
chartreuse $18.00
4166/757
Vase, 6", bud
crystal $18.00
silver mist amber $20.00
silver mist amethyst $20.00
silver mist milk glass $18.00
2724/779
Vase, 7½", goblet
silver mist amber $15.00
silver mist spruce $15.00
2577/792
Vase, 8½",
crystal $20.00
silver mist $20.00
silver mist amber $22.00
silver mist amethyst $22.00
silver mist milk glass $20.00

Garland, Etching 237
1915 – 1928
Stemware, 20, 28, 35

766 Goblet $15.00
766 Saucer Champagne $15.00
766 Sherbet $15.00
766 Fruit $15.00
766 Parfait $15.00
766 Cocktail $15.00
766 Claret $20.00
766 Rhine Wine $20.00
766 Wine $14.00
766 Burgundy $14.00
766 Sherry $14.00
766 Crème de Menthe $12.00
766 Brandy $25.00
766 Cordial $25.00
766 Sorbet $8.00
766 Ice Tea, footed, handled $20.00
766 Custard, handled $7.00
766 Grapefruit and Liner $25.00
863 Goblet, 10½ oz. $15.00
863 Goblet, 9 oz. $12.00
863 Saucer Champagne $12.00
863 Fruit $9.00
863 Cocktail, 3½ oz. $9.00
863 Claret $15.00
863 Rhine Wine $15.00
863 Wine $15.00
863 Sherry $9.00
863 Crème de Menthe $9.00
863 Brandy, pousse-café $20.00
863 Cordial $22.00
863 Champagne, hollow stem, CF .. $12.00
863 Champagne, tall $12.00
880 Goblet, 11 oz. $12.00
880 Goblet, 10 oz. $12.00
880 Goblet, 9 oz. $10.00
880 Goblet, 8 oz. $10.00
880 Saucer Champagne, 7 oz. $10.00
880 Saucer Champagne, 5½ oz. .. $10.00
880 Sherbet $9.00
880 Cocktail, 3½ oz. $9.00
880 Claret, 6½ oz. $12.00
880 Claret, 4½ oz. $12.00
880 Rhine Wine $12.00
880 Wine, 3½ oz. $12.00
880 Wine, 2¾ oz. $12.00
880 Sherry $10.00
880 Crème de Menthe $10.00
880 Brandy, pousse-café, 1 oz. $20.00
880 Cordial, 1 oz. $22.00
880 Champagne, hollow stem $12.00
880 Champagne, tall $10.00
880 Grapefruit, tall, and liner $25.00
880 Grapefruit, short, and liner ... $20.00
880 Hot Whiskey $10.00
880 Ale, tall $12.00
701 Tumbler .... $6.00 – 15.00
820 Tumbler .... $6.00 – 15.00
833 Tumbler .... $6.00 – 15.00
887 Tumbler .... $6.00 – 15.00
889 Tumbler .... $6.00 – 15.00
4011 Tumbler .... $6.00 – 15.00
4061 Tumbler, handled $18.00
899 Parfait $15.00
300 Tankard $95.00
724 Tankard $125.00
303 Jug $60.00
318 Jug $95.00
1236 Jug $115.00

Garland, Cutting 859
1958 – 1959
Stemware, 115

6077 Goblet $35.00
6077 Sherbet $32.00
6077 Cocktail/Wine $36.00
6077 Cordial $48.00
6077 Ice Tea, footed $35.00
6077 Juice, footed $32.00
2337 Plate, 7" $10.00
2337 Plate, 8" $12.00

Gazebo, 6126
1980 – 1982
Stemware 142

6126 Goblet,
ebony base $26.00
6126 Champagne,
ebony base $24.00
6126 Wine,
ebony base $28.00
6126 Ice Tea, footed, ebony base .. $26.00

Gazebo Rust, 6126
1981 – 1982
See illustration above
Stemware, 15, 142

6126 Goblet, rust base $20.00
6126 Champagne, rust base $20.00
6126 Wine, rust base $20.00
6126 Ice Tea, rust base $20.00

Geneva, Cutting 135
1918 – 1926
Stemware, 29, 36

863 Goblet, 9 oz..... $12.00
863 Saucer Champagne $10.00
863 Fruit $6.00
880 Goblet, 9 oz. $12.00
880 Saucer Champagne, 5½ oz. .. $10.00
880 Sherbet $7.00
880 Cocktail, 3½ oz. $7.00
701 Tumbler, 14 oz. and 5" plate .. $12.00
820 Tumbler, table $8.00
4011 Tumbler, 12 oz. $10.00
4011 Tumbler, 8 oz. $8.00
822 Parfait $14.00
4061 Lemonade, footed, handled .. $18.00
481 Custard $8.00
880 Bonbon $20.00
803 Comport, 5" $20.00

803 Comport, 6" $22.00
1769 Bowl, finger and plate $20.00
303 Jug, 7 ....$50.00
724 Jug, 7 ....$85.00
1968 Marmalade and Cover $26.00
2138 Mayonnaise, plate, ladle $45.00
1831 Mustard and Cover $24.00
803 Nappy, 5" $22.00
803 Nappy, 6" $24.00
803 Nappy, 7", footed $28.00
1227 Nappy, 4½" $20.00
1227 Nappy, 8" $28.00
1465 Oil, 7 oz., cut neck $46.00
1848 Plate, 9", sandwich $10.00
880 Salt Dip, footed $20.00
2022 Shaker, FGT, pair $35.00
2133 Sugar and Cream $35.00
922 Toothpick $23.00
4069 Vase, 9" $70.00

George and Martha Washington Plaques

1975 – 1976

Useful & Ornamental, 147

2913/597
George and Martha Washington plaques .$125.00 pair

Georgetown, Cutting 906

1961 – 1973

Stemware, 130

6105 Goblet $35.00
6105 Sherbet $32.00
6105 Claret $38.00
6105 Wine $38.00
6105 Cordial $42.00
6105 Ice Tea, footed $35.00
2337 Plate, 7" $10.00
2337 Plate, 8" $12.00

Georgian, Cutting 791

1939 – 1943

Stemware, 96

6025 Goblet $32.00
6025 Sherbet $28.00
6025 Cocktail $30.00
6025 Claret-Wine $35.00
6025 Cordial $42.00
6025 Oyster Cocktail $22.00
6025 Ice Tea, footed $32.00
6025 Juice, footed $24.00
2337 Plate, 6", no cut flutes $8.00
2337 Plate, 7", no cut flutes $10.00
2337 Plate, 8", no cut flutes $12.00
6011 Jug $175.00

Georgian, Cutting 885

1961 – 1982

Stemware, 122

6097 Goblet $30.00
6097 Sherbet $26.00
6097 Claret $35.00
6097 Wine/Cocktail $30.00
6097 Cordial $40.00
6097 Ice Tea, footed $30.00
6097 Juice, footed $24.00
833½ Highball $26.00
833½ Old Fashioned Cocktail, double $26.00

Glacier, 2510, see Sunray

Glacier, 2807

1969 – 1972

Tableware II, 102

2807 Ashtray, 3¾", small $9.00
2807 Ashtray, 5½", medium $12.00
2807 Ashtray, 8¾", large $15.00
2807 Cigarette Lighter, gold or silver fitting $18.00
Cigarette Lighter Set $30.00
Included cigarette lighter and 5½", medium ashtray $30.00

Glamour, 6103

1964 – 1982

Stemware, 128

6103 Goblet
crystal/green mist $22.00
gray mist/blue/onyx $24.00

6103 Sherbet
crystal/green mist $20.00
gray mist/blue/onyx $22.00

6103 Claret
crystal/green mist $22.00
gray mist/blue/onyx $24.00

6103 Tulip Wine
crystal/green mist $24.00
gray mist/blue/onyx $26.00

6103 Brandy
crystal/green mist $22.00
gray mist/blue/onyx $24.00

6013 Ice Tea, footed
crystal/green mist $22.00
gray mist/blue/onyx $24.00

2512 Glass Fruit

1934 – 1937

Useful & Ornamental, 150

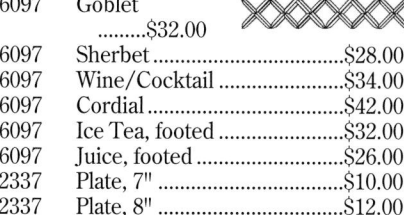

Grape
regal blue $57.00
burgundy $57.00
empire green $57.00
silver decoration $50.00

Orange
regal blue $57.00
burgundy $57.00
silver decoration $50.00

Banana
regal blue $57.00
burgundy $57.00
empire green $57.00
silver decoration $50.00

Apple
regal blue $57.00
burgundy $57.00
empire green $57.00
silver decoration $50.00

Pear
regal blue $57.00
burgundy $57.00
empire green $57.00
silver decoration $50.00

Peach
regal blue $57.00
burgundy $57.00
silver decoration $50.00

Glendale, Cutting 919

1967 – 1972

Stemware, 134

6110 Goblet $28.00
6110 Sherbet $25.00
6110 Wine $32.00
6110 Liqueur $40.00
6110 Ice Tea, footed $28.00
2337 Plate, 7" $8.00
2337 Plate, 8" $10.00

Gloucester, Cutting 898

1963 – 1969

Stemware, 122

6097 Goblet $32.00
6097 Sherbet $28.00
6097 Wine/Cocktail $34.00
6097 Cordial $42.00
6097 Ice Tea, footed $32.00
6097 Juice, footed $26.00
2337 Plate, 7" $10.00
2337 Plate, 8" $12.00

Gold Band Decoration

Note: These pieces were intended to be used with patterns that had Gold Band Decoration.

Tableware II, 195

4185 Bowl, dessert/finger $18.00
2785 Bowl, 10", footed $35.00
2364 Bowl, 10½", salad $35.00
2364 Bowl, 12", lily pond $50.00
2364 Bowl, 13", fruit $58.00
2324 Candlestick, 4", pair $48.00
6023 Candlestick, duo, pair $95.00
2350½ Cup and Saucer $26.00
2364 Mayonnaise, plate, spoon $58.00
2337 Plate, 6" $9.00
2337 Plate, 7" $12.00
2337 Plate, 8" $15.00
2364 Plate, 14", torte $45.00
2785 Relish, 2-part $30.00
2785 Relish, 4-part $35.00
2785 Relish, 5-part $42.00
2350½ Sugar and Cream $45.00
2785 Sugar and Cream $45.00

Golden Belle, Decoration 677

1967 – 1974

Stemware, 134

6110 Goblet $28.00
6110 Sherbet $25.00
6110 Wine $32.00
6110 Liqueur $38.00
6110 Ice Tea, footed $28.00
2337 Plate, 7" $10.00
2337 Plate, 8" $12.00

Golden Flair, Decoration 643

1959 – 1967

Stemware, 118

6087 Goblet $28.00
6087 Sherbet $26.00
6087 Wine/Cocktail $32.00
6087 Cordial $40.00
6087 Ice Tea, footed $28.00
6087 Juice, footed $24.00
2337 Plate, 7" $10.00
2337 Plate, 8" $12.00

Golden Garland, Decoration 664

1964 – 1967

Stemware, 127

6102 Goblet....$34.00
6102 Sherbet....$30.00
6102 Claret....$35.00
6102 Tulip Wine....$35.00
6102 Brandy....$38.00
6102 Ice Tea, footed....$34.00
2337 Plate, 7"....$10.00
2337 Plate, 8"....$12.00

Golden Glow, Decoration 513 (see Sunray)

Golden Grail, Decoration 644

1959 – 1970

Stemware, 117

6083 Goblet....$40.00
6083 Sherbet....$36.00
6083 Wine/Cocktail....$45.00
6083 Cordial....$54.00
6083 Ice Tea, footed....$40.00
6083 Juice, footed....$35.00
2337 Plate, 7"....$14.00
2337 Plate, 8"....$16.00

Golden Lace, Decoration 645

1959 – 1975

Stemware, 117

6085 Goblet....$42.00
6085 Sherbet....$38.00
6085 Wine/Cocktail....$48.00
6085 Cordial....$57.00
6085 Ice Tea, footed....$42.00
6085 Juice, footed....$38.00
2337 Plate, 7"....$12.00
2337 Plate, 8"....$14.00

Golden Love, Decoration 640

1958 – 1965

Stemware, 115

6074 Goblet....$36.00
6074 Sherbet....$34.00
6074 Cocktail/Wine/Seafood....$36.00
6074 Cordial....$48.00
6074 Ice Tea, footed....$36.00
6074 Juice, footed....$32.00
2337 Plate, 7"....$12.00
2337 Plate, 8"....$14.00

Golden Song, Decoration 662

1964 – 1968

Stemware, 123

6099 Goblet....$35.00
6099 Sherbet....$32.00
6099 Wine/Cocktail....$38.00
6099 Cordial....$48.00
6099 Ice Tea, footed....$35.00
6099 Juice, footed....$30.00
2337 Plate, 7"....$12.00
2337 Plate, 8"....$14.00

Golden Swirl, Decoration 614 (see Whirlpool)

Golden Twilight, Crystal Print 12 Tumbler

1958 – 1962

Stemware, 155

4180 Tumbler, 12 oz. flat, Fawn....$12.00
4180 Juice, 7 oz. flat, Fawn....$14.00

Gold Lace, Decoration 514 (see also Italian Lace)

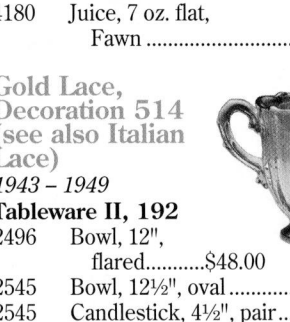

1943 – 1949

Tableware II, 192

2496 Bowl, 12", flared....$48.00
2545 Bowl, 12½", oval....$54.00
2545 Candlestick, 4½", pair....$65.00
2545 Candlestick, duo, pair....$87.00
2496 Candlestick, 5½", pair....$68.00
2496 Candlestick, duo, pair....$85.00
2496 Box, candy and cover....$95.00
2496 Celery....$30.00
2496 Cheese and Cracker....$75.00
2496 Comport, 5½"....$37.00
2496 Ice Bucket, gold handle....$68.00
2496 Mayonnaise, 2-part....$40.00
2496½ Mayonnaise, plate, ladle....$65.00
2496 Nappy, handled, flared....$24.00
2496 Nappy, handled, square....$24.00
2496 Nappy, handled, 3-cornered....$24.00
2496 Pickle....$24.00
2496 Plate, 10", cake....$52.00
2496 Plate, 14", torte....$65.00
2496 Relish, 2-part....$35.00
2496 Relish, 3-part....$50.00
2496 Dish, sauce and tray....$65.00
2496 Sugar and Cream....$55.00
2496 Sweetmeat....$32.00
2467 Vase, 7½"....$75.00
2545 Vase, 10"....$125.00

Gold Triumph, 6112

1968 – 1972

Stemware, 136

6112 Goblet....$25.00
6112 Sherbet....$25.00
6112 Tulip Wine....$28.00
6112 Ice Tea, footed....$25.00
2336 Plate, 7"....$8.00
2337 Plate, 8"....$10.00

Goldwood, Decoration 50 (see Woodland)

Gossamer, Cutting 746

1935 – 1939

Stemware, 84

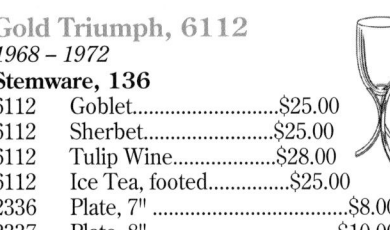

6012 Goblet....$28.00
6012 Sherbet, high....$26.00
6012 Sherbet, low....$22.00
6012 Cocktail....$22.00
6012 Claret....$28.00
6012 Wine....$28.00
6012 Cordial....$38.00
6012 Oyster Cocktail....$18.00
6012 Ice Tea, footed....$27.00
6012 Tumbler, 10 oz., footed....$20.00
6012 Juice, footed....$18.00

Tableware I, 287

1769 Bowl, finger....$14.00
2536 Bowl, 9", handled....$52.00
2535 Candlestick, 5½", pair....$60.00
2400 Comport, 6"....$27.00
6011 Jug....$185.00
2337 Plate, 6"....$6.00
2337 Plate, 7"....$7.00
2337 Plate, 8"....$8.00

Gossamer, Cutting 852

1957 – 1962

Stemware, 113

6068 Goblet....$22.00
6068 Sherbet....$20.00
6068 Cocktail/Wine/Seafood....$22.00
6068 Cordial....$30.00
6068 Ice Tea, footed....$22.00
6068 Juice, footed....$20.00

Tableware II, 190

2666 Bonbon....$28.00
2337 Plate, 7"....$10.00
2337 Plate, 8"....$12.00
2364 Plate, 14", torte....$35.00
2364 Relish, 2-part....$30.00
2364 Relish, 3-part....$38.00
2666 Sugar and Cream....$45.00

Gothic, Cutting 774

1938 – 1957

Stemware, 92

6020 Goblet....$32.00
6020 Saucer Champagne....$28.00
6020 Sherbet, low....$24.00
6020 Parfait....$32.00
6020 Cocktail....$28.00
6020 Claret....$35.00
6020 Wine....$34.00
6020 Cordial....$45.00
6020 Oyster Cocktail....$20.00
6020 Ice Tea, footed....$32.00
6020 Tumbler, 9 oz., footed....$26.00
6020 Juice, footed....$26.00

Tableware I, 298

869 Bowl, finger....$12.00
2560 Bowl, handled....$67.00
2430 Bowl, 11"....$60.00
2430 Candlestick, 2", pair....$65.00
2560 Candlestick, 4½", pair....$50.00
2560 Candlestick, duo, pair....$70.00
2400 Comport, 6"....$27.00
5000 Jug....$185.00
2337 Plate, 6"....$6.00
2337 Plate, 7"....$7.00
2337 Plate, 8"....$8.00
2560 Sugar and Cream....$40.00

Gourmet, 2785

1964 – 1970

Tableware II, 100

2785 Bowl, 10", footed....$35.00
2785 Plate, 14", torte, not decorated....$40.00
2785 Relish, 2-part....$30.00
2785 Relish, 4-part....$35.00
2785 Relish, 5-part....$42.00
2785 Shaker, chrome top A, decorated, pair....$35.00
2785 Sugar and Cream, footed....$38.00

Gourmet Service, GO05

1977 – 1978
Crystal, brown, green
Tableware II, 256

GO05/064
Tumbler, 5⅛", 14 oz. $7.00
GO05/159
Salad/Soup, 6¼" $7.00
GO05/396
Cup, handled $7.00
GO05/554
Plate, 10½", dinner $10.00
GO05/666
Snack Set: boxed plate, soup, and cup $24.00

Granada, Cutting 923

1971 – 1972
Stemware, 141

6124 Goblet $35.00
6124 Sherbet $35.00
6124 Wine $35.00
6124 Ice Tea, footed $35.00
2337 Plate, 7" $10.00

Grand Majesty, Etching GR03/GR04

1979 – 1980
Stemware, 79

6009 Goblet
crystal $38.00
blue $46.00
6009 Dessert/Champagne
crystal $34.00
blue $42.00
6009 Wine
crystal $42.00
blue $48.00
6009 Magnum
crystal $58.00
blue $70.00
6009 Ice Tea, 16 oz., footed
crystal $48.00
blue $54.00

Grape, Brocade Etching 287

1927 – 1929
Tableware I, 124 – 127

2375 Bonbon
green $54.00
2339 Bowl D, 7½",
blue $175.00
orchid $150.00
green $110.00
2297 Bowl A, 10½", shallow
blue $145.00
orchid $125.00
green $110.00
2297 Bowl C, 10½", deep
blue $145.00
orchid $135.00
green $135.00
2297 Bowl A, 12", deep
blue $147.00
orchid $135.00
green $135.00
2362 Bowl, 12", low
blue $185.00
orchid $165.00
green $150.00
2297 Bowl E, 12½", deep
blue $175.00
orchid $165.00
green $165.00
2372 Candlestick, 2", pair
blue $140.00
orchid $135.00
green $125.00
2362 Candlestick, 3", pair
blue $150.00
orchid $140.00
green $130.00
2324 Candlestick, 4", pair
blue $140.00
orchid $135.00
green $125.00
2331 Box, candy and cover
blue $225.00
orchid $195.00
green $175.00
2329 Centerpiece, 11", round
blue $195.00
orchid $175.00
green $65.00
2329 Centerpiece, 13", round
blue $225.00
orchid $210.00
green $195.00
2371 Centerpiece, 13", oval and 2371 Flower Holder
blue $500.00
orchid $400.00
green $400.00
2327 Comport, 7"
blue $135.00
orchid $125.00
green $110.00
2362 Comport, 11", footed
blue $250.00
orchid $225.00
green $200.00
2378 Ice Bucket, NP handle
blue $175.00
orchid $175.00
green $165.00
2378 Ice Bucket, NP handle, drainer, tongs
blue $225.00
orchid $225.00
green $225.00
2375 Lemon, handled
green $52.00
2375 Sweetmeat, handled
green $54.00
2387 Tray, handled, lunch
blue $195.00
orchid $185.00
green $175.00
2342 Tray, handled, lunch (2370)
blue $195.00
orchid $185.00
green $175.00
4103 Vase, 3", RO
blue $135.00
orchid $125.00
green $98.00
4103 Vase, 4", RO
blue $145.00
orchid $135.00
green $135.00
4103 Vase, 5", RO
blue $160.00
orchid $145.00
green $145.00
4103 Vase, 6", RO
blue $175.00
orchid $160.00
green $160.00
4100 Vase, 6", RO
blue $175.00
orchid $165.00
green $160.00
4100 Vase, 8", RO
blue $225.00
orchid $200.00
green $190.00
2369 Vase, 7", RO
blue $200.00
orchid $185.00
green $175.00
2369 Vase, 9", RO
blue $265.00
orchid $250.00
green $250.00
2292 Vase, 8"
blue $200.00
orchid $185.00
green $185.00
2375 Whip Cream, handled
green $56.00

Grape, Decoration 517

1939 – 1947
Tableware I, 329

4116 Bubble Ball, 4" $46.00
4116 Bubble Ball, 5" $50.00
4116 Bubble Ball, 6" $55.00
4116 Bubble Ball, 7" $64.00

Grape Leaf, 2513

1935 – 1943
Tableware I, 108

Almond, individual
crystal $15.00
regal blue $54.00
burgundy $54.00
empire green $54.00
Jar, candy and cover,
crystal $48.00
Mayonnaise, plate, ladle,
crystal $65.00
Mint, handled,
crystal $20.00
Plate, 7",
crystal $20.00
Preserve, 5",
crystal $22.00
Relish, 2-part,
crystal $24.00
Relish, 3-part,
crystal $28.00

Grape Stem, Decoration 61, 62, 63, 64

1926
Stemware, 32

870 Goblet
Decoration 62, white and yellow gold on crystal $45.00
Decoration 63, yellow gold on green $75.00
870 Saucer Champagne
Decoration 62, white and yellow gold

on crystal.........................$40.00
Decoration 63,
yellow gold on green......$60.00
870 Fruit
Decoration 62,
white and yellow gold
on crystal.........................$35.00
Decoration 63,
yellow gold on green......$45.00
870 Parfait
Decoration 62,
white and yellow gold
on crystal.........................$40.00
Decoration 63,
yellow gold on green......$60.00
870 Wine
Decoration 62,
white and yellow gold
on crystal.........................$40.00
Decoration 63,
yellow gold on green......$50.00
870 Cordial
Decoration 62,
white and yellow gold
on crystal.........................$65.00
Decoration 63,
yellow gold on green........$85.00
5084 Tumbler, 12 oz., footed
Decoration 62,
white and yellow gold
on crystal.........................$35.00
Decoration 63,
yellow gold on green......$45.00
5084 Tumbler, 9 oz., footed
Decoration 62,
white and yellow gold
on crystal.........................$30.00
Decoration 63,
yellow gold on green......$40.00
5084 Tumbler, 5 oz., footed
Decoration 62,
white and yellow gold
on crystal.........................$30.00
Decoration 63,
yellow gold on green......$40.00
5084 Tumbler, 2½ oz., footed
Decoration 62,
white and yellow gold
on crystal.........................$35.00
Decoration 63,
yellow gold on green......$45.00

Tableware I, 325

4095 Nappy, 5", footed
Decoration 61,
white gold on crystal......$35.00
Decoration 62,
white and yellow gold
on crystal.........................$45.00
Decoration 63,
yellow gold on green......$45.00
2384 Comport, 7",
Decoration 61,
white gold on crystal....$150.00
Decoration 62,
white and yellow gold
on crystal.......................$150.00
Decoration 63,
yellow gold on green....$225.00
Decoration 64,
amber, blue, or ebony..$150.00
2384 Candlestick, 9", pair
Decoration 61,
white gold on crystal....$225.00
Decoration 62,
white and yellow gold
on crystal.......................$225.00
Decoration 63,
yellow gold on green....$450.00
Decoration 64,
amber, blue, or ebony..$225.00
5084 Jug, footed
Decoration 61,
white gold on crystal....$195.00
Decoration 62,
white and yellow gold
on crystal.......................$195.00
Decoration 63,
yellow gold on green....$375.00

Greek, Etching 45

Pre-1900 – 1932

Stemware, 35, 67

880 Goblet, 11 oz. $8.00
880 Goblet, 10 oz. $8.00
880 Goblet, 9 oz. $7.00
880 Goblet, 8 oz. $7.00
880 Saucer Champagne,
7 oz...$8.00
880 Saucer Champagne,
5½ oz. $7.00
880 Sherbet $7.00
880 Cocktail, 3½ oz. $7.00
880 Cocktail, 3 oz...........................$7.00
880 Claret, 6½ oz. $12.00
880 Claret, 4½ oz. $8.00
880 Rhine Wine................................$9.00
880 Wine, 3½ oz. $8.00
880 Wine, 2¾ oz. $8.00
880 Sherry $7.00
880 Crème de Menthe $8.00
880 Brandy, pousse-café,
1 oz.......................................$15.00
880 Brandy, pousse-café,
¾ oz. $15.00
880 Cordial, 1 oz. $15.00
880 Cordial, ¾ oz. $15.00
880 Champagne,
hollow stem...........................$8.00
880 Champagne, tall.......................$8.00
880 Grapefruit and Liner,
tall $22.00
880 Grapefruit and Liner,
short.....................................$20.00
880 Hot Whiskey $7.00
880 Ale, tall.......................................$8.00
5097 Goblet
amber/green.........................$38.00
rose $48.00
5097 Sherbet, high
amber/green.........................$35.00
rose $45.00
5097 Sherbet, low
amber/green.........................$28.00
rose $32.00
5097 Parfait
amber/green.........................$38.00
rose $48.00
5097 Cocktail
amber/green.........................$30.00
rose $40.00
5097 Claret
amber/green.........................$40.00
rose $54.00
5097 Wine
amber/green.........................$40.00
rose $50.00
5097 Cordial
amber/green.........................$55.00
rose $60.00
5000 Oyster Cocktail
amber/green.........................$25.00
rose $30.00
5000 Tumbler, 12 oz., footed
amber/green.........................$38.00
rose $48.00
5000 Tumbler, 9 oz., footed
amber/green.........................$35.00
rose $45.00
5000 Tumbler, 5 oz., footed
amber/green.........................$28.00
rose $32.00
5000 Tumbler, 2½ oz., footed
amber/green.........................$38.00
rose $48.00
822 Parfait $18.00
945 Grapefruit and 945½"
Liner $25.00
945½ Grapefruit and Liner $30.00
701 Tumbler.........................$5.00 – 8.00
820 Tumbler.........................$5.00 – 8.00
833 Tumbler.........................$5.00 – 8.00
887 Tumbler.........................$5.00 – 8.00
889 Tumbler.........................$5.00 – 8.00
4011 Tumbler.........................$5.00 – 8.00

Tableware I, 120

880 Bonbon, 4½" $20.00
863 Almond $20.00
803 Comport, 5"............................$15.00
481 Custard $6.00
300 Decanter.................................$50.00
303/7 Jug...$60.00
318/7 Jug...$65.00
1236/6
Jug...$65.00
5000 Jug
rose, green, amber $225.00
300 Jug...$75.00
1227 Jug...$75.00
1236 Jug...$75.00
2018 Jug...$75.00
2018 Jug...$75.00
300½ Jug and Cover $85.00
317½ Jug and Cover $85.00
724 Tankard $95.00
803 Nappy, 5", footed $20.00
803 Nappy, 6", footed $20.00
2283 Plate, 5" $6.00
2283 Plate, 6" $6.00
2283 Plate, 7"
rose, green, amber $12.00
2283 Plate, 8"
rose, green, amber $14.00
300½ Oil, small $36.00
1478 Sugar and Cream...................$35.00
858 Sweetmeat.............................$15.00
880 Sweetmeat.............................$15.00
869 Bowl, finger and 2283 6" Plate,
RO
amber.....................................$24.00
rose/green $26.00
5097½ Grapefruit and 945½ Liner
amber.....................................$50.00
rose/green $58.00

Greek Key, Cutting 819

1942 – 1943

Stemware, 101

6032 Goblet $36.00
6032 Saucer Champagne $34.00
6032 Sherbet, low $28.00
6032 Cocktail $30.00
6032 Claret $38.00
6032 Wine $38.00
6032 Cordial $45.00
6032 Oyster Cocktail $25.00
6032 Ice Tea, footed $36.00
6032 Juice, footed $26.00

Tableware I, 306

766 Bowl, finger $12.00
2596 Bowl, 11", oblong, shallow $65.00
2596 Candlestick, 5", pair $65.00
6011 Jug $175.00
2337 Plate, 6" $6.00
2337 Plate, 7" $7.00
2337 Plate, 8" $8.00

Greenbriar, 6026

1940 – 1973

Stemware, 97

6026 Goblet $24.00
6026 Goblet, low $22.00
6026 Saucer Champagne $24.00
6026 Sherbet, low $18.00
6026 Cocktail $22.00
6026 Claret-Wine $28.00
6026 Cordial $32.00
6026 Oyster Cocktail $15.00
6026 Ice Tea, footed $24.00
6026 Juice, footed $18.00

Greenbriar, Crystal Print 14 Tumblers

1958 – 1962

Stemware, 155

4180 Tumbler, 12 oz., flat, mint green $12.00
4180 Juice, 7 oz., flat, mint green $12.00

Greenfield, Cutting 916

1967 – 1968

Stemware, 134

6110 Goblet $28.00
6110 Sherbet $25.00
6110 Wine $32.00
6110 Liqueur $40.00
6110 Ice Tea, footed $28.00
2337 Plate, 7" $10.00
2337 Plate, 8" $12.00

Greenfield, Cutting 935

1976 – 1982

Stemware, 54

2916 Goblet $20.00
2916 Champagne $18.00
2916 Wine $18.00
2916 Ice Tea, footed $20.00
2916 Cordial $18.00

Greyhounds, Carving 25

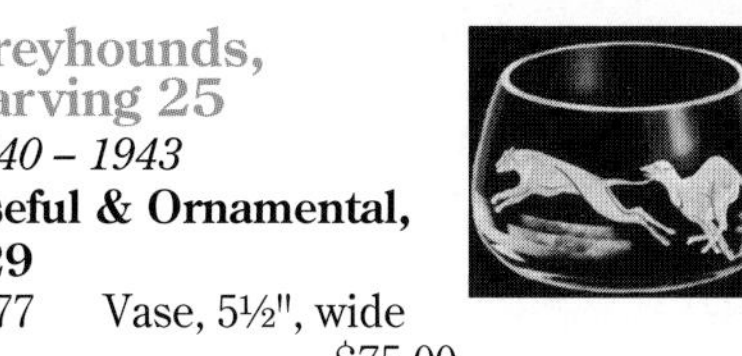

1940 – 1943

Useful & Ornamental, 129

2577 Vase, 5½", wide $75.00

Grille, Etching 236

1913 – 1924

Stemware, 37

882 Goblet, 11 oz. $10.00
882 Goblet, 10 oz. $10.00
882 Goblet, 9 oz. $9.00
882 Goblet, 8 oz. $9.00
882 Saucer Champagne, 7 oz. $10.00
882 Saucer Champagne, 5½ oz. $10.00
882 Sherbet $9.00
820 Tumbler $6.00 – 8.00
833 Tumbler $6.00 – 8.00
887 Tumbler $6.00 – 8.00
300 Tankard, cut flutes $50.00
880 Cocktail, 3½ oz. $9.00
880 Cocktail, 3 oz. $9.00
880 Claret, 6½ oz. $14.00
880 Claret, 4½ oz. $10.00
880 Rhine Wine $10.00
880 Wine, 3½ oz. $10.00
880 Wine, 2¾ oz. $10.00
880 Sherry $9.00
880 Crème de Menthe $9.00
880 Brandy, pousse-café $15.00
880 Cordial, 1 oz. $15.00
880 Cordial, ¾ oz. $15.00
880 Champagne, hollow stem $10.00
880 Champagne, tall $10.00
880 Grapefruit and Liner $22.00
880 Custard $7.00
880 Hot Whiskey $9.00
880 Ale, tall $10.00

Grosse Pointe, Carving 43

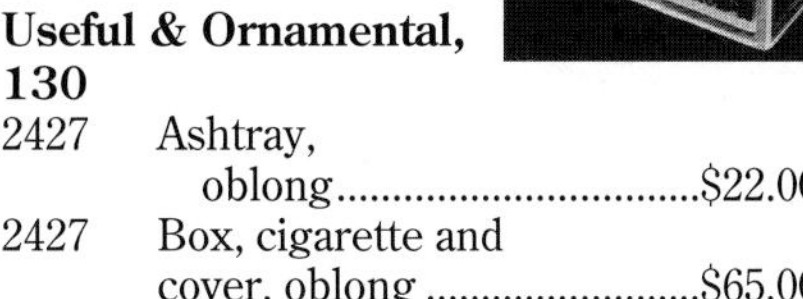

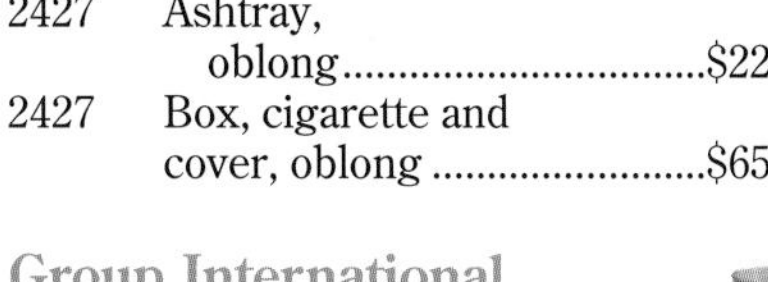

1940 – 1943

Useful & Ornamental, 130

2427 Ashtray, oblong $22.00
2427 Box, cigarette and cover, oblong $65.00

Group International

1967 – 1968

Fern green, Mayan blue, Tangerine

Tableware II, 258 – 259

2795/250 Bowl, 12" $75.00
2795/234 Bowl, 16" $120.00
2795/325 Candleholder, 8", pair $100.00
2795/330 Candleholder, 12", pair $150.00
2795/833 Candle Vase, 18" $145.00
2795/835 Candle Vase, 22" $165.00
2796/325 Candleholder, 8", pair $96.00
2796/384 Comport, 10" $95.00
2796/459 Candle Lamp, 19" $150.00

- H -

Halo, Decoration 689

1970 – 1971

Stemware, 139

6122 Goblet $22.00
6122 Sherbet $22.00
6122 Wine $22.00
6122 Ice Tea, footed $22.00

Hammered Silver, Decoration 66

1926

Amber and green

Stemware

870 Goblet $30.00
870 Saucer Champagne $30.00
870 Fruit $27.00
870 Parfait $34.00
870 Wine $34.00
870 Cocktail $27.00
870 Cordial $50.00
945½ Grapefruit and Liner $38.00
5084 Tumbler, 12 oz. $30.00
5084 Tumbler, 9 oz. $28.00
5084 Tumbler, 5 oz. $26.00
5084 Tumbler, 2½ oz. $26.00

Tableware I, 325

2350 Bouillon $15.00
869 Bowl, finger, and 2283 Plate $25.00
2350 Bowl, fruit $15.00
2350 Bowl, cereal $18.00
2350 Bowl, 9", oval, baker $28.00
2350 Bowl, 10½", oval, baker $37.00
2324 Bowl, 10" $38.00
2297 Bowl A, deep $45.00
2350 Butter and Cover $85.00
2324 Candlestick, 4", pair $46.00
2324 Candlestick, 9", pair $88.00
2350 Celery $34.00
2329 Centerpiece, 11" $85.00
2327 Comport, 7" $47.00
2350 Cream Soup $20.00
2350 Cup and Saucer $18.00
2350½ Cup, footed $12.00
5084 Jug, footed $175.00
2315 Mayonnaise $22.00
2350 Pickle $14.00
2350 Plate, 6" $6.00
2350 Plate, 7" $7.00
2350 Plate, 8" $9.00
2350 Plate, 7", soup $9.00
2350 Plate, 9" $18.00
2350 Plate, 10" $22.00
2350 Plate, 15", round $45.00
2350 Platter, 10½" $27.00
2350 Platter, 12" $30.00
2350 Platter, 15" $45.00
2350 Sugar and Cover $30.00
2350 Sugar and Cream $47.00
2287 Tray, handled, lunch $45.00

Hapsburg, 2750 (see Crown Collection)

Harvest, HA01, see 6097

1979 – 1982

Stemware, 122

HA01 Goblet, rust bowl, RO...........$26.00
HA01 Sherbet, rust bowl, RO.....................................$24.00
HA01 Claret, rust bowl, RO............$26.00
HA01 Magnum, rust bowl, RO $35.00
HA01 Ice Tea, footed, rust bowl, RO.....................................$26.00

Hawaiian, 2737

1961 – 1963

Tableware II, 96-97

2737 106 Appetizer Set: cracker plate and solid amber sauce dish ...$110.00
2737 126 Basket, 9" $54.00
2737 179 Bowl, 8", ruffled $58.00
2737 208 Bowl, 8", deep $67.00
2737 415 Bowl, 8", flower float $54.00
2737 188 Bowl, 9", handled $65.00
2737 239 Bowl, 11½", shallow $87.00
2737 266 Bowl, 15", oval $85.00
2737 500 Candy, 8", handled $56.00
2737 369 Cheese and Cracker, cracker plate and wooden cheese block.................................$85.00
2737 567 Plate, 14", torte, same as cracker...............................$75.00
2737 394 Shrimp and Dip, 2-piece: shrimp bowl and solid amber footed dip.....................................$125.00
2737 767 Vase, 6¾", ruffled $48.00
2737 807 Vase, 8⅞", pitcher $75.00

Hawthorn, Cutting 790

1939 – 1943

Stemware, 96

6025 Goblet $30.00
6025 Sherbet.................................$28.00
6025 Cocktail $28.00
6025 Claret-Wine $35.00
6025 Cordial..................................$45.00
6025 Oyster Cocktail......................$22.00
6025 Ice Tea, footed $30.00
6025 Juice, footed $24.00

Tableware I, 302

1769 Bowl, finger...........................$15.00
6023 Bowl, footed $65.00
2324 Candlestick, 6", pair $45.00
6011 Jug...$195.00
2337 Plate, 6" $7.00
2337 Plate, 7" $8.00
2337 Plate, 8" $10.00

Heather, Etching 343

1949 – 1971

Stemware, 104

6037 Goblet.............$36.00
6037 Goblet, low.......$30.00
6037 Sherbet, high......$32.00
6037 Sherbet, low...........$25.00
6037 Parfait $35.00
6037 Cocktail $30.00
6037 Claret-Wine $40.00
6037 Cordial....................................$45.00
6037 Oyster Cocktail.......................$24.00
6037 Ice Tea, footed $36.00
6037 Juice, footed $27.00

Tableware II, 146-147

2630 Basket, reed handle $120.00
2630 Bonbon, 3-toed......................$38.00
2630 Bowl, 4½", handled, nappy...$22.00
2630 Bowl, fruit..............................$22.00
2630 Bowl, cereal............................$26.00
2630 Bowl, 8", flared $36.00
2630 Bowl, 8½", salad $38.00
2630 Bowl, snack $28.00
2630 Bowl, 9", lily pond.................$47.00
2630 Bowl, oval, vegetable $45.00
2630 Bowl, oval, utility $64.00
2630 Bowl, handled, serving $52.00
2630 Bowl, 10¾", footed, flared...................................$65.00
2630 Bowl, 11", footed, rolled edge $68.00
2630 Bowl, 11¼", lily pond $58.00
2630 Bowl, 12", flared $68.00
2630 Butter, oblong and cover......$57.00
2630 Candlestick, 4½", single, pair.......................................$56.00
2630 Candlestick, duo, pair $75.00
2630 Candlestick, trindle, pair $125.00
2630 Jar, candy and cover.............$85.00
2630 Cheese and Cracker..............$85.00
2630 Comport $46.00
2630 Condiment Set $157.00
2630 Cup and Saucer......................$28.00
2630 Ice Bucket, metal handle....$125.00
2630 Jug, ice lip............................$225.00
2630 Jug...$165.00
2630 Mayonnaise, plate, ladle $65.00
2630 Mayonnaise, 2-part, 2 spoons.............................$65.00
2630 Mustard, cover, spoon $58.00
2630 Oil, 5 oz., DS $62.00
2630 Pickle, 8¾" $24.00
2630 Pitcher, pint, cereal $70.00
2630 Plate, 6" $16.00
2630 Plate, 7" $18.00
2630 Plate, 8" $22.00
2630 Plate, 9" $30.00
2630 Plate, 10½" $52.00
2630 Plate, crescent, salad............$55.00
2630 Plate, party and cup..............$40.00
2630 Plate, handled, cake $65.00
2630 Plate, 14", torte $75.00
2630 Plate, 16", torte $75.00
2630 Platter, 12", oval.....................$68.00
2630 Preserve and Cover, footed.................................$65.00
2630 Relish, 2-part $30.00
2630 Relish, 3-part $48.00
2630 Salad Set, 10½", 3-piece $125.00
2630 Salver, cake $110.00
2630 Shaker, chrome top B, pair $65.00
2630 Sugar and Cream...................$58.00
2630 Sugar and Cream, individual............................$57.00
2630 Sugar, cream, tray $20.00
2630 Tid Bit, 3-toed $36.00
2630 Tid Bit, 3-piece set.................$68.00
2630 Tray, 10½", snack...................$54.00
2630 Tray, handled, muffin............$65.00
2630 Tray, handled, utility.............$65.00
2630 Tray, handled, lunch $68.00
2630 Tricorne, 3-toed $38.00
4121 Vase, 5", blown $68.00
Vase, 6", bud $45.00
6021 Vase, 6", footed, bud, blown...$58.00
4143 Vase, 6", footed, blown..........$67.00
Vase, 7½", handled...............$85.00
2660 Vase, 8", flip, blown $92.00
5092 Vase, 8", footed, blown..........$95.00
Vase, 8½", oval.......................$87.00
2470 Vase, 10", footed, blown......$125.00

Heirloom

1959 – 1970

Tableware II, 260 – 270

2720 Basket
- yellow.....$75.00
- blue $65.00
- pink $65.00
- green...$65.00
- opal...$65.00
- bittersweet $60.00

2729 Bonbon
- yellow...$68.00
- blue $55.00
- pink $55.00
- green...$55.00
- opal...$50.00
- bittersweet $48.00
- ruby...$54.00

2720 Bowl, 5⅜", square, florette
- yellow...$57.00
- blue $43.00
- pink $43.00
- green...$43.00
- opal...$38.00
- bittersweet $36.00

2727 Bowl, 6", hanky
- yellow...$54.00
- blue $42.00
- pink $42.00
- green...$42.00
- opal...$38.00
- bittersweet $40.00
- ruby...$46.00

2727 Bowl, 6", square
- yellow...$58.00
- blue $50.00
- pink $50.00
- green...$50.00
- opal...$47.00
- bittersweet $45.00

2720 Bowl, 6½", crinkled
- yellow...$60.00
- blue $52.00
- pink $52.00
- green...$52.00
- opal...$47.00
- bittersweet $44.00

2183 Bowl, 7"
- yellow...$60.00
- blue $52.00
- pink $52.00
- green...$50.00
- opal...$47.00
- bittersweet $44.00
- ruby...$47.00

2720 Bowl, 8½", star
- yellow...$68.00
- blue $62.00
- pink $62.00
- green...$60.00
- opal...$58.00
- bittersweet $60.00

2727 Bowl, 9", square
- yellow...$89.00
- blue $75.00
- pink $75.00

green $75.00
opal $68.00
bittersweet $62.00

1515 Bowl, 10"
yellow $88.00
blue $74.00
pink $74.00
green $74.00
opal $70.00
bittersweet $68.00

2183 Bowl, 10", float
yellow $68.00
blue $62.00
pink $62.00
green $62.00
opal $57.00
bittersweet $57.00

2729 Bowl, 10", oval
yellow $70.00
blue $65.00
pink $65.00
green $65.00
opal $60.00
bittersweet $55.00
ruby $62.00

2727 Bowl, 11", shallow
yellow $125.00
blue $85.00
pink $85.00
green $80.00
opal $74.00
bittersweet $70.00

2727 Bowl, 11", crimped
yellow $135.00
blue $95.00
pink $95.00
green $90.00
opal $80.00
bittersweet $85.00
ruby $78.00

1515 Bowl, 15", oblong
yellow $175.00
blue $125.00
pink $125.00
green $125.00
opal $98.00
bittersweet $95.00

2183 Candle, flora, pair
yellow $185.00
blue $167.00
pink $167.00
green $165.00
opal $150.00
bittersweet $150.00

2726 Candleholder, pair
yellow $125.00
blue $95.00
pink $95.00
green $95.00
opal $85.00
bittersweet $85.00
ruby $85.00

2730 Candle, 6", pair
yellow $225.00
blue $195.00
pink $195.00
green $195.00
opal $175.00
bittersweet $175.00

1515 Centerpiece, 16", oval
yellow $225.00
blue $195.00
pink $195.00
green $195.00
opal $175.00
bittersweet $175.00

2730 Epergne, 12", small
yellow $275.00
blue $225.00
pink $225.00
green $225.00
opal $200.00
bittersweet $175.00

1515 Epergne, 16", large
yellow $400.00
blue $350.00
pink $350.00
green $350.00
opal $300.00
bittersweet $225.00

2727 Plate, 8"
yellow $50.00
blue $47.00
pink $47.00
green $47.00
opal $40.00
bittersweet $40.00

2727 Plate, 11"
yellow $75.00
blue $65.00
pink $65.00
green $65.00
opal $60.00
bittersweet $50.00

2570 Plate, 17"
yellow $125.00
blue $100.00
pink $100.00
green $100.00
opal $85.00
bittersweet $75.00

2728 Vase, 4½", handled
yellow $135.00
blue $135.00
pink $135.00
green $135.00
opal $125.00
bittersweet $95.00

1229 Vase, 6", bud
yellow $65.00
blue $50.00
pink $50.00
green $50.00
opal $42.00
bittersweet $50.00
ruby $42.00

2728 Vase, 9", pitcher
yellow $200.00
blue $165.00
pink $165.00
green $165.00
opal $125.00
bittersweet $135.00
ruby $125.00

1515 Vase, 10", candle, pair
yellow $300.00
blue $250.00
pink $250.00
green $250.00
opal $200.00
bittersweet $200.00

1515 Vase, 11"
yellow $67.00
blue $58.00
pink $58.00
green $58.00
opal $50.00
bittersweet $58.00
ruby $50.00

2728 Vase, 11", winged
yellow $365.00
blue $325.00
pink $325.00
green $325.00
opal $300.00
bittersweet $275.00

1002 Vase, 18"
yellow $600.00/market
blue $550.00/market
pink $550.00/market
green $550.00/market
opal $500.00/market

1002 Vase, 20"
yellow $400.00
blue $350.00
pink $350.00
green $350.00
opal $275.00
bittersweet $225.00

1002 Vase, 24"
yellow $600.00/market
blue $550.00/market
pink $550.00/market
green $550.00/market
opal $500.00/market

Heirloom, Cutting 751

1935 – 1938

Tableware I, 287 – 288

2394 Bowl, 12" $40.00
2447 Candlestick, duo, pair $75.00
2527 Candelabra, 2-light, UDP; pair $150.00
2440 Mayonnaise, 2-part $28.00
2440 Plate, 13", torte $52.00
2364 Plate, 16" $56.00
2440 Relish, 2-part $24.00
2440 Relish, 3-part $28.00
2514 Relish, 5-part $67.00
2440 Dish, sauce, oval $28.00
2440 Tray, oval $24.00
2470 Vase, 10" $95.00

Heirloom, Etching 36

1976 – 1982

Stemware, 143

6128 Goblet $26.00
6128 Champagne $24.00
6128 Wine $26.00
6128 Ice Tea, footed $26.00

Henry Ford Museum

(see also Argus, Exeter, Panelled Diamond Point)

1965 – 1977

Tableware II, 271-275

2776/327
Candlestick, 9", sandwich, pair
crystal $95.00
olive green $95.00
copper blue $150.00

2777/327
Candlestick, 9", Rebecca, pair
crystal mist $225.00
olive green mist $250.00

copper blue mist.............$300.00

2777/388
Comport, 12¾", Rebecca, Ribbon
crystal mist.......................$225.00
olive green mist..............$250.00
copper blue mist.............$395.00

2778/347
Candy and Cover, 8", 4-petal
crystal $40.00
olive green..........................$50.00
copper blue $65.00

2779/219
Bowl, 10½", footed, Pressed Block
crystal $78.00
olive green........................$100.00
copper blue $125.00

2780/388
Comport, 8", Dolphin
crystal mist.......................$150.00
olive green mist..............$165.00
copper blue mist.............$200.00

2786/803
Vase, 9", Sandwich, Draped
crystal $75.00
olive green..........................$85.00
copper blue $95.00

2787/387
Comport, 6½", Ribbon and cover
crystal $64.00
olive green..........................$64.00
copper blue $125.00

2788/389
Comport, Plume
crystal $64.00
olive green..........................$68.00
copper blue $90.00

2790/818
Vase, 10", footed, Tulip
crystal $78.00
olive green..........................$85.00
copper blue $120.00

2793/105
Salt, 3¼", Strawberry Diamond
crystal $22.00
olive green..........................$27.00
copper blue $30.00

Heraldry, Cutting 743

1935 – 1969

Stemware, 84

6012 Goblet $32.00
6012 Sherbet, high $28.00
6012 Sherbet, low $22.00
6012 Cocktail $25.00
6012 Claret $35.00
6012 Rhine Wine.............................$32.00
6012 Wine.......................................$35.00
6012 Sherry $32.00
6012 Creme de Menthe $22.00
6012 Brandy $35.00
6012 Cordial $40.00
6012 Oyster Cocktail......................$18.00
6012 Ice Tea, footed $32.00
6012 Tumbler, 10 oz., footed................................$22.00
6012 Juice, footed $22.00
701 Tumbler, 12 oz., sham $18.00
701 Tumbler, 10 oz. $15.00
1185 Old Fashioned Cocktail, 7 oz. $15.00

Tableware I, 285; II, 164 – 166

1769 Bowl, finger...........................$14.00
2400 Comport, 6"............................$25.00
6011 Jug...$185.00
6011 Decanter..............................$150.00
4185 Bowl, dessert/finger $22.00
2364 Bowl, 9", salad.......................$38.00
2364 Bowl, 12", flared $45.00
2364 Bowl, 12", lily pond...............$45.00
2324 Candlestick, 4", pair $46.00
6023 Candlestick, duo, pair $64.00
2666 Cup and 2350 Saucer............$22.00
2364 Mayonnaise, plate, ladle $48.00
2666 Pitcher, pint...........................$40.00
2666 Pitcher, quart $75.00
2666 Pitcher, 3-pint.........................$85.00
2364 Plate, 11", sandwich $28.00
2364 Plate, 14", torte $35.00
2364 Relish, 2-part $28.00
2364 Relish, 3-part $34.00
3264 Shaker, chrome top C, pair $55.00
2666 Sugar and Cream..................$45.00
2666 Sugar and Cream, individual...........................$35.00
2666 Tray, sugar and cream $14.00
2364 Tray, handled, lunch $38.00

Heritage, Cutting 849

1956 – 1957

Stemware, 112

6065 Goblet $35.00
6065 Sherbet $32.00
6065 Cocktail/Wine/ Seafood $34.00
6065 Cordial $40.00
6065 Ice Tea, footed $35.00
6065 Juice, footed $32.00
2337 Plate, 7" $10.00
2337 Plate, 8" $12.00

Heritage, 2887

1979 – 1982

Stemware, 53

2887 Goblet....................$20.00
2887 Sherbet..................$16.00
2887 Wine.......................$20.00
2887 Ice Tea, footed......$20.00
2887 Double Old Fashioned $18.00
2887 Highball.................................$20.00

Tableware II, 279, 291 – 294, 301

783 Tray...$22.00
973 Ice Bucket $35.00

HE04/344
Box, candy and cover, gold knob $18.00

HE03/578
Server, two-tiered, chrome.....$24.00

HE03/583
Tidbit, gold handle $20.00

HE03/313
Candleholder, pair................$16.00

HE03/380
Coaster, utility, set of four $15.00

HE03/382
Coaster, executive, set of four $18.00

HE03/894
Bowl, 5" $7.00

HE03/887
Plate, 8" $7.00

HE03/493
Napkin Rings $20.00

HE03/194
Bowl, large $22.00

HE03/639
Cake Stand or Chip and Dip ..$35.00

HE03/554
Platter, 10½" $22.00

HE03/738
Condiment Set, gold.............$18.00

HE03/742
Sauce Set, gold $18.00

HE03/556
Relish, divided $22.00

Heritage, 1871 Collection

1972 – 1973

Tableware II, 257

521 Bowl, 8⅜"................$20.00
506 Bowl, 5", fruit............$15.00
354 Box, candy and cover $22.00
899 Old Fashioned, double, boxed set of 4.....................$28.00
871 Highball, boxed set of 4........$32.00
454 Jug, quart...............................$45.00
869 Plate, 7", boxed set of 4.........$28.00
550 Plate, 8" $8.00
682 Sugar/Cover and Cream $25.00
583 Tidbit Set, 3-piece.................$30.00
567 Plate, torte $30.00

Hermitage, 2449

1932 – 1944

Stemware, 46

2449 Goblet
crystal................$24.00
green..................$30.00
amber................$24.00
azure..................$30.00
topaz/gold tint..................$30.00
wisteria $45.00

2449 Sherbet, high
crystal $20.00
green..................................$26.00
amber.................................$20.00
azure $26.00
topaz/gold tint..................$26.00
wisteria $40.00

2449 Sherbet, low
crystal $18.00
green..................................$20.00
amber.................................$18.00
azure $20.00
topaz/gold tint..................$20.00
wisteria $38.00

2449 Fruit Cocktail
crystal $16.00
green..................................$20.00
amber.................................$16.00
azure $20.00
topaz/gold tint..................$20.00
wisteria $35.00

2449 Cocktail
crystal $18.00
green..................................$18.00
amber.................................$18.00
azure $18.00
topaz/gold tint..................$18.00
wisteria $30.00

2449 Old Fashioned Cocktail
crystal $20.00

green $22.00
amber $20.00
azure $22.00
topaz/gold tint $22.00
wisteria $30.00

2449 Claret
crystal $25.00
green $34.00
amber $25.00
azure $34.00
topaz/gold tint $34.00

2449 Ice Tea, footed
crystal $24.00
green $30.00
amber $24.00
azure $30.00
topaz/gold tint $30.00
wisteria $45.00

2449 Tumbler, table, 9 oz., footed
crystal $20.00
green $20.00
amber $20.00
azure $20.00
topaz/gold tint $20.00
wisteria $40.00

2449 Juice, footed
crystal $16.00
green $20.00
amber $16.00
azure $20.00
topaz/gold tint $20.00
wisteria $35.00

2449 Whiskey, 2 oz., footed
crystal $15.00
green $20.00
amber $15.00
azure $20.00
topaz/gold tint $20.00

2449 Tumbler, 13 oz.
crystal $28.00
green $34.00
amber $28.00
azure $34.00
topaz/gold tint $34.00
wisteria $55.00

2449 Tumbler, 9 oz.
crystal $22.00
green $20.00
amber $22.00
azure $20.00
topaz/gold tint $20.00
wisteria $45.00

2449 Tumbler, 5 oz.
crystal $18.00
green $22.00
amber $18.00
azure $22.00
topaz/gold tint $22.00
wisteria $40.00

2449 Tumbler, 2 oz.
crystal $14.00
green $22.00
amber $14.00
azure $22.00
topaz/gold tint $22.00
wisteria $50.00

2449 Beer Mug, 12 oz. $48.00
2449 Beer Mug, 9 oz. $40.00

Tableware I, 78 – 82

2449 Ashtray
crystal $10.00
green $14.00
amber $12.00
azure $14.00
topaz/gold tint $14.00
ebony $12.00

2449 Ashtray Set
crystal $95.00
green $125.00
amber $110.00
azure $125.00
topaz/gold tint $115.00

2449 Bottle, bar, and stopper
crystal $165.00

2449 Bowl, finger
crystal $22.00
green $28.00
amber $24.00
azure $30.00
topaz/gold tint $25.00
wisteria $40.00

2449 Bowl, 5"
crystal $25.00
green $30.00
amber $30.00
topaz $30.00

2449½ Bowl, 5", fruit
crystal $22.00
green $25.00
amber $24.00
azure $25.00
topaz/gold tint $25.00
wisteria $40.00

2449½ Bowl, 6", cereal
crystal $24.00
green $30.00
amber $28.00
azure $30.00
topaz/gold tint $28.00
wisteria $45.00

2449½ Bowl, 6½", coup salad
crystal $24.00
green $30.00
amber $28.00
azure $32.00
topaz/gold tint $30.00
wisteria $50.00

2449½ Bowl, 7", nappy
crystal $24.00
amber $28.00
azure $38.00
topaz/gold tint $32.00

2449½ Bowl, 7", soup
crystal $26.00
amber $28.00
azure $38.00
topaz/gold tint $34.00

2449½ Bowl, 7½", coup salad
crystal $25.00
green $32.00
amber $30.00
azure $36.00
topaz/gold tint $32.00
wisteria $52.00

2449 Bowl, 8", deep, footed
crystal $45.00
green $65.00
amber $54.00
azure $75.00
topaz $65.00
wisteria $125.00

2449 Bowl, 10", flared
crystal $38.00
green $58.00
amber $54.00
topaz $58.00

2449 Bowl, 10", shallow
crystal $38.00
green $58.00
amber $45.00
azure $67.00
topaz $58.00
wisteria $95.00

2449 Candlestick, 6", pair
crystal $64.00
green $88.00
amber $80.00
azure $145.00
topaz $125.00
wisteria $200.00

2449 Celery, 11"
crystal $28.00
green $40.00
amber $32.00
azure $47.00
topaz/gold tint $42.00
wisteria $84.00

2449 Coaster
crystal $10.00
green $12.00
amber $12.00
azure $15.00
topaz/gold tint $12.00
wisteria $24.00

2449 Cocktail Shaker, similar to Bar Bottle
green $135.00
azure $145.00

2449 Comport, 6"
crystal $27.00
green $42.00
amber $38.00
azure $45.00
topaz/gold tint $42.00
wisteria $87.00

2449 Cup and Saucer
crystal $24.00
green $32.00
amber $30.00
azure $34.00
topaz/gold tint $32.00
wisteria $65.00

2449 Decanter and Stopper
crystal $125.00
green $150.00
amber $135.00
azure $165.00
topaz/gold tint $150.00
wisteria $275.00

2449 Grapefruit
crystal $30.00
green $40.00
amber $35.00
topaz $40.00

2449 Grapefruit Liner
crystal $20.00

2449 Dish, ice and plate
crystal $38.00
green $48.00
amber $46.00
azure $50.00
topaz/gold tint $48.00
wisteria $75.00

2451 Liner, blown, tomato juice, crab meat, fruit cocktail
crystal $20.00
green $25.00
amber $25.00
azure $28.00
topaz/gold tint $28.00
wisteria $38.00

2479 Liner, pressed (Tomato Juice, Crab Meat, Fruit Cocktail)
crystal $18.00

2449 Ice Tub
crystal $34.00
green $40.00
amber $38.00
azure $45.00
topaz $40.00
wisteria $95.00

2449 Mayonnaise and Plate
crystal $32.00
green $45.00
amber $40.00
topaz/gold tint $45.00

2449 Ladle/Mayonnaise (2375)
crystal $20.00

2449 Mustard and Cover
crystal $42.00
green $48.00
amber $45.00
topaz/gold tint $48.00

2449 Mustard Spoon
crystal $25.00

2449 Oil, 3 oz.
crystal $45.00
green $62.00
amber $58.00
topaz/gold tint $62.00

2449 Pickle, 8"
crystal $26.00
green $32.00
amber $30.00
azure $34.00
topaz, ...$32.00
wisteria $62.00

2449 Pitcher, pint, cereal
crystal $42.00
green $48.00
amber $45.00
azure $50.00
topaz/gold tint $45.00
wisteria $90.00

2449 Pitcher, Hall Boy Jug
crystal $95.00
green $110.00
amber $100.00
topaz $110.00
wisteria $225.00

2449 Pitcher, quart, ice jug
crystal $85.00
green $125.00
amber $100.00
topaz $125.00
wisteria $250.00

2449 Pitcher, 3-pint, jug
crystal $95.00
green $145.00
amber $125.00
azure $145.00
topaz $150.00
wisteria $300.00

2449½ Plate, 6"
crystal $7.00
green $12.00
amber $10.00
azure $12.00
topaz/gold tint $12.00
wisteria $28.00

2449½ Plate, 7"
crystal $12.00
green $15.00
amber $14.00
azure $16.00
topaz/gold tint $15.00
wisteria $36.00

2449½ Plate, 8"
crystal $12.00
green $16.00
amber $14.00
azure $16.00
topaz/gold tint $15.00
wisteria $38.00

2449 Plate, 8", ground bottom
crystal $13.00
green $17.00
amber $15.00
azure $17.00
topaz $15.00
wisteria $40.00

2449½ Plate, 9"
crystal $20.00
green $28.00
amber $25.00
azure $28.00
topaz/gold tint $27.00
wisteria $66.00

2449 Plate, crescent salad, star bottom
crystal $26.00
green $35.00
amber $32.00
azure $38.00
topaz $35.00
wisteria $65.00

2449½ Plate, crescent salad, plain bottom
crystal $22.00

2449 Plate, 12", sandwich
crystal $35.00
green $42.00
amber $40.00
topaz $42.00

2449 Relish, 2-part
crystal $24.00
green $30.00
amber $28.00
topaz/gold tint $30.00
wisteria $57.00

2449 Relish, 3-part
crystal $26.00
green $34.00
amber $30.00
topaz $34.00
wisteria $64.00

2449 Salt, individual
crystal $12.00
green $18.00
amber $16.00
topaz $18.00

2449 Salver, 11"
crystal $45.00
green $67.00
amber $58.00
azure $75.00
topaz $67.00
wisteria $150.00

2449 Shaker, priced individually
crystal $20.00
green $38.00
amber $35.00
azure $42.00
topaz/gold tint $38.00
wisteria $65.50

2449 Sugar and Cream
crystal $30.00
green $40.00
amber $36.00
azure $48.00
topaz/gold tint $40.00
wisteria $125.00

2449 Tray, condiment
crystal $18.00
green $23.00
amber $23.00
topaz/gold tint $23.00

2449 Vase, 6"
crystal $38.00
green $56.00
amber $45.00
topaz/gold tint $45.00

These sets were offered in 1933. Price depends on the colors chosen.

*Set B – 18-piece Refreshment Set: 6 tumblers, 13 oz.; 6 tumblers, 2 oz. ; 6 old fashioneds, 6 oz., all colors
*Set C – Cocktail Set: cocktail shaker; 6 cocktails, 4 oz. all colors
*Set D – Bar Set: 1 bar bottle and stopper; 6 tumblers, 2 oz., crystal
*Set E – Old Fashioned Set: 6 old fashioned cocktails, 6 oz., all colors
*Set F – Tall Drink Set: 6 tumblers, 13 oz., all colors
*Set G – Decanter Set: decanter and stopper; 6 tumblers, 2 oz., all colors
*Set H – Demitasse Set: 6 after dinner cups and saucers, all colors except wisteria
*Set I – Inspiration Set: 6 cocktails, 4 oz., all colors
*Set J – Sugar and Cream Set, all colors

**Also offered as "Rainbow Assortment."*

Heron, Carving 31

1940 – 1943

Useful & Ornamental, 131

2591 Vase, 15" $350.00

Highlighted Blue Spray, Decoration 631

1953 – 1957

Tableware II, 198, 199

2513 Jar, candy and cover....$150.00
2519 Cologne and Stopper $150.00
2519 Puff and Cover $145.00

Holiday, 2643

1949 – 1958

Stemware, 151

2643 Highball, 12 oz. $12.00
2643 Double Old Fashioned, 12 oz. $12.00
2643 Scotch and Soda, 9 oz. $10.00
2643 Old Fashioned, 6 oz. $8.00
2643 Cocktail, 4 oz. $6.00
2643 Whiskey, 1½ oz. $4.00

Tableware II, 79

2643 Coaster $10.00
2643 Cocktail Mixer, 20 oz., handled $45.00
2643 Cocktail Mixer, 30 oz., handled $64.00
2643 Decanter and Stopper $70.00
2643 Bowl, ice $30.00

Holly, Cutting 815

1942 – 1980

Stemware, 100

6030 Goblet $36.00
6030 Goblet, low $34.00
6030 Saucer Champagne $34.00
6030 Sherbet, low $26.00
6030 Cocktail $34.00
6030 Claret-Wine $42.00
6030 Cordial $56.00
6030 Oyster Cocktail $22.00
6030 Ice Tea, footed $36.00
6030 Juice, footed $27.00

Tableware II, 169-173

2364 Ashtray, individual $20.00
1769 Bowl, dessert/finger $32.00
2364 Bowl, 5", fruit $20.00
2364 Bowl, 6", baked apple $25.00
2364 Bowl, 8", rimmed, soup $30.00
2364 Bowl, 9", salad $52.00
6023 Bowl, 9", footed $95.00
2364 Bowl, 10½", salad $65.00
2364 Bowl, 12", flared $60.00
2364 Bowl, 12", lily pond $55.00
2364 Bowl, 13", fruit $68.00
2324 Candlestick, 4", pair $45.00
2324 Candlestick, 6", pair $68.00
6023 Candlestick, duo, pair $65.00
2364 Celery, 11" $32.00
2364 Cheese and Cracker $68.00
2364 Cigarette $35.00
2364 Comport, 8" $65.00
6030 Comport, 5" $40.00
2350½ Cup and 2350 Saucer $28.00
6011 Jug $295.00
2364 Mayonnaise, plate, ladle $52.00
2364 Pickle, 8" $20.00
2666 Pitcher, quart $195.00
2337 Plate, 6" $12.00
2337 Plate, 7" $15.00
2337 Plate, 8" $18.00
2364 Plate, 11" $34.00
2374 Plate, 14" $54.00
2364 Plate, 16", torte $65.00
2364 Relish, 2-part $34.00
2364 Relish, 3-part $45.00
2364 Salad Set, 4-piece $125.00
2364 Shaker, FGT, pair $58.00
2364 Shaker, chrome top C, pair $47.00
2364 Shaker, large, chrome top B $65.00
2350½ Sugar and Cream $54.00
2666 Sugar and Cream, individual $48.00
2666 Tray, sugar and cream, no etching $15.00
2364 Tray, handled, lunch $57.00
2619½ Vase, 6", ground bottom $75.00
2619½ Vase, 7½", ground bottom $85.00
2619½ Vase, 9½", ground bottom $95.00

Holly and Ruby Giftware

1981 – 1982

Tableware II, 289-290

HO02/211
Bowl, 10" $150.00
HO02/315
Candlestick, 4½", pair $95.00
HO02/506
Nappy, 5" $47.00
HO02/567
Plate, 14", torte $150.00
HO02/549
Plate, 7" $42.00
HO02/584
Party Server, two metal spoons $67.00
CA15/312
Candleholder, bird $48.00
CO15/682
Sugar and Cream (Colony) $125.00
CO15/762
Vase, 6", footed, bud (Colony) $62.00

Hollyhock, Carving 16

1940 – 1943

Useful & Ornamental, 123

1895½ Vase, 10" $135.00
5100 Vase, 10" $150.00
4126½ Vase, 11" $165.00

Homespun, 4183 Tumblers

1959 – 1965

Stemware, 155

4183 Ice Tea/Highball, 15 oz.
gold $28.00
moss green $28.00
teal blue $28.00
4183 Water/Scotch and Soda, 11½ oz.
gold $28.00
moss green $28.00
teal blue $28.00
4183 Juice/Old Fashioned, 9 oz.
gold $28.00
moss green $28.00
teal blue $28.00

Horizon, 2650

1951 – 1954

Tableware II, 80-82

2650 Bowl, dessert/finger
cinnamon $12.00
spruce $12.00
2650 Bowl, fruit
cinnamon $12.00
spruce $12.00
2650 Bowl, cereal
cinnamon $14.00
spruce $14.00
2650 Bowl, handled, serving
cinnamon $20.00
spruce $20.00
2650 Bowl, 8½", salad
cinnamon $22.00
spruce $22.00
2650 Bowl, 10½", salad
cinnamon $25.00
spruce $25.00
2650 Coaster
cinnamon $10.00
spruce $10.00
2650 Cup and Saucer
cinnamon $18.00
spruce $18.00
2650 Mayonnaise, plate, ladle
cinnamon $34.00
spruce $34.00
2650 Nappy and Cover, 5"
cinnamon $20.00
spruce $20.00
2650 Plate, 7"
cinnamon $8.00
spruce $8.00
2650 Plate, 10", dinner
cinnamon $18.00
spruce $18.00
2650 Plate, 11", sandwich
cinnamon $20.00
spruce $20.00
2650 Plate, 14", torte
cinnamon $35.00
spruce $35.00
2650 Platter, 12", oval
cinnamon $34.00
spruce $34.00
2650 Relish, 3-part
cinnamon $30.00
spruce $30.00
2650 Salad Set, 4-piece, with 8½" bowl
cinnamon $48.00
spruce $48.00
2650 Salad Set, 4-piece, with 10½" bowl
cinnamon $57.00
spruce $57.00
2650 Server, 4-part
cinnamon $40.00
spruce $40.00
2650 Sugar and Cream
cinnamon $30.00
spruce $30.00

Horizon, 5650 Tumblers

1951 – 1958

Stemware, 156

5650 Ice Tea/Highball
crystal $10.00
cinnamon/spruce $15.00
5650 Water/Scotch and Soda
crystal $10.00
cinnamon/spruce $15.00
5650 Sherbet/Old Fashioned
crystal $10.00
cinnamon/spruce $15.00
5650 Juice/Cocktail
crystal $10.00
cinnamon/spruce $15.00
5650 Bowl, dessert/finger
crystal $10.00
cinnamon/spruce $15.00

Horse, Carving 35

1940 – 1943

Useful & Ornamental, 130

4148 Ashtray, 2½", individual $22.00
4148 Cigarette Holder $35.00

Hostess Serveware

1985 – 1986

Tableware II, 291-294

HO04/503
Party Server, 2 gold spoons $16.00
HO04/163
Comport, hostess, footed $14.00

HO04/344
Hostess Candy and Cover, gold knob $15.00
HO04/509
Server and Spoon, hostess ...$12.00
HO04/987
Servers, salad, spoon and fork, stainless steel set....$50.00
HO04/733
Server, pastry, stainless steel and gold $35.00
HO04/732
Knife, cake, stainless steel and gold $35.00
HO04/304
Flame Snuffer, 24K gold, metal....$50.00
HO04/292
Mini Box, hinged cover $45.00

Note: The following are included because they do not fit elsewhere.

EX01/874
Magnifying Glass, 24K gold $50.00
EX01/875
Letter Opener, 24K gold....$45.00

Humpty Dumpty, 4146 Flat Tumblers

Stemware

4146 Scotch and Soda, 9 oz. $8.00
4146 Cocktail, 4 oz. $7.00
4146 Cordial, 1 oz. $7.00

Hunt, Carving 34

1940 – 1943

Useful & Ornamental, 124

4146 Cordial, 1 oz. $30.00
4146 Cocktail, 4 oz. $30.00
4146 Scotch and Soda, 9 oz. $35.00
4146 Above Set, nested $56.00

- I -

2378 Ice Buckets, Sugar Pails, Whip Cream Pails

1927 – 1930

Useful & Ornamental, 151

2378 Pail, sugar
NP handle
crystal $34.00
amber, ...$42.00
green $48.00
rose $48.00
azure $54.00
orchid $65.00
topaz $48.00

2378 Pail, sugar, SO
crystal $35.00
amber, ...$42.00
green $48.00
rose $52.00
azure $55.00
orchid $65.00

2378 Pail, whip cream
crystal $34.00
amber $42.00
green $48.00
rose $48.00
azure $54.00
orchid $65.00
topaz $48.00

2378 Pail, whip cream, SO
crystal $35.00
amber, ...$42.00
green $48.00
rose $52.00
azure $54.00
orchid $65.00

2378 Ice Bucket
crystal $45.00
amber, ...$48.00
green $54.00
rose $54.00
azure $56.00
orchid $75.00
blue $85.00

2378 Ice Bucket, SO
amber, ...$58.00
green $65.00
rose $70.00
azure $78.00

2451 Ice Dishes and Liners

1931 – 1971

Useful & Ornamental, 152

2451 Ice Dish
crystal $15.00
amber $20.00
green $23.00
rose $25.00
azure $27.00
topaz/gold tint $25.00
regal blue $45.00

2479 Liners, pressed, any size
crystal $18.00

2451 Liners, blown, any size
crystal $25.00
amber $30.00
green $34.00
rose $34.00
azure $38.00
topaz/gold tint $34.00
wisteria $45.00

Icicle, Carving 59

1982

Stemware, 145

6147 Goblet
crystal $25.00
blue $25.00
yellow $25.00

6147 Champagne
crystal $25.00
blue $25.00
yellow $25.00

6147 Wine
crystal $25.00
blue $25.00
yellow $25.00

6147 Ice Tea, footed
crystal $25.00
blue $25.00
yellow $25.00

Illusion, 6111

1968 – 1982

Stemware, 135

6111 Goblet $25.00
6111 Sherbet $25.00
6111 Claret $25.00
6111 Wine $25.00
6111 Cordial $25.00
6111 Ice Tea, footed $25.00

Images (Designer Collection)

1977 – 1978

Tableware II, 251-252

IM 02/724-L
Vase, 4⅞", crystal $65.00
IM 02/725-M,
Vase, opal $65.00
IM 02/727-N
Vase, 4¾", purple $95.00
IM 02/728-O
Vase, 6", opal $85.00
IM 02/731-P
Vase, 3¾", crystal $57.00
IM 02/739-S
Vase, 4⅜", brown $50.00
IM 02/740-T
Vase, 2¾", crystal mist $40.00

Imperial, Decoration 47

1925 – 1927

Tableware I, 322

2324 Bowl, 10", console $250.00
2297 Bowl A, 10¼", shallow $195.00
2315 Bowl A, 10½", console $225.00
2297 Bowl A, 12", deep $225.00
2324 Candlestick, 2", pair $135.00
2324 Candlestick, 4", pair $150.00
2324 Candlestick, 9", pair $250.00
2240 Jar, candy and cover, ½ pound $135.00
2331 Box, candy and cover $195.00
2329 Centerpiece, 11" $225.00
2322 Cologne $350.00
2323 Cologne $350.00
2327 Comport, 7" $125.00
2315 Grapefruit/Mayonnaise $85.00
2283 Plate, 7" $24.00
2283 Plate, 8" $27.00
2283 Plate, 10" $50.00
2316 Plate, 8", soup $45.00
2290 Plate, 13" $95.00
2338 Box, puff and cover $250.00
2315 Sugar and Cream $265.00
2287 Tray, handled, lunch $225.00
2276 Vanity Set $600.00

Impressions (Designer Collection)

1977 – 1978

Tableware II, 251-252

IM 01/711-A
Vase, 10¾", opal $175.00
IM 01/712-B
Vase, 7¾", crystal $145.00
IM 01/713-C
Vase, purple $185.00

IM 01/714-D
Vase, opal $135.00
IM 01/733-V
Vase, 5¼",
crystal mist....................$95.00

Inca, 4163 Tumblers

1955 – 1965

Stemware, 154

4163 Cooler, 21 oz.
crystal..........$15.00
pink..........$15.00
smoke..........$15.00
marine..........$15.00
amber..........$15.00
4163 Beverage, 14 oz.
crystal..........$14.00
pink..........$14.00
smoke..........$14.00
marine..........$14.00
amber..........$14.00
4163 Juice, 6 oz.
crystal..........$12.00
pink..........$12.00
smoke..........$12.00
marine..........$12.00
amber..........$12.00

Tableware

4163 Bowl, dessert/finger
crystal..........$12.00
pink..........$12.00
smoke..........$12.00
marine..........$12.00
amber..........$12.00
4163 Plate, dessert
crystal..........$12.00
pink..........$12.00
smoke..........$12.00
marine..........$12.00
amber..........$12.00

Ingrid, Cutting 794

1939 – 1943

Stemware, 40

892 Goblet..........$34.00
892 Saucer Champagne..........$32.00
892 Sherbet, low..........$30.00
892 Cocktail..........$32.00
892 Claret..........$42.00
892 Wine..........$40.00
892 Cordial..........$58.00
892 Oyster Cocktail..........$28.00
892 Ice Tea, footed..........$34.00
892 Juice, footed..........$30.00

Tableware I, 303

1769 Bowl, finger..........$15.00
6023 Bowl, footed..........$67.00
2324 Candlestick, 6", pair..........$45.00
6023 Candlestick, duo, pair..........$75.00
6011 Jug..........$200.00
2337 Plate, 6"..........$7.00
2337 Plate, 7".......... $8.00
2337 Plate, 8"..........$10.00

Ingrid, Cutting 836

1953 – 1970

Stemware, 107

6052½ Goblet..........$32.00
6052½ Sherbet..........$28.00
6052½ Cocktail..........$27.00
6052½ Claret-Wine..........$38.00
6052½ Cordial..........$45.00
6052½ Oyster Cocktail..........$20.00
6052½ Ice Tea, footed..........$32.00
6052½ Juice, footed..........$24.00

Tableware II, 184

2666 Bowl, oval..........$38.00
2666 Candle, flora, pair..........$56.00
2364 Mayonnaise, plate, ladle..........$58.00
2337 Plate, 7"..........$12.00
2337 Plate, 8"..........$16.00
2666 Plate, 10", snack..........$24.00
2364 Plate, 14", torte..........$48.00
2364 Relish, 2-part..........$30.00
2364 Relish, 3-part..........$38.00
2364 Shaker, large, chrome top B, pair..........$65.00
2666 Sugar and Cream..........$52.00
2666 Sugar and Cream, individual and tray..........$55.00

Inspiration, 6107

1966 – 1971

Stemware, 132

6107 Goblet..........$22.00
6107 Sherbet..........$22.00
6107 Claret..........$22.00
6107 Tulip Wine..........$22.00
6107 Liqueur..........$27.00
6107 Ice Tea, footed..........$22.00

Interpretations (Designer Collection)

1977 – 1978

Tableware II, 251-252

IN 03/715-E
Vase, opal..........$95.00
IN 03/716-F
Vase, 6¼", opal..........$95.00
IN 03/717-G
Vase, 6½", opal..........$95.00
IN 03/718-H
Vase, purple..........$150.00
IN 03/719-I
Vase, 6¾", crystal,..........$125.00
IN 03/721-J
Vase, 8", purple..........$150.00
IN 03/722-K
Vase, crystal..........$145.00
IN 03/735-U
Vase, 5", crystal..........$95.00
IN 03/736-R
Vase, 6½", brown..........$67.00

Intimate, Crystal Print 31

1971 – 1974

Stemware, 140

6123 Goblet
..........$35.00
6123 Sherbet..........$30.00
6123 Wine..........$35.00
6123 Ice Tea, footed..........$35.00

Inverness, Cutting 711

1933 – 1935

Stemware, 77

6007 Goblet
..........$35.00
6007 Sherbet, high..........$32.00
6007 Sherbet, low..........$28.00
6007 Cocktail..........$30.00
6007 Claret..........$38.00
6007 Wine..........$35.00
6007 Cordial..........$48.00
6007 Oyster Cocktail..........$28.00
6007 Ice Tea, footed..........$34.00
6007 Tumbler, footed, 9 oz...........$28.00
6007 Juice, footed..........$28.00
6007 Whiskey, footed..........$30.00

Tableware I, 276

2470 Bowl, 12"..........$45.00
2470 Candlestick, 5½", pair..........$65.00
2470 Comport, 6"..........$48.00
2451 Ice Dish and Plate..........$28.00
2470 Plate, 10", cake..........$45.00
2440 Plate, 13", torte..........$48.00
2283 Plate, 7"..........$8.00
2283 Plate, 8"..........$10.00

Invitation, Decoration 660

1963 – 1982

Stemware, 127

6102 Goblet
..........$32.00
6102 Sherbet..........$26.00
6102 Claret..........$32.00
6102 Tulip Wine..........$32.00
6102 Brandy..........$26.00
6102 Ice Tea, footed..........$32.00

Tableware II,
see Platinum Band Decoration

Irish Lace, Etching 36

1898 – 1928

*Note: * denotes pieces still offered in 1928.*

Stemware, 20, 34, 35

766 Goblet..........$10.00
766 Saucer Champagne..........$10.00
766 Sherbet..........$8.00
766 Fruit..........$8.00
766 Parfait..........$10.00
766 Cocktail..........$10.00
766 Claret..........$10.00
766 Rhine Wine..........$12.00
766 Wine..........$10.00
766 Burgundy..........$12.00
766 Sherry..........$12.00
766 Creme de Menthe..........$12.00
766 Brandy..........$15.00
766 Cordial..........$15.00
766 Sorbet..........$8.00
766 Ice Tea, footed, handled..........$16.00
766 Custard, handled..........$8.00
766 Grapefruit and Liner..........$20.00
879 Goblet..........$12.00
879 Saucer Champagne..........$12.00
879 Fruit..........$10.00
879 Cocktail..........$10.00
879 Claret..........$14.00
879 Wine..........$14.00
879 Sherry..........$10.00
879 Crème de Menthe..........$10.00
879 Brandy, pousse-café..........$18.00
879 Cordial..........$20.00
880 Goblet, 9 oz...........$12.00
880 Saucer Champagne, 6 oz...........$12.00
880 Sherbet..........$10.00
880 Cocktail, 3½ oz...........$10.00
880 Claret, 4½ oz...........$12.00
880 Wine, 2¾ oz...........$12.00

880 Sherry $10.00
880 Crème de Menthe $10.00
880 Cordial, 1 oz. $15.00
701 Tumbler, 14 oz......................$14.00
701 Tumbler, 12 oz. $12.00
701 Tumbler, 10 oz. $12.00
701 Tumbler, 8 oz. $10.00
701 Plate, 5", tumbler....................$5.00
766 Ice Tea, footed, handled $20.00
820 Tumbler, table $10.00
833 Tumbler, 8 oz. $10.00
858 Tumbler, table $10.00
858 Tumbler, 14 oz. $16.00
858 Tumbler, 12 oz. $14.00
858 Tumbler, 10 oz. $14.00
858 Tumbler, 8 oz. $12.00
858 Tumbler, 5 oz. $8.00
887 Tumbler, 2½ oz. $8.00
889 Tumbler, 5 oz. $8.00
4011 Tumbler, 15 oz. $20.00
4011 Tumbler, 12 oz. $14.00
4011 Tumbler, 10 oz. $12.00
4011 Tumbler, 8 oz. $10.00
4011 Tumbler, 5 oz. $8.00
4011 Tumbler, 12 oz., handled $20.00
4061 Lemonade, footed, handled ..$20.00
4077 Tumbler, 12 oz. $14.00
4077 Tumbler, 8 oz. $10.00
4077 Tumbler, 5 oz. $8.00
880, 880½ Grapefruit and Liner $24.00
5039 Grapefruit and Liner $24.00
837 Oyster Cocktail.....................$10.00
767 Parfait $32.00
5054 Parfait $10.00

Tableware I, 120

*766 Almond $20.00
5051 Almond, small.......................$20.00
5051 Almond, large $22.00
766 Bonbon $24.00
766 Comport, 5", footed $20.00
*803 Comport, 5".......................... $20.00
766 Comport, 6", footed $22.00
803 Comport, 6"...........................$22.00
766 Custard $8.00
810 Custard and 200 5" Plate........ $5.00
*300 Decanter, quart, cut neck $50.00
*766 Bowl, finger and 2283 6" Plate $15.00
810 Bowl, finger and 200 6" Plate $15.00
300/5 Jug, claret.............................$65.00
1236/6 Jug.. $60.00
*300/7 Jug, tankard $60.00
*303/7 Jug.. $50.00
317½ /7 Jug and plain Cover..............$65.00
*318/7 Jug..$57.00
724/7 Jug, tankard $57.00
766 Nappy, 4½", footed...............$10.00
803 Nappy, 4½", deep $10.00
1227 Nappy, 4½"............................$10.00
766 Nappy, 5", footed..................$10.00
803 Nappy, 5", deep.....................$10.00
*803 Nappy, 5", footed..................$10.00
766 Nappy, 6", footed..................$12.00
803 Nappy, 7", deep.....................$12.00
803 Nappy, 8", footed.................. $14.00
1227 Nappy, 8"............................... $18.00
300½ Oil, small $30.00
*300½ Oil, large............................... $35.00
1465 Oil, 7 oz., large, cut neck $40.00
2283 Plate, 5" $4.00
1897 Plate, 7" $6.00
*2283 Plate, 7" $6.00
1165½ Shaker, SPT, pair..................$35.00
858 Short Cake $10.00
*1480 Sugar and Cream..................$22.00
858 Sweetmeat.............................$10.00
*880 Sweetmeat.............................$12.00
922 Toothpick $20.00
160½ Bottle, water, cut neck $40.00

Italian Lace, Decoration 514 (see Gold Lace)

Ivy, Etching 235

1913 – 1917

Stemware, 37

882 Goblet, 11 oz. $10.00
882 Goblet, 10 oz. $10.00
882 Goblet, 9 oz. $9.00
882 Goblet, 8 oz. $9.00
882 Saucer Champagne, 7 oz..................................$10.00
882 Saucer Champagne, 5½ oz. $10.00
882 Sherbet $9.00
882 Cocktail, 3½ oz. $9.00
882 Cocktail, 3 oz.............................$9.00
882 Claret, 6½ oz..........................$14.00
882 Claret, 4½ oz..........................$10.00
882 Rhine Wine............................$10.00
882 Wine, 3½ oz. $10.00
882 Wine, 2¾ oz. $10.00
882 Sherry $9.00
882 Crème de Menthe $9.00
882 Brandy, pousse-café $15.00
882 Cordial, 1 oz. $15.00
882 Cordial, ¾ oz.........................$15.00
882 Champagne, hollow stem $10.00
882 Champagne, tall.....................$10.00
882 Grapefruit and Liner $22.00
882 Custard $7.00
882 Hot Whiskey $9.00
882 Ale, tall..................................$10.00
701 Tumbler........................$6.00 – 8.00
858 Tumbler........................$6.00 – 8.00
887 Tumbler........................$6.00 – 8.00
1558 Bottle, water, cut neck $40.00
300 Decanter, quart, cut neck $40.00
1464 Decanter, 18 oz., cut neck $40.00
1465 Oil, cut neck..........................$35.00
300 7 Tankard, cut flutes $50.00

Ivy, Cutting 745

1935 – 1943

Stemware, 84

6012 Goblet $28.00
6012 Sherbet, high $26.00
6012 Sherbet, low $22.00
6012 Cocktail $22.00
6012 Claret $28.00
6012 Rhine Wine............................$28.00
6012 Wine.......................................$28.00
6012 Sherry $26.00
6012 Creme de Menthe $22.00
6012 Brandy $32.00
6012 Cordial $38.00
6012 Oyster Cocktail.....................$18.00
6012 Ice Tea, footed $27.00
6012 Tumbler, footed 10 oz.....................................$20.00
6012 Juice, footed $18.00

Tableware I, 287

1769 Bowl, finger...........................$14.00
2536 Bowl, 9", handled $50.00
2535 Candlestick, 5½", pair...........$60.00
2400 Comport, 6"...........................$27.00
6011 Jug..$185.00
2337 Plate, 6" $7.00
2337 Plate, 7" $8.00
2337 Plate, 8" $10.00
701 Tumbler, 12 oz. $12.00
701 Tumbler, 10 oz. $10.00
1185 Old Fashioned Cocktail, 7 oz. $9.00

– J –

Jamestown, 2719

1958 – 1982

Stemware, 50

2719 Goblet
- crystal............$22.00
- amber.............$15.00
- blue................$30.00
- green.............$30.00
- pink $30.00
- amethyst...............................$30.00
- brown...................................$15.00
- ruby......................................$37.00

2719 Sherbet
- crystal $16.00
- amber....................................$12.00
- blue $24.00
- green.....................................$24.00
- pink $24.00
- amethyst................................$24.00
- brown....................................$12.00
- ruby.......................................$32.00

2719 Wine
- crystal $22.00
- amber....................................$15.00
- blue $28.00
- green.....................................$28.00
- pink $28.00
- amethyst................................$28.00
- brown....................................$15.00
- ruby.......................................$37.00

2719 Ice Tea, footed
- crystal $24.00
- amber....................................$15.00
- blue $30.00
- green.....................................$30.00
- pink $30.00
- amethyst................................$30.00
- brown....................................$15.00
- ruby.......................................$38.00

2719 Juice, footed
- crystal $16.00
- amber....................................$12.00
- blue $24.00
- green.....................................$24.00
- pink $24.00
- amethyst................................$24.00
- brown....................................$12.00
- ruby.......................................$30.00

2719 Tumbler, 12 oz.
- crystal $20.00
- amber....................................$15.00
- blue $34.00
- green.....................................$34.00
- pink $34.00

amethyst $34.00
brown $15.00
ruby $35.00

2719 Tumbler, 9 oz.
crystal $20.00
amber $12.00
blue $30.00
green $30.00
pink $30.00
amethyst $30.00
brown $12.00
ruby $35.00

Tableware II, 92-95

2719 Bowl, 4½", dessert
crystal $30.00
blue $32.00
green $32.00
amber $25.00
pink $34.00
amethyst $32.00
brown $20.00
ruby $37.00

2719 Bowl, 10", salad
crystal $65.00
green $85.00
amber $65.00
blue $85.00
amethyst $75.00

2719 Butter, oblong and cover
crystal $75.00
blue $135.00
green $135.00
amber $65.00
amethyst $95.00

2719 Celery, 9¼"
crystal $38.00
blue $56.00
green $85.00
amber $42.00
amethyst $54.00

2719 Cream
crystal $32.50
blue $37.50
green $35.00
amber $25.00
pink $48.00
amethyst $35.00
brown $20.00

2719 Dish, handled, serving
crystal $65.00
blue $85.00
green $85.00
amber $65.00
amethyst $85.00

2719 Jelly and Cover, 6⅛"
crystal $70.00
amber $70.00
blue $85.00
green $85.00
amethyst $95.00

2719 Jug, 3-pint
crystal $135.00
blue $185.00
green $175.00
amber $135.00
pink $200.00
amethyst $165.00
brown $95.00

2719 Pickle, 8⅜"
crystal $34.00
blue $47.00
green $47.00
amber $34.00
amethyst $52.00

2719 Relish, 2-part
crystal $42.00
blue $58.00
green $58.00
amber $36.00
amethyst $75.00

2719 Plate, 8"
crystal $18.00
blue $36.00
green $32.00
amber $18.00
pink $32.00
amethyst $32.00
brown $15.00
ruby $38.00

2719 Plate, 9½", handled, cake
crystal $65.00
blue $90.00
green $85.00
amber $65.00
amethyst $95.00

2719 Plate, 14", torte
crystal $65.00
blue $95.00
green $85.00
amber $65.00
amethyst $95.00

2719 Salad Set: 10" salad bowl, 14" torte, and wooden salad fork and spoon
crystal $130.00
green $170.00
amber $130.00
blue $175.00
amethyst $170.00

2719 Salver, 10", round
crystal $150.00
blue $225.00
green $225.00
amber $150.00
amethyst $195.00

2719 Dish, 4½", sauce and cover
crystal $54.00
blue $75.00
green $68.00
amber $60.00
amethyst $75.00

2719 Shaker, chrome top A, pair
crystal $65.00
blue $85.00
green $85.00
amber $65.00
pink $85.00
amethyst $75.00
brown $55.00

2719 Sugar
crystal $32.50
blue $37.50
green $37.50
amber $25.00
pink $48.00
amethyst $38.00
brown $20.00

2719 Tray, 9⅜", handled, muffin
crystal $65.00
blue $90.00
green $85.00
amber $65.00
amethyst $95.00

Jefferson, 6104, 6104½

1964 – 1972

Stemware, 129

6104 Goblet $22.00
6104 Sherbet $22.00
6104 Claret $22.00
6104 Wine $22.00
6104 Cordial $22.00
6104 Ice Tea, footed $22.00

Jellies, see Comports, Nappies and Jellies

Jenny Lind, Milkglass

1955 – 1965

Tableware II, 216-219

824 Tray, comb and brush
white $95.00
aqua $225.00
peach $225.00

826 Tray, pin
white $34.00
aqua $45.00
peach $45.00

827 Flask, cologne and stopper
white $165.00
aqua $295.00
peach $295.00

828 Box, pin and cover
white $68.00
aqua $98.00
peach $98.00

829 Puff and Cover
white $75.00
aqua $135.00
peach $135.00

830 Pomade and Cover
white $70.00
aqua $125.00
peach $125.00

831 Box, handkerchief and cover
white $94.00
aqua $150.00
peach $150.00

832 Box, glove and cover
white $150.00
aqua $250.00
peach $250.00

833 Box, jewel and cover
white $65.00
aqua $125.00
peach $125.00

834 Pitcher, blown, see Garden Center Items
white $165.00
aqua $295.00
peach $295.00

835 Tumbler, blown
white $65.00
aqua $85.00
peach $85.00

Jewelry (see Boudoir Accessories and Jewelry)

Jubilee, Decoration 699

1981 – 1982

Stemware, 145

6147 Goblet $21.00
6147 Champagne $21.00

6147 Wine....$21.00
6147 Ice Tea, footed....$21.00

Jugs and Tankards

Pre-1920 – 1940

Stemware, 166

Useful & Ornamental, 153-158

300 Jug....$75.00
300½ Jug....$80.00
303 Jug....$65.00
316 Jug, see 318
317-7 Jug, plain or CN....$65.00
317½-7 Jug, plain or CN, and cover....$75.00
318 Jug, optic....$78.00
724 Jug....$80.00
890-7 Jug
- crystal....$125.00
- solid rose....$250.00
- solid green....$250.00

1227-7 Jug, plain or CN....$65.00
1236 Jug
- crystal....$95.00
- blue....$250.00
- green....$175.00
- amber....$150.00

1518 Jug, automatic removable top; 6, 8, 12, 16, 24, or 32 oz. ...$12.00 – 45.00
1761 Tankard, claret....$125.00
1787 Tankard....$75.00
1793 Jug, 75 oz....$75.00
1852-6, 1852-8 Jug....$75.00
1992 Jug, 3-pint pressed....$58.00
1992 Jug, quart, pressed....$48.00
2010 Jug, 63 oz., plain or optic....$65.00
2018-7 Jug, plain or CN....$65.00
2040 Jug....$65.00
2082 Jug, plain or spiral optic; 37, 47, or 60 oz.
- crystal....$65.00
- solid green, SO....$95.00

2100 Tankard....$85.00
2104 Jug and Tumbler....$125.00
2230-7 Jug and Cover....$95.00
2270-7 Jug, plain or optic
- crystal....$75.00
- amber....$90.00
- blue....$125.00
- green....$110.00

2270-7 Jug and Cover, plain or optic
- crystal....$84.00
- amber....$95.00
- blue....$145.00
- green....$125.00

2464 Jug, ice
- crystal....$175.00
- rose....$315.00
- green....$295.00
- amber....$250.00
- topaz....$315.00

2503 Jug, wine, see Bar and Refreshment
2518 Jug, see Bar and Refreshment
2666 Jug, see Contour
4020 Jug, ½ gallon
- crystal....$150.00
- ebony base....$195.00
- green base....$250.00
- amber base....$225.00
- wisteria base....$495.00
- green bowl....$350.00
- rose bowl....$350.00
- topaz bowl....$350.00
- wisteria bowl....$700.00

4095-4, -5, -7 Jug, footed
- crystal, RO....$175.00
- solid green, SO....$275.00
- green base, SO....$250.00
- amber base, LO....$225.00
- blue base, RO....$300.00
- green bowl, RO....$295.00
- azure bowl, RO....$325.00
- rose bowl, RO....$295.00

4140, 4141, 4142 Refreshment Set, see Bar and Refreshment
5000-7 Jug, footed, RO
- crystal....$150.00
- solid green....$250.00
- green base....$200.00
- green bowl....$225.00
- amber base....$200.00
- amber bowl....$250.00
- solid amber....$250.00
- blue base....$400.00
- solid blue....$700.00
- orchid bowl....$600.00
- solid orchid....$600.00
- solid azure....$375.00
- azure bowl....$375.00
- rose bowl....$350.00
- topaz/gold tint bowl....$350.00

5084-7 Jug, footed, RO
- crystal....$145.00
- rose....$350.00
- green....$300.00
- amber....$250.00
- blue....$700.00

6011 Jug, footed
- crystal....$145.00
- regal blue bowl....$600.00
- burgundy bowl....$600.00
- empire green bowl....$600.00
- amber base....$195.00
- gold tint bowl....$325.00
- azure bowl....$350.00

Juliet, Cutting 865

1959 – 1969

Stemware, 117

6085 Goblet....$28.00
6085 Sherbet....$26.00
6085 Wine/Cocktail....$32.00
6085 Cordial....$42.00
6085 Ice Tea, footed....$28.00
6085 Juice, footed....$25.00
2337 Plate, 7"....$10.00
2337 Plate, 8"....$12.00

June, Etching 279

1928 – 1951

Stemware, 68

5098 Goblet
- crystal....$45.00
- rose....$85.00
- azure....$85.00
- topaz/gold tint....$75.00

5098 Sherbet, high
- crystal....$35.00
- rose....$70.00
- azure....$70.00
- topaz/gold tint....$60.00

5098 Sherbet, low
- crystal....$25.00
- rose....$55.00
- azure....$55.00
- topaz/gold tint....$35.00

5098 Parfait
- crystal....$68.00
- rose....$125.00
- azure....$125.00
- topaz/gold tint....$75.00

5098 Cocktail
- crystal....$35.00
- rose....$58.00
- azure....$58.00
- topaz/gold tint....$50.00

5098 Claret
- crystal....$65.00
- rose....$135.00
- azure....$135.00
- topaz/gold tint....$95.00

5098 Wine
- crystal....$50.00
- rose....$125.00
- azure....$125.00
- topaz/gold tint....$70.00

5098 Cordial
- crystal....$85.00
- rose....$165.00
- azure....$165.00
- topaz/gold tint....$125.00

5098 Oyster Cocktail
- crystal....$30.00
- rose....$45.00
- azure....$45.00
- topaz/gold tint....$35.00

5098 Ice Tea, footed
- crystal....$40.00
- rose....$75.00
- azure....$75.00
- topaz/gold tint....$60.00

5098 Tumbler, 9 oz., footed
- crystal....$30.00
- rose....$48.00
- azure....$48.00
- topaz/gold tint....$45.00

5098 Juice, footed
- crystal....$34.00
- rose....$45.00
- azure....$45.00
- topaz/gold tint....$45.00

5098 Whiskey, footed
- crystal....$35.00
- rose....$65.00
- azure....$65.00
- topaz/gold tint....$58.00

5082½ Grapefruit and 945½ Liner
- crystal....$95.00
- rose....$125.00
- azure....$125.00
- topaz/gold tint....$110.00

Tableware I, 174 – 179

2350 Ashtray, small
- crystal....$40.00
- rose....$56.00
- azure....$60.00
- topaz....$48.00

2375 Bonbon
- crystal....$38.00
- rose....$58.00
- azure....$62.00
- topaz/gold tint....$55.00

2375 Bouillon
- crystal....$30.00
- rose....$44.00

azure $44.00
topaz/gold tint $34.00

869 Bowl, finger and 2283 Plate
crystal $75.00
rose $125.00
azure $125.00
topaz/gold tint $100.00

2375 Bowl, 5", fruit
crystal $34.00
rose $47.00
azure $50.00
topaz/gold tint $45.00

2375 Bowl, 6", cereal
crystal $40.00
rose $58.00
azure $58.00
topaz.....................................$56.00

2394 Bowl, 6", same as mint
rose $58.00
azure $60.00
topaz.....................................$58.00

2375 Bowl, 7", soup
crystal $52.00
rose $125.00
azure $145.00
topaz...................................$125.00

2375 Bowl, 7", round, nappy
crystal, ...$54.00
rose $165.00
azure $175.00
topaz...................................$165.00

2375 Bowl, 9", baker/vegetable
crystal $65.00
rose $135.00
azure $135.00
topaz/gold tint $125.00

2395 Bowl, 10", Grecian
crystal $225.00
rose $295.00
azure $295.00
topaz/gold tint $245.00

2375 Bowl, large, dessert
crystal $110.00
rose $165.00
azure $185.00
topaz...................................$154.00

2375 Bowl, 12"
crystal $95.00
rose $135.00
azure $135.00
topaz/gold tint $125.00

2394 Bowl A, 12"
crystal $115.00
rose $150.00
azure $150.00
topaz/gold tint $145.00

2394 Candlestick, 2", pair
crystal $85.00
rose $145.00
azure $150.00
topaz/gold tint $125.00

2375½ Candlestick, mushroom, pair
crystal $125.00
rose $175.00
azure $185.00
topaz...................................$175.00

2375 Candlestick, 3", , pair
crystal $95.00
rose $135.00
azure $150.00
topaz/gold tint $140.00

2395 Candlestick, 3", Grecian, pair
rose $250.00
azure $250.00
topaz, may not have been made $250.00

2395½ Candlestick, 5", Grecian, pair
crystal $175.00
rose $250.00
azure $250.00
topaz/gold tint $225.00

2394 Candy and Cover, ½ lb.
crystal $325.00
rose $575.00
azure $600.00
topaz...................................$550.00

2331 Box, candy, and cover, 3-part
rose $550.00
azure $550.00
topaz...................................$550.00

2375 Celery, 11½"
crystal $95.00
rose $137.00
azure $125.00
topaz/gold tint $125.00

2375 Centerpiece, 12"
crystal $200.00
rose $265.00
azure $265.00
topaz...................................$250.00

2375½ Centerpiece, 13", oval and flower holder
crystal $395.00
rose $550.00
azure $550.00

2375 Cheese and Cracker
crystal $165.00
rose $200.00
azure $225.00
topaz/gold tint $200.00

2368 Cheese and Cracker
crystal $165.00
rose $200.00
azure $225.00
topaz...................................$200.00

5098 Comport, 5"
crystal $120.00
rose $150.00
azure $165.00
topaz...................................$145.00

2400 Comport, 6"
crystal $110.00
rose $165.00
azure $150.00
topaz/gold tint $145.00

2375 Comport, 7"
rose $165.00
azure $165.00
topaz...................................$150.00

2400 Comport, 8"
rose $225.00
azure $235.00
topaz...................................$225.00

2375 Cream Soup and Plate
crystal $87.00
rose $125.00
azure $138.00
topaz/gold tint $125.00

2375 Cup and Saucer, after dinner
crystal $95.00
rose $135.00
azure $150.00
topaz/gold tint $125.00

2375½ Cup and Saucer
crystal $38.00
rose $58.00
azure $64.00
topaz/gold tint $54.00

2439 Decanter
crystal ....market
rose ....market
azure ....market
topaz ....market

2375 Bucket, ice, NP handle
crystal $165.00
rose $225.00
azure $250.00
topaz/gold tint $225.00

2378 Bucket, ice, NP handle
crystal $195.00
rose $250.00
azure $265.00
topaz...................................$250.00

2451 Dish, ice, unetched liners
crystal $87.00
rose $135.00
azure $135.00
topaz/gold tint $125.00

2451 Plate, ice dish
crystal $20.00
rose $25.00
azure $25.00
topaz.....................................$25.00

5000 Jug
crystal $495.00
rose.................$1,100.00/market
azure...............$1,200.00/market
topaz/gold tint $800.00

2375 Dish, lemon
crystal $48.00
rose $60.00
azure $65.00
topaz/gold tint $57.00

2375 Mayonnaise, plate, ladle
crystal $115.00
rose $185.00
azure $200.00
topaz/gold tint $165.00

2394 Mint
rose $48.00
azure $58.00
topaz.....................................$48.00

5098 Nappy, 6", footed
crystal $135.00
rose $175.00
azure $185.00

2375 Oil, footed
crystal $450.00
rose,...................$800.00/market
azure................$1000.00/market
topaz $800.00/market

2375 Plate, 6"
crystal $22.00
rose $28.00
azure $30.00
topaz/gold tint $25.00

2375 Plate, 7"
crystal $22.00
rose $35.00
azure $35.00
topaz/gold tint $32.00

2375 Plate, 8"
crystal $25.00
rose $42.00
azure $42.00
topaz/gold tint $38.00

2375 Plate, 9"
crystal $47.00
rose $58.00
azure $67.00
topaz/gold tint $58.00

2375 Plate, 10"
crystal $68.00
rose $150.00
azure $150.00
topaz/gold tint $140.00
2375 Plate, 10", grill
crystal $75.00
rose $125.00
azure $125.00
topaz....$100.00
2375 Plate, 10", cake
crystal $87.00
rose $165.00
azure $175.00
topaz/gold tint $135.00
2375 Plate, 13", chop
crystal, ...$135.00
rose $200.00
azure, ...$250.00
topaz/gold tint $200.00
2440 Plate, 13", torte
crystal $135.00
rose $200.00
azure $250.00
topaz....$250.00
2375 Platter, 12"
crystal $135.00
rose $195.00
azure $225.00
topaz/gold tint $185.00
2375 Platter, 15"
crystal $195.00
rose $250.00
azure $275.00
topaz/gold tint $250.00
2375 Relish, 8½"
crystal $52.00
rose $58.00
azure $65.00
topaz/gold tint $58.00
2083 Bottle, salad dressing
crystal....$700.00/market
rose....$900.00/market
azure....$1,100.00/market
topaz/gold tint...$800.00/market
2375 Bottle, salad dressing
crystal....$700.00/market
rose....$900.00/market
azure....$1,000.00/market
topaz/gold tint...$900.00/market
2375 Sauce Boat and Plate
crystal $300.00
rose $495.00
azure $525.00
topaz....$475.00
2375 Shaker, footed, FGT, pair
crystal $250.00
rose $395.00
azure $375.00
topaz/gold tint $375.00
2375½ Sugar and Cream
crystal $165.00
rose $225.00
azure $195.00
topaz/gold tint $195.00
2375½ Sugar and Cover
crystal $175.00
rose $225.00
azure $200.00
topaz....$200.00
2375½ Sugar and Cream, tea
crystal $135.00
rose $200.00
azure $200.00
topaz/gold tint $175.00
2378 Pail, sugar, NP handle
crystal $400.00
rose $450.00
azure $465.00
topaz....$450.00
2375 Sweetmeat
crystal $58.00
rose $64.00
azure $67.00
topaz/gold tint $62.00
2375 Tray, handled, lunch
crystal $135.00
rose $200.00
azure $238.00
topaz/gold tint $195.00
2429 Tray, service, and lemon insert
crystal $300.00
rose $350.00
azure $400.00
topaz....$350.00
2417 Vase, 8", RO
topaz....$700.00
4100 Vase, 8", RO
rose $600.00
azure $650.00
2385 Vase, 8½", fan
rose $900.00
azure $900.00
2375 Whip Cream
crystal $58.00
rose $64.00
azure $67.00
topaz/gold tint $62.00
2378 Pail, whip cream, NP handle
crystal $400.00
rose $450.00
azure $465.00
topaz....$465.00

Juniper, JU05

1983 – 1986

Stemware, 186

JU05 Goblet, 10 oz. $20.00
JU05 Champagne, 8 oz. $18.00
JU05 Wine, 7 oz. $20.00
JU05 Flute/Parfait, 8 oz....$26.00
JU05 Ice Tea, 14 oz., footed $20.00
JU05 Double Old Fashioned....$16.00
JU05 Highball....$16.00

K

Karnak, 4161 Tumblers

1955 – 1965

Stemware, 154

4161 Cooler, 21 oz.
crystal....$15.00
pink....$15.00
smoke....$15.00
marine....$15.00
amber....$15.00
4161 Beverage, 14 oz.
crystal $14.00
pink $14.00
smoke $14.00
marine....$14.00
amber....$14.00
4161 Juice, 6 oz.
crystal $12.00
pink $12.00
smoke $12.00
marine....$12.00
amber....$12.00
4161 Bowl, dessert/finger
crystal $12.00
pink $12.00
smoke $12.00
marine....$12.00
amber....$12.00
4161 Plate, dessert
crystal $12.00
pink $12.00
smoke $12.00
marine....$12.00
amber....$12.00

Kashmir, Plate Etching 283

1930 – 1933

Stemware, 57, 70

4020 Goblet, green base....$48.00
4020 Sherbet, high, green base....$42.00
4020 Sherbet, low, 7 oz., green base....$35.00
4020 Sherbet, low, 5 oz., green base....$35.00
4020 Cocktail, 4 oz., green base (4020½) $32.00
4020 Cocktail, 3½ oz., green base....$32.00
4020 Ice Tea, footed, green base....$48.00
4020 Tumbler, 13 oz., footed, green base....$44.00
4020 Tumber, 10 oz., footed, green base....$35.00
4020 Juice, footed, green base....$35.00
4020 Whiskey, footed, green base....$35.00
5099 Goblet
azure $84.00
topaz....$45.00
5099 Sherbet, high
azure $70.00
topaz....$40.00
5099 Sherbet, low
azure $56.00
topaz....$36.00
5099 Parfait
azure $85.00
topaz....$48.00
5099 Cocktail
azure $65.00
topaz....$40.00
5099 Claret
azure $87.00
topaz....$56.00
5099 Wine
azure $80.00
topaz....$55.00
5099 Cordial
azure $135.00
topaz....$95.00
5099 Oyster Cocktail
azure $50.00
topaz....$35.00

5099 Ice Tea, footed
azure $75.00
topaz....................$45.00
5099 Tumbler, 9 oz., footed
azure $54.00
topaz....................$35.00
5099 Juice, footed
azure $54.00
topaz....................$35.00
5099 Whiskey, footed
azure $65.00
topaz....................$64.00

Tableware I, 186 – 188

5082½ Grapefruit and 945½ Liner
azure $87.00
topaz....................$75.00
2375 Bonbon
azure $48.00
topaz....................$42.00
869 Bowl, finger and 2283 6" Plate
azure $85.00
topaz....................$75.00
4021 Bowl, finger
green base....................$65.00
2375 Bowl, 5", fruit
azure $40.00
topaz....................$36.00
2375 Bowl, 6", cereal
azure $42.00
topaz....................$38.00
2394 Bowl, 6"
azure $45.00
topaz....................$42.00
2375 Bowl, 7", soup
azure $75.00
topaz....................$65.00
2375 Bouillon
azure $38.00
topaz....................$32.00
2375 Bowl, large, dessert
azure $125.00
topaz....................$95.00
2375 Bowl, 9", baker
azure $95.00
topaz....................$75.00
2395 Bowl, 10"
azure $250.00
topaz....................$200.00
2430 Bowl, 11"
azure $165.00
topaz....................$150.00
2394 Bowl A, 12"
azure $165.00
topaz....................$145.00
2375 Bowl, 12"
azure $165.00
topaz....................$145.00
2394 Candlestick, 2", pair
azure $85.00
topaz....................$64.00
2375½ Candlestick , pair
azure $125.00
topaz....................$95.00
2375 Candlestick, 3", pair
azure $85.00
topaz....................$65.00
2395½ Candlestick, 5", pair
azure $150.00
topaz....................$125.00
2430 Candlestick, 9½", pair
azure $250.00
topaz....................$195.00
2430 Jar, candy, and cover
azure $175.00
topaz....................$146.00
2375 Celery, 11½"
azure $110.00
topaz....................$85.00
2375 Centerpiece, 12"
azure $200.00
topaz....................$175.00
2375 Cheese and Cracker
azure $165.00
topaz....................$135.00
5099 Comport, 6"
azure $95.00
topaz....................$85.00
2375 Cream Soup and Plate
azure $125.00
topaz....................$85.00
2375 Cup and Saucer, after dinner
azure $135.00
topaz....................$110.00
2375½ Cup and Saucer
azure $52.00
topaz....................$40.00
2350½ Cup and 2419 Saucer
green....................$48.00
2350 Cup and 2419 Saucer, after dinner,
green....................$95.00
2375 Ice Bucket, NP handle
azure $175.00
topaz....................$145.00
2430 Jelly, 7"
azure $50.00
topaz....................$36.00
4020 Jug, green base....................$500.00
5000 Jug
azure....................$800.00/market
topaz....................$675.00
2375 Dish, lemon
azure $48.00
topaz....................$42.00
2430 Mint, 5½"
azure $45.00
topaz....................$32.00
2375 Oil, footed
azure $750.00
topaz....................$600.00
2375 Pickle, 8½"
azure $48.00
topaz....................$42.00
2375 Plate, 6"
azure $20.00
topaz....................$16.00
2375 Plate, 7"
azure $22.00
topaz....................$16.00
2375 Plate, 8"
azure $28.00
topaz....................$22.00
2375 Plate, 9"
azure $50.00
topaz....................$42.00
2375 Plate, 10"
azure $115.00
topaz....................$85.00
2419 Plate, 6"
green....................$16.00
2419 Plate, 7"
green....................$22.00
2419 Plate, 8"
green....................$28.00
2375 Plate, 10", cake
azure $125.00
topaz....................$95.00
2375 Plate, 13", chop
azure $175.00
topaz....................$145.00
2375 Platter, 12"
azure $165.00
topaz....................$150.00
2375 Platter, 15"
azure $250.00
topaz....................$195.00
2375 Relish, 8½"
azure $60.00
topaz....................$54.00
2375 Sauce Boat and Plate
azure $275.00
topaz....................$225.00
2375 Shaker, FGT, pair
azure $240.00
topaz....................$235.00
2375 Sugar and Cream, tea
azure $175.00
topaz....................$150.00
2375½ Sugar and Cream
azure $175.00
topaz....................$150.00
2375 Sweetmeat
azure $54.00
topaz....................$48.00
2375 Tray, handled, lunch
azure $175.00
topaz....................$147.00
2417 Vase, 8"
azure $600.00
topaz....................$495.00
2430 Vase, 8"
azure $300.00
topaz....................$250.00
4105 Vase, 8"
azure $500.00
topaz....................$400.00

Kenmore, Cutting 176

1925 – 1927

Stemware, 64

5082 Goblet,
blue base $54.00
5082 Sherbet, high,
blue base $45.00
5082 Sherbet, low,
blue base $35.00
5082 Parfait,
blue base $55.00
5082 Cocktail,
blue base $40.00
5082 Wine,
blue base $55.00
5082 Cordial....................$75.00
820 Tumbler, table,
crystal only....................$12.00
701 Tumbler, 13 oz.,
crystal only....................$14.00
887 Tumbler, 2½ oz.,
crystal only....................$6.00
889 Tumbler, 5 oz.,
crystal only....................$6.00
4011 Tumbler, 12 oz., handled,
crystal only....................$18.00
4095 Oyster Cocktail, 4 oz. $12.00
4095 Tumbler, 13 oz. $24.00
4095 Tumbler, 19 oz. $24.00
4095 Tumbler, 5 oz. $14.00

Tableware I, 268

4095 Almond, blue foot....................$35.00

1769 Bowl, finger and 1499 Plate $24.00
4095 Bowl, footed, finger, blue foot....$35.00
4095 Jar, candy and cover, blue foot....$78.00
1693½ Coaster, 3½" $10.00
303/7 Jug....$95.00
2082/7 Jug....$110.00
4095/7 Jug, blue foot....$270.00
2315 Mayonnaise and Plate....$32.00
2283 Plate, 6", blue....$16.00
2283 Plate, 8", blue....$22.00
2337 Plate, 7" $11.00
2337 Plate, 8" $12.00
2316 Plate, 8", soup, blue....$24.00
2283 Plate, 13" $30.00
2315 Sugar and Cream....$30.00
2287 Tray, lunch....$38.00

Kent, 2424

1939 – 1943

Tableware I, 65-67

2424 Almond, individual $18.00
2424 Ashtray, 3"....$18.00
2424 Bowl, 8", regular....$28.00
2424 Bowl, 9½", flared....$34.00
2424 Bowl, 11½", fruit....$36.00
2424 Candlestick, 3½" $27.00
2424 Candlestick, duo....$35.00
2424 Jar, candy and cover,....$38.00
2424 Box, cigarette and cover,....$45.00
2424 Comport, 5½", low, and cover....$48.00
2424 Mayonnaise, plate, ladle....$46.00
2424 Plate, 12" $36.00
2424 Salt, individual....$16.00
2424 Sweetmeat....$15.00
2424 Urn, 5", flared, footed....$42.00
2424 Urn, 5½", regular, footed....$42.00
2424 Urn, 6½", flared, footed....$45.00
2424 Urn, 7½", regular, footed....$48.00

Kent, 6079

1958 – 1970

Stemware, 116

6079 Goblet....$24.00
6079 Sherbet....$22.00
6079 Cocktail....$22.00
6079 Claret-Wine....$26.00
6079 Cordial....$32.00
6079 Ice Tea, footed....$24.00
6079 Juice, footed....$22.00

Kimberley, Cutting 775

1938 – 1943

Stemware, 92

6020 Goblet $30.00
6020 Saucer Champagne $30.00
6020 Sherbet, low....$26.00
6020 Parfait....$30.00
6020 Cocktail....$28.00
6020 Claret....$35.00
6020 Wine....$35.00
6020 Cordial....$50.00
6020 Oyster Cocktail....$24.00
6020 Ice Tea, footed....$30.00
6020 Tumbler, 9 oz., footed....$26.00
6020 Juice, footed....$26.00

Tableware I, 299

869 Bowl, finger....$12.00
2560 Bowl, handled....$65.00
2430 Bowl, 11" $60.00
2430 Candlestick, 2", pair....$65.00
2560 Candlestick, 4½", pair....$50.00
2560 Candlestick, duo, pair....$75.00
2400 Comport, 6"....$27.00
5000 Jug....$185.00
2337 Plate, 6" $6.00
2337 Plate, 7" $7.00
2337 Plate, 8" $8.00
2560 Sugar and Cream....$40.00
5100 Vase, 10", plain....$98.00

Kimberly, Cutting 855

1957 – 1965

Stemware, 114

6071 Goblet....$34.00
6071 Sherbet....$32.00
6071 Cocktail/Wine/Seafood....$35.00
6071 Cordial....$45.00
6071 Ice Tea, footed....$34.00
6071 Juice, footed....$30.00

Tableware II, 190

2574 Plate, 7" $10.00
2574 Plate, 8" $12.00
2574 Plate, 14", torte....$36.00
2574 Relish, 3-part....$38.00
2574 Sugar and Cream....$45.00

Kimberly, 2990

1979 – 1982

Stemware, 56;
Useful & Ornamental, 37

2990 Goblet....$18.00
2990 Sherbet....$18.00
2990 Wine....$18.00
2990 Wine Goblet, magnum....$25.00
2990 Flute/Parfait....$25.00
KI02/047 Bell, gold handle....$35.00

King George, Carving 11

1939 – 1940

Useful & Ornamental, 114

2424 Plate, 12"....$150.00

Kingsley, Cutting 192

1929

Stemware

877 Goblet $35.00
877 Sherbet, high....$32.00
877 Sherbet, low....$30.00
877 Parfait....$35.00
877 Wine....$35.00
877 Cocktail....$30.00
877 Tumbler, 12 oz., footed....$35.00
877 Tumbler, 9 oz., footed....$30.00
877 Tumbler, 5 oz., footed....$26.00
877 Tumbler, 2½ oz., footed....$24.00

Tableware I, 271

869 Bowl, finger and 2283 6" Plate....$28.00
2287 Bowl A, 12",
crystal....$48.00
rose....$67.00
azure....$70.00
2342 Bowl A, 12
crystal....$48.00
rose....$67.00
azure....$70.00
2375 Candlestick, 3", pair
crystal....$58.00
rose....$78.00
azure....$78.00
2375 Candlestick, 4", pair
crystal....$58.00
rose....$78.00
azure....$78.00

Kingston, Decoration 41

1928 – 1929

Note: Coin Gold Band, and Cambden Needle Etching 84, green bowl

Stemware, 69

5098 Goblet....$40.00
5098 Sherbet, high....$35.00
5098 Sherbet, low....$30.00
5098 Parfait....$40.00
5098 Cocktail....$35.00
5098 Claret....$45.00
5098 Wine....$40.00
5098 Cordial....$50.00
5098 Oyster Cocktail....$30.00
5098 Ice Tea, footed....$40.00
5098 Tumbler, 9 oz., footed....$30.00
5098 Juice, footed....$30.00
5098 Whiskey, footed....$38.00

Tableware I, 122

869 Bowl, finger....$22.00
5098 Comport, 5"....$38.00
4095 Jug, footed, solid color....$295.00
5098 Nappy, 6"....$48.00
2283 Plate, 6"....$14.00
2283 Plate, 7"....$16.00
2283 Plate, 8"....$20.00
5082½ Grapefruit and 945½ Liner....$44.00
5000 Jug....$295.00

Kismet, Crystal Print 10 4180 Tumblers

1958 – 1962

Stemware, 155

4180 Tumbler, 12 oz., flat, sky blue....$12.00
4180 Juice, 7 oz., flat, sky blue....$12.00

Kornflower, Etching 234

1913 – 1917

Stemware, 35

880 Goblet, 11 oz....$10.00
880 Goblet, 10 oz. $10.00
880 Goblet, 9 oz. $10.00
880 Goblet, 8 oz. $10.00
880 Saucer Champagne, 7 oz....$10.00
880 Saucer Champagne, 5½ oz. $10.00
880 Sherbet....$9.00
880 Cocktail, 3½ oz. $9.00

880 Claret, 6½ oz. $12.00
880 Claret, 4½ oz. $10.00
880 Rhine Wine $10.00
880 Wine, 3½ oz. $10.00
880 Wine, 2¾ oz. $10.00
880 Sherry $9.00
880 Crème de Menthe $9.00
880 Brandy, pousse-café, 1 oz. $14.00
880 Cordial, 1 oz. $14.00
880 Champagne, hollow stem $10.00
880 Champagne, tall $10.00
880 Grapefruit, tall and liner $15.00
880 Grapefruit, short and liner $12.00
880 Hot Whiskey $9.00
880 Tall Ale $10.00
701 Tumbler ....$7.00 – 10.00
820 Tumbler ....$7.00 – 10.00
858 Tumbler ....$7.00 – 10.00
303 Jug $54.00

–L–

Lacy Leaf, Crystal Print 6

1957 – 1958

Tableware II, 161, 162

2630 Bonbon, 3-toed $28.00
2630 Bowl, 10½", salad. $45.00
2630 Bowl, 12", flared $50.00
2630 Butter and cover, oblong $35.00
2630 Candlestick, 4½", pair $48.00
2630 Candlestick, duo, pair $68.00
2630 Jug, 3-pint, ice $94.00
2630 Lily Pond, 9" $38.00
2630 Mayonnaise, plate, ladle $47.00
2630 Nappy, 4½", handled $18.00
2630 Pickle, 8¾" $20.00
2630 Plate, handled, cake $45.00
2630 Relish, 2-part $22.00
2630 Relish, 3-part $35.00
2630 Salad Set, 4-piece $95.00
2630 Shaker, chrome top B, pair $48.00
2630 Sugar and Cream $45.00
2630 Sugar and Cream, individual and tray $56.00
2630 Tidbit, 3-toed $27.00
2630 Torte, 14" $50.00
2630 Tray, handled, lunch $54.00
2630 Tricorne, 3-toed $30.00

Ladles (see Spoons and Ladles)

Lafayette, 2440

1932 – 1942

Tableware I, 74 – 77

2440 Almond, individual
- crystal $26.00
- rose $37.00
- green $37.00
- amber $34.00
- topaz/gold tint $37.00
- wisteria $60.00

2440 Bonbon, 5", handled
- crystal $22.00
- rose $32.00
- green $32.00
- amber $28.00
- topaz/gold tint $30.00
- wisteria $65.00
- regal blue $60.00
- burgundy $60.00
- empire green $60.00

2440 Bowl, 5", fruit
- crystal $27.00
- topaz/gold tint $32.00
- wisteria $65.00

2440 Bowl, 6", cereal
- crystal $30.00
- topaz/gold tint $38.00
- wisteria $75.00

2440 Bowl D, 7"
- crystal $47.00
- rose $75.00
- green $75.00
- amber $65.00
- topaz/gold tint $68.00
- wisteria $135.00

2440 Bowl, 8", nappy
- crystal $44.00
- topaz/gold tint $52.00
- wisteria $125.00

2440 Bowl, 10", oval, baker
- crystal $38.00
- topaz/gold tint $57.00
- wisteria $150.00

2440 Bowl B, 10"
- crystal $38.00
- rose $75.00
- green $75.00
- amber $65.00
- topaz/gold tint $40.00

2440 Bowl, 12", salad
- crystal $45.00
- rose $85.00
- green $85.00
- amber $75.00
- topaz/gold tint $75.00
- wisteria $185.00

2440 Cake, 10½", oval
- crystal $44.00
- rose $65.00
- green $65.00
- amber $58.00
- topaz/gold tint $60.00
- regal blue $165.00
- burgundy $165.00
- empire green $165.00

2440 Celery, 11½"
- crystal, ...$38.00
- rose $54.00
- green $54.00
- amber $50.00
- topaz/gold tint $54.00
- wisteria $150.00

2440 Cream Soup
- crystal $40.00
- topaz $54.00
- wisteria $95.00

2440 Cup and Saucer
- crystal $22.00
- topaz/gold tint $34.00
- wisteria $65.00
- regal blue $65.00
- burgundy $65.00
- empire green $65.00

2440 Cup and Saucer, after dinner
- crystal $35.00
- topaz $55.00
- wisteria $165.00

2440 Lemon, 5", handled
- crystal $22.00
- rose $32.00
- green $32.00
- amber $26.00
- topaz/gold tint $30.00
- wisteria $58.00
- regal blue $58.00
- burgundy $58.00
- empire green $58.00

2440 Mayonnaise, 6½", 2-part
- crystal $42.00
- rose $54.00
- green $54.00
- amber $45.00
- topaz/gold tint $50.00
- wisteria $95.00
- regal blue $85.00
- burgundy $85.00
- empire green $85.00
- ruby $85.00
- silver mist $40.00

2440 Olive, 6½"
- crystal $24.00
- rose $35.00
- green $35.00
- amber $32.00
- topaz/gold tint $35.00
- wisteria $85.00

2440 Pickle, 8½"
- crystal $30.00
- rose $38.00
- green $38.00
- amber $32.00
- topaz/gold tint $35.00
- wisteria $85.00

2440 Plate, 6"
- crystal $10.00
- topaz/gold tint $14.00
- wisteria $34.00

2440 Plate, 7"
- crystal $10.00
- topaz/gold tint $16.00
- wisteria $45.00

2440 Plate, 8"
- crystal $12.00
- topaz/gold tint $16.00
- wisteria $50.00

2440 Plate, 9"
- crystal $26.00
- topaz/gold tint $32.00
- wisteria $84.00

2440 Plate, 10"
- crystal $45.00
- topaz $58.00
- wisteria $150.00

2440 Plate, 13", torte
- crystal $55.00
- rose $95.00
- green $95.00
- amber $75.00
- topaz/gold tint $78.00
- wisteria $225.00
- regal blue $195.00
- burgundy $195.00
- empire green $195.00
- ruby $195.00
- silver mist $60.00

2440 Platter, 12"
- crystal $54.00
- topaz/gold tint $65.00
- wisteria $195.00

2440 Platter, 15"
- crystal $67.00
- topaz $75.00

2440 Relish, 2-part, handled
crystal $32.00
rose $47.00
green $47.00
amber $40.00
topaz/gold tint $44.00
wisteria $95.00
regal blue $95.00
burgundy $85.00
empire green $85.00
ruby $85.00
silver mist $34.00

2440 Relish, 3-part, handled
crystal $42.00
rose $65.00
green $65.00
amber $52.00
topaz/gold tint $54.00
wisteria $135.00
regal blue $125.00
burgundy $110.00
empire green $110.00
ruby $110.00
silver mist $44.00

2440 Dish, sauce, 6½", oval
crystal $38.00
rose $48.00
green $48.00
amber $45.00
topaz/gold tint $47.00
wisteria $95.00
regal blue $125.00
burgundy $95.00
empire green $95.00
ruby $125.00
silver mist $38.00

2440 Sugar and Cream, footed
crystal $40.00
rose $62.00
green $62.00
amber $58.00
topaz/gold tint $60.00
wisteria $195.00
regal blue $185.00
burgundy $185.00
empire green $165.00

2440 Sweetmeat, 4½", handled
crystal $22.00
rose $26.00
green $26.00
amber $22.00
topaz/gold tint $24.00
wisteria $46.00
regal blue $42.00
burgundy $42.00
empire green $42.00

2440 Tray, 8½", oval
crystal $38.00
rose $48.00
green $48.00
amber $45.00
topaz/gold tint $47.00
wisteria $95.00
regal blue $125.00
burgundy $95.00
empire green $95.00
ruby $95.00
silver mist $38.00

2440 Vase, 7"
crystal $48.00
rose $67.00
green $67.00
amber $60.00
topaz $65.00

Lamps

pre-1910 – 1942

Note: This listing is merely a sampling of the lamps offered by the Fostoria Glass Company.

Useful & Ornamental, 159 – 171

No. 1 Banquet Lamp, 25" $400.00/market
No. 1½ Banquet Lamp, low standard $295.00
No. 2 Banquet Lamp, 18" $300.00
No. 21 Princess Lamp: No. 21 lustre base with font and chimney, shade with fringe beads ....market
2325 Electric Boudoir Lamp, large and small sizes, ebony ....$75.00 – 95.00
No. 1 Persian Red, 23½" $800.00/market
No. 2 Persian Red, 18½" $700.00/market
No. 5 Persian Red, 18½" $700.00/market
No. 17 Persian Red, 23½" $800.00/market
No. 19 Lamp, night $135.00
Lamp, Clover, night $225.00
No. 20 Lamp, night $250.00
No. 21 Lamp, night $150.00
No. 191 Lamp, squat $125.00
No. 191 Lamp A, B, C, D, or O, footed $135.00
No. 734 Lamp, flat $95.00
No. 734 Lamp, sewing $245.00
No. 734 Lamp A, B, C, D, or O $135.00
Hand-painted Lamps ....market

Lancaster, Cutting 719

1933 – 1935

Stemware, 79

6009 Goblet $34.00
6009 Sherbet, high $32.00
6009 Sherbet, low $28.00
6009 Cocktail $32.00
6009 Claret-Wine $38.00
6009 Cordial $47.00
6009 Oyster Cocktail $24.00
6009 Ice Tea, footed $32.00
6009 Tumbler, 9 oz., footed $26.00
6009 Juice, footed $25.00

Tableware I, 278

869 Bowl, finger $12.00
2470½ Bowl, 10½" $45.00
2470½ Candlestick, 5½", pair $45.00
2400 Comport, 6" $27.00
2337 Plate, 6" $6.00
2337 Plate, 7" $7.00
2337 Plate, 8" $8.00
4110 Vase, 7½" $75.00

Large Cloverleaf, Etching 47

1906 – 1927

Stemware, 22, 61

114 Goblet, 10 oz. $4.00
114 Champagne $4.00
114 Claret $4.00
114 Wine $4.00
114 Cordial $5.00
858 Goblet, 9 oz. $8.00
858 Saucer Champagne, 5½ oz. $8.00
858 Fruit $8.00
858 Wine, 2¾ oz. $8.00
5001 Goblet, 11 oz. $12.00
5001 Goblet, 8¾ oz. $10.00
5001 Goblet, 7½ oz. $10.00
5001 Saucer Champagne $10.00
5001 Cocktail, 4 oz. $10.00
5001 Cocktail, 3 oz. $10.00
5001 Cocktail, 2½ oz. $10.00
5001 Claret, 5½ oz. $12.00
5001 Claret, 4¾ oz. $12.00
5001 Rhine Wine, 4 oz. $12.00
5001 Rhine Wine, 2½ oz. $12.00
5001 Wine, 3½ oz. $12.00
5001 Wine, 2 oz. $12.00
5001 Sherry, 2½ oz. $12.00
5001 Sherry, 2 oz. $12.00
5001 Sherry, 1½ oz. $12.00
5001 Brandy, ¾ oz. $12.00
5001 Cordial, 1 oz. $12.00
5001 Cordial, ¾ oz. $12.00
5001 Champagne, tall, 5¾ oz. $10.00
5001 Hot Whiskey, 5 oz. $10.00
701 Tumbler ....$4.00 – 10.00
858 Tumbler ....$4.00 – 10.00
724 Tankard $87.00
300 Jug $65.00
303 Jug $48.00
316 Jug $75.00
317½ Jug $65.00
318 Jug $75.00
1227 Jug $65.00
1236 Jug $75.00
2918 Jug $65.00

Large Sunburst Star, Cutting 81

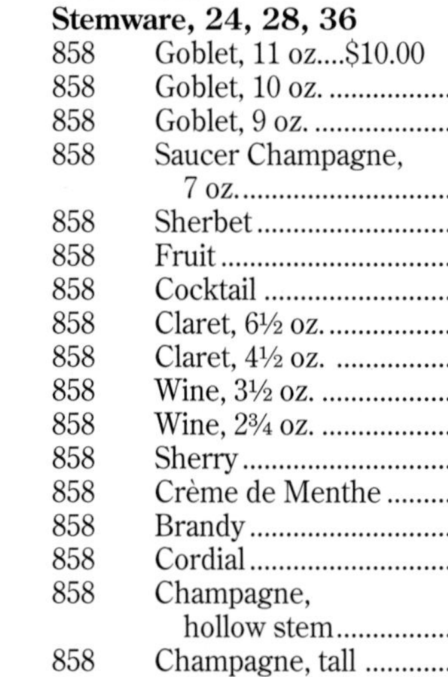

1904 – 1927

Stemware, 24, 28, 36

858 Goblet, 11 oz. $10.00
858 Goblet, 10 oz. $9.00
858 Goblet, 9 oz. $9.00
858 Saucer Champagne, 7 oz. $5.00
858 Sherbet $5.00
858 Fruit $5.00
858 Cocktail $5.00
858 Claret, 6½ oz. $5.00
858 Claret, 4½ oz. $5.00
858 Wine, 3½ oz. $5.00
858 Wine, 2¾ oz. $5.00
858 Sherry $5.00
858 Crème de Menthe $5.00
858 Brandy $8.00
858 Cordial $8.00
858 Champagne, hollow stem $8.00
858 Champagne, tall $8.00
858 Champagne, long stem $16.00
858 Hot Whiskey $5.00
863 Goblet, 10½ oz. $9.00
863 Goblet, 9 oz. $9.00
863 Goblet, 7 oz. $8.00
863 Saucer Champagne $9.00
863 Fruit $7.00
863 Cocktail, 3½ oz. $7.00
863 Claret $12.00
863 Rhine Wine $9.00
863 Wine $9.00
863 Sherry $8.00

863 Crème de Menthe $8.00
863 Brandy, pousse-café $15.00
863 Cordial $15.00
863 Champagne, tall $9.00
880 Goblet, 11 oz. $8.00
880 Goblet, 10 oz. $8.00
880 Goblet, 9 oz. $8.00
880 Goblet, 8 oz. $8.00
880 Saucer Champagne, 7 oz. $8.00
880 Saucer Champagne, 5½ oz. $7.00
880 Sherbet $7.00
880 Cocktail, 3½ oz. $7.00
880 Claret, 6½ oz. $10.00
880 Claret, 4½ oz. $9.00
880 Rhine Wine $9.00
880 Wine, 3½ oz. $9.00
880 Wine 2¾ oz. $9.00
880 Sherry $7.00
880 Crème de Menthe $7.00
880 Brandy, pousse-café, 1 oz. $7.00
880 Cordial, 1 oz. $15.00
880 Champagne, hollow stem $8.00
880 Champagne, tall $8.00
880 Grapefruit, tall and liner $30.00
880 Grapefruit, short and liner $25.00
880 Hot Whiskey $7.00
880 Ale, tall $8.00
766, 766½ Parfait $25.00
858 Tumbler ....$4.00 – 8.00
4011 Tumbler ....$4.00 – 8.00
945½ Grapefruit and Liner $28.00
303 Jug $50.00
1227 Jug $75.00
300 Tankard $75.00
724 Tankard $85.00

Lattice, Cutting 196

1929

Stemware, 33

877 Goblet $20.00
877 Sherbet, high $20.00
877 Sherbet, low $16.00
877 Parfait $22.00
877 Cocktail $18.00
877 Claret $24.00
877 Wine $22.00
877 Cordial $30.00
877 Oyster Cocktail $15.00
877 Ice Tea, footed $20.00
877 Tumbler, 9 oz., footed $15.00
877 Juice, footed $16.00
877 Whiskey, footed $16.00

Tableware I, 272

869 Bowl, finger and 2283 Plate $22.00
2394 Bowl, 12" $45.00
2394 Candlestick, 2", pair $45.00
2283 Plate, 6" $9.00
2283 Plate, 7" $10.00
2283 Plate, 8" $10.00

Laurel, Decoration 31

1920s

Stemware, 22

766 Goblet $12.00
766 Saucer Champagne $12.00
766 Fruit $10.00
766 Parfait $22.00
766 Cocktail $12.00
766 Wine $12.00
766 Cordial $20.00
766 Ice Tea, footed, handled $20.00
701 Tumbler, 14 oz. and plate $12.00
820 Tumbler, table $10.00
4011 Tumbler, 12 oz. $12.00
4011 Tumbler, 8 oz. $10.00
4011 Tumbler, 5 oz. $10.00
4011 Tumbler, 3 oz. $10.00

Tableware I, 317

766 Bowl, finger and plate $22.00
2244 Candlestick, 8¼", pair $95.00
2245 Candlestick, 8¼", pair $95.00
2219 Jar, candy and cover, ¼ pound $50.00
2219 Jar, candy and cover, ½ pound $54.00
2219 Jar, candy and cover, pound $62.00
2238 Jar, candy and cover, oblong, pound $85.00
2250 Jar, candy and cover, ¼ pound $50.00
2250 Jar, candy and cover, ½ pound $54.00
2250 Jar, candy and cover, pound $60.00
1697 Carafe Set $95.00
2241 Cologne, 2¼ oz., drip stopper $145.00
2243 Cologne, 2¼ oz., drip stopper $130.00
2242 Cologne, 3¼ oz., drip stopper $130.00
803 Comport, 5", footed $24.00
803 Comport, 6", footed $28.00
880 Comport, 5" $24.00
880 Comport and Cover, 5" $30.00
2252 Dish, 6", salad $22.00
1848 Dish, 9", salad, matt star base $36.00
825 Jelly
  with cover $45.00
  with no cover $37.00
2100/7 Jug $135.00
1968 Marmalade and cover $47.00
2138 Mayonnaise, plate, ladle, gold edge $58.00
803 Nappy, 5", deep, footed $27.00
803 Nappy, 6", deep, footed $32.00
803 Nappy, 7", deep, footed $35.00
803 Nappy, 5", and cover $30.00
1465 Oil, 5 oz., cut neck $48.00
1896 Plate, 7" $10.00
2238 Plate, 8¼" $12.00
2238 Plate, 11" $16.00
2290 Plate, 8", deep, salad $27.00
2290 Plate, 13", deep, salad $34.00
1848 Plate, 9", sandwich, matt star base $28.00
1719 Plate, 10½", sandwich, matt star base $30.00
2258 Plate, 11", sandwich $32.00
2258 Dish, 6", relish $16.00
2258 Dish, 8", relish $18.00
2258 Dish, 10", relish $25.00
2083 Bottle, salad dressing $84.00
858 Sweetmeat $24.00
2287 Tray, handled, lunch $58.00
1957 Vase, 7", center $54.00
2208 Vase, sweet pea $68.00
1465 Vinegar, 7 oz., cut neck $54.00
945½ Grapefruit and Liner, gold edge only $36.00

Laurel, Cutting 776

1938 – 1959

Stemware, 90, 91

6017 Goblet $30.00
6017 Sherbet, high $26.00
6017 Sherbet, low $22.00
6017 Cocktail $25.00
6017 Claret $36.00
6017 Wine $34.00
6017 Cordial $40.00
6017 Oyster Cocktail $20.00
6017 Ice Tea, footed $30.00
6017 Tumbler, 9 oz., footed $24.00
6017 Juice, footed $24.00
6019 Goblet $26.00
6019 Sherbet $23.00
6019 Parfait $26.00
6019 Cocktail $23.00
6019 Claret $28.00
6019 Wine $26.00
6019 Oyster Cocktail $16.00
6019 Ice Tea, footed $26.00
6019 Juice, footed $20.00

Tableware II, 167

4148 Ashtray, individual $20.00
2574 Bonbon $32.00
755 Bowl, finger $18.00
2574 Bowl, serving $34.00
6023 Bowl, footed $52.00
2574 Bowl, 9½", handled $38.00
2527 Candelabra, 2-light, UDP, pair $135.00
2574 Candlestick, 4", pair $58.00
2324 Candlestick, 6", pair $65.00
2574 Celery $30.00
4148 Cigarette Holder, 2¼" $35.00
2574 Comport, 5" $35.00
2451 Ice Dish $22.00
2451 Liner, ice dish (not cut) $20.00
2574 Ice Tub and 2510 Chrome Tongs $48.00
6011 Jug $265.00
2574 Lemon $28.00
2574 Mayonnaise, plate, ladle $47.00
2574 Olive $18.00
2574 Pickle $23.00
2337 Plate, 6" $10.00
2337 Plate, 7" $12.00
2337 Plate, 8" $12.00
2574 Plate, 14", torte $52.00
2574 Plate, cake $48.00
2574 Relish, 3-part $34.00
2586 Syrup, sani-cut $275.00
2574 Sugar and Cream $37.00
2574 Sugar and Cream, individual $35.00
2574 Sweetmeat $20.00
2574 Whip Cream $20.00

Lead Crystal Giftware

1970 – 1981

Tableware II, 295 – 300

LE04/123
Ashtray, 5½" $5.00
LE04/145
Ashtray A $4.00
LE04/147
Ashtray B, 2¾" $4.00
LE04/148
Ashtray C, 3⅛" $4.00
LE06/377
Candleholder, bird $16.00
675/118
Bowl, 8", round, serving, ... $12.00
LE04/521
Bowl, 8½" $18.00
LE04/2377/355
Bowl, 5⅝", snack $15.00
LE05/517
Bowl, 7½" $18.00
ST04/2377/433
Bowl, 6", Stratton $15.00
LE04/319
Candle, 6", pair $24.00
LE05/327
Candle B $4.00
ST06/327
Candleholder, star $10.00
2377/354
Box, candy and cover $40.00
LE04/377
Coaster A, 3½" $4.00
LE04/378
Coaster B, 3½" $4.00
LE04/379
Coaster C, 3½" $4.00
2377/382
Coaster D, set of 4 .... $20.00
LE05/2377/380
Coaster, Stratton $20.00
LE04/2183/297
Server, covered, Colonial Prism $47.00
LE04/680
Cream $12.00
CO11/8008/400
Decanter, quart, Coventry, Cut 928 .... $95.00
ST02/8008/400
Decanter, quart, Stratford, Cut 929 .... $95.00
LE04/509
Server and Spoon, hostess ... $12.00
2885/433
Ice Tub, 6", Stratton $35.00
LE06/676
Jar, candy and cover $42.00
2377/447
Jelly and cover, 8½" $32.00
JE 01/293
Box, jewelry and cover $27.00
2183/475
Marmalade and ladle, Colonial Prism $24.00
LE04/493
Napkin Ring A $4.00
LE04/494
Napkin Ring B $4.00
2183/506
Nappy, 5" $12.00
2222/536
Olive, 7", Colonial $10.00
LE04/540
Pickle, 8½" $10.00
LE04/554
Plate, 10", serving $15.00
LE04/2679/591
Preserve and Cover, 4½" $22.00
LE04/360
Tray, 10¼", relish $18.00
RI02/865
Ring Holder, silver or gold ... $25.00
LE04/623
Salt Dip, 2" $4.00
LE04/630
Salver, 10", round $145.00
LE04/654
Shaker, chrome top F, pair ... $20.00
1871 Shaker, chrome top F, pair ... $20.00
1883/654
Shaker, 4¾", chrome top F, pair $27.00
LE04/677
Sugar $12.00
2377/677
Sugar and Cream $24.00
LE04/2710/687 and 688
Sugar and Cream, individual, Daisy and Button $25.00
RA03/682
Sugar and Cream, Raleigh $24.00
VI06/682
Sugar and Cream, Virginia $28.00
LE04/512
Sweetmeat, 5½" $8.00
2878/583
Tid Bit, 7½", handled $24.00
LE04/583
Tid Bit, 7½", handled $18.00
LE04/2000/710
Toothpick Holder $22.00
LE04/2883/329
Urn and cover, 7⅝", footed $24.00
2326 /312
Candle Vase, 4⅜" $10.00
2870/755
Vase, 5½" $12.00
LE04/1300/751
Vase, 4¼", Drape $24.00
LE04/757
Vase, 6⅜", bud $12.00
LE04/761
Vase, 6", footed $22.00
LE04/2883/162
Bowl, wedding and cover, 8" $28.00
LE04/2864/380
Coaster, wine $6.00

Legacy, Decoration 635

1956 – 1967

Stemware, 112

6065 Goblet $36.00
6065 Sherbet $32.00
6065 Cocktail/Wine/Seafood $34.00
6065 Cordial $42.00
6065 Ice Tea, footed $36.00
6065 Juice, footed $32.00

Tableware II, 196

2364 Bowl, 9", salad $32.00
2324 Candlestick, 4", pair $35.00
2666 Cup and Saucer $26.00
2364 Mayonnaise, plate, ladle $58.00
2337 Plate, 7" $10.00
2337 Plate, 8" $12.00
2666 Sugar and Cream $40.00
2666 Sugar and Cream, individual $35.00
2666 Tray, sugar and cream, individual $10.00

Legion, Plate Etching 309

1933 – 1939

Stemware, 72

6000 Goblet $34.00
6000 Sherbet, high $30.00
6000 Sherbet, low $25.00
6000 Cocktail $30.00
6000 Wine $35.00
6000 Oyster Cocktail $20.00
6000 Ice Tea, footed $34.00
6000 Juice, footed $30.00

Tableware I, 206

2470 Bonbon
crystal $37.00
rose $45.00
topaz $40.00
2424 Bowl, 8"
crystal $57.00
rose $75.00
topaz $70.00
2440 Bowl, 10½"
crystal $69.00
rose $87.00
topaz $80.00
2440 Bowl, 12", salad
crystal $85.00
rose $125.00
topaz $100.00
2470 Bowl, 12"
crystal $125.00
rose $175.00
topaz $145.00
2375 Candlestick, 3", pair
crystal $68.00
rose $85.00
topaz $75.00
2470 Candlestick, 5½", pair
crystal $165.00
rose $225.00
topaz $195.00
2456 Jar, candy and cover, ½ lb.
crystal $125.00
rose $165.00
topaz $135.00
2470 Comport, 6", low
crystal $57.00
rose $74.00
topaz $65.00
2470 Comport, 6", tall
crystal $125.00
rose $145.00
topaz $135.00
2419 Comport, 6"
crystal $65.00
rose $85.00
topaz $75.00
2375½ Cup and Saucer
crystal $30.00
2470 Dish, lemon
crystal $37.00

rose $45.00
topaz...................................$40.00
2375 Plate, 6"
crystal $11.00
2375 Plate, 7"
crystal $14.00
2375 Plate, 8"
crystal $16.00
2375 Plate, 9"
crystal $36.00
2470 Plate, 10", cake
crystal $75.00
rose $98.00
topaz...................................$88.00
2440 Plate, 13", torte
crystal $87.00
rose $125.00
topaz...................................$95.00
2470 Relish, 3-part, round
crystal $68.00
rose $87.00
topaz...................................$75.00
2470 Dish, 9", service
crystal $60.00
rose $74.00
topaz...................................$65.00
2375½ Sugar and Cream
crystal $75.00
2470 Sweetmeat
crystal $38.00
rose $45.00
topaz...................................$40.00
2470 Tray, sugar and cream
crystal $38.00
rose $47.00
topaz...................................$45.00
2440 Vase, 7"
crystal $95.00
rose $150.00
topaz.................................$125.00
2454 Vase, 8"
crystal $125.00
rose $195.00
topaz.................................$175.00
887 Tumbler, 2½ oz.,
crystal only.........................$12.00
889 Tumbler, 13 oz.,
crystal only.........................$18.00
889 Tumbler, 5 oz.,
crystal only $14.00
4076 Tumbler, 9 oz.,
crystal only.........................$16.00

Leicester, Cutting 722½

1933 – 1934

Stemware, 80

6010 Goblet.......$35.00
6010 Sherbet, high $32.00
6010 Sherbet, low $28.00
6010 Cocktail $32.00
6010 Claret-Wine $38.00
6010 Cordial $47.00
6010 Oyster Cocktail.......................$24.00
6010 Ice Tea, footed $32.00
6010 Tumbler, 9 oz., footed...........$26.00
6010 Juice, footed $25.00

Tableware I, 279

869 Bowl, finger...........................$12.00
2470½ Bowl, 10½"................................$45.00
2470½ Candlestick, 5½", pair...........$45.00
2400 Comport, 6"...........................$27.00
2337 Plate, 6" $6.00
2337 Plate, 7" $7.00
2337 Plate, 8" $8.00
2440 Plate, 13", torte $35.00
4110 Vase, 7½" $75.00

Lenore, Needle Etching 73

1923 – 1930

Stemware, 22

858 Goblet, 9 oz. $10.00
858 Saucer Champagne, 5½ oz...$10.00
858 Sherbet $10.00
858 Fruit $10.00
858 Cocktail $10.00
858 Claret, 4½ oz. $10.00
858 Parfait $20.00
858 Wine, 2¾ oz. $10.00
858 Cordial $15.00
701 Ice Tea, 12 oz. and 5" plate...$10.00
858 Tumbler, 14 oz. $12.00
858 Tumbler, 12 oz. $12.00
858 Tumbler, 8 oz. $8.00
858 Tumbler, 5½ oz. $6.00
858 Tumbler, 3 oz. $4.00
869 Tumbler, 12 oz., handled, ...$12.00

Tableware I, 121

880 Bonbon $24.00
858 Bowl, finger, and
underplate $18.00
5078 Comport, 5", or 6"..................$20.00
1236/4 Jug...$56.00
1236/6 Jug...$65.00
303/7 Jug...$60.00
318/7 Jug...$65.00
858 Mayonnaise, plate, ladle $18.00
5078 Nappy, 5"..................................$18.00
5078 Nappy, 6"..................................$20.00
5078 Nappy, 7"..................................$22.00
312 Oil...$42.00
840 Plate, 5", tumbler......................$6.00
2133 Sugar and Cream...................$35.00
858 Sweetmeat..............................$24.00
2270 Jug and cover..........................$85.00
300 Tankard $75.00

Lenox, Etching 330

1937 – 1943

Stemware, 89

6017 Goblet.............$28.00
6017 Sherbet, high......$24.00
6017 Sherbet, low............$20.00
6017 Cocktail $24.00
6017 Claret $30.00
6017 Wine...$30.00
6017 Cordial $42.00
6017 Oyster Cocktail.......................$20.00
6017 Tumbler, 14 oz., footed $34.00
6017 Ice Tea, footed $28.00
6017 Tumbler, 9 oz., footed $24.00
6017 Juice, footed $22.00
4132 Tumbler....................$10.00 – 12.00
6011 Jug..$175.00
2337 Plate, 6" $8.00
2337 Plate, 7" $10.00
2337 Plate, 8" $12.00

Lexington, 2449

1974

Note: Reintroduction of Hermitage in olive green, brown, and yellow

Tableware II, 51

2449 199 Bowl, 8", footed...............$32.00
2449 224 Bowl, 10", footed
flared $32.00
2449 319 Candleholder, 6"............$64.00
2449 421 Bowl, 5", fruit $15.00
2449 622 Relish, 3-part $26.00
2449 679 Sugar, footed...................$13.50
2449 81 Cream, footed $13.50
2449 758 Vase, 6", footed..............$38.00

Liana Gold (Imported Stemware)

1984 – 1986

Tableware II, 280 – 281

Goblet......................$22.00
Wine.........................$22.00
Flute.........................$22.00
Ice Tea.....................$22.00

Liana Platinum (Imported Stemware)

1984 – 1986

See Liana Gold image

Tableware II, 280 – 281

Goblet $22.00
Wine.......................................$22.00
Flute.......................................$22.00
Ice Tea $22.00

Lido, Plate Etching 329

1937 – 1954

Stemware, 89

6017 Goblet
crystal $32.00
azure $75.00
6017 Sherbet, high
crystal $30.00
azure $70.00
6017 Sherbet, low
crystal $22.00
azure $55.00
6017 Cocktail
crystal $30.00
azure $65.00
6017 Claret
crystal $38.00
azure $85.00
6017 Wine
crystal $35.00
azure $75.00
6017 Cordial
crystal $44.00
azure $110.00
6017 Oyster Cocktail
crystal $22.00
azure $50.00
6017 Ice Tea, footed
crystal $36.00
azure $75.00
6017 Tumbler, 9 oz., footed
crystal $32.00
azure $55.00
6017 Juice, footed
crystal $25.00
azure $75.00
6017 Tumbler, 14 oz.
crystal $25.00
azure $55.00
4132 Tumbler
crystal ....$32.00 – 36.00

Tableware I, 249 – 253

2496 Bonbon
- crystal $40.00
- azure $68.00

766 Bowl, finger
- crystal $37.00
- azure $65.00

2496 Bowl, regular, handled, nappy
- crystal $34.00
- azure $58.00

2496 Bowl, flared, handled, nappy
- crystal $34.00
- azure $58.00

2496 Bowl, square, handled, nappy
- crystal $34.00
- azure $58.00

2496 Bowl, 3-cornered, handled, nappy
- crystal $34.00
- azure $58.00

2496 Bowl, 3-toed, nut
- crystal $50.00
- azure $70.00

2496 Bowl, 8½", handled, serving
- crystal $60.00
- azure $125.00

2496 Bowl, 10½", handled
- crystal $115.00
- azure $225.00

2496 Bowl, 12", flared
- crystal $85.00
- azure $135.00

2545 Bowl, 12½", Flame
- crystal $87.00
- azure $150.00

2496 Candlestick, 4", pair
- crystal $68.00
- azure $130.00

2496 Candlestick, 5½", pair
- crystal $95.00
- azure $175.00

2496 Candlestick, duo, pair
- crystal $125.00
- azure $200.00

2545 Candlestick, duo, pair
- crystal $145.00
- azure $265.00

2545 Candlestick, lustre, pair
- crystal $150.00
- azure $225.00

2545 Candelabra, 2-light, B prisms, pair
- crystal $295.00
- azure $400.00

2496 Box, candy and cover, 3-part
- crystal $125.00
- azure $200.00

2496 Celery, 11"
- crystal $75.00
- azure $135.00

2496 Cheese and Cracker
- crystal $115.00
- azure $200.00

2496 Comport, 5½"
- crystal $69.00
- azure $125.00

2496 Comport, 6½"
- crystal $85.00
- azure $135.00

2496 Cup and Saucer
- crystal $34.00
- azure $52.00

2496 Ice Bucket, metal handle
- crystal $125.00
- azure $200.00

2496 Jelly and Cover
- crystal $125.00
- azure $195.00

6011 Jug
- crystal $325.00
- azure $600.00

2496 Mayonnaise, 2-part
- crystal $58.00
- azure $88.00

2496½ Mayonnaise, plate, ladle
- crystal $75.00
- azure $135.00

2496 Oil, 3½ oz.
- crystal $125.00
- azure $300.00

2496 Pickle, 8"
- crystal $38.00
- azure $65.00

2496 Plate, 6"
- crystal $12.00
- azure $22.00

2496 Plate, 7"
- crystal $16.00
- azure $25.00

2496 Plate, 8"
- crystal $22.00
- azure $32.00

2496 Plate, 9"
- crystal $48.00
- azure $75.00

2496 Plate, 10", handled, cake
- crystal $85.00
- azure $150.00

2496 Plate, 14", torte
- crystal $94.00
- azure $165.00

2496 Relish, 2-part
- crystal $40.00
- azure $72.00

2496 Relish, 3-part
- crystal $65.00
- azure $125.00

2419 Relish, 5-part
- crystal $95.00

2496 Dish, sauce, 6½", oval
- crystal $75.00
- azure $135.00

2496 Shaker, FGT, pair
- crystal $150.00
- azure $245.00

2496 Sugar and Cream
- crystal $65.00
- azure $125.00

2496 Sugar and Cream, individual
- crystal $65.00
- azure $125.00

2496 Sweetmeat
- crystal $52.00
- azure $95.00

2496 Tid Bit, 3-toed
- crystal $5800
- azure $95.00

2496½ Tray, 6½", individual, sugar and cream
- crystal $32.00
- azure $65.00

2496 Tray, 8", oblong
- crystal $57.00
- azure $95.00

4128 Vase, 5"
- crystal $140.00
- azure $200.00

2470 Vase, 10"
- crystal $275.00
- azure $395.00

Light Show Giftware (see Hermitage, Hostess Giftware and Virginia)

1985 – 1986

Tableware II, 301

L101/467 Glass Light
- crystal $30.00
- cobalt $40.00
- opal $35.00

Lily of the Valley, Carving 19

1940 – 1943

Useful & Ornamental, 124

4143½ Vase, 6", footed $85.00

4143½ Vase, 7½", footed $125.00

4132½ Vase, 8" $150.00

2568 Vase, 9", footed $185.00

Lily of the Valley, Plate Etching 241

1915 – 1927

Stemware, 23

858 Goblet, 10 oz $25.00

858 Saucer Champagne, 5½ oz $25.00

858 Sherbet $25.00

858 Fruit $25.00

858 Cocktail $25.00

858 Claret, 4½ oz. $30.00

858 Wine, 2¾ oz. $25.00

858 Sherry $25.00

858 Crème de Menthe $25.00

858 Brandy $45.00

858 Cordial $45.00

858 Oyster Cocktail $20.00

858 Champagne, hollow stem $30.00

858 Champagne, tall $45.00

879 Goblet $35.00

879 Saucer Champagne $32.00

879 Fruit $27.00

879 Cocktail $30.00

879 Claret $38.00

879 Wine $35.00

879 Crème de Menthe $30.00

879 Brandy, pousse-café $42.00

879 Cordial $48.00

701 Tumbler, 14 oz. and plate $10.00

820 Tumbler .... $8.00 – 12.00

833 Tumbler .... $8.00 – 12.00

858 Tumbler .... $8.00 – 12.00

887 Tumbler .... $8.00 – 12.00

889 Tumbler .... $8.00 – 12.00

4061 Lemonade, footed, handled $35.00

4065 Tumbler .... $8.00 – 12.00

4077 Tumbler .... $8.00 – 12.00

Tableware I, 140

810 Bowl, finger and plate $22.00

858 Bowl, finger and plate $22.00

1697 Carafe $94.00

4023 Tumbler, 6 oz., carafe $15.00

803 Comport, 5" $22.00

803 Comport, 6" $24.00

300/7 Jug $95.00

303/7 Jug....$75.00
318/7 Jug....$85.00
1968 Marmalade and cover, plain....$42.00
1831 Mustard and cover, plain....$35.00
1227 Nappy, 4½"....$15.00
803 Nappy, 5"....$18.00
803 Nappy, 6"....$20.00
803 Nappy, 7"....$22.00
1227 Nappy, 8"....$27.00
300½ Oil, small....$65.00
1465 Oil, 7 oz., cut neck....$76.00
1848 Plate, 9", sandwich....$24.00
1719 Plate, 10½", sandwich, plain...$30.00
2083 Bottle, salad dressing....$88.00
1480 Sugar and Cream....$45.00
858 Sweetmeat....$34.00
922 Toothpick, Cut 19....$26.00
810 Custard and Plate....$8.00
858 Custard and Plate....$8.00
945, 945½ Grapefruit and Liner....$45.00
822 Parfait....$38.00
863 Almond....$22.00
1558 Bottle, water....$58.00
300 Decanter, quart....$58.00
1464 Decanter, 18 oz.....$50.00
2018 Jug....$85.00
300½ Oil, large....$75.00
1165 Shaker, pair....$47.00
300 Tankard....$75.00
724 Tankard....$125.00

Lineal, Cutting 899

1963 – 1965

Stemware, 127

6102 Goblet....$32.00
6102 Sherbet....$30.00
6102 Claret....$35.00
6102 Tulip Wine....$35.00
6102 Brandy....$35.00
6102 Ice Tea, footed....$32.00
2337 Plate, 7"....$10.00
2337 Plate, 8"....$12.00

Lines, Decoration 609

1931 – 1932

Tableware I, 331

2350 Ashtray, small....$18.00
2297 Bowl A, 12'....$48.00
2324 Candlestick, 4", pair....$48.00
2400 Comport, 6"....$34.00
2375 Dish, lemon....$22.00
2375 Plate, 10", cake....$54.00
4105 Vase, 8"....$75.00

Living Rose, Crystal Print 5

1956 – 1958

Stemware, 112

6065 Goblet....$38.00
6065 Sherbet....$35.00
6065 Cocktail/Wine/Seafood....$40.00
6065 Cordial....$50.00
6065 Ice Tea, footed....$38.00
6065 Juice, footed....$34.00
2337 Plate, 7"....$10.00
2337 Plate, 8"....$12.00

Lotus, Etching 232

1913 – 1927

Stemware, 20, 63

766 Goblet....$12.00
766 Saucer Champagne....$12.00
766 Sherbet....$10.00
766 Fruit....$10.00
766 Parfait....$22.00
766 Cocktail....$12.00
766 Claret....$12.00
766 Rhine Wine....$12.00
766 Wine....$12.00
766 Burgundy....$15.00
766 Sherry....$12.00
766 Crème de Menthe....$12.00
766 Brandy....$15.00
766 Cordial....$24.00
766 Sorbet....$10.00
766 Ice Tea, footed, handled....$20.00
766 Custard....$8.00
766 Grapefruit and Liner....$25.00
5070 Goblet, 10 oz.....$14.00
5070 Goblet, 9 oz.....$12.00
5070 Goblet, 8 oz.....$12.00
5070 Saucer Champagne....$12.00
5070 Sherbet....$10.00
5070 Cocktail, 3½ oz.....$10.00
5070 Cocktail, 3 oz.....$10.00
5070 Claret, 6 oz.....$16.00
5070 Claret, 4½ oz.....$15.00
5070 Rhine Wine....$16.00
5070 Wine....$15.00
5070 Sherry....$15.00
5070 Crème de Menthe....$12.00
5070 Brandy, pousse-café, 1 oz.....$20.00
5070 Brandy, pousse-café, ¾ oz.....$20.00
5070 Cordial, 1 oz.....$25.00
5070 Cordial, ¾ oz.....$25.00
5070 Champagne, hollow stem....$16.00
5070 Champagne, tall....$15.00
5070 Hot Whiskey....$12.00
837 Oyster Cocktail....$10.00
945½ Grapefruit and Liner....$28.00
820 Tumbler....$6.00 – 12.00
858 Tumbler....$6.00 – 12.00
887 Tumbler....$6.00 – 12.00
889 Tumbler....$6.00 – 12.00
4011 Tumbler....$6.00 – 12.00
303 Jug....$57.00
300 Tankard....$75.00
318 Tankard....$75.00

Lotus, 6144

1980 – 1982

Stemware, 145

6144 Goblet
crystal mist....$35.00
peach mist....$45.00
ebony bases....$45.00
6144 Champagne
crystal mist....$32.00
peach mist....$42.00
ebony bases....$42.00
6144 Claret, large
crystal mist....$38.00
peach mist....$48.00
ebony bases....$48.00
6144 Ice Tea, footed
crystal mist....$35.00
peach mist....$45.00
ebony bases....$45.00
6144 Flute, champagne
crystal mist....$38.00
peach mist....$48.00
ebony base....$48.00

Tableware II, 302

6144/318 Candlestick, 5½", low....$45.00
6144/323 Candlestick, 7½", high....$45.00
6144/789 Vase, 8", bud....$50.00

Louisa, Cutting 168

1922 – 1924

Stemware, 19

661 Goblet....$10.00
661 Saucer Champagne....$10.000
661 Fruit/Sherbet, low....$8.00
661 Parfait....$10.00
661 Cocktail....$10.00
661 Wine....$10.00
4011 Tumbler....$6.00 – 10.00
4085 Tumbler....$6.00 – 10.00

Tableware I, 265

880 Bonbon....$18.00
1769 Bowl, finger and 1736 plate..$18.00
2250 Jar, candy and cover, ¼ pound....$22.00
2250 Jar, candy and cover, ½ pound....$26.00
2250 Jar, candy and cover, pound....$30.00
1697 Carafe, and 6 oz. 4023 Tumbler....$45.00
2241 Cologne and Stopper....$52.00
803 Comport, 5"....$16.00
803 Comport, 6"....$17.00
803 Comport and cover, 5"....$23.00
825 Jelly....$18.00
825 Jelly and cover....$25.00
317 Jug, cut neck....$95.00
317½ Jug and cover....$125.00
1852/6 Jug....$95.00
303/7 Jug....$95.00
4087 Marmalade and cover....$28.00
2138 Mayonnaise, plate, ladle....$45.00
803 Nappy, 5"....$12.00
803 Nappy, 6"....$14.00
803 Nappy, 7"....$15.00
803 Nappy and cover, 5"....$20.00
1465 Oil, 5 oz., cut neck....$30.00
1465 Oil, 7 oz., cut neck....$35.00
840 Plate, 5", tumbler....$6.00
2283 Plate, 8¼"....$10.00
2283 Plate, 11"....$14.00
2263 Salt, individual....$14.00
2235 Shaker, FGT or pearl top, pair....$30.00
1480 Sugar and Cream....$28.00
2194 Syrup, 8 oz., nickel top....$37.00
2194 Syrup, 12 oz., nickel top....$48.00
2209 Vase, 9"....$35.00
945½ Grapefruit and Liner....$24.00

Lovelight, Decoration 671

1966 – 1970

Stemware, 132

6107 Goblet....$28.00
6107 Sherbet....$25.00
6107 Claret....$30.00
6107 Tulip Wine....$30.00

Lovelight, Decoration 671

6107 Liqueur $38.00
6107 Ice Tea, footed $28.00
2337 Plate, 7" $10.00
2337 Plate, 8" $12.00

Love Song, Decoration 655

1961 – 1973

Stemware, 123

6099 Goblet $35.00
6099 Sherbet $32.00
6099 Wine/Cocktail $38.00
6099 Cordial $48.00
6099 Ice Tea, footed $35.00
6099 Juice, footed $30.00
2337 Plate, 7" $10.00
2337 Plate, 8" $12.00

Lucerne, Cutting 778

1938 – 1939

Stemware, 90

6017 Goblet $30.00
6017 Sherbet, high $28.00
6017 Sherbet, low $24.00
6017 Cocktail $28.00
6017 Claret $35.00
6017 Wine $35.00
6017 Cordial $45.00
6017 Oyster Cocktail $22.00
6017 Ice Tea, footed $30.00
6017 Tumbler, 9 oz., footed $24.00
6017 Juice, footed $22.00
4132 Tumbler .... $10.00 – 12.00

Tableware I, 299 – 300

766 Bowl, finger $12.00
4132 Decanter $85.00
4132 Ice Bowl $45.00
6011 Jug $175.00
2337 Plate, 6" $7.00
2337 Plate, 7" $8.00
2337 Plate, 8" $10.00

Luxemburg, 2766 (see Crown Collection)

Lynn, Cutting 180

1925 – 1926

Stemware, 65

5083 Goblet $18.00
5083 Sherbet, high $18.00
5083 Sherbet, low $15.00
5083 Parfait $18.00
5083 Cocktail $15.00
5083 Wine $20.00
701 Tumbler .... $6.00 – 10.00
820 Tumbler .... $6.00 – 10.00
889 Tumbler .... $6.00 – 10.00
4011 Tumbler .... $6.00 – 10.00

Tableware I, 269

1769 Bowl, finger and 2283 Plate $18.00
2327 Comport, 7" $24.00
2040/3 Jug $55.00
2082/7 Jug $85.00
2315 Mayonnaise and Plate $20.00
2222 Plate, 7" $8.00
2222 Plate, 8" $10.00
2222 Plate, 10" $14.00
2315 Sugar and Cream $28.00

Lynwood, Crystal Print 4

1956 – 1965

Stemware, 112

6065 Goblet $36.00
6065 Sherbet $34.00
6065 Cocktail/Wine/Seafood $34.00
6065 Cordial $45.00
6065 Ice Tea, footed $36.00
6065 Juice, footed $32.00
2337 Plate, 7" $10.00
2337 Plate, 8" $12.00

Lyre, Carving 30

1940 – 1943

Useful & Ornamental, 130

2427 Ashtray, oblong $22.00
2427 Box, cigarette and cover $75.00

Lyric, 6061

1955 – 1965

Stemware, 110

6016 Goblet
crystal $32.00
pink base $38.00
6016 Sherbet
crystal $28.00
pink base $34.00
6016 Cocktail/Wine/Seafood
crystal $28.00
pink base $43.00
6016 Cordial
crystal $38.00
pink base $44.00
6016 Ice Tea, footed
crystal $32.00
pink base $38.00
6016 Juice, footed
crystal $26.00
pink base $34.00

Lyric, Cutting 796

1939 – 1943

Stemware, 40

892 Goblet $30.00
892 Saucer Champagne $28.00
892 Sherbet, low $25.00
892 Cocktail $25.00
892 Claret $32.00
892 Wine $30.00
892 Cordial $38.00
892 Oyster Cocktail $20.00
892 Ice Tea, footed $30.00
892 Juice, footed $25.00

Tableware I, 303

1769 Bowl, finger $15.00
6023 Bowl, footed $65.00
2324 Candlestick, 6", pair $45.00
6011 Jug $175.00
2337 Plate, 6" $7.00
2337 Plate, 7" $8.00
2337 Plate, 8" $10.00

--M--

Mademoiselle, 6033

1949 – 1971

Stemware, 102

6033 Goblet $120.00
6033 Sherbet, high $18.00
6033 Sherbet, low $14.00
6033 Parfait $18.00
6033 Cocktail $18.00
6033 Claret-Wine $23.00
6033 Cordial $25.00
6033 Oyster Cocktail $10.00
6033 Ice Tea, footed $18.00
6033 Juice, footed $10.00

Manhattan, Cutting 725

1933 – 1938

Stemware, 60

4024 Goblet, 11 oz. $26.00
4024 Goblet, 10 oz. $26.00
4024 Saucer Champagne $26.00
4024 Sherbet $20.00
4024 Cocktail $20.00
4024 Claret-Wine $30.00
4024 Rhine Wine $30.00
4024 Sherry $30.00
4024 Cordial $40.00
4024 Oyster Cocktail $20.00
4024 Ice Tea, footed $26.00
4024 Tumbler, 8 oz., footed $22.00
4024 Juice, footed $22.00
4024 Whiskey, footed $30.00
701 Tumbler .... $10.00 – 14.00
887 Tumbler .... $10.00 – 14.00
1184 Tumbler .... $10.00 – 14.00

Tableware I, 279

869 Bowl, finger $14.00
4024 Comport, 5" $20.00
2337 Plate, 6" $7.00
2337 Plate, 7" $8.00
2337 Plate, 8" $10.00

Manor, Plate Etching 286

1931 – 1943

Stemware, 74, 77

6003 Goblet
crystal $38.00
green bowl $54.00
topaz bowl $54.00
wisteria base $125.00
6003 Sherbet, high
crystal $35.00
green bowl $48.00
topaz bowl $48.00
wisteria base $110.00
6003 Sherbet, low
crystal $26.00
green bowl $35.00
topaz bowl $35.00
wisteria base $60.00
6003 Cocktail
crystal $34.00
green bowl $40.00
topaz bowl $40.00
wisteria base $85.00

6003 Cordial
crystal $60.00
green bowl $85.00
topaz bowl $85.00
wisteria base $145.00
6003 Oyster Cocktail
crystal $25.00
green bowl $34.00
topaz bowl $34.00
wisteria base $48.00
6003 Ice Tea, footed
crystal $40.00
green bowl $54.00
topaz bowl $54.00
wisteria base $125.00
6003 Tumbler, 10 oz., footed
crystal $30.00
green bowl $35.00
topaz bowl $35.00
wisteria base $62.00
6003 Juice, footed
crystal $30.00
green bowl $37.00
topaz bowl $37.00
wisteria base $60.00
6003 Whiskey, footed
crystal $34.00
green bowl $54.00
topaz bowl $54.00
wisteria base $110.00
6007 Goblet $45.00
6007 Sherbet, high $42.00
6007 Sherbet, low $34.00
6007 Cocktail $40.00
6007 Claret $54.00
6007 Wine........$54.00
6007 Cordial $75.00
6007 Oyster Cocktail........$30.00
6007 Ice Tea, footed $45.00
6007 Tumbler, 9 oz.,
footed $34.00
6007 Juice, footed $34.00
6007 Whiskey, footed $47.00

Tableware I, 197 – 202

4020 Almond, individual
crystal $32.00
green........$36.00
topaz........$32.00
2419 Ashtray
crystal $32.00
green........$36.00
topaz........$32.00
2419 Bonbon
crystal $32.00
green........$36.00
topaz........$32.00
4020 Bowl, finger
crystal $32.00
green........$50.00
topaz........$45.00
wisteria $75.00
2419 Bowl, 5", fruit
crystal $32.00
green........$36.00
topaz........$32.00
2419 Bowl, 6", cereal
crystal $32.00
green........$40.00
topaz........$35.00
2419 Bowl, 7", soup
crystal $45.00
green........$55.00
topaz........$50.00
2419 Bowl, 10", baker
crystal $55.00
green........$76.00
topaz........$64.00
2443 Bowl, 10", oval
crystal $95.00
green........$145.00
topaz........$135.00
2470½ Bowl, 10½"
crystal $145.00
green........$250.00
topaz........$195.00
2394 Bowl A, 12"
crystal $95.00
green........$145.00
topaz........$125.00
2433 Bowl A, 12"
crystal $195.00
green........$350.00
topaz........$300.00
2394 Candlestick, 2", pair
crystal $75.00
green........$125.00
topaz........$95.00
2443 Candlestick, 3", pair
crystal $87.00
green........$125.00
topaz........$115.00
2433 Candlestick, 3", pair
crystal $125.00
green........$165.00
topaz........$145.00
2470½ Candlestick, 5½", pair
crystal $135.00
green........$165.00
topaz........$150.00
2430 Jar, candy and cover, ½ pound
crystal $110.00
green........$160.00
topaz........$145.00
2419 Celery, 11"
crystal $52.00
green........$68.00
topaz........$62.00
2419 Comport, 6"
crystal $55.00
green........$65.00
topaz........$60.00
2433 Comport, 6", low
crystal $75.00
green........$87.00
topaz........$82.00
2433 Comport, 6", tall
crystal $195.00
green........$250.00
topaz........$225.00
2419 Cream Soup
crystal $48.00
green........$60.00
topaz........$54.00
2419 Cup and Saucer, after dinner
crystal $55.00
green........$68.00
topaz........$60.00
2419 Cup and Saucer
crystal $35.00
green........$45.00
topaz........$40.00
4020 Decanter, footed
crystal........$500.00/market
green $800.00/market
topaz $600.00/market
2451 Dish, ice and liner
crystal $58.00
green........$70.00
topaz........$65.00
2451 Plate, ice dish
crystal $12.00
green........$15.00
topaz........$15.00
2443 Ice Tub, 6"
crystal $110.00
green........$145.00
topaz........$125.00
4020 Jug (foot in colors)
crystal $500.00
green........$595.00
topaz........$565.00
wisteria,........$1,000.00/market
2419 Jelly
crystal $40.00
green........$47.00
topaz........$42.00
2419 Dish, lemon
crystal $32.00
green........$38.00
topaz........$36.00
2419 Mayonnaise
crystal $34.00
green........$40.00
topaz........$37.00
2419 Pickle, 8½"
crystal $34.00
green........$42.00
topaz........$38.00
2419 Plate, 6"
crystal $12.00
green........$16.00
topaz........$14.00
2419 Plate, 7"
crystal $14.00
green........$18.00
topaz........$16.00
2419 Plate, 8"
crystal $18.00
green........$25.00
topaz........$22.00
2419 Plate, 9"
crystal $45.00
green........$85.00
topaz........$65.00
2419 Plate, cake
crystal $65.00
green........$125.00
topaz........$98.00
2440 Plate, 13", torte
crystal $125.00
2419 Platter, 12"
crystal $110.00
green........$135.00
topaz........$125.00
2419 Platter, 15"
crystal $125.00
green........$175.00
topaz........$150.00
2419 Relish, 8½"
crystal $40.00
green........$48.00
topaz........$45.00
2419 Relish, 4-part
crystal $59.00
green........$67.00
topaz........$62.00
2419 Bowl, sauce and stand
crystal $95.00
green........$125.00
topaz........$110.00

2419 Shaker, FGT, pair
crystal ... $110.00
green ... $165.00
topaz ... $150.00
4020 Shaker, footed, FGT, pair
crystal ... $125.00
green ... $185.00
topaz ... $175.00
2419 Sugar and Cream, Tea
crystal ... $65.00
green ... $95.00
topaz ... $85.00
2419 Sugar and Cream
crystal ... $75.00
green ... $125.00
topaz ... $110.00
2419½ Sugar and Cream, footed
crystal ... $85.00
green ... $135.00
topaz ... $125.00
2419 Syrup, cover, saucer
crystal ... $200.00
green ... $275.00
topaz ... $250.00
2419 Tray, handled, lunch
crystal ... $110.00
green ... $137.00
topaz ... $125.00
4108 Vase, 5"
crystal ... $165.00
green ... $200.00
topaz ... $185.00
4108 Vase, 6"
crystal ... $195.00
green ... $245.00
topaz ... $225.00
4108 Vase, 7"
crystal ... $225.00
green ... $300.00
topaz ... $275.00
4106 Vase, 7"
crystal ... $225.00
green ... $300.00
topaz ... $290.00
4107 Vase, 9"
crystal ... $300.00
green ... $400.00
topaz ... $375.00

Mantilla, Decoration 675

1966 – 1970

Stemware, 131

6106 Goblet ... $32.00
6106 Sherbet ... $30.00
6106 Claret ... $35.00
6106 Tulip Wine ... $35.00
6106 Liqueur ... $45.00
6106 Ice Tea, footed ... $32.00

Tableware

2337 Plate, 7" ... $10.00
2337 Plate, 8" ... $12.00

Mardi Gras, Cutting 765

1937 – 1943

Stemware, 82

6011 Goblet ... $30.00
6011 Saucer Champagne ... $25.00
6011 Sherbet, low ... $22.00
6011 Cocktail ... $25.00
6011 Claret ... $30.00
6011 Wine ... $30.00
6011 Cordial ... $34.00
6011 Oyster Cocktail ... $20.00
6011 Ice Tea, footed ... $28.00
6011 Tumbler, 10 oz., footed ... $24.00
6011 Juice, footed ... $24.00
6011 Jug ... $175.00
2337 Plate, 6" ... $8.00
2337 Plate, 7" ... $10.00
2337 Plate, 8" ... $12.00

Mardi Gras, Decoration 627

1954 – 1957

Milk Glass with colored glass added.

Tableware II, 198 – 200

2677 Ashtray ... $38.00
2666 Bowl, ribbon ... $74.00
2618 Box, cigarette and cover ... $125.00
2666 Comport ... $72.00
2666 Sweetmeat ... $60.00
2666 Tid Bit ... $67.00
2619 Vase, 6" ... $95.00
4116 Vase, 6" ... $125.00
2619 Vase, 9½" ... $167.00

Marilyn, 6055

1954 – 1974

loop optic

Stemware, 108

6055 Goblet ... $24.00
6055 Sherbet ... $22.00
6055 Cocktail ... $20.00
6055 Claret-Wine ... $26.00
6055 Cordial ... $30.00
6055 Oyster Cocktail ... $18.00
6055 Ice Tea, footed ... $24.00
6055 Juice, footed ... $18.00
2337 Plate, 7" ... $12.00

Marlboro, Cutting 717

1933 – 1938

Stemware, 78

6008 Goblet ... $35.00
6008 Sherbet, high ... $32.00
6008 Sherbet, low ... $28.00
6008 Cocktail ... $32.00
6008 Wine ... $38.00
6008 Cordial ... $48.00
6008 Oyster Cocktail ... $28.00
6008 Ice Tea, footed ... $34.00
6008 Tumbler, 9 oz., footed ... $28.00
6008 Juice, footed ... $28.00

Tableware I, 278

2470 Bonbon ... $18.00
869 Bowl, finger and plate ... $20.00
2470½ Bowl, 10½" ... $40.00
2470½ Candlestick, 5½", pair ... $57.00
2472 Candlestick, duo, pair ... $60.00
2482 Candlestick, trindle, pair ... $75.00
2400 Comport, 6" ... $27.00
2451 Dish, ice with liner, plate ... $42.00
2470 Dish, lemon ... $18.00
2470 Plate, cake ... $34.00
2283 Plate, 7" ... $9.00
2283 Plate, 8" ... $10.00
2364 Plate, 16", torte ... $48.00
2470 Sweetmeat ... $18.00
2440 Sugar and Cream ... $34.00
2467 Vase, 7½" ... $75.00
4107 Vase, 9" ... $95.00

Marmalades, Mustards, and Mayonnaise Sets

1922 – 1938

Useful & Ornamental, 172

1968 Marmalade, blown, plain ... $32.00
4087 Marmalade and Cover, plain or optic, silver-plated metal spoon, see Appetizers, Buffet, and Relish
crystal ... $47.00
amber ... $64.00
green ... $67.00
rose ... $67.00
azure ... $67.00
regal blue ... $68.00
burgundy ... $68.00
empire green ... $75.00
4089 Marmalade, plain or optic ... $32.00
1831 Mustard and Cover, blown, plain or optic, see Appetizers, Buffet, and Relish
crystal ... $28.00
regal blue ... $52.00
burgundy ... $52.00
empire green ... $52.00
2496 Mustard, see Baroque
810 Mayonnaise, 3-piece ... $35.00
858 Mayonnaise, 3-piece ... $35.00
1769 Mayonnaise, 3-piece ... $35.00
2138 Mayonnaise, plate, and 2138 Spoon
crystal ... $67.00
2315 Mayonnaise sets, see Twenty-Three Fifteen
2375 Mayonnaise, see Fairfax
2496 Mayonnaise, see Baroque

Marquette, Cutting 733

1934 – 1935

Stemware, 60

4024 Goblet, 11 oz. ... $28.00
4024 Goblet, 10 oz. ... $28.00
4024 Saucer Champagne ... $28.00
4024 Sherbet ... $24.00
4024 Cocktail ... $24.00
4024 Claret-Wine ... $30.00
4024 Rhine Wine ... $30.00
4024 Sherry ... $30.00
4024 Cordial ... $35.00
4024 Oyster Cocktail ... $20.00
4024 Ice Tea, footed ... $28.00
4024 Tumbler, 8 oz., footed ... $20.00
4024 Juice, footed ... $20.00
4024 Whiskey, footed ... $30.00
701 Tumbler, 12 oz. ... $8.00 – 12.00
701 Tumbler, 10 oz. ... $8.00 – 12.00
887 Whiskey ... $10.00
1184 Old Fashioned Cocktail, 7 oz. ... $10.00
4122 Whiskey ... $10.00

Tableware I, 280

869 Bowl, finger ... $12.00
4024 Bowl, 10", footed ... $30.00
4024 Candlestick, 6", pair ... $40.00
4024 Comport, 5" ... $20.00
6011 Decanter ... $135.00

6011 Jug ... $175.00
2337 Plate, 6" ... $7.00
2337 Plate, 7" ... $8.00
2337 Plate, 8" ... $10.00

Marquis, Decoration 692

1971 – 1974

Stemware, 140

6123 Goblet ... $25.00
6123 Sherbet ... $22.00
6123 Wine ... $25.00
6123 Ice Tea, footed ... $25.00
2337 Plate, 7" ... $10.00

Matrimony, Cutting 910

1966 – 1969

Stemware, 132

6107 Goblet ... $28.00
6107 Sherbet ... $25.00
6107 Claret ... $32.00
6107 Tulip Wine ... $32.00
6107 Liqueur ... $38.00
6107 Ice Tea, footed ... $38.00
2337 Plate, 7" ... $10.00
2337 Plate, 8" ... $12.00

Mayday, Plate Etching 312

1931

Green base

This pattern was found only in the July 1931 Supplementary Price List. It may never have been made.

Stemware, 76

6005 Goblet ... $24.00
6005 Sherbet, high ... $22.00
6005 Sherbet, low ... $18.00
6005 Parfait ... $24.00
6005 Cocktail ... $22.00
6005 Claret ... $28.00
6005 Wine ... $28.00
6005 Cordial ... $32.00
6005 Oyster Cocktail ... $18.00
6005 Ice Tea, footed ... $24.00
6005 Tumbler, 9 oz., footed ... $16.00
6005 Juice, footed ... $18.00
6005 Whiskey, footed ... $22.00

Tableware I, 212

869 Bowl, finger ... $35.00
2449 Bowl B, 10½" ... $75.00
2375 Candlestick, 3" ... $50.00
2400 Comport, 6" ... $38.00
2440 Cup and Saucer ... $28.00
2440 Plate, 6" ... $7.00
2440 Plate, 7" ... $8.00
2440 Plate, 8" ... $10.00
2440 Plate, 9" ... $22.00
2440 Sugar and Cream ... $64.00

Mayfair, 2419

1930 – 1943

Tableware 1, 58 – 64

2419 Ashtray
- crystal ... $20.00
- rose ... $24.00
- green ... $24.00
- amber ... $22.00
- topaz/gold tint ... $24.00
- wisteria ... $26.00
- regal blue ... $24.00
- burgundy ... $22.00
- empire green ... $24.00
- ruby ... $24.00
- ebony ... $22.00
- silver mist ... $20.00

2419 Bonbon, handled
- crystal ... $18.00
- rose ... $23.00
- green ... $23.00
- amber ... $23.00
- topaz ... $23.00
- wisteria ... $45.00

2419 Bowl, 5", fruit
- crystal ... $16.00
- rose ... $22.00
- green ... $22.00
- amber ... $20.00
- topaz/gold tint ... $20.00

2419 Bowl, 6", cereal
- crystal ... $17.00
- rose ... $24.00
- green ... $24.00
- amber ... $22.00
- topaz/gold tint ... $24.00

2419 Bowl, 7", soup
- crystal ... $20.00
- rose ... $24.00
- green ... $24.00
- amber ... $22.00
- topaz/gold tint ... $24.00

2419 Bowl, 10", baker
- crystal ... $28.00
- rose ... $46.00
- green ... $42.00
- amber ... $35.00
- topaz/gold tint ... $40.00

2419 Cake, handled
- crystal ... $42.00
- rose ... $55.00
- green ... $55.00
- amber ... $48.00
- topaz/gold tint ... $54.00
- wisteria ... $78.00
- ebony ... $48.00

2419 Celery, 11"
- crystal ... $30.00
- rose ... $47.00
- green ... $47.00
- amber ... $40.00
- topaz/gold tint ... $44.00

2419 Comport
- crystal ... $34.00
- rose ... $56.00
- green ... $50.00
- amber ... $42.00
- topaz/gold tint ... $48.00
- ebony ... $45.00

2419 Cream soup
- crystal ... $30.00
- rose ... $42.00
- green ... $38.00
- amber ... $35.00
- topaz/gold tint ... $38.00

2419 Cup, footed and saucer
- crystal ... $20.00
- rose ... $26.00
- green ... $26.00
- amber ... $22.00
- topaz/gold tint ... $24.00
- ebony, saucer only ... $9.00

2419 Cup, after dinner and saucer
- crystal ... $22.00
- rose ... $35.00
- green ... $34.00
- amber ... $28.00
- topaz/gold tint ... $32.00
- ebony, saucer only ... $12.00

2419 Jelly, handled
- crystal ... $20.00
- rose ... $28.00
- green ... $28.00
- amber ... $24.00
- topaz/gold tint ... $27.00
- ebony ... $22.00

2419 Lemon, handled
- crystal ... $18.00
- rose ... $26.00
- green ... $26.00
- amber ... $22.00
- topaz ... $24.00
- wisteria ... $46.00

2419 Mayonnaise, 5¾", handled
- crystal ... $20.00
- rose ... $28.00
- green ... $28.00
- amber ... $24.00
- topaz/gold tint ... $26.00

2419 Oil, 6 oz.
- crystal ... $58.00
- rose ... $85.00
- green ... $85.00
- amber ... $65.00
- topaz/gold tint ... $78.00

2419 Pickle, 8½"
- crystal ... $18.00
- rose ... $26.00
- green ... $26.00
- amber ... $22.00
- topaz/gold tint ... $24.00

2419 Plate, 6"
- crystal ... $8.00
- rose ... $12.00
- green ... $12.00
- amber ... $9.00
- topaz/gold tint ... $12.00
- wisteria ... $18.00
- ebony ... $9.00
- azure ... $14.00

2419 Plate, 7"
- crystal ... $9.00
- rose ... $14.00
- green ... $14.00
- amber ... $12.00
- topaz/gold tint ... $14.00
- wisteria ... $22.00
- ebony ... $12.00
- azure ... $18.00

2419 Plate 8"
- crystal ... $10.00
- rose ... $15.00
- green ... $15.00
- amber ... $12.00
- topaz/gold tint ... $14.00
- wisteria ... $24.00
- ebony ... $12.00

2419 Plate, 9"
- crystal ... $18.00
- rose ... $34.00
- green ... $34.00
- amber ... $27.00
- topaz/gold tint ... $32.00
- wisteria ... $75.00
- ebony ... $24.00

2419 Platter, 12"
- crystal ... $32.00
- rose ... $48.00
- green ... $48.00

	amber	$36.00
	topaz/gold tint	$43.00
2419	Platter, 15"	
	crystal	$45.00
	rose	$67.00
	green	$67.00
	amber	$55.00
	topaz/gold tint	$64.00
2419	Relish, 8½", 2-part	
	crystal	$20.00
	rose	$28.00
	green	$32.00
	amber	$22.00
	topaz/gold tint	$37.00
2419	Relish, 4-part	
	crystal	$24.00
	rose	$36.00
	green	$34.00
	amber	$30.00
	topaz/gold tint	$32.00
	ruby	$48.00
	ebony	$30.00
	silver mist	$24.00
2419	Relish, 5-part	
	crystal	$30.00
	rose	$65.00
	green	$65.00
	amber	$50.00
	topaz/gold tint	$56.00
	silver mist	$30.00
2419	Bowl, sauce and stand	
	crystal	$42.00
	rose	$75.00
	green	$75.00
	amber	$67.00
	topaz	$75.00
2419	Shaker, FGT, pair	
	crystal	$45.00
	rose	$74.00
	green	$74.00
	amber	$68.00
	topaz/gold tint	$74.00
	ebony	$80.00
2419	Sugar and Cream	
	crystal	$48.00
	rose	$67.00
	green	$67.00
	amber	$60.00
	topaz/gold tint	$64.00
2419	Sugar and Cream, footed	
	crystal	$48.00
	rose	$67.00
	green	$67.00
	amber	$60.00
	topaz/gold tint	$65.00
2419	Sugar and Cream, tea	
	crystal	$45.00
	rose	$68.00
	green	$65.00
	amber	$56.00
	topaz/gold tint	$60.00
	wisteria	$97.00
	regal blue	$85.00
	burgundy	$85.00
	empire green	$85.00
	ebony	$56.00
2419	Syrup, cover, saucer	
	crystal	$95.00
	rose	$145.00
	green	$140.00
	amber	$125.00
	topaz/gold tint	$135.00
2419	Tray, condiment	
	crystal	$30.00
	rose	$45.00
	green	$45.00
	amber	$38.00
	topaz	$45.00
2419	Tray, handled, lunch	
	crystal	$75.00
	rose	$95.00
	green	$85.00
	amber	$74.00
	topaz	$90.00
	ebony	$84.00

Mayflower, Etching 332

1938 – 1954

Stemware, 92

6020	Goblet	$40.00
6020	Saucer Champagne	$36.00
6020	Sherbet, low	$30.00
6020	Parfait.	$40.00
6020	Cocktail	$36.00
6020	Claret	$45.00
6020	Wine	$45.00
6020	Cordial	$54.00
6020	Oyster Cocktail	$28.00
6020	Ice Tea, footed	$40.00
6020	Tumbler, 9 oz., footed	$32.00
6020	Juice, footed	$32.00

Tableware II, 115 – 123

2560	Bonbon	$42.00
2560	Bonbon, 3-toed	$65.00
869	Bowl, finger	$34.00
2560	Bowl, 5", fruit	$32.00
2560	Bowl, 6", cereal	$34.00
2560	Bowl, 3-toed nut	$65.00
2560	Bowl, 8½", serving	$54.00
2560	Bowl, 10", salad	$65.00
2430	Bowl, 11"	$85.00
2560	Bowl, 11", handled	$125.00
2496	Bowl, 10½", handled	$125.00
2560	Bowl, 11½", crimped	$125.00
2560	Bowl, 12", flared	$95.00
2545	Bowl, 12½", oval	$95.00
2560	Bowl, 13", fruit	$95.00
2430	Candlestick, 2", pair	$80.00
2560½	Candlestick, 4", pair	$88.00
2545	Candlestick, 4½", pair	$75.00
2545	Candlestick, lustre, UDP, pair	$225.00
2496	Candlestick, duo, pair	$120.00
2545	Candlestick, duo, pair	$135.00
2560	Candlestick, duo, pair	$125.00
2545	Candelabra, 2-light, B prisms, pair	$275.00
2430	Jar, candy and cover	$125.00
2560	Celery, 11"	$45.00
2560	Cheese and Cracker	$135.00
2560	Comport, 6"	$75.00
2560	Cup and Saucer	$34.00
2560	Ice Bucket, chrome handle and tongs	$167.00
2430	Jelly, 7"	$65.00
4140	Jug	$625.00
5000	Jug	$575.00
2560	Lemon	$38.00
2560	Mayonnaise, plate, ladle	$68.00
2560	Mayonnaise, 2-part, 2 ladles	$95.00
2430	Mint, 5½"	$37.00
2560	Oil, 3½ oz.	$165.00
2560	Olive, 6¾"	$30.00
2560	Pickle, 8¾"	$35.00
2560	Plate, 6"	$12.00
2560	Plate, 7"	$22.00
2560	Plate, 8"	$26.00
2560	Plate, 9"	$60.00
2560	Plate, cake	$75.00
2560	Plate, 14", torte	$95.00
2560	Relish, 2-part	$38.00
2560	Relish, 3-part	$75.00
2560	Relish, 4-part	$95.00
2560	Relish, 5-part	$125.00
2560	Salad Set, 4-piece	$175.00
2586	Server, sani-cut	$235.00/market
2560	Shaker, FGT, , pair	$135.00
2560	Sugar and Cream	$75.00
2560	Sugar, cream, tray, individual	$97.00
2560	Sweetmeat	$42.00
2560	Tid Bit, 3-toed	$60.00
2560	Tray, handled, lunch	$200.00
2560	Tray, handled, muffin	$85.00
2276	Vanity Set	$225.00/market
2430	Vase, 3¾"	$54.00
2560	Vase, 6", handled	$175.00
2430	Vase, 8"	$125.00
2545	Vase, 10"	$195.00
5100	Vase, 10"	$195.00
2560	Whip Cream	$42.00
2560	Tray, sugar and cream	$34.00

Mayonnaise (See Marmalades, Mustards and Mayonnaise Sets)

Maypole, 6149

1982

Stemware, 146

6149	Goblet	
	light blue	$32.00
	yellow	$32.00
	peach	$32.00
6149	Champagne	
	light blue	$30.00
	yellow	$30.00
	peach	$30.00
6149	Wine	
	light blue	$32.00
	yellow	$32.00
	peach	$32.00
6149	Ice Tea, footed	
	light blue	$32.00
	yellow	$32.00
	peach	$32.00

Tableware II, 303

195	Bowl, 9"	
	light blue	$95.00
	yellow	$95.00
	peach	$95.00
314	Candle, 3", pair	
	light blue	$95.00
	yellow	$95.00
	peach	$95.00
319	Candle, 9", pair	
	light blue	$150.00
	yellow	$150.00
	peach	$150.00
567	Plate, 12", torte	
	light blue	$110.00
	yellow	$110.00
	peach	$110.00
764	Vase, 6", bud	
	light blue	$58.00
	yellow	$58.00
	peach	$58.00

Meadow Rose, Plate Etching 328

1936 – 1975

Stemware, 87

6016 Goblet
crystal $38.00
azure $120.00
6016 Saucer Champagne
crystal $34.00
azure $95.00
6016 Sherbet, low
crystal $30.00
azure $55.00
6016 Cocktail
crystal $34.00
azure $60.00
6016 Claret
crystal $45.00
azure $135.00
6016 Wine
crystal $45.00
azure $135.00
6016 Cordial
crystal $65.00
azure $165.00
6016 Oyster Cocktail
crystal $30.00
azure $50.00
6016 Ice Tea, footed
crystal $38.00
azure $125.00
6016 Tumbler, 10 oz., footed
crystal $30.00
azure $60.00
6016 Juice, footed
crystal $32.00
azure $65.00

Tableware I, 240 – 248

2496 Bonbon, 3-toed
crystal $65.00
azure $130.00
869 Bowl, finger
crystal $35.00
azure $67.00
2496 Bowl, 8½", serving
crystal $64.00
azure $130.00
2496 Bowl, 10", floating garden
crystal $150.00
azure $300.00
2496 Bowl, 10½", handled
crystal $145.00
azure $350.00
2496 Bowl, 12", flared
crystal $95.00
azure $200.00
2545 Bowl, 12½", oval
crystal $110.00
azure $225.00
2510 Candelabra, 2-light, UDP, pair
crystal $400.00
2545 Candelabra, 2-light, B prisms, pair
crystal $400.00
azure $800.00/market
2496 Candlestick, 4", pair
crystal $84.00
azure $150.00
2496 Candlestick, 5½", pair
crystal $125.00
azure $265.00
2496 Candlestick, duo, pair
crystal $170.00
azure $375.00
2545 Candlestick, duo, pair
crystal $225.00
azure $500.00
2496 Candlestick, trindle, pair
crystal $225.00
azure $500.00
2496 Candy, 3-part and cover
crystal $125.00
azure $300.00
2496 Celery
crystal $78.00
azure $150.00
2496 Cheese and Cracker
crystal $115.00
azure $225.00
2496 Comport, 5½"
crystal $77.00
azure $135.00
2496 Cup and Saucer
crystal $34.00
azure $67.00
2496 Ice Bucket, metal handle
crystal $154.00
azure $325.00
2496 Jelly and cover
crystal $150.00
azure $325.00
5000 Jug
crystal $575.00
azure $1,200.00/market
2375 Mayonnaise, plate, ladle
crystal $115.00
azure $275.00
2496 Mayonnaise, 2-part
crystal $64.00
azure $130.00
2496½ Mayonnaise, plate, ladle
crystal $125.00
azure $300.00
2496 Nappy, 3-cornered, handled
crystal $3200
azure $60.00
2496 Nappy, handled, flared
crystal $32.00
azure $60.00
2496 Pickle
crystal $42.00
azure $85.00
2666 Pitcher, quart
crystal $350.00
2337 Plate, 7"
crystal $24.00
2496 Plate, 6"
crystal $14.00
azure $26.00
2496 Plate, 7"
crystal $1800
azure $40.00
2496 Plate, 8"
crystal $24.00
azure $47.00
2496 Plate, 9"
crystal $60.00
azure $128.00
2496 Plate, 10", cake
crystal $95.00
azure $200.00
2496 Plate, 14", torte
crystal $125.00
azure $250.00
2364 Plate, 16"
crystal $145.00
azure $335.00
2496 Relish, 2-part
crystal $58.00
azure $125.00
2496 Relish, 3-part
crystal $75.00
azure $195.00
2440 Relish, 3-part
crystal $85.00
2419 Relish, 5-part
crystal $125.00
2083 Bottle, salad dressing
crystal $450.00
2586 Server, sani-cut
crystal $700.00/market
2496 Sauce and Tray
crystal $150.00
azure $365.00
2364 Shaker, chrome top C, pair
crystal $75.00
2375 Shaker, footed, FGT, pair
crystal $200.00
azure $425.00
2496 Sugar and Cream
crystal $85.00
azure $200.00
2496 Sugar and Cream, individual
crystal $85.00
azure $200.00
2496 Tray, sugar and cream
crystal $35.00
2496 Sweetmeat
crystal $54.00
azure $125.00
2496 Tid Bit, 3-toed
crystal $59.00
azure $130.00
2375 Tray, handled, lunch
crystal $125.00
azure $245.00
4128 Vase, 5"
crystal $195.00
azure $275.00
2470 Vase, 10"
crystal $350.00
azure $500.00

Melba, Cutting 761

1936 – 1943

Stemware, 87

6016 Goblet $30.00
6016 Saucer Champagne $27.00
6016 Sherbet, low $24.00
6016 Cocktail $27.00
6016 Claret $35.00
6016 Wine $33.00
6016 Cordial $45.00
6016 Oyster Cocktail $22.00
6016 Ice Tea, footed $28.00
6016 Tumbler, 10 oz., footed $25.00
6016 Juice, footed $24.00

Tableware I, 290

869 Bowl, finger $12.00
2470½ Bowl, 10½" $40.00
2472 Candlestick, duo, pair $70.00
2400 Comport, 6" $27.00
5000 Jug $185.00
2337 Plate, 6" $8.00
2337 Plate, 7" $9.00
2337 Plate, 8" $10.00

Melody, 6020

1938 – 1957

Stemware, 92

6020 Goblet....................$32.00
6020 Saucer Champagne $28.00
6020 Sherbet, low...........$24.00
6020 Parfait....................$32.00
6020 Cocktail...................$28.00
6020 Claret......................................$35.00
6020 Wine..$34.00
6020 Cordial.....................................$45.00
6020 Oyster Cocktail.........................$20.00
6020 Ice Tea, footed.........................$32.00
6020 Tumbler, 9 oz., footed...........$26.00
6020 Juice, footed............................$26.00

Melody, Cutting 881

1960 – 1965

Stemware, 114

6072 Goblet $34.00
6072 Sherbet $32.00
6072 Cocktail/Wine/Seafood........$35.00
6072 Cordial.....................................$40.00
6072 Ice Tea, footed.........................$34.00
6072 Juice, footed............................$30.00
2337 Plate, 7"..................................$10.00
2337 Plate, 8"..................................$12.00

Melrose, Plate Etching 268

1924 – 1929

Stemware, 19

661 Goblet $12.00
661 Saucer Champagne...........................$12.00
661 Fruit/Sherbet, low................$12.00
661 Parfait...$18.00
661 Cocktail.......................................$12.00
661 Claret..$18.00
661 Wine..$15.00
661 Cordial...$22.00
4023 Tumbler, 6 oz. $8.00
4085 Tumbler, 13 oz. $15.00
4085 Tumbler, 6 oz. $8.00
4085 Tumbler, 2½ oz. $6.00
4095 Tumbler, 13 oz. ....$6.00 – 15.00
837 Oyster Cocktail and Liner....$10.00
5039 Oyster Cocktail and Liner....$10.00
945½ Grapefruit and Liner.............$30.00

Tableware I, 147

1769 Bowl, finger and 2283 Plate.....................................$22.00
1697 Carafe and Tumbler..............$70.00
803 Comport, 5"...............................$24.00
803 Comport, 6"...............................$26.00
300 Decanter, quart, cut neck.....$64.00
825 Jelly and cover........................$32.00
303/7 Jug...$125.00
1852/6 Jug.......................................$135.00
4095/4 Jug.......................................$125.00
4095/7 Jug.......................................$140.00
4087 Marmalade and cover...........$42.00
2138 Mayonnaise, plate, ladle, plain...$48.00
803 Nappy, 5"..................................$20.00
803 Nappy, 6"..................................$22.00
803 Nappy, 7"..................................$26.00
1465 Oil, 5 oz., cut neck.................$48.00
2283 Plate, 7"......................................$8.00
2283 Plate, 8¼"..................................$10.00
2283 Plate, 11"...................................$18.00
2283 Plate, 11", cut matt star.........$20.00
2235 Shaker, FGT or pearl top, plain, pair.............................$47.00
1480 Sugar and Cream...................$36.00
2287 Tray, lunch, plain...................$48.00

Memories, Cutting 750

1935

Stemware, 72

6000 Goblet $32.00
6000 Sherbet, high.........................$30.00
6000 Sherbet, low..........................$24.00
6000 Cocktail.................................$30.00
6000 Wine..$35.00
2337 Plate, 7"..................................$10.00
2337 Plate, 11"................................$12.00

Mesa, 4186

1967 – 1974

Stemware, 61

4186 Goblet
- crystal..............$20.00
- olive green.......$20.00
- brown.............$20.00
- amber.............$20.00
- blue...................................$20.00
- ruby...................................$35.00

4186 Sherbet
- crystal.................................$15.00
- olive green..........................$15.00
- brown..................................$15.00
- amber..................................$15.00
- blue.....................................$15.00
- ruby.....................................$30.00

4186 Wine/On the Rocks
- crystal.................................$20.00
- olive green..........................$20.00
- brown..................................$20.00
- amber..................................$20.00
- blue.....................................$20.00
- ruby.....................................$35.00

4186 Ice Tea
- crystal.................................$20.00
- olive green..........................$20.00
- brown..................................$20.00
- amber..................................$20.00
- blue.....................................$20.00
- ruby.....................................$35.00

4186 Old Fashioned Cocktail, double
- crystal.................................$18.00
- olive green..........................$18.00
- brown..................................$18.00
- amber..................................$18.00
- blue.....................................$18.00
- ruby.....................................$30.00

4086 Juice
- crystal.................................$15.00
- olive green..........................$15.00
- brown..................................$15.00
- amber..................................$15.00
- blue.....................................$15.00
- ruby.....................................$30.00

Tableware II, 106 - 107

380 Coaster
- crystal...................................$8.00
- olive green..........................$10.00
- brown....................................$6.00
- amber..................................$10.00
- blue.....................................$12.00

495 Dessert, 4¾"
- crystal.................................$14.00
- olive green..........................$15.00
- brown..................................$12.00
- amber..................................$15.00
- blue.....................................$18.00
- ruby.....................................$22.00

454 Pitcher, quart
- crystal.................................$45.00
- olive green..........................$45.00
- brown..................................$35.00
- amber..................................$40.00
- blue.....................................$65.00

458 Pitcher, 2-quart
- crystal.................................$55.00
- olive green..........................$60.00
- brown..................................$45.00
- amber..................................$50.00
- blue.....................................$75.00

550 Plate, 8"
- crystal.................................$12.00
- olive green..........................$14.00
- brown....................................$8.00
- amber..................................$14.00
- blue.....................................$18.00
- ruby.....................................$28.00

653 Shaker, chrome top A, pair
- crystal.................................$28.00
- olive green..........................$34.00
- brown..................................$24.00
- amber..................................$35.00
- blue.....................................$48.00

673 Sugar and cover
- crystal.................................$27.00
- olive green..........................$30.00
- brown..................................$20.00
- amber..................................$28.00
- blue.....................................$37.00

680 Cream
- crystal.................................$20.00
- olive green..........................$23.00
- brown..................................$15.00
- amber..................................$20.00
- blue.....................................$38.00

Meteor, Cutting 726

1933 – 1939

Stemware, 60

4024 Goblet, 11 oz. $34.00
4024 Goblet, 10 oz. $34.00
4024 Saucer Champagne.................34.00
4024 Sherbet...................................$27.00
4024 Cocktail..................................$27.00
4024 Claret-Wine............................$38.00
4024 Rhine Wine.............................$38.00
4024 Sherry.....................................$35.00
4024 Cordial....................................$40.00
4024 Oyster Cocktail.......................$20.00
4024 Ice Tea, footed.......................$34.00
4024 Tumbler, 8 oz., footed...........$20.00
4024 Juice, footed...........................$20.00
4024 Whiskey, footed.....................$35.00
701 Tumbler......................$10.00 – 14.00
887 Tumbler......................$10.00 – 14.00
1184 Tumbler.....................$10.00 – 14.00

Tableware I, 279

6011 Decanter..............................$275.00

6011 Jug $275.00
2337 Plate, 6" $18.00
2337 Plate, 7" $20.00
2337 Plate, 8" $22.00

Miami, Decoration 42

1924 – 1929

Stemware, 19

661 Goblet, 9 oz. $18.00
661 Saucer Champagne $14.00
661 Fruit/Sherbet, low $12.00
661 Parfait $15.00
661 Cocktail $14.00
661 Claret $15.00
661 Wine $14.00
661 Cordial $22.00
4085 Tumbler, 13 oz. $15.00
4085 Tumbler, 8 oz. $10.00
4095 Tumbler .... $8.00 – 15.00

Tableware

1769 Bowl, finger and 6" plate $18.00
1852 Jug, 6 .... $75.00
2283 Plate, 7", ... $5.00
2238 Plate, 8¼" $6.00

Midnight Rose, Plate Etching 316

1933 – 1957

Stemware, 79

6009 Goblet $45.00
6009 Sherbet, high $42.00
6009 Sherbet, low $35.00
6009 Cocktail $40.00
6009 Claret-Wine $54.00
6009 Cordial $68.00
6009 Oyster Cocktail $32.00
6009 Ice Tea, footed $45.00
6009 Tumbler, 9 oz., footed $36.00
6009 Juice, footed $35.00
795 Champagne, 5½ oz., hollow stem $75.00
846 Sherry, 2 oz. $32.00
906 Brandy Inhaler $75.00
887 Whiskey Sham, 1¾ oz. $32.00
1184 Old Fashioned Cocktail, 7 oz. $38.00

Tableware I, 214, 216, 217

2440 Bonbon, 5" $45.00
869 Bowl, finger and plate $46.00
2470½ Bowl, 7" $47.00
2470½ Bowl, 10½" $95.00
2481 Bowl, 11" $145.00
2481 Candlestick, 5", pair $145.00
2470½ Candlestick, 5½", pair $125.00
2472 Candlestick, duo, pair $135.00
2482 Candlestick, trindle, pair $150.00
4099 Jar, candy and cover $157.00
2440 Celery, 11½" $50.00
2440 Cup and Saucer $35.00
2440 Lemon, 5" $36.00
2464 Jug, ice $500.00
2464 Tumbler, 10 oz. $35.00
2440 Mayonnaise, 2-part $35.00
2440 Olive, 7½" $25.00
2440 Pickle, 8½" $30.00
2440 Plate, 6" $12.00
2440 Plate, 7" $15.00
2440 Plate, 8" $18.00
2440 Plate, 9" $45.00
2375 Plate, cake $75.00
2440 Plate, 10½", cake $75.00
2496 Plate, handled, cake $65.00
2440 Plate, 13", torte $95.00
2440 Relish, 2-part $37.00
2440 Relish, 3-part $46.00
2419 Relish, 4-part $48.00
2470 Relish, 4-part $125.00
2419 Relish, 5-part $125.00
2462 Relish, metal handle $98.00
2462 Relish, 5-part $125.00
2440 Sauce and Tray $110.00
2440 Sugar and Cream $75.00
2470 Tray, sugar and cream $40.00
2440 Sweetmeat, 4½" $36.00
2485 Vase, 5", crescent $200.00
2486 Vase, 7", square $250.00
2485 Vase, 7", crescent $300.00
2486 Vase, 9", square $325.00
4111 Vase, 6½" $225.00
4110 Vase, 7½" $300.00
2467 Vase, 7½" $145.00
4112 Vase, 8½" $350.00
2470 Vase, 10" $295.00

Milady, Cutting 895

1963 – 1965

Stemware, 126

6102 Goblet $32.00
6102 Sherbet $30.00
6102 Claret $35.00
6102 Tulip Wine $35.00
6102 Brandy $35.00
6102 Ice Tea, footed $32.00
2337 Plate, 7" $10.00
2337 Plate, 8 .... $12.00

Milkweed, Crystal Print 7

1957 – 1958

Tableware II, 162

2630 Bonbon, 3-toed $28.00
2630 Bowl, 10½", salad $45.00
2630 Bowl, 12", flared $50.00
2630 Butter and cover, oblong $40.00
2630 Candlestick, 4½", pair $48.00
2630 Candlestick, duo, pair $68.00
2630 Jug, 3-pint, ice $94.00
2630 Lily Pond, 9" $38.00
2630 Mayonnaise, plate, ladle $45.00
2630 Nappy, 4½", handled $18.00
2630 Pickle, 8¾" $18.00
2630 Plate, handled, cake $45.00
2630 Relish, 2-part $22.00
2630 Relish, 3-part $30.00
2630 Salad Set, 4-piece $95.00
2630 Shaker, chrome top B, pair $35.00
2630 Sugar and Cream $40.00
2630 Sugar and Cream, individual and tray $48.00
2630 Tidbit, 3-toed $28.00
2630 Torte, 14" $48.00
2630 Tray, handled, lunch $54.00
2630 Tricorne, 3-toed $30.00

Millefleur, Cutting 195

1929 – 1939

Stemware, 58

4020 Goblet
- crystal $35.00
- ebony base $35.00

4020 Sherbet, high
- crystal $35.00
- ebony base $35.00

4020 Sherbet, 7 oz., low
- crystal $30.00
- ebony base $30.00

4020 Sherbet, 5 oz., low
- crystal $30.00
- ebony base $30.00

4020 Cocktail, 3½ oz.
- crystal $30.00
- ebony base $30.00

4020 Claret
- crystal $40.00
- ebony base $40.00

4020 Wine
- crystal $40.00
- ebony base $40.00

4020 Ice Tea, footed
- crystal $35.00
- ebony base $35.00

4020 Tumbler, 13 oz., footed
- crystal $35.00
- ebony base $35.00

4020 Tumbler, 10 oz., footed
- crystal $30.00
- ebony base $30.00

4020 Juice, footed
- crystal $30.00
- ebony base $30.00

4020 Whiskey, footed
- crystal $30.00
- ebony base $30.00

Tableware I, 272

2350½ Cup $12.00
2350 Cup, after dinner, and 2419 Saucer $24.00
4020 Jug
- crystal $195.00
- ebony base $225.00

2350 Plate, 6" $10.00
2350 Plate, 7" $10.00
2350 Plate, 9" $16.00
2419 Plate, 6" $10.00
2419 Plate, 7" $10.00
2419 Plate, 8" $12.00
2350 Saucer $10.00
2419 Saucer $10.00
4020 Sugar and Cream
- crystal $40.00
- ebony base $48.00

Mints and Nuts (see Small Bowls, Mints and Nuts)

Minuet, Plate Etching 285

1930 – 1933

Stemware, 57

4020 Goblet, green base $65.00
4020 Sherbet, high, green base $60.00

Minuet, Plate Etching 285

4020 Sherbet, 7 oz., low,
green base $48.00

4020 Sherbet, 5 oz., low,
green base $45.00

4020½ Cocktail, 4 oz.,
green base $38.00

4020 Cocktail, 3½ oz.,
green base $38.00

4020 Ice Tea, footed,
green base $45.00

4020 Tumbler, 13 oz., footed,
green base $65.00

4020 Tumbler, 10 oz., footed,
green base $45.00

4020 Juice, footed,
green base $45.00

4020 Whiskey, footed,
green base $55.00

6002 Goblet,
topaz bowl $56.00

6002 Sherbet, high,
topaz bowl $48.00

6002 Sherbet, low,
topaz bowl $35.00

6002 Claret,
topaz bowl $65.00

6002 Wine,
topaz bowl $58.00

6002 Cordial,
topaz bowl $94.00

6002 Oyster Cocktail,
topaz bowl, ... $35.00

6002 Ice Tea, footed,
topaz bowl $56.00

6002 Tumbler, 10 oz., footed,
topaz bowl $40.00

6002 Juice, footed,
topaz bowl $35.00

6002 Whiskey, footed,
topaz bowl $67.00

Tableware I, 193

2419 Bonbon
green $45.00
topaz $42.00

4020 Bowl, finger
green base $46.00

6002 Bowl, finger
topaz $46.00

2419 Bowl, 5", fruit
green $34.00
topaz $30.00

2419 Bowl, 6", cereal
green $40.00
topaz $35.00

2419 Bowl, 7", soup
green $55.00
topaz $50.00

2394 Bowl D, 7½"
green $250.00
topaz $195.00

2433 Bowl D, 7½"
green $350.00
topaz $285.00

2419 Bowl, 10", baker
green $75.00
topaz $64.00

2430 Bowl, 11"
green $135.00
topaz $110.00

2394 Bowl A, 12"
green $125.00
topaz $100.00

2433 Bowl A, 12"
green $350.00
topaz $285.00

2441 Bowl, 12"
green $150.00
topaz $115.00

2394 Candlestick, 2", pair
green $100.00
topaz $85.00

2375 Candlestick, 3", pair
green $125.00
topaz $100.00

2433 Candlestick, 3", pair
green $165.00
topaz $150.00

2430 Candlestick, 9½", pair
green, ... $250.00
topaz $225.00

2430 Jar, candy and cover
green $160.00
topaz $135.00

2419 Celery, 11"
green $68.00
topaz $64.00

2400 Comport, 6"
green $65.00
topaz $60.00

2433 Comport, low
green $85.00
topaz $78.00

2433 Comport, tall
green $225.00
topaz $200.00

2419 Cream Soup
green $67.00
topaz $60.00

2419 Cup and Saucer, after dinner
green $25.00
topaz $75.00

2419 Cup and Saucer
green $45.00
topaz $40.00

2439 Decanter
green $800.00/market
topaz $700.00/market

4020 Decanter
green foot $700.00/market
topaz bowl $600.00/market

2375 Ice Bucket, NP handle
green $145.00
topaz $134.00

2451 Dish, ice and liner
green $70.00
topaz $65.00

2419 Jelly, 2 handles
green $45.00
topaz $42.00

2430 Jelly, 7"
green $45.00
topaz $42.00

4020 Jug
green base $575.00

5000 Jug
topaz $600.00

2419 Lemon, 2 handles
green $45.00
topaz $42.00

2419 Mayonnaise, 2 handles
green $47.00
topaz $45.00

2430 Mint, 5½"
green $38.00
topaz $34.00

2375 Oil, footed
green $485.00
topaz $450.00

2419 Pickle, 8½"
green $44.00
topaz $40.00

2419 Plate, 6"
green $16.00
topaz $14.00

2419 Plate, 7"
green $18.00
topaz $16.00

2419 Plate, 8"
green $25.00
topaz $20.00

2419 Plate, 9"
green $95.00
topaz $85.00

2419 Plate, handled, cake
green $125.00
topaz $110.00

2419 Platter, 12"
green $95.00
topaz $90.00

2419 Platter, 15"
green $150.00
topaz $135.00

2419 Relish, 8½"
green $48.00
topaz $45.00

2419 Relish, 4-part
green $67.00
topaz $64.00

2083 Bottle, salad dressing
green $400.00
topaz $375.00

2419 Sauce and Stand
green $95.00
topaz $85.00

4020 Shaker, FGT, pair
green $165.00
topaz $150.00

2419 Sugar and Cream
green $125.00
topaz $95.00

2419 Sugar and Cream, tea
green $100.00
topaz $90.00

2419½ Sugar and Cream
green $135.00
topaz $125.00

4020 Sugar and Cream
green base $100.00
topaz bowl $90.00

2430 Vase, 8"
green $300.00
topaz $275.00

Minuet, Cutting 826

1950 – 1959

Stemware, 96

6025 Goblet $34.00
6025 Sherbet $28.00
6025 Cocktail $28.00
6025 Claret-Wine $38.00
6025 Cordial $47.00
6025 Oyster Cocktail $26.00
6025 Ice Tea, footed $34.00
6025 Juice, footed $28.00

Tableware II, 175 – 176

2574 Bowl, 12", flared $57.00
2574 Candlestick, duo, pair $78.00
2574 Cup and Saucer $28.00

2574 Plate, 7" $12.00
2574 Plate, 8" $16.00
2574 Plate, 10", handled, cake $54.00
2574 Plate, 14", torte $58.00
2574 Relish, 3-part $42.00
2574 Shaker, chrome top B, pair $65.00
2574 Sugar and Cream $54.00

Miscellaneous Milk Glass

1954 – 1965

Tableware II, 214 – 215

600 Vase, 6½", cupped white...$75.00 aqua...$125.00 peach ...$125.00
1121 Comport, 6¾", white $58.00
1121 Comport, 5¾", white $48.00
1200 Bowl, 4", rose
white $40.00
aqua $64.00
peach $64.00
1200 Bowl, crimped
white $35.00
aqua $60.00
peach $60.00
1200 Spoon Holder
white $35.00
aqua $60.00
peach $60.00
1200 Vase, 8½", celery
white $38.00
aqua $58.00
peach $58.00
1300 Bowl, 5", rose
white $35.00
aqua $64.00
peach $64.00
1300 Vase, planter
white $38.00
aqua $65.00
peach, $65.00
1886 Box, pin and cover
white $75.00
aqua $87.00
peach $87.00
1886 Tray, pin
white $44.00
aqua $57.00
peach $57.00
1886 Puff and Cover
white $88.00
aqua, $125.00
peach $125.00
2183 Bowl, 12", shallow
whit $48.00
2183 Bowl, 12", square
white $50.00
aqua $67.00
peach $67.00
2183 Candleholder, 2¾", pair
white $35.00
2183 Hurricane Lamp and Chimney, 11¼"
white $40.00
2493 Beer Mug, white $57.00
2513 Bowl, crimped
white $38.00
aqua $57.00
peach $57.00
2513 Jar, candy and cover, Maple Leaf
white $44.00
aqua $68.00
peach $68.00
2519 Cologne and Stopper, white $87.00
2519 Puff and Cover, white $87.00
2521 Bird, white $38.00
2589 Deer, white $58.00
2589½ Deer, white $56.00
2595 Sleigh, 3", white $38.00
2595 Sleigh, 4½" $48.00
2595 Sleigh, 6", white $57.00
2676 Hen and Nest
white $160.00
aqua $300.00
peach $300.00
2676 Hen and Nest, decorated
white $195.00
2679 Puff and Cover
white $65.00
2680 Stagecoach and Cover
white $250.00/market
2682 Nappy, fish
white $42.00
2693 Urn and Cover, footed, see Garden Club Items
white $95.00
2700 Basket, pansy
white $18.00
aqua $28.00
peach $28.00
2700 Bowl, violet
white $18.00
aqua $28.00
peach $28.00
2714 Pot, crocus and cover
white $78.00
aqua $125.00
peach $125.00
2720 Trivet
white $54.00
4165 Santa Claus, decorated,
white market

Mission, Cutting 116

1913 – 1928

Stemware, 24, 28

858 Goblet, 11 oz. $10.00
858 Goblet, 10 oz. $8.00
858 Goblet, 9 oz. $8.00
858 Goblet, 8 oz. $6.00
858 Saucer Champagne, 7 oz. $6.00
858 Saucer Champagne, 5½ oz. $6.00
858 Sherbet $6.00
858 Fruit $6.00
858 Parfait $18.00
858 Cocktail $6.00
858 Claret, 6½ oz. $6.00
858 Claret, 4½ oz. $6.00
858 Wine, 3½ oz. $6.00
858 Wine, 2¾ oz. $6.00
858 Sherry $6.00
858 Crème de Menthe $6.00
858 Brandy $12.00
858 Cordial $15.00
858 Oyster Cocktail $5.00
858 Champagne, hollow stem $10.00
858 Champagne, tall $6.00
858 Champagne, long stem $18.00
858 Champagne, long stem, Cutting R. $18.00
858 Bass Ale $15.00
858 Hot Whiskey $6.00
863 Goblet, 10½ oz. $8.00
863 Goblet, 9 oz. $8.00
863 Saucer Champagne $8.00
863 Fruit $6.00
863 Cocktail, 3½ oz. $6.00
863 Claret $8.00
863 Rhine Wine $8.00
863 Wine $8.00
863 Sherry $6.00
863 Crème de Menthe $6.00
863 Brandy, pousse-café $8.00
863 Cordial $15.00
863 Champagne, hollow stem, CF $8.00
863 Champagne, tall $8.00
863 Roemer, 5½ oz. $15.00
863 Roemer, 4½ oz. $15.00
945/945½ Grapefruit and Liner $25.00
1389 Oyster Cocktail $8.00
4061 Lemonade, handled and plate $18.00
701 Tumbler $4.00 – 8.00
820 Tumbler $4.00 – 8.00
833 Tumbler $4.00 – 8.00
858 Tumbler $4.00 – 8.00
887 Tumbler $4.00 – 8.00
889 Tumbler $4.00 – 8.00

Tableware

863 Almond $20.00
880 Bonbon $20.00
1904 Bonbon $78.00
1558 Water Bottle, cut neck $50.00
803 Comport, 5" $24.00
803 Comport, 6" $25.00
481 Custard $10.00
300 Decanter, quart $50.00
48 Flower Set, 3-piece $75.00
1132 Horseradish $54.00
1718 Ice Tub, 6" $32.00
303 Jug $75.00
1851 Jug $75.00
1733 Marmalade and Cover $30.00
1831 Mustard and Cover $27.00
803 Nappy, 5" $18.00
803 Nappy, 6" $20.00
803 Nappy, 7", footed $22.00
1227 Nappy, 4½ " $18.00
1227 Nappy, 8" $24.00
300½ Oil, small $42.00
1465 Oil, 7 oz., cut neck $45.00
1666 Puff and Cover $68.00
1227 Bowl, punch and stand $120.00
1478 Salts and Stopper, lavender $78.00
1848 Plate, 9", sandwich, cut star $9.00
1165½ Shaker, pearl top, pair $35.00
2022 Shaker, FGT, pair $35.00
1478 Sugar and Cream $30.00
1480 Sugar and Cream $30.00
1759 Sugar and Cream $30.00
1851 Sugar and Cream $30.00
2194 Syrup, 12 oz., nickle top $50.00
2194 Syrup, 8 oz., nickle top $45.00
300 Tankard $75.00
1761 Tankard $75.00
1787 Tankard $75.00
1852 Tankard $75.00
1743 Tankard and Cover $84.00

MISSION, CUTTING 116

1741 Tea Caddy and cover $48.00
922 Toothpick $18.00
725 Vase, 10" $65.00
725 Vase, 8" $60.00
1797½ Vase, 7" $54.00
1895 Vase, 10" $70.00

Misty, 6129
1978 – 1982
Stemware, 143

6129 Goblet
blue......................$20.00
yellow..................$20.00
brown..................$20.00
6129 Champagne
blue $20.00
yellow.................................$20.00
brown.................................$20.00
6129 Claret
blue $20.00
yellow.................................$20.00
brown.................................$20.00
6129 Magnum
blue $20.00
yellow.................................$20.00
brown.................................$20.00
6129 Ice Tea, footed
blue $20.00
yellow.................................$20.00
brown.................................$20.00

Misty Platinum, Decoration 695
1978 – 1980
Stemware, 143

6129 Goblet $25.00
6129 Champagne...........................$25.00
6129 Claret...................................$25.00
6129 Magnum................................$25.00
6129 Ice Tea, footed $25.00

Modern Vintage, Etching 255
1920 – 1928
Stemware, 20

766 Goblet.............$12.00
766 Saucer Champagne $9.00
766 Fruit $8.00
766 Parfait $22.00
766 Cocktail $9.00
766 Wine...$9.00
766 Cordial $20.00
766 Ice Tea, footed, handled $20.00

Tableware

837 Oyster Cocktail......................$10.00
945½ Grapefruit and Liner $22.00
701 Tumbler.......................$6.00 – 12.00
820 Tumbler.......................$6.00 – 12.00
4011 Tumbler.......................$6.00 – 12.00
300 Jug...$75.00
303 Jug...$54.00
318 Jug...$87.00

Module, 2824 Tumbler
1970 – 1972
Stemware, 152

2824 Ice Tea, 13 oz.
crystal $14.00
dusk $14.00
sunrise $14.00
2824 Goblet, 9 oz.
crystal $14.00
dusk $14.00
sunrise $14.00
2824 Wine/Juice, 5 oz.
crystal $12.00
dusk $12.00
sunrise $12.00

Molasses Cans (see Syrups and Molasses Cans)

Monaco, Crystal Print 24 (see Coventry)
1970 – 1971
Crystal or Honey Gold
Tableware

2834 135 Bonbon $12.00
2834 191 Bowl, 8" $18.00
2834 195 Bowl, 9" $20.00
2834 300 Butter and cover, oblong.............................$35.00
2834 540 Pickle, 8" $16.00
2834 60 Plate, 12", square.............$22.00
2834 567 Plate, 14", service $26.00
2834 620 Relish, 8", 2-part.............$18.00
2834 651 Shaker, chrome top E, pair $30.00
2834 677 Sugar and Cream............$30.00

Monarch, Decoration 60
1926 – 1928
Stemware, 32

870 Goblet $22.00
870 Sherbet, high $20.00
870 Sherbet, low.............................$18.00
870 Parfait $25.00
870 Cocktail $20.00
870 Wine..$22.00
870 Cordial.......................................$28.00
870 Oyster Cocktail.......................$18.00

Tableware

945½ Grapefruit and Liner $28.00
5084 Jug...$95.00
2283 Plate, 6" $6.00
2283 Plate, 7" $8.00
2283 Plate, 8" $10.00
5084 Tumbler....................$10.00 – 12.00

Monarch, 2903
1979 – 1986
Stemware, 54

2903 Goblet................$18.00
2903 Wine.....................$18.00
2903 Ice Tea, footed.......$18.00
2903 Double Old Fashioned........$15.00
2903 Highball...............................$18.00

Monarch (Imported Stemware)
1985 – 1986
Tableware II, 282, 283

Goblet........................$22.00
Wine..........................$22.00
Flute..........................$22.00
Ice Tea.......................$22.00
Salad Bowl.............................$20.00
Vase $20.00
Pitcher $25.00
Wine Carafe $25.00
Decanter.................................$25.00
Candy Box...............................$25.00

Monet, MO12
1985 – 1986
Crystal Mist, gray, dark blue, Peach, light blue, Lilac
Stemware, 187

Price range, $10.00 – 15.00
MO12 Goblet...................$12.00
MO12 Wine......................$12.00
MO12 Ice Tea, footed.......$12.00

Monroe, Etching 86
1933 – 1939
Stemware, 72

6000 Goblet $25.00
6000 Sherbet, high $23.00
6000 Sherbet, low $16.00
6000 Cocktail $20.00
6000 Wine...$28.00
6000 Oyster Cocktail.......................$15.00
6000 Ice Tea, footed $25.00
6000 Juice, footed $16.00
2283 Plate, 7" $10.00

Monroe, 2678 Milkglass
1954 – 1965
Tableware II, 208

2678 Bowl, shallow fruit $75.00
2678 Bowl, banana $125.00
2678 Bowl, footed fruit................$135.00
2678 Salver $135.00

Monte Carlo, Cutting 912
1967 – 1970
Stemware, 129

6104 Goblet...........$28.00
6104 Sherbet..........$25.00
6104 Claret..............$30.00
6104 Wine...$30.00
6104 Cordial.......................................$38.00
6104 Ice Tea, footed $28.00
2337 Plate, 7" $10.00
2337 Plate, 8" $12.00

Monticello, Cutting 886
1961 – 1970
Stemware, 122

6097 Goblet $30.00
6097 Sherbet $26.00
6097 Wine/Cocktail $34.00
6097 Cordial $40.00
6097 Ice Tea, footed $30.00
6097 Juice, footed $24.00

Moonbeam, Cutting 856
1957 – 1965
Stemware, 114

6072 Goblet.........$34.00
6072 Sherbet.........$32.00
6072 Cocktail/Wine/ Seafood $35.00
6072 Cordial.......................................$42.00

6072 Ice Tea, footed $34.00
6072 Juice, footed $30.00

Tableware II, 190

2337 Plate, 7" $10.00
2337 Plate, 8" $12.00
2574 Plate, 7" $12.00
2574 Plate, 8" $14.00
2574 Plate, 14", torte $38.00
2574 Relish, 3-part $40.00
2574 Sugar and Cream $48.00

Moonglow, Decoration 649

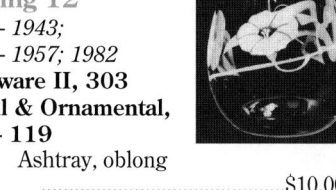

1960 – 1967

Stemware, 117

6085 Goblet $32.00
6085 Sherbet $30.00
6085 Wine/Cocktail $38.00
6085 Cordial $48.00
6085 Ice Tea, footed $32.00
6085 Juice, footed $30.00
2337 Plate, 7" $10.00
2337 Plate, 8" $12.00

Moon Mist, Decoration 684

1969 – 1972

Stemware, 136

6113 Goblet $45.00
6113 Sherbet $38.00
6113 Claret $52.00
6113 Wine $52.00
6113 Brandy $52.00
6113 Ice Tea, footed $45.00

Moon Ring, 6052

1953 – 1965

Stemware, 107

6052 Goblet, horizontal optic $22.00
6052 Sherbet, horizontal optic $20.00
6052 Cocktail, horizontal optic $20.00
6052 Claret-Wine, horizontal optic $25.00
6052 Cordial, horizontal optic $30.00
6052 Oyster Cocktail, horizontal optic $16.00
6052 Ice Tea, footed, horizontal optic $22.00
6052 Juice, footed, horizontal optic $18.00
4132 Tumbler, horizontal optic $18.00

Moonstone, 2882

1974 – 1982

Stemware, 52

2882 Goblet
crystal $18.00
apple green $18.00
pink $18.00
blue $14.00
yellow $18.00
dark blue $12.00
taupe (brown) $12.00

2882 Sherbet
crystal $14.00
apple green $14.00
pink $14.00
blue $12.00
yellow $14.00
dark blue $12.00
taupe (brown) $12.00

2882 Wine
crystal $18.00
apple green $18.00
pink $18.00
blue $14.00
yellow $18.00
dark blue $12.00
taupe (brown) $12.00

2882 Ice Tea, footed
crystal $18.00
apple green $18.00
pink $18.00
blue $14.00
yellow $18.00
dark blue $12.00
taupe (brown) $12.00

2882 Highball
crystal $20.00
apple green $20.00
pink $20.00
blue $15.00
yellow $20.00
dark blue $12.00
taupe (brown) $12.00

2882 Old Fashioned
crystal $20.00
apple green $20.00
pink $20.00
blue $14.00
yellow $20.00
dark blue $12.00
taupe (brown) $12.00

Morning Glory, Carving 12

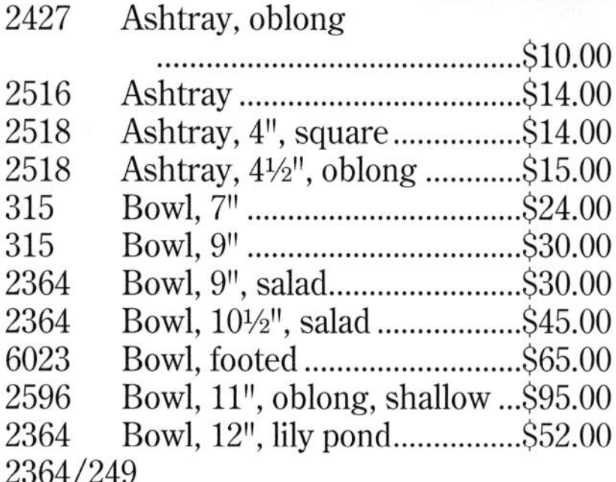

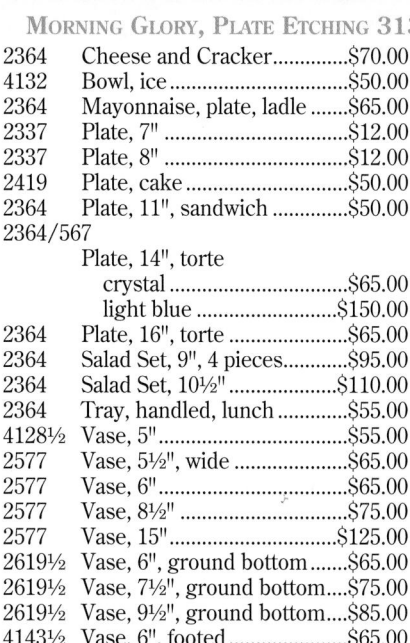

1939 – 1943; 1953 – 1957; 1982

Tableware II, 303

Useful & Ornamental, 114 – 119

2427 Ashtray, oblong $10.00
2516 Ashtray $14.00
2518 Ashtray, 4", square $14.00
2518 Ashtray, 4½", oblong $15.00
315 Bowl, 7" $24.00
315 Bowl, 9" $30.00
2364 Bowl, 9", salad $30.00
2364 Bowl, 10½", salad $45.00
6023 Bowl, footed $65.00
2596 Bowl, 11", oblong, shallow $95.00
2364 Bowl, 12", lily pond $52.00
2364/249 Bowl, 12", flared
crystal $52.00
light blue $125.00
2364 Bowl, 13", fruit $60.00
2324/314 Candlestick, 3", pair
crystal $56.00
light blue $95.00
2596 Candlestick, 5½", pair $80
2324/319 Candlestick, 6", pair
crystal $80.00
light blue $150.00
6023 Candlestick, duo, pair $95.00
2427 Box, cigarette and cover $68.00
2618 Box, cigarette and cover $57.00
2364 Cheese and Cracker $70.00
4132 Bowl, ice $50.00
2364 Mayonnaise, plate, ladle $65.00
2337 Plate, 7" $12.00
2337 Plate, 8" $12.00
2419 Plate, cake $50.00
2364 Plate, 11", sandwich $50.00
2364/567 Plate, 14", torte
crystal $65.00
light blue $150.00
2364 Plate, 16", torte $65.00
2364 Salad Set, 9", 4 pieces $95.00
2364 Salad Set, 10½" $110.00
2364 Tray, handled, lunch $55.00
4128½ Vase, 5" $55.00
2577 Vase, 5½", wide $65.00
2577 Vase, 6" $65.00
2577 Vase, 8½" $75.00
2577 Vase, 15" $125.00
2619½ Vase, 6", ground bottom $65.00
2619½ Vase, 7½", ground bottom $75.00
2619½ Vase, 9½", ground bottom $85.00
4143½ Vase, 6", footed $65.00
4143½ Vase, 7½", footed $75.00
4132½ Vase, 8" $80.00
5100 Vase, 10" $95.00
4126½ Vase, 11" $110.00
2612 Vase, 13" $125.00
2591 Vase, 15" $150.00
789 Vase, 8" bud, Lotus
crystal mist $84.00

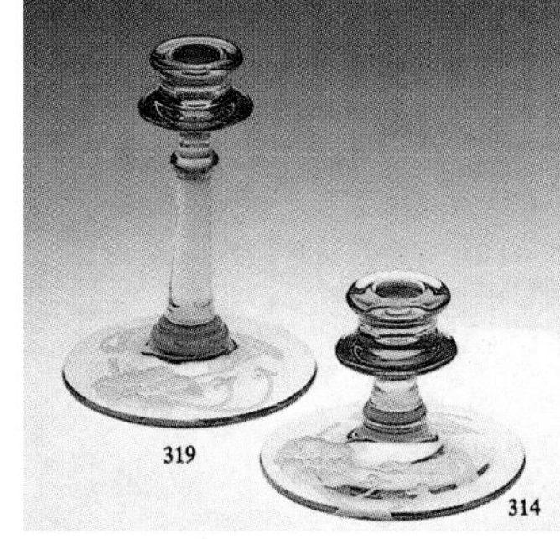

Morning Glory, Plate Etching 313

1933 – 1943

Stemware, 77

6007 Goblet
crystal $45.00
amber $48.00
6007 Sherbet, high
crystal $42.00
amber $45.00
6007 Sherbet, low
crystal $32.00
amber $37.00
6007 Cocktail
crystal $42.00
amber $42.00
6007 Claret
crystal $50.00
amber $56.00
6007 Wine
crystal $50.00
amber $54.00
6007 Cordial
crystal $68.00
amber $75.00

6007 Oyster Cocktail
crystal $30.00
amber....$35.00
6007 Ice Tea, footed
crystal $45.00
amber....$48.00
6007 Tumbler, 9 oz., footed
crystal $34.00
amber....$38.00
6007 Juice, footed
crystal $34.00
amber....$38.00
6007 Whiskey, footed
crystal $48.00
amber....$48.00

Tableware I, 212 – 214

2470 Bonbon,
crystal $42.00
869 Bowl, finger,
crystal $32.00
2440 Bowl, 5", fruit,
crystal $30.00
2440 Bowl, 6", cereal,
crystal $34.00
2440 Bowl, 10", baker,
crystal $58.00
2470½ Bowl, 10",
crystal $85.00
2470 Bowl, 12"
crystal $95.00
amber base....$125.00
2470 Candlestick, 5½", pair
crystal $135.00
amber base....$150.00
2470½ Candlestick, 5½", pair,
crystal $95.00
2440 Celery, 11½",
crystal $50.00
2470 Comport, low
crystal $57.00
amber base....$65.00
2440 Cream Soup,
crystal $50.00
2440 Cup and Saucer,
crystal $35.00
2440 Cup and Saucer, after dinner,
crystal $45.00
2451 Dish, ice and liner,
crystal $58.00
2451 Dish, ice and plate,
crystal $18.00
2270 Jug,
crystal $265.00
2470 Lemon,
crystal $42.00
2440 Olive, 6½",
crystal $36.00
2440 Pickle, 8½",
crystal $42.00
2440 Plate, 6",
crystal $9.00
2440 Plate, 7",
crystal $12.00
2440 Plate, 8",
crystal $15.00
2440 Plate, 9",
crystal $32.00
2440 Plate, 10",
crystal $45.00
2470 Plate, 10", cake,
crystal $70.00
2440 Plate, 13", torte,
crystal $88.00
2440 Platter, 12",
crystal $85.00
2470 Relish, 3-part,
crystal $65.00
2419 Relish, 4-part,
crystal $65.00
2440 Sugar and Cream,
crystal $87.00
2470 Tray, sugar and cream,
crystal $36.00
2470 Sweetmeat,
crystal $42.00
2440 Vase, 7",
crystal $125.00
2467 Vase, 7½",
crystal $135.00

Mount Vernon, Cutting 817

1942 – 1955

Stemware, 101

6031 Goblet $24.00
6031 Goblet, low $20.00
6031 Saucer Champagne $20.00
6031 Sherbet, low $16.00
6031 Cocktail $16.00
6031 Claret-Wine $26.00
6031 Cordial $35.00
6031 Oyster Cocktail $16.00
6031 Ice Tea, footed $22.00
6031 Juice, footed $16.00

Tableware I, 306

1769 Bowl, finger $12.00
2364 Bowl, 13", fruit $55.00
6023 Candlestick, duo, pair $76.00
6011 Jug....$175.00
2337 Plate, 6" $7.00
2337 Plate, 7" $8.00
2337 Plate, 8" $10.00

Mulberry, Cutting 799

1940 – 1959

Stemware, 97

6026 Goblet......$34.00
6026 Goblet, low $26.00
6026 Saucer Champagne $30.00
6026 Sherbet, low $24.00
6026 Cocktail $30.00
6026 Claret-Wine $43.00
6026 Cordial $55.00
6026 Oyster Cocktail $22.00
6026 Ice Tea, footed $34.00
6026 Juice, footed $25.00

Tableware I, 303

869 Bowl, finger $15.00
2563 Bowl, handled $95.00
2563 Candlestick, 4½", pair $95.00
5000 Jug....$275.00
2337 Plate, 6" $10.00
2337 Plate, 7" $12.00
2337 Plate, 8" $16.00

Mustards (see Marmalades, Mustards and Mayonnaise Sets)

Myriad, 2592

1941 – 1944

Tableware I, 115 – 116

2592 Ashtray,
individual....$14.00
2592 Ashtray, oblong $16.00
ebony $22.00
ebony with gold $25.00
2592 Bonbon, handled $27.00
2592 Bowl, 8½" $45.00
2592 Bowl, 10½", lily pond $57.00
2592 Bowl, 11", fruit $54.00
2592 Bowl, 11", oblong $64.00
2592 Candlestick, 4", pair $75.00
2592 Candlestick, duo, pair $85.00
2592 Box, candy and cover....$85.00
2592 Box, cigarette and cover....$84.00
with ebony cover $95.00
2592 Console Set, 3-piece $150.00
2592 Jelly, handled $27.00
2592 Lemon, handled....$27.00
2592 Salver, 12" $60.00
2592 Sweetmeat, handled....$27.00
2592 Vase, 7", oval....$75.00
2592 Vase, 9", flared....$85.00
2592 Whip Cream, handled....$27.00

Mystic, Plate Etching 270

1924 – 1928

Stemware, 17

660 Goblet,
crystal...........$25.00
660 Saucer Champagne,
crystal $20.00
660 Sherbet, low,
crystal $20.00
660 Parfait,
crystal $25.00
660 Cocktail,
crystal $20.00
660 Claret,
crystal $30.00
660 Wine,
crystal $25.00
660 Cordial,
crystal $35.00
5082 Goblet,
green....$45.00
5082 Sherbet, high,
green....$40.00
5082 Sherbet, low,
green....$35.00
5082 Parfait,
green....$48.00
5082 Cocktail,
green....$38.00
5082 Wine,
green....$48.00
837 Oyster Cocktail,
crystal $20.00
4095 Tumbler
crystal ....$18.00 – 25.00
green....$26.00 – 40.00

Tableware I, 149

4095 Bowl, finger and plate
crystal $28.00
green....$34.00
4095/4 Jug
crystal $350.00
4095/7 Jug
crystal $350.00
green....$575.00
2283 Plate, 6"
crystal $14.00
2283 Plate, 7", 8"
crystal $16.00
green....$20.00

2283 Plate, 13"
crystal $95.00
green $125.00
4095 Vase, 8½"
crystal $350.00

--N--

Nairn, Cutting 708

1933 – 1943

Stemware, 75

6004 Goblet $34.00
6004 Sherbet, high $30.00
6004 Sherbet, low $25.00
6004 Cocktail $30.00
6004 Claret $37.00
6004 Wine $37.00
6004 Oyster Cocktail $25.00
6004 Ice Tea, footed $34.00
6004 Tumbler, 9 oz., footed $25.00
6004 Juice, footed $25.00
6004 Whiskey, footed $32.00

Tableware I, 276

2470½ Bowl, 10½" $50.00
2470½ Candlestick, 5½", pair $58.00
2451 Dish, ice and plate $28.00
2283 Plate, 7" $9.00
2283 Plate, 8" $12.00

Nappies, see Comports, Nappies, and Jellies

National, Cutting 727

1933 – 1943

Stemware, 60

4024 Goblet, 11 oz. $28.00
4024 Goblet, 10 oz. $28.00
4024 Saucer Champagne $28.00
4024 Sherbet $24.00
4024 Cocktail $24.00
4024 Claret-Wine $30.00
4024 Rhine Wine $30.00
4024 Sherry $30.00
4024 Cordial $35.00
4024 Oyster Cocktail $20.00
4024 Ice Tea, footed $28.00
4024 Tumbler, 8 oz., footed $20.00
4024 Juice, footed $20.00
4024 Whiskey, footed $32.00
701 Tumbler, 12 oz. $10.00
701 Tumbler, 10 oz. $8.00
887 Whiskey, 1¾ oz. $8.00
1184 Old Fashioned Cocktail, 7 oz. $8.00
4115 Cocktail, 3 oz. $6.00

Tableware I, 279

869 Bowl, finger $12.00
4024 Bowl, 10", footed $47.00
4024 Candlestick, 6", pair $50.00
4024 Comport, 5" $25.00
6011 Decanter $145.00
6011 Jug $165.00
2337 Plate, 6" $8.00
2337 Plate, 7" $9.00
2337 Plate, 8" $12.00

Navarre, Plate Etching 327

1936 – 1982

Stemware, 87, 88

6016 Goblet
crystal $45.00
pink $125.00
blue $125.00
6016 Saucer Champagne
crystal $36.00
pink $85.00
blue $85.00
6016 Sherbet, low
crystal $30.00
6016 Cocktail
crystal $36.00
6016 Claret
crystal $65.00
pink $135.00
blue $125.00
6016 Cordial
crystal $95.00
6016 Oyster Cocktail
crystal $30.00
6016 Ice Tea, footed
crystal $45.00
pink $125.00
blue $95.00
6016 Tumbler, 10 oz., footed
crystal $35.00
6016 Juice, footed
crystal $32.00
6016 Claret, large
crystal $68.00
pink $150.00
blue $125.00
6016 Magnum
crystal $135.00
blue $195.00
6016 Champagne, Continental
crystal $125.00
6016 Brandy Inhaler
crystal $155.00
6016 Cocktail/Sherry
crystal $175.00
6016 Old Fashioned, double
crystal $65.00
6016 Highball
crystal $70.00
6016 Wine
crystal $65.00

Tableware I, 232 – 239; II, 109 – 114

2496 Bonbon $65.00
869 Bowl, finger $42.00
2496 Bowl, regular, nappy $37.00
2496 Bowl, flared, nappy $32.00
2496 Bowl, square, nappy $37.00
2496 Bowl, 3-cornered, nappy $34.00
2496 Bowl, 3-toed, nut $68.00
2496 Bowl, 8½", handled, serving ..$85.00
2496 Bowl, 10", floating garden $150.00
2470½ Bowl, 10½" $125.00
2496 Bowl, 12", flared $95.00
2545 Bowl, 12½", Flame $125.00
2545 Candelabra, 2-light, pair $650.00
2545 Candlestick, lustre, pair $300.00
2496 Candlestick, 4", pair $88.00
2496 Candlestick, 5½", pair $135.00
2496 Candlestick, duo, pair $135.00
2496 Candlestick, trindle, pair $200.00
2472 Candlestick, duo, pair $175.00
2482 Candlestick, trindle, pair $250.00
2545 Candlestick, duo, pair $200.00
2496 Candy and Cover $225.00
2440 Celery, 11½" $95.00
2496 Cheese and Cracker $165.00
2496 Comport, 5½" $68.00
2400 Comport, 6" $74.00
2440 Cup and Saucer $34.00
2496 Ice Bucket and Tongs $195.00
2375 Ice Bucket and Tongs $365.00
2496 Jelly $57.00
5000 Jug $595.00
2375 Mayonnaise, plate, ladle $125.00
2496 Mayonnaise, 2-part $75.00
2496½ Mayonnaise, plate, ladle $125.00
2440 Pickle, 8½" $42.00
2496 Pickle, 8" $39.00
2666 Pitcher, quart $500.00/market
2440 Plate, 6" $18.00
2440 Plate, 7" $20.00
2440 Plate, 8" $25.00
2440 Plate, 9" $76.00
2496 Plate, 10", cake $95.00
2440 Plate, oval, cake $125.00
2496 Plate, 14", torte $125.00
2364 Plate, 16", torte $150.00
2496 Relish, 2-part, ...$48.00
2496 Relish, 3-part $74.00
2496 Relish, 4-part $165.00
2419 Relish, 5-part $168.00
2083 Bottle, salad dressing $525.00/market
2586 Syrup, sani-cut $800.00/market
2496 Sauce, 6½", oval $120.00
2364 Shaker, chrome top C, pair $75.00
2375 Shaker, footed, FGT, pair ...$225.00
2496 Sugar and Cream, individual $75.00
2440 Sugar and Cream $65.00
2496 Sugar and Cream and Tray ..$130.00
2496 Sweetmeat, 6" $50.00
2496 Tid Bit, 3-toed $64.00
2496 Tray, 8½", oval $68.00
4121 Vase, 5" $225.00
4128 Vase, 5" $245.00
4143 Vase, 6" $500.00/market
2470 Vase, 10" $350.00
2660 Vase, 8", flip $250.00
NA01/790
Carafe/Vase, table, 65 oz. ...market
NA01/750
Carafe/Vase, mini, 10½ oz. ..market
NA01/580
Box, puff and cover ....market
NA01/842
Bottle, perfume and stopper ....market

Navarre, 2751, see Crown Collection

Nectar, Etching 322

1936 – 1942

Stemware, 81 – 82

6011 Goblet $30.00
6011 Saucer Champagne $20.00
6011 Sherbet, low $18.00
6011 Cocktail $20.00
6011 Claret $30.00
6011 Rhine Wine $35.00
6011 Wine $30.00
6011 Sherry $25.00
6011 Crème de Menthe $25.00
6011 Brandy $35.00

6011 Cordial $37.00
6011 Oyster Cocktail $15.00
6011 Ice Tea, footed $28.00
6011 Tumbler, 10 oz., footed $20.00
6011 Juice, footed $20.00
6011 Whiskey, footed $30.00
906 Brandy Inhaler $20.00
4122 Whiskey, 1½ oz. $18.00
2337 Plate, 11" $30.00
795 Champagne, hollow stem $20.00
701 Tumbler, 12 oz. $20.00
701 Tumbler, 10 oz. $18.00
1184 Old Fashioned Cocktail $20.00

Tableware I, 221 – 222

1769 Bowl, finger $22.00
4024 Bowl, 10", footed $75.00
4024 Candlestick, 6", pair $85.00
4024 Comport, 5" $42.00
2350½ Cup and Saucer $24.00
6011 Decanter $175.00
6011 Jug $225.00
2337 Plate, 6" $9.00
2337 Plate, 7" $10.00
2337 Plate, 8" $12.00
2235 Shaker, FGT, pair $45.00
2350½ Sugar and Cream $45.00
2440 Torte, 13" $40.00
2350 Cup and Saucer, after dinner ..$37.00

Needlepoint, 4184 Tumbler

1959 – 1965

Stemware, 156

4184 Ice Tea/Highball, 16½ oz.
gold $30.00
moss green $30.00
teal blue $30.00
4184 Water/Scotch and Soda, 12¼ oz.
gold $30.00
moss green $30.00
teal blue $30.00
4184 Juice/Old Fashioned, 8 oz.
gold $30.00
moss green $30.00
teal blue $30.00

Neo Classic, 6011

1934 – 1964

Stemware, 81

6011 Goblet
crystal $20.00
amber $35.00
burgundy/amethyst $75.00
empire green $75.00
regal blue $68.00
ruby $68.00
silver mist $35.00
6011 Saucer Champagne
crystal $15.00
amber $32.00
burgundy/amethyst $50.00
empire green $50.00
regal blue $50.00
ruby $50.00
silver mist $32.00
6011 Sherbet, low
crystal $12.00
amber $28.00
burgundy/amethyst $34.00
empire green $34.00
regal blue $37.00
ruby $37.00
silver mist $28.00
6011 Cocktail
crystal $15.00
amber $32.00
burgundy/amethyst $45.00
empire green $45.00
regal blue $45.00
ruby $45.00
silver mist $32.00
6011 Claret
crystal $20.00
amber $48.00
burgundy/amethyst $70.00
empire green $70.00
regal blue $70.00
ruby $70.00
silver mist $48.00
6011 Rhine Wine
crystal $22.00
amber $40.00
burgundy/amethyst $68.00
empire green $68.00
regal blue $68.00
ruby $68.00
silver mist $40.00
6011 Wine
crystal $20.00
amber $45.00
burgundy/amethyst $65.00
empire green $65.00
regal blue $65.00
ruby $65.00
silver mist $45.00
6011 Sherry
crystal $18.00
amber $42.00
burgundy/amethyst $55.00
empire green $55.00
regal blue $55.00
ruby $55.00
silver mist $42.00
6011 Crème de Menthe
crystal $15.00
amber $32.00
burgundy/amethyst $50.00
empire green $50.00
regal blue $50.00
ruby $50.00
silver mist $32.00
6011 Brandy
crystal $20.00
amber $40.00
burgundy/amethyst $58.00
empire green $58.00
regal blue $58.00
ruby $58.00
silver mist $40.00
6011 Cordial
crystal $25.00
amber $47.00
burgundy/amethyst $75.00
empire green $75.00
regal blue $75.00
ruby $75.00
silver mist $47.00
6011 Oyster Cocktail
crystal $12.00
amber $27.00
burgundy/amethyst $34.00
empire green $34.00
regal blue $34.00
ruby $34.00
silver mist $27.00
6011 Ice Tea, footed
crystal $20.00
amber $35.00
burgundy/amethyst $70.00
empire green $70.00
regal blue $65.00
ruby $65.00
silver mist $35.00
6011 Tumbler, 10 oz., footed
crystal $15.00
amber $30.00
burgundy/amethyst $40.00
empire green $40.00
regal blue $40.00
ruby $40.00
silver mist $30.00
6011 Juice, footed
crystal $12.00
amber $30.00
burgundy/amethyst $37.00
empire green $37.00
regal blue $37.00
ruby $37.00
silver mist $30.00
6011 Whiskey, footed
crystal $20.00
amber $45.00
burgundy/amethyst $50.00
empire green $50.00
regal blue $52.00
ruby $52.00
silver mist $45.00

Tableware

6011 Decanter
crystal $250.00
regal blue bowl $750.00
burgundy bowl $750.00
empire green bowl $750.00
amber base $325.00
6011 Jug
crystal $145.00
amber base $195.00
burgundy bowl $600.00
regal blue bowl $600.00
empire green bowl $600.00

New Adam, Etching 252

1918 – 1927

Note: also made with gold trim

Stemware, 24

858 Goblet, 9 oz. $8.00
858 Saucer Champagne $8.00
858 Fruit $8.00
858 Cocktail $8.00
858 Claret, 4½ oz. $8.00
858 Wine, 2¾ oz. $8.00
858 Sherry $8.00
858 Cordial $15.00
701 Tumbler, 14 oz.
handled $8.00
no handle $6.00
833 Tumbler, 8 oz. $6.00
858 Tumbler ....$4.00 – 8.00
4061 Lemonade, footed, handled ..$18.00
858 Custard $8.00
837 Oyster Cocktail $7.00
822 Parfait $22.00
945½ Grapefruit and Liner $28.00

Tableware

863 Almond $20.00
880 Bonbon $20.00

160½ Bottle, water $47.00
896 Bowl and cover $26.00
1697 Carafe and Tumbler $68.00
803 Comport, 5" $20.00
803 Comport, 6" $20.00
300 Decanter, quart $47.00
858 Bowl, finger, and plate $20.00
979 Horseradish $45.00
300 Jug $78.00
303 Jug $75.00
318 Jug $85.00
724-7 Jug $88.00
300½-5 Jug $60.00
1236-6 Jug $77.00
2104 Jug and Tumbler $95.00
1968 Marmalade and cover $27.00
2138 Mayonnaise, plate, ladle $42.00
1831 Mustard and cover $22.00
803 Nappy, 5" $20.00
803 Nappy, 6" $22.00
803 Nappy, 7", footed $25.00
1227 Nappy, 8" $28.00
1227 Nappy, 4½" $16.00
1465 Oil, 7 oz., cut neck $44.00
1465 Oil, 5 oz. cut neck $37.00
1897 Plate, 7", salad $5.00
1848 Plate, 9", sandwich $10.00
1719 Plate, 10½", sandwich $12.00
2083 Bottle, salad dressing $58.00
2022 Shaker, FGT, pair $35.00
2015 Spoon Tray $28.00
2133 Sugar and Cream $30.00
858 Sweetmeat $18.00
2194 Syrup, 12 oz., nickle top $65.00
2194 Syrup, 8 oz., nickle top $57.00
922 Toothpick $22.00

New Garland, Plate Etching 284

1930 – 1933

Stemware, 57

4020 Goblet
- amber base $35.00
- rose bowl $45.00
- topaz bowl $45.00

4020 Sherbet, high
- amber base $32.00
- rose bowl $40.00
- topaz bowl $40.00

4020 Sherbet, 7 oz., low
- amber base $30.00
- rose bowl $30.00
- topaz bowl $30.00

4020 Sherbet, 5 oz., low
- amber base $30.00
- rose bowl $30.00
- topaz bowl $30.00

4020 Cocktail, 4 oz. (4020½)
- amber base $30.00
- rose bowl $35.00
- topaz bowl $35.00

4020 Cocktail, 3½ oz.
- amber base $30.00
- rose bowl $30.00
- topaz bowl $30.00

4020 Ice Tea, footed
- amber base $35.00
- rose bowl $45.00
- topaz bowl $45.00

4020 Tumbler, 13 oz., footed
- amber base $35.00
- rose bowl $45.00
- topaz bowl $45.00

4020 Tumbler, 10 oz., footed
- amber base $30.00
- rose bowl $35.00
- topaz bowl $35.00

4020 Juice, footed
- amber base $35.00
- rose bowl $35.00
- topaz bowl $35.00

4020 Whiskey, footed
- amber base $35.00
- rose bowl $45.00
- topaz bowl $45.00

6002 Goblet,
- rose bowl $56.00

6002 Sherbet, high,
- rose bowl $48.00

6002 Sherbet, low,
- rose bowl $35.00

6002 Claret,
- rose bowl $65.00

6002 Wine,
- rose bowl $58.00

6002 Cordial,
- rose bowl $94.00

6002 Oyster Cocktail,
- rose bowl $35.00

6002 Ice Tea, footed,
- rose bowl $56.00

6002 Tumbler, 10 oz., footed,
- rose bowl $40.00

6002 Juice, footed,
- rose bowl $38.00

6002 Whiskey, footed,
- rose bowl $67.00

Tableware I, 189 – 193

4020 Almond
- amber $30.00
- rose $36.00
- topaz $34.00

2419 Bonbon
- amber $36.00
- rose $40.00
- topaz $38.00

4020 Bowl, finger
- amber base $36.00
- rose bowl $45.00
- topaz bowl $40.00

6002 Bowl, finger
- rose bowl $50.00

2419 Bowl, 5", fruit
- amber $22.00
- rose $28.00
- topaz $25.00

2419 Bowl, 6", cereal
- amber $24.00
- rose $30.00
- topaz $28.00

2419 Bowl, 7", soup
- amber $28.00
- rose $36.00
- topaz $32.00

2394 Bowl D, 7½"
- amber $75.00
- rose $125.00
- topaz $110.00

2433 Bowl D, 7½"
- amber $150.00
- rose $350.00
- topaz $275.00

2419 Bowl, 10", baker
- amber $48.00
- rose $65.00
- topaz $57.00

2430 Bowl, 11"
- amber $74.00
- rose $96.00
- topaz $85.00

2394 Bowl A, 12"
- amber $95.00
- rose $125.00
- topaz $115.00

2433 Bowl A, 12"
- amber $135.00
- rose $300.00
- topaz $225.00

2441 Bowl, 12"
- amber $95.00
- rose $125.00
- topaz $115.00

2394 Candlestick, 2", pair
- amber $75.00
- rose $88.00
- topaz $82.00

2375 Candlestick, 3", pair
- amber $65.00
- rose $85.00
- topaz $75.00

2433 Candlestick, 3", pair
- amber $90.00
- rose $115.00
- topaz $100.00

2430 Candlestick, 9½", pair
- amber $185.00
- rose $225.00
- topaz $200.00

2430 Jar, candy and cover
- amber $110.00
- rose $150.00
- topaz $125.00

2419 Celery, 11"
- amber $58.00
- rose $67.00
- topaz $62.00

2400 Comport, 6"
- amber $60.00
- rose $70.00
- topaz $65.00

2433 Comport, low
- amber $58.00
- rose $78.00
- topaz $74.00

2433 Comport, tall
- amber $125.00
- rose $150.00
- topaz $135.00

2419 Cream Soup
- amber $54.00
- rose $65.00
- topaz $60.00

2419 Cup and Saucer, after dinner
- amber $50.00
- rose $60.00
- topaz $55.00

2419 Cup and Saucer
- amber $38.00
- rose $45.00
- topaz $42.00

2439 Decanter
- amber $600.00/market
- rose $700.00/market
- topaz $650.00/market

4020 Decanter
- amber $600.00
- rose $800.00
- topaz $700.00

2375 Ice Bucket
- amber $100.00

No.	Item	Price
	rose	$145.00
	topaz	$125.00
2451	Dish, ice and liner	
	amber	$58.00
	rose	$68.00
	topaz	$65.00
2419	Jelly, 2-handled	
	amber	$38.00
	rose	$45.00
	topaz	$42.00
2430	Jelly, 7"	
	amber	$35.00
	rose	$45.00
	topaz	$40.00
4020	Jug	
	amber	$375.00
	rose	$495.00
	topaz	$450.00
5000	Jug	
	rose	$600.00/market
2419	Lemon	
	amber	$35.00
	rose	$42.00
	topaz	$40.00
2419	Mayonnaise	
	amber	$38.00
	rose	$45.00
	topaz	$42.00
2430	Mint, 5½"	
	amber	$30.00
	rose	$34.00
	topaz	$32.00
2375	Oil, footed	
	amber	$395.00
	rose	$495.00
	topaz	$450.00
2419	Pickle, 8½"	
	amber	$38.00
	rose	$47.00
	topaz	$42.00
2419	Plate, 6"	
	amber	$12.00
	rose	$16.00
	topaz	$14.00
2419	Plate, 7"	
	amber	$14.00
	rose	$18.00
	topaz	$16.00
2419	Plate, 8"	
	amber	$14.00
	rose	$22.00
	topaz	$18.00
2419	Plate, 9"	
	amber	$20.00
	rose	$38.00
	topaz	$32.00
2419	Plate, 10", cake	
	amber	$70.00
	rose	$88.00
	topaz	$78.00
2419	Platter, 12"	
	amber	$68.00
	rose	$87.00
	topaz	$80.00
2419	Relish, 8½"	
	amber	$42.00
	rose	$47.00
	topaz	$44.00
2419	Relish, 4-part	
	amber	$55.00
	rose	$67.00
	topaz	$64.00
2083	Bottle, salad dressing	
	amber	$295.00
	rose	$350.00
	topaz	$325.00
2419	Sauce and Stand	
	amber	$75.00
	rose	$95.00
	topaz	$85.00
2419	Shaker, FGT , pair	
	amber	$125.00
	rose	$158.00
	topaz	$147.00
4020	Shaker, FGT , pair	
	amber	$135.00
	rose	$175.00
	topaz	$150.00
2419	Sugar and Cream, tea	
	amber	$58.00
	rose	$75.00
	topaz	$64.00
2419½	Sugar and Cream	
	amber	$60.00
	rose	$78.00
	topaz	$67.00
4020	Sugar and Cream	
	amber	$68.00
	rose	$80.00
	topaz	$75.00
2430	Vase, 8"	
	amber	$195.00
	rose	$275.00
	topaz	$250.00

Newport, Decoration 9

1920s

Stemware, 21

No.	Item	Price
766	Goblet	$12.00
766	Saucer Champagne	$12.00
766	Sherbet	$12.00
766	Fruit	$12.00
766	Parfait	$22.00
766	Cocktail	$12.00
766	Ice Tea, footed, handled,	$20.00
4011	Tumbler	$10.00 – 12.00

Tableware I, 311

No.	Item	Price
766	Almond	$26.00
766	Bowl, finger and plate	$18.00
2244	Candlestick, 6"	$24.00
1697	Carafe and 4023 Tumbler	$38.00
803	Comport, 5"	$22.00
803	Comport and cover, 5"	$26.00
825	Jelly	$20.00
825	Jelly and cover	$24.00
300½	Jug	$95.00
803	Nappy, 5"	$20.00
803	Nappy and cover	$24.00
1897	Plate, 7"	$9.00
1478	Sugar and Cream	$26.00

New Vintage, Etching 227

1913 – 1927

Stemware, 23

No.	Item	Price
858	Goblet, 11 oz.	$12.00
858	Goblet, 10 oz.	$10.00
858	Goblet, 9 oz.	$10.00
858	Saucer Champagne, 7 oz.	$6.00
858	Saucer Champagne, 5½ oz.	$6.00
858	Sherbet	$6.00
858	Fruit	$6.00
858	Parfait	$14.00
858	Cocktail	$6.00
858	Claret, 6½ oz.	$6.00
858	Claret, 4½ oz.	$6.00
858	Wine, 3½ oz.	$6.00
858	Wine, 2¾ oz.	$6.00
858	Sherry	$6.00
858	Crème de Menthe	$6.00
858	Brandy	$6.00
858	Cordial	$15.00
858	Oyster Cocktail	$6.00
858	Champagne, hollow stem	$10.00
858	Champagne, tall	$10.00
858	Champagne, long stem	$18.00
858	Champagne, long stem, Cutting R	$18.00
858	Hot Whiskey	$6.00
863	Goblet, 10½ oz.	$10.00
863	Goblet, 9 oz.	$10.00
863	Goblet, 7 oz.	$10.00
863	Goblet, 5½ oz.	$10.00
863	Saucer Champagne	$10.00
863	Fruit	$8.00
863	Cocktail, 3½ oz.	$8.00
863	Cocktail, 3 oz.	$8.00
863	Claret	$12.00
863	Rhine Wine	$10.00
863	Wine	$10.00
863	Sherry	$8.00
863	Crème de Menthe	$8.00
863	Brandy, pousse-café	$15.00
863	Cordial	$15.00
863	Champagne, hollow stem, CF	$10.00
863	Champagne, tall	$10.00
863	Roemer, 5½ oz.	$18.00
863	Roemer, 4½ oz.	$18.00
880	Goblet, 11 oz.	$10.00
880	Goblet, 10 oz.	$10.00
880	Goblet, 9 oz.	$8.00
880	Goblet, 8 oz.	$8.00
880	Saucer Champagne, 7 oz.	$8.00
880	Saucer Champagne, 5½ oz.	$7.00
880	Sherbet	$7.00
880	Cocktail, 3½ oz.	$7.00
880	Claret, 6½ oz.	$12.00
880	Claret, 4½ oz.	$10.00
880	Rhine Wine	$10.00
880	Wine, 3½ oz.	$10.00
880	Wine, 2¾ oz.	$10.00
880	Sherry	$7.00
880	Crème de Menthe	$8.00
880	Brandy, pousse-café, 1 oz.	$15.00
880	Cordial, 1 oz.	$15.00
880	Champagne, hollow stem	$10.00
880	Champagne, tall	$10.00
880	Grapefruit, tall and liner	$25.00
880	Grapefruit, short and liner	$20.00
880	Hot Whiskey	$7.00
880	Tall Ale	$10.00
766	Ice Tea, footed, handled	$18.00
4061	Lemonade, footed, handled	$18.00
5039	Oyster Cocktail	$6.00
822	Parfait	$14.00
5036	Parfait	$14.00
5054	Parfait	$14.00
701	Tumbler	$5.00 – 14.00
833	Tumbler	$5.00 – 12.00
858	Tumbler	$6.00 – 16.00
887	Tumbler	$5.00 – 9.00
889	Tumbler	$5.00 – 18.00

4011 Tumbler $6.00 – 18.00
880, 880½
Grapefruit and Liner $25.00
945½ Grapefruit and Liner $25.00
300 Jug $85.00
303 Jug $75.00
318 Jug $94.00
724 Jug $100.00
1236 Jug $100.00
1852 Jug $95.00
317½ Jug and cover $100.00
300 Tankard $85.00
724 Tankard $100.00
1743 Tankard $100.00

New Yorker, Cutting 703

1930 – 1943

Stemware, 58

4020 Goblet
crystal $40.00
green base $45.00
ebony base $45.00
4020 Sherbet, high
crystal $40.00
green base $45.00
ebony base $45.00
4020 Sherbet, 7 oz., low
crystal $25.00
green base $35.00
ebony base $35.00
4020 Cocktail, 4 oz.
crystal $35.00
green base $35.00
ebony base $35.00
4020 Claret
crystal $45.00
green base $48.00
ebony base $48.00
4020 Wine
crystal $45.00
green base $48.00
ebony base $48.00
4020 Ice Tea, footed
crystal $40.00
green base $45.00
ebony base $45.00
4020 Tumbler, 13 oz., footed
crystal $40.00
green base $45.00
ebony base $45.00
4020 Tumbler, 10 oz., footed
crystal $35.00
green base $35.00
ebony base $35.00
4020 Juice, footed
crystal $35.00
green base $35.00
ebony base $35.00
4020 Whiskey, footed
crystal $35.00
green base $35.00
ebony base $35.00

Tableware I, 274

4021 Bowl, finger
crystal $20.00
green base $24.00
ebony base $24.00
4020 Decanter
crystal $125.00
green base $150.00
4020 Jug
crystal $165.00
green base $225.00
ebony base $195.00
2419 Plate, 6" $6.00
2419 Plate, 7" $7.00
2419 Plate, 8" $8.00
4020 Sugar and Cream
crystal $45.00
green base $65.00

Niagara Optic, 6026½

1940 – 1965

Stemware, 97

6026½ Goblet $26.00
6026½ Goblet, low $22.00
6026½ Saucer Champagne $24.00
6026½ Sherbet, low $18.00
6026½ Cocktail $22.00
6026½ Claret-Wine $28.00
6026½ Cordial $34.00
6026½ Oyster Cocktail $16.00
6026½ Ice Tea, footed $26.00
6026½ Juice, footed $18.00
2337/2 Plate, 7", Niagara optic $10.00

Nightmare, Carving 39, Decoration 621

1940 – 1943

Useful & Ornamental, 128

4146 Scotch and Soda, 9 oz. $35.00
4146 Cocktail, 4 oz. $25.00
4146 Cordial, 1 oz. $30.00
4146 Set, 3 piece, nested $85.00
2306 Smoker Set, 4-piece $75.00
2306 Ashtray, 2¾" $15.00
2306 Ashtray, 3" $17.50
2306 Ashtray, 3½" $20.00
2306 Ashtray, 4" $25.00

Nineteenth Hole, Carving 15

1940 – 1943

Useful & Ornamental, 122

2419 Ashtray, Approaching $18.00
2427 Ashtray, Putting $18.00
2391 Box, cigarette and cover, Driving $45.00
4132 Decanter, Driving $85.00
4132 Bowl, ice, Putting $65.00
4132 Tumbler, whiskey, Approaching $18.00
4132 Tumbler, Old Fashioned Cocktail, Putting $18.00
4132 Tumbler, 5 oz., Exploding $20.00
4132½ Tumbler, 9 oz., scotch and soda, Exploding $22.00
4132 Tumbler, 12 oz., Driving $24.00

Nome, Decoration 40

1924 – 1929

Stemware, 19

661 Goblet $15.00
661 Saucer Champagne $10.00
661 Fruit/Sherbet, low $10.00
661 Parfait $15.00
661 Cocktail $10.00
661 Wine $10.00
661 Cordial $20.00

Tableware I, 320

1769 Bowl, finger and plate $24.00
803 Comport, 5", deep, footed $18.00
803 Nappy, 5", deep, footed $18.00
803 Nappy, 6", deep, footed $22.00
1897 Plate, 7", salad $10.00
1852/6 Tankard $200.00
945½ Grapefruit and Liner $25.00
701 Tumbler $4.00 – 18.00
4085 Tumbler, 13 oz., handled and plate $22.00
4085 Ice Tea, 13 oz. and plate $20.00
4085 Tumbler, table $10.00
863 Almond $18.00

Nordic, 892

1939 – 1943

Stemware, 40

892 Goblet $22.00
892 Saucer Champagne $20.00
892 Sherbet, low $18.00
892 Cocktail $20.00
892 Claret $25.00
892 Wine $22.00
892 Cordial $35.00
892 Oyster Cocktail $16.00
892 Ice Tea, footed $22.00
892 Juice, footed $18.00

Nordic, 6077

1958 – 1965

Stemware, 115

6077 Goblet $24.00
6077 Sherbet $22.00
6077 Cocktail/Wine $24.00
6077 Cordial $32.00
6077 Ice Tea, footed $24.00
6077 Juice, footed $22.00

Northampton (Imported Stemware)

1984 – 1986

Tableware II, 280 – 281

Goblet $22.00
Wine $22.00
Flute $22.00
Ice Tea $22.00

Nosegay, Cutting 834

1953 – 1972

Stemware, 106

6051½ Goblet $32.00
6051½ Sherbet $28.00
6051½ Cocktail $26.00
6051½ Claret-Wine $38.00
6051½ Cordial $45.00
6051½ Oyster Cocktail $22.00
6051½ Ice Tea, footed $32.00
6051½ Juice, footed $26.00

Tableware II, 182

4185 Bowl, finger/dessert $24.00
2666 Bowl, oval $38.00
2666 Candle, flora, pair $48.00
2364 Mayonnaise, plate, ladle $47.00
2337 Plate, 7" $10.00
2337 Plate, 8" $12.00

2666 Plate, 10", snack $22.00
2364 Plate, 14", torte $35.00
2666 Relish, 2-part $30.00
2666 Relish, 3-part $37.00
2364 Shaker, large, chrome top B, pair $48.00
2666 Sugar and Cream..................$52.00
2666 Tray, sugar and cream..........$20.00

Nottingham, Cutting 720

1933 – 1934

Stemware, 79

6009 Goblet $34.00
6009 Sherbet, high $32.00
6009 Sherbet, low $28.00
6009 Cocktail $32.00
6009 Claret-Wine $38.00
6009 Cordial $47.00
6009 Oyster Cocktail.......................$24.00
6009 Ice Tea, footed $32.00
6009 Tumbler, 9 oz., footed...........$26.00
6009 Juice, footed $25.00

Tableware I, 278, 279

869 Bowl, finger...........................$14.00
2470½ Bowl, 10½" $52.00
2470½ Candlestick, 5½", pair...........$54.00
2400 Comport, 6" $27.00
2337 Plate, 6" $6.00
2337 Plate, 7" $7.00
2337 Plate, 8" $8.00
2470 Vase, 10" $95.00

Nouveau, Etching 42

1980 – 1982

Stemware, 144

6143 Goblet
crystal $34.00
gray bowl.......$35.00
6143 Champagne
crystal $30.00
gray bowl...........................$32.00
6143 Wine
crystal $35.00
gray bowl...........................$36.00
6143 Ice Tea, footed
crystal $34.00
gray bowl...........................$35.00

Nova, Cutting 934

1976 – 1978

Stemware, 143

6128 Goblet $25.00
6128 Champagne $25.00
6128 Wine.......................................$25.00
6128 Ice Tea, footed $25.00

Nugget, Decoration 507

1931

Gold on Ebony

Tableware I, 328

2350 Ashtray, large.........................$34.00
2297 Bowl, 12" $145.00
2324 Candlestick, 4", pair $95.00
2447 Candlestick, duo.................$160.00
2456 Jar, candy and cover, ½ pound $150.00
2391 Cigarette and Cover, large $125.00
2400 Comport, 6" $75.00
2375 Dish, lemon...........................$46.00
2375 Plate, cake $95.00
5088 Vase, bud...............................$48.00
4105 Vase, 8" $165.00

Nuptial, Crystal Print 21

1969 – 1974

Stemware, 128

6103 Goblet.........$25.00
6103 Sherbet.........$22.00
6103 Claret...............$26.00
6103 Tulip Wine............................$26.00
6103 Brandy $26.00
6103 Ice Tea, footed $25.00

Nuts, see Small Bowls, Mints and Nuts

--O--

Oak Leaf, Brocade Etching 290

1928 – 1930

Stemware, 33

877 Goblet
crystal.......$70.00
green...$70.00
877 Sherbet, high
crystal $65.00
green...$65.00
877 Sherbet, low
crystal $35.00
green...$35.00
877 Parfait
crystal $65.00
green...$65.00
877 Cocktail
crystal $55.00
green...$55.00
877 Claret
crystal $75.00
green...$75.00
877 Wine
crystal $65.00
green...$65.00
877 Cordial
crystal $125.00
green.......................................$125.00
877 Oyster Cocktail
crystal $35.00
green...$35.00
877 Grapefruit and Liner
crystal $85.00
green...$85.00
877 Ice Tea, footed
crystal $65.00
green...$65.00
877 Tumbler, 9 oz., footed
crystal $35.00
green...$35.00
877 Juice, footed
crystal $35.00
green...$35.00
877 Whiskey, footed
crystal $40.00
green...$40.00

Tableware I, 133 – 135

2375 Bonbon
crystal $48.00
rose $56.00
green.................................$56.00
869 Bowl, finger and 2283 Plate
crystal $75.00
green.................................$85.00
2395 Bowl, 10"
crystal $325.00
rose $350.00
green...............................$350.00
ebony $350.00
2398 Bowl, 11"
crystal $225.00
rose $250.00
green...............................$250.00
2342 Bowl, 12"
crystal $165.00
rose $175.00
green...............................$175.00
2394 Bowl, 12"
crystal $165.00
rose $185.00
green...............................$185.00
2375 Bowl, dessert, large
crystal $135.00
rose $154.00
green...............................$154.00
2415 Bowl, combination
crystal $300.00
rose $300.00
green.............................$1300.00
2394 Candlestick, 2", pair
crystal $150.00
rose $175.00
green...............................$175.00
2375 Candlestick, 3", pair
crystal $145.00
rose $160.00
green...............................$160.00
2395 Candlestick, 3", pair
crystal $175.00
rose $185.00
green...............................$185.00
ebony $175.00
2375½ Candlestick, pair
crystal $185.00
rose $225.00
green...............................$225.00
2331 Box, candy and cover
crystal $175.00
rose $185.00
green...............................$185.00
ebony $175.00
2375 Centerpiece, 12"
crystal $145.00
rose $158.00
green...............................$158.00
2375½ Centerpiece, oval
crystal $295.00
rose $325.00
green...............................$325.00
2368 Cheese and Cracker
crystal $150.00
rose $165.00
green...............................$165.00
2391 Cigarette and Cover, small
crystal $95.00
rose $125.00
green...............................$125.00
ebony $115.00
2391 Cigarette and Cover, large
crystal $125.00

rose $160.00
green $160.00
ebony $150.00
2350 Comport, 8"
crystal $87.00
rose $115.00
green $115.00
2400 Comport, 8"
crystal $95.00
rose $125.00
green $125.00
2380 Confection and Cover
crystal $150.00
rose $165.00
green $165.00
2395 Confection and Cover, oval
rose $200.00
green $200.00
2378 Ice Bucket, NP handle
crystal $165.00
rose $175.00
green $175.00
5000 Jug
crystal $775.00/market
green $800.00/market
2375 Dish, lemon
crystal $48.00
rose $56.00
green $56.00
2315 Mayonnaise
crystal $95.00
rose $145.00
green $145.00
2394 Mint
crystal $44.00
rose $50.00
green $50.00
2332 Plate, 7", mayonnaise
crystal $30.00
rose $44.00
green $44.00
2283 Plate, 7"
crystal $30.00
rose $44.00
green $44.00
2283 Plate, 8"
crystal $30.00
rose $44.00
green $44.00
2375 Plate, 10", cake
crystal $95.00
rose $135.00
green $1350.00
2315 Plate, 13", lettuce/mayonnaise
crystal $95.00
rose $125.00
green $125.00
2315 Salver, 12"
crystal $150.00
rose $195.00
green $195.00
2378 Pail, sugar
crystal $275.00
rose $450.00
green $450.00
2375 Sweetmeat
crystal $48.00
rose $56.00
green $56.00
2342 Tray, handled, lunch
crystal $145.00
rose $175.00
green $175.00

2413 Urn and Cover
rose $325.00
green $325.00
4103 Vase, 3", optic
crystal $75.00
rose $95.00
green $95.00
4105 Vase, 6", optic
crystal $140.00
rose $175.00
green $175.00
4105 Vase, 8", optic
crystal $225.00
rose $275.00
green $275.00
2369 Vase, 7", optic
crystal $225.00
rose $275.00
green $275.00
2369 Vase, 9", optic
crystal $300.00
rose $360.00
green $310.00
2292 Vase, 8"
crystal $250.00
rose $285.00
green $285.00
ebony $265.00
2387 Vase, 8"
crystal $250.00
rose $285.00
green $285.00
2385 Vase, 8½", fan
crystal $400.00
rose $595.00
green $585.00
ebony $450.00
2373 Vase, small, window box and cover
crystal $500.00
rose $595.00
green $575.00
ebony $575.00
2373 Vase, large, window box and cover
crystal $600.00
rose $675.00
green $650.00
ebony $650.00
2375 Whip Cream
crystal $54.00
rose $60.00
green $60.00
2378 Pail, whip cream
crystal $275.00
rose $465.00
green $450.00

Oakwood, Decoration 72

1928 – 1929

Stemware, 33

877 Goblet
orchid $150.00
azure $150.00
877 Sherbet, high
orchid $125.00
azure $125.00
877 Sherbet, low
orchid $75.00
azure $75.00
877 Parfait
orchid $125.00
azure $125.00
877 Cocktail
orchid $85.00
azure $85.00
877 Claret
orchid $165.00
azure $165.00
877 Wine
orchid $135.00
azure $135.00
877 Cordial
orchid $195.00
azure $195.00
877 Oyster Cocktail
orchid $65.00
azure $65.00
877 Grapefruit and Liner
orchid $175.00
azure $175.00
877 Ice Tea, footed
orchid $125.00
azure $125.00
877 Tumbler, 9 oz., footed
orchid $75.00
azure $75.00
877 Juice, footed
orchid $68.00
azure $68.00
877 Whiskey, footed
orchid $75.00
azure $75.00

Tableware I, 135 – 137

2375 Bonbon
orchid $135.00
azure $135.00
869 Bowl, finger and 2283 Plate
orchid $195.00
azure $195.00
2398 Bowl, 11"
orchid $400.00
azure $400.00
2342 Bowl, 12"
orchid $375.00
azure $375.00
2394 Bowl, 12"
orchid $395.00
azure $395.00
2375 Bowl, dessert, large
azure $225.00
2415 Bowl, combination
azure $690.00
2394 Candlestick, 2", pair
orchid $275.00
azure $275.00
2375 Candlestick, 3", pair
orchid $265.00
azure $265.00
2375½ Candlestick, pair
orchid $325.00
azure $325.00
2331 Box, candy and cover
orchid $700.00
azure $700.00
2375 Centerpiece, 12"
orchid $575.00
azure $550.00
2375½ Centerpiece, 13", oval and 2371 Flower Holder
orchid $750.00
azure $750.00
2368 Cheese and Cracker
crystal $135.00
orchid $175.00
azure $175.00
2391 Cigarette and Cover, small
orchid $285.00
azure $285.00

2391 Cigarette and Cover, large
orchid $450.00
azure $450.00
2400 Comport, 8"
orchid $545.00
azure $545.00
2380 Confection and Cover
orchid $525.00
azure $525.00
2395 Confection and Cover, oval
azure $525.00
2378 Ice Bucket, NP handle
orchid $800.00
azure $800.00
5000 Jug
orchid $1,600.00/market
azure $1,600.00/market
2375 Dish, lemon
orchid $150.00
azure $150.00
2315 Mayonnaise, plate, ladle
orchid $395.00
azure $395.00
2332 Plate, 7", mayonnaise
orchid $74.00
azure $74.00
2283 Plate, 7"
orchid $75.00
azure $75.00
2283 Plate, 8"
orchid $85.00
azure $85.00
2375 Plate, 10", cake
azure $450.00
2315 Plate, 13", lettuce/mayonnaise
orchid $235.00
azure $235.00
2315 Salver, 12"
orchid $750.00
azure $750.00
2378 Pail, sugar
orchid $595.00
azure $595.00
2375 Sweetmeat
orchid $150.00
azure $150.00
2342 Tray, handled, lunch
orchid $465.00
azure $465.00
2413 Urn and cover
azure $800.00/market
4105 Vase, 6", optic
orchid $425.00
azure $425.00
4105 Vase, 8", optic
orchid $800.00/market
azure $800.00/market
2387 Vase, 8"
orchid $850.00/market
azure $850.00/market
2385 Vase, 8½", fan
orchid $1,000.00/market
azure $1,000.00/market
2373 Vase, small, window box and cover
orchid $950.00
azure $950.00
2373 Vase, large, window box and cover
orchid $1,000.00
azure $1,000.00
2375 Whip Cream
orchid $165.00
azure $165.00
2375 Pail, whip cream
orchid $595.00
azure $595.00

Oil and Vinegar, Carving 38, see Salad Dressing and Oil Bottles

Oil Bottles, see Salad Dressing and Oil Bottles

Olympic Gold, Decoration 680

1968 – 1970

Stemware, 135

6111 Goblet $35.00
6111 Sherbet $32.00
6111 Claret $38.00
6111 Wine $38.00
6111 Cordial $45.00
6111 Ice Tea, footed $35.00
2337 Plate, 7" $10.00
2337 Plate, 8" $12.00

Olympic Platinum, Decoration 679

1968 – 1970

See Olympic Gold for design

Stemware, 135

6111 Goblet $35.00
6111 Sherbet $32.00
6111 Claret $38.00
6111 Wine $38.00
6111 Cordial $45.00
6111 Ice Tea, footed $35.00
2337 Plate, 7" $10.00
2337 Plate, 8" $12.00

Onyx Lustre Decoration

1926

Tableware I, 332

2367 Bowl, 7", bulb $165.00
2367 Bowl, 8", bulb $175.00
2297 Bowl A, 10", shallow $175.00
2297 Bowl A, 12", deep $195.00
2324 Candlestick, 4", pair $225.00
2269 Candlestick, 6", pair $250.00
2331 Box, candy and cover $265.00
2329 Centerpiece, 11" $225.00
2329 Centerpiece, 13" $275.00
2327 Comport, 7" $168.00
2283 Plate, 13", cupped $187.00
2276 Vanity Set $295.00
1681 Vase, wall $225.00

Orange Blossom, Cutting 911

1966 – 1967

Stemware, 132

6107 Goblet $30.00
6107 Sherbet $28.00
6107 Claret $35.00
6107 Tulip Wine $35.00
6107 Liqueur $42.00
6107 Ice Tea, footed $30.00
2337 Plate, 7" $9.00
2337 Plate, 8" $10.00

Orbit, Cutting 742

1934 – 1936

Stemware, 84

6012 Goblet $35.00
6012 Sherbet, high $32.00
6012 Sherbet, low $26.00
6012 Cocktail $32.00
6012 Claret $38.00
6012 Rhine Wine $40.00
6012 Wine $38.00
6012 Sherry $35.00
6012 Crème de Menthe $32.00
6012 Brandy $42.00
6012 Cordial $54.00
6012 Oyster Cocktail $26.00
6012 Ice Tea, footed $34.00

Tableware I, 285

319 Bottle, bar $125.00
1769 Bowl, finger $14.00
2525 Cocktail Shaker $125.00
2400 Comport, 6" $30.00
2525 Decanter $95.00
6011 Decanter $125.00
6011 Jug $185.00
2337 Plate, 6" $6.00
2337 Plate, 7" $7.00
2337 Plate, 8" $8.00
2350½ Sugar and Cream $56.00
863 Champagne, hollow stem $24.00
701 Tumbler $4.00 – 18.00
1185 Tumbler $6.00 – 14.00
4122 Tumbler $6.00 – 14.00

Orchid, Carving 48

1941 – 1943

Stemware, 40

892 Goblet $65.00
892 Saucer Champagne $62.00
892 Sherbet, low $54.00
892 Cocktail $60.00
892 Claret $75.00
892 Wine $65.00
892 Cordial $125.00
892 Oyster Cocktail $45.00
892 Ice Tea, footed $65.00
892 Juice, footed $60.00
1769 Bowl, finger $35.00
2337 Plate, 7" $26.00
2337 Plate, 8" $32.00

Orient, Etching 265

1922 – 1928

Stemware, 18

661 Goblet $8.00
661 Saucer Champagne $8.00
661 Fruit/Sherbet, low $7.00
661 Parfait $8.00
661 Cocktail $8.00
661 Claret $9.00
661 Wine $10.00
837 Oyster Cocktail $12.00
945½ Grapefruit and Liner $20.00
889 Tumbler, 5 oz. $5.00
4085 Tumbler, 13 oz., table $8.00
4085 Tumbler, 13 oz., handled, plate $8.00

Tableware

880 Bonbon $20.00
1697 Carafe and Tumbler $57.00
803 Comport, 5" $20.00
803 Comport, 6" $22.00
300 Decanter, quart, cut neck ... $125.00
825 Jelly and cover $26.00
317-7 Jug, cut neck $95.00
318-7 Jug $95.00
1852-6 Jug $90.00
317½ Jug and cover $100.00
4085 Marmalade and Cover $32.00
803 Nappy, 5", and cover $23.00
803 Nappy, 6" $22.00
803 Nappy, 7" $24.00
1465 Oil, 7 oz., cut neck $42.00
1465 Oil, 5 oz., cut neck $40.00
2083 Bottle, salad dressing $54.00
2283 Plate, 11", salad $14.00
2283 Plate, 8¼", salad $12.00
2022 Shaker, FGT or pearl top, pair $37.00
2133 Sugar and Cream $30.00

Oriental, Plate Etching 250

1918 – 1928

Stemware, 20

766 Goblet $25.00
766 Saucer Champagne $20.00
766 Sherbet $10.00
766 Fruit $10.00
766 Parfait $30.00
766 Cocktail $12.00
766 Claret $35.00
766 Wine $28.00
766 Sherry $12.00
766 Brandy $25.00
766 Cordial $35.00
766 Ice Tea, footed, handled $30.00
766 Custard $8.00
837 Oyster Cocktail $12.00
945½ Grapefruit and Liner $67.00
701 Tumbler, 14 oz. $20.00
701 Tumbler, 8 oz. $18.00
701 Tumbler, 14 oz., handled and plate $35.00
820 Tumbler, table $18.00
887 Tumbler, 3 oz. $35.00
889 Tumbler, 5 oz. $16.00
4011 Tumbler, 15 oz. $22.00
4011 Tumbler, 12 oz. $20.00
4011 Tumbler, 8 oz. $18.00
4011 Tumbler, 5 oz. $16.00
4011 Tumbler, 3 oz. $35.00
4061 Lemonade, footed, handled .. $27.00

Tableware I, 140-141

766 Almond $25.00
880 Bonbon, 4½" $32.00
766 Bowl, finger and 1736 Plate $25.00
1697 Carafe and 4023 6 oz. Tumbler $95.00
1691 Carafe, 981 Whiskey, 2½ oz. $95.00
2618 Box, cigarette and cover $62.00
803 Comport, 5" $28.00
803 Comport, 6" $30.00
766 Cup, 4 oz., custard $15.00
300 Decanter, quart, cut neck ... $125.00
979 Horseradish $58.00
300/7 Jug $225.00
303/7 Jug $200.00
317½ Jug and cover $245.00
724/7 Jug $250.00
1761 Jug, claret $250.00
2104 Jug and Tumbler $225.00
1968 Marmalade and cover $54.00
2138 Mayonnaise, plate, ladle $65.00
1831 Mustard and Cover $45.00
803 Nappy, 5" $20.00
803 Nappy, 6" $20.00
803 Nappy, 7" $22.00
1227 Nappy, 4½" $20.00
1227 Nappy, 8" $25.00
1465 Oil, 5 oz., cut neck $65.00
1465 Oil, 7 oz., cut neck $75.00
701 Plate, 5", tumbler $10.00
1897 Plate, 7", salad $14.00
1848 Plate, 9", sandwich $20.00
1719 Plate, 10½", sandwich $25.00
1227 Bowl, punch and foot $435.00
2083 Bottle, salad dressing $95.00
2169 Bottle, salad dressing $95.00
2022 Shaker, FGT, pair $64.00
2133 Sugar and Cream $48.00
851 Sugar and Cream $48.00
858 Sweetmeat $35.00
2194 Syrup, 8 oz. $165.00

Orleans, 6089

1960 – 1974

Stemware, 119

6089 Goblet $25.00
6089 Sherbet $23.00
6089 Wine/Cocktail $27.00
6089 Brandy $36.00
6089 Ice Tea, footed $25.00
6089 Juice, footed $22.00

Orleans, Cutting 194

1929

Tableware I, 272

2375 Bonbon
topaz $32.00
azure $38.00
2375 Bowl, large, dessert
topaz $44.00
azure $56.00
2395 Bowl, 10"
topaz $125.00
azure $150.00
2375 Bowl, 12"
topaz $95.00
azure $110.00
2394 Bowl, 12"
topaz $95.00
azure $115.00
2394 Candlestick, 2", pair
topaz $75.00
azure $95.00
2375 Candlestick, 3", pair
topaz $75.00
azure $95.00
2395½ Candlestick, 5", pair
topaz $125.00
azure $150.00
2394 Jar, candy and cover, ½ pound
topaz $125.00
azure $138.00
2395 Jar, candy and cover, oval, confection
azure $150.00
topaz $125.00
2368 Cheese and Cracker
topaz $67.00
azure $75.00
2400 Comport, 6"
topaz $46.00
azure $52.00
2375 Ice Bucket, NP handle
topaz $76.00
azure $94.00
2375 Dish, lemon
topaz $27.00
azure $35.00
2375 Plate, 10", cake
topaz $75.00
azure $87.00
2375 Sweetmeat
topaz $32.00
azure $38.00
2375 Tray, handled, lunch
topaz $64.00
azure $76.00
2417 Vase, 8", optic
topaz $95.00
azure $125.00
4105 Vase, 8", optic
topaz $94.00
azure $120.00

Our American States

1971 – 1973

Tableware II, 241

2838/552 Ohio $50.00
2845/552 California $50.00
2846/552 New York $50.00
2850/552 Pennsylvania $50.00
2851/552 Texas $50.00
2852/552 Massachusetts $50.00
2853/552 Florida $50.00
2854/552 Hawaii $50.00
2871/555 Michigan $50.00

Overture, Cutting 867

1959 – 1960

Stemware, 118

6086 Goblet $28.00
6086 Sherbet $25.00
6086 Wine/Cocktail $30.00
6086 Cordial $38.00
6086 Ice Tea, footed $28.00
6086 Juice, footed $23.00
2337 Plate, 7" $8.00
2337 Plate, 8" $10.00

Oxford, Cutting 714

1933 – 1943

Stemware, 77

6007 Goblet $35.00
6007 Sherbet, high $32.00
6007 Sherbet, low $28.00
6007 Cocktail $30.00
6007 Claret $38.00
6007 Wine $35.00

6007 Cordial $48.00
6007 Oyster Cocktail $28.00
6007 Ice Tea, footed $34.00
6007 Tumbler, 9 oz., footed $28.00
6007 Juice, footed $28.00
6007 Whiskey, footed $30.00

Tableware I, 277

2470½ Bowl, 10½" $40.00
2470½ Candlestick, 5½", pair $45.00
2482 Candlestick, trindle, pair $85.00
2430 Jar, candy and cover, ½ pound $54.00
2400 Comport, 6" $27.00
2451 Dish, ice with liner and plate $42.00
2337 Plate, 7" $7.00
2337 Plate, 8" $8.00
2440 Plate, 13", torte $35.00
2419 Relish, 5-part $35.00
2440 Sugar and Cream $34.00
2467 Vase, 7½" $75.00

--P--

Pagoda, Etching 90

1935 – 1943

Stemware, 17

660 Goblet $15.00
660 Saucer Champagne $12.00
660 Sherbet, low $10.00
660 Cocktail $10.00
660 Claret $16.00
660 Wine $15.00
660 Cordial $22.00
4095 Oyster Cocktail $12.00
4095 Tumbler $9.00 – 15.00
2337 Plate, 6" $8.00
2337 Plate, 7" $9.00
2337 Plate, 8" $10.00

Pails, see Ice Buckets, Sugar Pails, Whip Cream Pails

Palmetto, Cutting 755

1935 – 1939

Stemware, 86

6014 Goblet $30.00
6014 Saucer Champagne $27.00
6014 Sherbet, low $22.00
6014 Cocktail $27.00
6014 Claret $35.00
6014 Wine $34.00
6014 Cordial $45.00
6014 Oyster Cocktail $20.00
6014 Ice Tea, footed $30.00
6014 Tumbler, 9 oz., footed $25.00
6014 Juice, footed $22.00

Tableware I, 291

869 Bowl, finger $12.00
2533 Bowl, 9", handled $95.00
2533 Candlestick, duo, pair $95.00
5000 Jug $235.00
2337 Plate, 6" $6.00
2337 Plate, 7" $7.00
2337 Plate, 8" $8.00

Palm Leaf, Decoration 73

1929

Green or Rose

Tableware I, 137

2375 Bonbon $125.00
2375 Bowl, dessert, large $225.00
2395 Bowl, 10" $575.00
2394 Bowl, 12" $350.00
2415 Bowl, combination $650.00
2394 Candlestick, 2", pair $275.00
2375 Candlestick, 3", pair $275,00
2395½ Candlestick, 5", pair $575.00
2383 Candlestick, trindle, pair $400.00/market
2375 Centerpiece, 11" $395.00
2400 Comport, 6" $225.00
2395 Confection and cover, oval $465.00
2378 Ice Bucket, GF handle $650.00
2375 Lemon $125.00
2419 Plate, 8", square $95.00
2375 Plate, 10", cake $400.00
2378 Pail, sugar, handle $565.00
2375 Sweetmeat $125.00
2342 Tray, handled, lunch $450.00
2413 Urn and cover $500.00 to market
2408 Vase, 8" $750.00
4105 Vase, 8" $700.00
2385 Vase, 8½", fan $875.00
2373 Vase, small, window and cover $765.00
2373 Vase, large, window and cover $845.00
2421 Vase, 10½", footed $800.00/market
2375 Whip Cream $160.00
2378 Pail, whip cream $600.00

Panelled Diamond Point, 2860

1973 – 1974

Henry Ford Museum

Stemware, 52

2860 Goblet $25.00
2860 Champagne $20.00
2860 Wine $25.00
2860 Ice Tea, footed $25.00
2860 Plate, 8" $15.00

Papyrus, Cutting 795

1939 – 1943

Stemware, 40

892 Goblet $34.00
892 Saucer Champagne $32.00
892 Sherbet, low $30.00
892 Cocktail $32.00
892 Claret $42.00
892 Wine $38.00
892 Cordial $48.00
892 Oyster Cocktail $28.00
892 Ice Tea, footed $34.00
892 Juice, footed $30.00

Tableware I, 303

1769 Bowl, finger $15.00
6023 Bowl, footed $65.00
2324 Candlestick, 6", pair $45.00
6023 Candlestick, duo, pair $65.00
6011 Jug $225.00
2337 Plate, 6" $7.00
2337 Plate, 7" $8.00
2337 Plate, 8" $10.00

Paradise, Brocade Etching 289

1927 – 1929

Tableware I, 130-132

2297 Bowl A, 10½", shallow
 green $125.00
 orchid $125.00
2297 Bowl A, 12", deep
 green $125.00
 orchid $125.00
2315 Bowl C, 10½", footed
 green $125.00
 orchid $125.00
2342 Bowl, 12"
 green $110.00
 orchid $110.00
2362 Bowl, 12"
 green $125.00
 orchid $125.00
2372 Candlestick, 2", block, pair
 green $75.00
 orchid $75.00
2362 Candlestick, 3", pair
 green $95.00
 orchid $95.00
2324 Candlestick, 4", pair
 green $85.00
 orchid $85.00
2331 Box, candy and cover
 green $175.00
 orchid $175.00
2329 Centerpiece, 11"
 green $125.00
 orchid $125.00
2329 Centerpiece, 13"
 green $150.00
 orchid $150.00
2371 Centerpiece, 13", oval, 2371 Flower Holder
 green $195.00
 orchid $195.00
2327 Comport, 7"
 green $95.00
 orchid $95.00
2350 Comport, 8"
 green $85.00
 orchid $85.00
2362 Comport, 11"
 green $135.00
 orchid $135.00
2380 Confection and Cover
 green $135.00
 orchid $135.00
2378 Ice Bucket, NP handle, drainer, and tongs
 green $135.00
 orchid $135.00
2342 Tray, handled, lunch
 green $115.00
 orchid $115.00
4100 Vase, 6", optic
 green $135.00
 orchid $135.00
4100 Vase, 8", optic
 green $150.00
 orchid $150.00
4103 Vase, 3", optic
 green $75.00
 orchid $75.00
4103 Vase, 5", optic
 green $95.00
 orchid $95.00
2369 Vase, 7", optic
 green $125.00
 orchid $125.00
2369 Vase, 9", optic
 green $145.00
 orchid $145.00

Parisian, Etching 53

1904 – 1927

Stemware, 30

867 Goblet, 10 oz. $10.00
867 Saucer Champagne $10.00
867 Fruit $8.00
867 Sherbet $8.00
867 Cocktail $8.00
867 Claret $10.00
867 Wine $10.00
867 Sherry $8.00
867 Cordial $15.00
822 Parfait $22.00
701 Tumbler $4.00 – 18.00
820 Tumbler $3.00 – 12.00
833 Tumbler $4.00 – 12.00
858 Tumbler $4.00 – 14.00
887 Tumbler $3.00 – 12.00
889 Tumbler $3.00 – 12.00
4011 Tumbler $4.00 – 14.00
300 Jug $75.00
303 Jug $68.00
318 Jug $75.00

Pasadena, Decoration 52

1925 – 1926

Tableware I, 323

2267 Bowl, 7", console, gold or silver band on ebony $42.00
2297 Bowl A, 10¼", shallow, gold or silver band on ebony $50.00
2297 Bowl A, 12", deep, gold or silver band on ebony $58.00
2324 Candlestick, 4", pair, gold or silver band on ebony $45.00
2299 Candlestick, 5", pair, gold or silver band on ebony $50.00
2269 Candlestick, 6", pair, gold or silver band on ebony $56.00
2297 Candlestick, 7", pair, gold or silver band on ebony $60.00
2331 Box, candy and cover, gold or silver band on ebony $65.00
2329 Centerpiece, 11", gold or silver band on ebony $60.00
2349 Holder, cigarette and ashtray, gold or silver band on ebony $57.00
2327 Comport, 7", gold or silver band on ebony $45.00
2290 Plate, 7", gold or silver band on ebony $7.00
2290 Plate, 8", gold or silver band on ebony $10.00
2276 Vanity Set, gold or silver band on ebony $135.00
1491 Vase, small, 6", gold or silver band on ebony $47.00
1491 Vase, large, 8½", gold or silver band on ebony $58.00
1681 Vase, wall pocket, gold or silver band on ebony $135.00
2288 Vase, Tut, gold or silver band on ebony $85.00

Patrician, 6064

1956 – 1970

Stemware, 111

6064 Goblet $30.00
6064 Champagne $27.00
6064 Sherbet, low $25.00
6064 Cocktail $27.00
6064 Claret $34.00
6064 Wine $32.00
6064 Cordial $35.00
6064 Seafood Cocktail $24.00
6064 Ice Tea, footed $30.00
6064 Juice, footed $25.00

Pavillion, 6143

1980 – 1982

Stemware, 144

6143 Goblet
- crystal $25.00
- gray $30.00

6143 Champagne
- crystal $22.00
- gray $28.00

6143 Wine
- crystal $27.00
- gray $34.00

6143 Ice Tea, footed
- crystal $25.00
- gray $30.00

Pebble Beach, 2806

1969 – 1970

Stemware, 51

2806 Goblet
- crystal ice $15.00
- pink lady $15.00
- mocha $15.00
- black pearl $15.00
- lemon twist $15.00
- flaming orange $15.00

2806 Sherbet
- crystal ice $12.00
- pink lady $12.00
- mocha $12.00
- black pearl $12.00
- lemon twist $12.00
- flaming orange $12.00

2806 Wine/On the Rocks
- crystal ice $12.00
- pink lady $12.00
- mocha $12.00
- black pearl $12.00
- lemon twist $12.00
- flaming orange $12.00

2806 Tumbler, ice tea
- crystal ice $15.00
- pink lady $15.00
- mocha $15.00
- black pearl $15.00
- lemon twist $15.00
- flaming orange $15.00

2806 Tumbler, juice
- crystal ice $12.00
- pink lady $12.00
- mocha $12.00
- black pearl $12.00
- lemon twist $12.00
- flaming orange $12.00

Tableware II, 101

211 Bowl, 10", salad $40.00
600 Bowl, 11½", salad/punch, crystal only $65.00
615 Cup, 6½ oz., punch, crystal only $15.00
421 Dessert $14.00
also made in Flaming Orange
550 Plate, 8" $14.00
also made in Flaming Orange
558 Plate, 11", cake $50.00
567 Plate, 14", torte $65.00
454 Pitcher, quart $75.00
622 Relish, 10", 3-part $65.00
652 Shaker, chrome top E, pair $34.00
676 Sugar and Cover $22.00
680 Cream $20.00

Persian, Etching 253

1920 – 1927

Stemware, 28

863 Goblet, 9 oz. $12.00
863 Goblet, 7 oz. $12.00
863 Saucer Champagne $10.00
863 Fruit $9.00
863 Cocktail, 3½ oz. $9.00
863 Wine $12.00
863 Cordial $20.00
899 Parfait $25.00
945½ Grapefruit and Liner $28.00
701 Tumbler, 14 oz., plate $8.00
701 Tumbler, 8 oz. $6.00
820 Tumbler, table $6.00
889 Tumbler, 5 oz. $5.00
4061 Lemonade, footed, handled $18.00

Tableware

880 Bonbon, 4½" $24.00
1769 Bowl, finger and plate $22.00
2219 Jar, candy and cover ¼ lb. $48.00
2219 Jar, candy and cover ½ lb. $54.00
2219 Jar, candy and cover 1 lb. $65.00
2241 Cologne and Stopper $97.00
2242 Cologne and Stopper $88.00
2243 Cologne and Stopper $88.00
803 Comport, 5" $20.00
803 Comport, 6" $22.00
303-7 Jug $96.00
803 Nappy, 5" $22.00
803 Nappy, 6" $25.00
803 Nappy, 7", footed $28.00
2283 Plate, 8", salad $6.00
2465 Oil, 5 oz., cut neck $47.00
2214 Sugar and Cover, Cream and Cover set $48.00

Persian, Decoration 34

1924

Gold Coin on Etching 253

Tableware I, 318

2419 Jar, candy and cover, ¼ pound $64.00
2419 Jar, candy and cover, ½ pound $75.00
2419 Jar, candy and cover, pound $85.00
2241 Cologne, 2¼ oz., drip stopper $150.00
2243 Cologne, 2¼ oz., drip stopper $135.00
2242 Cologne, 3¼ oz., drip stopper $135.00

Personalized Giftware

1985

Tableware II, 304

SMALL CRYSTAL ROCK:

PE01/541 Paperweight, plain $7.25
PE01/545 Grandpa paperweight.................$9.25
PE01/546 Pen Stand $13.75

HEART SHAPED CRYSTAL:

PE02/541 Paperweight, plain..................$7.25
PE02/542 Paperweight, Friends Forever $9.75
PE02/543 Paperweight, Mom.................$9.75
PE02/544 Paperweight, Love..................$9.75
PE02/546 Pen Stand, Love.....................$16.75

LARGE CRYSTAL FORM:

PE03/541 Paperweight, plain..................$7.75
PE03/546 Pen Stand $14.25
PE03/547 Pen Stand, Dad $16.75

Petite, 6085

1959 – 1975

Stemware, 117

6085 Goblet.................$25.00
6085 Sherbet................$23.00
6085 Wine/Cocktail......$28.00
6085 Cordial................$37.00
6085 Ice Tea, footed.....$25.00
6085 Juice, footed..........................$22.00
2337 Plate, 7" $7.00
2337 Plate, 8" $8.00

Petit Fleur, Cutting 922

1971 – 1972

Stemware, 140

6123 Goblet....$22.00
6123 Sherbet $22.00
6123 Wine.......................................$22.00
6123 Ice Tea, footed $22.00
2337 Plate, 7" $8.00

Pierrette, Cutting 764

1937 – 1939

Stemware, 84

6012 Goblet $25.00
6012 Sherbet, high $22.00
6012 Sherbet, low $18.00
6012 Cocktail $22.00
6012 Claret......................................$28.00
6012 Wine..$28.00
6012 Cordial $34.00
6012 Oyster Cocktail $16.00
6012 Ice Tea, footed $22.00
6012 Tumbler, 10 oz., footed $18.00
6012 Juice, footed $18.00
6011 Jug...$175.00
2337 Plate, 6" $6.00
2337 Plate, 7" $8.00
2337 Plate, 8" $10.00

Pilgrim, Cutting 787

1935 – 1951

Stemware, 93

6023 Goblet...$25.00
6023 Saucer Champagne $20.00
6023 Sherbet, low $20.00
6023 Cocktail $22.00
6023 Claret-Wine $28.00
6023 Cordial $38.00
6023 Oyster Cocktail.......................$18.00
6023 Ice Tea, footed $20.00
6023 Tumbler, 9 oz., footed $20.00
6023 Juice, footed $20.00

Tableware II, 168

2574 Bonbon $30.00
766 Bowl, finger $22.00
2574 Bowl, 8½", serving $34.00
2574 Bowl, 9½", handled $45.00
6023 Bowl, footed $78.00
2574 Bowl, 12", flared $48.00
2574 Bowl, 13", fruit $52.00
2574 Candlestick, 4", pair $58.00
2324 Candlestick, 6", pair $65.00
2574 Celery, 10½" $30.00
2574 Comport, 5" $35.00
6023 Comport, 5" $35.00
2574 Cup and Saucer.......................$28.00
2574 Ice Tub and Tongs $48.00
6011 Jug..$275.00
2574 Lemon.......................................$28.00
2574 Mayonnaise, plate, ladle $38.00
2574 Oil, 4½ oz., GS $54.00
2574 Olive, 6" $18.00
2574 Pickle, 8" $23.00
2574 Plate, 6" $6.00
2574 Plate, 7" $8.00
2574 Plate, 8" $12.00
2574 Plate, 9" $28.00
2574 Plate, 10", cake $40.00
2574 Plate, 14", torte $52.00
2574 Relish, 3-part $37.00
2586 Server, sani-cut $275.00
2574 Sugar and Cream, individual...........................$35.00
2574 Sugar and Cream....................$37.00
2574 Sweetmeat..............................$22.00
2567 Vase, 6"...................................$68.00
2567 Vase, 7½" $75.00
2567 Vase, 8½" $85.00
2574 Whip Cream............................$24.00

Pine, Cutting 835

1953 – 1972

Stemware, 107

6052½ Goblet $30.00
6052½ Sherbet $26.00
6052½ Cocktail $26.00
6052½ Claret-Wine $34.00
6052½ Cordial $28.00
6052½ Oyster Cocktail......................$38.00
6052½ Ice Tea, footed $20.00
6052½ Juice, footed $30.00

Tableware II, 183

2666 Bonbon $28.00
4185 Bowl, finger/dessert............$32.00
2666 Bowl, oval................................$38.00
2666 Bowl, 10½", salad $45.00
2666 Butter and cover, oblong...............................$47.00
2666 Candle, flora, pair $48.00
2666 Cup and Saucer.......................$25.00
2666 Mayonnaise, plate, ladle $54.00
2666 Pitcher, quart........................$145.00
2337 Plate, 7" $10.00
2337 Plate, 8" $12.00
2666 Plate, 10", snack $25.00
2666 Plate, 14", serving..................$44.00
2666 Relish, 2-part $30.00
2666 Relish, 3-part $37.00
2666 Salad Set, 4-piece $95.00
2685 Salver $75.00
2364 Shaker, large, chrome top B, pair $55.00
2666 Sugar and Cream.....................$45.00
2666 Sugar and Cream, individual and tray.............................$55.00

Pinnacle, Cutting 753

1935 – 1937

Stemware, 18

660 Goblet. $15.00
660 Saucer Champagne $9.00
660 Sherbet, low $6.00
660 Cocktail $9.00
660 Claret $9.00
660 Wine...$9.00
660 Cordial $20.00
4095 Tumbler, 13 oz., footed $18.00
4095 Tumbler, 10 oz., footed $16.00
4095 Tumbler, 5 oz., footed $12.00
869 Bowl, finger $14.00
2337 Plate, 6" $6.00
2337 Plate, 7" $8.00
2337 Plate, 8" $10.00

Pioneer, 2350

1926 – 1959

Tableware I, 41-46

2350 Ashtray, small, 3¾"
- crystal $16.00
- amber....................................$18.00
- green.....................................$20.00
- ebony $18.00
- rose $20.00
- azure $26.00
- topaz/gold tint $20.00
- orchid....................................$27.00

2350 Ashtray, large
- crystal $16.00
- amber....................................$20.00
- green.....................................$22.00
- ebony $18.00
- rose $26.00
- azure $27.00
- topaz/gold tint $25.00

2350 Bouillon and Saucer
- crystal $16.00
- amber....................................$16.00
- green.....................................$18.00
- blue $22.00

2350½ Bouillon, footed
- crystal $8.00
- amber....................................$10.00
- green.....................................$16.00

Bowl, 5", fruit
crystal $7.00
amber $8.00
green $10.00
blue $18.00
Bowl, 6", cereal
crystal $8.00
amber $9.00
green $12.00
blue $22.00
Bowl, 7", soup
crystal $11.00
amber $14.00
green $16.00
blue $24.00
Bowl, 9", oval, baker
crystal $20.00
amber $22.00
green $24.00
blue $26.00
Bowl, 10", salad
crystal $22.00
amber $22.00
green $27.00
blue $35.00
Bowl, 10½", oval, baker
crystal $22.00
amber $24.00
green $27.00
blue $40.00
Butter and Cover
crystal $65.00
amber $70.00
green $75.00
blue $125.00
Celery, 11"
crystal $18.00
amber $20.00
green $22.00
blue $28.00
Comport, 8"
crystal $25.00
amber $27.00
green $30.00
blue $40.00
rose $30.00
azure $34.00
orchid $30.00
Cream Soup
crystal $14.00
amber $16.00
green $20.00
blue $28.00
2350½ Cream Soup, footed
crystal $15.00
amber $18.00
green $22.00
2350 Plate, cream soup
crystal $5.00
amber $6.00
green $7.00
blue $8.00
ebony $6.00
2350 Cup and Saucer
crystal $11.00
amber $12.00
green $12.00
blue $16.00
2350½ Cup, footed and saucer
crystal $10.00
amber $12.00
green $14.00
blue $18.00
ebony $12.00
regal blue $28.00
burgundy $26.00
empire green $26.00
ruby $26.00
2350 Cup and Saucer, after dinner
crystal $24.00
amber $27.00
green $35.00
blue $48.00
ebony $40.00
regal blue $64.00
burgundy $60.00
empire green $60.00
ruby $65.00
2350 Egg Cup
crystal $22.00
amber $25.00
green $27.00
rose $30.00
azure $30.00
2350 Grapefruit and crystal Liner
crystal $28.00
amber $32.00
green $34.00
blue $40.00
2350 Nappy, 8"
crystal $15.00
amber $18.00
green $18.00
blue $22.00
2350 Nappy, 9"
crystal $16.00
amber $18.00
green $20.00
blue $25.00
2350 Pickle
crystal $10.00
amber $16.00
green $18.00
blue $22.00
2350 Plate, 6"
crystal $5.00
amber $6.00
green $7.00
blue $10.00
ebony $6.00
2350 Plate, 7"
crystal $5.00
amber $6.00
green $7.00
blue $12.00
ebony $6.00
2350 Plate, 8"
crystal $6.00
amber $9.00
green $10.00
blue $18.00
ebony $10.00
2350 Plate, 9"
crystal $14.00
amber $18.00
green $20.00
blue $30.00
ebony $15.00
2350 Plate, 10"
crystal $20.00
amber $25.00
green $32.00
blue $45.00
ebony $22.00
2350 Plate, 12", chop
crystal $22.00
amber $27.00
green $34.00
blue $45.00
2350 Plate, 13", chop
crystal $24.00
amber $28.00
green $36.00
blue $47.00
2350 Plate, 15", round
crystal $30.00
amber $37.00
green $48.00
blue $65.00
2350 Platter, 10½"
crystal $22.00
amber $25.00
green $34.00
blue $45.00
2350 Platter, 12"
crystal $24.00
amber $27.00
green $35.00
blue $48.00
2350 Platter, 15"
crystal $35.00
amber $45.00
green $54.00
blue $75.00
2350 Relish, 3-part
crystal $12.00
amber $16.00
green $18.00
rose $20.00
azure $24.00
topaz $24.00
2350 Sauce Boat and Plate
crystal $30.00
amber $32.00
green $40.00
blue $56.00
2350 Sugar and Cream
crystal $20.00
amber $24.00
green $32.00
blue $58.00
2350 Sugar Cover
crystal $18.00
amber $18.00
green $20.00
blue $32.00
2350½ Sugar and Cream, footed
crystal $20.00
amber $26.00
green $30.00
blue $60.00
ebony $26.00
rose $37.00
ruby $75.00
2350½ Sugar and Cover
crystal $30.00
amber $34.00
green $38.00
blue $65.00
2350 Salad Set: six 7" plates and a 12" plate
crystal $48.00
amber $56.00
green $65.00
blue $88.00
2350 Cold Meat Set: six 8" plates, six footed cups and saucers, and a 12" oval platter
crystal $118.00
amber $135.00
green $135.00
blue $200.00

Pioneer, 2350

2350 Bridge Set: six 8" plates, six footed cups and saucers, a footed sugar and cream, and 13" plate
- crystal $135.00
- amber $140.00
- green $154.00
- blue $265.00

2350 Breakfast Set: six 8", plates, six footed cups and saucers, six 6" cereals, a 10½" platter, a 9" plate, and a footed sugar and cream
- crystal $215.00
- amber $250.00
- green $300.00
- blue $395.00

Pitchers (see Jugs and Tankards)

Plain 'n Fancy, Crystal Print 11 Tumblers

1958 – 1962

Stemware, 155

4180 Tumbler, 12 oz., flat, harvest yellow $12.00

4180 Juice, 7 oz., flat, harvest yellow $12.00

Planet, Cutting 734

1934 – 1935

Stemware, 81

6011 Goblet $35.00
6011 Saucer Champagne $32.00
6011 Sherbet, low $25.00
6011 Cocktail $32.00
6011 Claret $45.00
6011 Rhine Wine $48.00
6011 Wine $45.00
6011 Sherry $42.00
6011 Crème de Menthe $38.00
6011 Brandy $50.00
6011 Cordial $55.00
6011 Oyster Cocktail $28.00
6011 Ice Tea, footed $34.00
6011 Tumbler, 10 oz., footed $28.00
6011 Juice, footed $28.00
6011 Whiskey, footed $45.00

Tableware I, 280

1769 Bowl, finger $14.00
4024 Bowl, 10", footed $35.00
4024 Candlestick, 6", pair $45.00
6011 Decanter $155.00
6011 Jug $195.00
2337 Plate, 6" $6.00
2337 Plate, 7" $7.00
2337 Plate, 8" $8.00

Plates

Useful & Ornamental, 173-177

2283 Plate, 5"
- crystal $6.00
- amber $8.00
- green $9.00
- blue $12.00

2283 Plate, 6"
- crystal $7.00
- amber $9.00
- green $9.00
- blue $12.00
- canary $14.00
- orchid $12.00
- rose $10.00
- azure $12.00

22283 Plate, 7"
- crystal $10.00
- amber $12.00
- green $14.00
- blue $20.00
- canary $20.00
- orchid $20.00
- rose $18.00
- azure $18.00

22283 Plate, 7", Cut 175, 177, or 178
- crystal $12.00
- amber $14.00
- green $16.00
- canary $25.00

2283 Plate, 8"
- crystal $10.00
- amber $14.00
- green $18.00
- blue $22.00
- canary $22.00
- orchid $22.00
- rose $20.00
- azure $20.00

2283 Plate, 9"
- crystal $12.00
- amber $18.00
- green $20.00
- blue $28.00

2283 Plate, 10"
- crystal $16.00
- amber $22.00
- green $25.00
- blue $35.00

2283 Plate, 11"
- crystal $16.00
- amber $22.00
- green $28.00
- blue $35.00
- canary $40.00

2283 Plate, 12"
- amber $26.00
- green $30.00
- blue $45.00

2283 Plate, 13", flared
- amber $35.00
- green $38.00
- blue $50.00
- canary $50.00
- orchid $50.00
- rose $40.00

2283 Plate, 6", RO
- crystal $6.00
- amber $9.00
- green $9.00
- blue $15.00
- topaz $10.00
- orchid $15.00
- rose $10.00
- azure $10.00

2283 Plate, 7", RO
- crystal $10.00
- amber $12.00
- green $14.00
- blue $20.00

2283 Plate, 8", RO
- crystal $10.00
- amber $14.00
- green $14.00
- blue $22.00

2283 Plate, 6", SO
- crystal $8.00
- amber $8.00
- green $14.00
- blue $16.00
- orchid $18.00
- rose $14.00
- azure $14.00

2283 Plate, 7", SO
- crystal $10.00
- amber $12.00
- green $14.00
- blue $20.00
- canary $22.00
- orchid $20.00
- rose $16.00
- azure $16.00

2283 Plate, 8", SO
- crystal $12.00
- amber $14.00
- green $16.00
- blue $22.00
- canary $25.00
- orchid $25.00
- rose $18.00
- azure $20.00

2283 Plate, 9", SO
- amber $16.00
- green $18.00
- azure $20.00
- rose $20.00

2283 Plate, 10", SO
- amber $22.00
- green $32.00
- rose $35.00
- azure $40.00

2283 Plate, 13", SO
- amber $47.00
- green $52.00
- blue $65.00
- canary $68.00
- orchid $68.00
- rose $57.00
- azure $57.00

2290 Plate, 7", deep, salad
- amber $10.00
- green $14.00
- blue $18.00
- canary $18.00
- ebony $12.00

2290 Plate, 8", deep, salad
- amber $16.00
- green $18.00
- blue $24.00
- canary $24.00
- ebony $16.00

2290 Plate, 13", flared, RO
- amber $48.00
- green $55.00
- blue $67.00
- canary $75.00

2290 Plate, 13", cupped, used with the 2284 3-piece Epergne, see Vases

2316 Plate, 8", soup
- crystal $14.00
- amber $20.00
- green $24.00
- blue $28.00

2330 Plate/Sherbet, 6", one piece, green $24.00

2332 Plate, 7", mayonnaise, used with 2315 Mayonnaise, although most of the time the mayonnaise was shown without a plate.

crystal $10.00
amber....$12.00
green....$14.00
blue $18.00
canary $18.00
orchid....$16.00
rose $16.00
azure $16.00

2337 Plate, 6"
crystal $6.00
regal blue $18.00
burgundy....$18.00
empire green....$18.00
ruby....$18.00

2337 Plate, 7"
crystal $8.00
amber....$16.00
green....$16.00
blue $18.00
regal blue $32.00
burgundy....$32.00
empire green....$32.00
ruby....$34.00
amethyst....$32.00
gold $16.00
lilac....$16.00
gray mist....$14.00
pink $16.00
green mist $14.00
onyx $12.00
blue $18.00
plum....$16.00

2337 Plate, 8"
crystal $10.00
amber....$18.00
green....$20.00
blue $24.00
regal blue $34.00
burgundy....$34.00
empire green....$34.00
ruby....$36.00

2337 Plate, 11"
crystal $12.00
regal blue $38.00
burgundy....$38.00
empire green....$38.00
ruby....$46.00

2337 Plate, 6", RO $6.00
2337 Plate, 7", RO $9.00
2337 Plate, 8", RO $10.00
2337 Plate, 9", ...$12.00
2337 Plate, 10", dinner $18.00
2337 Plate, 6", LO $8.00
2337 Plate, 7", LO $10.00
2337 Plate, 8", LO $14.00
2337 Plate, 7", Niagara optic....$15.00
2337 Plate, 7", narrow optic....$15.00

2341 Plate, 8", figured edge
amber....$22.00
green....$24.00
blue $28.00
canary, ...$30.00

2342 Plate, 6", octagon
amber....$6.00
green....$8.00
azure $8.00
rose $10.00

2342 Plate, 7", octagon
crystal $6.00
amber....$7.00
green....$10.00
blue $12.00
canary $14.00
orchid....$12.00
rose $12.00

2342 Plate, 8", octagon
crystal $7.00
amber....$10.00
green....$12.00
blue $15.00
canary $18.00
orchid....$15.00
rose $15.00
azure $15.00

2342 Plate, 13", octagon
amber....$44.00
green....$48.00
blue $55.00
canary $55.00
orchid....$50.00
rose $47.00
azure $47.00

2348 Plate, 8"
amber....$14.00
green....$16.00
blue $20.00
canary $25.00

2356 Plate, 8"
amber....$12.00
green....$15.00
blue $18.00
canary $18.00
orchid....$16.00

2364 Plate, 14", torte, see Sonata
2364 Plate, 16", Sonata
crystal $45.00
amber....$70.00
green....$74.00
ebony $55.00
rose, ...$75.00
topaz/gold tint....$65.00
regal blue $125.00
burgundy....$120.00
empire green....$135.00

2492 Plate, 8½", fish canape, see Bar and Refreshment
2541 Plate, snack $12.00
2665 Plate, 7" $10.00
2665 Plate, 8" $10.00

Platina Rose, Decoration 663

1964 – 1974

Stemware, 127

6102 Goblet....$35.00
6102 Sherbet....$30.00
6102 Claret....$38.00
6102 Tulip Wine....$38.00
6102 Brandy....$45.00
6102 Ice Tea, footed....$35.00
2337 Plate, 7" $10.00
2337 Plate, 8" $12.00

Platinum Band Decoration

1952 – 1975

Note: These pieces were intended to be used with patterns that had Platinum Band Decoration.

Tableware II, 195 – 197

4185 Bowl, dessert/finger....$18.00
2364 Bowl, 9", salad....$32.00
2785 Bowl, 10", footed....$35.00
2324 Candlestick, 4", pair $48.00
2666 Cup and Saucer....$26.00
2364 Mayonnaise, plate, ladle $58.00
2337 Plate, 7" $9.00
2337 Plate, 8" $12.00
2785 Relish, 2-part $32.00
2785 Relish, 4-part $35.00
2785 Relish, 5-part $42.00
2666 Sugar and Cream....$40.00
2666 Sugar and Cream, individual....$35.00
2666 Sugar and Cream, individual, and tray $45.00
2785 Sugar and Cream....$40.00

Plume, Cutting 839

1954 – 1960

Stemware, 106

6051½ Goblet $30.00
6051½ Sherbet $26.00
6051½ Cocktail $26.00
6051½ Claret-Wine $34.00
6051½ Cordial $40.00
6051½ Oyster Cocktail....$20.00
6051½ Ice Tea, footed $30.00
6051½ Juice, footed $24.00

Tableware II, 186

2666 Bowl, oval....$38.00
2666 Candle, flora, pair $48.00
2666 Mayonnaise, plate, ladle $52.00
2337 Plate, 7" $10.00
2337 Plate, 8" $12.00
2666 Plate, canape....$22.00
2666 Plate, 10", snack $24.00
2666 Plate, 14", serving....$35.00
2666 Relish, 2-part $30.00
2666 Relish, 3-part $38.00
2364 Shaker, large, chrome top B, pair....$55.00
2666 Sugar and Cream....$45.00
2666 Sugar and Cream, individual and tray....$55.00

Plymouth, Etching 336

1939 – 1944

Stemware, 96

6025 Goblet $38.00
6025 Sherbet....$34.00
6025 Cocktail $32.00
6025 Claret-Wine $45.00
6025 Cordial....$65.00
6025 Oyster Cocktail....$28.00
6025 Ice Tea, footed $38.00
6025 Juice, footed $28.00

Tableware II, 132

2574 Bonbon $42.00
766 Bowl, finger....$27.00
2574 Bowl, 8½", serving $54.00
6023 Bowl, 9½", footed $125.00
2574 Bowl, 9½", handled $75.00
2574 Bowl, 12", flared $60.00
2574 Bowl, 13", fruit $75.00
2574 Candlestick, 4", pair $80.00
2324 Candlestick, 6", pair $90.00
2374 Celery, 10½" $48.00
2574 Comport, 5" $68.00
6023 Comport, 5" $68.00
2574 Cup and Saucer....$34.00
2574 Ice Tub $64.00
6011 Jug....$395.00
2574 Lemon....$38.00
2574 Mayonnaise, plate, ladle $75.00
2574 Oil, 4½ oz., GS $125.00

Plymouth, Etching 336

2574	Olive, 6"	$27.00
2574	Pickle, 8"	$34.00
2574	Plate, 6"	$15.00
2574	Plate, 7"	$20.00
2574	Plate, 8"	$26.00
2574	Plate, 9"	$52.00
2574	Plate, 10", cake	$76.00
2574	Plate, 14", torte,	$85.00
2475	Relish, 3-part	$68.00
2574	Shaker, FGT, pair	$125.00
2574	Sugar and Cream, individual	$75.00
2574	Sugar and Cream	$85.00
2574	Sweetmeat	$42.00
2574	Tray, handled, muffin	$75.00
2574	Whip Cream	$42.00

Poetry, Crystal Print 32

1972 – 1982

Stemware, 140

6123	Goblet	$27.00
6123	Sherbet	$25.00
6123	Wine	$30.00
6123	Ice Tea, footed	$27.00

Poinsetta, Decoration 36

1924

Encrusted gold and blue

Tableware I, 319

2136	Bonbon and Cover	$175.00
2252	Bowl, 6", salad	$25.00
2267	Bowl, 7", console	$95.00
2267	Bowl, 9", console	$125.00
2269	Candlestick, 6", pair	$175.00
2244	Candlestick, 8¼", pair	$250.00
2245	Candlestick, 8¼", pair	$195.00
2275	Candlestick, 9¼", pair	$250.00
2250	Jar, candy and cover, ¼ pound	$95.00
2250	Jar, candy and cover, ½ pound	$125.00
2264	Cheese and Cover	$67.00
2250	Cracker Plate, 9"	$37.00
2136	Cold Cream and Cover	$145.00
2135	Hair Receiver and Cover	$157.00
2138	Mayonnaise and Plate	$74.00
1897	Plate, 7", salad	$24.00
2238	Plate, 8½", salad	$32.00
1848	Plate, 9", sandwich, cut matt star base	$36.00
1719	Plate, 10½", sandwich, cut matt star base	$40.00
2238	Plate, 11", sandwich	$40.00
2258	Plate, 11", sandwich	$40.00
2258	Dish, relish, 6", cut matt star base	$27.00
2258	Dish, relish, 8", cut matt star base	$38.00
2258	Dish, relish, 10", cut matt star base	$45.00
2276	Vanity Set	$350.00
2208	Vase, 5"	$68.00
1957	Vase, 7"	$85.00

Poinsetta, Decoration 67

1926

Decoration on Ebony

Tableware I, 326

2367	Bowl, 8", bulb	$50.00
2297	Bowl A, 10", shallow	$75.00
2297	Bowl A, 12", deep	$85.00
2324	Candlestick, 4", pair	$125.00
2298	Candlestick, pair	$125.00
2324	Candlestick, 9", pair	$185.00
2331	Box, candy and cover	$135.00
2250	Jar, candy and cover, ½ pound	$110.00
2329	Centerpiece, 11"	$95.00
2298	Clock	$375.00
2327	Comport, 7"	$85.00
2347	Box, puff and cover	$195.00
2306	Smoker Set, 4-piece	$95.00
2286	Tray, 5", Pin	$48.00
2286	Tray, 10", comb and brush	$75.00
2287	Tray, lunch	$125.00
2276	Vanity Set	$300.00
1681	Vase, wall	$225.00
2292	Vase, 8"	$150.00

Polar Bear, Carving 29

1941 – 1943

Useful & Ornamental, 131

2577	Vase, 6"	$135.00

Polka Dot, Decoration 607

1931 – 1932

Stemware, 59

4020	Goblet ebony base	$45.00
4020	Sherbet, high, ebony base	$45.00
4020	Sherbet, 7 oz., low, ebony base	$45.00
4020	Sherbet, 5 oz., low, ebony base	$45.00
4020	Cocktail, 3½ oz., ebony base	$45.00
4020	Ice Tea, footed, ebony base	$45.00
4020	Tumbler, 13 oz., footed, ebony base	$45.00
4020	Tumbler, 10 oz., footed, ebony base	$45.00
4020	Juice, footed, ebony base	$45.00
4020	Whiskey, footed, ebony base	$45.00

Tableware I, 331

4021	Bowl, finger	$35.00
4020	Jug	$395.00
4020	Sugar and Cream	$85.00

Poupee Etching 231

1906 – 1927

(pronounced "poppy")

Stemware, 63

5070	Goblet, 10 oz	$14.00
5070	Goblet, 9 oz.	$12.00
5070	Goblet, 8 oz.	$12.00
5070	Saucer Champagne	$12.00
5070	Sherbet	$10.00
5070	Cocktail, 3½ oz.	$10.00
5070	Cocktail, 3 oz.	$10.00
5070	Claret, 6 oz.	$16.00
5070	Claret, 4½ oz.	$15.00
5070	Rhine Wine	$16.00
5070	Wine	$15.00
5070	Sherry	$15.00
5070	Crème de Menthe	$12.00
5070	Brandy, pousse-café, 1 oz.	$20.00
5070	Brandy, pousse-café, ¾ oz.	$20.00
5070	Cordial, 1 oz.	$25.00
5070	Cordial, ¾ oz.	$25.00
5070	Champagne, hollow stem	$16.00
5070	Champagne, tall	$18.00
5070	Hot Whiskey	$12.00
945½	Grapefruit and Liner	$25.00
822	Parfait	$22.00
701	Tumbler, 14 oz.	$14.00
701	Tumbler, 12 oz.	$12.00
701	Tumbler, 10 oz.	$12.00
701	Tumbler, 8 oz.	$10.00
701	Tumbler, 5 oz.	$8.00
701	Tumbler, 4 oz.	$8.00
820	Tumbler	$5.00
887	Tumbler, 3 oz.	$4.00
889	Tumbler, 14 oz.	$12.00
889	Tumbler, 10 oz.	$8.00
889	Tumbler, 9 oz.	$8.00
889	Tumbler, 8 oz.	$7.00
889	Tumbler, 5 oz.	$6.00
4015	Tumbler, 14 oz.	$12.00

Tableware

481	Custard and Plate	$12.00
863	Almond	$12.00
803	Comport, 5"	$18.00
803	Comport, 6"	$20.00
300	Decanter, quart, handled,	$50.00
1195	Decanter, large, cut neck	$55.00
1491	Decanter, cut neck, optic	$58.00
1499	Bowl, finger, plate	$15.00
1769	Bowl, finger, plate	$15.00
303-7	Jug	$80.00
803	Nappy, 5", deep	$15.00
803	Nappy, 6", deep	$16.00
803	Nappy, 7", deep	$18.00
300½	Oil	$35.00
1465	Oil, cut neck	$40.00
1719	Plate, sandwich	$10.00
1848	Plate, sandwich	$12.00
1478	Sugar and Cream	$30.00
858	Sweetmeat	$15.00
300-7	Tankard	$75.00
724-6	Tankard	$75.00
724 -7	Tankard	$75.00

Precedence, 6108

1967 – 1974

Stemware, 133

6108	Goblet	
	crystal	$32.00
	gray mist bowl	$45.00
	onyx bowl	$45.00
6108	Champagne	
	crystal	$30.00
	gray mist bowl	$42.00
	onyx bowl	$42.00

6108 Claret
crystal ...$35.00
gray mist bowl ...$50.00
onyx bowl ...$50.00
6108 Tulip Wine
crystal ...$35.00
gray mist bowl ...$50.00
onyx bowl ...$50.00
6108 Liqueur
crystal ...$45.00
gray mist bowl ...$57.00
onyx bowl ...$57.00
6108 Ice Tea, footed
crystal ...$32.00
gray mist bowl ...$45.00
onyx bowl ...$45.00
2337 Plate, 7"
crystal ...$8.00
gray mist ...$14.00
2337 Plate, 8", crystal only ...$10.00

Prelude, 6071

1957 – 1969

Stemware, 114

6071 Goblet ...$24.00
6071 Sherbet ...$22.00
6071 Cocktail/Wine/Seafood ...$24.00
6071 Cordial ...$32.00
6071 Ice Tea, footed ...$24.00
6071 Juice, footed ...$22.00

President's House, The, 7780

1971 – 1973

Stemware, 146

7780 Goblet ...$24.00
7780 Saucer Champagne ...$22.00
7780 Sherbet ...$20.00
7780 Tulip Champagne ...$24.00
7780 Burgundy Wine ...$27.00
7780 Wine, 8 oz. ...$27.00
7780 Wine, 5 oz. ...$24.00
7780 Whiskey Sour/Parfait ...$27.00
7780 Ice Tea, footed ...$24.00
7780 Highball ...$16.00
7780 Juice ...$12.00
7780 Old Fashioned ...$16.00

Princess, 6123

1971 – 1982

Stemware, 140

6123 Goblet
crystal ...$20.00
green mist bowl ...$20.00
blue bowl ...$20.00
gray mist bowl/onyx base ...$20.00
6123 Champagne
crystal ...$20.00
green mist bowl ...$20.00
blue bowl ...$20.00
gray mist bowl/onyx base ...$20.00
6123 Wine
crystal ...$20.00
green mist bowl ...$20.00
blue bowl ...$20.00
gray mist bowl/onyx base ...$20.00
6123 Ice Tea, footed
crystal ...$20.00
green mist bowl ...$20.00
blue bowl ...$20.00
gray mist bowl/onyx base ...$20.00
2337 Plate, 7"
crystal ...$8.00
green mist ...$14.00
gray mist ...$14.00
onyx ...$12.00

Princess, Decoration 43

1925 – 1928

Stemware, 65

5082 Goblet ...$25.00
5082 Sherbet, high ...$25.00
5082 Sherbet, low ...$18.00
5082 Parfait ...$25.00
5082 Cocktail ...$20.00
5082 Claret ...$30.00
5082 Wine ...$30.00
5082 Cordial ...$35.00
945½ Grapefruit and Liner ...$25.00
4095 Tumbler ...$8.00 – 12.00
2270 Jug ...$175.00
2283 Plate, 6" ...$8.00
2283 Plate, 7" ...$10.00

Princess, Cutting 824

1950 – 1951

Stemware, 98

6027 Goblet ...$26.00
6027 Sherbet, low ...$24.00
6027 Cocktail ...$22.00
6027 Wine ...$30.00
6027 Cordial ...$38.00
6027 Oyster Cocktail ...$18.00
6027 Ice Tea, footed ...$26.00
6027 Juice, footed ...$20.00
2337 Plate, 7" ...$10.00
2337 Plate, 8" ...$12.00

Princess Ann, Cutting 893

1962 – 1967

Stemware, 1124

6100 Goblet ...$28.00
6100 Sherbet ...$26.00
6100 Claret ...$32.00
6100 Tulip Wine ...$32.00
6100 Brandy ...$32.00
6100 Ice Tea, footed ...$28.00
2337 Plate, 7", ...$9.00
2337 Plate, 8" ...$10.00

Princess Platinum, Decoration 690

1971 – 1982

Stemware, 140

6123 Goblet ...$25.00
6123 Champagne ...$22.00
6123 Wine ...$25.00
6123 Ice Tea, footed ...$25.00
2337 Plate, 7" ...$10.00

Priscilla, Cutting 130

1918 – 1927

Stemware, 21

766 Goblet ...$12.00
766 Saucer Champagne ...$12.00
766 Sherbet ...$9.00
766 Fruit ...$9.00
766 Parfait ...$22.00
766 Cocktail ...$10.00
766 Claret ...$12.00
766 Rhine Wine ...$12.00
766 Wine ...$12.00
766 Burgundy ...$12.00
766 Sherry ...$12.00
766 Crème de Menthe ...$12.00
766 Brandy, pousse-café ...$15.00
766 Cordial ...$22.00
766 Sorbet ...$7.00
766 Ice Tea, footed, handled ...$15.00
766 Custard ...$7.00
766 Grapefruit and Liner ...$22.00
820 Tumbler ...$5.00 – 10.00
833 Tumbler ...$5.00 – 10.00
4011 Tumbler ...$5.00 – 10.00
303 Jug ...$52.00
2283 Plate, 8¼" ...$8.00

Priscilla, 2321

1925 – 1930

Stemware, 45

2321 Goblet, 9 oz.
crystal ...$12.00
amber ...$20.00
green ...$20.00
blue ...$30.00
2321 Goblet, 7 oz.
crystal ...$10.00
amber ...$20.00
green ...$20.00
blue ...$25.00
2321 Saucer Champagne
crystal ...$10.00
amber ...$20.00
green ...$20.00
blue ...$30.00
2321 Sherbet
crystal ...$10.00
amber ...$20.00
green ...$20.00
blue ...$25.00
2321 Tumbler, footed
crystal ...$12.00
amber ...$22.00
green ...$22.00
blue ...$30.00
2321 Tumbler, footed, handled
crystal ...$12.00
amber ...$30.00
green ...$30.00
blue ...$35.00
2321 Custard, footed, handled
crystal ...$12.00
amber ...$30.00
green ...$30.00
blue ...$30.00
2321 Bouillon
crystal ...$8.00
amber ...$10.00
green ...$14.00
blue ...$18.00
rose ...$18.00
azure ...$18.00

2321 Bridge Set: mah jongg plate and sherbet or handled custard
amber $22.00
green $28.00
blue $34.00
canary $36.00

2321 Cream
crystal $8.00
amber $10.00
green $14.00
blue $18.00
rose $18.00
azure $18.00

2321 Cream and Bouillon on 2000 Condiment Tray
amber $55.00
green, $58.00
rose $65.00
azure $65.00

Cream Soup, also used as mayonnaise
crystal $15.00
amber $16.00
green $16.00
blue $18.00
canary $20.00

Cup and Saucer
crystal $14.00
amber $16.00
green $18.00
blue $20.00

Mah Jongg with Sherbet
crystal $22.00
amber $28.00
green $34.00
blue $36.00
ebony $28.00
canary $36.00

Jug, 3-pint
crystal $95.00
amber $100.00
green $125.00
blue $165.00

Plate, 8"
crystal $8.00
amber $9.00
green $10.00
blue $15.00
ebony $9.00
canary $22.00

Priscilla, 6092

1960 – 1982

Stemware, 120

6092 Goblet $25.00
6092 Sherbet $23.00
6092 Wine/Cocktail $27.00
6092 Cordial $36.00
6092 Ice Tea, footed $25.00
6092 Juice, footed $22.00

Promise, 6110

1967 – 1974

Stemware, 134

6110 Goblet $25.00
6110 Sherbet $23.00
6110 Wine $30.00
6110 Liqueur $38.00
6110 Ice Tea, footed $25.00

Puritan, 6068

1957 – 1971

Stemware, 113

6068 Goblet $22.00
6068 Sherbet $20.00
6068 Cocktail/Wine/Seafood $22.00
6068 Cordial $28.00
6068 Ice Tea, footed $22.00
6068 Juice, footed $18.00

Pussywillow, Cutting 769

1937 – 1943

Tableware I, 248

1769 Bowl, finger $14.00
4132 Decanter and Stopper $75.00
4132 Bowl, ice $40.00
4132 Tumbler, 14 oz., sham $15.00
4132 Tumbler, 12 oz., sham $14.00
4132 Tumbler, 9 oz., sham $12.00
4132 Tumbler, 5 oz., sham $9.00
4132 Old Fashioned Cocktail, 7½ oz., sham $10.00
4132 Whiskey, 1½ oz., sham $10.00
2337 Plate, 7" $7.00

--Q--

Queen Anne, 2412, see also Colony

1926 – 1927

Tableware I, 57

2412 Bowl, 9", shallow, low foot, solid color $250.00
2412 Bowl, 9", shallow, high foot, solid color $285.00
2412 Bowl, 9", shallow, high foot, colored base $225.00
2412 Candelabra, 2-light, colored pedestal, pair $600.00/market
2412 Candlestick, 9", solid color, pair $350.00
2412 Centerpiece, 11", solid color $225.00
2412 Lustre, 14½", colored pedestal, pair $500.00
2412 Vase, 12", solid color $250.00
2412 Vase, 14", solid color market

Queen Anne, Plate Etching 306

1929 – 1933

Stemware, 57

4020 Goblet
crystal $35.00
amber $45.00

4020 Sherbet, high
crystal $30.00
amber $40.00

4020 Sherbet, 7 oz., low
crystal $25.00
amber $30.00

4020 Sherbet, 5 oz., low
crystal $25.00
amber $30.00

4020½ Cocktail, 4 oz.
crystal $25.00
amber $32.00

4020 Cocktail, 3½ oz.
crystal $25.00
amber $30.00

4020 Ice Tea, footed
crystal $35.00
amber $45.00

4020 Tumbler, 13 oz., footed
crystal $35.00
amber $45.00

4020 Tumbler, 10 oz., footed
crystal $32.00
amber $40.00

4020 Juice, footed
crystal $32.00
amber $40.00

4020 Whiskey, footed
crystal $35.00
amber $45.00

Tableware I, 204

4020 Bowl, finger
crystal $32.00
amber $37.00

2350 Cream Soup and Plate
crystal $48.00
amber $55.00

2350 Cup and Saucer, after dinner
crystal $48.00
amber $55.00

2350½ Cup and 2350 Saucer
crystal $32.00
amber $38.00

4020 Jug
crystal $325.00
amber $350.00

2350 Plate, 6"
crystal $9.00
amber $12.00

2350 Plate, 7"
crystal $12.00
amber $16.00

2350 Plate, 9"
crystal $40.00
amber $45.00

2419 Plate, 6"
crystal $10.00
amber $14.00

2419 Plate, 7"
crystal $15.00
amber $20.00

2419 Plate, 8"
crystal $18.00
amber $22.00

2419 Saucer, after dinner
crystal $12.00
amber $15.00

2419 Saucer
crystal $12.00
amber $15.00

4020 Shaker, FGT , pair
crystal $95.00
amber $125.00

4020 Sugar and Cream
crystal $75.00
amber $87.00

Queen Anne, Cutting 905
1965 – 1970

Stemware, 129

6104 Goblet $28.00
6104 Sherbet $25.00
6104 Claret $30.00
6104 Wine $30.00
6104 Cordial $38.00
6104 Ice Tea, footed $28.00
2337 Plate, 7" $8.00
2337 Plate, 8" $10.00

Quinfoil, Cutting 737
1934 – 1937

Stemware, 81 – 82

6011 Goblet $30.00
6011 Saucer Champagne $25.00
6011 Sherbet, low $22.00
6011 Cocktail $25.00
6011 Claret $30.00
6011 Rhine Wine $30.00
6011 Wine $30.00
6011 Sherry $28.00
6011 Crème de Menthe $24.00
6011 Brandy $32.00
6011 Cordial $34.00
6011 Oyster Cocktail $20.00
6011 Ice Tea, footed $28.00
6011 Tumbler, 10 oz., footed $24.00
6011 Juice, footed $24.00
6011 Whiskey, footed $30.00

Tableware I, 281

319 Bottle, bar $95.00
1769 Bowl, finger $14.00
4024 Bowl, 10", footed $30.00
4024 Candlestick, 6", pair $35.00
2518 Cocktail Shaker, 32 oz. $84.00
2518½ Cocktail Shaker, 28 oz. $75.00
2400 Comport, 6" $27.00
2518 Decanter $75.00
6011 Decanter $95.00
6011 Jug $185.00
2337 Plate, 6" $6.00
2337 Plate, 7" $7.00
2337 Plate, 8" $8.00
2350½ Sugar and Cream $30.00

--R--

Radiance, 2700
1956 – 1957

Stemware, 49

2700 Goblet $15.00
2700 Sherbet $12.00
2700 Juice, footed $12.00

Tableware II, 88 – 89

Basket, Pansy
- white $18.00
- aqua $22.00
- peach $22.00

Bowl, serving $15.00
Bowl, cereal/dessert $10.00
Bowl, 12", salad $20.00
Bowl, violet
- white $18.00
- aqua $22.00
- peach $22.00

Cup and Saucer $14.00
Plate, 7" $4.00
Plate, 10" $16.00
Plate, 14", buffet $18.00
Platter, 15" $20.00
Salad Set $45.00
Bowl, sauce and plate and ladle $26.00
Server, 3-part $18.00
Shaker, gold top, pair $18.00
Sugar and Cream $22.00

Radiance, 3113
1981 – 1982

Lead crystal

Stemware, 56

3113 Goblet $18.00
3113 Sherbet $15.00
3113 Wine $15.00
3113 Ice Tea, footed $18.00

Rainbow, Decoration 638
1957 – 1963

Stemware, 113

6068½ Goblet $28.00
6068½ Sherbet $26.00
6068½ Cocktail/Wine/Seafood $28.00
6068½ Cordial $35.00
6068½ Ice Tea, footed $28.00
6068½ Juice, footed $25.00
2337 Plate, 7", narrow optic $10.00

Raleigh, 2574
1939 – 1965

Tableware II, 61-64

Bonbon $20.00
Bowl, 8½", serving dish $28.00
Bowl, 9½", handled $35.00
Bowl, 12", flared $34.00
Bowl, 13", fruit $37.00
Candlestick, 4", pair $45.00
Candlestick, duo, pair $55.00
Celery, 10½" $20.00
Comport, 5", $22.00
Cup and Saucer $14.00
Ice Tub and Tongs $37.00
Lemon $20.00
Mayonnaise, plate, ladle $36.00
Oil, 4¼ oz., ground stopper $35.00
Olive, 6" $12.00
Pickle, 8" $14.00
Plate, 6" $5.00
Plate, 7" $6.00
Plate, 8" $8.00
Plate, 9" $18.00
Plate, 10", cake $30.00
Plate, 14", torte $30.00
Relish, 3-part $30.00
Shaker, pair $45.00
Sugar and Cream, $22.00
Sugar and Cream, individual $22.00
Sugar and Cream Set $34.00
Tray, sugar and cream $12.00
Sweetmeat $20.00
Tray, handled, muffin $30.00
Whip Cream $20.00

Rambler, Plate Etching 323 and Rambler, Decoration 615

1935 – 1957

Stemware, 83-84

6012 Goblet
- crystal $38.00
- Decoration 615 $30.00

6012 Sherbet, high
- crystal $32.00
- Decoration 615 $28.00

6012 Sherbet, low
- crystal $28.00
- Decoration 615 $22.00

6012 Cocktail
- crystal $32.00
- Decoration 615 $28.00

6012 Claret
- crystal $45.00
- Decoration 615 $35.00

6012 Rhine Wine
- crystal $42.00
- Decoration 615 $35.00

6012 Wine
- crystal $45.00
- Decoration 615 $35.00

6012 Sherry
- crystal $34.00
- Decoration 615 $32.00

6012 Crème de Menthe
- crystal $32.00
- Decoration 615 $28.00

6012 Brandy
- crystal $42.00
- Decoration 615 $35.00

6012 Cordial
- crystal $48.00
- Decoration 615 $45.00

6012 Oyster Cocktail
- crystal $28.00
- Decoration 615 $20.00

6012 Ice Tea, footed
- crystal $36.00
- Decoration 615 $30.00

6012 Tumbler, 10 oz., footed
- crystal $28.00
- Decoration 615 $25.00

6012 Juice, footed
- crystal $28.00
- Decoration 615 $20.00

701 Tumbler, 12 oz.
- crystal $28.00
- Decoration 615 $20.00

701 Tumbler, 10 oz.
- crystal $25.00
- Decoration 615 $20.00

1184 Old Fashioned Cocktail
- crystal $24.00
- Decoration 615 $18.00

4122 Whiskey, 1½ oz.
- crystal $28.00
- Decoration 615 $20.00

Tableware I, 223 – 224

2440 Bonbon $30.00
1769 Bowl, finger $25.00
2484 Bowl, 10", handled $135.00
2470½ Bowl, 10½" $85.00
- Decoration 615 $85.00

2470½ Candlestick, 5½", pair $95.00
2472 Candlestick, duo, pair $145.00
- Decoration 615 $145.00

2482 Candlestick, trindle, pair $165.00
with Decoration 615........$165.00
2496 Candlestick, trindle, pair $150.00
4117 Jar, candy, Bubble..............$135.00
with Decoration 615........$175.00
2524 Cocktail Mixer....................$140.00
2525 Cocktail Shaker, gold top ...$250.00
2525½ Cocktail Shaker, gold top ...$295.00
2350½ Cup and Saucer......................$32.00
6011 Decanter..............................$275.00
6011 Jug.......................................$285.00
with Decoration 615 ....$275.00
2440 Lemon, 5" $30.00
2440 Mayonnaise, 2-part................$40.00
with Decoration 615..........$45.00
2337 Plate, 6" $7.00
with Decoration 615............$7.00
2337 Plate, 7" $12.00
with Decoration 615..........$12.00
2337 Plate, 8" $16.00
with Decoration 615..........$16.00
2440 Plate, 13", torte $85.00
with Decoration 615..........$85.00
2440 Relish, 2-part..........................$37.00
with Decoration 615..........$37.00
2440 Relish, 3-part..........................$43.00
with Decoration 615..........$47.00
2419 Relish, 4-part..........................$54.00
with Decoration 615..........$58.00
2419 Relish, 5-part..........................$75.00
with Decoration 615..........$75.00
2514 Relish, 5-part..........................$75.00
2440 Sauce and Tray $75.00
with Decoration 615..........$75.00
2235 Shaker, FGT, pair...................$95.00
2350½ Sugar and Cream...................$60.00
with Decoration 615..........$60.00
2440 Sweetmeat, 4½".....................$30.00
2470 Vase, 11½" $250.00
with Decoration 615........$275.00

Randolph, 2675 Milkglass

1954 – 1965

Tableware II, 207 – 227

Ashtray............$20.00
Bowl, 10", footed and cover............$67.00
Bowl, 10", shallow footed.................................$48.00
aqua..................................$58.00
peach $58.00
Candleholder, 1½", pair $34.00
aqua..................................$48.00
peach $48.00
Candleholder, 6", pair $64.00
aqua..................................$85.00
peach $85.00
Box, cigarette and cover.......$75.00
Cup and Saucer......................$24.00
Egg Cup, 4½".........................$28.00
Egg Plate $75.00
Hurricane Lamp, 1½", candle and shade $65.00
Nappy, 6", square $22.00
aqua..................................$30.00
peach $30.00
Nappy, 6"...............................$24.00
aqua..................................$34.00
peach $34.00
Nappy, 5⅜", cupped $22.00
aqua..................................$30.00
peach $30.00
Nappy, 5", oblong $22.00
aqua..................................$30.00
peach $30.00
Nappy, 6"...............................$22.00
Plate, 9" $22.00
Plate, 12½", buffet $47.00
aqua..................................$60.00
peach $60.00
Preserve, footed and cover...$56.00
aqua..................................$75.00
peach $75.00
Shaker, chrome top A, pair.....$48.00
aqua..................................$67.00
peach $67.00
Sugar and Cover and Cream ..$65.00
aqua..................................$85.00
peach $85.00
Tray, 7".................................$22.00
Tumbler, 9 oz., footed...........$22.00
Urn and Cover $64.00

Raynel, Cutting 777

1938 – 1939

Stemware, 90

6017 Goblet $30.00
6017 Sherbet, high $28.00
6017 Sherbet, low...........................$24.00
6017 Cocktail $28.00
6017 Claret.....................................$35.00
6017 Wine.......................................$35.00
6017 Cordial....................................$45.00
6017 Oyster Cocktail.......................$22.00
6017 Ice Tea, footed $30.00
6017 Tumbler, 9 oz., footed...........$24.00
6017 Juice, footed $22.00
4132 Tumbler, 12 oz.........................$22.00
4132 Tumbler, 9 oz. $20.00
4132 Tumbler, 7½ oz. $18.00
4132 Tumbler, 5 oz..........................$15.00
4132 Tumbler, 1½ oz. $22.00

Tableware I, 299

766 Bowl, finger............................$12.00
4132 Decanter...................................$85.00
4132 Ice Bowl...................................$45.00
6011 Jug...$175.00
2337 Plate, 6" $7.00
2337 Plate, 7" $8.00
2337 Plate, 8" $10.00

Reception, Decoration 676

1967 – 1974

Stemware, 134

6110 Goblet......................................$28.00
6110 Sherbet.....................................$25.00
6110 Wine...$32.00
6110 Liqueur.....................................$38.00
6110 Ice Tea, footed $28.00
2337 Plate, 7" $10.00
2337 Plate, 8" $12.00

Reflection, Decoration 625

1952 – 1971

Stemware, 102

6033 Goblet....$20.00
6033 Sherbet, high $18.00
6033 Sherbet, low...........................$14.00
6033 Parfait $18.00
6033 Cocktail $14.00
6033 Claret-Wine $25.00
6033 Cordial.....................................$28.00
6033 Oyster Cocktail.......................$10.00
6033 Ice Tea, footed $18.00
6033 Juice, footed $10.00

Tableware II, 196

2364 Bowl, 9", salad.........................$32.00
2324 Candlestick, 4", pair $48.00
2666 Cup and Saucer.......................$26.00
2364 Mayonnaise, plate, ladle $58.00
2337 Plate, 7" $9.00
2337 Plate, 8" $12.00
2666 Sugar and Cream...................$40.00
2666 Sugar and Cream, individual...........................$35.00
2666 Tray, individual sugar and cream $10.00

Regal, Cutting 782

1937 – 1942

Stemware, 95

6024 Goblet..........$34.00
6024 Saucer Champagne $30.00
6024 Sherbet, low $25.00
6024 Cocktail $30.00
6024 Claret......................................$38.00
6024 Wine..$36.00
6024 Cordial.....................................$48.00
6024 Oyster Cocktail.......................$22.00
6024 Ice Tea, footed $34.00
6024 Tumbler, 9 oz., footed...........$25.00
6024 Juice, footed $26.00
5000 Jug...$245.00
2337 Plate, 6" $8.00
2337 Plate, 7" $10.00
2337 Plate, 8" $12.00

Regal, Cutting 842

1955 – 1958

Stemware, 110

6061 Goblet......................................$32.00
6061 Sherbet.....................................$28.00
6061 Cocktail/Wine/ Seafood..............................$28.00
6061 Cordial.....................................$40.00
6061 Ice Tea, footed $32.00
6061 Juice, footed $26.00

Tableware II, 187, 188

2691 Ashtray, individual $18.00
2666 Bowl, oval $38.00
2666 Candle, flora, pair $48.00
2691 Cigarette Holder, individual............................$26.00
2337 Plate, 7" $10.00
2337 Plate, 8" $12.00
2364 Plate, 11", sandwich $24.00
2364 Plate, 14", torte $34.00
691 Preserve, handled....................$24.00
2691 Bowl, sauce with plate and ladle $52.00
2691 Server, 2-part..........................$30.00
2691 Server, 3-part..........................$38.00
2691 Shaker, chrome top A, pair $48.00
2691 Sugar and Cover....................$26.00
2691 Sugar and Cream...................$45.00
2691 Sugar and Cream, individual and tray...............................$52.00

Regal, Decoration 693

1972 – 1973

Stainless steel on crystal

Stemware, 120

6092 Goblet....$26.00
6092 Sherbet....$24.00
6092 Wine/Cocktail....$28.00
6092 Ice Tea, footed....$26.00

Regency, Cutting 744

1935 – 1943

Stemware, 84

6012 Goblet....$28.00
6012 Sherbet, high....$26.00
6012 Sherbet, low....$22.00
6012 Cocktail....$22.00
6012 Claret....$28.00
6012 Rhine Wine....$28.00
6012 Wine....$28.00
6012 Sherry....$26.00
6012 Crème de Menthe....$22.00
6012 Brandy....$32.00
6012 Cordial....$38.00
6012 Oyster Cocktail....$14.00
6012 Ice Tea, footed....$27.00
6012 Tumbler, 10 oz., footed....$20.00
6012 Juice, footed....$18.00
701 Tumbler, 12 oz....$20.00
701 Tumbler, 10 oz....$18.00
1185 Old Fashioned Cocktail, 7 oz....$15.00

Tableware I, 285

1769 Bowl, finger....$14.00
2470½ Bowl, 10½"....$45.00
2472 Candlestick, duo, pair....$60.00
6011 Jug....$185.00
2337 Plate, 6"....$6.00
2337 Plate, 7"....$7.00
2337 Plate, 8"....$8.00
2440 Plate, 13", torte....$40.00

Regency, 6128

1976 – 1977

Stemware, 143

6128 Goblet....$24.00
6128 Champagne....$20.00
6128 Wine....$24.00
6128 Ice Tea, footed....$24.00

Regent, Decoration 32

1920s

Stemware, 22

766 Goblet....$15.00
766 Saucer Champagne....$15.00
766 Fruit....$10.00
766 Parfait....$20.00
766 Cocktail....$15.00
766 Wine....$15.00
766 Cordial....$25.00
766 Ice Tea, footed, handled....$22.00
701 Tumbler, 14 oz. and plate....$15.00
820 Tumbler....$10.00
4011 Tumbler, 12 oz....$12.00
4011 Tumbler, 8 oz....$12.00
4011 Tumbler, 5 oz....$10.00
4011½ Tumbler, table....$10.00

Tableware I, 318

766 Bowl, finger and plate....$25.00
2244 Candlestick, 8¼", pair....$225.00
2245 Candlestick, 8¼", pair....$150.00
2219 Jar, candy and cover, ¼ pound....$64.00
2219 Jar, candy and cover, ½ pound....$74.00
2219 Jar, candy and cover, pound....$85.00
2228 Jar, candy and cover, pound, square....$95.00
2250 Jar, candy and cover, ¼ pound....$64.00
2250 Jar, candy and cover, ½ pound....$74.00
2250 Jar, candy and cover, pound....$85.00
1697 Carafe Set....$125.00
2241 Cologne, 2¼ oz. , drip stopper....$145.00
2242 Cologne, 3¼ oz., drip stopper....$130.00
2243 Cologne, 2½ oz., drip stopper....$130.00
803 Comport, 5", footed....$47.00
803 Comport, 6", footed....$52.00
803 Comport and Cover, 5"....$52.00
880 Comport, 5"....$45.00
1848 Dish, 7", salad, matt star base....$37.00
825 Jelly and Cover, or no cover....$48.00
2100/7 Jug....$225.00
1968 Marmalade and Cover....$48.00
2138 Mayonnaise and Plate, flared....$60.00
803 Nappy and Cover, 5"....$38.00
803 Nappy, 5", footed, deep....$40.00
803 Nappy, 6", footed, deep....$45.00
803 Nappy, 7", footed, deep....$45.00
1897 Plate, 7"....$8.00
2283 Plate, 8¼"....$10.00
2283 Plate, 11"....$15.00
2290 Plate, 8", deep, salad....$16.00
2290 Plate, 13", deep ,salad....$32.00
1848 Plate, 9", sandwich, matt star base....$25.00
1719 Plate, 10½", sandwich, matt star base....$28.00
2258 Plate, 11", sandwich....$28.00
858 Sweetmeat....$20.00
2287 Tray, handled, lunch....$58.00

Regis, Decoration 697

1980 – 1982

Stemware, 88

6016 Goblet....$25.00
6016 Saucer Champagne....$22.00
6016 Claret, large....$25.00
6016 Ice Tea, footed....$25.00

Rehearsal, Decoration 667

1964 – 1974

Stemware, 128

6103 Goblet....$25.00
6103 Sherbet....$22.00
6103 Claret....$27.00
6103 Tulip Wine....$27.00
6103 Brandy....$25.00
6103 Ice Tea, footed....$25.00

Tableware II, 100

2785 Bowl, gourmet, 10", footed....$35.00
2785 Relish, gourmet, 2-part....$30.00
2785 Relish, gourmet, 4-part....$35.00
2785 Relish, gourmet, 5-part....$42.00
2785 Sugar and Cream, gourmet....$38.00

Relish, see Appetizer, Buffet and Relish

Remembrance, Decoration 670

1966 – 1968

Stemware, 132

6107 Goblet....$25.00
6107 Sherbet....$25.00
6107 Claret....$25.00
6107 Tulip Wine....$25.00
6107 Liqueur....$30.00
6107 Ice Tea, footed....$25.00
2337 Plate, 7"....$10.00
2337 Plate, 8"....$12.00

Renaissance Gold, Decoration 678

1968 – 1982

Stemware, 135

6111 Goblet....$65.00
6111 Sherbet....$54.00
6111 Claret....$68.00
6111 Wine....$68.00
6111 Cordial....$75.00
6111 Ice Tea, footed....$65.00
2337 Plate, 7"....$14.00
2337 Plate, 8"....$16.00

Renaissance Platinum, Decoration 682

1969 – 1982

See illustration above

Stemware, 135

6111 Goblet....$55.00
6111 Sherbet....$50.00
6111 Claret....$58.00
6111 Wine....$58.00
6111 Cordial....$65.00
6111 Ice Tea, footed....$55.00
2337 Plate, 7"....$14.00
2337 Plate, 8"....$16.00

Repeal, Blown Stemware

1934 – 1942

Stemware, 184, 185

Blank 795

Champagne, hollow stem, 5½ oz.
- regal blue base....$58.00
- burgundy base....$58.00
- empire green base....$58.00
- amber base....$58.00
- crystal....$16.00
- mother-of-pearl....$16.00

Blank 846

Sherry, 2 oz.
- regal blue base....$65.00
- burgundy base....$65.00
- empire green base....$65.00
- amber base....$65.00
- crystal....$14.00
- mother-of-pearl....$14.00

Blank 858
Brandy, 1 oz.; champagne, 7 oz., long stem; cordial, 1 oz.
regal blue base ... $125.00
burgundy base ... $125.00
empire green base ... $125.00
amber base ... $75.00
crystal ... $35.00
mother-of-pearl ... $35.00

Blank 863
Champagne, 5 oz., hollow stem
regal blue base ... $58.00
burgundy base ... $58.00
empire green base ... $58.00
amber base ... $58.00
crystal ... $12.00
mother-of-pearl ... $12.00

Blank 877
Saucer Champagne, 6 oz.
regal blue base ... $95.00
burgundy base ... $95.00
empire green base ... $95.00
amber base ... $95.00
crystal ... $22.00
mother-of-pearl ... $22.00

Blank 877½
Goblet, 10 oz.
regal blue base ... $125.00
burgundy base ... $125.00
empire green base ... $125.00
amber base ... $125.00
crystal ... $25.00
mother-of-pearl ... $25.00

Blank 902
Wine, 5 oz.
regal blue base ... $58.00
burgundy base ... $58.00
empire green base ... $58.00
amber base ... $58.00
crystal ... $22.00
mother-of-pearl ... $22.00

Blank 906
Brandy Inhaler, 4¾ oz.
regal blue base ... $95.00
burgundy base ... $95.00
empire green base ... $95.00
amber base ... $95.00
crystal ... $26.00
mother-of-pearl ... $26.00

Blank 952
Cocktail, 3 oz.
regal blue base ... $54.00
burgundy base ... $54.00
empire green base ... $54.00
amber base ... $54.00
crystal ... $20.00
mother-of-pearl ... $20.00

Blank 963
Rhine Wine, 4½ oz.; cocktail, 3½ oz.; créme de menthe, 2 oz.
regal blue base ... $75.00
burgundy base ... $75.00
empire green base ... $75.00
amber base ... $75.00
crystal ... $25.00
mother-of-pearl ... $25.00

Blank 887
Whiskey Sham, 1¾ oz.
regal blue ... $34.00
burgundy ... $34.00
empire green ... $34.00
amber ... $34.00
crystal ... $12.00
mother-of-pearl ... $12.00
ruby ... $34.00

Blank 902
Martini Cocktail, 3 oz.
regal blue base ... $75.00
burgundy base ... $75.00
empire green base ... $75.00
crystal ... $25.00
mother-of-pearl ... $25.00

Blank 963
Cordial, 1 oz.
regal blue base ... $75.00
empire green base ... $75.00
crystal ... $30.00
mother-of-pearl ... $30.00

Blank 932
Saucer Champagne, 5½ oz.
regal blue ... $58.00
burgundy base ... $58.00
crystal ... $20.00

Blank 1184
Old Fashioned Cocktail, 7oz.
azure ... $35.00
gold tint ... $35.00
crystal ... $20.00
mother-of-pearl ... $20.00
wisteria ... $35.00

Blank 4122
Sham, 1½ oz., whiskey
crystal ... $18.00
mother-of-pearl ... $18.00

Blank 1554
Champagne, 5 oz., pressed hollow stem
crystal ... $10.00

Revere, Cutting 825

1950 – 1960

Stemware, 94

6023	Goblet	$25.00
6023	Saucer Champagne	$23.00
6023	Sherbet, low	$20.00
6023	Cocktail	$23.00
6023	Claret-Wine	$28.00
6023	Cordial	$38.00
6023	Oyster Cocktail	$20.00
6023	Ice Tea, footed	$25.00
6023	Juice, footed	$22.00
2337	Plate, 7"	$8.00
2337	Plate, 8"	$10.00

Rhapsody, 6055½

1954 – 1971

Stemware, 108

6055½ Goblet
crystal ... $22.00
turquoise ... $24.00

6055½ Sherbet
crystal ... $20.00
turquoise ... $20.00

6055½ Cocktail
crystal ... $20.00
turquoise ... $20.00

6055½ Claret-Wine
crystal ... $25.00
turquoise ... $28.00

6055½ Cordial
crystal ... $30.00
turquoise ... $35.00

6055½ Oyster Cocktail
crystal ... $16.00
turquoise ... $18.00

6055½ Ice Tea, footed
crystal ... $22.00
turquoise ... $24.00

6055½ Juice, footed
crystal ... $18.00
turquoise ... $18.00

Rheims, Cutting 803

1940 – 1943

Stemware, 97

6026	Goblet	$35.00
6026	Goblet, low	$26.00
6026	Saucer Champagne	$30.00
6026	Sherbet, low	$24.00
6026	Cocktail	$30.00
6026	Claret-Wine	$43.00
6026	Cordial	$55.00
6026	Oyster Cocktail	$22.00
6026	Ice Tea, footed	$35.00
6026	Juice, footed	$26.00
5000	Jug	$275.00
2337	Plate, 7"	$8.00
2337	Plate, 8"	$10.00

Rhythm, Cutting 773

1938 – 1942

Stemware, 58

4020	Goblet	$30.00
4020	Sherbet, high	$30.00
4020	Sherbet, 7 oz., low	$28.00
4020	Sherbet, 5 oz., low	$28.00
4020	Cocktail, 4 oz.	$28.00
4020	Cocktail, 3½ oz.	$28.00
4020	Claret	$35.00
4020	Wine	$35.00
4020	Tumbler, 13 oz., footed	$30.00
4020	Tumbler, 10 oz., footed,	$28.00
4020	Juice, footed	$28.00
4020	Whiskey, footed	$30.00
4020	Jug	$250.00
2419	Plate, 7"	$8.00
2419	Plate, 8"	$10.00

Richelieu, Decoration 515

1938 – 1939

Stemware, 88

6016	Goblet	$65.00
6016	Saucer Champagne	$50.00
6016	Sherbet, low	$35.00
6016	Cocktail	$50.00
6016	Claret	$65.00
6016	Wine	$60.00
6016	Cordial	$85.00
6016	Oyster Coctail	$35.00
6016	Ice Tea, footed	$60.00
6016	Tumbler, 10 oz., footed	$50.00
6016	Juice, footed	$40.00

Tableware II, 193

2560	Bonbon, 2 handled	$45.00
2560	Bonbon, 3-toed	$45.00
869	Bowl, finger	$38.00
2430	Bowl, 11"	$75.00

2560 Bowl, 11½", crimped............$95.00
2560 Bowl, 12", flared $85.00
2560 Bowl, 13", fruit $110.00
2430 Candlestick, 2", pair $65.00
2560 Candlestick, 4½", pair..........$95.00
2560 Candlestick, duo, pair $125.00
2430 Jar, candy and cover.............$95.00
2560 Cheese and Cracker.............$95.00
2560 Comport, 6"..........................$75.00
2560 Ice Bucket, gold handle and tongs...............................$125.00
2430 Jelly, 7" $42.00
5000 Jug $595.00/market
2560 Lemon...................................$45.00
2560 Mayonnaise, plate, ladle $85.00
2430 Mint, 5½" $38.00
2337 Plate, 7" $30.00
2337 Plate, 8" $35.00
2560 Plate, handled, cake $85.00
2560 Plate, 14", torte $95.00
2560 Relish, 2-part.........................$45.00
2560 Relish, 3-part.........................$75.00
2560 Sugar and Cream..................$95.00
2560 Sugar and Cream, individual..........................$85.00
2560 Sweetmeat............................$45.00
2467 Vase, 7½" $165.00
2430 Vase, 8"...............................$157.00
2545 Vase, 10"..............................$225.00
5100 Vase, 10"..............................$225.00
2560 Whip Cream..........................$45.00

Richmond, Needle Etching 74

1924 – 1943

Stemware, 64

5082 Goblet $25.00
5082 Sherbet, high $20.00
5082 Sherbet, low $18.00
5082 Parfait $25.00
5082 Cocktail $18.00
5082 Claret $30.00
5082 Wine..$25.00
5082 Cordial $35.00
4095 Oyster Cocktail $15.00
945½ Grapefruit and Liner $25.00
701 Tumbler, 13 oz. $10.00
701 Tumbler, 8 oz...........................$8.00
869 Tumbler, 12 oz., handled, plate $10.00
869 Tumbler, 5 oz. $6.00
4095 Tumbler.......................$6.00 – 10.00

Tableware I, 121

1769 Bowl, finger and plate $18.00
5078 Comport, 5"...........................$18.00
303/7 Jug..$65.00
318/7 Jug..$75.00
2270/7 Jug..$75.00
2270 Jug and Cover.......................$85.00
5078 Nappy, 5"...............................$15.00
5078 Nappy, 6"...............................$18.00
701 Plate, 5", tumbler.....................$5.00
2283 Plate, 7" $7.00
858 Sweetmeat............................$24.00

Richmond, Decoration 654

1961 – 1982

Stemware, 122

6097 Goblet.....................................$30.00
6097 Sherbet $26.00
6097 Claret $34.00
6097 Wine/Cocktail $30.00
6097 Cordial $40.00
6097 Ice Tea, footed $30.00
6097 Juice, footed $28.00
6097 Magnum $50.00

Tableware

2785 Bowl, gourmet, 10", footed $35.00
2337 Plate, 7" $8.00
2337 Plate, 8" $10.00
2785 Relish, gourmet, 2-part $30.00
2785 Relish, gourmet, 4-part $35.00
2785 Relish, gourmet, 5-part $42.00
2785 Sugar and Cream, gourmet............................$38.00

Ringlet, Tracing 95

1940 – 1943

Stemware, 40

892 Goblet....................................$25.00
892 Saucer Champagne $22.00
892 Sherbet, low $20.00
892 Cocktail $22.00
892 Claret $28.00
892 Wine..$25.00
892 Cordial $38.00
892 Oyster Cocktail......................$18.00
892 Ice Tea, footed $25.00
892 Juice, footed $20.00
2337 Plate, 7" $8.00

Ringlet, 6051

1953 – 1965

Stemware, 106

6051 Goblet...........$22.00
6051 Sherbet...........$20.00
6051 Cocktail.............$20.00
6051 Claret-Wine...........$25.00
6051 Cordial $30.00
6051 Oyster Cocktail......................$16.00
6051 Ice Tea, footed $22.00
6051 Juice, footed $18.00

Ring O' Roses, Crystal Print 9 Tumbler

1958 – 1962

Stemware, 155

4180 Tumbler, 12 oz., flat, fawn $12.00
4180 Juice, 7 oz., flat, fawn..................................$12.00

Ripple, Cutting 766

1937 – 1943

Stemware, 89

6017 Goblet $22.00
6017 Sherbet, high $20.00
6017 Sherbet, low $16.00
6017 Cocktail $20.00
6017 Claret $27.00
6017 Wine..$27.00
6017 Cordial $32.00
6017 Oyster Cocktail......................$16.00
6017 Tumbler, 14 oz., footed.................................$20.00
6017 Ice Tea, footed $20.00
6017 Tumbler, 9 oz., footed.................................$16.00
6017 Juice, footed $16.00
4132 Tumbler.....................$14.00 – 20.00

Tableware I, 297

766 Bowl, finger...........................$12.00
2545 Bowl, 12½" $57.00
2545 Candelabra, 2-light, pair......$175.00
2545 Candlestick, duo, pair $95.00
6011 Jug...$175.00
2337 Plate, 6" $6.00
2337 Plate, 7" $7.00
2337 Plate, 8" $8.00
2350½ Sugar and Cream..................$30.00
4132 Decanter.................................$65.00
4132 Bowl, ice $32.00

Rivera, Decoration 44

1924

Encrusted Gold on green, Amber, Canary, and Ebony

Tableware I, 320

2297 Bowl A, 10¼", shallow.........$165.00
2297 Bowl C, 10½", deep $185.00
2219 Jar, candy and cover, ½ pound $150.00
2250 Jar, candy and cover, ½ pound $145.00
2241 Cologne, 2¼ oz. $200.00
2321 Mah Jongg Set.......................$95.00
2286 Tray, 5", pin, ebony $48.00
2286 Tray, 10½", comb and brush, ebony $95.00
2276 Vanity Set............................$465.00
2269 Candle, 6", pair $250.00

Rocket, Cutting 729

1934 – 1943

Stemware, 81

6011 Goblet $35.00
6011 Saucer Champagne $30.00
6011 Sherbet, low $25.00
6011 Cocktail $30.00
6011 Claret $40.00
6011 Rhine Wine.............................$40.00
6011 Wine..$35.00
6011 Sherry $38.00
6011 Crème de Menthe $34.00
6011 Brandy $47.00
6011 Cordial $48.00
6011 Oyster Cocktail......................$25.00
6011 Ice Tea, footed $32.00
6011 Tumbler, 10 oz., footed.................................$25.00
6011 Juice, footed $25.00
6011 Whiskey, footed.....................$38.00

Tableware I, 280

1769 Bowl, finger...........................$14.00
4024 Bowl, 10", footed....................$35.00
4024 Candlestick, 6", pair $45.00
6011 Decanter...............................$155.00
6011 Jug...$195.00
2337 Plate, 6" $6.00
2337 Plate, 7" $7.00
2337 Plate, 8" $8.00

Rock Garden, Cutting 739

1934 – 1943

Stemware, 83

6012 Goblet $35.00
6012 Sherbet, high $32.00
6012 Sherbet, low $26.00
6012 Cocktail $32.00
6012 Claret $38.00
6012 Rhine Wine $40.00
6012 Wine $38.00
6012 Sherry $35.00
6012 Crème de Menthe $32.00
6012 Brandy $42.00
6012 Cordial $54.00
6012 Oyster Cocktail $25.00
6012 Ice Tea, footed $34.00
6012 Tumbler,10 oz., footed $30.00
6012 Juice, footed $30.00
863 Champagne, hollow stem $25.00
701 Tumbler ....$8.00 – 10.00
4122 Tumbler $8.00

Tableware I, 283

319 Bottle, bar $95.00
1769 Bowl, finger $14.00
4024 Bowl, 10", footed $30.00
4024 Candlestick, 6", pair $35.00
4117 Jar, candy and cover $67.00
2525 Cocktail Shaker $95.00
2400 Comport, 6" $27.00
2525 Decanter $95.00
6011 Decanter $125.00
6011 Jug $185.00
2337 Plate, 6" $6.00
2337 Plate, 7" $7.00
2337 Plate, 8" $8.00
2440 Plate, 13", torte $40.00
2364 Plate, 16", torte $54.00
2350½ Sugar and Cream $35.00
2470 Vase, 10" $95.00

Rogene, Plate Etching 269

1924 – 1929

Stemware, 64

5082 Goblet...$35.00
5082 Sherbet, high $30.00
5082 Sherbet, low $26.00
5082 Parfait $35.00
5082 Cocktail $30.00
5082 Claret $38.00
5082 Wine $35.00
5082 Cordial $47.00
5082 Grapefruit and Liner $50.00
837 Oyster Cocktail $12.00
945½ Grapefruit and Liner $40.00
869 Tumbler, 13 oz. $20.00
869 Tumbler, 8 oz. $18.00
869 Tumbler, 5 oz. $15.00
869 Tumbler, 12 oz., handled and plate $25.00
887 Tumbler, 2½ oz. $20.00
4023 Tumbler, 6 oz. $15.00
4076 Tumbler, 9 oz., table $18.00
4095 Tumbler ....$15.00 – 20.00

Tableware I, 148

766 Bowl, finger and 2283 Plate $25.00
1697 Carafe and Tumbler $95.00
5078 Comport, 5" $30.00
5078 Comport, 6" $35.00
300 Decanter, quart, cut neck $85.00
825 Jelly and Cover $37.00
4095/4 Jug $135.00
1852/6 Jug $175.00
318/7 Jug $245.00
2270/7 Jug $245.00
2270/7 Jug and Cover $268.00
4095/7 Jug $295.00
1968 Marmalade and Cover $54.00
766 Mayonnaise, plate, ladle $65.00
2138 Mayonnaise, plate, ladle, plain $95.00
5078 Nappy, 5" $24.00
5078 Nappy, 6" $26.00
5078 Nappy, 7" $30.00
4095 Nut $25.00
1465 Oil, 5 oz., cut neck $56.00
2283 Plate, 7" $10.00
2283 Plate, 8¼" $15.00
2283 Plate, 11" $24.00
2283 Plate, 11", cut matt star $27.00
2235 Shaker, FGT or pearl top, plain, pair $67.00
1851 Sugar and Cream $48.00
4095 Vase, medium, rolled edge, plain $135.00

Romance, Etching 341

1942 – 1971

Stemware, 89

6017 Goblet $35.00
6017 Sherbet, high $32.00
6017 Sherbet, low $28.00
6017 Cocktail $32.00
6017 Claret $45.00
6017 Wine $42.00
6017 Cordial $55.00
6017 Oyster Cocktail $25.00
6017 Ice Tea, footed $35.00
6017 Tumbler, 9 oz., footed $28.00
6017 Juice, footed $28.00

Tableware II, 139 – 143

2364 Ashtray $42.00
766 Bowl, finger $38.00
2364 Bowl, 6", baked apple $54.00
2364 Bowl, rim soup $57.00
6023 Bowl, 9¼", footed $125.00
2364 Bowl, 9", salad $65.00
2594 Bowl, 10", handled $150.00
2364 Bowl, 10½", salad $75.00
2596 Bowl, 11", oblong $125.00
2364 Bowl, 12", flared $78.00
2364 Bowl, 12", lily pond $78.00
2364 Bowl, 13", fruit $94.00
2324 Candlestick, 4", pair $76.00
2596 Candlestick, 5", pair $150.00
2594 Candlestick, 5½", pair $125.00
6023 Candlestick, duo, pair $150.00
2594 Candlestick, trindle, pair $225.00
2364 Box, candy and cover $265.00/market
2364 Celery, 11" $52.00
2364 Cheese and Cracker $115.00
2364 Cigarette Holder $74.00
6030 Comport, 5" $68.00
2364 Comport, 8" $120.00
2350½ Cup and Saucer $34.00
4132 Bowl, ice $300.00
6011 Jug $500.00
2364 Mayonnaise, plate, ladle $85.00
2364 Pickle, 8" $42.00
2666 Pitcher, quart $425.00
2337 Plate, 6" $16.00
2337 Plate, 7" $20.00
2337 Plate, 8" $24.00
2337 Plate, 9" $45.00
2364 Plate, crescent, salad $55.00
2364 Plate, 11", sandwich $50.00
2364 Plate, 14", torte $75.00
2364 Plate, 16", torte $85.00
2364 Relish, 2-part $75.00
2364 Relish, 3-part $75.00
2364 Salad Set, 9", 3-piece $150.00
2364 Salad Set, 10½", 3-piece $175.00
2364 Fork and Spoon, salad wood $25.00
2364 Shaker, FGT, pair $85.00
silver top C, pair $75.00
2350½ Sugar and Cream $75.00
2364 Tray, handled, lunch $115.00
4121 Vase, 5" $150.00
2619½ Vase, 6", ground, bottom $175.00
4143 Vase, 6", footed $110.00
6021 Vase, 6", footed, bud $87.00
2619½ Vase, 7½" $150.00
4143 Vase, 7½", footed $325.00
2660 Vase, 8", flip $250.00
2619½ Vase, 9½", ground bottom $300.00
2470 Vase, 10" $225.00
2614 Vase, 10" $400.00/market

Rondeau, Cutting 740

1934 – 1935

Stemware, 83

6012 Goblet $35.00
6012 Sherbet, high $32.00
6012 Sherbet, low $26.00
6012 Cocktail $32.00
6012 Claret $38.00
6012 Rhine Wine $40.00
6012 Wine $38.00
6012 Sherry $35.00
6012 Crème de Menthe $32.00
6012 Brandy $42.00
6012 Cordial $58.00
6012 Oyster Cocktail $26.00
6012 Ice Tea, footed $35.00
863 Champagne, hollow stem $25.00
701 Tumbler ....$8.00 – 10.00
4122 Tumbler $8.00

Tableware I, 283

1769 Bowl, finger $14.00
4024 Bowl, 10", footed $30.00
4024 Candlestick, 6", pair $35.00
4117 Jar, candy and cover $67.00
2525 Cocktail Shaker, 42 oz. $95.00
2525½ Cocktail Shaker, 30 oz. $85.00
2400 Comport, 6" $27.00
2525 Decanter $95.00
6011 Decanter $125.00
6011 Jug $185.00
2337 Plate, 6" $6.00
2337 Plate, 7" $7.00

2337 Plate, 8" $8.00
2440 Plate, 13", torte $40.00
2470 Vase, 10" $125.00

Rondel, 6019
1937 – 1943
Stemware, 91
6019 Goblet
crystal $25.00
azure $30.00
gold tint $30.00
6019 Sherbet
crystal $23.00
azure $26.00
gold tint $26.00
6019 Parfait
crystal $25.00
6019 Cocktail
crystal $22.00
azure $26.00
gold tint $26.00
6019 Claret
crystal $25.00
azure $30.00
gold tint $30.00
6019 Wine
crystal $23.00
azure $30.00
gold tint $30.00
6019 Oyster Cocktail
crystal $15.00
azure $20.00
gold tint $20.00
6019 Ice Tea, footed
crystal $25.00
azure $30.00
gold tint $30.00
6019 Juice, footed
crystal $18.00
azure $23.00
gold tint $23.00

Rondo, Cutting 830
1952 – 1954
Stemware, 104
6045 Goblet $22.00
6045 Sherbet $20.00
6045 Cocktail $20.00
6045 Claret-Wine $22.00
6045 Cordial $25.00
6045 Ice Tea, footed $22.00
6045 Juice, footed $20.00
2665 Plate, 8" $10.00

Rooster, Carving 37
1940 – 1943
Useful & Ornamental, 130
4148 Ashtray, 2½", individual $22.00
4148 Cigarette Holder $35.00

Rosalie, Crystal Print 19
1963 – 1975
Stemware, 126
6102 Goblet $35.00
6102 Sherbet $32.00
6102 Claret $38.00
6102 Tulip Wine $42.00
6102 Brandy $45.00
6102 Ice Tea, footed $35.00
2337 Plate, 7" $8.00
2337 Plate, 8" $10.00

Rose, Cutting 827
1951 – 1973
Stemware, 103
6036 Goblet $36.00
6036 Sherbet, high $32.00
6036 Sherbet, low $24.00
6036 Parfait $35.00
6036 Cocktail $30.00
6036 Claret-Wine $36.00
6036 Cordial $45.00
6036 Oyster Cocktail $22.00
6036 Ice Tea, footed $36.00
6036 Juice, footed $26.00
Tableware II, 177 – 178
4185 Bowl, finger/dessert $35.00
2666 Bowl, individual salad/dessert $30.00
2666 Bowl, 11", salad $48.00
2666 Celery $36.00
2666 Cup and Saucer $36.00
6011 Jug $325.00
2666 Mayonnaise, plate, ladle $68.00
2666 Pickle $28.00
2666 Pitcher, quart $195.00
2337 Plate, 7" $14.00
2337 Plate, 8" $18.00
2666 Plate, 14", serving $68.00
2666 Relish, 2-part $35.00
2666 Relish, 3-part $47.00
2666 Salad Set $125.00
2364 Shaker, chrome top C, pair $54.00
2666 Sugar and Cream $54.00
2666 Sugar and Cream, individual and tray $65.00

Rosemary, Plate Etching 339
1940 – 1943
Stemware, 40
892 Goblet $30.00
892 Saucer Champagne $28.00
892 Sherbet, low $24.00
892 Cocktail $26.00
892 Claret $35.00
892 Wine $32.00
892 Cordial $40.00
892 Oyster Cocktail $20.00
892 Ice Tea, footed $30.00
892 Juice, footed $25.00
Tableware I, 261
1769 Bowl, finger $38.00
6023 Bowl, 9", footed $145.00
2364 Bowl, 10½", salad $95.00
2364 Bowl, 12", flared $95.00
2364 Bowl, 13", fruit $100.00
6023 Candlestick, duo, pair $195.00
6011 Jug $295.00
2337 Plate, 6" $10.00
2337 Plate, 7" $14.00
2337 Plate, 8" $20.00
2364 Plate, 14", torte $85.00
4143 Vase, 6", footed $145.00
4143 Vase, 7½", footed $175.00

Rosette, 2501
1936 – 1943;
1970 – 1972
Tableware I, 97, 98
Useful & Ornamental, 111
2496 Ashtray, oblong $16.00
2501 Ashtray, individual $15.00
2510 Ashtray, individual $15.00
2510 Ashtray, square $12.00
2501 Ashtray, 5", large $20.00
2501 Bowl, 9", flared $35.00
2501 Box, cigarette and cover $68.00
2501 Relish, crescent $38.00
2501 Plate, 7" $15.00
2496 Plate, 7" $15.00
2501 Plate, 8" $16.00
2501 Plate, oval, cake $52.00
2501 Plate, 13", torte $65.00
2496 Plate, 14", torte $65.00
2501 Tray, oval $45.00
2510 Tray, sugar and cream $35.00
Useful & Ornamental, 111
2371 Ashtray, 7½" $28.00
2364 Bowl, 9", salad $35.00
2364 Bowl, 9", lily pond $35.00
2364 Plate, 11", sandwich $40.00
2364 Plate, 14", torte $55.00

Rosette, Crystal Print 3
1956
Stemware, 111
6064 Goblet $35.00
6064 Champagne $30.00
6064 Sherbet, low $27.00
6064 Cocktail $30.00
6064 Claret $38.00
6064 Wine $36.00
6064 Cordial $42.00
6064 Seafood Cocktail $24.00
6064 Ice Tea, footed $35.00
6064 Juice, footed $27.00
2337 Plate, 7" $8.00
2337 Plate, 8" $10.00

Rosilyn, Etching 249
1918 – 1926
Stemware, 36
880 Goblet, 10 oz. $12.00
880 Saucer Champagne, 5½ oz. $12.00
880 Sherbet $10.00
880 Cocktail, 4½ oz. $10.00
880 Claret, 4½ oz. $12.00
880 Wine, 2¾ oz. $12.00
880 Sherry $10.00
880 Cordial, 1 oz. $15.00
837 Oyster Cocktail $9.00
822 Parfait $22.00
801 Rhine Wine $10.00
481 Custard $8.00
945½ Grapefruit and Liner $25.00
701 Tumbler, 14 oz. and plate $8.00
701 Tumbler, 8 oz. $6.00
701 Tumbler, 14 oz., handled $8.00
820 Tumbler $8.00
833 Tumbler, 8 oz. $6.00
889 Tumbler, 5 oz. $5.00

Rosilyn, Etching 249

No.	Item	Price
4011	Tumbler, 12 oz.	$8.00
4011	Tumbler, 8 oz.	$6.00
4061	Lemonade, footed, handled	$22.00
5051	Almond, small	$20.00
5051	Almond, large	$24.00
880	Bonbon, 4½"	$20.00
1607	Carafe and Tumbler	$67.00
981	Carafe Whiskey, 2½ oz.	$16.00
803	Comport, 5"	$20.00
803	Comport, 6"	$22.00
1769	Bowl, finger and plate	$20.00
300-7	Jug	$95.00
303-7	Jug	$87.00
318-7	Jug	$95.00
724-7	Jug	$95.00
803	Nappy, 5"	$22.00
803	Nappy, 6"	$25.00
803	Nappy, 7", footed	$27.00
2083	Bottle, salad dressing	$58.00
1848	Plate, 9", sandwich	$12.00
1480	Sugar and Cream	$36.00
1806	Bottle, water, cut neck	$48.00

Roulette, 2739

1968 (New Goods)

Tableware II, 98

No.	Item	Price
208	Bowl, Star, 5", tall	
	ebony/crystal	$65.00
	ruby/crystal	$75.00
231	Bowl, 11", tall, quadrangle	
	ebony/crystal	$95.00
	ruby/crystal	$135.00
316	Candlestick, pair	
	ebony/crystal	$125.00
	ruby/crystal	$130.00
248	Bowl, tricorne, 3½", tall	
	ebony/crystal	$65.00
	ruby/crystal	$87.00
266	Centerpiece, 17", oval	
	ebony/crystal	$150.00
	ruby/crystal	$225.00
267	Vase, 7", Petal	
	ebony/crystal	$78.00
	ruby/crystal	$95.00
785	Vase, 8", Basket	
	ebony/crystal	$100.00
	ruby/crystal	$140.00
792	Vase, 8½", Trident	
	ebony/crystal	$100.00
	ruby/crystal	$140.00
832	Vase, 15", Flame	
	ebony/crystal	$150.00
	ruby/crystal	$225.00

Royal, Decoration 39

1924

Tableware I, 319

No.	Item	Price
2267	Bowl, 7"	$95.00
2267	Bowl, 9"	$125.00
2267	Bowl, 9", deep, rolled edge	$125.00
2297	Bowl C, 9¾", shallow, rolled edge	$135.00
2297	Bowl A, 10¼", flared	$145.00
2297	Bowl C, 10½", deep, rolled edge	$165.00
2297	Bowl A, 12", deep, flared	$165.00
2245	Candlestick, 6"	$175.00
2269	Candlestick, 6"	$175.00
2275	Candlestick, 7"	$175.00
2297	Candlestick, 7"	$200.00
2245	Candlestick, 8"	$195.00
2275	Candlestick, 9"	$225.00
2250	Jar, candy and cover, ¼ pound	$95.00
2250	Jar, candy and cover, ½ pound	$125.00
2250	Jar, candy and cover, pound	$150.00
2249	Jar, candy and cover, ¼ pound	$95.00
2249	Jar, candy and cover, ½ pound	$125.00
2249	Jar, candy and cover, pound	$150.00
2244	Cologne	$175.00
2283	Plate, 6"	$30.00
2283	Plate, 7"	$36.00
2238	Plate, 8¼"	$40.00
2238	Plate, 11"	$54.00
2290	Plate, 8¼", deep, salad	$45.00
2290	Plate, 13½", deep, salad	$65.00
2287	Tray, handled, lunch	$125.00
2276	Vanity Set	$450.00

Royal, Plate Etching 273

1925 – 1938

Stemware, 31

No.	Item	Price
869	Goblet	
	crystal	$25.00
	amber	$40.00
	green	$40.00
	blue	$85.00
869	Saucer Champagne	
	crystal	$20.00
	amber	$35.00
	green	$35.00
	blue	$75.00
869	Sherbet, high	
	crystal	$20.00
	amber	$35.00
	green	$35.00
	blue	$75.00
869	Sherbet, low	
	crystal	$10.00
	amber	$30.00
	green	$30.00
	blue	$64.00
869	Fruit	
	crystal	$10.00
	amber	$30.00
	green	$30.00
	blue	$64.00
869	Parfait	
	crystal	$20.00
	amber	$45.00
	green	$45.00
	blue	$96.00
869	Cocktail	
	crystal	$20.00
	amber	$32.00
	green	$32.00
	blue	$72.00
869	Wine	
	crystal	$22.00
	amber	$40.00
	green	$40.00
	blue	$95.00
869	Cordial	
	crystal	$35.00
	amber	$45.00
	green	$45.00
	blue	$125.00
869	Oyster Cocktail	
	crystal	$10.00
	amber	$27.00
	green	$27.00
	blue	$48.00
945½	Grapefruit	
	crystal	$70.00
	amber	$75.00
	green	$80.00
	blue	$95.00
869	Tumbler	
	crystal	$25.00
	amber	$28.00
	green	$32.00
	blue	$37.00
5000	Tumbler	
	crystal	$22.00
	amber	$25.00
	green	$25.00
	blue	$35.00

Tableware I, 150 – 155

No.	Item	Price
2350	Ashtray, small	
	crystal	$22.00
	amber	$24.00
	green	$26.00
2350½	Bouillon	
	crystal	$12.00
	amber	$18.00
	green	$18.00
	blue	$22.00
869	Bowl, finger and plate	
	crystal	$22.00
	amber	$27.00
	green	$30.00
	blue	$38.00
2350	Bowl, 5", fruit	
	crystal	$27.00
	amber	$30.00
	green	$34.00
	blue	$43.00
2350	Bowl, 6", cereal	
	crystal	$28.00
	amber	$34.00
	green	$37.00
	blue	$46.00
2350	Bowl, 7", soup	
	crystal	$30.00
	amber	$38.00
	green	$42.00
	blue	$50.00
2267	Bowl, 7", low foot	
	crystal	$34.00
	amber	$38.00
	green	$45.00
	blue	$56.00
	ebony	$45.00
2350	Bowl, 8", nappy	
	crystal	$45.00
	amber	$48.00
	green	$50.00
	blue	$64.00
2350	Bowl, 9", nappy	
	crystal	$48.00
	amber	$54.00
	green	$57.00
	blue	$70.00

2350 Bowl, 9", oval, baker
crystal $48.00
amber..........$54.00
green..........$57.00
blue $75.00

2324 Bowl, 10", footed
crystal $95.00
amber..........$125.00
green..........$135.00
blue $195.00

2350 Bowl, 12", salad
crystal $110.00
amber..........$125.00
green..........$145.00
blue $165.00

2350 Bowl, 10½", oval, baker
crystal $58.00
amber..........$65.00
green..........$68.00
blue $95.00

2315 Bowl A, 10½", footed, flared
crystal $85.00
amber..........$110.00
green..........$125.00

2297 Bowl A, 12", deep
crystal $85.00
amber..........$110.00
green..........$125.00
blue $195.00
ebony $150.00

2324 Bowl, 13", footed
crystal $125.00
amber..........$165.00
green..........$178.00
blue $235.00

2350 Butter and Cover
crystal $148.00
amber..........$165.00
green..........$195.00
blue $287.00

2324 Candlestick, 2", pair
crystal $65.00
amber..........$87.00
green..........$94.00
blue $125.00

2324 Candlestick, 4", pair
crystal $75.00
amber..........$85.00
green..........$94.00
blue $125.00
ebony $95.00

2324 Candlestick, 9", pair
crystal $120.00
amber..........$135.00
green..........$150.00
blue $194.00

2324 Candlestick, 12", pair
crystal $168.00
amber..........$185.00
green..........$200.00
blue $250.00

2331 Box, candy and cover
crystal $115.00
amber..........$130.00
green..........$145.00
blue $225.00
ebony $150.00

2250 Candy and Cover, ½ pound
crystal $94.00
amber..........$120.00
green..........$125.00
blue $145.00

2350 Celery
crystal $38.00
amber..........$48.00
green..........$54.00
blue $62.00

2329 Centerpiece, 11"
crystal $75.00
amber..........$94.00
green..........$98.00
blue $165.00
ebony $110.00

2329 Centerpiece, 13"
crystal $90.00
amber..........$124.00
green..........$135.00
blue $200.00

2371 Centerpiece, 13", oval
crystal $120.00
amber..........$150.00
green..........$165.00
blue $225.00

2276 Cheese (Cover) and Cracker
amber..........$125.00
green..........$135.00

2322 Cologne, tall
crystal $125.00
amber..........$147.00
green..........$158.00
blue $235.00

2323 Cologne, squat
crystal $125.00
amber..........$145.00
green..........$168.00
blue $237.00

2327 Comport, 7"
crystal $85.00
amber..........$94.00
green..........$97.00
blue $125.00
ebony $100.00

2350 Comport, 8"
crystal $85.00
amber..........$92.00
green..........$95.00
blue $125.00

2350 Cream Soup
crystal $30.00
amber..........$35.00
green..........$38.00
blue $48.00

2350 Cup and Saucer
crystal $22.00
amber..........$25.00
green..........$27.00
blue $36.00

2350 Cup and Saucer, after dinner
crystal $30.00
amber..........$37.00
green..........$45.00
blue $65.00

2350½ Cup and Saucer
crystal $22.00
amber..........$25.00
green..........$27.00
blue $36.00

2378 Ice Bucket
crystal $95.00
amber..........$125.00
green..........$135.00
blue $225.00

1861½ Jelly, 6"
crystal $70.00
amber..........$78.00
green..........$80.00
blue $110.00

1236 Jug, optic
crystal $275.00
amber..........$295.00
green..........$325.00
blue $775.00

5000 Jug
crystal $275.00
amber..........$295.00
green..........$350.00
blue $850.00

2315 Mayonnaise/Grapefruit
crystal $32.00
amber..........$40.00
green..........$48.00
blue $57.00

2350 Pickle
crystal $24.00
amber..........$28.00
green..........$30.00
blue $40.00

2283 Plate, 6"
crystal $12.00
amber..........$16.00
green..........$18.00
blue $22.00

2350 Plate, 6"
crystal $12.00
amber..........$16.00
green..........$18.00
blue $22.00

2290 Plate, 7"
crystal $12.00
amber..........$20.00
green..........$22.00
blue $25.00

2283 Plate, 7"
crystal $12.00
amber..........$20.00
green..........$22.00
blue $25.00

2350 Plate, 7"
crystal $12.00
amber..........$20.00
green..........$22.00
blue $25.00

2290 Plate, 8"
crystal $14.00
amber..........$22.00
green..........$25.00
blue $28.00

2283 Plate, 8"
crystal $14.00
amber..........$22.00
green..........$25.00
blue $28.00

2350 Plate, 8"
crystal $14.00
amber..........$22.00
green..........$25.00
blue $28.00

2283 Plate, 9"
crystal $24.00
amber..........$28.00
green..........$34.00
blue $46.00

2350 Plate, 9"
crystal $24.00
amber..........$28.00
green..........$34.00
blue $45.00

2283 Plate, 10"
crystal $45.00
amber..........$52.00

green $64.00
blue $80.00

2350 Plate, 10"
crystal $45.00
amber $52.00
green $64.00
blue $80.00

2290 Plate, 13"
crystal $67.00
amber $72.00
green $85.00
blue $125.00

2321 Plate, 8", salad
crystal $14.00
amber $20.00
green $25.00
blue $28.00

2316 Plate, 8", soup
crystal $14.00
amber $20.00
green $24.00
blue $28.00

2350 Plate, 13", chop
crystal $67.00
amber $72.00
green $85.00
blue $125.00

2350 Plate, 15", chop
crystal $75.00
amber $95.00
green $110.00
blue $135.00

2350 Platter, 10½"
crystal $45.00
amber $56.00
green $68.00
blue $87.00

2350 Platter, 12"
crystal $48.00
amber $60.00
green $68.00
blue $95.00

2350 Platter, 15"
crystal $75.00
amber $95.00
green $110.00
blue $135.00

2350 Sauce Boat and Plate
crystal $60.00
amber $72.00
green $85.00
blue $150.00

5000 Shaker, FGT, pair
crystal $95.00
amber $125.00
green $135.00
blue $200.00

2315 Sugar and Cream
crystal $75.00
amber $125.00
green $150.00
blue $200.00

2350 Sugar and Cream
crystal $58.00
amber $64.00
green $70.00
blue $135.00

2350½ Sugar, with cover and cream
crystal $75.00
amber $85.00
green $94.00
blue $150.00

2287 Tray, handled, lunch
crystal $120.00
amber $145.00
green $157.00
blue $195.00

2324 Urn, small
crystal $130.00
amber $150.00
green $165.00
blue $195.00

2276 Vanity Set
crystal $195.00
amber $264.00
green $300.00
blue $450.00
ebony $300.00

2292 Vase, 8", footed, flared
crystal $175.00
amber $220.00
green $265.00
blue $395.00

Royal Garden, Cutting 704

1931 – 1932

Tableware I, 274

2430 Bowl, 11"
crystal $50.00
topaz $55.00

2394 Bowl A, 12"
crystal $54.00
topaz $60.00

2433 Bowl A, 12"
crystal $95.00
topaz $110.00

2394 Candlestick, 2", pair
crystal $65.00
topaz $72.00

I2433 Candlestick, 3", pair
crystal $110.00
topaz $125.00

2430 Candlestick, 9½", pair
crystal $140.00
topaz $165.00

2447 Candlestick, duo, pair
crystal $95.00
topaz $115.00

2430 Jar, candy and cover, ½ pound
crystal $75.00
topaz $87.00

2433 Comport, 6", tall
crystal $125.00
topaz $140.00

2443 Ice Tub, 6"
crystal $64.00
topaz $75.00

2375 Plate, 10", cake
crystal $64.00
topaz $75.00

2419 Tray, handled, lunch
crystal $75.00
topaz $87.00

2430 Vase, 8"
crystal $88.00
topaz $100.00

4107 Vase, 12"
crystal $150.00
topaz $195.00

4108 Vase, 6"
crystal $65.00
topaz $76.00

Rutledge, 6036

1951 – 1973

Stemware, 103

6036 Goblet $20.00
6036 Sherbet, high $18.00
6036 Sherbet, low $14.00
6036 Parfait $18.00
6036 Cocktail $18.00
6036 Claret-Wine $23.00
6036 Cordial $25.00
6036 Oyster Cocktail $10.00
6036 Ice Tea, footed $20.00
6036 Juice, footed $10.00

Rye, Plate Etching 321

1935 – 1936

Useful & Ornamental, 2526

319 Bottle, bar and stopper, 29 oz. $65.00
322 Bottle, bar and stopper, 26 oz. $65.00
1918 Decanter and Stopper, 24 oz. $68.00
1918 Decanter and Stopper, 24 oz., handled $75.00
1928 Bottle, pinch and stopper, 24 oz. $67.00
2052 Bottle, pinch and stopper, 29 oz. $68.00

—S—

St. Regis, Decoration 616

1939 – 1943

Stemware, 84

6012 Goblet $38.00
6012 Sherbet, high $34.00
6012 Sherbet, low $28.00
6012 Cocktail $34.00
6012 Claret $42.00
6012 Wine $42.00
6012 Cordial $45.00
6012 Oyster Cocktail $26.00
6012 Ice Tea, footed $38.00
6012 Tumbler, 10 oz., footed $28.00
6012 Juice, footed $30.00
4132 Tumbler .... $15.00 – 30.00

St. Regis, Cutting 873

1939 – 1943

Stemware, 117

6083 Goblet $24.00
6083 Sherbet $22.00
6083 Wine/Cocktail $26.00
6083 Cordial $28.00
6083 Ice Tea, footed $24.00
6083 Juice, footed $20.00
2337 Plate, 7" $8.00
2337 Plate, 8" $10.00

Salad Dressing and Oil Bottles

Pre-1924 – 1943

Useful & Ornamental, 178

312 Plain or CN, optic $32.00
1465 Plain or CN, 5 oz., optic $32.00
1465 Plain or CN, 7 oz., optic $32.00
2083 Bottle, salad dressing, plain or optic, "Vinegar and Oil" optional
crystal $58.00
amber $64.00
green $85.00
rose $125.00
azure $125.00
topaz $95.00
2056 see American
2169 Bottle, salad dressing $67.00
2375 see Fairfax
2412 see Colony
2449 see Hermitage
2510 see Sunray
2560 see Coronet
2574 see Raleigh
2630 see Century
2666 see Contour

Salon, Cutting 804

1940 – 1943

Stemware, 98

6027 Goblet $25.00
6027 Saucer Champagne $24.00
6027 Sherbet, low $20.00
6027 Cocktail $24.00
6027 Wine $28.00
6027 Cordial $35.00
6027 Oyster Cocktail $16.00
6027 Ice Tea, footed $25.00
6027 Juice, footed $20.00

Tableware I, 304

4024 Bowl, finger $18.00
2364 Bowl, 13", fruit $65.00
6023 Candlestick, duo, pair $75.00
6011 Jug $195.00
2337 Plate, 7" $8.00
2337 Plate, 8" $10.00

Salts, Open, see Shakers and Open Salts

Sampler, Etching 337

1939 – 1943

Stemware, 96

6025 Goblet $34.00
6025 Sherbet $32.00
6025 Cocktail $32.00
6025 Claret-Wine $36.00
6025 Cordial $45.00
6025 Oyster Cocktail $28.00
6025 Ice Tea, footed $34.00
6025 Juice, footed $30.00

Tableware II, 133

2574 Bonbon $34.00
766 Bowl, finger $26.00
2574 Bowl, 8½", serving $45.00
6023 Bowl, 9¼", footed $97.00
2574 Bowl, 9½", handled $58.00
2574 Bowl, 12", flared $67.00
2574 Bowl, 13", fruit $75.00
2574 Candlestick, 4", pair $76.00
2324 Candlestick, 6", pair $85.00
2574 Celery, 10½" $38.00
2574 Comport, 5" $58.00
6023 Comport, 5" $58.00
2574 Cup and Saucer $28.00
2574 Ice Tub $48.00
2574 Lemon $30.00
2574 Mayonnaise, plate, ladle $67.00
2574 Oil, 4½ oz, GS $85.00
2574 Olive, 6" $20.00
2574 Pickle, 8" $25.00
6011 Jug $295.00
2574 Plate, 6" $12.00
2574 Plate, 7" $18.00
2574 Plate, 8" $20.00
2574 Plate, 9" $42.00
2574 Plate, 10", cake $54.00
2574 Plate, 14", torte $65.00
2574 Relish, 3-part $60.00
2574 Shaker, FGT, pair $85.00
2574 Sugar and Cream $65.00
2574 Sugar and Cream, individual $65.00
2574 Sweetmeat $34.00
2574 Tray, handled, muffin $54.00
2574 Whip Cream $34.00

San Francisco (Imported Stemware)

1984 – 1986

Tableware II, 282 – 283

Goblet $22.00
Wine $22.00
Flute $22.00
Ice Tea $22.00
Salad Bowl $22.00
Vase $22.00
Pitcher $25.00
Carafe, wine $25.00
Decanter $25.00
Box, candy $25.00

Satin Mist/Swirl

1978 – 1979

Tableware II, 304

Satin Mist

238 Bowl, 11", salad
crystal $22.00
pink $22.00
blue $22.00
504 Salad/Dessert, 6"
crystal $12.00
pink $12.00
blue $12.00

Swirl

223 Bowl, 10¾", salad
crystal $22.00
apple green $22.00
amber $22.00
504 Salad/Dessert, 6"
crystal $12.00
apple green $12.00
amber $12.00

Satin Ribbons, SA05

Year

Stemware, 186

SA05 Goblet, 10 oz. $30.00
SA05 Champagne, 8 oz. $28.00
SA05 Wine, 7 oz. $32.00
SA05 Flute/Parfait, 8 oz. $45.00
SA05 Ice Tea, 14 oz., footed $30.00

Tableware II, 294

SA05/293 Box, jewel and cover $25.00
SA05/293 Place Card Holder $15.00

Saturn, Decoration 69

1927

Tableware I, 326

2324 Bowl, 10"
amber $54.00
blue $58.00
green $54.00
2297 Bowl A, 10¼", shallow bowl
amber $54.00
blue $58.00
green $54.00
2297 Bowl C, 10½", deep
amber $54.00
blue $58.00
green $54.00
2315 Bowl A, 10½"
amber $56.00
blue $60.00
green $56.00
2297 Bowl A, 12", deep
amber $56.00
blue $60.00
green $56.00
2362 Bowl, 12½"
amber $58.00
blue $65.00
green $60.00
2362 Candlestick, 3", pair
amber $65.00
blue $78.00
green $67.00
2324 Candlestick, 4", pair
amber $65.00
blue $75.00
green $65.00
2324 Candlestick, 6", pair
amber $74.00
blue $80.00
green $74.00
2324 Candlestick, 9", pair
amber $95.00
blue $110.00
green $95.00
2331 Box, candy and cover
amber $85.00
blue $120.00
green $95.00

2219	Jar, candy and cover, ½ pound	
	amber	$85.00
	blue	$95.00
	green	$85.00
2350	Jar, candy and cover, ½ pound	
	amber	$80.00
	blue	$90.00
	green	$84.00
2329	Centerpiece, 11"	
	amber	$85.00
	blue	$95.00
	green	$90.00
371	Centerpiece, oval	
	amber	$115.00
	blue	$135.00
	green	$120.00
2368	Cheese and Cracker	
	amber	$78.00
	blue	$95.00
	green	$84.00
2327	Comport, 7"	
	amber	$54.00
	blue	$65.00
	green	$58.00
2350	Comport, 8"	
	amber	$54.00
	blue	$65.00
	green	$58.00
2380	Confection and Cover	
	amber	$65.00
	blue	$78.00
	green	$68.00
2315	Mayonnaise and Plate	
	amber	$37.00
	blue	$46.00
	green	$40.00
2347½	Puff and Cover	
	amber	$145.00
	blue	$165.00
	green	$154.00
2287	Tray, lunch	
	amber	$82.00
	blue	$95.00
	green	$87.00
2276	Vanity Set	
	amber	$175.00
	blue	$250.00
	green	$195.00
2292	Vase, 8"	
	amber	$95.00
	blue	$125.00
	green	$110.00

Saturn, Decoration 605

1931 – 1932

Ebony base, black enamel lines

Stemware, 59

4020	Goblet	$45.00
4020	Sherbet, high	$45.00
4020	Sherbet, 7 oz., low	$40.00
4020	Sherbet, 5 oz., low	$40.00
4020	Cocktail, 3½ oz.	$40.00
4020	Ice Tea, footed	$45.00
4020	Tumbler, 13 oz., footed	$45.00
4020	Tumbler, 10 oz., footed	$40.00
4020	Juice, footed	$40.00
4020	Whiskey, footed	$45.00

Tableware I, 330

4021	Bowl, finger	$35.00
2350	Cup, after dinner and 2419 Saucer, after dinner	$47.00
2350½	Cup and 2419 Saucer	$32.00
4020	Jug, footed	$395.00
2419	Plate, 6"	$14.00
2419	Plate, 7"	$16.00
2419	Plate, 8"	$20.00
4020	Sugar and Cream, footed	$85.00

Savannah, Cutting 902

1964 – 1968

Stemware, 129

6104	Goblet	$28.00
6104	Sherbet	$26.00
6104	Claret	$30.00
6104	Wine	$30.00
6104	Cordial	$38.00
6104	Ice Tea, footed	$28.00
2337	Plate, 7"	$8.00
2337	Plate, 8"	$10.00

Saybrooke, Cutting 813

1941 – 1943

Stemware, 99

6029	Goblet	$22.00
6029	Saucer Champagne	$20.00
6029	Cocktail	$18.00
6029	Claret	$24.00
6029	Wine	$24.00
6029	Cordial	$30.00
6029	Oyster Cocktail	$14.00
6011	Jug	$175.00
2337	Plate, 6"	$7.00
2337	Plate, 7"	$8.00
2337	Plate, 8"	$10.00

Sceptre, 6017

1939 – 1991

Stemware, 89

6017	Goblet	
	crystal	$22.00
	azure bowl	$40.00
	gold tint bowl	$40.00
6017	Sherbet, high	
	crystal	$20.00
	azure bowl	$35.00
	gold tint bowl	$35.00
6017	Sherbet, low	
	crystal	$18.00
	azure bowl	$30.00
	gold tint bowl	$30.00
6017	Cocktail	
	crystal	$20.00
	azure bowl	$35.00
	gold tint bowl	$35.00
6017	Claret	
	crystal	$24.00
	azure bowl	$45.00
	gold tint bowl	$45.00
6017	Wine	
	crystal	$24.00
	azure bowl	$42.00
	gold tint bowl	$42.00
6017	Cordial	
	crystal	$30.00
	azure bowl	$52.00
	gold tint bowl	$52.00
6017	Oyster Cocktail	
	crystal	$14.00
	azure bowl	$28.00
	gold tint bowl	$28.00
6017	Tumbler, 14 oz., footed	
	crystal	$20.00
6017	Ice Tea, footed	
	crystal	$20.00
	azure bowl	$40.00
	gold tint bowl	$40.00
6017	Tumbler, 9 oz., footed	
	crystal	$18.00
	azure bowl	$30.00
	gold tint bowl	$30.00
6017	Juice, footed	
	crystal	$18.00
	azure bowl	$30.00
	gold tint bowl	$30.00
4132	Tumbler	
	crystal	$10.00
	azure	$20.00
	gold tint	$20.00
6011	Jug	
	crystal	$145.00

Sculpture, 2570 – 2745

1961 – 1971

Crystal, Gray Mist

Tableware II, 59 – 60

2570/795	Basket, 17"	$38.00
2745/208	Bowl, 5¾", ruffled	$21.00
2756/208	Bowl, 5¾", Triton	$22.00
2740/168	Bowl, 8", Spire	$28.00
2745/183	Bowl, 8½", trindle	$26.00
2743/179	Bowl, 10¾", Petal	$32.00
2740/126	Bowl, 13½", oblong	$35.00
2744/174	Bowl, 13½", Tricorne	$35.00
2741/266	Bowl, 14", oval	$35.00
2570/189	Bowl, 14", Shell	$38.00
2740/415	Bowl, 14", float	$35.00
2741/279	Bowl, 18", lineal	$38.00
2742/311	Candleholder, 3½", pair	$22.00
2757/313	Candle Twist, 2", pair	$22.00
2756/168	Cosmic, 8½"	$28.00
2743/767	Vase, 7¼", Star	$24.00
2745/758	Vase, 8¼", Florette	$24.00
2741/755	Vase, 11½", pinch	$32.00
2744/830	Vase, 12½", swung	$48.00

Seascape, 2685 Vintage, Plate Etching 237

1954 – 1997

Caribee Blue, Coral Sand

Asterisk indicates made with Vintage etching.

Tableware II, 83 – 86

2685 Bowl, square $85.00
*Bowl, footed $110.00
2685 Bowl, Pansy $30.00
*Bowl, 10", salad $55.00
*Bowl, 8", shallow $75.00
*Bowl, 11½", shallow $95.00
*Candleholder, pair $125.00
2685 Mayonnaise, plate, ladle $125.00
*Plate, 14", buffet $130.00
*Preserve, handled $88.00
2685 Relish, 2-part $60.00
Relish, 3-part $74.00
2685 *Salver $157.00
2685 Sugar and Cream $98.00
2685 Sugar and Cream, individual $98.00
2685 Tray, sugar and cream $25.00
2685 Sugar and Cream and Tray, individual set $125.00
*Tray, mint $58.00
*Tray, oval $64.00

Sea Shells Line, 2844

1971 – 1973

Tableware II, 103, 105 – 106

2844/172
Bowl, 7", rolled edge
crystal $30.00
copper blue $48.00
green $48.00
2844/758
Bowl, 7½", shallow
crystal $30.00
copper blue $45.00
green $45.00
2844/193
Bowl, 8½", rolled edge
crystal $38.00
copper blue $50.00
green $50.00
2844/208
Bowl, 10", flared edge
crystal $65.00
copper blue $125.00
green $125.00
2844/231
Bowl, 11", flared
crystal $65.00
copper blue $125.00
green $125.00
2844/257
Bowl, 12½", rolled edge
crystal $85.00
copper blue $175.00
green $175.00
2844/275
Bowl, 15", rolled edge
crystal $75.00
copper blue $157.00
green $157.00
2844/311
Candlestick, 2⅝", flora, pair
crystal $54.00
copper blue $87.00
green $87.00
2844/317
Candlestick, 3½", flared, pair
crystal $54.00
copper blue $84.00
green $84.00
2803/380
Coaster, Shell
crystal $8.00
black pearl $12.00
lemon twist $12.00
2823/421
Dessert, Shell
crystal luster $12.00
black pearl luster $15.00
lemon twist luster $15.00
2825/201
Shell, 9½", small
crystal $40.00
copper blue $55.00
green $55.00
2825/259
Shell, 13", medium
crystal $65.00
copper blue $78.00
green $78.00
2825/280
Shell, 18", large
crystal $78.00
copper blue $125.00
green $125.00
2844/575
Plate, 17", torte
crystal $78.00
copper blue $125.00
green $125.00
2844/751
Vase, 4"
crystal $30.00
copper blue $35.00
green $35.00
2844/785
Vase, 8"
crystal $57.00
copper blue $68.00
green $68.00
2825/139
Seashell, small, pair $150.00
2825/140
Seashell, large, pair $185.00

Seaweed, Cutting 732

1934 – 1935

Stemware, 60

4024 Goblet, 11 oz. $28.00
4024 Goblet, 10 oz. $28.00
4024 Saucer Champagne $28.00
4024 Sherbet $24.00
4024 Cocktail $24.00
4024 Claret-Wine $30.00
4024 Rhine Wine $30.00
4024 Sherry $30.00
4024 Cordial $35.00
4024 Oyster Cocktail $20.00
4024 Ice Tea, footed $28.00
4024 Tumbler, 8 oz., footed $20.00
4024 Juice, footed $20.00
4024 Whiskey, footed $32.00
906 Brandy Inhaler $35.00
795 Champagne, hollow stem $30.00
701 Tumbler, 12 oz. $20.00
701 Tumbler, 10 oz. $18.00
887 Tumbler, 1¾ oz., whiskey $18.00
1184 Old Fashioned Cocktail, 7 oz. $16.00
4122 Whiskey, 1½ oz. $16.00

Tableware I, 280

869 Bowl, finger $16.00
4024 Bowl, 10", footed $45.00
4024 Candlestick, 6", pair $48.00
4024 Comport, 5" $20.00
6011 Decanter $135.00
6011 Jug $265.00
2337 Plate, 6" $7.00
2337 Plate, 7" $8.00
2337 Plate, 8" $10.00

Selma, Cutting 800

1940 – 1943

Stemware, 97

6026 Goblet $35.00
6026 Goblet, low $26.00
6026 Saucer Champagne $30.00
6026 Sherbet, low $24.00
6026 Cocktail $30.00
6026 Claret-Wine $43.00
6026 Cordial $55.00
6026 Oyster Cocktail $22.00
6026 Ice Tea, footed $35.00
6026 Juice, footed $26.00

Tableware I, 304

869 Bowl, finger $15.00
6023 Bowl, footed $77.00
6023 Candlestick, duo, pair $75.00
5000 Jug $275.00
2337 Plate, 7" $10.00
2337 Plate, 8" $16.00

Sentimental, Crystal Print 25

1971 – 1975

Stemware, 122

6097 Goblet $28.00
6097 Sherbet $26.00
6097 Claret $30.00
6097 Ice Tea, footed $28.00
2337 Plate, 7" $8.00

Serenade, Cutting 864

1959 – 1965

Stemware, 118

6086 Goblet $28.00
6086 Sherbet $25.00
6086 Wine/Cocktail $30.00
6086 Cordial $38.00
6086 Ice Tea, footed $28.00
6086 Juice, footed $23.00

Serendipity Line

1972 – 1974

Tableware II, 276 – 277

2825/139
Bookends, Shell, small, pair $135.00
2825/140
Bookends, Shell, large, pair $165.00

Serendipity Line

2842/112
Ashtray/Candle, 2" $30.00
2842/124
Ashtray, 9½" $38.00
2842/311
Candleholder, individual, pair .. $38.00
2842/327
Candleholder, 9½", pair $38.00
2842/539
Paperweight $34.00
2856/117
Ashtray B, 7" $38.00
2856/118
Ashtray D, 7" $38.00
2856/139
Bookend A, 5", pair $65.00
2856/140
Bookend B, 5", pair $65.00
2856/141
Bookend E, 5", pair $75.00
2856/539
Paperweight A, 6" $35.00
2856/545
Paperweight B, 6" $35.00
2856/546
Paperweight C, 6" $35.00
2856/547
Paperweight D, 6" $35.00
2857/124
Ashtray, 10" $40.00
2857/117
Ashtray, 7" $37.00
2858/152
Bowl, 5", crimp $28.00
2858/178
Bowl, 8", crimp $38.00
2858/207
Bowl, 10", crimp $45.00
2866/313
Candle, 2", pair $30.00
2866/315
Candle, 4", pair $34.00
2866/319
Candle, 6", pair $38.00
2868/539
Paperweight, Family, 4", Child, ... $95.00
2868/545
Paperweight, Family 5½", Mother, ... $115.00
2868/546
Paperweight, Family 7½", Father $125.00

Serenity, Etching 35

1975 – 1982

Stemware, 142

6127 Goblet
crystal $34.00
yellow bowl $35.00
blue bowl $38.00
6127 Champagne
crystal $32.00
yellow bowl $34.00
blue bowl $35.00
6127 Wine
crystal $38.00
yellow bowl $4000
blue bowl $40.00
6127 Ice Tea, footed
crystal $34.00
yellow bowl $35.00
blue bowl $38.00

Serenity, Cutting 868

1958 – 1965

Stemware, 114

6072 Goblet $30.00
6072 Sherbet $27.00
6072 Cocktail/Wine/Seafood $30.00
6072 Cordial $40.00
6072 Ice Tea, footed $30.00
6072 Juice, footed $26.00

Tableware

2337 Plate, 7" $8.00
2337 Plate, 8" $10.00

Seville, Plate Etching 274

1926 – 1933

Stemware, 32

870 Goblet
crystal $30.00
amber $30.00
green $32.00
870 Sherbet, high
crystal $28.00
amber $28.00
green $30.00
870 Sherbet, low
crystal $26.00
amber $26.00
green $27.00
870 Parfait
crystal $32.00
amber $32.00
green $35.00
870 Cocktail
crystal $26.00
amber $26.00
green $28.00
870 Wine
crystal $32.00
amber $32.00
green $36.00
870 Cordial
crystal $45.00
amber $45.00
green $52.00
870 Oyster Cocktail
crystal $22.00
amber $22.00
green $26.00
5084 Tumbler, 12 oz., footed
crystal $30.00
amber $30.00
green $32.00
5084 Tumbler, 9 oz., footed
crystal $26.00
amber $26.00
green $27.00
5084 Tumbler, 5 oz., footed
crystal $22.00
amber $22.00
green $26.00
5084 Tumbler, 2 oz., footed
crystal $30.00
amber $30.00
green $32.00

Tableware I, 156 – 158

2350 Ashtray, small
crystal $20.00
amber $22.00
green $24.00
2350½ Bouillon
crystal $12.00
amber $15.00
green $15.00
2350 Bowl, 5", fruit
crystal $24.00
amber $26.00
green $28.00
2350 Bowl, 6", cereal
crystal $25.00
amber $28.00
green $30.00
2350 Bowl, 7", soup
crystal $26.00
amber $30.00
green $32.00
2350 Bowl, 8", nappy
crystal $34.00
amber $37.00
green $42.00
2350 Bowl, 9", nappy
crystal $36.00
amber $40.00
green $45.00
2350 Bowl, 9", oval, baker
crystal $40.00
amber $44.00
green $52.00
869 Bowl, finger and 2283 Plate
crystal $20.00
amber $22.00
green $26.00
2267 Bowl, 7", low, footed
crystal $34.00
amber $38.00
green $45.00
2324 Bowl, 10", footed
crystal $85.00
amber $95.00
green $115.00
2350 Bowl, 10", salad
crystal $70.00
amber $75.00
green $87.00
2315 Bowl, 10½", flared
crystal $75.00
amber $80.00
green $88.00
2350 Bowl, 10½", oval, baker
crystal $54.00
amber $58.00
green $67.00
2297 Bowl A, 12"
crystal $80.00
amber $85.00
green $94.00
2350 Butter and Cover
crystal $115.00
amber $130.00
green $145.00
2324 Candlestick, 2", pair
crystal $58.00
amber $64.00
green $70.00
2324 Candlestick, 4", pair
crystal $58.00
amber $65.00
green $74.00

2324 Candlestick, 9", pair
crystal $78.00
amber $85.00
green $94.00

2250 Jar, candy and cover, ½ pound
crystal $85.00
amber $95.00
green $110.00

2329 Centerpiece, 11", round
crystal $85.00
amber $95.00
green $110.00

2329 Centerpiece, 13", round
crystal $95.00
amber $125.00
green $135.00

2371 Centerpiece, 13", oval and flower holder
crystal $135.00
amber $160.00
green $174.00

2350 Celery
crystal $38.00
amber $43.00
green $46.00

2368 Cheese and Cracker
crystal $95.00
amber $110.00
green $125.00

2327 Comport, 7"
crystal $67.00
amber $75.00
green $85.00

2350 Comport, 8"
crystal $65.00
amber $72.00
green $80.00

2350 Cream Soup and Plate
crystal $30.00
amber $36.00
green $40.00

2350 Cup and Saucer
crystal $22.00
amber $25.00
green $28.00

2350 Cup and Saucer, after dinner
crystal $26.00
amber $32.00
green $37.00

2350½ Cup and Saucer
crystal $22.00
amber $25.00
green $27.00

2315 Grapefruit, same as Mayonnaise
crystal $28.00
amber $34.00
green $42.00

2378 Ice Bucket, NP handle
crystal $88.00
amber $95.00
green $98.00

5084 Jug
crystal $225.00
amber $260.00
green $275.00

2315 Mayonnaise, same as Grapefruit
crystal $28.00
amber $34.00
green $42.00

2350 Pickle
crystal $24.00
amber $28.00
green $30.00

2350 Plate, 6"
crystal $12.00
amber $16.00
green $18.00

2350 Plate, 7"
crystal $12.00
amber $18.00
green $20.00

2350 Plate, 8"
crystal $12.00
amber $20.00
green $22.00

2350 Plate, 9"
crystal $22.00
amber $30.00
green $35.00

2350 Plate, 10"
crystal $35.00
amber $45.00
green $50.00

2350 Plate, 13", chop
crystal $60.00
amber $70.00
green $76.00

2350 Plate, 15", round
crystal $68.00
amber $76.00
green $85.00

2350 Platter, 10½"
crystal $42.00
amber $48.00
green $57.00

2350 Platter, 12"
crystal $48.00
amber $57.00
green $64.00

2350 Platter, 15"
crystal $75.00
amber $87.00
green $98.00

2350 Sauce Boat and Plate
crystal $58.00
amber $67.00
green $75.00

5000 Shaker, FGT, pair
crystal $95.00
amber $125.00
green $140.00

2315½ Sugar and Cream
crystal $60.00
amber $68.00
green $72.00

2350½ Sugar and Cream
crystal $60.00
amber $68.00
green $72.00

2350½ Sugar and Cover
crystal $47.00
amber $54.00
green $58.00

2287 Tray, handled, lunch
crystal $85.00
amber $95.00
green $110.00

2324 Urn, small
crystal $95.00
amber $120.00
green $135.00

2292 Vase, 8"
crystal $137.00
amber $175.00
green $200.00

2331 Box, candy and cover
crystal $95.00
amber $125.00
green $138.00

Shakers and Open Salts, Shaker Collection

Pre-1924 – 1982
Tableware II, 305; Useful & Ornamental, 179 – 182
Priced as pair

614 Shaker, FGT
crystal $32.00

713½ Shaker, FGT
crystal $32.00
amber $37.00
green $39.00

800 Shaker, FGT
crystal $32.00

880 Salt, footed, open
crystal $22.00

1913½ Salt, open
amber $22.00
green $22.00
blue $26.00

2022 Shaker $45.00
2056 Shaker, see American

2111 Shaker, FGT
crystal $28.00
amber $32.00
blue $45.00
green $34.00
canary $45.00
rose $35.00
azure $37.00
topaz/gold tint $35.00
orchid $35.00

2127 Shaker, FGT
crystal $28.00
amber $32.00
blue $45.00
green $34.00
canary $45.00

2128 Shaker, FGT
crystal $28.00
amber $32.00
blue $45.00
green $34.00
canary $45.00

2222 Salt, footed, Colonial $18.00

2235 Shaker, FGT or plated top
crystal $32.00
regal blue $45.00
burgund $45.00
empire green $45.00

2236 Shaker, FGT
amber $38.00
green $40.00
rose $45.00
topaz/gold tint $40.00

2263 Salt, individual, open
crystal $20.00

2364 Shaker, see Sonata
2375 Shaker, footed, FGT, see Fairfax
2412 Shaker, see Colony
2419 Shaker, FGT, see Mayfair
2449 Shaker, see Hermitage
2496 Shaker, FGT, see Baroque
2510 Shaker, see Sunray

2521 Salt, Bird
crystal $20.00
regal blue $38.00

burgundy ... $38.00
empire green ... $38.00
ruby ... $38.00
Milk glass, see Milk Glass
2560 Shaker, see Coronet
2574 Shaker, see Raleigh
2593 Salt, individual
crystal ... $22.00
2630 Shaker, see Century
2666 Shaker, see Contour
2719 Shaker, see Jamestown
4020 Shaker, SPT
crystal ... $77.00
amber base ... $98.00
green base ... $125.00
rose bowl ... $125.00
topaz bowl ... $125.00
ebony base ... $110.00
wisteria base ... $145.00
4095 Salt, individual footed
crystal, RO ... $20.00
crystal, SO ... $22.00
amber, RO ... $25.00
amber foot, LO ... $25.00
green, RO, SO ... $28.00
green foot, SO ... $28.00
blue, RO ... $35.00
blue foot, RO ... $30.00
rose bowl, RO ... $28.00
azure bowl, RO ... $30.00
topaz bowl ... $30.00
5100 Shaker, optic, SPT, FGT
crystal ... $64.00
amber foot ... $95.00
solid amber ... $95.00
blue foot ... $125.00
solid blue ... $125.00
green foot ... $110.00
solid green ... $110.00
AM01/649
American, chrome top A ... $32.00
AM01/650
American, individual, chrome top C ... $38.00
CE01/649
Century, chrome top B ... $28.00
CE01/650
Century, individual, chrome top C ... $32.00
CO01/649
Coin, chrome top E ... $54.00
CO13/649
Colonial Prism, chrome top G ... $28.00
FA04/649
Facet, chrome top A ... $45.00
LE07/649
Leonardo, chrome top F ... $27.00
MA07/649
Madison, chrome top G ... $27.00
RE12/649
Revere, chrome top F ... $15.00
RO06/649
Rosby, chrome top G ... $36.00
SA04/649
Salem, chrome top F ... $27.00
TE02/659
Teardrop, chrome top C ... $25.00
TR05/649
Transition, chrome top G ... $26.00
WO01/659
Woodland, chrome top A ... $27.00
YO01/659
York, chrome top C ... $25.00

Sheffield, Decoration 653

1961 – 1982

Stemware, 122

6097 Goblet ... $34.00
6097 Sherbet ... $30.00
6097 Claret ... $45.00
6097 Wine/Cocktail ... $40.00
6097 Cordial ... $45.00
6097 Ice Tea, footed ... $34.00
6097 Juice, footed ... $29.00
6097 Magnum ... $55.00

Tableware II, 196 – 197

4185/495
Bowl, dessert/finger ... $18.00
2364/195
Bowl, 9", salad ... $32.00
2785/224
Bowl, 10", footed ... $35.00
2324/315
Candlestick, 4", pair ... $48.00
2666/396
Cup and Saucer ... $26.00
2364/477
Mayonnaise, plate, ladle ... $58.00
2337/549
Plate, 7" ... $9.00
2337/549
Plate, 8" ... $12.00
2785/620
Relish, 2-part ... $32.00
2785/643
Relish, 4-part ... $35.00
2785/644
Relish, 5-part ... $42.00
2666/677
Sugar and Cream ... $40.00
2666/686
Sugar and Cream, individual ... $35.00
2666 Tray, individual sugar and cream ... $10.00

Shell Pearl, Decoration 633

1954 – 1974

Mother-of-pearl decoration

Stemware, 108

6055 Goblet ... $35.00
6055 Sherbet ... $30.00
6055 Cocktail ... $30.00
6055 Claret-Wine ... $40.00
6055 Cordial ... $45.00
6055 Oyster Cocktail ... $22.00
6055 Ice Tea, footed ... $35.00
6055 Juice, footed ... $25.00

Tableware II, 200

2666 Bowl, oval ... $45.00
2666 Candle, flora, pair ... $56.00
2666 Mayonnaise, plate, ladle ... $68.00
2337 Plate, 7", LO ... $18.00
2666 Plate, canape ... $35.00
2666 Plate, 10", snack ... $45.00
2666 Plate, 14", serving ... $67.00
2666 Relish, 2-part ... $38.00
2666 Relish, 3-part ... $50.00
2364 Shaker, large, chrome top B, pair ... $75.00
2666 Sugar and Cream ... $58.00
2666 Sugar and Cream, individual and tray ... $65.00

Sheraton, Etching 317

1933 – 1938

Stemware, 80

6010 Goblet ... $34.00
6010 Sherbet, high ... $28.00
6010 Sherbet, low ... $25.00
6010 Cocktail ... $28.00
6010 Claret-Wine ... $36.00
6010 Cordial ... $48.00
6010 Oyster Cocktail ... $22.00
6010 Ice Tea, footed ... $34.00
6010 Tumbler, 9 oz., footed ... $22.00
6010 Juice, footed ... $22.00
869 Bowl, finger ... $22.00
2283 Plate, 5" ... $6.00
2337 Plate, 7" ... $8.00
2337 Plate, 8" ... $10.00

Sheraton, 6097

1961 – 1982

Stemware, 122

6097 Goblet ... $24.00
6097 Sherbet ... $22.00
6097 Claret ... $27.00
6097 Wine/Cocktail ... $26.00
6097 Cordial ... $36.00
6097 Ice Tea, footed ... $24.00
6097 Juice, footed ... $22.00
833½ Highball ... $22.00
833½ Old Fashioned, double ... $24.00

Sherman, Needle Etching 77

1925 – 1930

Stemware, 31

869 Goblet ... $20.00
869 Saucer Champagne ... $20.00
869 Sherbet, high ... $20.00
869 Sherbet, low ... $10.00
869 Fruit ... $10.00
869 Parfait ... $22.00
869 Cocktail ... $10.00
869 Wine ... $12.00
869 Cordial ... $25.00
869 Oyster Cocktail ... $8.00
4095 Oyster Cocktail ... $10.00
869 Tumbler, 12 oz., table, handled, ... $14.00
869 Tumbler, 12 oz. ... $12.00
869 Tumbler, 5 oz. ... $8.00
869 Tumbler, 2 oz. ... $10.00
4095 Tumbler, footed ... $8.00 – 14.00
5000 Tumbler, 12 oz., footed ... $12.00
5000 Tumbler, 9 oz., footed ... $10.00
5000 Tumbler, 5 oz., footed ... $8.00
5000 Tumbler, 2½ oz., footed ... $12.00

Tableware I, 122

869 Bowl, finger and 2283 Plate ... $18.00
5078 Comport, 5" ... $18.00
945½ Grapefruit and Liner ... $30.00
4095/7 Jug ... $85.00
2270/7 Jug and Cover ... $90.00
4095 Nappy, 5" ... $10.00
4095 Nappy, 6" ... $12.00
4095 Nappy, 7" ... $15.00
2283 Plate, 7" ... $6.00

2283 Plate, 8" $7.00

Shirley, Plate Etching, 331

1938 – 1956

Stemware, 89

6017 Goblet $35.00
6017 Sherbet, high $32.00
6017 Sherbet, low $28.00
6017 Cocktail $32.00
6017 Claret $45.00
6017 Wine $45.00
6017 Cordial $55.00
6017 Oyster Cocktail $25.00
6017 Tumbler, 14 oz., footed $28.00
6017 Ice Tea, footed $35.00
6017 Tumbler, 9 oz., footed $28.00
6017 Juice, footed $28.00

Tableware I, 254 – 256

2496 Bonbon $52.00
766 Bowl, finger $40.00
2496 Bowl, 5", fruit $32.00
2496 Bowl, 3-toed, nut $60.00
2496 Bowl, 9½", oval, vegetable $60.00
2496 Bowl, 10½", handled $125.00
2496 Bowl, 12", flared $80.00
2545 Bowl, 12½", oval $95.00
2496 Box, candy and cover $140.00
2545 Candelabra, 2-light, B prisms, pair $300.00
2496 Candlesticks, 4", pair $95.00
2545 Candlestick, 4½", pair $85.00
2545 Candlestick, lustre, UDP, pair $165.00
2496 Candlestick, duo, pair $145.00
2545 Candlestick, duo, pair $200.00
2496 Celery, 11" $58.00
2496 Cheese and Cracker $115.00
2496 Comport, 5½" $60.00
2496 Cream Soup and Plate $64.00
2496 Ice Bucket $125.00
6011 Jug $425.00
2496 Mayonnaise, 6½", 2-part $58.00
2496½ Mayonnaise, plate, ladle $125.00
2496 Nappy, 3-cornered $30.00
2496 Nappy, flared $30.00
2496 Nappy, regular $36.00
2496 Nappy, square $36.00
2496 Pickle, 8" $40.00
2337 Plate, 6" $14.00
2337 Plate, 7" $18.00
2337 Plate, 8" $24.00
2337 Plate, 9" $45.00
2496 Plate, 10", cake $85.00
2496 Plate, 14", torte $115.00
2496 Platter, 12" $125.00
2496 Relish, 2-part $54.00
2496 Relish, 3-part $68.00
2496 Sauce, oblong $125.00
2496 Shaker, FGT, pair $187.00
2496 Sugar and Cream $65.00
2496 Sugar and Cream, individual $65.00
2496 Tray, sugar and cream $50.00
2496 Sweetmeat $50.00
2545 Vase, 10" $265.00

Shooting Stars, Cutting 735

1934 – 1943

Stemware, 82

6011 Goblet $30.00
6011 Saucer Champagne $28.00
6011 Sherbet, low $24.00
6011 Cocktail $28.00
6011 Claret $34.00
6011 Rhine Wine $35.00
6011 Wine $34.00
6011 Sherry $32.00
6011 Crème de Menthe $28.00
6011 Brandy $35.00
6011 Cordial $40.00
6011 Oyster Cocktail $20.00
6011 Ice Tea, footed $28.00
6011 Tumbler, 10 oz., footed $28.00
6011 Juice, footed $24.00
6011 Whiskey, footed $32.00

Tableware I, 281

1769 Bowl, finger $14.00
4024 Bowl, 10", footed $35.00
4024 Candlestick, 6", pair $45.00
6011 Decanter $155.00
6011 Jug $195.00
2337 Plate, 6" $7.00
2337 Plate, 7" $8.00
2337 Plate, 8" $10.00

Sierra, 2816 Sierra Ice, Cutting 921

1969 – 1970

Tableware II, 103

110 Ashtray, 4½" $12.00
111 Ashtray, 5½" $15.00
178 Bowl, 8", accent $24.00
219 Centerpiece, 10", footed $60.00
325 Pedestal, 8", candle, single $75.00
630 Server, 11½", footed $60.00
645 Tri-Server, 6½" $26.00
757 Vase, 6", flora $30.00
768 Urn, 7", footed $54.00

Silhouette, 6102

1963 – 1982

Stemware, 126

6102 Goblet, 10 oz.
 crystal $28.00
 pink $35.00
6102 Goblet, 11 oz.
 crystal $32.00
6102 Sherbet
 crystal $26.00
 pink $32.00
6102 Claret
 crystal $30.00
 pink $40.00
6102 Tulip Wine
 crystal $30.00
 pink $40.00
6102 Brandy
 crystal $30.00
 pink $40.00
6102 Ice Tea, footed
 crystal $28.00
 pink $35.00
6102 Sherry
 crystal $35.00
6102 Flute, champagne
 crystal $35.00
6102 Claret, 10 oz., large
 crystal $35.00

SILHOUETTE CLASSICS (1980 – 1982)

Goblet, 11 oz.
 blue $34.00
 ebony $34.00
Sherry
 blue $40.00
 ebony $40.00
Flute, champagne
 blue $40.00
 ebony $40.00
Claret, 10 oz., large
 blue $40.00
 ebony $40.00

2337 Plate, 7", pink $12.00

Silver Flutes, 6037

1949 – 1971

Stemware, 104

6037 Goblet $30.00
6037 Goblet, low $28.00
6037 Sherbet, high $28.00
6037 Sherbet, low $24.00
6037 Parfait $34.00
6037 Cocktail $28.00
6037 Claret-Wine $36.00
6037 Cordial $45.00
6037 Oyster Cocktail $24.00
6037 Ice Tea, footed $30.00
6037 Juice, footed $24.00

Silver Mist Decoration 525

1934 – 1943

Useful & Ornamental, 183 – 184

2419 Ashtray $16.00
2457 Ashtray $16.00
2520 Ashtray $12.00
2534 Ashtray $12.00
2538 Ashtray/Place Card Holder $15.00
2538 Berry Set, 9 pieces: 11" nappy and eight 4½" nappies $65.00
2521 Bird $32.00
2494 Bottle, bitters $75.00
2517 Bonbon $18.00
2536 Bowl, 9", handled $65.00
2484 Bowl, 10", handled $110.00
4024 Bowl, 10", footed $75.00
4024 Candlestick, 6", silver mist base $85.00
2472 Candlestick, duo $87.00
2496 Candlestick, duo $75.00
2496 Candlestick, trindle $95.00
2484 Candlestick, 2-light $200.00
2484 Candlestick, 2-light with drip, see Candlesticks for photograph
2484½ Candle Drips, 3½" $12.00
2535 Candlestick, 5½" $48.00
4099 Jar, candy and cover $70.00
2511 Cheese and Cracker $38.00
2391 Box, cigarette, large and cover $47.00

5092 Cigarette $48.00
2518 Cocktail, 3 oz., footed $18.00
4115½ Cocktail, 4 oz., footed $15.00
2518 Cocktail Shaker, gold top $100.00
2518½ Cocktail Shaker, gold top $100.00
2525 Cocktail Shaker, gold top $78.00
2525½ Cocktail Shaker, gold top $78.00
2519 Cologne and Stopper $85.00
2589 Colt, standing $64.00
2589 Colt, reclining $64.00
4024 Comport, 5", silver mist base $38.00
4024 Cordial $85.00
2494 Cordial Set, 10 pieces: cordial tray, cordial bottle, 8 cordials $250.00
2494 Cordial Set, 7 pieces: Cordial Bottle, and six 4024 Cordials $235.00
2494 Decanter and Stopper $125.00
2502 Decanter and Stopper $125.00
2518 Decanter and Stopper $95.00
2502 Decanter Set, 7 pieces: Decanter and six 2502 Whiskeys $225.00
2589 Deer, standing $58.00
2589 Deer reclining $58.00
2585 Bookend,eagle, pair $500.00
2585 Bookend, eagle with stars carving, pair $550.00
2580 Bookend, elephant, pair $450.00
2492 Canape, fish, see Bar and Refreshment
2564 Bookend, horse, pair $300.00
2518 Jug $75.00
2517 Lemon $18.00
2440 Mayonnaise, 2-part, see Lafayette
2513 Mayonnaise, plate, crystal ladle $65.00
2513 Mint, 4", handled $22.00
2538 Nappy, 4½" $8.00
2538 Nappy, 6" $8.00
2538 Nappy, 11" $40.00
2531 Pelican $135.00
2531 Penguin $135.00
2440 Plate, 13", torte, see Lafayette
2531 Polar Bear $95.00
2513 Preserve, 5", handled $25.00
2519 Puff and Cover $85.00
2440 Relish, 2-part handled, see Lafayette
2440 Relish, 3-part handled, see Lafayette
2419 Relish, 4-part, see Mayfair
2419 Relish, 5-part, see Mayfair
2513 Relish, 2-part $27.00
2513 Relish, 3-part $30.00
2538 Salad Set, 9 pieces: 11", nappy and eight 6" nappies $88.00
2440 Dish, sauce, 6½", oval, see Lafayette
2497 Seafood Cocktail $25.00
2531 Seal $110.00
4024 Sherry $26.00
2497½ Sugar and Cream $64.00
2517 Sweetmeat $20.00
2429 Tray, cordial $88.00
2440 Tray, 8½", oval, see Lafayette
2518 Tumbler, 10 oz. $18.00
2404 Vase, 6" $30.00
2428 Vase, 9" $64.00
2428 Vase, 13" $75.00
2489 Vase, 5½" $36.00
2522 Vase, 8" $50.00
2523 Vase, 6½" $34.00
4103 Vase, 4" $24.00
4110 Vase, 7½" $45.00
4116 Vase, 4", Bubble Ball $16.00
4116 Vase, 5", Bubble Ball $18.00
4116 Vase, 6", Bubble Ball $20.00
4116 Vase, 7", Bubble Ball $24.00
4116 Vase, 8", Bubble Ball $27.00
4116 Vase, 9", Bubble Ball $30.00
4129 Vase, 2½", Bubble Ball $16.00
5088 Vase, 8", bud $34.00
5091 Vase, 6½", bud $30.00
887 Whiskey, 1¾ oz, optic $22.00
2502 Whiskey $20.00
2518 Whiskey, 2 oz. $18.00
2494 Whiskey Set, 7 pieces: Decanter and six 887 Whiskeys, 1¾ oz., optic $225.00
2518 Wine, 5 oz. $18.00
2503 Wine Jug, quart wine $75.00
2494 Wine Set: 7 pieces: decanter and six 4024 Sherries $275.00
2496 Candy and Cover, 3-part $115.00

Silver Triumph, 6112

1968 – 1972

Note: Similar to Caribbean in design.

Stemware, 15, 136

6112 Goblet $25.00
6112 Sherbet $25.00
6112 Tulip Wine $28.00
6112 Ice Tea, footed $25.00
2337 Plate, 7" $8.00
2337 Plate, 8" $10.00

Simplicity, Decoration 618

1938 – 1967

Stemware, 90

6017 Goblet $35.00
6017 Sherbet, high $32.00
6017 Sherbet, low $24.00
6017 Cocktail $32.00
6017 Claret $40.00
6017 Wine $40.00
6017 Cordial $45.00
6017 Oyster Cocktail $22.00
6017 Ice Tea, footed $35.00
6017 Tumbler, 9 oz., footed $24.00
6017 Juice, footed $24.00

Tableware II, 194

6023 Bowl, salad, $35.00
6023 Bowl, footed $65.00
2364 Bowl, 13", fruit $58.00
6023 Candlestick, duo, pair $64.00
2324 Candlestick, 4", pair $35.00
2527 Candelabra, 2-light, pair $125.00
2350 Celery $25.00
2364 Cheese and Cracker $48.00
2350½ Cup and 2350 Saucer $26.00
6011 Jug $150.00
2364 Lily Pond, 12" $38.00
2364 Mayonnaise, plate, ladle $58.00
2350 Pickle $22.00
2337 Plate, 6" $9.00
2337 Plate, 7" $12.00
2337 Plate, 8" $15.00
2350 Plate, 10" $30.00
2350½ Sugar and Cream $45.00
2364 Torte, 14" $45.00
4143 Vase, 6", footed $64.00
4143 Vase, 7½", footed $70.00

Skater, Carving 9

1938 – 1943

Useful & Ornamental, 113

4132½ Vase, 8" $110.00

Ski, Carving 2

1938 – 1943

Useful & Ornamental, 111, 112

2550 Ashtray, round $18.00
2391 Box, cigarette and cover $57.00
4132 Decanter $95.00
4132 Bowl, ice $64.00
2337 Plate, 7" $12.00
4139 Tumbler, whiskey $18.00
4139 Tumbler, old fashioned cocktail $18.00
4139 Tumbler, 5 oz. $18.00
4139 Tumbler, 9 oz., water $18.00
4139 Tumbler, 10 oz. $20.00
4139 Tumbler, 12 oz. $20.00
4139 Tumbler, 14 oz. $22.00
4139 Tumbler, 16 oz. $22.00

Skyflower, Crystal Print 2

1955 – 1958

Stemware, 110

6061 Goblet $34.00
6061 Sherbet $30.00
6061 Cocktail/Wine/ Seafood $34.00
6061 Cordial $38.00
6061 Ice Tea, footed $34.00
6061 Juice, footed $30.00

Tableware II, 159 – 160

2666 Bonbon $30.00
2666 Bowl, oval $34.00
2666 Butter and Cover, oblong $48.00
2666 Candle, flora, pair $48.00
2666 Celery $22.00
2666 Cup and Saucer $25.00
2666 Mayonnaise, plate, ladle $58.00
2666 Plate, 7" $12.00
2666 Plate, 10" $24.00
2666 Plate, canape $18.00
2666 Plate, 10", snack $24.00
2666 Plate, 14", serving $52.00
2685 Preserve, handled $32.00
2666 Relish, 2-part $30.00
2666 Relish, 3-part $38.00
2685 Salver $54.00
2364 Shaker, large, chrome top B, pair $65.00
2666 Sugar and Cream $52.00
2666 Sugar and Cream, individual and tray $58.00

Skylark, Cutting 846

1956 – 1958

Stemware, 111

6064 Goblet $34.00
6064 Champagne $30.00
6064 Sherbet, low $26.00
6064 Cocktail $28.00
6064 Claret $36.00

6064 Wine $35.00
6064 Cordial $42.00
6064 Seafood Cocktail $25.00
6064 Ice Tea, footed $34.00
6064 Juice, footed $26.00
2337 Plate, 7" $8.00
2337 Plate, 8" $10.00

Small Bowls, Mints and Nuts

pre 1924 – 1963

Useful & Ornamental, 185, 186

315 Bowl, thin, 4½", 5", 6", 7", or 8" .... $10.00 – 25.00
766 Almond, small $24.00
766 Bonbon, 4½", plain or optic $18.00
858 Sweetmeat, 4½", plain or optic $18.00
863 Almond, small $20.00
880 Bonbon, 4½", plain or optic $18.00
2374 Bowl, 6", nut, see Comports, Nappies, and Jellies
- crystal $28.00
- amber $40.00
- green $45.00
- rose $45.00
- azure $45.00

2374 Bowl, individual, nut
- crystal $20.00
- amber $22.00
- green $24.00
- rose $25.00
- azure $25.00
- topaz/gold tint $24.00
- regal blue $32.00
- burgund $32.00
- empire green $32.00

2394 Bowl, 6"
- crystal $30.00
- amber $32.00
- green $34.00
- rose $36.00
- azure $36.00
- topaz $34.00

2394 Bowl, 4½", mint
- crystal $18.00
- amber $20.00
- green $25.00
- rose $25.00
- azure $25.00
- topaz $25.00

2402 Bowl, 6", mint
- crystal $18.00
- amber $18.00
- green $22.00
- rose $22.00
- azure $22.00
- topaz $22.00
- ebony $20.00

2513 Bowl, individual. almond, see Milk Glass
- crystal $16.00
- regal blue $30.00
- burgund $30.00
- empire green $30.00

2517 Sweetmeat, see Appetizers, Buffet, and Relish
- crystal $16.00
- regal blue $25.00
- burgundy $25.00
- empire green $25.00
- ruby $28.00

2517 Bonbon, see Appetizers, Buffet, and Relish
- crystal $16.00
- regal blue $25.00
- burgundy $25.00
- empire green $25.00
- ruby $26.00

2517 Lemon, see Appetizers, Buffet, and Relish
- crystal $16.00
- regal blue $25.00
- burgundy $25.00
- empire green $25.00
- ruby $26.00

2521 Salt or Almond, Bird, see Shakers and Open Salts
2546 Bowl, quadrangle, see Bowls, Centerpieces, and Console Bowls
4020 Almond, individual
- crystal $22.00
- amber $25.00
- green $27.00
- ebony $27.00
- rose $32.00
- topaz $30.00
- wisteria $45.00

4095 Almond
- crystal, RO $20.00
- amber, RO $22.00
- amber foot, LO $24.00
- green, SO $26.00
- green bowl, RO $26.00
- green foot, SO $26.00
- blue foot, RO $28.00
- rose bowl, RO $28.00
- azure bowl, RO $28.00

4152 Bowl, snack
- crystal $15.00
- cinnamon $18.00
- spruce $18.00
- chartreuse $18.00
- ebony $18.00

Small Cloverleaf, Etching 67

1898 – 1927

Stemware, 27

863 Goblet, 10½ oz. $8.00
863 Goblet, 9 oz. $8.00
863 Goblet, 7 oz. $8.00
863 Goblet, 5½ oz. $8.00
863 Saucer Champagne $8.00
863 Fruit $8.00
863 Cocktail, 3½ oz. $8.00
863 Cocktail, 3 oz. $8.00
863 Claret $8.00
863 Rhine Wine $8.00
863 Wine $8.00
863 Sherry $8.00
863 Crème de Menthe $8.00
863 Brandy, pousse-café $8.00
863 Cordial $15.00
863 Champagne, hollow stem $8.00
863 Champagne, tall $8.00
810 Tumbler .... $4.00 – 8.00

Smoking Accessories

1924 – 1968

Useful & Ornamental, 187 – 197

1372 see Coin
2056 see American
2106 Box, cigarette and cover, small
- amber $85.00
- blue $125.00
- green $95.00
- canary $150.00

2106 Box, cigarette and cover, large
- amber $110.00
- blue $150.00
- green $125.00
- canary $175.00

2106 Box, match and cover
- amber $85.00
- blue $125.00
- green $95.00
- canary $150.00

2306 Smoker Set, 4-piece
- crystal $20.00
- amber $40.00
- blue $45.00
- green $40.00
- ebony $40.00
- rose, ... $40.00
- azure $40.00

2306 Ashtray, 2¾", 3⅛", 3½", or 4"
- crystal $5.00
- amber $8.00
- blue $12.00
- green $8.00
- ebony $10.00
- rose, ... $10.00
- azure $10.00

2349 Cigarette Holder/round Ashtray
- amber $45.00
- blue $54.00
- green $47.00
- canary $58.00
- ebony $45.00

2351 Cigarette Holder/Ashtray
- crystal $67.00
- amber $84.00
- blue $75.00
- green $75.00
- canary $125.00
- ebony $67.00

2351 Cigarette Holder/oval Ashtray, colored foot
- amber $67.00
- blue $84.00
- green $45.00
- canary $125.00

2354 Cigarette
- crystal $58.00
- amber $67.00
- blue $84.00
- green $75.00
- ebony $67.00
- orchid $95.00

2354 Cigarette, colored foot
- amber $67.00
- blue $84.00
- green $75.00

2391 Cigarette and Cover, small
- crystal $34.00
- amber $45.00
- green $48.00

No.	Item	Price
	ebony	$45.00
	orchid	$60.00
	rose	$48.00
	azure	$60.00
2391	Cigarette and Cover, large	
	crystal	$42.00
	amber	$57.00
	green	$60.00
	ebony	$57.00
	orchid	$85.00
	rose	$67.00
	azure	$85.00
	regal blue	$125.00
	burgundy	$150.00
	empire green	$125.00
	ruby	$125.00
2391	Cigarette and Cover Cut A, B, or C in azure, green, or rose	
	small	$74.00
	large	$125.00
2420	Ashtray Set, 3 pieces: small, medium, and large, ebony	$75.00
2424	Ashtrays, see Kent	
2427	Box, cigarette, divided and cover	
	crystal, ridged	$65.00
	amber	$78.00
	green	$95.00
	ebony	$95.00
	rose	$125.00
	azure	$125.00
	topaz	$125.00
	crystal, plain	$48.00
2427	Ashtray, oblong, crystal	$10.00
2457	Ashtray	
	crystal	$15.00
	amber	$22.00
	regal blue	$38.00
	burgundy	$38.00
	empire green	$45.00
2496	Smoker Set, see Baroque	
2510	see Sunray	
2515	Ashtray	$10.00
2516	Ashtray	$18.00
2520	Ashtray	$10.00
2530	Ashtray	
	crystal	$12.00
	ebony	$15.00
2534	Ashtray	
	crystal	$15.00
	regal blue	$32.00
	burgundy	$32.00
	empire green	$32.00
2538	Ashtray/Place Card Holder	
	crystal	$15.00
	silver mist	$26.00
	ebony	$26.00
	azure	$36.00
2550	Spool, see Spool	
2566	Ashtray, fish	$54.00
2596	Box, cigarette and cover	$57.00
2596	Ashtray, 4", square	$16.00
2592	see Myriad	
2608	Ashtray, 4½", round	$12.00
2609	Ashtray, 4", oblong	$10.00
2610	Ashtray, 3½", Shell	$14.00
2618	Box, cigarette and cover	
	crystal	$45.00
	ebony	$54.00
2618	Ashtray, 4", square	$10.00
2618	Ashtray, 4½", oblong	$10.00
2622	Ashtray, 4½"	$8.00
2623	Ashtray, 5"	$10.00
2625	Ashtray, 5"	$12.00
2625	Ashtray, 6½"	$15.00
2625	Ashtray Set, 2-piece	$25.00
2628	Box, cigarette and cover	$75.00
2628	Ashtray, 4¼"	$15.00
2667	Cigarette Holder	
	crystal	$18.00
	ebony	$25.00
2667	Ashtray, 5"	
	crystal	$6.00
	ebony	$12.00
2667	Ashtray, 7"	
	crystal	$10.00
	ebony	$16.00
2667	Ashtray, 9"	
	crystal	$12.00
	ebony	$18.00
2667	Ashtray Set, 3-piece	$30.00
2667	Smoking Set, 3-piece	$32.00
2667	Smoking Set, 4-piece	$45.00
2691	Cigarette, individual	$20.00
2691	Ashtray, individual	$14.00
2731	Box, cigarette and cover	$48.00
2731	Ashtray, 4", oblong	$5.00
2731	Ashtray, 5", round	$6.00
2731	Ashtray, 7½", round	
	crystal	$12.00
	amber	$15.00
	green	$24.00
	blue	$24.00
2746	Ashtray, 6", footed	
	ruby mist	$48.00
	green texture	$64.00
2747	Ashtray, 4½"	
	crystal	$8.00
	amber	$10.00
	green	$12.00
2747	Ashtray, 6"	
	crystal	$12.00
	amber	$16.00
	green	$20.00
2747	Ashtray Set, 2-piece	
	crystal	$20.00
	amber	$26.00
	green	$32.00
2748	Ashtray, mortar	
	amber mist	$28.00
	pink mist	$38.00
2752	see Facets	
2753	Ashtray, 5½"	
	crystal	$8.00
	brown	$10.00
	gold	$10.00
2753	Ashtray, 7½"	
	crystal,	$10.00
	brown	$12.00
	gold	$15.00
2753	Ashtray, 10½"	
	crystal	$14.00
	brown	$15.00
	gold	$15.00
2753	Ashtray Set, 3-piece	
	crystal	$32.00
	brown	$35.00
	gold	$37.00
4148	Cigarette Holder	$35.00
4148	Ashtray	$10.00
5092	Cigarette Holder/Ashtray, blown	
	crystal	$65.00
	amber	$75.00
	blue	$95.00
	green	$85.00
	rose	$85.00
	azure	$88.00
5092	Cigarette Holder/Ashtray, colored foot	
	amber	$75.00
	blue	$105.00
	green	$95.00
5092	Cigarette Holder/Ashtray, colored bowl	
	ruby	$165.00
	regal blue	$145.00
	burgundy	$125.00
	empire green	$125.00
FU01	Functional Sculptures/Ashtrays, see Figurals	
2354	Cigarette, etched, dog	
	crystal	$87.00
	amber	$125.00
	blue	$150.00
	green	$135.00
	ebony	$135.00
2354	Cigarette, etched, horse	
	crystal	$94.00
	amber	$135.00
	blue	$165.00
	green	$150.00
	ebony	$135.00
2354	Cigarette, etched, Cupid	
	crystal	$125.00
	amber	$145.00
	blue	$175.00
	green	$165.00
	ebony	$157.00
2354	Cigarette, etched, deer	
	crystal	$125.00
	amber	$145.00
	blue	$175.00
	green	$165.00
	ebony	$157.00

MISCELLANEOUS ROCK CRYSTAL CUTTINGS

CUT 808:

No.	Item	Price
2427	Ashtray, oblong	$12.00
2427	Cigarette, oblong and cover	$56.00
2516	Ashtray	$18.00
2550	Ashtray	$10.00
2550½	Cigarette and Cover	$52.00

CUT 809:

No.	Item	Price
2427	Ashtray, oblong	$12.00
2427	Cigarette, oblong and cover	$56.00

CUT 810:

No.	Item	Price
2427	Cigarette, oblong and cover	$56.00

CUT 811:

No.	Item	Price
2306	Smoker Set, 3-piece	$22.00

Snow Crystal, Carving 42

1940 – 1943

Useful & Ornamental, 130

No.	Item	Price
2427	Ashtray, oblong	$22.00
2427	Box, cigarette and cover, oblong	$65.00

Snow Drop, Decoration 526

1955 – 1956

Tableware II, 194

No.	Item	Price
2691	Ashtray, individual	$16.00
2691	Holder, cigarette, individual	$22.00
2691	Cup and Saucer, Demitasse	$27.00
2691	Bowl, sauce with plate and ladle	$38.00

2691 Server, 2-part $22.00
2691 Server, 3-part $30.00
2691 Sugar and Cream $32.00
2691 Sugar and Cover $18.00
2691 Tray, sugar and cream $14.00

Society, Cutting 757

1935 – 1937

Stemware, 85

6013 Goblet $32.00
6013 Goblet, low $30.00
6013 Saucer Champagne $30.00
6013 Sherbet, low $26.00
6013 Cocktail $30.00
6013 Claret $45.00
6013 Wine $40.00
6013 Cordial $56.00
6013 Oyster Cocktail $24.00
6013 Ice Tea, footed $30.00
6013 Juice, footed $25.00

Tableware I, 292

766 Bowl, finger $16.00
2527 Bowl, 9", footed $64.00
2527 Candelabra, 2-light, UDP, pair $125.00
6013 Comport, 5" $32.00
5000 Jug $200.00
2337 Plate, 6" $7.00
2337 Plate, 7" $8.00
2337 Plate, 8" $10.00

Something Blue, Decoration 685

1970 – 1975

Blue bowl

Stemware, 128

6103 Goblet $28.00
6103 Sherbet $26.00
6103 Claret $30.00
6103 Tulip Wine $30.00
6103 Brandy $28.00
6103 Ice Tea, footed $28.00

Sommelier Collection, 6115 - 6119

1970 – 1973

Stemware, 137

6115 Continental $22.00
6116 Grande $28.00
6117 Vin Blanc $24.00
6118 Sherry $24.00
6119 Tulip Wine $24.00

Sonata, 2364

1940 – 1976

Tableware II, 34 - 37

6023 Almond, individual $7.00
6023 Ashtray, individual $7.00
6023 Bowl, 5", fruit $12.00
2350 Bowl, 6", baked apple $15.00
2350 Bowl, 8", rim soup $18.00
6023 Bowl, oval, sauce $30.00
6023 Bowl, 9", salad $30.00
6023 Bowl, 9", lily pond $32.00
6023 Bowl, 10½", salad $35.00
6023 Bowl, 12", flared, $40.00
6023 Bowl, 12", lily pond $40.00
6023 Bowl, 13", fruit $45.00
6023 Candlestick, duo $48.00
2364 Box, candy and cover $67.00
2364 Celery, 11" $22.00
2364 Cheese and Cracker $34.00
2364 Cigarette Holder $22.00
2400 Comport, 6" $22.00
2364 Comport, 8" $30.00
2364 Mayonnaise, plate, ladle $46.00
2364 Mayonnaise, 2-part, with plate and ladle $48.00
2364 Pickle, 8" $18.00
2364 Plate, crescent, salad $18.00
2364 Plate, 11", sandwich $20.00
2364 Plate, 14", torte $40.00
2364 Plate, 16", torte $45.00
2364 Relish, 2-part $22.00
2364 Relish, 3-part $45.00
2364 Salad Set, 9" $65.00
2364 Salad Set, 10½" $75.00
2364 Shaker, individual, E top, pair $18.00
2364 Shaker, large, B top, pair $25.00
2364 Tray, handled, lunch $45.00

Sorrento, 2832

1971 – 1974

Stemware, 51

2832 Goblet
- blue $12.00
- green $12.00
- brown $12.00
- plum $12.00
- pink $12.00

2832 Sherbet
- blue $10.00
- green $10.00
- brown $10.00
- plum $10.00
- pink $10.00

2832 Wine
- blue $12.00
- green $12.00
- brown $12.00
- plum $12.00
- pink $12.00

2832 Ice Tea, footed
- blue $12.00
- green $12.00
- brown $12.00
- plum $12.00
- pink $12.00

2832 Old Fashioned, double
- blue $10.00
- green $10.00
- brown $10.00
- plum $10.00
- pink $10.00

2832 Highball
- blue $10.00
- green $10.00
- brown $10.00
- plum $10.00
- pink $10.00

2832 Plate, 8" $8.00

Spartan, Etching 80

1927 – 1943

Stemware, 67

5097 Goblet
- crystal $30.00
- green bowl $35.00
- amber bowl $35.00
- orchid bowl $40.00

5097 Sherbet, high
- crystal $28.00
- green bowl $30.00
- amber bowl $30.00
- orchid bowl $38.00

5097 Sherbet, low
- crystal $20.00
- green bowl $25.00
- amber bowl $25.00
- orchid bowl $34.00

5097 Parfait
- crystal $30.00
- green bowl $37.00
- amber bowl $37.00
- orchid bowl $40.00

5097 Cocktail
- crystal $28.00
- green bowl $30.00
- amber bowl $30.00
- orchid bowl $35.00

5097 Claret
- crystal $34.00
- green bowl $38.00
- amber bowl $38.00
- orchid bowl $45.00

5097 Wine
- crystal $30.00
- green bowl $35.00
- amber bowl $35.00
- orchid bowl $40.00

5097 Cordial
- crystal $36.00
- green bowl $48.00
- amber bowl $48.00
- orchid bowl $55.00

5000 Oyster Cocktail
- crystal $20.00
- green bowl $25.00
- amber bowl $25.00
- orchid bowl $34.00

5097½ Grapefruit and Liner
- crystal $45.00
- green bowl $50.00
- amber bowl $50.00
- orchid bowl $58.00

869 Tumbler, 12 oz., table
- crystal $10.00
- green bowl $12.00
- amber bowl $12.00
- orchid bowl $15.00

869 Tumbler, 5 oz., table
- crystal $8.00
- green bowl $10.00
- amber bowl $10.00
- orchid bowl $12.00

869 Tumbler, 2 oz., table
- crystal $6.00
- green bowl $8.00
- amber bowl $8.00
- orchid bowl $10.00

5000 Tumbler, 12 oz., footed
- crystal $30.00
- green bowl $35.00
- amber bowl $35.00
- orchid bowl $40.00

5000 Tumbler, 9 oz., footed
- crystal $28.00
- green bowl $30.00
- amber bowl $30.00
- orchid bowl $38.00

5000 Tumbler, 5 oz., footed
- crystal $20.00
- green bowl $25.00
- amber bowl $25.00
- orchid bowl $34.00

5000 Tumbler, 2½ oz. footed
- crystal $28.00
- green bowl $30.00
- amber bowl $30.00
- orchid bowl $38.00

869 Bowl, finger and plate
- crystal $18.00
- green bowl $35.00
- amber bowl $35.00
- orchid bowl $40.00

2283 Plate, 7"
- crystal $10.00
- green bowl $14.00
- amber bowl $12.00
- orchid bowl $20.00

2283 Plate, 8"
- crystal $12.00
- green bowl $16.00
- amber bowl $14.00
- orchid bowl $25.00

Spencerian, Tracing 94

1940 – 1943

Stemware, 93

6023 Goblet $20.00
6023 Saucer Champagne $18.00
6023 Sherbet, low $15.00
6023 Cocktail $16.00
6023 Claret-Wine $20.00
6023 Cordial $25.00
6023 Oyster Cocktail $12.00
6023 Ice Tea, footed $20.00
6023 Tumbler, 9 oz., footed $16.00
6023 Juice, footed $16.00
2337 Plate, 7" $8.00

Sphere, 6122

1971 – 1972

Stemware, 139

6122 Goblet
- terra bowl $20.00
- gray mist bowl $20.00
- green mist bowl $20.00

6122 Sherbet
- terra bowl $15.00
- gray mist bowl $15.00
- green mist bowl $15.00

6122 Wine
- terra bowl $20.00
- gray mist bowl $20.00
- green mist bowl $20.00

6122 Ice Tea, footed
- terra bowl $20.00
- gray mist bowl $20.00
- green mist bowl $20.00

Spinet, Cutting 821

1950 – 1960

Stemware, 102

6033 Goblet $30.00
6033 Sherbet, high $28.00
6033 Sherbet, low $22.00
6033 Parfait $28.00
6033 Cocktail $27.00
6033 Claret-Wine $34.00
6033 Cordial $42.00
6033 Oyster Cocktail $18.00
6033 Ice Tea, footed $30.00
6033 Juice, footed $22.00
2337 Plate, 7" $8.00
2337 Plate, 8" $10.00

Spire, Cutting 793

1939 – 1943

Stemware, 94

6023 Goblet $25.00
6023 Saucer Champagne $23.00
6023 Sherbet, low $20.00
6023 Cocktail $22.00
6023 Claret-Wine $28.00
6023 Cordial $38.00
6023 Oyster Cocktail $18.00
6023 Ice Tea, footed $25.00
6023 Tumbler, 9 oz., footed $20.00
6023 Juice, footed $20.00

Tableware I, 302

766 Bowl, finger $12.00
6023 Bowl, footed $85.00
2324 Candlestick, 6", pair $54.00
6023 Comport, 5" $30.00
6011 Jug $175.00
2337 Plate, 6" $7.00
2337 Plate, 7" $8.00
2337 Plate, 8" $9.00

Splendor, 6124

1971 – 1973

Stemware, 141

6124 Goblet $32.00
6124 Sherbet $32.00
6124 Wine $32.00
6124 Ice Tea, footed $32.00

Splendor, 6131

1978 – 1982

Stemware, 144

6131 Goblet
- blue $22.00
- rust $20.00

6131 Champagne
- blue $22.00
- rust $20.00

6131 Claret
- blue $22.00
- rust $20.00

6131 Ice Tea, footed
- blue $22.00
- rust $20.00

Spool, 2550

1937 – 1943

Tableware I, 110 – 114

2250 Ashtray, 3¼", round
- crystal $8.00
- azure $12.00
- gold tint $12.00

2550½ Ashtray, individual
- crystal $8.00
- azure $22.00
- gold tint $22.00

2550½ Ashtray, 4½"
- crystal $10.00

2550½ Ashtray, 5½"
- crystal $12.00
- azure $22.00
- gold tint $20.00

2550½ Ashtray Set, 3-piece, crystal or assorted colors $35.00

2550 Bowl, 8", straight
- crystal $21.00
- azure $40.00
- gold tint $38.00

2550 Bowl, 9½", flared
- crystal $28.00
- azure $42.00
- gold tint $44.00

2550 Bowl, 10½", centerpiece
- crystal $40.00
- azure $52.00
- gold tint $48.00

2550 Bowl, 11", oval
- crystal $32.00
- azure $50.00
- gold tint $47.00

2550 Candlestick, 3"
- crystal $25.00
- azure $45.00
- gold tint $40.00

2550½ Candlestick, 3"
- crystal $30.00
- azure $48.00
- gold tint $50.00

2550½ Candle Lamp, 3-piece
- crystal, $48.00

Cigarette and Cover
- crystal $42.00
- azure $115.00
- gold tint $95.00

2550½ Box, cigarette, oblong and cover
- crystal $95.00
- azure $125.00
- gold tint $95.00

2550 Coaster, 3⅛"
- crystal $6.00
- azure $12.00
- gold tint $12.00

2550 Comport, 6", low
- crystal $24.00
- azure $45.00
- gold tint $40.00

2550 Decanter and Stopper
- crystal $225.00
- azure $275.00
- gold tint $275.00

2550 Decanter Set, 7-piece, includes 2518 Tumbler
- crystal $295.00
- azure $350.00
- gold tint $350.00

2550 Mayonnaise, plate, ladle
- crystal $58.00

2550 Nappy, 6½"
- crystal $45.00
- azure $50.00
- gold tint $50.00

2550 Plate, 13"
- crystal $45.00
- azure $58.00
- gold tint $58.00

2550 Plate, 14", buffet
- crystal $45.00
- azure $64.00
- gold tint $64.00

2550 Sweetmeat
- crystal $24.00

2518 Tumbler, whiskey, sham
- crystal $10.00
- azure $16.00

gold tint $16.00
2550 Vase, 5½", straight
crystal $54.00
azure $75.00
gold tint $75.00
2550 Vase, 5½", flared
crystal $50.00
azure $75.00
gold tint $75.00
2550 Vase, 6", straight
crystal $55.00
azure $87.00
gold tint $85.00
2550 Vase, 6", flared
crystal $55.00
azure $88.00
gold tint $85.00

Spoons and Ladles

1924 – 1972

Useful & Ornamental, 198, 199

Sanitary Spoons
Mustard, 3½" $28.00
Horseradish, 4" $32.00
Highball, 6" $20.00
Ice Tea, 8" $22.00
Most Perfect Dipper ....market
2056 Spoon, crushed fruit, 9", see American
979 Ladle, plastic $15.00
2138 Ladle, used with 2138 Mayonnaise Set $45.00
2375 Ladle, mayonnaise, see Fairfax
crystal $24.00
amber $45.00
green $45.00
rose $52.00
azure $60.00
topaz/gold tint $47.00
orchid $75.00
2449 Spoon, mustard, see Hermitage
987 Fork and Spoon, salad, wooden, see Bowls, Centerpieces, and Console Bowls $25.00

Spray, Cutting, 841

1954 – 1972

Stemware, 108

6055½ Goblet $32.00
6055½ Sherbet $25.00
6055½ Cocktail $25.00
6055½ Claret-Wine $35.00
6055½ Cordial $40.00
6055½ Oyster Cocktail $22.00
6055½ Ice Tea, footed $32.00
6055½ Juice, footed $24.00

Tableware II, 187

4185 Bowl, dessert/finger $24.00
2666 Bowl, 8¼", oval $38.00
2666 Bowl, 10½", salad $45.00
2666 Butter and Cover, oblong $48.00
2666 Candle, flora, pair $48.00
2666 Cup and Saucer $24.00
2666 Mayonnaise, plate, ladle $54.00
2666 Pitcher, quart $155.00
2337 Plate, 7" $10.00
2337 Plate, 8" $12.00
2666 Plate, canape $22.00
2666 Plate, 10", snack $24.00
2666 Plate, 14", serving $40.00
2666 Relish, 2-part $30.00
2666 Relish, 3-part $38.00
2666 Salad Set, 4-piece $95.00
2685 Salver $75.00
2364 Shaker, large, chrome top B, pair $55.00
2666 Sugar and Cream $50.00
2666 Sugar and Cream, individual, and tray $55.00

Spread Eagle, Carving 32

1941 – 1943

Useful & Ornamental, 131

4143½ Vase, 6" $175.00
4143½ Vase, 7½" $225.00

Spring, Cutting 844

1955 – 1958

Stemware, 110

6060 Goblet $30.00
6060 Sherbet $26.00
6060 Cocktail/Wine/Seafood $30.00
6060 Cordial $40.00
6060 Ice Tea, footed $30.00
6060 Juice, footed $26.00
2337 Plate, 7" $10.00
2337 Plate, 8" $12.00

Spring Song, Cutting 884

1961 – 1962

Stemware, 120

6092 Goblet $35.00
6092 Sherbet $32.00
6092 Wine/Cocktail $38.00
6092 Cordial $42.00
6092 Ice Tea, footed $35.00
6092 Juice, footed $30.00
2337 Plate, 7" $10.00
2337 Plate, 8" $12.00

Springtime, Plate Etching 318

1933 – 1943

Stemware, 39, 83

891 Goblet
crystal $35.00
topaz $42.00
891 Sherbet, high
crystal $30.00
topaz $40.00
891 Sherbet, low
crystal $20.00
topaz $32.00
891 Cocktail
crystal $30.00
topaz $35.00
891 Claret
crystal $40.00
topaz $50.00
891 Cordial
crystal $45.00
topaz $65.00
891 Oyster Cocktail
crystal $20.00
topaz $28.00
891 Ice Tea, footed
crystal $35.00
topaz $40.00
891 Tumbler, 9 oz., footed
crystal $30.00
topaz $30.00
891 Juice, footed
crystal $30.00
topaz $30.00
6012 Goblet $35.00
6012 Sherbet, high $32.00
6012 Sherbet, low $28.00
6012 Cocktail $32.00
6012 Claret $40.00
6012 Rhine Wine $35.00
6012 Wine $40.00
6012 Sherry $35.00
6012 Crème de Menthe $32.00
6012 Brandy $36.00
6012 Cordial $42.00
6012 Oyster Cocktail $25.00
6012 Ice Tea, footed $35.00
6012 Tumbler, 10 oz., footed $22.00
6012 Juice, footed $22.00

Tableware I, 216, 218 – 219

2440 Bonbon, 5"
crystal $36.00
869 Bowl, finger
crystal $30.00
topaz $38.00
2440 Bowl, 5", fruit
crystal $25.00
topaz $34.00
2440 Bowl, 6", cereal
crystal $28.00
topaz $40.00
2470½ Bowl, 7"
crystal $34.00
topaz $42.00
2470½ Bowl, 10½"
crystal $96.00
topaz $127.00
2481 Bowl, 11", oblong
crystal $110.00
topaz $125.00
2481 Candlestick, 5", pair
crystal $120.00
topaz $150.00
2470½ Candlestick, 5½", pair
crystal $100.00
topaz $135.00
2482 Candlestick, trindle, pair
crystal $150.00
topaz $250.00
2440 Celery, 11½"
crystal $52.00
topaz $65.00
2400 Comport, 6"
crystal $64.00
topaz $75.00
2440 Cream Soup
crystal $58.00
topaz $75.00
2440 Cup and Saucer
crystal $35.00
topaz $47.00
6011 Jug
crystal $500.00

SPRINGTIME, PLATE ETCHING 318

2440 Lemon, 5"
crystal $35.00
2470 Lemon
crystal $35.00
topaz..................................$46.00
2440 Mayonnaise, 2-part
crystal $45.00
2440 Olive, 6½"
crystal $32.00
topaz..................................$44.00
2440 Pickle, 8½"
crystal $42.00
topaz..................................$48.00
2440 Plate, 6"
crystal $12.00
topaz..................................$16.00
2440 Plate, 7"
crystal $16.00
topaz..................................$20.00
2440 Plate, 8"
crystal $24.00
topaz..................................$38.00
2440 Plate, 9"
crystal $48.00
topaz..................................$67.00
2470 Plate, cake
crystal $75.00
topaz..................................$88.00
2440 Plate, 13", torte
crystal $95.00
topaz..................................$135.00
2440 Relish, 2-part
crystal $47.00
2440 Relish, 3-part
crystal $50.00
2470 Relish, 4-part, oval
crystal $68.00
topaz..................................$95.00
2419 Relish, 4-part
crystal $54.00
topaz..................................$68.00
2419 Relish, 5-part
crystal $94.00
2440 Sauce and Tray
crystal $96.00
2440 Sugar and Cream
crystal $87.00
topaz..................................$125.00
2440 Sweetmeat, 4½"
crystal $35.00
2470 Sweetmeat
crystal $35.00
topaz..................................$44.00
4111 Vase, 6½"
crystal $200.00
topaz..................................$250.00
4112 Vase, 8½"
crystal $300.00
topaz..................................$425.00
2470 Vase, 10"
crystal $325.00
topaz..................................$450.00

Sprite, Cutting 823

1950 – 1968

Stemware, 102

6033 Goblet
......$30.00
6033 Sherbet, high
.......$28.00
6033 Sherbet, low $22.00
6033 Parfait $28.00
6033 Cocktail $27.00
6033 Claret-Wine $34.00
6033 Cordial $42.00
6033 Oyster Cocktail.......................$18.00
6033 Ice Tea, footed $30.00
6033 Juice, footed $22.00

Tableware II, 173 - 174

2630 Bonbon, 3-toed.......................$32.00
2630 Bowl, 10¾", footed, flared $64.00
2630 Candle, duo, pair $135.00
2630 Candle, trindle, pair............$175.00
2630 Comport $36.00
2630 Cup and Saucer......................$27.00
6011 Jug..$250.00
2630 Mayonnaise, plate, ladle $58.00
2666 Pitcher, quart......................$145.00
2337 Plate, 7" $12.00
2337 Plate, 8" $16.00
2630 Plate, handled, cake $47.00
2630 Plate, 14", torte $54.00
2630 Relish, 2-part $30.00
2630 Shaker, large, chrome
top B, pair..........................$65.00
2630 Sugar and Cream...................$54.00

Stallion, Carving 10

1938 – 1943

Useful & Ornamental, 113

2567 Vase, 7½"
.....................$125.00

Standish, 4132 Tumbler

1938 – 1982

Stemware, 154

4132 Tumbler, sham, 14 oz.
crystal...........$10.00
azure.............$20.00
gold tint...........$20.00
4132 Old Fashioned, 13 oz., double
crystal $10.00
azure $18.00
gold tint $18.00
4132 Highball, 12 oz.
crystal $10.00
azure $17.00
gold tint $17.00
4132 Scotch and Soda, 9 oz.
crystal $10.00
azure $15.00
gold tint $15.00
4132 Old Fashioned Cocktail, 7½ oz.
crystal $10.00
azure $15.00
gold tint $15.00
4132 Tumbler, 5 oz., sham
crystal $8.00
azure $15.00
gold tint $15.00
4132 Whiskey Sour, 5 oz.
crystal $8.00
azure $15.00
gold tint $15.00
4132 Whiskey, 1½ oz.
crystal $10.00
azure $20.00
gold tint $20.00

Stardust, Cutting 851

1957 – 1970

Stemware, 113

6068 Goblet
.........$22.00
6068 Sherbet
.................$20.00
6068 Cocktail/Wine/
Seafood $22.00
6068 Cordial $30.00
6068 Ice Tea, footed $22.00
6068 Juice, footed $20.00

Tableware II, 189

2666 Bonbon $28.00
4185 Bowl, dessert/finger.............$24.00
2337 Plate, 7" $10.00
2337 Plate, 8" $12.00
2364 Plate, 14", torte $36.00
2364 Relish, 2-part $30.00
2364 Relish, 3-part $37.00
2666 Sugar and Cream...................$45.00

Starflower, Etching 345

1952 – 1957

Stemware, 105

6049 Goblet
....$22.00
6049 Sherbet, high $20.00
6049 Sherbet, low $18.00
6049 Parfait $20.00
6049 Cocktail $18.00
6049 Claret $25.00
6049 Wine...$25.00
6049 Cordial $30.00
6049 Oyster Cocktail.......................$14.00
6049 Ice Tea, footed $20.00
6049 Juice, footed $14.00

Tableware II, 153 - 154

2630 Basket, reed handle $110.00
2630 Bonbon $30.00
2630 Bowl, 4½", handled, nappy...$18.00
2630 Bowl, fruit...............................$18.00
2630 Bowl, cereal.............................$20.00
2630 Bowl, snack $25.00
2630 Bowl, 8", flared $30.00
2630 Bowl, 8½", salad $32.00
2630 Bowl, handled, serving $45.00
2630 Bowl, oval, vegetable $40.00
2630 Bowl, oval, utility $48.00
2630 Bowl, 9", lily pond.....................$40.00
2630 Bowl, 10½", salad $47.00
2630 Bowl, 10¾", footed, flared $50.00
2630 Bowl, 11", rolled edge............$57.00
2630 Bowl, 11¼", lily pond $54.00
2630 Bowl, 12", flared $55.00
2630 Butter and Cover, oblong $56.00
2630 Candlestick, 4½", pair...........$50.00
2630 Candlestick, duo, pair $125.00
2630 Candlestick, trindle $145.00
2630 Jar, candy and cover..............$80.00
2630 Cheese and Cracker..............$75.00
2630 Comport, 4⅜"........................$40.00
2630 Condiment Set, 3-piece $125.00
2630 Cup and Saucer......................$26.00
2630 Ice Bucket, metal handle......$75.00
2630 Jug, 3-pint, ice $125.00
2630 Mayonnaise, plate, ladle $56.00
2630 Mayonnaise, 2-part,
2 spoons.............................$56.00
2630 Mustard, cover, spoon $58.00
2630 Oil, 5 oz., DS $56.00

2630 Pickle, 8¾" $22.00
2630 Pitcher, pint, cereal $64.00
2630 Plate, 6" $10.00
2630 Plate, 7" $12.00
2630 Plate, 8" $16.00
2630 Plate, 9" $24.00
2630 Plate, 10½", dinner $40.00
2630 Plate, crescent, salad....$40.00
2630 Plate, Party, and cup $40.00
2630 Plate, handled, cake $55.00
2630 Plate 14", torte $60.00
2630 Plate, 16", torte $65.00
2630 Platter, 12", oval....$60. 00
2630 Preserve and Cover, footed ..$58.00
2630 Relish, 2-part....$20.00
2630 Relish, 3-part....$32.00
2630 Salad Set, 4-piece....$95.00
2630 Salver....$85.00
2630 Shaker, chrome top B, pair....$55.00
2630 Sugar and Cream....$54.00
2630 Sugar and Cream, individual, and tray....$64.00
2630 Tid Bit, 3-toed $30.00
2630 Tid Bit, 3-piece....$54.00
2630 Tray, handled, muffin....$55.00
2630 Tray, handled, utility....$55.00
2630 Tray, handled, lunch....$57.00
2630 Tray, 10½", snack....$40.00
2630 Tricorne, 3-toed $35.00
4121 Vase, 5"....$60.00
2630 Vase, 6", bud $42.00
4143 Vase, 6", footed....$64.00
6021 Vase, 6", footed bud $55.00
2630 Vase, 7½", handled....$75.00
2660 Vase, 8", flip $75.00
5092 Vase, 8", footed, bud $75.00
2630 Vase, 8½", oval....$75.00
2470 Vase, 10", footed....$95.00
2657 Vase, 10½", footed....$157.00

Starlight
1985
Tableware II, 305

ST07/179 Bowl, 8" $25.00
ST07/255 Tray, 12" x 6" $25.00
ST07/344 Box, candy and cover....$25.00
ST07/560 Tray, 12", round, serving....$25.00
ST07/686 Sugar and Cream and Tray ..$25.00
ST07/810 Vase, 9"....$25.00

Stars, Carving 14
1940 – 1943
Usefule & Ornamental, 120

2518 Bookend, eagle, pair $450.00

Stars and Bars, Carving 47
1940 – 1943
Useful & Ornamental, 127

2596 Ashtray, 4", square $25.00
2596 Bowl, 11", oblong, shallow .$125.00
2596 Candlestick, 5", pair $125.00
2596 Box, cigarette and cover....$95.00
2596 Bowl, 7½", square $115.00

Star Song, Cutting 871
1959 – 1965
Stemware, 118

6086 Goblet $30.00
6086 Sherbet $27.00
6086 Wine/Cocktail $35.00
6086 Cordial $40.00
6086 Ice Tea, footed $30.00
6086 Juice, footed $25.00
2337 Plate, 7" $10.00
2337 Plate, 8" $12.00

Staunton, Cutting 707
1933 – 1943
Stemware, 75

6004 Goblet $34.00
6004 Sherbet, high $30.00
6004 Sherbet, low $25.00
6004 Cocktail $30.00
6004 Claret $37.00
6004 Wine....$37.00
6004 Oyster Cocktail....$25.00
6004 Ice Tea, footed $34.00
6004 Tumbler, 9 oz., footed....$25.00
6004 Juice, footed $25.00
6004 Whiskey, footed....$32.00

Tableware I, 276

2470½ Bowl, 10½"....$48.00
2470½ Candlestick, 5½", pair....$58.00
2451 Dish, ice and plate....$28.00
2283 Plate, 7" $10.00
2283 Plate, 8" $12.00

Stockholm, 6093
1960 – 1968
Stemware, 121

6093 Goblet....$24.00
6093 Sherbet....$20.00
6093 Wine....$28.00
6093 Cocktail....$20.00
6093 Cordial....$30.00
6093 Ice Tea, footed $22.00
6093 Juice, footed $16.00

Stowe, 2862 Tumbler
1974 – 1982
Stemware, 152

2862 Highball, 13 oz., pressed lead, crystal....$16.00
2862 Old Fashioned, 11 oz., double, pressed lead, crystal....$16.00

Stratford, Cutting 914
1967 – 1968
Stemware, 130

6105 Goblet $35.00
6105 Sherbet....$32.00
6105 Claret....$38.00
6105 Wine....$38.00
6105 Cordial....$42.00
6105 Ice Tea, footed $35.00
2337 Plate, 7" $10.00
2337 Plate, 8" $12.00

Stratton, 2885
1974 – 1982
lead crystal
Stemware, 53

2885 Goblet....$20.00
2885 Sherbet....$16.00
2885 Wine....$18.00
2885 Ice Tea, footed....$20.00
2885 Old Fashioned, double....$18.00
2885 Highball....$18.00

Suffolk, Cutting 789
1939 – 1959
Stemware, 96

6025 Goblet $30.00
6025 Sherbet....$28.00
6025 Cocktail $28.00
6025 Claret-Wine $35.00
6025 Cordial....$45.00
6025 Oyster Cocktail....$22.00
6025 Ice Tea, footed $30.00
6025 Juice, footed $24.00
6011 Jug....$175.00
2337 Plate, 6" $8.00
2337 Plate, 7" $10.00
2337 Plate, 8" $12.00

Sugar Pails, see Ice Buckets, Sugar Pails, Whip Cream Pails

Sunburst Star, large, see Large Sunburst Star

Sunglow, Decoration 650
1960 – 1967
Stemware, 117

6085 Goblet....$32.00
6085 Sherbet....$30.00
6085 Wine/Cocktail $38.00
6085 Cordial....$48.00
6085 Ice Tea, footed $32.00
6085 Juice, footed $30.00
2337 Plate, 7" $10.00
2337 Plate, 8" $12.00

Sunray, 2510; Glacier, 2510; Golden Glow, Decoration 513
1935 – 1943
Stemware, 47

2510 Goblet
- Sunray....$15.00
- Glacier $16.00
- azure/green $24.00
- amber/topaz $24.00

2510 Sherbet
- Sunray....$12.00
- Glacier $14.00
- azure/green $20.00
- amber/topaz $20.00

2510 Fruit Cocktail
- Sunray....$12.00
- Glacier $14.00

2510 Cocktail, footed
- Sunray....$12.00
- Glacier $14.00

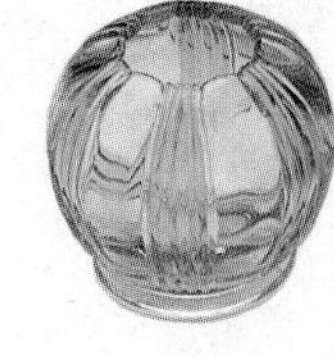

2510 Claret
Sunray................................$15.00
Glacier...............................$16.00
2510 Ice Tea, footed
Sunray................................$15.00
Glacier...............................$17.00
2510 Tumbler, 9 oz., footed
Sunray................................$12.00
Glacier...............................$15.00
azure/green/amber/topaz.$20.00
2610 Juice, footed
Sunray................................$12.00
Glacier...............................$15.00
2510 Tumbler, 13 oz.
Sunray................................$14.00
Glacier...............................$16.00
2510 Tumbler, 9 oz.
Sunray................................$10.00
Glacier...............................$12.00
2510 Tumbler, 5 oz.
Sunray................................$10.00
Glacier...............................$12.00
2510 Old Fashioned
Sunray................................$10.00
Glacier...............................$12.00
2510 Tumbler, whiskey
Sunray................................$18.00
Glacier...............................$20.00

Tableware I, 99 – 107

2510 Almond, individual, footed
Sunray................................$24.00
2510 Ashtray, individual
Sunray................................$20.00
Glacier...............................$22.00
2510 Ashtray, square
Sunray................................$16.00
Glacier...............................$18.00
Golden Glow.......................$22.00
2510 Bonbon, handled
Sunray................................$20.00
ruby...................................$45.00
2510 Bonbon, 3-toed
Sunray................................$28.00
ruby...................................$54.00
2510 Bowl, frozen, dessert
Sunray................................$20.00
Glacier...............................$23.00
azure.................................$28.00
green.................................$28.00
amber,................................$27.00
topaz/gold tint..................$28.00
2510 Bowl, 5", fruit
Sunray................................$20.00
Glacier...............................$22.00
2510 Bowl, handled, nappy, regular
Sunray................................$16.00
ruby...................................$45.00
Glacier...............................$22.00
Golden Glow.......................$28.00
2510 Bowl, handled, nappy, flared
Sunray................................$16.00
ruby...................................$45.00
Glacier...............................$22.00
Golden Glow.......................$28.00
2510 Bowl, handled, nappy, square
Sunray................................$16.00
ruby...................................$22.00
Glacier...............................$45.00
Golden Glow.......................$28.00
2510 Bowl, 9½", nappy, flared
Sunray................................$27.00

2510 Bowl, 10", handled
Sunray................................$45.00
Glacier...............................$48.00
2510 Bowl, 13", rolled edge
Sunray................................$45.00
Glacier...............................$48.00
2510 Bowl, 12", salad
Sunray................................$45.00
2510 Candlestick, 3", priced each
Sunray................................$48.00
Glacier...............................$56.00
2510 Candlestick, 5½", priced each
Sunray................................$65.00
Glacier...............................$75.00
2510 Candlestick, duo, priced each
Sunray..............................$135.00
Glacier.............................$145.00
2510 Candelabra, 2-light, UDP, priced each
Sunray..............................$235.00
Glacier.............................$250.00
2510 Candy and Cover
Sunray................................$65.00
Glacier...............................$75.00
Golden Glow.......................$85.00
2510 Celery, 10", handled
Sunray................................$38.00
Glacier...............................$42.00
Golden Glow.......................$48.00
2510 Cigarette and Cover
Sunray................................$88.00
Glacier...............................$95.00
Golden Glow.....................$120.00
2510 Cigarette, oblong
Sunray................................$85.00
Glacier...............................$90.00
2510 Cheese and Cover or Butter and Cover
Sunray................................$56.00
Glacier...............................$60.00
2510 Coaster, 4"
Sunray................................$10.00
2510 Comport
Sunray................................$36.00
Glacier...............................$42.00
Golden Glow.......................$50.00
2510 Tray, condiment, 8½"
Sunray................................$65.00
Glacier...............................$70.00
2510 Condiment Set, 5-piece
Sunray..............................$275.00
Glacier.............................$295.00
2510 Cream Soup and Plate
Sunray................................$58.00
Glacier...............................$62.00
2510 Cup and Saucer
Sunray................................$16.00
Glacier...............................$20.00
2510 Decanter, oblong
Sunray..............................$125.00
Glacier.............................$150.00
2510 Decanter, 18 oz., oval
Sunray..............................$225.00
Glacier.............................$265.00
2510 Decanter Set, 8-piece
Sunray..............................$450.00
2510 Decanter Set: oval decanter, six 2-oz. whiskeys and oblong tray
Sunray..............................$450.00
Glacier.............................$500.00
2510 Ice Bucket with chrome handle and tongs
Sunray................................$87.00
ruby.................................$150.00
Glacier...............................$94.00

2510 Ice Bucket with silver-plated handle and tongs
Sunray................................$95.00
Glacier.............................$100.00
2510 Jelly and Cover
Sunray................................$67.00
Glacier...............................$72.00
Golden Glow.......................$94.00
2510 Jug, 2-quart
Sunray................................$95.00
Glacier.............................$100.00
2510 Jug, ice
Sunray................................$95.00
2510 Mayonnaise, plate, ladle
Sunray................................$58.00
Glacier...............................$65.00
Golden Glow.......................$75.00
2510 Mustard, cover, spoon
Sunray................................$64.00
Glacier...............................$68.00
2510 Oil and Stopper, 3 oz.
Sunray................................$60.00
Glacier...............................$68.00
2510 Onion Soup and Cover
Sunray................................$58.00
Glacier...............................$65.00
2510 Pitcher, pint, cereal
Sunray................................$37.00
2510 Plate, 6"
Sunray..................................$8.00
Glacier.................................$9.00
2510 Plate, 7"
Sunray................................$10.00
Glacier...............................$12.00
2510 Plate, 8"
Sunray................................$10.00
Glacier...............................$12.00
2510 Plate, 9"
Sunray................................$18.00
Glacier...............................$22.00
2510 Plate, 11", torte
Sunray................................$38.00
ruby...................................$95.00
Glacier...............................$42.00
Golden Glow.......................$47.00
2510 Plate, 12", sandwich
Sunray................................$40.00
ruby...................................$98.00
Glacier...............................$42.00
Golden Glow.......................$48.00
2510 Plate, 15", torte
Sunray................................$44.00
ruby.................................$125.00
Glacier...............................$53.00
Golden Glow.......................$60.00
2510 Plate, 16", flat
Sunray................................$47.00
ruby.................................$125.00
Glacier...............................$54.00
Golden Glow.......................$60.00
2510 Relish, 2-part
Sunray................................$32.00
ruby...................................$64.00
Glacier...............................$40.00
Golden Glow.......................$47.00
2510 Relish, 3-part
Sunray................................$38.00
ruby...................................$65.00
Glacier...............................$43.00
Golden Glow.......................$52.00
2510 Relish, 4-part
Sunray................................$40.00
ruby...................................$70.00

Glacier $45.00
Golden Glow $55.00
2510 Salad Set, 3-piece
Sunray....$110.00
Glacier $125.00
2510 Salt Dip
Sunray....$22.00
Glacier $24.00
2510 Shaker, FGT, pair
Sunray....$56.00
Glacier $64.00
2510 Shaker, individual, FGT, pair
Sunray....$48.00
Glacier $57.00
2510 Smoker Set, 5-piece: cigarette and cover and four individual ashtrays
Sunray....$165.00
Glacier $175.00
2510 Smoker Set, 5-piece: cigarette and cover, and four square ashtrays
Sunray....$150.00
Glacier $160.00
2510 Smoker Set, No. 3: two individual ashtrays, cigarette and cover on tray, sugar and cream
Sunray....$135.00
Glacier $150.00
2510 Sugar and Cream, footed
Sunray....$36.00
Glacier $42.00
2510 Sugar and Cream, individual
Sunray....$36.00
Glacier $42.00
2510 Tray, sugar and cream
Sunray....$22.00
Glacier $25.00
2510 Sugar and Cream Set
Sunray....$58.00
Glacier $67.00
2510 Sweetmeat, divided
Sunray....$28.00
Glacier $30.00
Golden Glow $35.00
2510 Tray, 7", oval handled
Sunray....$26.00
Glacier $28.00
Golden Glow $32.00
2510 Tray, 8½", condiment
Sunray....$65.00
Glacier $70.00
2510 Tray, 10", square
Sunray....$125.00
Glacier $135.00
2510 Tray, 10½", oblong
Sunray....$125.00
Glacier $140.00
2510 Vase, 3½", rose bowl
Sunray....$48.00
Glacier $57.00
Golden Glow $68.00
2510 Vase, 5", rose bowl
Sunray....$64.00
Glacier $68.00
Golden Glow $75.00
Vase, 6", crimped
Sunray....$58.00
Glacier $65.00
2510 Sweet Pea Vase, 5¼"....$68.00
2510 Vase, 7"....$75.00
2510 Vase, 8", square, footed $95.00

Sun Valley, Crystal Print 15 Tumbler

1958 – 1962

Stemware, 155

4180 Tumbler, 12 oz., flat, harvest yellow....$12.00
4180 Juice, 7 oz., flat, harvest yellow....$12.00

Sweetbriar, Cutting 857

1958 – 1959

Stemware, 115

6074 Goblet $34.00
6074 Sherbet....$32.00
6074 Cocktail/Wine/ Seafood....$34.00
6074 Cordial....$40.00
6074 Ice Tea, footed....$34.00
6074 Juice, footed....$30.00
2337 Plate, 7"....$10.00
2337 Plate, 8"....$12.00

Sweetheart Rose, Cutting 877

1960 – 1974

Stemware, 120

6092 Goblet ...$35.00
6092 Sherbet $33.00
6092 Wine/Cocktail....$38.00
6092 Cordial....$42.00
6092 Ice Tea, footed....$35.00
6092 Juice, footed....$30.00
2337 Plate, 7"....$10.00
2337 Plate, 8"....$12.00

Swirl, Cutting 848

1956 – 1965

Stemware, 112

6065 Goblet $35.00
6065 Sherbet....$32.00
6065 Cocktail/Wine/ Seafood....$34.00
6065 Cordial....$40.00
6065 Ice Tea, footed....$35.00
6065 Juice, footed....$32.00
2337 Plate, 7"....$10.00
2337 Plate, 8"....$12.00

Swirl Giftware, see Satin Mist/Swirl

Sylvan, Crystal Print 1

1955 – 1965

Stemware, 110

6060 Goblet $30.00
6060 Sherbet....$26.00
6060 Cocktail/Wine/ Seafood....$30.00
6060 Cordial....$40.00
6060 Ice Tea, footed....$30.00
6060 Juice, footed....$26.00

Tableware II, 159

2666 Bonbon....$26.00
2666 Bowl, oval....$32.00
2666 Butter and Cover, oblong....$45.00
2666 Candle, flora, pair....$58.00
2666 Celery....$22.00
2666 Cup and Saucer....$20.00
2666 Mayonnaise, plate, ladle....$56.00
2666 Plate, 7"....$12.00
2666 Plate, 10"....$24.00
2666 Plate, canape....$18.00
2666 Plate, 10", snack....$24.00
2666 Plate, 14", serving....$52.00
2685 Preserve, handled....$34.00
2666 Relish, 2-part....$30.00
2666 Relish, 3-part....$38.00
2685 Salver....$60.00
2364 Shaker, large, chrome top B, pair....$58.00
2666 Sugar and Cream....$58.00
2666 Sugar and Cream, individual and tray....$65.00

Symphony, 6065

1959 – 1970

Stemware, 112

6065 Goblet....$35.00
6065 Sherbet....$32.00
6065 Cocktail/Wine/ Seafood....$35.00
6065 Cordial....$44.00
6065 Ice Tea, footed....$35.00
6065 Juice, footed....$32.00

Syrups and Molasses Cans, see also American and Mayfair

pre-1924 – 1943

Useful & Ornamental, 200 – 201

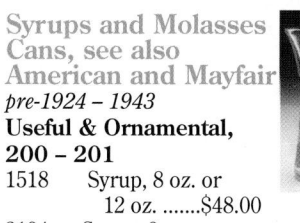

1518 Syrup, 8 oz. or 12 oz. $48.00
2194 Syrup, 8 oz. or 12 oz.....$48.00
2017 Molasses, 7 oz., plain or optic....$48.00
2586 Syrup, 9 oz., sani-cut....$125.00

–T–

Table Charms (see Bowls, Centerpieces, and Console Bowls)

Tankards (see Jugs and Tankards)

Tapestry, Cutting 701

1930

Stemware, 58

4020 Goblet $35.00
4020 Sherbet, high $35.00
4020 Sherbet, 7 oz., low....$30.00
4020 Sherbet, 5 oz., low....$30.00
4020 Cocktail, 3½ oz.....$30.00
4020 Ice Tea, footed....$35.00
4020 Tumbler, 13 oz., footed....$35.00
020 Tumbler, 10 oz., footed....$35.00
4020 Juice, footed....$30.00
4020 Whiskey, footed....$35.00

Tableware I, 273

4020 Bowl, finger....$24.00

Tapestry, Cutting 701

2350½ Cup, footed $16.00
2350 Cup, after dinner $18.00
2419 Plate, 6" $8.00
2419 Plate, 7" $10.00
2419 Plate, 8" $14.00
2419 Saucer $8.00
2419 Saucer, after dinner $10.00

Tara, Etching 34

1974 – 1982

Stemware, 142

6126 Goblet $35.00
6126 Champagne $32.00
6126 Wine $37.00
6126 Ice Tea, footed $35.00

Tempo, 6032

1942 – 1943

Stemware, 101

6032 Goblet $34.00
6032 Saucer Champagne $32.00
6032 Sherbet, low $28.00
6032 Cocktail $30.00
6032 Claret-Wine $36.00
6032 Cordial $42.00
6032 Oyster Cocktail $24.00
6032 Ice Tea, footed $34.00
6032 Juice, footed $36.00

Tenderness, Decoration 691

1971 – 1974

Green Mist bowl

Stemware, 140

6123 Goblet $25.00
6123 Sherbet $22.00
6123 Wine $25.00
6123 Ice Tea, footed $25.00
2337 Plate, 7", green mist, decorated $18.00

The President's House, 7780 (see President's House, The)

Thelma, Cutting 186

1928

Tableware I, 271

2297 Bowl A, 12", deep
amber $57.00
green $68.00
rose $68.00
orchid $68.00

2342 Bowl A, 12½", deep
amber $85.00
green $95.00
rose $95.00
orchid $95.00

2362 Bowl, 12½"
amber $70.00
green $85.00
rose $85.00
orchid $85.00

2362 Candlestick, 3", pair
amber $65.00
green $78.00
rose $78.00
orchid $78.00

2324 Candlestick, 4", pair
amber $65.00
green $78.00
rose $78.00
orchid $78.00

2331 Box, candy and cover
amber $84.00
green $97.00
rose $97.00
orchid $97.00

2329 Centerpiece, 11"
amber $80.00
green $94.00
rose $94.00
orchid $94.00

2329 Centerpiece, 13"
amber $87.00
green $100.00
rose $100.00
orchid $100.00

2368 Cheese and Cracker
amber $70.00
green $85.00
rose $85.00
orchid $85.00

2327 Comport, 7"
amber $64.00
green $75.00
rose $75.00
orchid $75.00

2378 Ice Bucket, NP handle
amber $87.00
green $98.00
rose $98.00
orchid $98.00

2378 Sugar Pail, NP handle
amber $175.00
green $200.00
rose $200.00
orchid $200.00

2287 Tray, 11", handled, lunch
amber $64.00
green $70.00
rose $70.00
orchid $70.00

2342 Tray, 12", handled, lunch
amber $64.00
green $70.00
rose $70.00
orchid $70.00

4103 Vase, 4", optic
amber $54.00
green $65.00
rose $65.00
orchid $65.00

4103 Vase, 5", optic
amber $60.00
green $68.00
rose $68.00
orchid $68.00

4103 Vase, 6", optic
amber $65.00
green $74.00
rose $74.00
orchid $74.00

4100 Vase, 6", optic
amber $65.00
green $74.00
rose $74.00
orchid $74.00

4100 Vase, 8", optic
amber $85.00
green $125.00
rose $125.00
orchid $125.00

2369 Vase, 7", optic
amber $94.00
green $135.00
rose $135.00
orchid $135.00

2369 Vase, 9", optic
amber $140.00
green $175.00
rose $175.00
orchid $175.00

Thistle, Etching 346

1953 – 1970

Stemware, 107

6052½ Goblet ... $30.00
6052½ Sherbet $26.00
6052½ Cocktail $26.00
6052½ Claret-Wine $34.00
6052½ Cordial $40.00
6052½ Oyster Cocktail $20.00
6052½ Ice Tea, footed $30.00
6052½ Juice, footed $24.00

Tableware II, 155 – 158

2666 Bonbon $30.00
2666 Bowl, individual salad/dessert $20.00
2666 Bowl, 8¼", oval $35.00
2666 Bowl, 9", salad $42.00
2666 Bowl, 11", salad $45.00
2666 Butter Pat $18.00
2666 Candle, flora, pair $44.00
2666 Celery $22.00
2666 Cup and Saucer $25.00
2666 Mayonnaise, plate, ladle $58.00
2666 Pickle $22.00
2666 Pitcher, pint $42.00
2666 Pitcher, quart $85.00
2666 Pitcher, 3-pint $110.00
2666 Plate, 7" $12.00
2666 Plate, 7⅜", canape $16.00
2666 Plate, 10" $24.00
2666 Plate 10", snack $24.00
2666 Plate, 14", serving $52.00
2666 Relish, 2-part $32.00
2666 Relish, 3-part $38.00
2666 Salad Set, 11", 4-piece $97.00
2364 Shaker, large, chrome top C, pair $65.00
2666 Sugar and Cream $52.00
2666 Sugar and Cream, individual $48.00
2666 Tray, sugar and cream $15.00
6021 Vase, 6", footed, bud $54.00
2660 Vase, 8", flip $80.00
2470 Vase, 10" $95.00

Thoroughbred, Carving 40

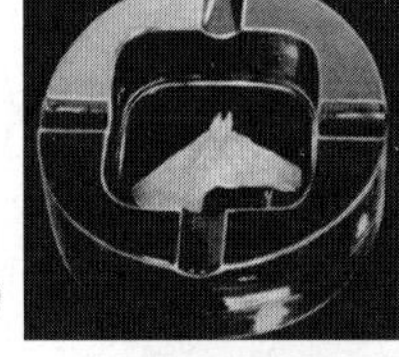

1940 – 1943

Useful & Ornamental, 130

2516 Ashtray $30.00

Three Geese, Carving 26

1940 – 1943

Useful & Ornamental, 129

4132½ Vase, 8" $125.00

Tiara, 6044 Tumbler
1957 – 1958
Stemware, 156
6044 Ice Tea/Highball
crystal.............$14.00
cinnamon bowl............$14.00
spruce bowl $14.00
6044 Water/Scotch and Soda
crystal $14.00
cinnamon bowl..................$14.00
spruce bowl.......................$14.00
6044 Sherbet/Old Fashioned
crystal $14.00
cinnamon bowl..................$14.00
spruce bowl.......................$14.00
6044 Juice/Cocktail
crystal $14.00
cinnamon bowl..................$14.00
spruce bowl.......................$14.00
6044 Dessert/Finger Bowl
crystal $14.00
cinnamon bowl..................$14.00
spruce bowl.......................$14.00

Tiara, Cutting 903
1964 – 1970
Stemware, 129
6104 Goblet $28.00
6104 Sherbet $26.00
6104 Claret $30.00
6104 Wine..$30.00
6104 Cordial $38.00
6104 Ice Tea, footed $28.00
2337 Plate, 7" $10.00
2337 Plate, 8" $12.00

Tiger Lily, Carving 18
1940 – 1943
Useful & Ornamental, 123
4132 Vase, 5".........$65.00
2577 Vase, 5½", wide $70.00
2577 Vase, 6"..........$75.00

Toy, Carving 33, Decoration 620
1940 – 1943
Useful & Ornamental, 128
4146 Scotch and Soda, 9 oz. 46.00
4146 Cocktail, 4 oz.........................$34.00
4146 Cordial, 1 oz. $40.00
2306 Smoker Set, 4 piece:
Ashtray, 2¾" $28.00
Ashtray, 3"..........................$32.00
Ashtray, 3½" $37.00
Ashtray, 4"..........................$40.00

Transition, 2936
1978 – 1986
Stemware, 55
2936 Wine/Juice $10.00
2936 Old Fashioned, double $10.00
2936 Highball.................................$12.00
Tableware II, 306
TR05/123 Ashtray, 5"..............................$25.00
TR05/179 Bowl, 8", serving....................$25.00
TR05/319 Candleholder, pair.................$25.00
TR05/504 Salad/Dessert, 5" $25.00
TR05/557 Plate, 11", buffet.....................$25.00
TR05/665 Chip and Dip, 5", salad and 11" plate $35.00
TR05/686 Sugar and Cream..................$25.00

Trellis, Cutting 169
1924 – 1928
Stemware, 18
660 Goblet ..$20.00
660 Saucer Champagne $15.00
660 Sherbet, low $12.00
660 Parfait $15.00
660 Cocktail $15.00
660 Wine..$15.00
660 Cordial $30.00
Tableware I, 265
766 Bonbon $18.00
766 Bowl, finger and plate $18.00
810 Bowl, finger and plate $18.00
2250 Jar, candy and cover, ¼ pound $28.00
2250 Jar, candy and cover, ½ pound $32.00
2250 Jar, candy and cover, pound...................................$36.00
1697 Carafe $38.00
4023 Carafe Tumbler $12.00
5078 Comport, 5"............................$22.00
5078 Comport and Cover, 5" $27.00
5078 Comport, 6"............................$24.00
5078 Comport and Cover, 6" $30.00
300 Decanter, quart, cut neck $50.00
825 Jelly $20.00
825 Jelly and Cover $25.00
303/7 Jug..$88.00
724/7 Jug..$95.00
1787/3 Jug..$95.00
2270 Jug..$95.00
2270 Jug and Cover....................$110.00
1968 Marmalade and Cover $30.00
810 Mayonnaise Set, 3-piece $47.00
1831 Mustard and Cover $24.00
5078 Nappy, 5"..................................$20.00
5078 Nappy and Cover, 5" $24.00
5078 Nappy, 6"..................................$20.00
5078 Nappy and Cover, 6" $24.00
5078 Nappy, 7"..................................$22.00
5078 Nappy and Cover, 7" $28.00
5078 Nappy, 8"..................................$24.00
5078 Nappy and Cover, 8" $32.00
1465 Oil, 5 oz., CN, polished stopper $46.00
1465 Oil, 7 oz., CN, polished stopper $49.00
2283 Plate, 5" $4.00
840 Plate, 5" $4.00
2283 Plate, 6" $7.00
2283 Plate, 7" $8.00
1897 Plate, 7" $8.00
2283 Plate, 8" $10.00
2238 Plate, 8½" $10.00
1848 Plate, 9", cut matt star...........$12.00
2235 Shaker, FGT............................$35.00
2235 Shaker, pearl top $36.00
1851 Sugar and Cream...................$34.00
2194 Syrup, 8 oz..............................$85.00
2276 Vanity Set $125.00
837 Oyster Cocktail......................$12.00
945½ Grapefruit and Liner $30.00
887 Tumbler, 2½ oz. $6.00
889 Tumbler, 13 oz. $15.00
889 Tumbler, 8 oz. $10.00
889 Tumbler, 5 oz. $7.00
4011 Tumbler, 12 oz., handled......$20.00
4076 Tumbler, 9 oz. $7.00
4095 Tumbler, 13 oz., footed $20.00
4095 Tumbler, 10 oz., footed $16.00
4095 Tumbler, 5 oz., footed $12.00

Trellis, Cutting 822
1950 – 1954
Stemware, 100
6030 Goblet $30.00
6030 Goblet, low $28.00
6030 Saucer Champagne $28.00
6030 Sherbet, low $24.00
6030 Cocktail $26.00
6030 Claret-Wine $34.00
6030 Cordial $40.00
6030 Oyster Cocktail......................$22.00
6030 Ice Tea, footed $30.00
6030 Juice, footed $24.00
2337 Plate, 7" $10.00
2337 Plate, 8" $12.00

Triangle, Decoration 610
1931 – 1932
Silver on ebony
Tableware I, 331
2375 Bonbon $28.00
2395 Bowl, 10" $150.00
2395½ Candlestick, 5".......................$140.00
2391 Cigarette and Cover, large ...$95.00
2375 Dish, lemon..............................$28.00
2375 Plate, 10", cake $85.00
2385 Vase, 8½", fan $295.00
2373 Vase and Cover, large, window $275.00

Triumph, Silver, Gold (see Gold Triumph, Silver Triumph)

Trojan, Plate Etching 280
1929 – 1943

Stemware, 70
5099 Goblet
topaz..$65.00
rose...$125.00
5099 Sherbet, high
topaz..................................$60.00
rose $95.00
5099 Sherbet, low
topaz..................................$37.00
rose $48.00

5099 Parfait
topaz $75.00
rose $125.00

5099 Cocktail
topaz $58.00
rose $90.00

5099 Claret
topaz $85.00
rose $135.00

5099 Wine
topaz $85.00
rose $125.00

5099 Cordial
topaz $95.00
rose $150.00

5099 Oyster Cocktail
topaz $35.00
rose $48.00

5099 Ice Tea, footed
topaz $60.00
rose $120.00

5099 Tumbler, 9 oz., footed
topaz $35.00
rose $57.00

5099 Juice, footed
topaz $35.00
rose $57.00

5099 Whiskey, footed
topaz $68.00
rose $95.00

Tableware I, 180 – 183

2350 Ashtray, small
topaz $47.00
rose $47.00

2350 Ashtray, large
topaz $50.00
rose $54.00

2375 Bonbon
topaz $48.00
rose $57.00

2375 Bouillon
topaz $30.00
rose $38.00

869 Bowl, finger and 2283 Plate, 6"
topaz $95.00
rose $125.00

2375 Bowl, 5", fruit
topaz $32.00
rose $45.00

2375 Bowl, 6", cereal
topaz $48.00
rose $57.00

2394 Bowl, 6"
topaz $52.00
rose $58.00

2375 Bowl, 7", soup
topaz $95.00
rose $110.00

2375 Bowl, 7", round, nappy
topaz $140.00
rose $156.00

2375 Bowl, 9", baker
topaz $94.00
rose $125.00

2395 Bowl, 10"
topaz $235.00
rose $350.00

2375 Bowl, dessert, large
topaz $95.00
rose $125.00

2375 Bowl, 12"
topaz $115.00
rose $175.00

2394 Bowl A, 12"
topaz $125.00
rose $200.00

2394 Candlestick, 2", pair
topaz $98.00
rose $150.00

2375 Candlestick, 3", pair
topaz $98.00
rose $150.00

2375½ Candlestick, pair
topaz $150.00
rose $165.00

2395½ Candlestick, 5", pair
topaz $160.00
rose $200.00

2394 Jar, candy and cover
topaz $150.00
rose $185.00

2375 Celery, 11½"
topaz $85.00
rose $125.00

2375 Centerpiece, 12"
topaz $250.00
rose $265.00

2368 Cheese and Cracker
topaz $130.00
rose $150.00

2375 Cheese and Cracker
topaz $150.00
rose $185.00

2400 Comport, 6"
topaz $98.00
rose $135.00

5099 Comport, 6"
topaz $125.00
rose $150.00

2375 Cream Soup and Plate
topaz $85.00
rose $125.00

2375 Cup and Saucer, after dinner
topaz $125.00
rose $150.00

2375½ Cup and Saucer
topaz $45.00
rose $57.00

2439 Decanter and Stopper
topaz market
rose market

2375 Ice Bucket, NP handle
topaz $185.00
rose $250.00

2451 Dish, ice and liner
topaz $85.00
rose $95.00

5000 Jug
topaz $595.00
rose $1200.00/market

2375 Lemon
topaz $48.00
rose $57.00

2375 Mayonnaise, plate, ladle
topaz $135.00
rose $150.00

2394 Mint
topaz $47.00
rose $58.00

2375 Oil
topaz $650.00
rose $700.00

2375 Plate, 6"
topaz $20.00
rose $28.00

2375 Plate, 7"
topaz $22.00
rose $32.00

2375 Plate, 8"
topaz $24.00
rose $35.00

2375 Plate, 9"
topaz $35.00
rose $58.00

2375 Plate, 10", dinner
topaz $85.00
rose $138.00

2375 Plate, 10", cake
topaz $125.00
rose $165.00

2375 Plate, 10", grill
topaz $80.00
rose $125.00

2375 Plate, canape
topaz $37.00
rose $50.00

2375 Plate, 13", chop
topaz $145.00
rose $175.00

2375 Platter, 12"
topaz $145.00
rose $168.00

2375 Platter, 15"
topaz $160.00
rose $200.00

2375 Relish, 8½"
topaz $58.00
rose $76.00

2350 Relish, 3-part
topaz $75.00
rose $110.00

2375 Sauce and Plate
topaz $225.00
rose $300.00

2375 Shaker, FGT , pair
topaz $250.00
rose $335.00

2375½ Sugar and Cream, tea
topaz $145.00
rose $168.00

2375½ Sugar and Cream
topaz $125.00
rose $175.00

2375½ Sugar and Cover
topaz $115.00
rose $160.00

2378 Pail, sugar, NP handle
topaz $425.00
rose $450.00

2375 Sweetmeat
topaz $48.00
rose $57.00

2375 Tray, handled, lunch
topaz $175.00
rose $195.00

2429 Tray, service, and lemon insert
topaz $295.00
rose $350.00

2417 Vase, 8", RO
topaz $500.00
rose $650.00

4105 Vase, 8", RO
topaz $500.00
rose $650.00

2375 Whip Cream
topaz $48.00
rose $57.00

2378 Pail, whip cream, NP handle
topaz $425.00
rose $450.00

Trousseau, Decoration 642

1958 – 1982

Stemware, 116

6080 Goblet $35.00
6080 Sherbet $32.00
6080 Cocktail $32.00
6080 Claret-Wine $37.00
6080 Cordial $45.00
6080 Ice Tea, footed $35.00
6080 Juice, footed $32.00
6080 Claret, 8 oz., large $45.00
6080 Claret, 6 oz., large $45.00
2337 Plate, 7" $10.00
2337 Plate, 8" $12.00

True Love, Cutting 862

1958 – 1967

Stemware, 116

6080 Goblet $34.00
6080 Sherbet. $32.00
6080 Cocktail $32.00
6080 Claret-Wine $38.00
6080 Cordial $42.00
6080 Ice Tea, footed $34.00
6080 Juice, footed $30.00
2337 Plate, 7" $10.00
2337 Plate, 8" $12.00

Tulip, Cutting 772

1937 – 1943

Stemware, 91

6019 Goblet $26.00
6019 Sherbet $23.00
6019 Parfait $26.00
6019 Cocktail $23.00
6019 Claret $28.00
6019 Wine $26.00
6019 Oyster Cocktail $16.00
6019 Ice Tea, footed $26.00
6019 Juice, footed $20.00
4132 Tumbler, 13 oz., standish $12.00
4132 Tumbler, 12 oz., standish $12.00
4132 Tumbler, 9 oz., standish $10.00
4132 Tumbler, 7½ oz., standish $8.00
4132 Tumbler, 5 oz.,standish $8.00
4132 Tumbler, 1½ oz., standish $10.00

Tableware I, 298

766 Bowl, finger $12.00
4132 Bowl, ice $40.00
2496 Bowl, 10½", handled $75.00
2430 Bowl, 11 $65.00
2430 Candlestick, 2", pair $65.00
2496 Candlestick, 5½", pair $48.00
4132 Decanter and Stopper $85.00
2430 Jelly, 7" $28.00
2430 Mint, 5½" $22.00
2337 Plate, 6" $6.00
2337 Plate, 7" $7.00
2337 Plate, 8" $8.00
2430 Vase, 8" $60.00

Tumblers

Blank 127 Tumbler

Stemware, 148

127 Tumbler, 9 oz., flat $6.00
127 Tumbler, 9 oz., handled, $10.00

Blank 701 Tumbler

RO, NO, SO, No Optic
Crystal, rose, green, amber, topaz, wisteria

Stemware, 148

701 Tumbler, 21 oz., flat
- crystal $14.00
- regular colors $18.00
- wisteria $50.00

701 Tumbler, 20 oz., flat
- crystal $14.00
- regular colors $18.00
- wisteria $50.00

701 Tumbler, 19 oz., flat
- crystal $14.00
- regular colors $18.00
- wisteria $50.00

701 Tumbler, 18 oz., flat
- crystal $14.00
- regular colors $18.00
- wisteria $50.00

701 Tumbler, 16 oz., flat
- crystal $14.00
- regular colors $18.00
- wisteria $50.00

701 Tumbler, 17 oz., flat
- crystal $14.00
- regular colors $18.00
- wisteria $50.00

701 Tumbler, 15 oz., flat
- crystal $14.00
- regular colors $18.00
- wisteria $50.00

701 Tumbler, 14 oz., flat
- crystal $14.00
- regular colors $18.00
- wisteria $50.00

701 Tumbler, 13 oz., flat
- crystal $12.00
- regular colors $16.00
- wisteria $45.00

701 Tumbler, 12 oz., flat
- crystal $12.00
- regular colors $16.00
- wisteria $45.00

701 Tumbler, 11½ oz., flat
- crystal $12.00
- regular colors $16.00
- wisteria $45.00

701 Tumbler, 11 oz., flat
- crystal $12.00
- regular colors $16.00
- wisteria $45.00

701 Tumbler, 10 oz., flat
- crystal $12.00
- regular colors $16.00
- wisteria $45.00

701 Tumbler, 9 oz., flat
- crystal $10.00
- regular colors $14.00
- wisteria $40.00

701 Tumbler, 8 oz., flat
- crystal $10.00
- regular colors $14.00
- wisteria $40.00

701 Tumbler, 8 oz., handled
- crystal $10.00
- regular colors $14.00
- wisteria $40.00

701 Tumbler, 7½ oz., flat
- crystal $8.00
- regular colors $12.00
- wisteria $25.00

701 Tumbler, 7 oz., flat
- crystal $8.00
- regular colors $12.00
- wisteria $25.00

701 Tumbler, 6½ oz., flat
- crystal $8.00
- regular colors $12.00
- wisteria $25.00

701 Tumbler, 6 oz., flat
- crystal $8.00
- regular colors $12.00
- wisteria $25.00

701 Tumbler, 5 oz., flat
- crystal $8.00
- regular colors $12.00
- wisteria $25.00

701 Tumbler, 4 oz., flat
- crystal $8.00
- regular colors $12.00
- wisteria $25.00

Blank 766 Tumbler

(see Blank 766)

Blank 810 Tumbler

Stemware, 148

810 Tumbler, 10 oz., tall, flat
- regular $8.00
- no optic $8.00

810 Tumbler, 8 oz., tall, flat
- regular $7.00
- no optic $7.00

810 Tumbler, 5 oz., tall, flat
- regular $5.00
- no optic $5.00

810 Tumbler, 3 oz., tall, flat
- regular $4.00
- no optic $4.00

810 Tumbler, 11 oz., flat
- regular $9.00
- no optic $9.00

810 Tumbler, 9 oz., flat
- regular $8.00
- no optic $8.00

810 Tumbler, 8 oz., flat
- regular $7.00
- no optic $7.00

810 Tumbler, 6 oz., flat
- regular $6.00
- no optic $6.00

810 Tumbler, 5 oz., flat
- regular $5.00
- no optic $5.00

810 Tumbler, 3 oz., flat
- regular $4.00
- no optic $4.00

Blank 820/ 820½ Tumbler

Stemware, 149

820 Tumbler, flat, table, no optic $5.00
820½ Tumbler, flat, table, cut flutes, no optic $6.00

Blank 833 Tumbler

Stemware, 149

833 Tumbler, 14 oz., flat,
- narrow optic $10.00
- no optic $10.00

833 Tumbler, 12 oz., flat
narrow optic $9.00
no optic $9.00
833 Tumbler, 10 oz., flat
narrow optic $8.00
no optic $8.00
833 Tumbler, 9 oz., flat
narrow optic $7.00
no optic $7.00
833 Tumbler, 8 oz., flat
narrow optic $5.00
no optic $5.00
833 Tumbler, 7 oz., flat
narrow optic $4.00
no optic $4.00
833 Tumbler, 6 oz., flat
narrow optic $3.00
no optic $3.00
833 Tumbler, 5 oz., flat
narrow optic $3.00
no optic $3.00
833 Tumbler, 4 oz., flat
narrow optic $4.00
no optic $4.00
833 Tumbler, 3 oz., flat
narrow optic $4.00
no optic $4.00
833 Tumbler, 2 oz., flat
narrow optic $6.00
no optic $6.00
833 Tumbler, 1½ oz., flat
narrow optic $7.00
no optic $7.00
833 Tumbler, 1 oz., flat
narrow optic $7.00
no optic $7.00

Blank 833½, Sham Bottoms

Note: Named Heatherbell

Stemware

833½ Tumbler, 14 oz., sham $10.00
833½ Tumbler, 12 oz., sham $10.00
833½ Tumbler, 10 oz., sham $10.00
833½ Tumbler, 8 oz., sham $6.00
833½ Old Fashioned Cocktail, 7 oz., sham $5.00
833½ Tumbler, 5 oz., sham $4.00
833½ Whiskey, 1½ oz., sham $7.00

Blank 835 Tumbler, see Jenny Lind

Blank 837 Tumbler

Stemware, 149

837 Oyster Cocktail $10.00
837 Tumbler, 9 oz., flat $6.00
837 Tumbler, 5 oz., flat $5.00
837 Tumbler, 3 oz., flat $5.00
837 Tumbler, 12 oz., handled $10.00

Blank 858 Tumbler, see Blank 858

Blank 869 Tumbler, see Blank 869

Blank 877 Tumbler, see Blank 877

Blank 887 Tumbler and Sham, Tumbler

Stemware, 150

887 Tumbler, 5 oz., flat
regular $5.00
narrow $6.00
no optic $5.00
887 Tumbler, 4½ oz., flat $5.00
887 Tumbler, 4¼ oz., flat $5.00
887 Tumbler, 4 oz., flat $5.00
887 Tumbler, 3½ oz., flat $4.00
887 Tumbler, 3 oz., flat $4.00
887 Tumbler, 2¾ oz., flat $4.00
887 Tumbler, 2½ oz., flat, narrow optic
rose $22.00
green $22.00
amber $22.00
topaz $22.00
wisteria $36.00
azure $22.00
887 Tumbler, 2¼ oz., flat $4.00
887 Tumbler, 2 oz., flat $5.00
887 Tumbler, 1 ¾ oz., flat $5.00
887 Tumbler, 1½ oz., flat $6.00
887 Whiskey, 1¾ oz., no optic
regal blue $34.00
burgundy $34.00
empire green $34.00
ruby $34.00
887 Whiskey, RO, 1¾ oz.
crystal $7.00
amber $22.00
887 Whiskey Sham, 1¾ oz.
crystal only $7.00

Blank 889 Tumbler

No optic, narrow optic, cut flutes
Made in crystal except as noted

Stemware, 150

889 Tumbler, 21 oz., flat $14.00
889 Tumbler, 18 oz., flat $13.00
889 Tumbler, 16 oz., flat $13.00
889 Tumbler, 15 oz., flat $12.00
889 Tumbler, 14 oz., flat $12.00
889 Tumbler, no optic, 13 oz., flat $10.00
889 Tumbler, 13 oz., RO, flat
crystal $10.00
amber $12.00
889 Tumbler, 12 oz., flat $9.00
889 Tumbler, 11 oz., flat $9.00
889 Tumbler, 10 oz., flat $8.00
889 Tumbler, 10 oz., flat, sham, NO
amber $12.00
topaz $14.00
889 Tumbler, 9 oz., flat $8.00
889 Tumbler, 8 oz., flat $7.00
889 Tumbler, 7 oz., flat $7.00
889 Tumbler, 6 oz., flat $6.00
889 Tumbler, 5½ oz., flat $6.00
889- Tumbler, 5 oz. flat
crystal, plain, RO, NO $6.00
amber, RO, NO $16.00
empire green, plain $34.00
regal blue, plain $34.00
burgundy, plain $34.00
ruby, plain $34.00
green, NO $22.00
rose, NO $22.00
topaz, NO $22.00
wisteria, NO $36.00
889 Tumbler, 4½ oz., flat $5.00
889 Tumbler, 4 oz., flat $4.00
889 Tumbler, 3 oz., flat $4.00
889 Tumbler, 14 oz., handled $16.00
889 Tumbler, 8 oz., handled $14.00

Blank 923

Stemware, 150

Tumbler, 7 oz., handled $12.00

Blank 1184 Tumbler

No optic, narrow optic

Stemware, 150

1184 Old Fashioned Cocktail, 7 oz., NO
no optic $8.00
narrow optic $22.00
crystal $22.00
rose $22.00
amber $22.00
green $22.00
topaz $22.00
wisteria $34.00
azure $24.00
1184 Tumbler, 6 oz., flat $7.00
1184 Tumbler, 5 oz., flat $6.00
1184 Tumbler, 4½ oz., flat $6.00
1184 Tumbler, 4¼ oz., flat $6.00
1184 Tumbler, 4 oz., flat $6.00
1184 Tumbler, 3½ oz., flat $5.00
1184 Tumbler, 3 oz., flat $5.00
1184 Tumbler, 2¾ oz., flat $4.00
1184 Tumbler, 2¼ oz., flat $4.00
1184 Tumbler, 2 oz., flat $4.00
1184 Tumbler, 1¾ oz., flat $4.00
1184 Tumbler, 5 oz., handled $8.00

Blank 1185 Tumbler

Stemware, 151

1185 Old Fashioned Cocktail, 8 oz., sham
crystal $8.00
regal blue $34.00
burgundy $34.00
empire green $34.00
ruby $34.00
1185 Whiskey Sour, 5 oz., sham
crystal only $7.00

Blank 1704 Tumbler, see Winburn

Blank 2643 Tumbler, see Holiday

Blank 2670 Tumbler, see Dawn

Blank 2671 Tumbler, see Dusk

Blank 2675 Tumbler, see Randolph

Blank 2824 Tumbler, see Module

Blank 2861 Tumbler, see Aspen

Blank 2862 Tumbler, see Stowe

Blank 2863 Tumbler, see Alta and Vale

Blank 2934 Tumbler, see York

Blank 4005 Tumbler

Regular optic

4005 Tumbler, 12 oz., flat $20.00
4005 Tumbler, 9 oz., flat $18.00
4005 Tumbler, 5 oz., flat $12.00
4005 Tumbler, 2½ oz., flat $12.00

Blank 4011, 4011½ Tumbler

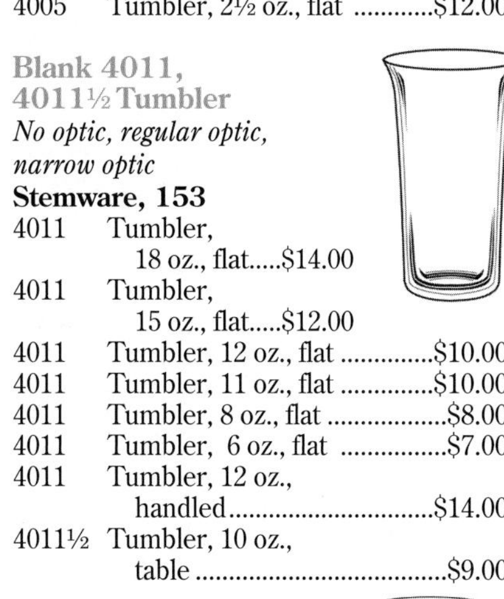

No optic, regular optic, narrow optic

Stemware, 153

4011 Tumbler, 18 oz., flat....$14.00
4011 Tumbler, 15 oz., flat....$12.00
4011 Tumbler, 12 oz., flat $10.00
4011 Tumbler, 11 oz., flat $10.00
4011 Tumbler, 8 oz., flat $8.00
4011 Tumbler, 6 oz., flat $7.00
4011 Tumbler, 12 oz., handled....$14.00
4011½ Tumbler, 10 oz., table $9.00

Blank 4061

Stemware, 153

4061 Lemonade, footed, handled....$18.00

Blank 4076 9 oz. Flat Tumbler

Regular optic
Made in the colors of the pattern

Stemware, 153

4076 Tumbler, 10 oz., flat $20.00
4076 Tumbler, 9 oz., flat
amber....$20.00
green....$22.00
rose $22.00
topaz....$22.00

Blank 4077 Tumbler

Regular optic

Stemware, 153

4077 Tumbler, 15 oz., table....$14.00
4077 Tumbler, 12½ oz., table....$14.00
4077 Tumbler, 11 oz., table $12.00
4077 Tumbler, 9½ oz., table $10.00
4077 Tumbler, 9 oz., table $8.00
4077 Tumbler, 8 oz., table $7.00
4077 Tumbler, 5½ oz., table $6.00
4077 Tumbler, 3 oz., table $5.00

Blank 4085 Tumbler

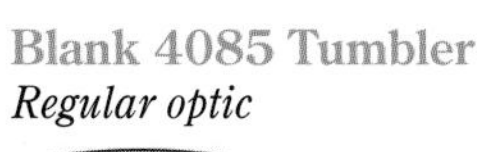

Regular optic

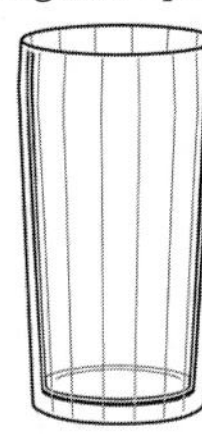

Stemware, 153

4085 Tumbler, 6 oz., flat $6.00
4085 Tumbler, 2½ oz., flat $6.00
4085 Tumbler, 13 oz., table $14.00
4085 Tumbler, 13 oz., handled....$18.00

Blank 4095 Footed Tumbler

1923 – 1929

Stemware, 154

Regular optic, spiral optic, loop optic

4095 Oyster Cocktail, 4 oz.
crystal....$12.00
green....$18.00
azure bowl....$20.00
green bowl....$18.00
rose bowl....$20.00
amber base....$16.00
green base....$18.00
blue base....$22.00

4095 Parfait, 6 oz.
crystal....$20.00
green....$26.00
azure bowl....$28.00
green bowl....$26.00
rose bowl....$28.00
amber base....$22.00
green base....$24.00
blue base....$30.00

4095 Tumbler, 13 oz., footed
crystal....$22.00
green....$28.00
azure bowl....$30.00
green bowl....$28.00
rose bowl....$30.00
amber base....$25.00
green base....$26.00
blue base....$32.00

4095 Tumbler, 10 oz., footed
crystal....$18.00
green....$22.00
azure bowl....$25.00
green bowl....$22.00
rose bowl....$25.00
amber base....$20.00
green base....$22.00
blue base....$26.00

4095 Tumbler, 5 oz., footed
crystal....$14.00
green....$22.00
azure bowl....$25.00
green bowl....$22.00
rose bowl....$25.00
amber base....$20.00
green base....$20.00
blue base....$26.00

4095 Tumbler, 2½ oz., footed
crystal....$14.00
green....$22.00
azure bowl....$25.00
green bowl....$24.00
rose bowl....$25.00
amber base....$22.00
green base....$23.00
blue base....$26.00

Blank 4115/4115½ Tumbler

Used with Fish Canape

4115 Tumbler, 3 oz., footed....$4.00
4115½ Tumbler, 4 oz. footed....$5.00

Blank 4122 Tumbler

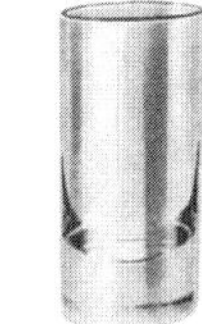

4115 Whiskey, 15 oz., sham....$12.00

Blank 4132 Tumbler, see Standish

Blank 4139 Tumbler, see Esquire

Blank 4140 Tumbler, see Blank 4140

Blank 4141 Tumbler, see Blank 4141

Blank 4142 Tumbler, see Blank 4142

Blank 4146 Tumbler, see Humpty Dumpty

Blank 4161 Tumbler, see Karnak

Blank 4162 Tumbler, see Congo

Blank 4163 Tumbler, see Inca

Blank 4180 Tumbler, see Casual Flair, Blue Meadow, Ring O'Roses, Kismet, Plain 'N Fancy, Golden Twilight, Country Garden, Greenbriar, Sun Valley

Blank 4183 Tumbler, see Homespun

Blank 4184 Tumbler, see Needlepoint

Blank 5000 Tumbler, see also Jugs and Tankards

1927 – 1943

Regular, spiral, loop optic

Stemware, 156

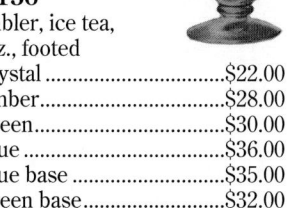

5000 Tumbler, ice tea, 12 oz., footed
crystal....$22.00
amber....$28.00
green....$30.00
blue....$36.00
blue base....$35.00
green base....$32.00
amber base....$30.00
amber bowl....$32.00
green bowl....$34.00

orchid bowl $36.00
rose bowl $38.00
azure bowl $38.00
amber base with
mother-of pearl bowl....$32.00
green base with
mother-of pearl bowl....$32.00

5000 Tumbler, 9 oz., footed
crystal $18.00
amber........................$22.00
green........................$24.00
blue $28.00
blue base $28.00
green base........................$24.00
amber base........................$22.00
amber bowl $22.00
green bowl $24.00
orchid bowl $27.00
rose bowl........................$28.00
azure bowl........................$28.00
amber base with
mother-of-pearl bowl....$22.00
green base with
mother-of-pearl bowl....$24.00

5000 Tumbler, 7 oz., footed
crystal $14.00
amber........................$18.00
green........................$20.00
blue $26.00
blue base $26.00
green base........................$20.00
amber base........................$18.00
amber bowl $18.00
green bowl $20.00
rose bowl........................$25.00
azure bowl........................$25.00
amber base with
mother-of-pearl bowl....$18.00
green base with
mother-of-pearl bowl....$20.00

5000 Parfait, 6 oz., footed
crystal $20.00
amber........................$22.00
green........................$26.00
blue $30.00
blue base $30.00
green base........................$76.00
amber base........................$22.00
amber bowl $22.00
green bowl $26.00
orchid bowl $28.00
rose bowl........................$28.00
azure bowl........................$28.00
amber base with
mother-of-pearl bowl....$22.00
green base with
mother-of-pearl bowl....$26.00

5000 Juice, 5 oz., footed
crystal $14.00
amber........................$22.00
green........................$22.00
blue $26.00
blue base $26.00
green base........................$22.00
amber base........................$22.00
amber bowl $22.00
green bowl $24.00
orchid bowl $26.00
rose bowl........................$25.00
azure bowl........................$25.00
amber base with
mother-of-pearl bowl....$22.00
green base with
mother-of-pearl bowl....$22.00

5000 Oyster Cocktail, 4½ oz., footed
crystal $12.00
amber........................$18.00
green........................$20.00
blue $25.00
blue base $25.00
green base........................$20.00
amber base........................$18.00
amber bowl $18.00
green bowl $20.00
orchid bowl $24.00
rose bowl........................$24.00
azure bowl........................$24.00
amber base with
mother-of-pearl bowl....$18.00
green base with
mother-of-pearl bowl....$20.00

5000 Whiskey, 2½ oz., footed
crystal $14.00
amber........................$20.00
green........................$22.00
blue $26.00
blue base $26.00
green base........................$22.00
amber base........................$20.00
amber bowl $22.00
green bowl $24.00
orchid bowl $26.00
rose bowl........................$26.00
azure bowl........................$26.00
amber base with
mother-of-pearl bowl....$20.00
green base with
mother-of-pearl bowl....$22.00

Blank 5084 Tumbler, see also Jugs and Tankards

Used with 870 stemware

Stemware, 156

5084 Ice Tea, 12 oz., footed
crystal..........$22.00
green...........$34.00
amber..........$32.00
rose $40.00
blue $42.00

5084 Tumbler, 9 oz., footed
crystal $18.00
green........................$28.00
amber........................$26.00
rose $28.00
blue $30.00

5084 Tumbler, 5 oz., footed
crystal $15.00
green........................$22.00
amber........................$20.00
rose $24.00
blue $25.00

5084 Tumbler, 2½ oz., footed
crystal $14.00
green........................$22.00
amber........................$20.00
rose $26.00
blue $28.00

5084 Oyster Cocktail, 4¾ oz.
crystal $12.00
green........................$20.00
amber........................$18.00
rose $22.00
blue $24.00

Blank 5650 Tumbler, see Horizon

Blank 6044 Tumbler, see Tiara

Blank 6046 Tumbler, see Catalina

Twenty-Four Twenty-Nine

1929 – 1936

Tableware I, 68

Tray, service and lemon dish insert
crystal $125.00
amber........................$140.00
green........................$156.00
rose $185.00
azure $225.00
topaz,........................$175.00

Tray, cordial
crystal $125.00
silver mist........................$140.00
regal blue $225.00
empire green........................$225.00
burgundy,........................$225.00

Twenty-Four Thirty-Three

1931 – 1932

Tableware I, 71 – 73

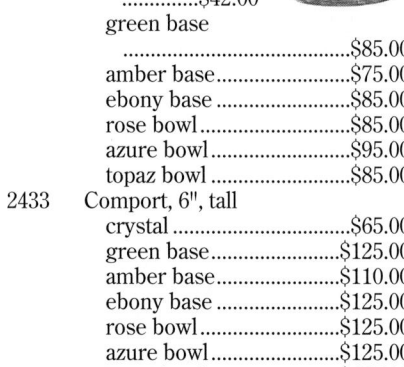

2433 Comport, 6", low
crystal
.............$42.00
green base
........................$85.00
amber base........................$75.00
ebony base $85.00
rose bowl........................$85.00
azure bowl........................$95.00
topaz bowl $85.00

2433 Comport, 6", tall
crystal $65.00
green base........................$125.00
amber base........................$110.00
ebony base $125.00
rose bowl........................$125.00
azure bowl........................$125.00
topaz bowl $125.00
wisteria bowl........................$195.00

2433 Candlestick, 3", pair........................
crystal $74.00
green base........................$125.00
amber base........................$110.00
ebony base $125.00
rose bowl........................$125.00
azure bowl........................$135.00
topaz bowl $125.00
wisteria bowl........................$225.00

2433 Bowl A, 12"
crystal $125.00
green base........................$150.00
amber base........................$145.00
ebony base $150.00
rose bowl........................$165.00
azure bowl........................$175.00
topaz bowl $150.00
wisteria bowl........................$345.00

Bowl D, 7½"
crystal $150.00
green base........................$165.00
amber base........................$165.00
ebony base $165.00
rose bowl........................$175.00
azure bowl........................$175.00
topaz bowl $165.00

Twenty-Four Seventy

1933 – 1945

Tableware I, 83 – 85

2470 Bonbon
- crystal $20.00
- rose $24.00
- green $24.00
- amber $22.00
- topaz $24.00

2470 Bowl, 7"
- crystal $28.00
- rose $45.00
- green $40.00
- amber $34.00
- topaz $35.00
- wisteria $65.00

2470 Bowl, 9", service dish
- crystal $38.00
- rose $65.00
- green $65.00
- amber $60.00

2470½ Bowl, 10½"
- crystal $55.00
- rose $85.00
- green $85.00
- amber $75.00
- topaz/gold tint $85.00
- wisteria $145.00
- ruby $145.00

2470 Bowl, 12"
- crystal $65.00
- rose $125.00
- green $125.00
- amber $110.00
- topaz/gold tint $125.00
- wisteria $325.00

2470 Candlestick, 5½", pair
- crystal $95.00
- rose bowl $150.00
- green base, ... $165.00
- amber base $150.00
- topaz bowl $150.00
- wisteria base $325.00

2470½ Candlestick, 5½", pair
- crystal $87.00
- rose $150.00
- green $125.00
- amber $115.00
- topaz/gold tint $125.00
- wisteria $295.00
- regal blue $325.00
- burgundy $300.00
- empire green $300.00
- ruby $250.00

2470 Comport, 6", low
- crystal $35.00
- rose bowl $48.00
- green base $45.00
- amber base $42.00
- topaz/gold tint bowl $45.00
- wisteria base $125.00

2470 Comport, 6", tall
- crystal $65.00
- rose bowl $125.00
- green base $135.00
- amber base $110.00
- topaz bowl $120.00
- wisteria base $225.00

2470 Lemon, 2-handled
- crystal $20.00
- rose $24.00
- green $24.00
- amber $22.00
- topaz $24.00

2470 Plate, 10", cake
- crystal $45.00
- rose $74.00
- green $74.00
- amber $70.00
- topaz $74.00

2470 Relish, 3-part, round
- crystal $42.00
- rose $70.00
- green $70.00
- amber $62.00
- topaz $65.00

2470 Relish, 4-part, oval
- crystal $48.00
- rose $85.00
- green $85.00
- amber $75.00
- topaz $75.00

2470 Sweetmeat, 2-handled
- crystal $20.00
- rose $24.00
- green $24.00
- amber $22.00
- topaz/gold tint $22.00

2470 Tray, sugar and cream
- crystal $22.00
- rose $28.00
- green $28.00
- amber $25.00
- topaz/gold tint $25.00

2470 Tray, 9¾", round
- rose $65.00
- green $65.00
- amber $60.00
- topaz $65.00
- ebony $60.00

2470 Vase, 8"
- crystal $54.00
- regal blue bowl $85.00
- burgundy bowl $75.00
- empire green bowl $85.00
- ruby bowl $85.00

2470 Vase, 10"
- crystal $60.00
- green bowl, ... $95.00
- topaz/gold tint bowl $75.00
- wisteria bowl $158.00
- regal blue bowl $115.00
- burgundy bowl $95.00
- empire green bowl $95.00
- ruby bowl $115.00
- azure bowl $150.00

2470 Vase, 11½"
- crystal $65.00
- regal blue bowl $125.00
- burgundy bowl $115.00
- empire green bowl $115.00

Twenty-Three Fifteen

1925 – 1934

Tableware I, 37 – 39

2315 Bowl A, 10½", footed, console
- crystal.... $20.00
- amber..... $30.00
- amber spiral optic...... $34.00
- blue $35.00
- blue spiral optic $40.00
- green $28.00
- green spiral optic $38.00
- orchid $30.00
- orchid spiral optic $40.00
- canary $38.00

2315 Bowl B, 11½", footed, console
- crystal $20.00
- amber $22.00
- blue $30.00
- green $24.00
- orchid $28.00
- canary $34.00

2315 Bowl C, 10½", footed, console
- crystal $20.00
- amber $32.00
- amber spiral optic $34.00
- blue $37.00
- blue spiral optic $45.00
- green $30.00
- green spiral optic $37.00
- canary $38.00
- orchid $34.00

2315 Bowl D, 8¾"
- crystal $20.00
- amber $30.00
- amber spiral optic $34.00
- blue $36.00
- blue spiral optic $45.00
- green $30.00
- green spiral optic $38.00
- canary $38.00
- orchid $34.00

2315 Cream, footed
- crystal $15.00
- amber $22.00
- green $26.00
- blue $34.00
- canary $35.00

2315½ Cream, footed
- crystal $15.00
- amber $18.00
- green $22.00
- blue $35.00
- orchid $35.00

2315 Sugar, footed
- crystal $15.00
- amber $22.00
- green $26.00
- orchid $34.00
- rose $35.00
- azure $35.00

2315 Grapefruit, footed and 2283 Plate, 7"
- crystal $22.00
- amber $25.00
- green $27.00
- orchid $30.00
- rose $34.00
- azure $30.00

2315 Mayonnaise, footed and 2332 Plate, 7", also used as a grapefruit
- crystal $22.00
- amber $25.00
- green $27.00
- orchid $40.00
- rose $40.00
- azure $42.00
- blue $30.00
- canary $34.00

2315 Mayonnaise with 13" lettuce plate
- crystal $30.00
- amber $34.00
- green $36.00
- orchid $40.00
- rose $40.00
- azure $42.00

2315 Plate, 13", lettuce
- crystal $15.00
- amber $15.00
- green $18.00
- orchid $20.00
- rose $18.00
- azure $18.00

2315 Salver
- crystal $35.00
- amber $40.00
- green $45.00
- orchid $54.00
- rose $49.00
- azure $54.00

2315 Sugar and Cream
- crystal $35.00
- amber $40.00
- blue $69.00
- green $48.00
- canary $74.00

Twilight, Cutting 883

1961 – 1962

Stemware, 120

6092 Goblet $35.00
6092 Sherbet $32.00
6092 Wine/Cocktail $38.00
6092 Cordial $42.00
6092 Ice Tea, footed $35.00
6092 Juice, footed $30.00
2337 Plate, 7" $10.00
2337 Plate, 8" $12.00

--U--

USA Map, Carving 44

1941 – 1943

Useful & Ornamental, 131

2577 Vase, 6" $175.00

--V--

Vale, 2863 Tumbler

1974 – 1975

Stemware, 152

2863 Highball, 13 oz., pressed, lead crystal $15.00
2863 Old Fashioned, double, 11 oz., pressed, lead crystal $15.00

Vase and Scroll, Decoration 25

1924

Decoration 25, blue tinted glass. Glass was etched on top and painted blue on its underside. Gold bands.

Tableware I, 315

2267 Bowl, 7" $95.00
2267 Bowl, 9" $125.00
2269 Candlestick, 6" $185.00
2275 Candlestick, 9" $250.00
2250 Jar, candy and cover ¼ pound $95.00
2250 Jar, candy and cover ½ pound $125.00
2283 Plate, 7" $38.00
2238 Plate 8¼" $45.00
2290 Plate , 8¼", deep, salad $60.00
2238 Plate, 11" $55.00
2290 Plate, 13½", deep, salad $84.00
2276 Vanity Set $375.00

Vase and Scroll, Decoration 37

1924

Decoration 37: rose, light blue, or green tint and encrusted gold, also encrusted gold on amber

Tableware I, 315 – 316

2267 Bowl, 7", console $97.00
2267 Bowl, 9", console $125.00
2269 Candlestick, 6", pair $135.00
2275 Candlestick, 9½", pair $200.00
2238 Plate, 8¼", salad $45.00
1848 Plate, 9", sandwich $48.00
2238 Plate, 11", sandwich, cut matt star base $58.00
2276 Vanity Set $395.00

Vase Collection

1985

Tableware II, 307

GR04/757 Vase, 4¾", Grace $10.00
ME03/757 Vase, 4¾", Melissa $10.00
NO03/758 Vase, 7½", Nostalgia $18.00
RE11/758 Vase, 7½", Reflection $18.00

Vases and Bouquet Holders

1900 – 1963

Useful & Ornamental, 202 – 239

45-3 Flower Set $95.00
300 Vase, 12", etched $175.00
622 Vase, 6½" $22.00
725 Vase, 9" $37.00
725 Vase, 10" $45.00
760 Vase, 12"
- crystal $50.00
- regal blue bowl $175.00
- burgundy bowl $150.00
- ruby bowl $175.00
- empire green bowl $150.00

761 Vase, 10", footed $195.00
762 Vase, 8", footed $65.00
763 Vase, 9", footed $125.00
764 Vase, 8", footed $95.00
765 Vase, 10", bud $38.00
864 Vase, 7½" $75.00
1001 Vase, 7", 9", or 11" $75.00 – $95.00
1002A Vase, 18 to 21", swung $45.00
1002B Vase, 12 to 14", swung $40.00
1002C Vase, 9 to 10", swung $25.00
1106 Vase, 4", violet
- crystal $32.00
- green $47.00

1106 Vase, 5", violet
- crystal $35.00
- amber $45.00
- green $45.00

1106 Vase, 6½", orchid $65.00
1106 Vase, 8", orchid $75.00
1106 Vase, 15", E shape
- crystal $95.00
- amber $125.00
- green $125.00

1120 Vase, 12", RO, LO
- crystal $47.00
- amber $58.00
- green $74.00

1120 Vase, 15", RO, LO
- crystal $75.00
- amber $85.00
- green $95.00

1120 Vase, 18", RO, LO
- crystal $95.00
- amber $125.00
- green $135.00

1120 Vase, 24", LO $300.00
1120 Vase, 36", LO $500.00
1120 Vase, 50", 2 pieces $800.00/market
1479 Vase, 6", RO
- crystal $32.00
- amber $38.00
- green $46.00

1479 Vase, 7", RO
- crystal $35.00
- amber $48.00
- green $56.00

1479 Vase, 9", RO $48.00
1491 Vase, 6", ebony $47.00
1491 Vase, 8½", ebony $55.00
1630 Vase, Alexis $54.00
1663 Vase, 9", pressed $40.00
1663 Vase, 16", pressed $65.00
1681 Vase, wall
- crystal $65.00
- amber $85.00
- green $95.00
- blue $125.00
- ebony $95.00

1699A Vase, 13", pressed $50.00
1699B Vase, 11", pressed $40.00
1699C Vase, 9", pressed $35.00
1761 Vase, 10½" $60.00
1796 Vase, 9", Engraving 5 $75.00
1797½ Vase, 7", Cut 116 $54.00
1798 Vase, 9", footed $75.00
1799½ Vase, 7¼", deep etched, poppy $65.00
1827/801 Vase, see Centennial II
1840 Vase, 10½", RO, $58.00
1840 Vase, 15", RO $65.00
1873 Vase, 8" $45.00
1895 Vase, 8", RO
- crystal $35.00
- topaz $48.00

1895 Vase, 10", RO
- crystal $40.00
- topaz $55.00

1895 Vase, 12", RO
- crystal $44.00
- topaz $75.00

1895½ Vase, 10", heavy $37.00
1939 Vase, center, set $250.00
2056 see American
2072 Vase, 8" $57.00
2081 Vase, 12" or tall aquarium, plain or optic $47.00
2081 Vase, 15" or tall aquarium, plain or optic $55.00

2081 Vase, 18" or tall aquarium, plain or optic, 1928 ....$68.00
2137 Vase, brush, cut or decorated $95.00
2208 Vase, 5" $26.00
2209 Vase, 9", etched $54.00
2210 Vase, 10", etched $60.00
2211 Vase, 10", etched $60.00
2212 Vase, 10", etched $60.00
2218 Vase, sweet pea $45.00
2222 Vase, 8" $48.00
2222 Vase, 10" $55.00
2265 Vase, 12" $75.00
2284 Vase, 12"
- amber $125.00
- green $125.00

2284 Epergne Set: 2284 Vase, 2284 12" Bowl, and 2290 13" Plate
- amber $295.00
- green $295.00

2288 Vase, Tut
- crystal $37.00
- amber $60.00
- green $62.00
- blue $87.00
- canary $125.00
- ebony $68.00

2292 Vase, 8", flared
- crystal $47.00
- amber $55.00
- green $60.00
- blue $75.00
- orchid $85.00
- azure $75.00
- rose $70.00

2292 Vase, 8", cupped
- crystal $47.00
- green $60.00
- azure $125.00
- rose $70.00

2292 Vase, 8", SO
- amber $62.00
- green $65.00
- blue $95.00
- orchid $95.00

2297 Vase, 8", square top
- crystal, ...$45.00
- amber $85.00
- green $95.00
- canary $125.00

2297 Vase, 8", rolled edge
- crystal $45.00
- amber $65.00
- green $70.00
- blue $85.00
- canary $100.00

2300 Vase, 12"
- amber $85.00
- green $95.00
- blue $125.00
- canary $150.00
- ebony $85.00

2312 Vase, 10", bud, ebony $60.00
2312 Vase, 12", bud, ebony $65.00
2312 Vase, 14", bud, ebony $70.00
2326 Vase, 7"
- crystal $42.00
- amber $54.00
- green $65.00
- blue $75.00
- canary $125.00

2360 Vase, 8", RO
- amber $77.00
- green $85.00
- blue $125.00
- orchid $125.00

2360 Vase, 10", RO
- amber $85.00
- green $94.00
- blue $150.00
- ebony, plain $85.00
- orchid $165.00

2369 Vase, 5", RO
- crystal $35.00
- amber $47.00
- green $50.00
- blue $75.00
- orchid $75.00

2369 Vase, 7", footed, RO
- crystal $35.00
- amber $50.00
- green $57.00
- orchid $95.00
- azure $68.00
- rose $68.00

2369 Vase, 9"
- crystal $48.00
- amber $56.00
- green $65.00
- azure $75.00
- rose $75.00

2369 Vase, 11", RO
- crystal $87.00
- amber $125.00
- green $125.00
- blue $175.00
- orchid $160.00
- azure $160.00

2373 Vase, small, window, offered with or without cover, priced with cover
- crystal $85.00
- amber $95.00
- green $110.00
- orchid $135.00
- azure $125.00
- rose $125.00
- ebony $110.00

2373 Vase, large, window, offered with or without cover, priced with cover
- crystal $95.00
- amber $115.00
- green $125.00
- orchid $150.00
- azure $145.00
- rose $145.00
- ebony $120.00

2385 Vase, 8½", fan
- crystal $65.00
- green $98.00
- orchid $200.00
- azure $125.00
- rose $125.00
- ebony $100.00

2385 Vase, 8½", Fan, Cut A, B, or C in azure, green, or rose, see Smoker Items $250.00
2387 Vase, 8"
- crystal $85.00
- green $125.00
- orchid $165.00
- azure $150.00
- rose $125.00
- ebony $125.00

2387½ Vase, 8", heavy $65.00
2396 Vase, 7", RO
- crystal $55.00
- amber $60.00
- green $65.00
- blue $75.00
- orchid $70.00

2396 Vase, 9", RO
- crystal $60.00
- green $70.00
- blue $80.00
- orchid $75.00
- rose $70.00

2397 Vase, 4", footed, RO
- green $65.00
- azure $75.00
- rose $75.00

2397 Vase, 6", footed, RO
- green $75.00
- azure $85.00
- rose $85.00

2397 Vase, 8", footed, RO
- green $95.00
- azure $125.00
- rose $125.00

2404 Vase, 6", RO
- crystal $40.00
- amber $66.00
- green $74.00
- azure $68.00
- rose $68.00
- ebony $68.00
- topaz $75.00
- regal blue $135.00
- empire green 135.00

2408 Vase, 8", RO
- amber $75.00
- green $95.00
- azure $97.00
- rose $95.00
- topaz $95.00

2409 Vase, 7½", RO
- amber $75.00
- green $85.00
- azure $97.00
- rose $95.00
- ebony $85.00
- topaz $95.00

2417 Vase, RO, SO
- crystal $75.00
- amber $85.00
- green $96.00
- azure $125.00
- rose $100.00
- topaz $100.00

2421 Vase, 10½", footed, RO
- amber $95.00
- green $125.00
- azure $150.00
- rose $150.00
- ebony $98.00

2425 Vase, 8"
- crystal $74.00
- amber $85.00
- green $92.00
- azure $125.00
- rose $125.00
- ebony $90.00
- topaz $95.00

2428 Vase, 6", NO
- amber $54.00
- green $65.00
- rose $65.00
- ebony $75.00
- topaz $75.00
- wisteria $200.00

2428 Vase, 7½"
- crystal $65.00
- amber $74.00

green $80.00
azure $87.00
rose $80.00
ebony $84.00
topaz $80.00

2428 Vase, 9", NO
crystal $77.00
amber $84.00
green $96.00
rose $95.00
ebony $98.00
topaz/gold tint $86.00
wisteria $375.00

2428 Vase, 10"
crystal $85.00
amber $94.00
green $120.00
azure $150.00
rose $150.00
ebony $135.00
topaz $135.00

2428 Vase, 13"
crystal $110.00
amber $150.00
green $185.00
rose $185.00
ebony $165.00
topaz $160.00
wisteria $600.00/market

2430 see Diadem

2431 Vase, 7½", wall
amber $131.00
green $150.00
azure $165.00
rose $150.00
ebony $150.00

2440 Vase, 7", see Lafayette

2449 Vase, 6", see Hermitage

2454 Vase, 8"
crystal $75.00
amber $95.00
green $97.00
rose $97.00
ebony $97.00
topaz/gold tint $97.00
ruby $195.00

2467 Vase, 7½"
crystal $48.00
green $67.00
ebony $68.00
topaz/gold tint $65.00

2470 Vase, 8"
crystal $68.00
regal blue $120.00
empire green $120.00
burgundy $115.00
ruby $120.00

2470 Vase, 10"
crystal $74.00
green $150.00
azure $195.00
topaz/gold tint $130.00
wisteria $300.00
empire green $125.00
burgundy $125.00
ruby $135.00
cinnamon $95.00
spruce $95.00

2470 Vase, 11½"
crystal $84.00
regal blue $158.00
empire green $158.00
burgundy $158.00

2484 Vase, 7", see Baroque

2485 Vase, 5", crescent
crystal $100.00
green $125.00
topaz $125.00
ebony $125.00

2486 Vase, 7", square
crystal $125.00
green $150.00
topaz $150.00
ebony $150.00

2485 Vase, 7", crescent
crystal $125.00
green $150.00
topaz $150.00

2486 Vase, 9", square
crystal $150.00
green $175.00
topaz $175.00

2489 Vase, 5½"
crystal $45.00
green $54.00
topaz $54.00
wisteria $95.00

2489 Vase, 6½"
crystal $48.00
green $60.00
topaz/gold tint $60.00
wisteria $125.00

2503 Vase, 7", crimped
regal blue $98.00
empire green $98.00
burgundy $125.00
ruby $150.00

2503 Vase, 8", crystal handles
regal blue $165.00
empire green $165.00
burgundy $200.00

2510 see Sunray

2518 Vase, 10"
regal blue $150.00
empire green $150.00
burgundy $150.00
ruby $150.00

2522 Vase, 8", similar to 4100
Silver Mist $47.00

2523 Vase, 6½", similar to 4105
Silver Mist $32.00

2545 Vase, 10", see Flame

2550 see Spool

2560 see Coronet

2567 Vase, 6", footed, heavy $50.00

2567 Vase, 7½", footed, heavy
crystal $54.00
ebony base $85.00

2567 Vase, 8½", footed, heavy $60.00

2568 Vase, 9", footed, heavy $65.00

2569 Vase, 9", footed, heavy $70.00

2570 Vase, 6¾", flared $46.00

2570 Vase, 7", regular $48.00

2577 Vase, 15" $75.00

2579 Vase, 6", Cornucopia $50.00

2577 Vase, 5½", wide $35.00

2577 Vase, 6" $40.00

2577 Vase, 8½" $45.00

2591 Vase, 8½" $48.00

2591 Vase, 11½" $65.00

2591 Vase, 15", heavy $95.00

2592 see Myriad

2600 Vase, Acanthus $97.00

2611 Vase, 14" $85.00

2612 Vase, 13" $65.00

2614 Vase, 10" $75.00

2619½ Vase, 6", ground bottom $34.00

2619½ Vase, 7½", ground bottom $40.00

2619½ Vase, 9½", ground bottom $48.00

2654 Vase, 9½", footed $54.00

2656 Vase, 10", footed
crystal $50.00
spruce $64.00

2657 Vase, 10½", footed
crystal $55.00
cinnamon $65.00

2658 Vase, 10½", footed
crystal $95.00
spruce $95.00

2659 Vase, 10", footed
crystal $65.00
cinnamon $75.00

2659 Vase, 8", footed
crystal $57.00
cinnamon $67.00

2660 Vase, 8", flip
crystal $37.00
cinnamon $45.00
spruce $45.00

2692 see Garden Center Items

2702 Candleholder/Vase, brass and glass, 6¾", 8", or 9½" ....$22.00 – $28.00

2723 Epergne Set: 10" bowl and three 8" trumpet vases
crystal $150.00
amber $175.00
amethyst $200.00

2724 Vase, see Garden Center Items

4020 Vase, 7½", bud, SO
crystal $35.00
amber base $40.00
green, base $44.00
rose bowl $50.00
ebony base $44.00
topaz bowl $50.00

4055D Vase, 7½", Cut B $45.00

4056 Vase, 5" $24.00

4056 Vase, 5½" $24.00

4056 Vase, 6½" $30.00

4056 Vase, 7½" $35.00

4069 Vase, 9"
crystal $47.00
amber $52.00
blue $75.00
green $65.00

4095 Vase, 7", SO
amber $52.00
blue $65.00
green $47.00
orchid $65.00

4095 Vase, 8", small, flared, LO
crystal $54.00
amber $57.00
blue $78.00
green $65.00

4095 Vase, 8", small, flared SO
amber $57.00
blue $78.00
green $65.00
orchid $75.00

4095 Vase, 8", small, rolled top, plain or LO
crystal $58.00
amber $60.00
blue $75.00

4095 Vase, 9", medium flared, plain or LO
crystal $64.00
amber $68.00
blue $87.00

green....$75.00
4095 Vase, 9", LO
amber....$68.00
blue....$87.00
green....$75.00
4095 Vase, 10", large, flared
crystal....$67.00
amber....$74.00
blue....$96.00
green....$80.00
4095 Vase, 9", rolled edge
crystal....$67.00
amber....$70.00
blue....$90.00
green....$80.00
4095 Vase, 10", rolled edge
crystal....$70.00
amber....$78.00
blue....$100.00
green....$85.00
canary, listed in catalog but not price list
4095½ Vase, 8", plain, RO, SO, LO
crystal....$47.00
amber....$57.00
amber foot, LO....$58.00
green....$65.00
green foot, SO....$67.00
blue....$78.00
blue foot, RO....$80.00
4100 Vase, 6", RO, LO
crystal, RO only....$32.00
amber....$38.00
blue....$55.00
green....$45.00
orchid....$55.00
4100 Vase, 8", RO, LO
crystal, RO only....$36.00
amber....$45.00
blue....$65.00
green....$50.00
orchid....$65.00
rose....$56.00
azure....$60.00
4100 Vase, 10", RO, LO
crystal....$44.00
amber....$57.00
blue....$75.00
green....$65.00
orchid....$75.00
rose....$70.00
4100 Vase, 12", RO
crystal....$50.00
amber....$60.00
blue....$80.00
green....$68.00
orchid....$80.00
rose....$75.00
4100 Vase, 12", LO
crystal....$50.00
amber....$60.00
blue....$80.00
green....$68.00
4101 Vase, 5½"
amber....$38.00
green....$46.00
rose,....$46.00
topaz....$46.00
4103 Vase, 3", RO
crystal....$22.00
amber....$27.00
blue....$35.00
green....$30.00
orchid....$35.00
rose....$35.00
azure....$35.00
regal blue....$48.00
empire green....$48.00
burgundy....$48.00
4103 Vase, 4", RO
crystal....$25.00
amber....$30.00
blue....$46.00
green....$35.00
orchid....$40.00
rose....$40.00
regal blue....$54.00
empire green....$54.00
burgundy....$54.00
ruby....$54.00
4103 Vase, 5", RO
crystal....$28.00
amber....$32.00
blue....$54.00
green....$38.00
orchid....$54.00
rose....$42.00
4103 Vase, 6", RO
crystal....$32.00
amber....$35.00
blue....$60.00
green....$42.00
rose....$54.00
4103½ Vase, 5", ribbed, heavy
crystal....$28.00
4105 Vase, 6", RO
crystal....$35.00
green....$45.00
orchid....$57.00
rose....$54.00
azure....$60.00
4105 Vase, 6", LO
green....$50.00
rose....$50.00
azure....$55.00
4105 Vase, 8", RO
crystal....$45.00
green....$58.00
orchid....$65.00
ebony....$58.00
rose....$60.00
azure....$65.00
topaz....$60.00
4105 Vase, 8", LO
green....$60.00
rose....$60.00
azure....$65.00
4105 Vase, 10", RO, LO
green....$75.00
rose....$75.00
azure....$95.00
4106 Vase, 7"
crystal....$48.00
amber....$57.00
green....$65.00
ebony....$57.00
rose....$75.00
topaz....$60.00
4107 Vase, 9"
crystal....$60.00
amber....$70.00
green....$75.00
rose....$78.00
topaz....$78.00
wisteria....$195.00
4107 Vase, 12"
crystal....$70.00
amber....$75.00
green....$85.00
ebony....$75.00
rose....$95.00
topaz....$85.00
4107 Vase, 15"
crystal....$78.00
amber....$95.00
green....$125.00
rose....$150.00
topaz/gold tint....$125.00
4108 Vase, 5"
crystal....$37.00
amber....$45.00
green....$48.00
rose....$50.00
topaz....$50.00
wisteria....$125.00
4108 Vase, 6"
crystal....$42.00
amber....$48.00
green....$54.00
ebony....$48.00
rose....$54.00
topaz....$54.00
4108 Vase, 7"
crystal....$48.00
amber....$55.00
green....$60.00
rose....$60.00
topaz....$60.00
4110 Vase, 7½"
crystal....$50.00
green....$60.00
topaz....$60.00
wisteria....$195.00
regal blue....$125.00
empire green....$125.00
burgundy....$125.00
4111 Vase, 6½"
crystal....$42.00
green....$56.00
ebony....$50.00
topaz....$56.00
wisteria....$165.00
4112 Vase, 8½"
crystal....$57.00
green....$68.00
topaz/gold tint....$68.00
wisteria....$225.00
regal blue....$150.00
empire green....$150.00
burgundy....$150.00
4116 Vase, 4", Bubble Ball
crystal....$16.00
ebony....$22.00
azure....$38.00
regal blue....$38.00
empire green....$38.00
burgundy....$38.00
ruby....$40.00
cinnamon....$22.00
spruce....$22.00
4116 Vase, 5", Bubble Ball
crystal....$18.00
azure....$45.00
regal blue....$45.00
empire green....$45.00
burgundy....$45.00
4116 Vase, 6", Bubble Ball
crystal....$20.00
azure....$50.00
regal blue....$50.00
empire green....$50.00
burgundy....$50.00

ruby....................................$50.00
cinnamon...........................$30.00
spruce...............................$30.00
4116 Vase, 7", Bubble Ball
crystal...............................$22.00
azure.................................$55.00
regal blue..........................$55.00
empire green......................$55.00
burgundy...........................$55.00
ruby....................................$55.00
4116 Vase, 8", Bubble Ball
crystal...............................$25.00
regal blue..........................$60.00
empire green......................$60.00
burgundy...........................$60.00
ruby....................................$60.00
4116 Vase, 9", Bubble Ball
crystal...............................$27.00
azure.................................$65.00
regal blue..........................$65.00
empire green......................$65.00
burgundy...........................$65.00
ruby....................................$65.00
4116½ Vase, 5", heavy, ribbed $20.00
4121 Vase, 5", RO, crystal.............$28.00
4121 Vase, 5", plain
regal blue..........................$68.00
empire green......................$65.00
burgundy...........................$65.00
cinnamon...........................$35.00
spruce...............................$35.00
chartreuse.........................$35.00
4123 Vase, Pansy
crystal...............................$18.00
azure.................................$27.00
regal blue..........................$27.00
empire green......................$27.00
burgundy...........................$27.00
ruby....................................$27.00
cinnamon...........................$20.00
spruce...............................$18.00
chartreuse.........................$20.00
4124 Vase, 4½", RO
crystal...............................$20.00
azure.................................$30.00
4124 Vase, 4½", plain
regal blue..........................$34.00
empire green......................$34.00
burgundy...........................$34.00
4125 Vase, 7", RO..........................$45.00
4125 Vase, 7", plain
regal blue..........................$75.00
empire green......................$75.00
burgundy...........................$75.00
4126 Vase, 11", LO.........................$95.00
4126 Vase, 11", plain, colored bowl
regal blue........................$175.00
empire green....................$185.00
burgundy.........................$165.00
4126½ Vase, 11", footed, heavy........$65.00
4128 Vase, 5", RO
crystal...............................$28.00
azure.................................$54.00
regal blue..........................$60.00
empire green......................$60.00
burgundy...........................$58.00
4129 Vase, 2½", Bubble Ball
crystal...............................$14.00
azure.................................$30.00
regal blue..........................$58.00
empire green......................$58.00
burgundy...........................$58.00
ruby....................................$58.00
4130 Vase, Violet
crystal...............................$20.00
azure.................................$32.00
regal blue..........................$38.00
empire green......................$38.00
burgundy...........................$38.00
ruby....................................$38.00
cinnamon...........................$25.00
spruce...............................$25.00
chartreuse,........................$25.00
4128½ Vase, 5", heavy......................$28.00
4132½ Vase, 8", heavy......................$38.00
4133 Vase, 4", LO
crystal...............................$37.00
azure.................................$55.00
gold tint............................$55.00
4134 Vase, 6", LO
crystal...............................$42.00
azure.................................$60.00
gold tint............................$60.00
4136 Vase, 6", bud
crystal...............................$34.00
azure.................................$56.00
regal blue..........................$65.00
empire green......................$60.00
burgundy...........................$60.00
4137 Vase, 3¾"
crystal...............................$20.00
azure.................................$35.00
regal blue..........................$40.00
empire green......................$40.00
burgundy...........................$40.00
4138 Vase, 3½", plain
crystal...............................$20.00
azure.................................$32.00
regal blue..........................$35.00
empire green......................$35.00
burgundy...........................$35.00
4143 Vase, 6", footed.....................$34.00
4143 Vase, 7½", footed...................$45.00
4143½ Vase, 6", heavy, footed..........$34.00
4143½ Vase, 7½", heavy,
footed...............................$45.00
4144 Vase, 3"
crystal...............................$18.00
regal blue..........................$30.00
empire green......................$30.00
burgundy...........................$30.00
4145 Vase, 3"
crystal...............................$18.00
regal blue..........................$30.00
empire green......................$30.00
burgundy...........................$30.00
4152 see Garden Center Items
4166 Vase, 6", bud
silver mist.........................$20.00
silver mist spruce..............$20.00
5079 Vase, 9", bud..........................$35.00
5085 Vase, 8", bud
crystal...............................$42.00
amber.................................$48.00
green.................................$54.00
blue...................................$65.00
5085 Vase, 8", bud, SO
amber.................................$52.00
green.................................$58.00
blue...................................$75.00
orchid................................$70.00
rose...................................$58.00
azure.................................$65.00
5086 Vase, 9", bud
crystal...............................$50.00
amber.................................$68.00
green.................................$75.00
blue...................................$85.00
5086 Vase, 9", bud, SO
amber.................................$60.00
green.................................$65.00
blue...................................$88.00
orchid................................$85.00
rose...................................$65.00
5087 Vase, 8", bud
crystal...............................$42.00
amber.................................$52.00
blue...................................$65.00
5087 Vase, 8", bud, SO
crystal...............................$48.00
amber.................................$52.00
green.................................$58.00
blue...................................$75.00
orchid................................$70.00
rose...................................$58.00
5088 Vase, 5", bud
crystal...............................$32.00
ebony.................................$35.00
green base.........................$38.00
wisteria base.....................$67.00
ebony base,........................$38.00
topaz bowl.........................$42.00
regal blue bowl..................$48.00
empire green bowl............$48.00
5088 Vase, 8", bud
crystal...............................$36.00
ebony.................................$38.00
green base.........................$45.00
ebony base.........................$45.00
topaz/gold tint bowl..........$45.00
wisteria base.....................$75.00
regal blue bowl..................$64.00
empire green bowl............$64.00
burgundy bowl...................$68.00
5088 Vase, 8", bud, RO
crystal...............................$36.00
ebony.................................$38.00
amber base,........................$52.00
green base.........................$58.00
ebony base.........................$52.00
wisteria base.....................$75.00
regal blue bowl..................$64.00
empire green bowl............$64.00
burgundy bowl...................$68.00
5090 Vase, 8", bud
crystal...............................$38.00
regal blue..........................$64.00
empire green......................$64.00
burgundy...........................$64.00
ruby....................................$68.00
5091 Vase, 6½", bud
crystal...............................$32.00
regal blue..........................$57.00
empire green......................$57.00
burgundy...........................$57.00
ruby....................................$65.00
5092 Vase, 8", bud
crystal...............................$40.00
regal blue bowl..................$67.00
empire green bowl............$67.00
burgundy bowl...................$67.00
ruby bowl...........................$75.00
5100 Vase, 10", footed, RO
crystal, plain......................$50.00
amber.................................$72.00
green.................................$95.00
orchid..............................$125.00
5300 Vase, 7", footed, bud............$47.00
5301 Vase, 8", footed, bud............$56.00
6021 Vase, 6", footed, bud
crystal...............................$28.00
azure.................................$54.00

regal blue $58.00
burgundy..........................$58.00
empire green $58.00
cinnamon.... $35.00
6021 Vase, 9", bud .. $38.00

Venise, Decoration 688

1970 – 1974

Stemware, 138

6120 Goblet $45.00
6120 Sherbet $45.00
6120 Claret $52.00
6120 Liqueur $60.00
6120 Ice Tea, footed $45.00
2337 Plate, 7" $10.00

Venture, 6114

1969 – 1970

Gray Mist base

Stemware, 137

6114 Goblet.................$28.00
6114 Sherbet...............$26.00
6114 Wine....................$30.00
6114 Brandy................$35.00

Venus, Cutting 896

1963 – 1974

Stemware, 126

6102 Goblet............$28.00
6102 Sherbet...........$26.00
6102 Claret.................$30.00
6102 Tulip Wine...........$30.00
6102 Brandy..................$30.00
6102 Ice Tea, footed $28.00
2337 Plate, 7" $10.00
2337 Plate, 8" $12.00

Vermeil, Decoration 661

1963 – 1974

Stemware, 127

6102 Goblet $30.00
6102 Sherbet $28.00
6102 Claret $32.00
6102 Tulip Wine $32.00
6102 Brandy $30.00
6102 Ice Tea, footed $30.00
2785 Bowl, 10", footed $40.00
2337 Plate, 7" $10.00
2337 Plate, 8" $12.00
2785 Relish, 2-part $35.00
2785 Relish, 4-part $40.00
2785 Relish, 5-part $45.00
2785 Sugar and Cream..................$42.00

Vernon, Plate Etching 277

1937 – 1933

Stemware, 33

877 Goblet
crystal.....$35.00
orchid........$65.00
green.............$45.00
amber...............................$45.00
azure $65.00

877 Sherbet, high
crystal $30.00
orchid...............................$58.00
green...............................$42.00
amber...............................$42.00
azure $58.00

877 Sherbet, low
crystal $20.00
orchid...............................$48.00
green...............................$32.00
amber...............................$32.00
azure $48.00

877 Parfait
crystal $35.00
orchid...............................$65.00
green...............................$45.00
amber...............................$45.00
azure $65.00

877 Cocktail
crystal $30.00
orchid...............................$58.00
green...............................$40.00
amber...............................$40.00
azure $58.00

877 Claret
crystal $40.00
orchid...............................$75.00
green...............................$50.00
amber...............................$50.00
azure $75.00

877 Wine
crystal $35.00
orchid...............................$65.00
green...............................$45.00
amber...............................$45.00
azure $65.00

877 Cordial
crystal $50.00
orchid.............................$125.00
green...............................$58.00
amber...............................$58.00
azure $125.00

877 Oyster Cocktail
crystal $25.00
orchid...............................$40.00
green...............................$32.00
amber...............................$32.00
azure $40.00

877 Grapefruit and Liner
crystal $50.00
orchid.............................$125.00
green...............................$68.00
amber...............................$68.00
azure $125.00

877 Ice Tea, footed
crystal $35.00
orchid...............................$60.00
green...............................$42.00
amber...............................$42.00
azure $60.00

877 Tumbler, 9 oz., footed
crystal $22.00
orchid...............................$48.00
green...............................$34.00
amber...............................$34.00
azure $48.00

877 Juice, footed
crystal $22.00
orchid...............................$45.00
green...............................$28.00
amber...............................$28.00
azure $45.00

877 Whiskey, footed
crystal $22.00
orchid...............................$48.00
green...............................$28.00
amber...............................$28.00
azure $48.00

Tableware I, 164 – 167

2350 Ashtray, small
azure $22.00
green...............................$18.00
amber...............................$18.00
orchid,..............................$24.00

2375 Bonbon
azure $37.00
green...............................$30.00
amber...............................$26.00

2375 Bouillon
azure $26.00
green...............................$20.00
amber...............................$18.00
orchid...............................$26.00

869 Bowl, finger and 2283 Plate
crystal $32.00
azure $45.00
green...............................$38.00
amber...............................$35.00
orchid...............................$45.00

2375 Bowl, 5", fruit
azure $37.00
green...............................$24.00
amber...............................$22.00
orchid...............................$38.00

2375 Bowl, 6", cereal
azure $38.00
green...............................$32.00
amber...............................$28.00
orchid...............................$40.00

2375 Bowl, 7", soup
azure $34.00
green...............................$32.00
amber...............................$30.00
orchid...............................$35.00

2375 Bowl, 9", baker
azure $75.00
green...............................$55.00
amber...............................$52.00
orchid...............................$95.00

2375 Bowl, 12"
azure $125.00
green...............................$95.00
amber...............................$87.00
orchid.............................$135.00

2384 Bowl A, 12"
azure $165.00
green.............................$125.00
amber.............................$110.00
orchid.............................$225.00

2415 Bowl, combination
azure $270.00
green.............................$225.00
amber.............................$195.00

2394 Candlestick, 2", pair
azure $87.00
green...............................$78.00
amber...............................$70.00

orchid...............................$125.00
2375 Candlestick, 3", pair
azure.................................$80.00
green.................................$72.00
amber.................................$65.00
orchid...............................$145.00
2375½ Candlestick , pair
azure.................................$95.00
green.................................$88.00
amber.................................$80.00
orchid...............................$125.00
2331 Box, candy and cover
azure................................$195.00
green................................$165.00
amber................................$150.00
orchid...............................$225.00
2375½ Celery, 11½"
azure.................................$78.00
green.................................$68.00
amber.................................$64.00
orchid.................................$85.00
2375½ Centerpiece, 13", oval, flower holder
azure................................$400.00
green................................$350.00
amber................................$300.00
orchid...............................$500.00
2368 Cheese and Cracker
azure................................$145.00
green................................$115.00
amber.................................$95.00
2375 Comport, 7"
azure.................................$76.00
green.................................$65.00
amber.................................$58.00
2400 Comport, 8"
crystal...............................$75.00
azure................................$125.00
green.................................$95.00
amber.................................$85.00
orchid...............................$150.00
2375 Cream Soup and Plate
azure.................................$74.00
green.................................$68.00
amber.................................$62.00
orchid.................................$78.00
2375 Cup and Saucer, after dinner
azure.................................$52.00
green.................................$45.00
amber.................................$40.00
orchid.................................$67.00
2375½ Cup and Saucer
crystal...............................$32.00
azure.................................$40.00
green.................................$38.00
amber.................................$34.00
orchid.................................$48.00
2375 Ice Bucket
azure................................$130.00
green................................$115.00
amber.................................$98.00
2378 Ice Bucket
azure................................$130.00
green................................$115.00
amber.................................$98.00
orchid...............................$150.00
5000 Jug
crystal..............................$265.00
azure................................$575.00
green................................$385.00
amber................................$295.00
orchid...............................$650.00
2375 Lemon
azure.................................$37.00
green.................................$30.00
amber.................................$26.00
orchid.................................$40.00
2375 Oil, footed
azure................................$225.00
green................................$175.00
amber................................$160.00
2375 Plate, 6"
azure,................................$20.00
green.................................$18.00
amber.................................$16.00
orchid.................................$23.00
2375 Plate, 7"
crystal...............................$16.00
azure.................................$24.00
green.................................$22.00
amber.................................$20.00
orchid.................................$26.00
2375 Plate, 8"
crystal...............................$18.00
azure.................................$30.00
green.................................$28.00
amber.................................$25.00
orchid.................................$32.00
2375 Plate, 9"
azure.................................$60.00
green.................................$56.00
amber.................................$52.00
orchid.................................$65.00
2375 Plate, 10"
azure.................................$68.00
green.................................$64.00
amber.................................$60.00
orchid.................................$75.00
2375 Plate, 13", chop
azure.................................$95.00
green.................................$77.00
amber.................................$70.00
orchid...............................$115.00
2375 Platter, 12"
azure.................................$94.00
green.................................$87.00
amber.................................$75.00
orchid.................................$98.00
2375 Platter, 15"
azure................................$145.00
green................................$140.00
amber................................$125.00
2375 Relish, 8½"
azure.................................$68.00
green.................................$62.00
amber.................................$57.00
orchid.................................$70.00
2375 Sauce Boat and Plate
azure................................$110.00
green.................................$95.00
amber.................................$85.00
2375 Shaker, FGT, pair
azure................................$157.00
green................................$145.00
amber................................$130.00
5000 Shaker, FGT, pair
green................................$122.00
amber................................$100.00
orchid...............................$150.00
2375½ Sugar and Cream
crystal...............................$90.00
azure................................$135.00
green................................$115.00
amber.................................$95.00
orchid...............................$135.00
2375½ Sugar and Cover
azure.................................$95.00
green.................................$85.00
amber.................................$72.00
orchid.................................$95.00
2375 Tray, handled, lunch
azure................................$150.00
green................................$135.00
amber................................$125.00
orchid...............................$150.00
2375 Whip Cream
azure.................................$47.00
green.................................$44.00
amber.................................$40.00

Verona, Plate Etching 281

1929 – 1931

Stemware, 38

890 Goblet
crystal......$35.00
green..........$45.00
rose...............$45.00
890 Saucer Champagne
crystal...............................$32.00
green.................................$40.00
rose..................................$40.00
890 Sherbet, low
crystal...............................$26.00
green.................................$30.00
rose..................................$30.00
890 Parfait
crystal...............................$35.00
green.................................$45.00
rose..................................$45.00
890 Cocktail
crystal...............................$32.00
green.................................$40.00
rose..................................$40.00
890 Claret
crystal...............................$40.00
green.................................$52.00
rose..................................$52.00
890 Wine
crystal...............................$35.00
green.................................$45.00
rose..................................$45.00
890 Cordial
crystal...............................$45.00
green.................................$75.00
rose..................................$75.00
890 Oyster Cocktail
crystal...............................$18.00
green.................................$30.00
rose..................................$30.00
890 Ice Tea, footed
crystal...............................$32.00
green.................................$42.00
rose..................................$42.00
890 Tumbler, 9 oz., footed
crystal...............................$20.00
green.................................$35.00
rose..................................$35.00
890 Juice, footed
crystal...............................$20.00
green.................................$35.00

890 Jug
crystal $450.00
green/rose $600.00
2375 Plate, 6"
crystal $12.00
green/rose $14.00
2375 Plate, 7"
crystal $14.00
green/rose $16.00
2375 Plate, 8"
crystal $18.00
green/rose $22.00
2375 Plate, 13"
crystal $85.00
green/rose $110.00
2375½ Sugar and Cover and Cream
890 crystal $110.00
green/rose $145.00
877 Grapefruit and 945½ Liner
crystal $65.00
green/rose $75.00

Versailles, Blank 6113

1969 – 1972

Stemware, 136

6113 Goblet....$50.00
6113 Sherbet....$45.00
6113 Claret....$54.00
6113 Wine....$54.00
6113 Brandy....$54.00
6113 Ice Tea, footed....$50.00

Versailles, Plate Etching 278

1928 – 1943

Stemware, 68-70

5098 Goblet
green bowl...$85.00
rose bowl....$85.00
azure bowl....$95.00
5099 topaz bowl....$75.00
5098 Sherbet, high
green bowl $70.00
rose bowl $70.00
azure bowl $75.00
5099 topaz bowl $65.00
5098 Sherbet, low
green bowl $52.00
rose bowl $52.00
azure bowl $55.00
5099 topaz bowl $45.00
5098 Parfait
green bowl $95.00
rose bowl $95.00
azure bowl $125.00
5099 topaz bowl $85.00
5098 Cocktail
green bowl $58.00
rose bowl $58.00
azure bowl $64.00
5099 topaz bowl $58.00
5098 Claret
green bowl $135.00
rose bowl $135.00
azure bowl $140.00
5099 topaz bowl $95.00
5098 Wine
green bowl $110.00
rose bowl $110.00
azure bowl $125.00
5099 topaz bowl $90.00
5098 Cordial
green bowl $165.00
rose bowl $165.00
azure bowl $175.00
5099 topaz bowl $125.00
5098 Oyster Cocktail
green bowl $48.00
rose bowl $48.00
azure bowl $50.00
5099 topaz bowl $40.00
5098 Ice Tea, footed
green bowl $75.00
rose bowl $75.00
azure bowl $84.00
5099 topaz bowl $70.00
5098 Tumbler, 9 oz., footed
green bowl $48.00
rose bowl $48.00
azure bowl $55.00
5099 topaz bowl $42.00
5098 Juice, footed
green bowl $48.00
rose bowl $48.00
azure bowl $55.00
5099 topaz bowl $42.00
5098 Whiskey, footed
green bowl $68.00
rose bowl $68.00
azure bowl $95.00
5099 topaz bowl $68.00
5082½ Grapefruit and 945½ Liner
green bowl $135.00
rose bowl $135.00
azure bowl $165.00

Tableware I, 169 – 174

2350 Ashtray, small
rose $48.00
azure $48.00
green....$40.00
topaz....$40.00
2375 Bonbon
rose $60.00
azure $67.00
green....$65.00
topaz/gold tint $48.00
2375 Bouillon
rose $48.00
azure $52.00
green....$48.00
topaz....$40.00
869 Bowl, finger and 2283 Plate
rose $95.00
azure $95.00
green....$100.00
topaz/gold tint $85.00
2375 Bowl, 5", fruit
rose $42.00
azure $42.00
green....$54.00
topaz/gold tint $40.00
2375 Bowl, 6", cereal
rose $57.00
azure $62.00
green....$57.00
topaz....$54.00
2394 Bowl, 6"
topaz....$58.00
2375 Bowl, 7", soup
rose $125.00
azure $145.00
green....$145.00
topaz....$125.00
2375 Bowl, 9", baker
rose $135.00
azure $135.00
green....$140.00
topaz/gold tint $125.00
2375 Bowl, large, dessert
rose $165.00
azure $187.00
green....$175.00
topaz....$154.00
2395 Bowl, 10"
rose $250.00
azure $275.00
green....$325.00
topaz/gold tint $225.00
2394 Bowl A, 12"
rose $150.00
azure $157.00
green....$165.00
topaz/gold tint $135.00
2394 Candlestick, 2", pair
rose $150.00
azure $150.00
green....$165.00
topaz/gold tint $120.00
2375 Candlestick, 3", pair
rose $150.00
azure $150.00
green....$165.00
topaz....$125.00
2375½ Candlestick, pair
rose $165.00
azure $165.00
green....$165.00
topaz....$160.00
2395 Candlestick, 3", pair
rose $225.00
azure $250.00
green....$225.00
2395½ Candlestick, 5", pair
rose $240.00
azure $250.00
green....$275.00
topaz/gold tint $225.00
2331 Box, candy and cover
rose $295.00
azure $330.00
green....$295.00
2394 Jar, candy and cover, ½ pound
topaz....$550.00
2375 Celery, 11½"
rose $125.00
azure $135.00
green....$125.00
topaz/gold tint $95.00
2375 Centerpiece, 12"
rose $225.00
azure $250.00
green....$250.00
topaz....$225.00
2375½ Centerpiece, 13", oval and flower holder
rose $450.00
azure $500.00
green....$450.00
2368 Cheese and Cracker
rose $175.00
azure $190.00
green....$175.00
topaz....$164.00
2375 Cheese and Cracker
rose $200.00
azure $225.00
green....$225.00

topaz......$195.00

5098 Comport, 5"
rose......$150.00
azure......$165.00
green......$165.00

2400 Comport, 6"
rose......$165.00
azure......$175.00
green......$165.00
topaz......$150.00

5099 Comport, 6"
topaz......$150.00

2375 Comport, 7"
rose......$150.00
azure......$165.00
green......$165.00

2400 Comport, 8"
rose......$195.00
azure......$225.00
green......$225.00

2375 Cream Soup and Plate
rose......$125.00
azure......$125.00
green......$150.00
topaz/gold tint......$120.00

2375 Cup and Saucer, after dinner
rose......$135.00
azure......$150.00
green......$135.00
topaz......$125.00

2375½ Cup and Saucer
rose......$54.00
azure......$58.00
green......$58.00
topaz/gold tint......$54.00

2439 Decanter and Stopper
rose......market
azure......market
green......market

2375 Ice Bucket
rose......$250.00
azure......$295.00
green......$275.00
topaz/gold tint......$185.00

2378 Ice Bucket
rose......$250.00
azure......$295.00
green......$275.00

2451 Dish, ice with plate and liners
rose......$135.00
azure......$150.00
green......$140.00
topaz......$125.00

5000 Jug
rose......$875.00
azure......$950.00
green......$1,000.00
topaz/gold tint......$695.00

2375 Dish, lemon
rose......$60.00
azure......$65.00
green......$65.00
topaz/gold tint......$58.00

2375 Mayonnaise, plate, ladle
rose......$150.00
azure......$165.00
green......$150.00
topaz......$150.00

2394 Mint
rose......$48.00
azure......$56.00
green......$52.00
topaz......$48.00

5098 Nappy, 6", footed
rose......$156.00
azure......$156.00
green......$165.00

2375 Oil, footed
rose......$750.00
azure......$850.00
green......$800.00
topaz......$750.00

2375 Plate, 6"
rose......$28.00
azure......$30.00
green......$30.00
topaz......$25.00

2375 Plate, 7"
rose......$35.00
azure......$35.00
green......$35.00
topaz......$30.00

2375 Plate, 8"
rose......$42.00
azure......$52.00
green......$56.00
topaz......$38.00

2375 Plate, 9"
rose......$58.00
azure......$67.00
green......$75.00
topaz......$50.00

2375 Plate, 10"
rose......$150.00
azure......$175.00
green......$175.00
topaz......$150.00

2375 Plate, canape
rose......$47.00
azure......$50.00
green......$50.00
topaz......$47.00

2375 Plate, 10", grill
rose......$125.00
azure......$150.00
green......$150.00

2375 Plate, 10", cake
rose......$125.00
azure......$175.00
green......$175.00
topaz/gold tint......$95.00

2375 Plate, 13", chop
rose......$175.00
azure......$225.00
green......$195.00
topaz......$175.00

2375 Platter, 12"
rose......$175.00
azure......$225.00
green......$250.00
topaz/gold tint......$165.00

2375 Platter, 15"
rose......$250.00
azure......$275.00
green......$300.00
topaz/gold tint......$250.00

2375 Relish, 8½"
rose......$58.00
azure......$65.00
green......$62.00
topaz......$58.00

2083 Bottle, salad dressing
rose......$900.00/market
azure......$1,100.00/market
green......$900.00/market
topaz......$900.00/market

2375 Bottle, salad dressing
rose......$1,100.00/market
azure......$1,200.00/market
green......$1,000.00/market
topaz......$900.00/market

2375 Sauce Boat and Plate
rose......$495.00
azure......$550.00
green......$550.00
topaz......$475.00

2375 Shaker, FGT, pair
rose......$350.00
azure......$365.00
green......$375.00
topaz......$350.00

2375½ Sugar and Cover
rose......$235.00
azure......$250.00
green......$235.00
topaz......$225.00

2375½ Sugar and Cream, tea
rose......$165.00
azure......$175.00
green......$165.00
topaz......$165.00

2375½ Sugar and Cream
rose......$195.00
azure......$225.00
green......$250.00
topaz......$195.00

2378 Pail, sugar, NP handle
rose......$450.00
azure......$475.00
green......$465.00
topaz......$465.00

2375 Sweetmeat
rose......$58.00
azure......$64.00
green......$67.00
topaz......$57.00

2375 Tray, handled, lunch
rose......$165.00
azure......$185.00
green......$175.00
topaz/gold tint......$135.00

2429 Tray, service and lemon
rose......$300.00
azure......$350.00
green......$300.00
topaz......$300.00

2417 Vase, 8", RO
topaz......$560.00

4100 Vase, 8", RO
rose......$600.00
azure......$650.00
green......$625.00

2385 Vase, 8½", fan
rose......$795.00
azure......$850.00
green......$785.00

2375 Whip Cream
rose......$60.00
azure......$67.00
green......$67.00
topaz......$57.00

2378 Pail, whip cream, NP handle
rose......$465.00
azure......$500.00
green......$485.00
topaz......$450.00

Vesper, Plate Etching 275

1926 – 1933

Stemware, 66

5093 Goblet
amber.............$40.00
green..............$40.00
blue...............$125.00

5093 Sherbet, high
amber................................$35.00
green................................$35.00
blue $95.00

5093 Sherbet, low
amber................................$28.00
green................................$28.00
blue $45.00

5093 Parfait
amber................................$40.00
green................................$40.00
blue $95.00

5093 Cocktail
amber................................$30.00
green................................$30.00
blue $54.00

5093 Wine
amber................................$40.00
green................................$40.00
blue $95.00

5093 Cordial
amber................................$75.00
green................................$75.00
blue $150.00

5082½ Grapefruit and 945½ Liner
amber................................$95.00
green................................$95.00
blue $150.00

5000 Oyster Cocktail
amber................................$25.00
green................................$25.00
blue $35.00

5000 Tumbler, 12 oz., footed
amber................................$40.00
green................................$40.00
blue $95.00

5000 Tumbler, 9 oz., footed
amber................................$35.00
green................................$35.00
blue $75.00

5000 Tumbler, 5 oz., footed
amber................................$30.00
green................................$30.00
blue $54.00

5000 Tumbler, 2 oz., footed
amber................................$35.00
green................................$35.00
blue $75.00

Tableware I, 158-161

2350 Ashtray
amber................................$23.00
green................................$24.00

2350 Bouillon and Saucer
amber................................$24.00
green................................$26.00
blue $30.00

2350½ Bouillon, footed
amber................................$18.00
green................................$20.00

869 Bowl, finger and 2283 Plate
amber................................$26.00
green................................$30.00
blue $38.00

2350 Bowl, 5", fruit
amber................................$35.00
green................................$38.00
blue $54.00

2350 Bowl, 6", cereal
amber................................$42.00
green................................$37.00
blue $48.00

2350 Bowl, 7", soup
amber................................$38.00
green................................$42.00
blue $65.00

2267 Bowl, 7", low foot
amber................................$42.00
green................................$46.00
blue $54.00

2350 Bowl, 8", nappy
amber................................$50.00
green................................$52.00
blue $65.00

2350 Bowl, 9", nappy
amber................................$54.00
green................................$57.00
blue $70.00

2350 Bowl, 9", oval, baker
amber................................$54.00
green................................$57.00
blue $74.00

2324 Bowl, 10", footed
amber..............................$125.00
green..............................$145.00
blue $195.00

2350 Bowl, 10", salad
amber................................$87.00
green................................$95.00
blue $125.00

2315 Bowl, 10½", footed, flared
amber..............................$110.00
green..............................$125.00
blue $175.00

2350 Bowl, 10½", oval, baker
amber................................$65.00
green................................$70.00
blue $95.00

2297 Bowl A, 12", deep
amber..............................$175.00
green..............................$220.00
blue $300.00

2350 Butter and Cover
amber..............................$345.00
green..............................$345.00
blue $465.00

2324 Candlestick, 2", pair
amber................................$68.00
green................................$75.00
blue $95.00

2324 Candlestick, 4", pair
amber................................$85.00
green................................$94.00
blue $145.00

2324 Candlestick, 9", pair
amber..............................$150.00
green..............................$165.00
blue $200.00

2250 Box, candy and cover
amber..............................$120.00
green..............................$125.00
blue $145.00

2331 Box, candy and cover
amber..............................$237.00
green..............................$250.00
blue $365.00

2350 Celery
amber................................$52.00
green................................$57.00
blue $95.00

2329 Centerpiece, 11"
amber................................$94.00
green..............................$120.00
blue $175.00

2329 Centerpiece, 13"
amber..............................$125.00
green..............................$165.00
blue $225.00

2371 Centerpiece, 13", oval
amber..............................$150.00
green..............................$185.00
blue $235.00

2368 Cheese and Cracker
amber................................$95.00
green..............................$110.00
blue $168.00

2327 Comport, 7"
amber................................$94.00
green................................$97.00
blue $125.00

2350 Comport, 8"
amber................................$90.00
green................................$96.00
blue $135.00

2315½ Cream
amber................................$38.00
green................................$42.00

2350 Cream Soup and Plate
amber................................$40.00
green................................$45.00
blue $56.00

2350½ Cream Soup and Plate
amber................................$40.00
green................................$45.00

2350 Cup and Saucer, after dinner
amber................................$35.00
green................................$45.00
blue $65.00

2350 Cup and Saucer
amber................................$25.00
green................................$27.00
blue $36.00

2350½ Cup and Saucer
amber................................$25.00
green................................$27.00
blue $38.00

2378 Ice Bucket, NP handle
amber..............................$135.00
green..............................$165.00
blue $400.00

5000 Jug
amber..............................$325.00
green..............................$400.00
blue................$1,200.00/market

2315 Mayonnaise/Grapefruit
amber................................$42.00
green................................$50.00
blue $58.00

2350 Pickle
amber................................$28.00
green................................$32.00
blue $45.00

2350 Plate, 6"
amber................................$16.00
green................................$18.00
blue $22.00

2350 Plate, 7"
amber................................$20.00
green................................$22.00
blue $25.00

2350 Plate, 8"
amber................................$22.00
green................................$25.00
blue $30.00

2350 Plate, 9"
- amber $32.00
- green $37.00
- blue $55.00

2350 Plate, 10"
- amber $56.00
- green $67.00
- blue $84.00

2321 Plate, 6"
- amber $16.00
- green $18.00
- blue $22.00

2321 Plate, 7"
- amber $20.00
- green $22.00
- blue $25.00

2321 Plate, 8"
- amber $22.00
- green $25.00
- blue $28.00

2321 Plate 9"
- amber $36.00
- green $38.00
- blue $55.00

2321 Plate, 10"
- amber $56.00
- green $67.00
- blue $84.00

2350 Plate, 12", chop
- amber $56.00
- green $68.00
- blue $125.00

2350 Plate, 15", round
- amber $95.00
- green $125.00
- blue $157.00

2350 Platter, 10½"
- amber $58.00
- green $70.00
- blue $94.00

2350 Platter, 12"
- amber $58.00
- green $72.00
- blue $98.00

2350 Platter, 15"
- amber $98.00
- green $125.00
- blue $160.00

2350 Sauce Boat and Plate
- amber $72.00
- green $85.00
- blue $150.00

5000 Shaker, footed, FGT , pair
- amber $135.00
- green $145.00
- blue $250.00

2315 Sugar and Cream
- amber $125.00
- green $150.00
- blue $250.00

2350 Sugar and Cover and Cream
- amber $84.00
- green $94.00
- blue $150.00

2350½ Sugar and Cream
- amber $84.00
- green $94.00
- blue $150.00

2350½ Sugar and Cover
- amber $57.00
- green $67.00
- blue $94.00

2287 Tray, handled, lunch
- amber $145.00
- green $157.00
- blue $225.00

2276 Vanity Set
- amber $335.00
- green $375.00
- blue $475.00

2292 Vase, 8"
- amber $295.00
- green $325.00
- blue $450.00

2324 Vase, small, urn
- amber $165.00
- green $185.00
- blue $220.00

2350 Egg Cup
- amber $35.00
- green $37.00

Vesper, 6086

1959 – 1965

Stemware, 118

6086 Goblet $25.00
6086 Sherbet $23.00
6086 Wine/Cocktail $28.00
6086 Cordial $32.00
6086 Ice Tea, footed $25.00
6086 Juice, footed $22.00

Victoria, Decoration 71

(See Paradise for image)

1927

Mother-of-pearl on crystal brocade

Tableware I, 130

2297 Bowl A, 10½", shallow $125.00
2297 Bowl A, 12", deep $125.00
2315 Bowl C, 10½", footed $125.00
2342 Bowl, 12" $110.00
2372 Candlestick, 2", block, pair $95.00
2331 Box, candy and cover $175.00
2329 Centerpiece, 11" $125.00
2329 Centerpiece, 13" $150.00
2371 Centerpiece, 13", oval and 2371 Flower Holder $195.00
2327 Comport, 7" $95.00
2350 Comport, 8" $85.00
2362 Comport, 11" $125.00
2380 Confection and Cover $135.00
2378 Ice Bucket, NP handle, drainer and tongs $135.00
2342 Tray, handled, lunch $115.00
4100 Vase, 6", optic $115.00
4100 Vase, 8", optic $135.00
4103 Vase, 5", optic $95.00

Victoria, Decoration 696

1980 – 1982

Stemware, 88

6016 Goblet $25.00
6016 Saucer Champagne $22.00
6016 Claret, large $25.00
6016 Ice Tea, footed $25.00

Victorian, 4024

1933 – 1943

Stemware, 60

4024 Goblet, 11 oz.
- crystal $30.00
- burgundy bowl $35.00
- empire green bowl $35.00
- regal blue bowl $45.00
- silver mist $26.00
- silver mist base $26.00

4024 Goblet, 10 oz.
- crystal $30.00
- burgundy bowl $35.00
- empire green bowl $35.00
- regal blue bowl $45.00
- silver mist $26.00
- silver mist base $26.00

4024 Saucer Champagne
- crystal $25.00
- burgundy bowl $30.00
- empire green bowl $30.00
- regal blue bowl $40.00
- silver mist $24.00
- silver mist base $24.00

4024 Sherbet
- crystal $20.00
- burgundy bowl $22.00
- empire green bowl $22.00
- regal blue bowl $32.00
- silver mist $22.00
- silver mist base $22.00

4024 Cocktail
- crystal $20.00
- burgundy bowl $22.00
- empire green bowl $22.00
- regal blue bowl $32.00
- silver mist $22.00
- silver mist base $22.00

4024 Claret-Wine
- crystal $34.00
- burgundy bowl $40.00
- empire green bowl $40.00
- regal blue bowl $45.00
- silver mist $26.00
- silver mist base $26.00

4024 Rhine Wine
- crystal $34.00
- burgundy bowl $35.00
- ruby bowl $50.00
- empire green bowl $35.00
- regal blue bowl $50.00
- silver mist $26.00

4024 Sherry
- crystal $30.00
- burgundy bowl $35.00
- ruby bowl $50.00
- empire green bowl $35.00
- regal blue bowl $45.00
- silver mist $26.00
- silver mist base $26.00
- mother-of-pearl bowl $30.00

4024 Cordial
- crystal $40.00
- burgundy bowl $45.00
- ruby bowl $55.00
- empire green bowl $45.00
- regal blue bowl $55.00
- silver mist $30.00
- silver mist base $30.00
- mother-of-pearl bowl $40.00

4024 Oyster Cocktail
- crystal $20.00

burgundy bowl....................$22.00
empire green bowl $22.00
regal blue bowl $32.00
silver mist...........................$22.00
silver mist base $22.00
4024 Ice Tea, footed
crystal $30.00
burgundy bowl....................$35.00
empire green bowl $35.00
regal blue bowl $45.00
silver mist...........................$26.00
silver mist base $26.00
4024 Tumbler, 8 oz., footed
crystal $25.00
burgundy bowl....................$28.00
empire green bowl $28.00
regal blue bowl $30.00
silver mist...........................$22.00
silver mist base $22.00
4024 Juice, footed
crystal $25.00
burgundy bowl....................$28.00
empire green bowl $28.00
regal blue bowl $30.00
silver mist...........................$22.00
silver mist base $22.00
4024 Whiskey, footed
crystal $30.00
burgundy bowl....................$35.00
empire green bowl $35.00
regal blue bowl $40.00
silver mist...........................$22.00
silver mist base $22.00

Victory, Etching 257

1922 – 1928

Stemware, 21

766 Goblet, 9 oz. $15.00
766 Goblet, 7 oz. $10.00
766 Saucer Champagne $10.00
766 Sherbet......................................$8.00
766 Fruit $8.00
766 Parfait $22.00
766 Cocktail $10.00
766 Claret $15.00
766 Wine..$10.00
766 Ice Tea, footed, handled..............................$18.00
766 Grapefruit and Liner $30.00
837 Oyster Cocktail......................$11.00
945½ Grapefruit and Liner $24.00
300 Jug...$75.00
303 Jug...$57.00
318 Jug...$87.00
2100 Jug...$95.00
2283 Plate, 8¼" $14.00
2283 Plate, 11" $18.00
701 Tumbler......................$6.00 – 12.00
820 Tumbler......................$6.00 – 12.00
4011 Tumbler......................$6.00 – 12.00

Viennese, Decoration 506

1931 – 1932

Gold on ebony

Tableware I, 328

2375 Bonbon $42.00
2395 Bowl, 10" $195.00
2297 Bowl A, 12", deep $135.00
2324 Candlestick, 4", pair $85.00
2383 Candlestick, trindle, pair $125.00
2430 Jar, candy and cover............$130.00
2391 Cigarette and Cover, large $125.00
2375 Dish, lemon............................$42.00
2375 Plate, cake $120.00
4105 Vase, 8".................................$150.00
2421 Vase, 10½" $250.00

Vintage, Etching 204

1904 – 1928

Stemware, 23, 27

858 Goblet, 11 oz. $6.00
858 Goblet, 10 oz. ....$ 6.00
858 Goblet, 9 oz. $6.00
858 Saucer Champagne, 7 oz. $6.00
858 Saucer Champagne, 5½ oz. $6.00
858 Sherbet $6.00
858 Fruit $6.00
858 Parfait $18.00
858 Cocktail $6.00
858 Claret, 6½ oz. $6.00
858 Claret, 4½ oz. $6.00
858 Wine, 3½ oz. $6.00
858 Wine, 2¾ oz. $6.00
858 Sherry $6.00
858 Crème de Menthe $6.00
858 Brandy $6.00
858 Cordial $15.00
858 Oyster Cocktail........................$5.00
858 Champagne, hollow stem............................$10.00
858 Champagne, tall......................$10.00
858 Champagne, long stem $18.00
858 Champagne, long stem, Cutting R. $18.00
858 Hot Whiskey $7.00
863 Goblet, 10½ oz. $9.00
863 Goblet, 9 oz. $9.00
863 Goblet, 7 oz. $9.00
863 Saucer Champagne, 5½ oz. $9.00
863 Fruit $7.00
863 Cocktail, 3½ oz. $7.00
863 Claret $9.00
863 Rhine Wine...............................$9.00
863 Wine...$9.00
863 Sherry $7.00
863 Crème de Menthe $7.00
863 Brandy, pousse-café $9.00
863 Cordial $20.00
863 Champagne, hollow stem, CF...$9.00
863 Champagne, tall.........................$9.00
837 Oyster Cocktail........................$6.00
5039 Oyster Cocktail and Liner $35.00
945½ Grapefruit and Liner $30.00
822 Parfait $22.00
863 Parfait $22.00
5054 Parfait $22.00
701 Tumbler.........................$5.00 – 8.00
820 Tumbler.........................$5.00 – 8.00
833 Tumbler.........................$5.00 – 8.00
858 Tumbler.........................$5.00 – 8.00
887 Tumbler.........................$5.00 – 8.00
889 Tumbler.........................$5.00 – 8.00
300 Jug...$65.00
303 Jug...$50.00
318 Jug...$85.00
724 Jug...$110.00
1236 Jug...$85.00
1761 Jug...$75.00
1851 Jug...$65.00
1852 Jug...$65.00

Vintage, Etching 347, see Seascape

Vintage, 2713 Milk Glass

1958 – 1965

Stemware, 49

2713 Goblet.................$35.00
2713 Sherbet...............$30.00
2713 Ice Tea, footed $35.00

Tableware II, 213

2713 Bowl, wedding and cover, white...................................$58.00
2713 Bowl, 4½", berry
white $20.00
aqua $24.00
peach $24.00
2713 Bowl, 8", berry
white $38.00
aqua $48.00
peach $48.00
2713 Bowl, 8", crimped
white $48.00
aqua $65.00
peach $65.00
2713 Tray, bread, white $75.00
2713 Butter, oblong and cover, white...................................$65.00
2713 Candleholder, Leaf, pair white $65.00
2713 Candleholder, 4", pair white $64.00
2713 Jar, candy and cover white $57.00
2713 Nappy, 4", crimped
white $20.00
aqua $37.00
peach $37.00
2713 Nappy, 4", square
white $20.00
aqua $32.00
peach $32.00
2713 Plate, 8"
white $20.00
aqua $34.00
peach $34.00
2713 Planter, white..........................$42.00
2713 Shaker, chrome top A, pair white $52.00
2713 Sugar, cream, tray
white $68.00
aqua $125.00
peach $125.00
2713 Tray, Leaf, white....................$37.00

Virginia, Plate Etching 267

1923 – 1929

Stemware, 19

661 Goblet $15.00
661 Saucer Champagne $12.00

Virginia, Plate Etching 267

661 Fruit/Sherbet, low $12.00
661 Parfait $12.00
661 Cocktail $12.00
661 Claret $15.00
661 Wine $15.00
661 Cordial $25.00
837 Oyster Cocktail $10.00
945½ Grapefruit and Liner $25.00
837 Tumbler, 12 oz., handled, $10.00
4085 Tumbler, 13 oz., table $14.00
4085 Tumbler, 6 oz., table $12.00
4085 Tumbler, 2½ oz., table $10.00
4085 Tumbler, 13 oz., handled $18.00
4095 Tumbler, footed $10.00 – 22.00

Tableware I, 144

880 Bonbon $22.00
1769 Bowl, finger and 2283 Plate $22.00
2267 Bowl, 9", Console $45.00
2275 Candlestick, 9½" $38.00
2250 Jar, candy and cover, ¼ pound, optic $42.00
2250 Jar, candy and cover, ½ pound, optic $48.00
1697 Carafe and 4023 Tumbler $70.00
2241 Cologne $98.00
5078 Comport, 5" $26.00
5078 Comport, 6" $32.00
300 Decanter, quart, CN, optic $65.00
825 Jelly and Cover $32.00
303/3 Jug, optic $75.00
303/7 Jug, optic $145.00
318/7 Jug, optic $145.00
1852/6 Jug, optic $145.00
2270 Jug and Cover, optic $150.00
4089 Marmalade and Cover, optic $42.00
1769 Mayonnaise, plate, ladle $48.00
2138 Mayonnaise, plate, ladle $48.00
1831 Mustard and Cover, optic $36.00
5078 Nappy, 5" $20.00
5078 Nappy, 6" $22.00
5078 Nappy, 7" $27.00
5078 Nappy, 8" $30.00
5078 Nappy and Cover, 5" $25.00
5078 Nappy and Cover, 6" $27.00
5078 Nappy and Cover, 7" $30.00
5078 Nappy and Cover, 8" $35.00
1465 Oil, 5 oz., CN, optic $48.00
1465 Oil, 7 oz., CN, optic $54.00
2283 Plate, 5", sherbet, optic $5.00
2283 Plate, 7", optic $6.00
2283 Plate, 8¼", salad, optic $7.00
2283 Plate, 9", sandwich, cut matt star, optic $15.00
2283 Plate, 11", cut matt star, optic $20.00
2083 Bottle, salad dressing, optic $67.00
2235 Shaker, FGT, pair $38.00
2235 Shaker, pearl top, pair $45.00
2133 Sugar and Cream, optic $37.00
2194 Syrup, 8 oz., nickel top $95.00
4055 Vase D, optic $77.00

Virginia, 2977

1978 – 1986

Stemware, 55

2977 Goblet $15.00
2977 Sherbet $15.00
2977 Wine $15.00
2977 Ice Tea, footed $15.00

Tableware II, 307

VI05/171 Comport, footed $15.00
VI05/319 Candlesticks, 6", pair $30.00
VI05/466 Hurricane Globe, crystal $25.00
VI05/469 Hurricane Chimney, crystal $25.00
VI05/550 Plate, 7" $12.00
VI05/554 Plate, 10" $20.00
VI05/761 Vase, 7", also made in ruby $12.00 – 18.00

Vision, 3008

1971 – 1973

Note: an Old Morgantown pattern

Stemware, 56

3008 Goblet
- crystal $18.00
- ebony $18.00
- nutmeg $18.00
- midnight blue $25.00
- white $25.00

3008 Sherbet
- crystal $18.00
- ebony $18.00
- nutmeg $18.00
- midnight blue $22.00
- white $22.00

3008 Claret
- crystal $18.00
- ebony $18.00
- nutmeg $18.00
- midnight blue $25.00
- white $25.00

3008 Tulip Wine
- crystal $20.00
- ebony $20.00
- nutmeg $20.00
- midnight blue $26.00
- white $26.00

3008 Cordial
- crystal $22.00
- ebony $22.00
- nutmeg $22.00
- midnight blue $28.00
- white $28.00

3008 Ice Tea, footed
- crystal $18.00
- ebony $18.00
- nutmeg $18.00
- midnight blue $25.00
- white $25.00

Vogue, 2106

1916 – 1928

Stemware, 44

2106 Goblet $10.00
2106 Sherbet, 3 oz. $8.00
2106 Sherbet, 2½ oz. $8.00
2106 Parfait, 6¼oz. $10.00
2106 Parfait, 4⅜ oz. $10.00
2106 Wine $10.00
2106 Lemonade, footed handled $15.00
2106 Soda, 12 oz., footed $10.00
2106 Soda, 10 oz., footed $10.00
2106 Soda, 8 oz., footed $8.00
2106 Soda, 6 oz., footed $8.00
2106 Soda, 4 oz., footed $8.00
2106 Cocola $8.00
2106 Sundae $8.00

Tableware

2106 Tumbler, flat $4.00 – 8.00
2106 Serving Pieces $10.00 – 35.00
2106 Jug, 3-quart $45.00
2106 Jug, ½ gallon $65.00
2106 Jug, 3-quart and cover $65.00
2106 Jug, ½ gallon and cover $75.00

Vogue, 6099

1961 – 1974

Stemware, 123

6099 Goblet
- crystal $24.00
- gold tint $35.00

6099 Sherbet
- crystal $22.00
- gold tint $30.00

6099 Wine/Cocktail
- crystal $27.00
- gold tint $38.00

6099 Cordial
- crystal $32.00
- gold tint $48.00

6099 Ice Tea, footed
- crystal $24.00
- gold tint $35.00

6099 Juice, footed
- crystal $22.00
- gold tint $30.00

2337 Plate, 7", gold tint $10.00

—W—

Wakefield, Cutting 820

1942 – 1972

Stemware, 94

6023 Goblet $30.00
6023 Saucer Champagne $27.00
6023 Sherbet, low $22.00
6023 Cocktail $26.00
6023 Claret-Wine $34.00
6023 Cordial $45.00
6023 Oyster Cocktail $24.00
6023 Ice Tea, footed $30.00
6023 Tumbler, 9 oz., footed $26.00
6023 Juice, footed $26.00
6011 Jug $175.00
2337 Plate, 6" $8.00

2337 Plate, 7" ... $10.00
2337 Plate, 8" ... $12.00

Warwick, Cutting 198

1929 – 1932

Stemware, 38

890 Goblet ... $22.00
890 Saucer Champagne ... $20.00
890 Sherbet, low ... $15.00
890 Parfait ... $25.00
890 Cocktail ... $18.00
890 Claret Wine ... $25.00
890 Cordial ... $45.00
890 Oyster Cocktail ... $12.00
890 Ice Tea, footed ... $20.00
890 Tumbler, 9 oz., footed ... $15.00
890 Juice, footed ... $15.00
890 Whiskey, footed ... $15.00

Tableware I, 273

890 Bowl, finger and 2283 Plate, 6" ... $22.00
2430 Bowl, 11" ... $40.00
2394 Bowl, 12" ... $45.00
2394 Candlestick, 2", pair ... $45.00
2430 Jar, candy and cover, ½ pound ... $35.00
2400 Comport, 6" ... $22.00
2400 Comport, 8" ... $28.00
2350½ Cream Soup and Plate ... $30.00
2375 Ice Bucket, NP handle ... $38.00
2430 Jelly, 7" ... $16.00
890 Jug ... $135.00
2430 Mint, 5½" ... $15.00
2283 Plate, 7" ... $7.00
2283 Plate, 8" ... $8.00
2283 Plate, 13" ... $26.00
2350 Plate, 10" ... $18.00
2419 Plate, 6" ... $6.00
2419 Plate, 7" ... $7.00
2419 Plate, 8" ... $8.00
2350½ Sugar and Cream ... $36.00
2375 Tray, handled, lunch ... $38.00
2417 Vase, 8" ... $45.00
2430 Vase, 8" ... $45.00
4105 Vase, 8" ... $45.00

Washington, Plate Etching 266

1923 – 1928

Stemware, 17

660 Goblet ... $18.00
660 Saucer Champagne ... $12.00
660 Sherbet, low ... $10.00
660 Parfait ... $18.00
660 Cocktail ... $12.00
660 Claret ... $18.00
660 Wine ... $15.00
660 Cordial ... $22.00
837 Oyster Cocktail ... $10.00
4081 Custard ... $8.00
945½ Grapefruit and Liner ... $42.00
837 Tumbler, 2½ oz. ... $15.00
869 Tumbler, 12 oz., handled ... $15.00
889 Tumbler, 13 oz. ... $15.00
889 Tumbler, 8 oz. ... $10.00
889 Tumbler, 5 oz. ... $6.00
4095 Tumbler, footed ... $6.00 – 15.00

Tableware I, 142 – 143

766 Bonbon, sweetmeat ... $20.00
766 Bowl, finger and 2283 Plate ... $22.00
2267 Bowl, 9", console ... $46.00
2275 Candlestick, 9½", plain, pair ... $65.00
2250 Jar, candy and cover, ¼ pound, optic ... $42.00
2250 Jar, candy and cover, ½ pound, optic ... $48.00
1697 Carafe ... $57.00
4023 Carafe Tumbler, 6 oz. ... $12.00
5078 Comport, 5" ... $26.00
5078 Comport, 6" ... $32.00
5078 Comport and Cover, 5" ... $32.00
5078 Comport and Cover, 6" ... $38.00
300 Decanter, quart, cut neck ... $64.00
825 Jelly and Cover ... $32.00
300/7 Jug, tankard, optic ... $145.00
303/7 Jug ... $140.00
318/7 Jug ... $145.00
318/3½ Jug ... $54.00
2270 Jug and Cover ... $150.00
4089 Marmalade and Cover, optic ... $42.00
766 Mayonnaise, plate, spoon ... $48.00
2138 Mayonnaise, plate, ladle, plain ... $48.00
1831 Mustard and Cover ... $35.00
5078 Nappy, 5" ... $20.00
5078 Nappy, 6" ... $22.00
5078 Nappy, 7" ... $27.00
5078 Nappy, 8" ... $30.00
5078 Nappy and Cover, 5" ... $25.00
5078 Nappy and Cover, 6" ... $27.00
5078 Nappy and Cover, 7" ... $30.00
5078 Nappy and Cover, 8" ... $35.00
1465 Oil, 5 oz., cut neck ... $48.00
1465 Oil, 7 oz., cut neck ... $54.00
2283 Plate, 5", sherbet ... $5.00
2283 Plate, 7", salad ... $6.00
2238 Plate, 8¼", optic ... $7.00
1848 Plate, 9", cut matt star, optic ... $15.00
2238 Plate, 11", cut matt star ... $20.00
2083 Bottle, salad dressing ... $67.00
2235 Shaker, FGT, plain, pair ... $38.00
2234 Shaker, pearl top, plain, pair ... $45.00
1851 Sugar and Cream, optic ... $37.00
2194 Syrup, 8 oz., nickel top, plain ... $95.00
4095 Toothpick and 2½ oz. Tumbler, footed ... $27.00

Waterbury, Cutting 712

1933 – 1943

Stemware, 72

6000 Goblet ... $32.00
6000 Sherbet, high ... $30.00
6000 Sherbet, low ... $24.00
6000 Cocktail ... $30.00
6000 Wine ... $35.00
6000 Oyster Cocktail ... $20.00
6000 Ice Tea, footed ... $30.00
6000 Juice, footed ... $28.00

Tableware I, 277

2424 Bowl, 8", regular ... $25.00
2451 Dish, ice and plate ... $28.00
2453 Lustre, 7½", pair ... $125.00
2283 Plate, 7" ... $7.00
2283 Plate, 8" ... $8.00

Watercress, Cutting 741

1934 – 1943

Stemware, 83

6012 Goblet ... $35.00
6012 Sherbet, high ... $32.00
6012 Sherbet, low ... $26.00
6012 Cocktail ... $32.00
6012 Claret ... $38.00
6012 Rhine Wine ... $40.00
6012 Wine ... $38.00
6012 Sherry ... $35.00
6012 Crème de Menthe ... $32.00
6012 Brandy ... $42.00
6012 Cordial ... $54.00
6012 Oyster Cocktail ... $26.00
6012 Ice Tea, footed ... $35.00
6012 Tumbler, 10 oz., footed ... $27.00
6012 Juice, footed ... $27.00
863 Champagne, hollow stem ... $22.00
1185 Old Fashioned Cocktail ... $15.00
701 Tumbler, 12 oz. ... $15.00
701 Tumbler, 10 oz. ... $12.00
4122 Tumbler, 1½ oz., whiskey ... $10.00

Tableware I, 285

319 Bottle, bar ... $95.00
1769 Bowl, finger ... $14.00
4024 Bowl, 10", footed ... $30.00
2470½ Bowl, 10½" ... $40.00
4024 Candlestick, 6", pair ... $35.00
2472 Candlestick, duo, pair ... $60.00
2496 Candlestick, trindle, pair ... $75.00
4117 Jar, candy and cover, Bubble ... $67.00
2524 Cocktail Mixer ... $56.00
2525 Cocktail Shaker, 42 oz. ... $95.00
2525½ Cocktail Shaker, 30 oz. ... $80.00
2400 Comport, 6" ... $27.00
2525 Decanter ... $95.00
6011 Decanter ... $125.00
6011 Jug ... $185.00
2440 Dish, lemon ... $18.00
2440 Mayonnaise, 2-part ... $26.00
2337 Plate, 6" ... $7.00
2337 Plate, 7" ... $8.00
2337 Plate, 8" ... $10.00
2440 Plate, 13", torte ... $40.00
2364 Plate, 16", torte ... $48.00
2440 Relish, 2-part ... $24.00
2440 Relish, 3-part ... $30.00
2350½ Sugar and Cream ... $30.00
2440 Sweetmeat ... $20.00
2440 Tray, 8½", oval ... $22.00
2470 Vase, 10" ... $95.00

Waterfowl, Carving 1

1938 – 1943

Useful & Ornamental, 111 – 112

2550 Ashtray, round, Swan ... $18.00
2391 Box, cigarette and cover, Swan ... $57.00
4132 Decanter, Gull ... $95.00
4132 Bowl, ice, Goose ... $64.00
2337 Plate, 7", Swan ... $12.00

4132 Tumbler, 1½ oz. whiskey, Gull $18.00
4132 Tumbler, Old Fashioned Cocktail, Goose $18.00
4132 Tumbler, 5 oz., Duck $18.00
4132 Tumbler, 9 oz., Swan....$18.00
4132½ Tumbler, 9 oz., scotch and soda, Duck $18.00
4132 Tumbler, 12 oz., Crane $22.00
4132 Tumbler, 14 oz., Crane $22.00

Wave Crest, 6014½

1935 – 1943

Stemware, 86

6014½ Goblet, LO..$30.00
6014½ Saucer Champagne, LO...$28.00
6014½ Sherbet, low, LO $22.00
6014½ Cocktail, LO $28.00
6014½ Claret, LO $35.00
6014½ Wine, LO $35.00
6014½ Cordial, LO $45.00
6014½ Oyster Cocktail, LO $20.00
6014½ Ice Tea, footed, LO $28.00
6014½ Tumbler, 9 oz., footed, LO $24.00
6014½ Juice, footed, LO $22.00

Waveland, Decoration 57

1926

Tableware I, 324

2367 Bowl, 7", bulb, white gold on ebony....$45.00
2367 Bowl, 8", bulb, white gold on ebony....$50.00
2297 Bowl A, 10", shallow, white gold on ebony....$75.00
2297 Bowl A, 12", deep, white gold on ebony....$85.00
2298 Candlestick, pair, white gold on ebony....$125.00
2324 Candlestick, 4", pair, white gold on ebony....$125.00
2299 Candlestick, 5", pair, white gold on ebony....$135.00
2324 Candlestick, 9", pair, white gold on ebony....$175.00
2331 Box, candy and cover, white gold on ebony....$135.00
2250 Jar, candy and cover, ½ pound, white gold on ebony....$95.00
2329 Centerpiece, 11", white gold on ebony....$120.00
2298 Clock, white gold on ebony $350.00
2298 Clock Set, white gold on ebony....$475.00
2327 Comport, 7", white gold on ebony....$85.00
2317 Puff and Cover, white gold on ebony....$195.00
2306 Smoker Set, 4-piece, white gold on ebony....$95.00
2286 Tray, 5", pin, white gold on ebony....$48.00
2287 Tray, lunch, white gold on ebony....$125.00
2276 Vanity Set, white gold on ebony....$235.00
1681 Vase, wall pocket, white gold on ebony....$200.00
2292 Vase, 8", white gold on ebony....$150.00

Wavemere, 6030/3

1942 – 1943

Stemware, 100

6030/3 Goblet, LO....$25.00
6030/3 Goblet, low, LO....$25.00
6030/3 Saucer Champagne, LO....$22.00
6030/3 Sherbet, low, LO....$20.00
6030/3 Cocktail, LO $22.00
6030/3 Claret-Wine, LO....$28.00
6030/3 Cordial, LO....$35.00
6030/3 Oyster Cocktail, LO $18.00
6030/3 Ice Tea, footed, LO....$25.00
6030/3 Juice, footed, LO....$20.00

Wedding Flower, Cutting 920

1969 – 1970

Stemware, 127

6102 Goblet....$45.00
6102 Sherbet....$40.00
6102 Claret....$48.00
6102 Tulip Wine $48.00
6102 Brandy....$48.00
6102 Ice Tea, footed $45.00
2337 Plate, 7" $10.00
2337 Plate, 8" $12.00

Wedding Ring, Decoration 626

1953 – 1975

Stemware, 106

6051½ Goblet $30.00
6051½ Sherbet....$24.00
6051½ Cocktail $24.00
6051½ Claret-Wine $35.00
6051½ Cordial....$38.00
6051½ Oyster Cocktail....$22.00
6051½ Ice Tea, footed $30.00
6051½ Juice, footed $24.00

Tableware II, 196

2364 Bowl, 9", salad....$32.00
2324 Candlestick, 4", pair $48.00
2666 Cup and Saucer....$26.00
2364 Mayonnaise, plate, ladle $58.00
2337 Plate, 7" $9.00
2337 Plate, 8" $12.00
2666 Sugar and Cream....$40.00
2666 Sugar and Cream, individual....$35.00
2666 Tray, individual sugar and cream $10.00

Wellington, Cutting 722

1933 – 1942

Stemware, 80

6010 Goblet $35.00
6010 Sherbet, high $32.00
6010 Sherbet, low $28.00
6010 Cocktail $32.00
6010 Claret-Wine $38.00
6010 Cordial....$47.00
6010 Oyster Cocktail....$24.00
6010 Ice Tea, footed $32.00
6010 Tumbler, 9 oz., footed....$26.00
6010 Juice, footed $25.00

Tableware I, 279

869 Bowl, finger....$12.00
2470½ Bowl, 10½" $45.00
2470½ Candlestick, 5½", pair $45.00
2400 Comport, 6"....$27.00
2337 Plate, 6" $7.00
2337 Plate, 7" $8.00
2337 Plate, 8" $10.00
2440 Plate, 13", torte $40.00
4110 Vase, 7½" $75.00

Wentworth, Cutting 802

1940 – 1943

Stemware, 94

6023 Goblet $25.00
6023 Saucer Champagne....$23.00
6023 Sherbet, low $20.00
6023 Cocktail $22.00
6023 Claret-Wine $28.00
6023 Cordial....$38.00
6023 Oyster Cocktail....$18.00
6023 Ice Tea, footed $25.00
6023 Tumbler, 9 oz., footed....$26.00
6023 Juice, footed $20.00

Tableware II, 168

766 Bowl, finger....$22.00
2574 Bowl, 9½", handled $45.00
2574 Candlestick, duo, pair....$87.00
6023 Comport, 5"....$35.00
6011 Jug....$250.00
2337 Plate, 7" $8.00
2337 Plate, 8" $10.00

Westchester, 6012

1934 – 1970

Stemware, 83

6012 Goblet
crystal....$30.00
empire green bowl....$75.00
regal blue bowl....$75.00
ruby bowl $75.00
burgundy bowl....$75.00
mother-of-pearl bowl....$30.00

6012 Sherbet, high
crystal $26.00
empire green bowl $65.00
regal blue bowl $65.00
ruby bowl $65.00
burgundy bowl....................$65.00
mother-of-pearl bowl $26.00
6012 Sherbet, low
crystal $22.00
empire green bowl $48.00
regal blue bowl $48.00
ruby bowl $48.00
burgundy bowl....................$48.00
mother-of-pearl bowl $22.00
012 Cocktail
crystal $26.00
empire green bowl $65.00
regal blue bowl $65.00
ruby bowl $65.00
burgundy bowl....................$65.00
mother-of-pearl bowl $26.00
6012 Claret
crystal $35.00
empire green bowl $85.00
regal blue bowl $85.00
ruby bowl $85.00
burgundy bowl....................$85.00
mother-of-pearl bowl $35.00
6012 Rhine Wine
crystal $35.00
empire green bowl $80.00
regal blue bowl $80.00
ruby bowl $80.00
burgundy bowl....................$80.00
mother-of-pearl bowl $35.00
6012 Wine
crystal $35.00
empire green bowl $75.00
regal blue bowl $75.00
ruby bowl $75.00
burgundy bowl....................$75.00
mother-of-pearl bowl $35.00
6012 Sherry
crystal $37.00
empire green bowl $70.00
regal blue bowl $70.00
ruby bowl $70.00
burgundy bowl....................$70.00
mother-of-pearl bowl $37.00
6012 Crème de Menthe
crystal $26.00
empire green bowl $65.00
regal blue bowl $65.00
ruby bowl $65.00
burgundy bowl....................$65.00
mother-of-pearl bowl $26.00
6012 Brandy
crystal $40.00
empire green bowl $75.00
regal blue bowl $75.00
ruby bowl $75.00
burgundy bowl....................$75.00
mother-of-pearl bowl $40.00
6012 Cordial
crystal $45.00
empire green bowl $95.00
regal blue bowl $95.00
ruby bowl $95.00
burgundy bowl....................$95.00
mother-of-pearl bowl $45.00
6012 Oyster Cocktail
crystal $20.00
empire green bowl $45.00
regal blue bowl $45.00
ruby bowl $45.00
burgundy bowl....................$45.00
mother-of-pearl bowl $20.00
6012 Ice Tea, footed
crystal $28.00
empire green bowl $65.00
regal blue bowl $65.00
ruby bowl $65.00
burgundy bowl....................$65.00
mother-of-pearl bowl $28.00
6012 Tumbler, 10 oz., footed
crystal $24.00
empire green bowl $48.00
regal blue bowl $48.00
ruby bowl $48.00
burgundy bowl....................$48.00
mother-of-pearl bowl $24.00
6012 Juice, footed
crystal $22.00
empire green bowl $50.00
regal blue bowl $50.00
ruby bowl $50.00
burgundy bowl....................$50.00
mother-of-pearl bowl $22.00

Westminster, Cutting 723

1933 – 1938

Stemware, 80

6010 Goblet
....................$35.00
6010 Sherbet, high $32.00
6010 Sherbet, low $28.00
6010 Cocktail $32.00
6010 Claret-Wine $38.00
6010 Cordial $47.00
6010 Oyster Cocktail....................$24.00
6010 Ice Tea, footed $32.00
6010 Tumbler, 9 oz., footed....................$26.00
6010 Juice, footed $25.00

Tableware I, 279

869 Bowl, finger....................$12.00
2470½ Bowl, 10½" $45.00
2470½ Candlestick, 5½", pair....................$45.00
2400 Comport, 6" $27.00
2337 Plate, 6" $7.00
2337 Plate, 7" $8.00
2337 Plate, 8" $10.00
2470 Vase, 10" $95.00

Westminister, Cutting 872

1959 – 1972

Stemware, 117

6083 Goblet
........$28.00
6083 Sherbet....................$25.00
6083 Wine/Cocktail $30.00
6083 Cordial $38.00
6083 Ice Tea, footed $28.00
6083 Juice, footed $24.00
2337 Plate, 7" $10.00
2337 Plate, 8" $12.00

Weylin, Cutting 759

1936 – 1938

Stemware, 86

6014 Goblet
......$30.00
6014 Saucer Champagne $27.00
6014 Sherbet, low $22.00
6014 Cocktail $27.00
6014 Claret $35.00
6014 Wine....................$32.00
6014 Cordial $45.00
6014 Oyster Cocktail....................$20.00
6014 Ice Tea, footed $30.00
6014 Tumbler, footed, 9 oz. $25.00
6014 Juice, footed $22.00

Tableware I, 290

869 Bowl, finger....................$12.00
2470½ Bowl, 10½" $40.00
2472 Candlestick, duo, pair $70.00
2400 Comport, 6" $27.00
5000 Jug....................$185.00
2337 Plate, 6" $7.00
2337 Plate, 7" $8.00
2337 Plate, 8" $10.00

Wheat, Cutting 760

Year

Tableware I, 292 – 297

2496 Bonbon, 3-toed....................$32.00
2496 Bowl, 8½", serving $60.00
2496 Bowl, 10", floating garden $65.00
2496 Bowl, 10½", handled $94.00
2496 Bowl, 12", flared $65.00
2545 Bowl, 12½", oval....................$65.00
2545 Candelabra, 2-light, B prisms, pair $200.00
2496 Candlestick, 4", pair $45.00
2496 Candlestick, 5½", pair....................$55.00
2496 Candlestick, duo, pair $75.00
2545 Candlestick, duo, pair $125.00
2496 Candlestick, trindle, pair $95.00
2496 Box, candy and cover....................$55.00
2440 Celery $27.00
2496 Celery $27.00
2496 Cheese and Cracker....................$45.00
2496 Comport, 5½"....................$30.00
2496 Comport, 6½"....................$65.00
2375 Ice Bucket, NP handle....................$54.00
2496 Ice Bucket, gold handle....................$54.00
2496 Jelly and Cover $75.00
2496 Mayonnaise, 2-part....................$27.00
2496½ Mayonnaise and Plate....................$35.00
2449 Pickle....................$22.00
2496 Pickle....................$22.00
2440 Plate, 10", cake $40.00
2496 Plate, 10", handled, cake.......$45.00
2496 Plate, 14", torte $48.00
2496 Bowl, nut, 3-toed....................$38.00
2496 Relish, 2-part....................$25.00
2496 Relish, 3-part....................$35.00
2496 Relish, 4-part....................$45.00
2419 Relish, 5-part....................$55.00
2496 Sauce and Tray, oblong $57.00
2440 Sugar and Cream....................$45.00
2496 Sugar and Cream, individual....................$45.00
2496 Sweetmeat....................$27.00
2496 Tid Bit, 3-toed $30.00
2470 Vase, 10"....................$95.00

Wheat, Cutting 837
(see Fostoria Wheat)

Whip Cream Pails,
see Ice Buckets, Sugar Pails, Whip Cream Pails

Whirlpool, Cutting 730 and Golden Swirl, Decoration 614

1934 – 1939; 1935 – 1937

Stemware, 81-82

6011 Goblet
Whirlpool..........$30.00
Golden Swirl $32.00
6011 Saucer Champagne
Whirlpool..........$28.00
Golden Swirl $28.00
6011 Sherbet, low
Whirlpool..........$24.00
Golden Swirl $24.00
6011 Cocktail
Whirlpool..........$28.00
Golden Swirl $28.00
6011 Claret
Whirlpool..........$34.00
Golden Swirl $37.00
6011 Rhine Wine
Whirlpool..........$35.00
Golden Swirl $40.00
6011 Wine
Whirlpool..........$34.00
Golden Swirl $35.00
6011 Sherry
Whirlpool..........$32.00
6011 Crème de Menthe
Whirlpool..........$28.00
Golden Swirl $25.00
6011 Brandy
Whirlpool..........$35.00
Golden Swirl $37.00
795 Champagne, hollow stem
Whirlpool..........$25.00
863 Champagne, hollow stem
Whirlpool..........$25.00
6011 Cordial
Whirlpool..........$40.00
Golden Swirl $32.00
6011 Oyster Cocktail
Whirlpool..........$20.00
6011 Ice Tea, footed
Whirlpool..........$28.00
Golden Swirl $32.00
6011 Tumbler, 10 oz., footed
Whirlpool..........$24.00
Golden Swirl $25.00
6011 Juice, footed
Whirlpool..........$24.00
6011 Whiskey, footed
Whirlpool..........$32.00
Golden Swirl $30.00
906 Brandy Inhaler
Whirlpool..........$28.00
701 Tumbler, 12 oz.
Whirlpool..........$10.00
701 Tumbler, 10 oz.
Whirlpool..........$8.00
887 Tumbler, 1¾ oz., whiskey
Whirlpool..........$10.00
1184 Old Fashioned Cocktail, 7 oz.
Whirlpool..........$10.00
4122 Tumbler, 1½ oz., whiskey
Whirlpool..........$10.00

Tableware I, 281 - 282

1769 Bowl, finger..........$14.00
4024 Bowl, 10", footed..........$35.00
4024 Candlestick, 6", pair..........$45.00
4117 Jar, candy and cover, Bubble..........$95.00
2525 Cocktail Shaker..........$125.00
2525 Decanter..........$145.00
6011 Decanter..........$160.00
2337 Plate, 6"..........$14.00
2337 Plate, 7"..........$16.00
2337 Plate, 11"..........$24.00
4116 Vase, 4", Bubble Ball..........$24.00
4116 Vase, 5", Bubble Ball..........$27.00
4116 Vase, 6", Bubble Ball..........$30.00
4116 Vase, 7", Bubble Ball..........$35.00
6011 Jug
Whirlpool..........$195.00
2337 Plate, 8"
Whirlpool..........$18.00

Whisper, Cutting 875

1960 – 1970

Stemware, 119

6089 Goblet..........$32.00
6089 Sherbet..........$30.00
6089 Wine/Cocktail..........$36.00
6089 Brandy..........$40.00
6089 Ice Tea, footed..........$32.00
6089 Juice, footed..........$28.00
2337 Plate, 7"..........$10.00
2337 Plate, 8"..........$12.00

White Edge Decoration

1924

Tableware I, 333

2136 Bonbon..........$95.00
2267 Bowl, 7"..........$65.00
2267 Bowl, 9"..........$75.00
2297 Bowl A, 7", deep, flared..........$75.00
2297 Bowl C, 7", deep, rolled edge..........$75.00
2297 Bowl A, 7", shallow, flared..........$75.00
2297 Bowl C, 7", shallow, rolled edge..........$75.00
2267 Bowl, deep, rolled edge..........$75.00
2245 Candlestick, 6", pair..........$58.00
2245 Candlestick, 8", pair..........$75.00
2269 Candlestick, 6", pair..........$64.00
2297 Candlestick, 7", pair..........$75.00
2275 Candlestick, 7", pair..........$68.00
2275 Candlestick, 9", pair..........$95.00
2219 Jar, candy and cover, ¼ pound..........$65.00
2219 Jar, candy and cover, ½ pound..........$75.00
2219 Jar, candy and cover, pound..........$85.00
2250 Jar, candy and cover, ¼ pound..........$58.00
2250 Jar, candy and cover, ½ pound..........$65.00
2250 Jar, candy and cover, pound..........$75.00
2136 Cold Cream and Cover, 3"..........$75.00
2241 Cologne..........$125.00
2283 Plate, 6"..........$12.00
2283 Plate, 7"..........$14.00
2283 Plate, 8¼"..........$18.00
2283 Plate, 11"..........$35.00
2290 Plate, 8¼", deep, salad..........$32.00
2290 Plate, 13½", deep, salad..........$58.00
2136 Pomade and Cover, 2"..........$65.00
2287 Tray, handled, lunch..........$65.00
2276 Vanity Set..........$225.00

Wildflower, Plate Etching 308

1931 – 1932

Tableware I, 205, 206

2419 Bonbon
green....$45.00
amber...$95.00
2443 Bowl, 10", oval
green..........$195.00
amber..........$195.00
2433 Bowl A, 12"
green..........$325.00
amber..........$325.00
2433 Candle, 3", pair
green..........$150.00
amber..........$150.00
2443 Candle, 4", pair
green..........$125.00
amber..........$125.00
2447 Candle, duo, pair
green..........$225.00
amber..........$225.00
2430 Jar, candy and cover, ½ pound
green..........$175.00
amber..........$175.00
2375 Cheese and Cracker
green..........$187.00
amber..........$187.00
2400 Comport, 6"
green..........$75.00
amber..........$75.00
2433 Comport, 6", low
green..........$95.00
amber..........$95.00
2433 Comport, 6", tall
green..........$250.00
amber..........$250.00
4020 Decanter and 2 oz. Whiskey
green..........$800.00/market
amber..........$800.00/market
2443 Ice Tub, 6"
green..........$135.00
amber..........$135.00
2419 Jelly
green..........$47.00
amber..........$47.00
2419 Lemon
green..........$38.00
amber..........$38.00
2419 Mayonnaise
green..........$48.00
amber..........$48.00
2419 Plate, cake
green..........$125.00
amber..........$125.00
2364 Plate, 16"
green..........$200.00
amber..........$200.00
2419 Relish, 4-part
green..........$75.00
amber..........$75.00
4020 Sugar and Cream
green..........$95.00
amber..........$95.00
2419 Syrup and Cover and Saucer
green..........$250.00
amber..........$250.00
2419 Tray, handled, lunch
green..........$138.00
amber..........$138.00
4106 Vase, 7"
green..........$300.00
amber..........$300.00

4107 Vase, 9"
green $450.00
amber $450.00
4107 Vase, 12"
green $625.00
amber $625.00
4107 Vase, 15"
green $700.00/market
amber $700.00/market
4108 Vase, 5"
green $185.00
amber $185.00
4108 Vase, 6"
green $200.00
amber $200.00
4108 Vase, 7"
green $250.00
amber $250.00

Wildwood, Cutting 854

1957

Stemware, 114

6071 Goblet $30.00
6071 Sherbet $27.00
6071 Cocktail/Wine/Seafood $30.00
6071 Cordial $40.00
6071 Ice Tea, footed $30.00
6071 Juice, footed $25.00
2574 Plate, 7", Raleigh $10.00
2574 Plate, 8", Raleigh $12.00

Williamsburg, Cutting 874

1960 – 1969

Stemware, 116

6079 Goblet $34.00
6079 Sherbet $32.00
6079 Cocktail $32.00
6079 Claret-Wine $36.00
6079 Cordial $42.00
6079 Ice Tea, footed $34.00
6079 Juice, footed $30.00
2337 Plate, 7" $10.00
2337 Plate, 8" $12.00

Willow, Etching 335

1934 – 1944

Stemware, 93

6023 Goblet $38.00
6023 Saucer Champagne $36.00
6023 Sherbet, low $32.00
6023 Cocktail $35.00
6023 Claret-Wine $45.00
6023 Cordial $65.00
6023 Oyster Cocktail $30.00
6023 Ice Tea, footed $38.00
6023 Tumbler, 9 oz., footed $30.00
6023 Juice, footed $32.00

Tableware II, 127, 130, 131

2574 Bonbon $42.00
766 Bowl, finger $27.00
2574 Bowl, 8½", serving $54.00
6023 Bowl, 9½", footed $125.00
2574 Bowl, 9½", handled $75.00
2574 Bowl, 12", flared $60.00
2574 Bowl, 13", fruit $75.00
2574 Candlestick, 4", pair $84.00
2324 Candlestick, 6", pair $88.00
2374 Celery, 10½" $48.00
2574 Comport, 5" $67.00
6023 Comport, 5" $67.00
2574 Cup and Saucer $32.00
2574 Ice Tub $60.00
6011 Jug $375.00
2574 Lemon $38.00
2574 Mayonnaise, plate, ladle $75.00
2574 Oil, 4½ oz., GS $125.00
2574 Olive, 6" $27.00
2574 Pickle, 8" $34.00
2574 Plate, 6" $15.00
2574 Plate, 7" $20.00
2574 Plate, 8" $26.00
2574 Plate, 9" $52.00
2574 Plate, 10", cake $76.00
2574 Plate, 14", torte $85.00
2475 Relish, 3-part $68.00
2574 Shaker, FGT, pair $125.00
2574 Sugar and Cream, individual $75.00
2574 Sugar and Cream $95.00
2574 Sweetmeat $42.00
2574 Tray, handled, muffin $75.00
2574 Whip Cream $42.00

Willowmere, Etching 333

1938 – 1970

Stemware, 95

6024 Goblet $38.00
6024 Saucer Champagne $34.00
6024 Sherbet, low $26.00
6024 Cocktail $30.00
6024 Claret $45.00
6024 Wine $45.00
6024 Cordial $55.00
6024 Oyster Cocktail $24.00
6024 Ice Tea, footed $38.00
6024 Tumbler, 9 oz., footed $26.00
6024 Juice, footed $28.00

Tableware II, 124-126

2560 Bonbon $42.00
2560 Bonbon, 3-toed $65.00
869 Bowl, finger $34.00
2560 Bowl, 5", fruit $32.00
2560 Bowl, 6", cereal $34.00
2560 Bowl, 3-toed, nut $65.00
2560 Bowl, 8½", serving $54.00
2560 Bowl, 10", salad $78.00
2560 Bowl, 2-part, salad $125.00
2560 Bowl, 11", handled $125.00
2560 Bowl, 11½", crimped $95.00
2560 Bowl, 12", flared $86.00
2560 Bowl, 13", fruit $94.00
2560½ Candlestick, 4", pair $75.00
2560 Candlestick, 4½", pair $75.00
2560 Candlestick, duo, pair $125.00
2560 Celery, 11" $45.00
2560 Cheese and Cracker $135.00
2560 Comport, 6" $75.00
2560 Cup and Saucer $34.00
2560 Ice Bucket, chrome handle and tongs $165.00
5000 Jug $575.00
2560 Lemon $38.00
2560 Mayonnaise, plate, ladle $68.00
2560 Mayonnaise, 2-part, 2 ladles $95.00
2560 Oil, 3 oz. and stopper $165.00
2560 Olive, 6¾" $30.00
2560 Pickle, 8¾" $34.00
2666 Pitcher, quart $425.00
2560 Plate, 6" $12.00
2560 Plate, 7" $22.00
2560 Plate, 8" $26.00
2560 Plate, 9" $54.00
2560 Plate, 11½", cake $75.00
2560 Plate, 14", torte $95.00
2560 Relish, 2-part $38.00
2560 Relish, 3-part $74.00
2560 Relish, 4-part $77.00
2560 Relish, 5-part $125.00
2560 Salad Set, 3-piece $150.00
2586 Server, sani-cut $235.00/market
2364 Shaker, chrome top C, pair $95.00
2560 Shaker, FGT, pair $135.00
2560 Sugar and Cream $75.00
2560 Sugar and Cream, individual $75.00
2560 Tray, sugar and cream, 7½" $32.00
2560 Sweetmeat $42.00
2560 Tid Bit, 3-toed $65.00
2560 Tray, handled, lunch $125.00
2560 Tray, handled, muffin $85.00
2276 Vanity Set $225.00/market
2560 Vase, 6", handled $175.00
2567 Vase, 7½" $195.00
2568 Vase, 9" $225.00
2470 Vase, 10" $295.00
5100 Vase, 10" $275.00
2560 Whip Cream $42.00

Wilma, 6016

1936 – 1982

Stemware, 87

6016 Goblet
crystal $30.00
azure $60.00
blue $60.00
pink $60.00
6016 Saucer Champagne
crystal $26.00
azure $48.00
blue $48.00
pink $48.00
6016 Sherbet, low
crystal $22.00
azure $40.00
6016 Cocktail
crystal $26.00
azure $48.00
6016 Claret
crystal $35.00
azure $50.00
blue $50.00
pink $50.00
6016 Wine
crystal $34.00
azure $54.00
6016 Cordial
crystal $40.00
azure $65.00
6016 Oyster Cocktail
crystal $22.00
azure $38.00
6016 Ice Tea, footed
crystal $30.00

	azure	$58.00
	blue	$58.00
	pink	$58.00
6016	Tumbler, 10 oz., footed	
	crystal	$26.00
	azure	$50.00
6016	Juice, footed	
	crystal	$25.00
	azure	$40.00
6016	Claret, large	
	crystal	$40.00
	blue	$58.00
	pink	$58.00
6016	Champagne, continental	
	crystal	$54.00

Wimbledon, 6126 (see also Corsage Plum, Gazebo, and Gazebo Rust)

1974 – 1982

Stemware, 142

6126	Goblet	$24.00
6126	Champagne	$22.00
6126	Wine	$24.00
6126	Ice Tea, footed	$24.00

Winburn, 1704 Milk Glass

1954 – 1965

Tableware II, 204

1704	Butter and Cover, round,	
	white	$75.00
1704	Jar, cracker and cover	
	white	$75.00
1704	Jelly, 3-cornered	
	white	$25.00
	aqua	$34.00
	peach	$34.00
1704	Jelly, oblong	
	white	$25.00
	aqua	$34.00
	peach	$34.00
1704	Jelly, square	
	white	$25.00
	aqua	$34.00
	peach	$34.00
1704	Jug, ½-gallon, ice	
	white	$97.00
1704	Nappy, 3-cornered, handled	
	white	$24.00
	aqua	$34.00
	peach	$34.00
1704	Nappy, square, handled	
	white	$24.00
	aqua	$34.00
	peach	$34.00
1704	Oil and Stopper	
	white	$54.00
1704	Bowl, punch and foot, 16", plastic ladle and hooks	
	white	$335.00
1704	Cup, punch	
	white	$18.00
1704	Jar, pickle and cover	
	white	$48.00
1704	Shaker, FGT or chrome top D, milk glass tops, pair	
	white	$85.00
	aqua	$95.00
	peach	$95.00
1704	Sugar and Cover and Cream	
	white	$77.00
	aqua	$98.00
	peach	$98.00
1704	Tumbler, 7 oz., flat, water	$32.00

Windfall, Cutting 870

1958 – 1962

Stemware, 110

6060	Goblet	$28.00
6060	Sherbet	$25.00
6060	Cocktail/Wine/Seafood	$28.00
6060	Cordial	$40.00
6060	Ice Tea, footed	$28.00
6060	Juice, footed	$25.00
2337	Plate, 7"	$10.00
2337	Plate, 8"	$12.00

Windsor, 2749 (see Crown Collection)

Windsor, 6049

1952 – 1965

Stemware, 105

6049	Goblet	$20.00
6049	Sherbet, high	$18.00
6049	Sherbet, low	$14.00
6049	Parfait	$18.00
6049	Cocktail	$16.00
6049	Claret	$20.00
6049	Wine	$20.00
6049	Cordial	$22.00
6049	Oyster Cocktail	$12.00
6049	Ice Tea, footed	$18.00
6049	Juice, footed	$12.00

Wistar, 2620 (see also Betsy Ross)

1941 – 1943

Stemware, 48

2326	Goblet	$35.00
2326	Sherbet	$30.00
2326	Tumbler, 12 oz.	$34.00
2326	Tumbler, 5 oz.	$30.00

Tableware I, 117, 118

2326	Bonbon, 3-toed	$34.00
	Bowl, 3-toed, nut	$34.00
	Bowl, 3-toed, tricorne	$34.00
	Bowl, 10", salad	$47.00
	Bowl, 12", lily pond	$50.00
	Bowl, 13", fruit	$65.00
	Candlestick, 4"	$32.00
	Celery, 9½"	$36.00
	Mayonnaise, plate, ladle	$68.00
	Nappy, handled, regular	$22.00
	Nappy, handled, square	$22.00
	Nappy, handled, flared	$22.00
	Nappy, 3-cornered	$22.00
	Plate, 7"	$12.00
	Plate, 14", torte	$65.00
	Sugar and Cream	$67.00

Woodland, Etching 264 and Goldwood, Decoration 50

1922 – 1928

Note: Add 20% to prices for Goldwood

Stemware, 17

660	Goblet	$18.00
660	Saucer Champagne	$12.00
660	Sherbet, low	$10.00
660	Parfait	$18.00
660	Cocktail	$12.00
660	Claret	$18.00
660	Wine	$15.00
660	Cordial	$22.00
837	Oyster Cocktail	$10.00
945½	Grapefruit and Liner	$25.00
4011	Tumbler, 12 oz.	$10.00
4011	Tumbler, 3 oz.	$8.00
4011	Tumbler, 12 oz., handled, plate	$12.00
4011½	Tumbler	$10.00
4095	Tumbler, 13 oz., footed	$18.00
4095	Tumbler, 10 oz., footed	$15.00
4095	Tumbler, 5 oz., footed	$10.00
4095	Tumbler/Toothpick, 2½ oz., footed	$8.00

Tableware I, 142

766	Bowl, finger and 1736 Plate	$22.00
	with Goldwood Decoration 50	$22.00
2250	Jar, candy and cover, ¼ pound	$45.00
2250	Jar, candy and cover, ½ pound	$55.00
2250	Jar, candy and cover, pound	$65.00
1697	Carafe	$65.00
	with Goldwood Decoration 50	$65.00
4023	Carafe, 6 oz., tumbler	$10.00
803	Comport, 5"	$22.00
803	Comport, 6"	$22.00
300	Decanter, quart, cut neck	$65.00
825	Jelly and Cover	$32.00
300/7	Jug	$150.00
	with Goldwood Decoration 50	$150.00
303/7	Jug	$150.00
1743/4	Jug, grape juice and cover	$150.00
1743/7	Jug	$150.00
4089	Marmalade and Cover	$42.00
2138	Mayonnaise, plate, ladle	$50.00
1831	Mustard and Cover	$35.00
803	Nappy, 5"	$22.00
803	Nappy, 6"	$25.00
803	Nappy, 7"	$27.00
1465	Oil, 5 oz., cut neck	$48.00
1465	Oil, 7 oz., cut neck	$54.00
701	Plate, 5", tumbler	$5.00
	with Goldwood Decoration 50	$5.00
840	Plate, 5", sherbet	$5.00
	with Goldwood Decoration 50	$5.00
1897	Plate, 7", salad	$6.00
	with Goldwood Decoration 50	$6.00
2238	Plate, 8¼"	$7.00
	with Goldwood Decoration 50	$7.00
2238	Plate, 11"	$16.00
2083	Bottle, salad dressing	$68.00
	with Goldwood Decoration 50	$68.00
2022	Shaker, FGT, pair	$45.00
766	Sweetmeat	$32.00
2194	Syrup, 8 oz., nickel top	$115.00

Woodland, 2921

1975 – 1981

Stemware, 55

2921 Goblet
- crystal............$15.00
- blue...............$15.00
- brown............$15.00
- green.............$15.00

2921 Sherbet
- crystal $15.00
- blue $15.00
- brown...................................$15.00
- green...................................$15.00

2921 Wine
- crystal $15.00
- blue $15.00
- brown...................................$15.00
- green...................................$15.00

2921 Ice Tea, footed
- crystal $15.00
- blue $15.00
- brown...................................$15.00
- green...................................$15.00

Tableware II, 308

2921/517
Bowl, 7" $15.00

2921/317
Candle, 5", pair $20.00

2921/448
Jelly, 4⅝", footed $15.00

2921/505
Nappy and Cover, 5" $15.00

2921/554
Plate, 10", serving..................$15.00

2921/653
Shaker, chrome top A, pair $27.00

2921/506
Nappy, 5"................................$11.00

--Y--

Yachting, Carving 8

1938 – 1943

Useful & Ornamental, 113

4132½ Vase, 8" $95.00

York, 2934 Tumbler

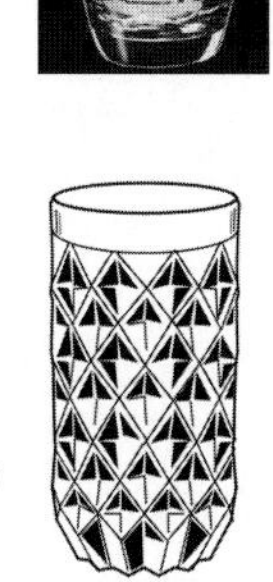

1979 – 1982

Stemware, 153

2934 Highball, 13 oz., pressed lead, crystal.............$14.00

2934 Old Fashioned, 10 oz., double, pressed, lead crystal.........................$14.00

York, Cutting 709

1933 – 1943

Stemware, 77

6007 Goblet....$35.00
6007 Sherbet, high $32.00
6007 Sherbet, low $28.00
6007 Cocktail $30.00
6007 Claret $38.00
6007 Wine...$35.00
6007 Cordial $48.00
6007 Oyster Cocktail.......................$28.00
6007 Ice Tea, footed $34.00
6007 Tumbler, 9 oz., footed..................................$28.00
6007 Juice, footed $28.00
6007 Whiskey, footed......................$30.00

Tableware I, 276

2470 Bowl, 12" $45.00
2470 Candlestick, 5½", pair...........$58.00
2470 Comport, 6"............................$45.00
2451 Dish, ice and plate..................$28.00
2283 Plate, 7" $7.00
2283 Plate, 8" $8.00
2470 Plate, 10", cake $45.00
2440 Plate, 13", torte $45.00

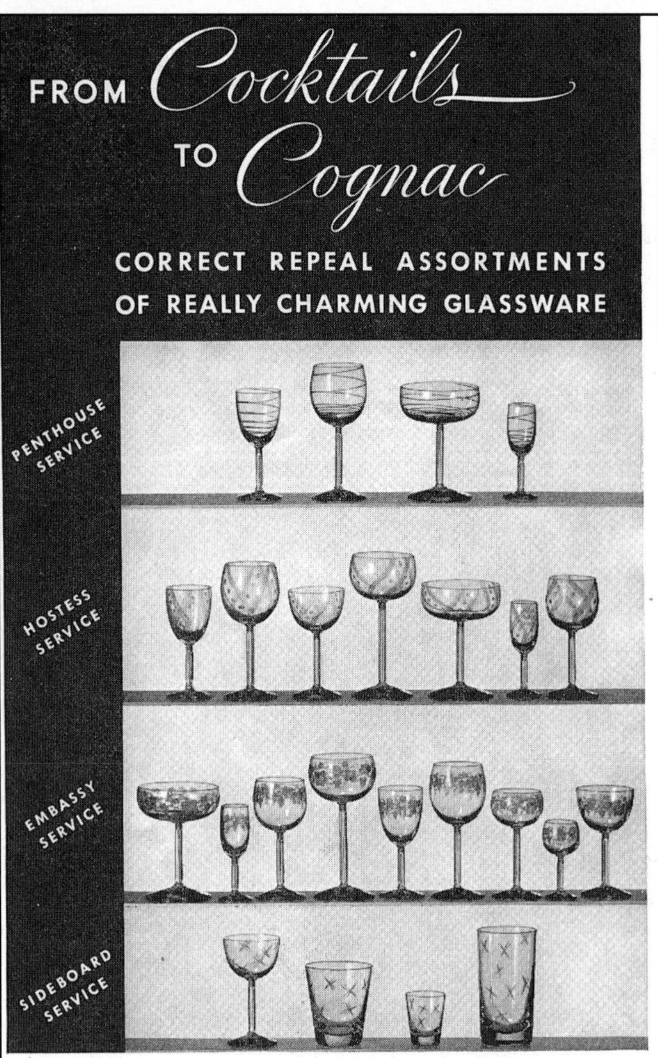

The four designs illustrated are (from top to bottom) Whirlpool, Celestial, Nectar and Rocket. Each service is available in any of these, as well as in many other designs and colors. Water goblets, tumblers and dinner pieces may be had to match.

penthouse service . . . The customary essentials for correct table service of wines and liqueurs. Penthouse No. 1 . . . (32 pieces) . . . 8 each—Sherry, Claret, Champagne and Brandy. Penthouse No. 2 . . . (48 pieces) . . . a dozen each of the same glasses.

hostess service . . . A satisfyingly adequate stock of glassware for those whose entertainment requirements assume more than ordinary proportions. Hostess No. 1 . . . (56 pieces) . . . 8 each —Sherry, Claret, Cocktail, Rhine Wine, Champagne, Brandy and Wine. Hostess No. 2 . . . (84 pieces) . . . a dozen each of the same glasses.

embassy service . . . For the occasional dinner of exceptional formality. Embassy No. 1 . . . (72 pieces) . . . 8 each—Champagne, Brandy, Wine, Rhine Wine, Sherry, Claret, Crème de Menthe, Cordial and Cocktail. Embassy No. 2 . . . (108 pieces) . . . a dozen each of the same glasses.

sideboard service . . . Standard equipment for every home. Sideboard No. 1 . . . (32 pieces) . . . 8 each—Cocktail, Old-Fashioned Cocktail, Whiskey-2 oz., Highball-10 oz. Sideboard No. 2 . . . (48 pieces) . . . a dozen each of the same glasses.

Write for our book on Correct Wine and Table Service. Fostoria Glass Co., Moundsville, W. Va.

1934 advertisement from *The American Home* magazine

American . . . the crystal that leads a *DOUBLE LIFE*

Sparkling *American* is a happy choice for family dinners. Extremely economical, it permits a complete table setting in *open stock*. For friendly, informal occasions, you will want to combine your *American* with the *American Lady* stemware. Here the rugged prismatic colonial base is combined with a more feminine motif in a lucent thin-blown bowl. Both patterns are *open stock*. For illustrated leaflet, write to Dept. 4225.

FOSTORIA

GLASS COMPANY · · · MOUNDSVILLE · WEST VIRGINIA

1934 advertisement from *The American Home* magazine

Fostoria Glass Company, Moundsville, West Virginia, Jan. 1, 1933

BLOWN TUMBLERS

NARROW OPTIC

Made in Solid Rose, Green, Amber, Topaz and Wisteria
(Except as noted below the item)

887—2½ oz. Tumbler
Height 2½ in.
Also made in Azure

889—5 oz. Tumbler
Height 3½ in.

1184—7 oz. Old Fashioned Cocktail
Height 3⅜ in.
Also made in Az-Crys

701—8 oz. Tumbler
Height 4⅜ in.

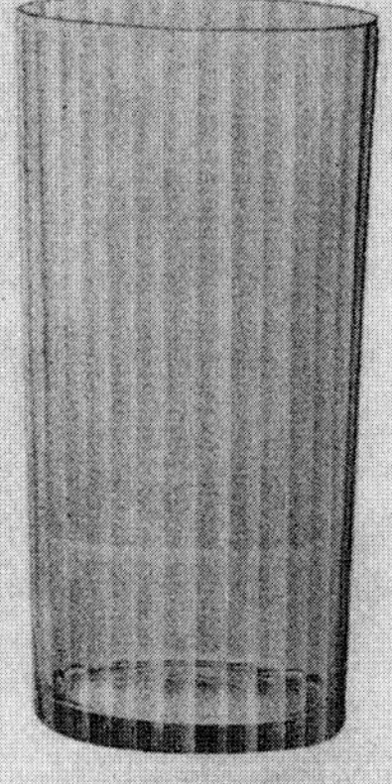

701—20 oz. Tumbler
Height 6 in.

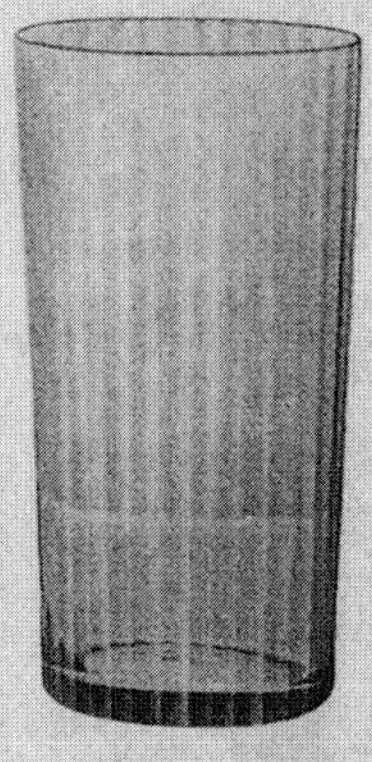

701—16 oz. Tumbler
Height 5⅝ in.
Also made in Azure

701—13 oz. Tumbler
Height 5¼ in.

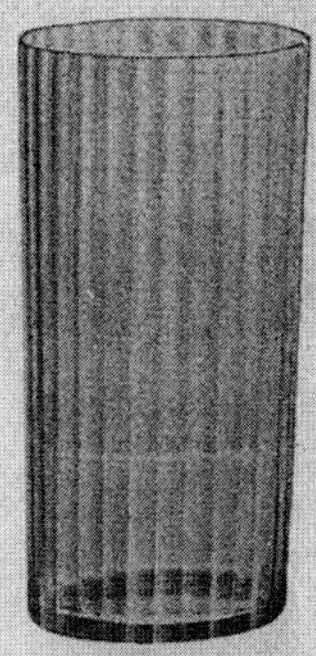

701—10 oz. Tumbler
Height 4¾ in.

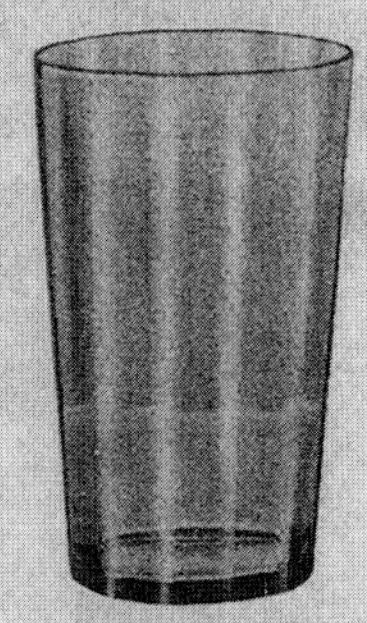

4076—9 oz. Tumbler
Height 4¼ in.
Not made in Wisteria
Made in Reg. Optic Only

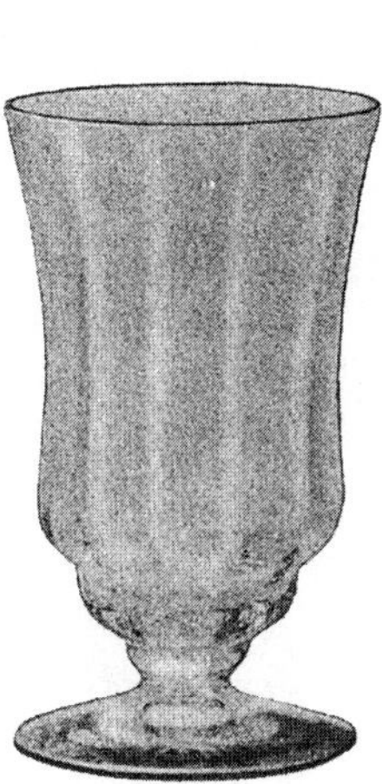

5084—9 oz. Footed Tumbler
Height 5 in.

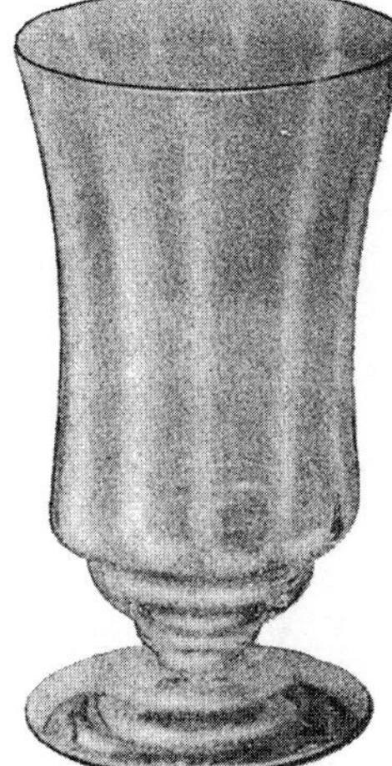

5084—12 oz. Footed Tumbler
Height 5⅝ in.

5084—4¾ oz. Oyster
Cocktail
Height 3⅜ in.

4005—12 oz. Tumbler
Height 4⅞ in.
Crystal only
4005—9 oz. Tumbler
Height 3⅞ in.
Crystal only
4005—5 oz. Tumbler
Height 3¼ in.
Crystal only
4005—2½ oz. Tumbler
Height 2½ in.
Crystal only

1933 Fostoria catalog page showing Tumblers.

1933 Fostoria catalog page showing Tumblers.

A variety of Fostoria Tumblers

889, 887 flat Tumblers; 5000, 4095 footed Oyster Cocktails.

4011 (flared tops) flat Tumblers and 701 (straight sided) flat Tumbler.

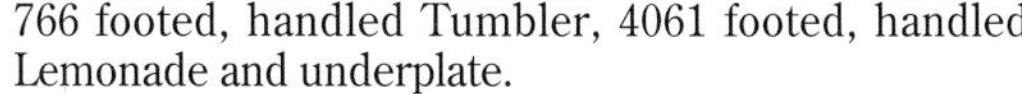

766 footed, handled Tumbler, 4061 footed, handled Lemonade and underplate.

5000, 4095, and 877 footed Tumblers.

An assortment of lovely Parfaits.

660, 5054, 5082, 661, and 889 Parfaits.

766½ short, 858½, 766 tall, 6033 Mademoiselle, and 5070 Parfaits.

Delicious butterscotch, chocolate, vanilla, and cherry layered parfait in a 5082 glass on a 2574 Raleigh plate.

5083, 766½ short, 5097, and 5098 Parfaits.

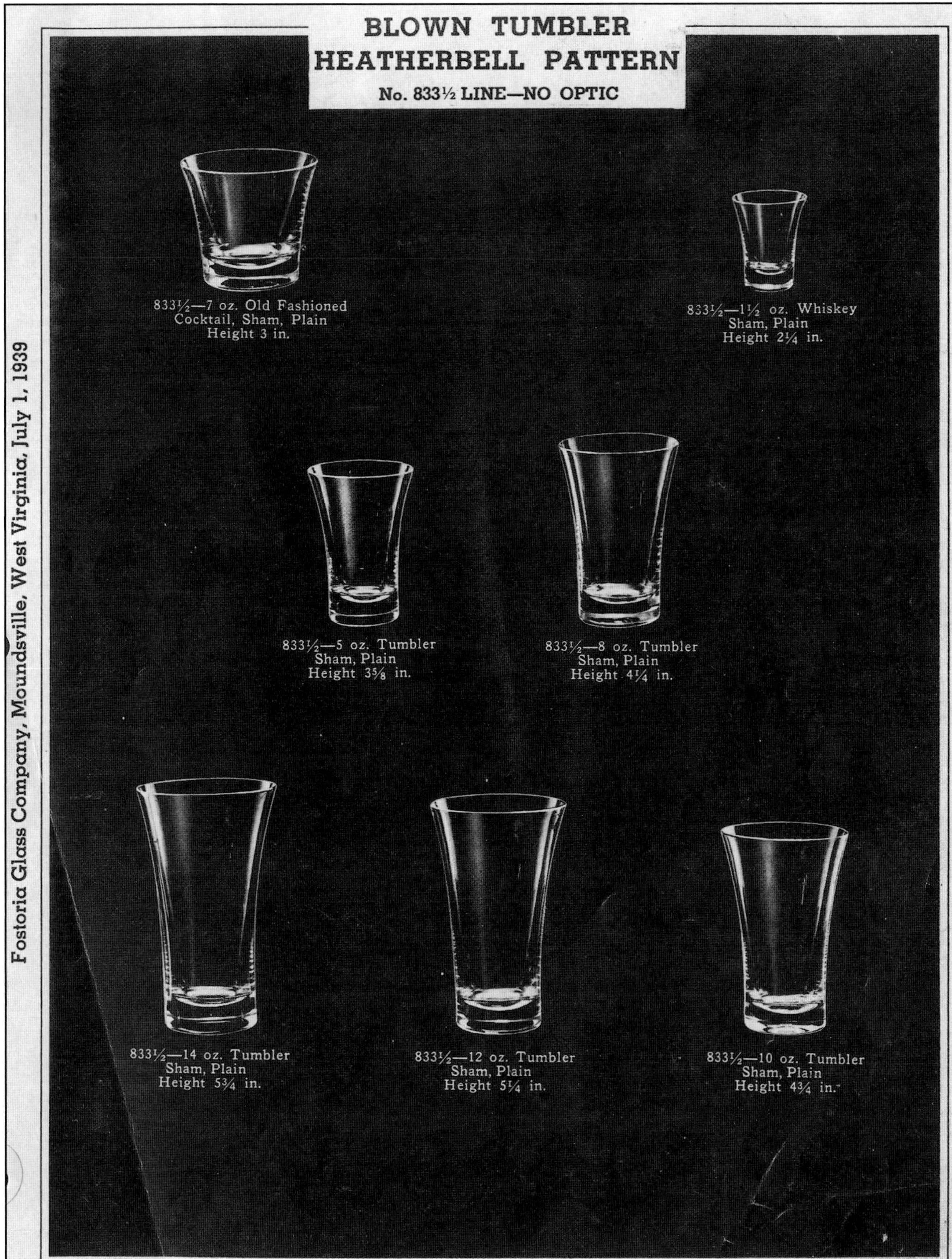

BLOWN TUMBLER
HEATHERBELL PATTERN
No. 833½ LINE—NO OPTIC
833½—7 oz. Old Fashioned Cocktail, Sham, Plain Height 3 in.
833½—1½ oz. Whiskey Sham, Plain Height 2¼ in.
833½—5 oz. Tumbler Sham, Plain Height 3⅝ in.
833½—8 oz. Tumbler Sham, Plain Height 4¼ in.
833½—14 oz. Tumbler Sham, Plain Height 5¾ in.
833½—12 oz. Tumbler Sham, Plain Height 5¼ in.
833½—10 oz. Tumbler Sham, Plain Height 4¾ in.
402A
Fostoria Glass Company, Moundsville, West Virginia, July 1, 1939

Heatherbell Tumblers from the 1939 catalog.

Fostoria Glass Company, Moundsville, West Virginia, July 1, 1940

BLOWN STEMWARE
ENVOY PATTERN

No. 6027 LINE—NO OPTIC

6027—10 oz. Goblet
Height 5¼ in.

6027—5½ oz. Saucer Champagne
Height 4¼ in.

6027—6 oz. Low Sherbet
Height 3¼ in.

6027—3½ oz. Cocktail
Height 3⅞ in.

6027·
4 oz. Wine
Height 4⅜ in.

6027—12 oz. Footed Tumbler
Height 5½ in.

6027—5 oz.
Footed Tumbler
Height 4 in.

6027—4 oz. Oyster or Fruit Cocktail
Height 3 in.

6027—1 oz. Cordial
Height 2¾ in.

HUMPTY DUMPTY PATTERN

No. 4146 LINE—NO OPTIC

4146—9 oz. Scotch & Soda
Height 3⅛ in.

4146—4 oz. Cocktail
Height 2½ in.

4146—1 oz. Cordial
Height 1½ in.

429

Envoy (top) and Humpty Dumpty (bottom) tumblers, from 1940 catalog.

ESQUIRE PATTERN

No. 4139 LINE—NO OPTIC

4139—7 oz. Old Fashioned Cocktail, Sham, Plain
Height 2¾ in.

4139—1¾ oz. Whiskey, Sham, Plain
Height 1⅞ in.

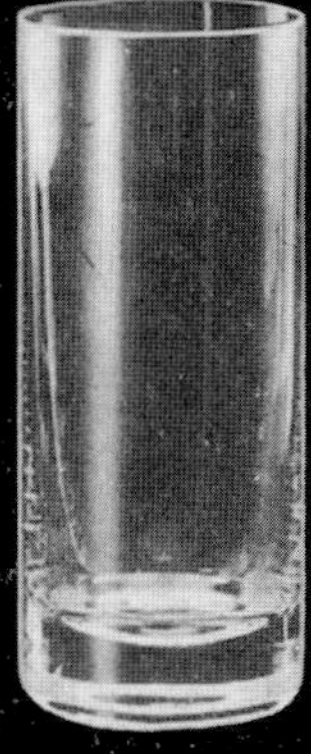

4139—10 oz. Tumbler, Sham, Plain
Height 5¼ in.

4139—9 oz. Water Tumbler, Sham, Plain
Height 3½ in.

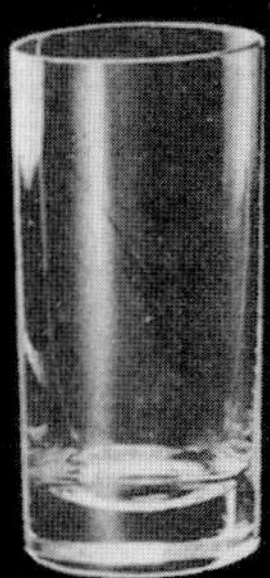

4139—5 oz. Tumbler, Sham, Plain
Height 4 in.

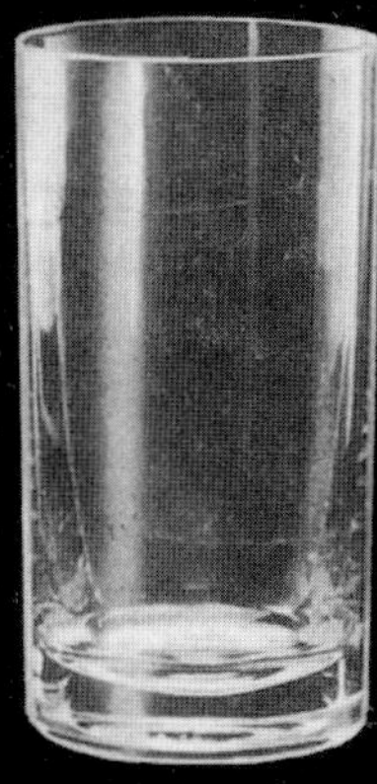

4139—16 oz. Tumbler, Sham, Plain
Height 5⅜ in.

4139—14 oz. Tumbler, Sham, Plain
Height 6¼ in.

4139—12 oz. Tumbler, Sham, Plain
Height 5⅝ in.

Blown Esquire pattern tumblers from Fostoria catalog.

Fostoria Glass Company, Moundsville, West Virginia, Jan. 1, 1937

BLOWN TUMBLERS STANDISH PATTERN

No. 4132 LINE—NO OPTIC

See Price List for Colors

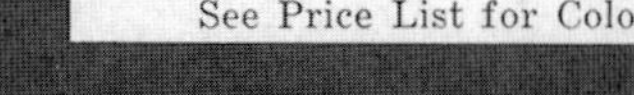

4132—7½ oz. Old Fashioned Cocktail, Sham, Plain
Height 3⅛ in.

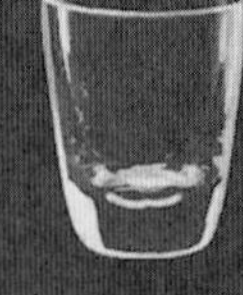

4132—1½ oz. Whiskey
Sham, Plain
Height 2⅛ in.

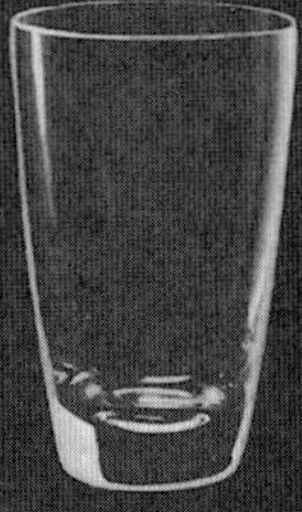

4132—7 oz. Tumbler
Sham, Plain
Height 4⅛ in.

4132—5 oz. Tumbler
Sham, Plain
Height 3¾ in.

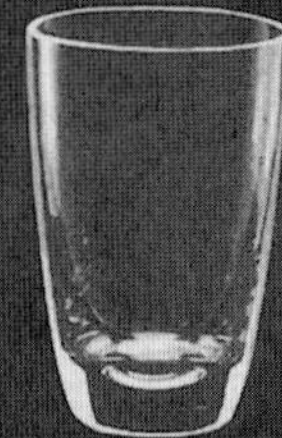

4132—4 oz. Tumbler
Sham, Plain
Height 3½ in.

4132—14 oz. Tumbler
Sham, Plain
Height 5⅜ in.

4132—9 oz. Tumbler
Sham, Plain
Height 3¾ in.

4132—12 oz. Tumbler
Sham, Plain
Height 4⅞ in.

Blown Standish pattern tumblers from 1937 catalog.

Coin Glass Wedding Bowl $7.25

4-Light Candelabra $75.00

Here you start a Christmas tradition

Right here. This page. Even in print, there's something about fine crystal that catches the eye. And, it being Christmas time, you may think, "Wouldn't this candelabra be the thing to give . . ." "And the Madonna — perfect for . . ."

Before you know it, you find yourself in a store, examining the Fostoria collection, deciding just who should be particularly favored this year.

And it's not the money. It's more a matter of taste—an appreciation of style and quality and beauty. A 75¢ Fostoria ash tray is just as truly handmade Fostoria crystal as a $95 candelabra. That's *our* tradition. An old one.

The point is—once you've given Fostoria and heard the applause, you'll want this lovely crystal sparkling for you *every* Christmas. Write the Fostoria Glass Company, Dept. HB, Moundsville, West Virginia.

Fine Crystal with Fashion Flair... made by hand in America

Fostoria

14" Torte Plate $5.75 Candleholders (Pair) $5.50 Petal Bowl $4.50 Bud Vase $3.25 Lighted Madonna $11.75 5" Ash Tray $1.75 Quart Pitcher $5.75 7½" Ash Tray $3.50 Cake Salver $7.50

(All prices slightly higher west)

Seasonal 1960s advertisement for Fostoria crystal.

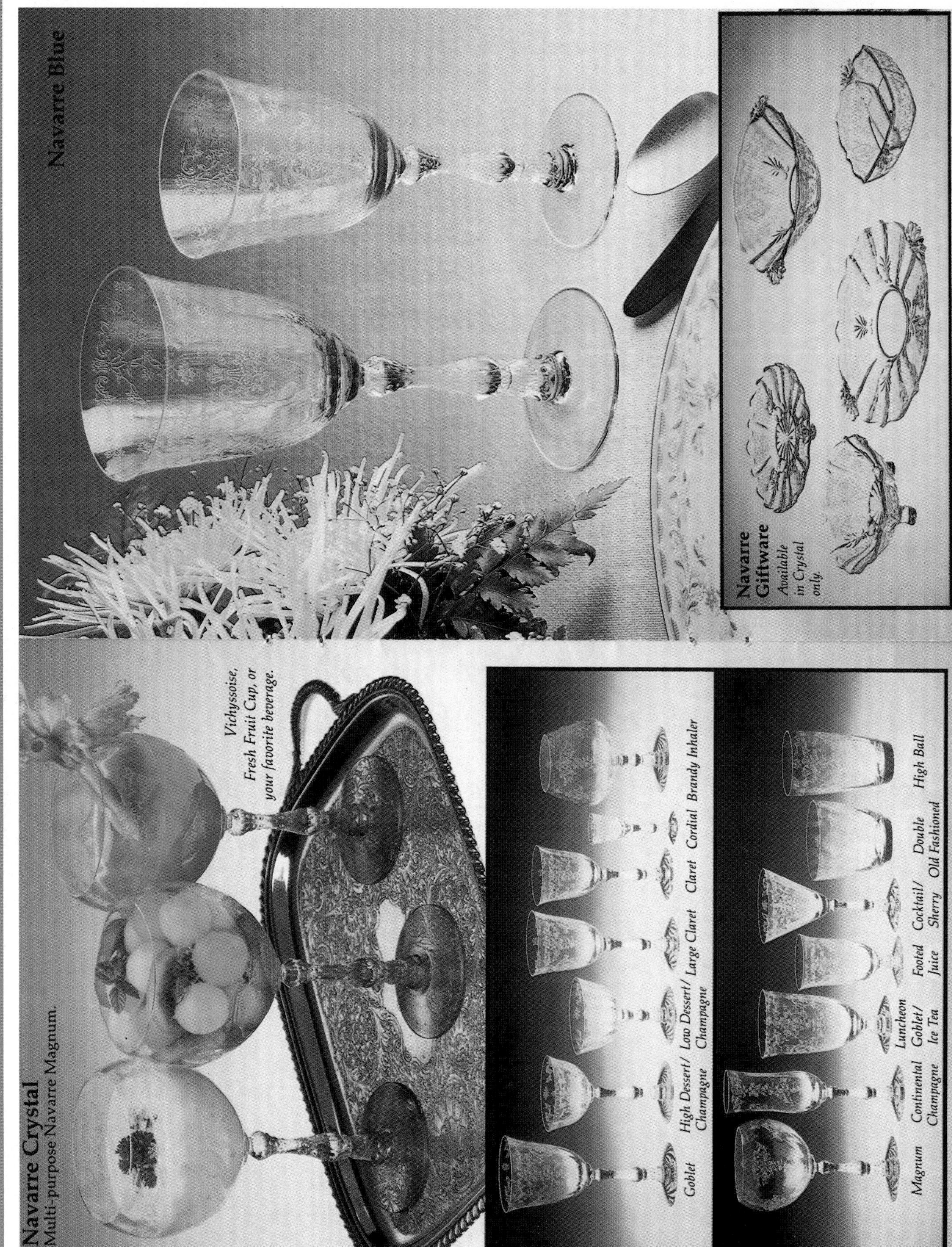

Navarre Crystal pages from Fostoria brochure.

Fine Fostoria crystal.

2510 Glacier oval Decanter Set.

6003 Cordial, 4020 Decanter, 6003 Whiskey.

2427 Cigarette Box and Cover, 2354 Cigarette with rare Cupid etching.

More crystal, functional and fabulous.

890 and 5000 jugs. Notice that the 890 is a little shorter and fatter than the 5000 jug.

Left:
1681 Wall Vase with silver deposit. This piece can be seen in the Fostoria Glass Museum, Moundsville, West Virginia.

Right:
870 High Sherbet with Grape Stem, Decoration 63, yellow gold on green.

2378 and 2375 Ice Buckets. Notice that the only difference between them is that the 2375 has an optic.

AMERICAN LADY PATTERN

No. 5056 Line

Blown Lead Glass Stemware
See Price List For Color

FOSTORIA GLASS COMPANY, MOUNDSVILLE, WEST VIRGINIA — 1953

5056—10 oz.
Goblet
Height 6⅛ in.

5056—5½ oz.
Sherbet
Height 4⅛ in.

5056—3½ oz.
Cocktail
Height 4 in.

5056—3½ oz
Claret
Height 4⅝ in.

5056—1 oz.
Cordial
Height 3⅛ in.

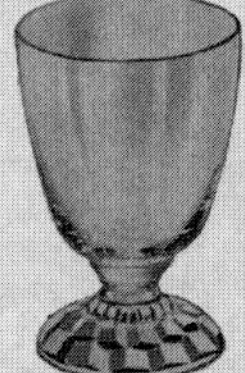

5056—4 oz.
Oyster Cocktail
Height 3½ in.

5056—12 oz.
Footed Tumbler
Height 5½ in.

5056—5 oz.
Footed Tumbler
Height 4⅛ in.

No. 2056- 4¼ inch Jelly Regular
Height 4¼ inches

No. 2056- 5 inch Jelly
Flared.
Height 3½ inches

American Lady stemware and jellies. The regular jelly was made from 1916 to 1982, but the flared jelly was only offered until 1928.

A. Cake stand/chip and dip (a single, reversible item, shown both ways), cake knife (on cake stand), pastry server
B. Kimberly bell
C. Crystal mini-box
D. Salad servers
E. Leonardo shakers (gold or chrome)
F. Party server with 24K gold-plated spoons
G. Condiment set
H. Sauce set
I. Handled tidbit (gold or chrome)
J. Captiva place card holders in a crystal box

Lovely giftware and service items.

Colonial Dame

FOR A MELODY OF COLOR

The quaint and charming *Colonial Dame* dressed with a gorgeous Empire Green bowl pendant to a swirling base. For you to give or get, there's nothing nicer than *Colony* in clear crystal and *Colonial Dame* resplendent in color . . . open stock at the better stores everywhere.

Fostoria
MADE IN U.S.A.

FOSTORIA GLASS COMPANY • • • MOUNDSVILLE • WEST VIRGINIA

ABOUT THE AUTHORS

With this volume, Milbra Long and Emily Seate combine their knowledge of the Fostoria Glass Company. A retired teacher, Milbra has been a researcher for years, offering articles to many publications including *Glass Collectors Digest* and *The Daze.* She volunteered her services as chair of the research committee for the Fostoria Glass Society of America, served on the board of directors, and often wrote articles for *Facets of Fostoria,* the organization's newsletter, before undertaking the Crystal for America project.

Milbra's love of glass is evident in each book of the series. Since 1994, when *Fostoria Stemware* was published, Milbra and Emily have scoured the countryside for glass to photograph, wanting to present the Fostoria Glass Company through both pictures and catalog illustrations. As they have often said, "The catalog gives the piece authenticity, but the photograph makes it real." In the process of gathering glass and information, they have made some remarkable discoveries about the company, and fondly call each discovery "a Fostoria moment."

Emily has been a writer of fiction and poetry for most of her life, with her "great American novel" still a work in progress. She is a philosopher, preferring long hours spent in thought to just about anything, except shopping for Fostoria glassware and the possibility of fresh discovery that doing so brings.

Together, they are mother and daughter, partners, and lifelong friends.

The Crystal for America Series

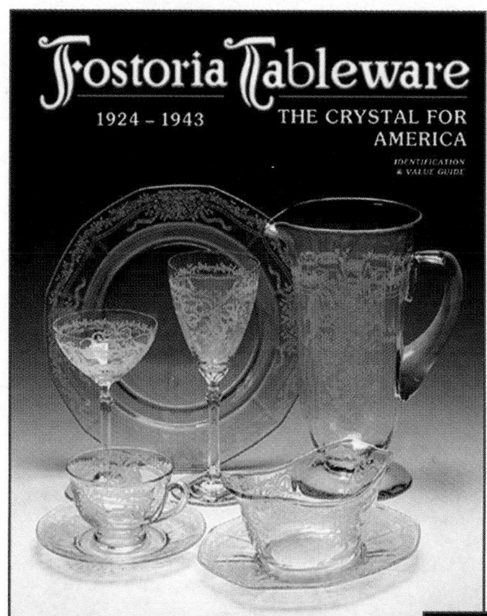

FOSTORIA Tableware and Useful and Ornamental *Milbra Long & Emily Seate*

The *Crystal for America Series* is the most complete reference available for the Fostoria Glass Company from 1924 to 1986. The first tableware volume is dedicated to Fostoria's golden age, 1924 – 1943, and the second volume covers 1944 – 1986. The final volume is devoted to useful and ornamental items, including compotes, candlesticks, bowls, syrups, and many more items used as accent pieces. A master index documents all three books and hundreds of color photos and vintage catalog illustrations are included.

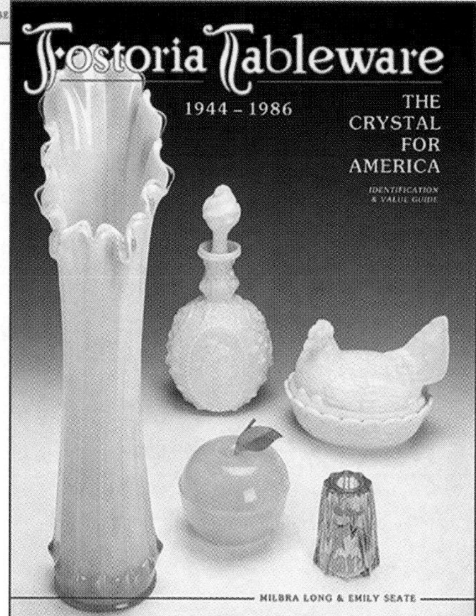

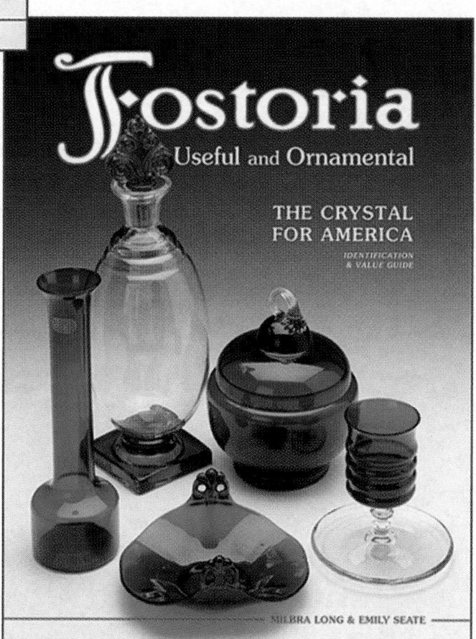

Tableware 1924 – 1943 • Item #5261 • ISBN: 1-57432-109-9
8½ x 11 • 336 Pgs. • HB • 1999 values • $24.95

Tableware 1944 – 1986 • Item #5361 • ISBN: 1-57432-143-9
8½ x 11 • 312 Pgs. • HB • 1999 values • $24.95

Useful and Ornamental • Item #5604 • ISBN: 1-57432-166-8
8½ x 11 • 256 Pgs. • HB • 2000 values • $29.95